European Media Governance: National and Regional Dimensions

Edited by Georgios Terzis

European Media Governance: National and Regional Dimensions

Edited by Georgios Terzis

intellect Bristol, UK / Chicago, USA

First Published in the UK in 2007 by
Intellect Books, The Mill, Parnall Road, Fishponds, Bristol, BS16 3JG, UK

First published in the USA in 2007 by
Intellect Books, The University of Chicago Press, 1427 E. 60th Street, Chicago,
IL 60637, USA

A catalogue record for this book is available from the British Library.

Cover Design: Gabriel Solomons
Copy Editor: Holly Spradling
Typesetting: Mac Style, Nafferton, E. Yorkshire

ISBN 978-1-84150-192-5

Printed and bound by Gutenberg Press, Malta.

To Myria

CONTENTS

FOREWORD

European Journalism Centre: 1992–2007

For fifteen years now, the European Journalism Centre has monitored, researched, reflected and conducted trainings on the present and future challenges facing the media in Europe. The EJC celebrates its 15th birthday at the service of the media community with this new publication: *European Media Governance: National and Regional Dimensions*.

The publication would not have been possible without the support of the Dutch Ministry of Education, Culture & Science (OCenW) to which the EJC would like to express its gratitude for the fruitful cooperation.

I would also like to thank the EJC Executive Committee: Ove Joanson (President), Vicent Partal (Vice-President), Hugh Stephenson (Founder) and Wilfried Ruetten (Director) for their invaluable guidance and constant input to our intellectual endeavours.

A final note of appreciation goes to Professor Georgios Terzis, EJC's dedicated and knowledgeable publications' editor, for his tireless efforts in the last two years and for his overall conception of this project.

Giuseppe Zaffuto
Director of Programmes, European Journalism Centre (EJC)

EDITOR'S PREFACE

Georgios Terzis
Associate Professor, Vesalius College-Vrije Universiteit Brussel
Chair, Journalism Studies Section, European Communication Research and Education Association

This volume concentrates on the analysis of the national dimensions of media governance in 32 European countries [the 27 EU Member States, the 2 candidate countries, Croatia and Turkey, as well as Iceland, Norway and Switzerland, which have special political relations with the EU and where most of the EU media governance-related regulations and programmes are applicable]. Further, the publication analyses four regional dimensions of media governance: the North Atlantic/Liberal, Northern European/ Democratic Corporatist, Mediterranean/Polarized Pluralist and Eastern European/Post-Communist, as defined by the criteria set by Hallin and Mancini (2004).

Governance, according to the European Union, consists of rules, processes and behaviour that affect the way in which powers are exercised, particularly as regards openness, participation, accountability, effectiveness and coherence.[1] Despite efforts of the EU to regulate part of the media industry, media governance is considerably different in the various national and regional domains in Europe.

A trip to the media landscapes of Europe offers us the variety of unique characteristics such as the Berlusconi phenomenon in Italy, pirate media in Ireland and a public broadcasting station (PBS) with audience rating quotas in Belgium. In Croatia the law forbids the media to promote war, while Turkey, with 5 hours daily viewing, has one of the highest TV audience ratings in the world. A German company is the biggest newspaper owner in Bulgaria, and almost all the daily newspapers in the Czech Republic and Hungary are foreign owned, while in Slovenia there is almost no foreign ownership of newspapers.

In Luxemburg the biggest newspaper belongs to the Catholic archbishop, and media activities have always been almost exclusively the domain of private initiatives, while in Malta 98 per cent of the population watches PBS or stations that belong to public institutions. In Switzerland private television does not exist, and PBS has the responsibility to promote cultural understanding among the different linguistic communities. On the other hand, in Poland the programmes of PBS should respect the Christian system of values, strengthen the family ties and combat 'social pathologies'.

At the same time that Finland sees the introduction of mobile television, Norway boasts the most successful newspaper website and one that has more readers on the Internet than on paper. In Sweden more than 80 per cent of the population reads a newspaper every day, while Greece and Portugal have some of the lowest newspaper readerships in the developed world. In Iceland there is home delivery of free sheets and in Spain newspapers are making more money from the sale of products than the sale of newspaper copies.

In Germany there is fierce competition among news agencies, while in Romania newspaper title numbers go up and competition is also fierce during election periods. Competition is also fierce in the second biggest media market in the world, the UK, where some newspapers saw circulation declines of up to 4.4 million. Finally, in the Netherlands one company owns almost all daily newspapers.

Four regional dimensions rest among these unique characteristics and Europe-wide trends described above. According to Hallin and Mancini, the social and political characteristics of a country shape its media system and, thus, there is a 'systemic parallelism'. As such, and despite their differences, European media landscapes share regional media dimensions parallel to their social and political regional dimensions. These are analysed in the introductory chapters of each section by the respective authors.

Despite those and other unique characteristics of the media landscapes of the 32 countries, the same voyage through their media landscape offers us a clear picture of the common characteristics that exist across all these national and regional dimensions such as commercialization, convergence, concentration, transnationalization and audience fragmentation. The introduction of cable, satellite and digital radio and television stations, for example, and the consequent channel proliferation and new types of media content, put 'must carry' regulations and public funding of PSBs under pressure, while digital convergence makes it hard to differentiate between sectors and, thus, hard to sustain sector-specific regulation.

In the meantime, ideological and social shifts such as the prevalence of neo-liberal thinking, the reliance on market forces for delivering choice and individualism and diversification of lifestyles put the whole concept of PSB and state policies of media governance in Europe into question (Iosifidis 2006). And as our journey to the different media landscapes reveals, market forces and technological developments do not necessarily protect media pluralism or the national public sphere and democratic participation. Instead, they might allow the flourishing of multiple identities across borders, since Europeans can now afford to take their media and politics with them, as well as their food, when they migrate to another European country.

External and internal media pluralism, however, depends not only on state policies as the country media landscapes reveal, but also on geographic and linguistic market sizes and the country's civil society organizations relating to media (the so-called 'fifth estate').[2] While freedom of expression is legally protected in each of the EU Member States and freedom of information is part of the legal and democratic framework in all Member States; normally through Constitutional Articles or Parliamentary Acts,

> their practical implementation includes on the one hand either voluntary or statutory rules for publishers that ensure the independence of journalistic output (codes on editorial independence, confidentiality of sources, privacy rules, defamation legislation etc); and on the other hand codes for journalists relating to standards of accuracy, fairness, honesty, respect for privacy and to ensure high professional standards, by avoiding plagiarism, defamation or the acceptance of bribes. Several companies have voluntarily introduced internal rules to protect their editorial staff from outside pressure and to separate managerial and editorial responsibilities.[3]

Finally, in regard to the market, the introduction, success and dominance of free sheets, like the *Metro*, almost everywhere in Europe are forcing traditional paid newspapers to rethink their business models. The dominance of traditional off-line media on Internet news also makes start-up Internet news companies rethink their business models and proves to the Internet utopians that the new medium does not necessarily change the old status quo and the power structures of the definition of the news agenda. Finally, the 'pleonastic excommunication' (Fortner 1995) from traditional television stations of the young population due to the introduction of the Internet, and general audience fragmentation of TV and radio audiences due to the introduction of a plethora of digital and satellite channels everywhere in Europe, forces the European broadcast industry to rethink its position too.

As a result, media governance in Europe is never static: instead there are constantly shifting media rules and regulations between exclusively governmental domains to others, such as the market and civil society organizations and from national policies to local, regional, multinational and international ones (McQuail 1997 and 2005; Bardoel & d'Haenens 2004).

Acknowledgments

I would like to thank all 45 of the contributors of this volume for their generous provision of time and energy in order to make this book a reality, as well as the Director of Programmes of the European Journalism Centre, Giuseppe Zaffuto, for trusting me with the editing.

Notes

1. European Commission (2001), EUROPEAN GOVERNANCE, A WHITE PAPER, Brussels, 25.7.2001, COM(2001) 428 final, p. 8. Available from: http://eur-lex.europa.eu/LexUriServ/site/en/com/2001/com2001_0428en01.pdf.

2. Civil society according to EU includes exactly those organizations: "trade unions and employers' organisations ('social partners'); nongovernmental organisations; professional associations; charities; grass-roots organisations; organisations that involve citizens in local and municipal life with a particular contribution from churches and religious communities". European Commission (2001), EUROPEAN GOVERNANCE, A WHITE PAPER, Brussels, 25.7.2001, COM(2001) 428 final, p. 14. Available from: http://eur-lex.europa.eu/LexUriServ/site/en/com/2001/com2001_0428en01.pdf.

3. Organization for Security and Co-operation in Europe, Representative on Freedom of Media, The Impact of Concentration on Professional Journalism, Vienna 2003, page 47 quoted at COMMISSION STAFF WORKING DOCUMENT, Media pluralism in the Member States of the European Union, {SEC(2007) 32}

References

Bardoel, J. & d'Haenens, L. (2004), Media responsibility and accountability: New conceptualizations and practices, *Communications: The European Journal of Communication Research* 29(1): 5-25.

European Commission, (2001), *European Governance, a white paper*, Brussels, 25.7.2001, COM(2001) 428 final, p. 8 and 14. Available from: http://eur-lex.europa.eu/LexUriServ/site/en/com/2001/com2001_0428en01.pdf.

Fortner, R. S. (1995), Excommunication in the Information Society. *Critical Studies in Mass Communication*, 12, 133-154.

Hallin, Daniel C. & Mancini, Paolo (2004), *Comparing Media Systems. Three Models of Media and Politics*. Cambridge: Cambridge University Press.

Iosifidis P. (2006), *Public TV in small EU countries: the Greek case*, Conference presentation at the Research Institute of Applied Communications, Cyprus, June 2006.

McQuail, D. (2005), *McQuail's Mass Communication Theory*, Sage.

McQuail, D. (1997), Accountability of Media to Society: Principles and Means, *European Journal of Communication*, vol. 12, no. 4, 511-529 (1997).

INTRODUCTION

THE CURRENT STATE OF MEDIA GOVERNANCE IN EUROPE

Denis McQuail

The fact that this book can deal with Europe as an entity in respect of media governance is itself a sign of changing times, although the title does not presume the existence of a European media system or even of pan-European media on any scale. Nevertheless, there are important respects in which the numerous separate national media systems can be framed and compared according to the same categories and issues. Despite the continuing and probably ineradicable differences arising from history, geography and national culture, a considerable convergence has been forged on the basis of shared technology and of much the same basic social, legal and political principles. Equally, it is not really open to doubt that the media institution has steadily advanced in its centrality for the public and private life of contemporary national societies, in Europe as elsewhere.

On Governance

In the present context, term 'governance' is particularly apposite, more so than regulation or control. It reflects first of all the lack of compulsion in respect of media conduct that would be incompatible with fundamental rights to freedom of publication and expression enshrined in one way or another in national constitutions as well as the European Convention on Human Rights. Its central meaning is one of steering or guidance, according to certain agreed principles or ground rules, with voluntary compliance by the main media participants. Secondly, it incorporates the notion of a network of various influences, claims and demands from many different groups and interests in the society. While media governance certainly allocates a key place to national media or press laws and other relevant legal and constitutional provisions it also refers to numerous forms of management and accountability that operate within the media and to the more or less institutionalized relations that exist between the media and the wider society. Of itself, governance does not imply any absolute barrier to freedom of the press, since it includes many forms of 'soft power' and influence as well as industry and professional self-regulation. Although governments still keep an eye on media developments and formulate and administer policies that often closely affect media, there is a new degree of distance between government and media.

From 'Old' to 'New Order'
These remarks point to a significant movement from the conditions that characterized the European scene as recently as thirty years ago, when television broadcasting had advanced to a dominant position in the spectrum of media provision and was very much within the scope of government policy and direct action in nearly every European country. The 'old order' of media governance that dated from the 1920s and began to dissolve only in the last two decades of the twentieth century was characterized by: a generally firm public (in effect governmental or political) control of radio and television broadcasting, run largely on monopoly lines together with a clear separation of these media from print media. The latter operated without any formal accountability to government and according to market principles although they were often as much entailed in political and ideological struggles on behalf of favoured clients as much as in seeking for profits. In many respects, the European press was more politicized than the media sector most directly within the power of government.

In fact, the separation of political control from ownership of the media in European democracies has never implied de-politicization of media. There has been (and remains) a considerable variety and strength of politicization, as captured by the work of Hallin and Mancini (2004), whose typology provides the basic classification system for this book. Apart from more or less formal regulatory arrangements, a miscellaneous and variable array of instruments for self-regulation or informal social control could be always found in different countries. Although the integrity of constitutionally guaranteed freedoms of press and expression was respected, the operating environment for all media was generally quite restrictive, especially in respect of sexual mores and where the integrity and security of the state was concerned. Political, social and religious establishments exerted more influence than direct power but, even so, they cast a long shadow.

The still emerging 'new order' of governance that is described in this volume is the outcome of several forces working together and often all quite closely interconnected. The fundamental direction and scope of change can be described according to different interpretations. In one version, technological change is credited as the main driving force, with three linked developments at its heart. The first of these is the rise and rise of computerization and the digitalization of all communication vehicles and contents; a second is the discovery and application of satellite communication; a third is the immense advance in wireless transmission technology and the accompanying steep decline in costs of electronic transmission of all kinds.

A second interpretation attributes the pace and scale of change in communications media to the unleashing of market forces that provided the investment and motivation to innovate and compete that were essential to the take-up and development of technology that might otherwise have been largely confined to military and state purposes, as had been the case of with earlier inventions in the field of communication. This change was linked to the triumph of liberalism and consumerism around the world in the latter part of the century and very evident in Europe, West and East. The transition to the market-dominated development of new media was not only the result of ideological preference or the influence of the European 'Common Market', but was also accelerated by the lack of success and the cost of attempts by national states to control and direct innovations in cable, satellite and telecommunications during the early 1980s (McQuail and Siune 1986).

A third narrative stresses the general globalization of social and cultural life as well as of economic arrangements that is now widely regarded as unstoppable and far-reaching in its consequences. The globalization of the media is both a reflection of larger trends and a stimulus towards greater inter-connection and the emergence of national and global 'network societies'. For mass media, globalization has produced a convergence of content of all kinds, especially of audio-visual material, by way of trade and imitative production. This has undermined the legitimacy and feasibility of claims to national communication sovereignty and exerted pressure for greater internationalization of regulatory systems and principles at the European level.

For present purposes it is unnecessary to choose between alternative explanations of change. We need only note that change in media governance is a reflection of all the trends mentioned. The 'new order' (although it has not reached any settled or final state) is clearly differentiated from the old by the relatively much greater centrality and pervasiveness of electronic media, by the much greater degree of commercialization or marketization of all forms of public communication and by the relative decline of national sovereignty over the content and flow of media content, both *de jure* and *de facto*.

Not least important is the simple fact that compared to our notional earlier status quo, the scale and complexity of media operation is much greater and the 'space' the media occupy in social affairs, however estimated, is also larger. These facts have direct consequences for systems of governance. They exert pressure towards a more extensive and differentiated form of societal management. Control of any kind, for any purpose has also simply become more difficult to achieve by former methods of regulation and institutional oversight and dominance within a limited national context. The changes mentioned also reflect the larger share of social power acquired by media in general, arising from their penetration into more and more aspects of social life and their increasing centrality for the activities of major social institutions. Paradoxically, along with the liberalization of forms of organization and relaxation of normative control in line with individualist, secular and consumerist trends has come a revived perception of the potential of media for influence that attracts the regulatory attention of social, political and economic elites that might otherwise welcome the changes that have been outlined.

It is worth noting that the 'old order' of governance was not as stable as it appeared at the time and was subject to tensions that would probably have led to major change, even without the levers of technology and liberal ideology. It was unlikely that the ambitions of radio and television operators and commercial entrepreneurs could have been indefinitely held back, especially when the governing elites could see national, sectional and personal advantages in permitting or encouraging change. Similarly, the ostensible rationale for denying equal freedom of publication to electronic media could not easily survive the gradual solution to technical problems of access and supply.

These comments on a change from new to old orders are made primarily with 'Western' Europe in mind (Van Cuilenburg and McQuail 2003). A quite different and more sudden form of change was experienced by Central and Eastern formerly Communist countries, but the essential line of direction and consequences for media governance have been much the same in the end. Privatization of media was required both for reasons intrinsic to the political changes from state-dominated systems and the transition to open societies and also for practical reasons of economics. The necessary expansion and innovation of media could only be financed from new sources on the basis of market principles. Economics aside, the main continuing difference between the two 'territories' of West and East was that for the East, direct government intervention by policy was delegitimated as well as unaffordable from state funds. The once powerful public broadcasting systems were tainted by previous association with state power as well as being impoverished. By contrast, the new free and private sector of print media was as yet untarnished by the critique of monopoly capitalism and could be seen as innovative and disrespectful of authority.

The European Context
The media in different parts of the world are based on much the same technologies and there is also a good deal that is held in common in what can be called 'media culture', in the professional practices of media work and in basic forms of organization and institutional arrangements. The trends of globalization and marketization mentioned above have brought Europe more into line with regulatory regimes elsewhere. Despite this, the media in Europe have retained some distinctive features compared with the rest of the world. However, this convergent trend has not eliminated several traditionally distinctive features of European media systems. These include: the acceptance of a transparent role for government as a positive (as well as inevitable) feature of the system; the significant position still occupied by public service broadcasting, alongside a commercial system as a key expression of this role; the high status still often attributed to print and print journalism in the spectrum of mass media, despite the sins of tabloidization and new signs of decline; the value attached to linguistic and cultural distinctiveness, according to national and regional identities; the acceptance in various degrees of an element of

'politicization' (or its explicit avoidance); the willingness to acknowledge an idea of the 'public interest' (sometimes 'national interest') that is unlikely to be revealed or achieved by market forces on their own; the continued attachment, for a mixture of these reasons, to protectionist measures, exceptional for global markets. It can be said generally of Europe that the mass media have remained within the scope of influence of cultural and political elites, much more so than the 'liberal model' prescribes.

A new factor has been the conscious 'Europeanization' of the media as a result of aspirations of the EU and other Europe-wide bodies to achieve both a more open market for media goods and services, and also a shared set of norms for content and control of media. The most concrete expression of the results has been by way of the European Television Directive that has established ground rules for trans-border broadcasting and for some aspects of internal organization which are on the whole observed. In the context of the Council of Europe, a wider grouping of countries has sought to establish recognition of basic rights and responsibilities of all those involved in public communication. Virtually all relevant professional, industry and sectional interests in the media field as well as many action groups are organized to cooperate and to exert influence on the European as well as national plane. The search for common grounds for the operation of broadcasting has encouraged some efforts (largely unsuccessful) to harmonize such regulation as applies to the press, either by way of law or the application of principles enshrined in international agreements on human rights. For some time there have also been attempts to provide a framework of principle for the operation of the Internet and to give Europe a more prominent voice in the global governance of the new system of communication.

There is something of a paradox in the fact that the acquisition of a more distinctive European identity for media systems has not yet reduced the many inter-country differences (see Kelly, Mazzoleni, McQuail 2004, as well as the following chapters). On a number of basic dimensions of media variation, European countries still differ a good deal. This reflects differences of national history and culture as well as economic, geographic and demographic differences. Not least important is the diversity of types of linkage between media and politics from one country to another that is anchored firmly in media and political systems (Hallin and Mancini 2004). There is further evidence for such differences in this book. Inevitably, they are reflected in the setting of goals for policy and their implementation by way of law and regulation. There is not only an interesting paradox here but also the seeds of a good deal of conflict when it comes to establishing common rules for essential features of the media systems that may have implications for other countries. It is clear at least that the field of media governance and associated policy-making in Europe is far from settled and harmonious and needs close and continuing examination.

A Comment on Changing Principles

Frameworks of media governance embody an intricate mixture of pragmatism and self-interest as well as being shaped by more fundamental values. There are continuous changes in the pragmatic considerations guiding media policy and regulation, but, as one would expect, it is less easy to discern great changes in principles, even if the order of importance changes. At the high watermark of the 'old order' when media policy seemed very much in control, around the mid-1970s, there was a good deal of consensus in Europe about fundamental issues. Diversity or pluralism had pride of place, although it was interpreted and applied in quite diverse ways. It was to be achieved negatively by limiting concentration of ownership and control and positively by way of public broadcasting and by promoting broad access to public media channels and choice for audiences in the media market. The diversity principle favoured media provision for alternative social, cultural and linguistic groups. Values of cultural identity and localism were included under the umbrella of diversity, involving resistance to the homogenizing effects of global media flows on domestic reception and production. A basic plank of diversity was to assure fair access for political parties for essential political communication purposes and to limit the media advantages that could be purchased by dominant economic interests.

A second basic principle, applying mainly to broadcasting, was that of maintaining a public service element in communication to ensure certain essential benefits to the society as a whole and its constituent groups. This overlaps with the principle of universal service that had long governed state intervention in post and telephone services, but was much extended to apply to the content as well simply access to send or receive. The public element also included the essential idea that there would be more or less direct control and accountability of the media to the public by way of government agencies or bodies set up by governments (for instance, public service broadcasting organizations) rather than simply by the market. This would also entail an element of public funding.

Although less clearly articulated, there was broad acceptance of the notion that a democratic society requires the means to circulate reliable information among citizens, sufficient to support informed political choice and maintain essential links between government and government. Somewhat paradoxically, the pursuit of the public service principle had a potential to conflict with that of diversity since public control and universal provision involved some restricted allocation of limited resources and also some need for neutrality (and, thus, uniformity) in the provision of information, if not of ideas. Access to channels and supply of content did not necessarily match the distribution of demand from would-be 'voices' or receivers.

Thirdly, the protection of order and decency and a commitment to notions of informational and cultural 'quality' of media provision carried much weight, both with influential public opinion and in the eyes of policy-makers. This led to various legal and regulatory limitations on content that might offend or potentially cause harm. Even the typical guarantees of freedom of publication for the press did not completely exempt the media from caution in these matters and some legal limitations. The order principle had a wider range than others, since it included an expectation – that could ultimately be backed by state power – that the media would not engage in (or aid) subversive or criminal activities harmful to the national interest, especially in matters relating to defence, state secrets and the threat of insurgent terrorism (already perceived as a significant problem in several countries). The value of order was both a pragmatic reason and a justifying principle for maintaining public control.

Fourthly, the principle of freedom was maintained in policy, although somewhat ambiguously, since it was hard to ignore the fact that most positive acts of media policy entailed some limitations on freedom of media and entrepreneurs. Even so we can account freedom as an overarching principle, to be achieved in respect of media not by removing all legal and governmental restraints but by positive action to promote access, competition, freedom of information and diversity of content. In addition the media would be encouraged to implement their own systems of self-regulation to remove the need for any enforced intervention So at least it appeared in the Europe of the 1970s.

This leads us to a fifth basic principle, one that concerns the safeguarding of individual rights against harm from possible defamation, invasion of privacy and some other kinds of offence. In some cases, similar rights can be claimed on behalf of clearly identifiable groups and minorities that may be victimized by treatment in the media. Such rights are a correlate of, and their respect a condition of, the claim to freedom. Essentially they call for media to act responsibly and accountably, preferably by voluntary agreement and self-regulation, but if necessary by way of outside pressure or legal resources.

These five basic principles indicate the main areas where some form of direction or limitation was and still is called for. They do not exhaust the full range of potential topics that fall within the scope of media governance. Amongst others, we can include: safeguarding the economic viability of different media sectors; promoting the accuracy and integrity of advertising and protecting media consumers more generally; protecting intellectual and artistic property rights and resolving problems caused by new forms of technology that affect these matters.

The changes that have taken place in the discourse of principle are subtle but real enough. Diversity is still valued but is likely to be interpreted in the first instance as diversity of supply and consumption, the outcome of a properly performing market in which all significant audience demands are likely to be satisfied because the range of services and content is very wide and always growing and competition maintains fair prices. The possibility of limited market failure is recognized and also of certain small minorities lacking market power and needing some subsidy or special provision. The 'public service' principle has been watered down where it seems to conflict with the logic and working of the market.

A free market is deemed capable of developing its own forms of accountability between suppliers and consumers and media and society, without clumsy forms of government intervention of limited effectiveness in a 'consumer society'. Universal service no longer seems to need to be guaranteed by state action, except very marginally and the virtues of direct public financing are no longer very apparent, nor appealing to governments. A qualification to this is the fact that pragmatic and political motives for public intervention in media may now be relatively more important than before, given the great freedom, globalization and liberalization of the media market as a whole.

It is quite obvious that the development and commercial exploitation of new communication technologies has upset the once reigning regulatory arrangements and also exacerbated the tension between public and private objectives. The digitalization of transmission and reception has introduced instability and uncertainty into systems of governance as well as media industry, especially with the gradual loss of public control over actual developments on the ground. There is a perceived decline of control and accountability. Most of the allegedly problematic features of the mass media for society, rightly or wrongly, have seemed to be accentuated, with not much in redeeming features to compensate (aside from abundance and choice). The arrival of the Internet has revived the recurrent fears that accompanied previous new media, without there being any obvious means of supervision or control at national (or regional) level. The media scene in Europe can be represented as distinctly more ungoverned, if not ungovernable, and generally more 'normless'.

The Emerging Agenda of Issues for Media Governance

The notion of an 'agenda of issues' is in many ways already an anachronism, since it employs the language of government, law and regulation, as if measures can be taken to 'deal with' known and circumscribed problems. In reality, the challenges posed to society by changing media in a changing global environment can no longer be tackled in the traditional way. Media institutions operate in an open and constantly shifting economic and social environment, subject to unforeseeable buffeting from technological innovation and economic events both close to and far from home. The degree of sovereignty possessed by agencies of democratic control has diminished. New forms of media governance have already begun to evolve in response to changed conditions. Decision-making is left more and more to marketplace judgments, with relatively independent public regulatory bodies at some distance from government and with legal and regulatory intervention reserved for maintaining basic ground rules as agreed nationally and internationally.

There are some large issues arising from the conditions of uncertainty mentioned above that are not really within the scope of any system of governance. These include especially the following matters: the extent and limits to globalization as it affects any given national or regional media system; the degree to which convergence is developing between media on a number of dimensions (technological, ownership, regulatory); the changing structure (and balance of functions) of media types or forms, with particular reference to the rise of online media and the adaptation of 'traditional' media forms (press, broadcasting, especially) to new conditions (which are being shaped by technologies such as the Internet and mobile telephony that have never really been on the map of regulatory ambitions); the particular forms that are being taken by 'commercialization' in the new conditions.

These are matters that will have to be settled by historical forces at work rather than by skilful forecasting or planned intervention in a delimited region or market. But within the limits set by flux uncertainty there remain a set of perennial problems arising from the nature of communication and the important (and probably increased) role it plays in organized social life, from local to global. The brief statement of these issues that follows indicates a significant degree of continuity with previous concerns and reminds us of the relevance of past experience and thinking as well as past attempts to manage communication for social purposes. These issues come down, at base, to the following matters, each of which has an international dimension as well as a national and local one:

- Achieving due accountability for ethical, moral and professional standards of media performance, as decided by the larger community;
- Protecting individuals and society from potential harm of many kinds that can occur by way of communication systems;
- Setting positive expectations and goals for public social and cultural communication and steering the development of systems accordingly;
- Maintaining essential freedoms of communication under conditions of total surveillance and registration;
- Managing relations between state and political power on the one hand and communicative power on the other, according to democratic principles.

This list is based on an acceptance of the fundamental principles outlined above and takes for granted a continued need for effective forms of governance, even if the locus of action no longer lies with state power. The items listed are formulated in very general terms and are open to numerous more specific and variable expression. The question of convergence and divergence is inevitably a central one in a book of this kind that provides comparisons between many countries that subscribe to approximately the same principles of human and legal rights. Even so we do not have to presume that convergence (e.g., of the kind towards which markets tend) is either good or necessary. It can also be a problematic condition when it reduces diversity and multiplicity, concentrates power and closes off lines of action that work in a given cultural and political context. This introduction is not the place to assess the progress of converging trends, but it is not out of place to record that European media still show very large differences on many dimensions and that the sources of these differences are not dried up by technological change and overarching regional cooperation and harmonization.

References

Hallin, D. and Mancini, P. (2004), *Comparing Media Systems*. Cambridge: Cambridge University Press.

Kelly, M., Mazzoleni, G. and McQuail, D. (eds.) (2004), *The Media in Europe*. London: Sage.

McQuail, D. and Siune, K. (1986), *New Media Politics*. London: Sage.

Van Cuilenburg, J. J. and McQuail, D. (2003), 'Media policy paradigm shifts'. *European Journal of Communication*, 18, 2: 181–207.

THE NORTH ATLANTIC OR LIBERAL MEDIA MODEL COUNTRIES

INTRODUCTION

Dan Hallin & Paolo Mancini

The Liberal, or as it is often called the Anglo-American, model of the mass media is in some sense the only model that has really been analyzed in media studies as such, as a coherent model. Indeed, while other media systems have rarely been conceptualized as coherent wholes, it could be said that the "Anglo-American" model has been treated as far more coherent and unitary than it actually is. There are, in fact, substantial differences between the US – which is a purer example of a liberal system – and Britain or Ireland.

Nevertheless, there are important common features of the media systems which distinguish Britain and Ireland along with the US and Canada from continental European media systems. In all these countries newspapers developed relatively early, expanded with relatively little state involvement and became overwhelmingly dominant, marginalizing party, trade union, religious and other kinds of non-commercial media. An informational style of journalism has become dominant, and traditions of political neutrality tend to be strong – though with a very important exception in the British press. Journalistic professionalism is relatively strongly developed. And the state plays a more limited role in the media system than in continental Europe.

Liberalism and the Development of a Commercial Mass-Circulation Press
The most distinctive characteristic of the media history of the North Atlantic countries is the early and strong development of commercial newspapers, which would dominate the press by the end of the nineteenth century, marginalizing other forms of media organization. Newspaper circulations fell from their peak in the Liberal countries following the introduction of television, and are not as high today as some countries of continental Europe and East Asia, but remain relatively strong. Commercialization not only expanded circulations but transformed newspapers from small-scale enterprises,

most of which lost money and required subsidies from wealthy individuals, communities of readers, political parties or the state, into highly capitalized and highly profitable businesses. This in turn transformed the political role of the press. The nature of this transformation and its implications for democracy has been the subject of one of the most important debates in media scholarship in the Liberal countries, a debate posed most explicitly in Britain, though it is present in some form in all four countries. The traditional interpretation, dominant in media scholarship for many years as well as in public discourse about the Liberal media system which has been diffused around the world, is the view that "the increasing value of newspapers as advertising mediums allow[ed] them gradually to shake off government or party control and to become independent voices of public sentiment" (Altick 1957: 322). This view was challenged by a revisionist scholarship which began to develop in the 1970s, which saw the commercialization of the press as undermining their role in democratic life, first by concentrating media power in the hands of particular social interests – those of business, especially – and, second, by shifting the purpose of the press from the expression of political viewpoints to the promotion of consumerism. The kinds of "representative media" that played central roles in the media history in continental Europe – media directly tied to political parties or other organized social groups, have been far more marginal in the Liberal countries.

Political Parallelism
The commercial press that developed so strongly in North America and in Britain played a pioneering role in developing what Chalaby (1996) calls a "fact-centred discourse". Commercial papers emphasized news at the expense of the political rhetoric and commentary which had dominated earlier papers. They were innovators in the development of organizational infrastructure to gather news rapidly and accurately, as well as in the development of the cultural forms of factual reporting

Often it is assumed that this kind of "fact-centred discourse" goes naturally with a stance of political neutrality and that a strong commercial press inevitably means a low level of political parallelism. In fact, there are significant differences among Liberal countries in the extent to which political neutrality or partisanship prevails. In the U.S., Canada and Ireland political neutrality has come to be the typical stance of newspapers. The British press, on the other hand, is still characterized by external pluralism; it is no coincidence that the concept of "party-press parallelism" was developed in Britain, where despite their commercial character and despite the importance of the fact-centred discourse stressed by Chalaby, the press has always mirrored the divisions of party politics fairly closely.

As in other countries, the party affiliations of British newspapers have become weaker over the post-war period. Newspapers became less consistent in their support for one party or another, less inclined to follow the agenda set by party leaders and less focused on the rhetoric of party politics.

Despite this general trend toward diminishing political parallelism, however, the political orientations of British newspapers today are as distinct as anywhere in Europe, with the possible exceptions of Italy and Greece. The spectrum of political views is surely not as wide – Britain is characterized by moderate pluralism, and its politics have a strong orientation toward the centre. Nevertheless, within the limits of the British political spectrum, strong, distinct political orientations are clearly manifested in news content. Strong political orientations are especially characteristic of the tabloid press. But the British quality papers also have distinct political identities. This can be seen in the political affinities of their readers. The readerships of British national papers, for example, are differentiated politically very much like those of newspapers in the Polarized Pluralist or Democratic Corporatist countries. In broadcasting, in contrast to the press, political neutrality is the rule; in Britain, both the BBC and the ITV companies are bound by requirements for impartiality and balance in news and public affairs.

Professionalization

Journalistic professionalism is relatively strongly developed in the Liberal countries. Certainly journalism has developed into a distinct occupational community and social activity, with a value system and standards of practice of its own, rooted in an ideology of public service, and with significant autonomy. At the same time, many contradictions in the nature and significance of professionalization emerge when we look at journalism in Liberal systems.

In Britain as in all the Liberal countries journalism is strongly professionalized in the sense that journalists have their own set of criteria for the selection and presentation of news; this is closely related to the strong development of the press as an industry in Britain, and in this way Britain is very different from, say, Italy, where the standards of journalistic practice are less separated from those of politics. With the development of the press as an industry, as Chalaby (1998: 107) puts it, "journalists began to report politics according to their own needs and interests, covering the topic from their own perspective and professional values." As far as journalistic autonomy is concerned, the picture is mixed. Broadcast journalists in Britain are probably more autonomous than their counterparts in the commercial media of the US or Canada. Donsbach (1995), however, reports that British journalists were second, after Italians, in the percentage reporting that their stories were changed "to give a political slant," 6 per cent saying that this happened at least occasionally, as compared with 8 per cent in Italy, 2 per cent in the US and Germany and 1 per cent in Sweden (a lower percent of the news in Britain concerns politics, compared with Italy, it might be noted). Another survey showed 44 per cent of British journalists saying they had suffered "improper editorial interference" with a story (Henningham & Delano 1998: 154).

Formal institutions of self-regulation of the media are less developed in the Liberal than in Democratic Corporatist countries, though more so than in the Mediterranean region. Ireland has no news council or press complaints commission. Britain moved in 1991 from a very weak Press Council to the Press Complaints Commission, a move intended to avoid continental-style privacy and right-of-reply legislation. The British tabloids, especially, have a heavy emphasis on sex scandals, about both public and private figures.

The PCC is clearly stronger than its predecessor, and its presence is a characteristic the British system now shares with the Democratic Corporatist countries, though it is still essentially run by the newspaper industry, "illustrative of the enduring British commitment to 'hands-off' self-regulation" (Humphreys 1996: 61).

The Role of the State

The Liberal countries are, by definition, those in which the social role of the state is relatively limited, and the role of the market and private sector relatively large. Britain was the birthplace of industrial capitalism, and the United States the centre of its twentieth-century growth. Market institutions and liberal ideology developed strongly in both countries – in general, and specifically in the media field, where they are manifested in the early development of commercial media industries and of the liberal theory of a free press rooted in civil society and the market.

In Britain, a strong liberal tradition is modified both by a legacy of conservative statism and by a strong labour movement, whose integration into the system of power in the 1940s shifted Britain in the direction of liberal. Britain, moreover, has no written constitution, and the doctrine of parliamentary sovereignty is central to its legal framework, so freedom of the press remains an important cultural tradition but not the privileged legal principle it is in the US. The press sector remains essentially liberal in character, with neither subsidies nor significant regulatory intervention, though the threat of such intervention did induce the formation of the Press Complaints Commission – and it continues to be discussed, as many argue that the PCC is ineffective. Important manifestations of Britain's strong state tradition include the D-notice system, which restricts reporting of information that affects "national security", and the Official Secrets Act, under which both journalists and public officials can be punished for "leaking" privileged information.

It is in the sphere of broadcasting, however, that the differences between the US and Britain have been most marked, with Britain building a strong public service broadcasting system. In 1954 Britain became the first major European country to introduce commercial broadcasting; even then, however, its broadcasting system retained a strong public service orientation. The BBC and ITV competed for audiences but not for revenue, with the BBC relying on the licence fee and ITV on advertising. And the Independent Broadcasting Authority, which regulated commercial broadcasting until the Broadcasting Act of 1990, was a far different, far stronger institution than the American FCC. Like the rest of Europe, British broadcasting, including the BBC, is increasingly affected by market logic, though the public service system remains stronger in Britain than in much of Europe.

In Ireland concerns about national culture have modified the logic of the Liberal model. Ireland is a postcolonial state, and also a small country proximate to a larger one with the same language. Its political culture combines a tradition of liberalism with a strong official ideology of nationalism. It also has a history of economic dependency and weak development of domestic capital, which like other postcolonial societies – Greece, for example – has resulted in a post-independence tradition of an interventionist state (Bell 1985). Public broadcasting has therefore been strongly dominant in Ireland, with free-to-air commercial television introduced only in 1998, although Irish public broadcasting has a high level of commercial funding, 66 per cent in 1998. Unlike Canada, Ireland has not protected its print industry. About 20 per cent of daily newspaper circulation today represents British titles. The Censorship of Publications Act, which lasted until 1967, resulted from the political conflicts of the civil war of the 1920s, and Ireland, like Britain, has restrictions on media related to the conflict in Northern Ireland.

Conclusion
The early consolidation of liberal institutions in Britain and its former colonies, together with a cluster of social and political characteristics related to this history – early industrialization, limited government, strong rational-legal authority, moderate and individualized pluralism and majoritarianism, are connected with a distinctive pattern of media–system characteristics. These include the strong development of a commercial press and its dominance over other forms of press organization, early development of commercial broadcasting, relatively strong professionalization of journalism, the development of a strong tradition of "fact-centred" reporting, and the strength of the objectivity norm. Media have been institutionally separate from political parties and other organized social groups, for the most part, since the late nineteenth century. And state intervention in the media sector has been limited by comparison with the Democratic Corporatist or Polarized Pluralist systems.

We have also seen that there are important differences among the four countries, enough that we should be careful about throwing around the notion of an "Anglo-American" media model too easily. The British and, to a lesser extent, the Irish and Canadian systems share important characteristics in common with continental European systems –particularly those of the Democratic Corporatist countries – both in their political institutions and cultures and in their media systems. This is manifested most obviously in the strength of public broadcasting and in the persistence of party-press parallelism in the British press. The latter also suggests that the common assumption that commercialization automatically leads to the development of politically neutral media is incorrect.

There are, finally, many tensions or contradictions in the Liberal media systems: there is a tension between the fact of private ownership and the expectation that the media will serve the public good and a closely related tension between the ethics of journalistic professionalism and the pressures of commercialism; there is also a tension between the liberal tradition of press freedom and the pressures of government control in societies where the "national security state" is strong.

Acknowledgments

This chapter is an extract from chapter 7 of the book *Comparing Media Systems. Three Models of Media and Politics*. Cambridge: Cambridge University Press, by Hallin, Daniel C. & Mancini, Paolo (2004), and it is published with the permission of the publisher.

References

Altick, R. (1957), *The English Common Reader: A social History of the Mass Reading Public, 1800–1900*. Columbus: Ohio State University Press.

Bell, D. (1985), Proclaiming the Republic: Broadcasting Policy and the Corporate State in Ireland, *West European Politics* 8(2): 26–49.

Chalaby, J. (1996), Journalism as an Anglo-American Invention: A Comparison of the Development of French and Anglo-American Journalism, 1830–1920s, *European Journal of Communication* 11(3): 303–26.

Donsbach, W. (1995), Lapdogs, Watchdogs and Junkyard Dogs, *Media Studies Journal* 9(4): 17–31.

Henningham, J. & A. Delano (1998), British Journalists, in D. H. Weaver, ed., *The Global Journalist: News People Around the World*, pp. 143–60. Cresskill, NJ: Hampton Press.

Humphreys, P. (1996), *Mass Media and Media Policy in Western Europe*, Manchester: Manchester University Press.

THE IRISH MEDIA LANDSCAPE

Wolfgang Truetzschler

From the mid–1990s onwards Ireland has witnessed an unparalleled economic boom with an accompanying increase in wealth and economic activity. Ireland's population has increased to approximately 4.2 million due to immigration, the Irish labour force has increased in order to meet the demand of an increased number of jobs, and the unemployment rate has fallen to 4.2 per cent of the labour force.

As is outlined below, the economic developments in Ireland have led to an increase in the number of media outlets, an increasing interest by foreign companies in the Irish media, an increasing consolidation in the media industry and an increase in spending in the media.

1. The Market

A. Print Media
Main features:

- Ireland's booming economy has led to an increase in newspaper sales
- Independent News and Media is the dominant actor
- Consolidation in the regional press
- Irish magazines continue to sell well despite competition from the UK

The press in Ireland consists of four national dailies: *Irish Independent*, *The Irish Times*, *The Star* and *The Irish Examiner*, and two national evening newspapers, *Evening Herald The Evening Echo*, five national Sunday newspapers: *Sunday Independent*, *Sunday World*, *Sunday*

Tribune, *Sunday Business Post* and *Ireland on Sunday*, around fifty regional and twelve local newspapers, as well as approximately thirty-two, mainly urban-based free (advertising-financed) newspapers. Newspapers other than the dailies tend to be published on a weekly basis. Roughly 600,000 national newspapers and 650,000 regional newspapers are sold in the Republic each day and week respectively.

Irish-language newspapers consist of two weekly newspapers (*Foinse* and *La*, subsidized to the tune of €120,000 in the case of *La* and €4,500 per issue of *Foinse*) by Foras Na Gailge, the state body responsible for the promotion of the Irish language throughout the whole island of Ireland.

Ireland's booming economy has had a positive effect on its newspaper industry in that there has been a modest increase of around 2.3 per cent in Irish newspaper sales in 2005/2006 (according to the World Association of Newspapers 2006). The daily readership of newspapers has also increased in a similar manner.

The only Irish tabloid newspapers are *Ireland on Sunday*, *Sunday World* and *The Star*, an Irish edition of the British *Daily Star*. This is probably due to the wide availability of British newspapers (especially the tabloid ones who tend to publish Irish editions), which can be bought all over Ireland. UK newspapers are cheaper in Ireland than Irish ones as Ireland (unlike Britain) imposes value added tax on the printing of newspapers. Approximately 25 per cent of daily and 33 per cent of Sunday newspapers sold in Ireland are British.

Independent News and Media is the dominant actor in the Irish newspaper industry in that around 80 per cent of Irish newspapers sold in Ireland in 2006 were sold by companies which are fully or partially Independent News and Media. This situation has been reviewed by the Irish Government and the Irish Competition Authority on a few occasions over the last five years. The conclusion reached by these reviews has usually been that the Irish newspaper industry shows sufficient editorial diversity not to warrant intervention in the Irish newspaper market.

This diversity is provided by Ireland's main quality broadsheet, *The Irish Times*, and to a lesser extent (lower circulation figures) by the daily *Irish Examiner* and by the quality Sunday *Business Post*, both owned by the Thomas Crosbie Group.

There has been considerable consolidation in the regional and local newspaper market in the last few years. Ireland's economic boom has led to a strong growth in advertising revenue of over 250 per cent in the years 1998 to 2004. Regional newspapers are particularly attractive acquisition targets due to their high level of profitability, loyal readership and their quasi-monopoly for advertising in regional markets.

In 2006 there are five main players in the regional press: Independent News and Media, Thomas Crosbie Holdings (publisher of 18 newspapers), the UK Johnston Press with 47 titles, Scotland's Dumfermline Press Group and Northern Ireland's Alpha Group.

Around 30 independent paid newspapers remain in the marketplace. Thus, further consolidation of the regional press is likely to occur.

Foreign ownership of Irish print media has traditionally been quite limited since the demise of one of the oldest Irish newspapers the *Irish Press*, 50 per cent of the shares of which were some years ago owned by a US company. However, the booming Irish economy and the healthy state of the Irish newspaper industry (increasing profitability due to higher advertising spending in Ireland) has changed the traditional lack of interest in the Irish newspaper market by foreign (British) investors.

In the magazine sector, Irish titles continue to sell well despite the strong competition from the United Kingdom. Irish periodical and magazine publishers are organized in the periodicals Publishers Association of Ireland (PPA). It has companies with a total of 200 magazines in membership.

The most successful magazine with 102,705 copies sold per issue in the period Jan-Jun 2006 is the *RTE Guide* the weekly guide to radio and television published by the public service broadcaster RTE. The highest selling magazine in the country with an audited circulation of 43,666 per issue in 2006 is the women's monthly *U Magazine*.

All Irish media are dependent on advertising revenue. In 2005 the total expenditure amounted to roughly €1,500 million. The profile of media expenditure is estimated by the Institute of Advertising Practitioners in Ireland (IAPI) to be press: 64 per cent, television: 20 per cent, radio: 7 per cent, outdoor: 8 per cent, cinema: 1 per cent, Internet: 0.3 per cent.

B. The Broadcast Media
Main features:

- Dominance by the public service broadcaster RTE
- Start up of new television channels
- No Irish digital television service
- Increase in radio advertising

Broadcasting in Ireland has been dominated since the 1920s by Ireland's public service broadcaster Radio Telifis Eireann (RTE) and this is still the situation in 2007 to the extent that RTE is a major player in Ireland's broadcasting scene. RTE operates two national television services: RTE 1, and Network 2. Since October 1996 Ireland has a third public service broadcasting channel, the Irish-language Telefis na Gailge (TG4). TG4 operates under the statutory and corporate aegis of RTE, but will be set up as a separate Broadcasting Authority according to the new Broadcasting Act 2001.

Apart from the public service broadcaster TG4, indigenous competition to RTE television is the private commercial general television channel TV3, which was awarded a licence to broadcast television as far back as 1988/89 but only commenced broadcasting in September 1998. In order to start up television broadcasting TV3 needed strong financial backers which it received in 1997 when CanWest Global, the Canadian television company, took a 45 per cent stake in TV3.

The Canadian company also owns 29.9 per cent of Ulster Television (UTV), the British independent television company of Northern Ireland. In September 2000 the British media group Granada Media also took a 45 per cent stake in TV3. Granada Media is the dominant player in the British private television sector in that it effectively controls the UK's ITV network and produces 47 per cent of the network's output. In early 2006 CanWest decided to sell its 45 per cent stake in TV3 to Doughty Hanson, one of Europe's largest media investors, for €265 m.

The year 2006 saw the start up of 3 additional commercial television channels: a sports channel Setanta Sports, Channel 6, a general entertainment channel aimed purely at the most lucrative market segment of people under 35 years of age, and the Dublin City Channel, a cable television channel. These 3 new television channels bear witness to the attractiveness of Ireland's TV advertising market. The economic prosperity has led to a significant growth in advertising expenditure over the last ten years (e.g. 14 per cent growth in advertising expenditure in 2005)

In terms of channel share of viewing in 2005 the two RTE channels are the most popular with over 30 per cent market share. The other main channels were TV3 (11.5%), BBC1 (8.6%), UTV (7.2%), Channel 4 (5.1%), BBC2 (4.3%), TG4 (2.7%), Sky1 (2.5%).

RTE operates four national radio channels. Radio 1 with traditional public service radio programming, 2 FM, a 24-hour music radio station, Raidio na Gaeltachta with public service radio programming in the Irish language, and Lyric FM, a 24-hour classical music and arts channel. The Irish public service broadcaster is excluded from the provision of local radio since the enactment of the Radio and Television Act 1988.

In early 2006 there are 54 licensed private commercial 'sound broadcasting services' (radio stations) in Ireland. These consist of one national independent commercial radio station, 1 regional commercial radio station, 25 local commercial, 19 Community/ Community of Interest and 1 special-interest radio station in Dublin. The remainder consist of hospital and college radio. The official Irish listenership figures for radio show that Radio 1 has lost its position as being the most popular Irish radio station in all parts of the country except Dublin.

The Irish radio advertising market has doubled in revenue between 1998 and 2004. The local radio market is still quite fragmented with 12 of the country's 28 radio stations currently under independent ownership. The other stations are owned by the UK companies Emap, Ulster Television (UTV) and Communicorp Group owned by Denis O'Brien, one of Ireland's leading entrepreneurs. Consolidation may not have been any more extensive due to ownership and the control restrictions set by Ireland's regulator the Broadcasting Commission of Ireland (BCI) that not more than 29 per cent of the shares in a radio station can be bought by another station or any other communications company without approval by the BCI. In 2006 the listener/radio enthusiast will find on any day of the year 50 or 60 pirate radio stations operating in different parts of the Republic.

At the end of 2005, there were approximately 568,500 subscribers to cable/MMDS television services in Ireland. The cable/MMDS market has seen a migration of customers from analogue to digital subscriptions, with digital subscribers now representing 38 per cent of cable/MMDS subscribers. In December 2005, BSkyB had 393,000 Irish subscribers, a 6 per cent increase in subscriptions for the quarter, and a 16 per cent increase in subscriptions year on year. The total number of pay-TV subscribers in Ireland (cable/MMDS and satellite) stood at almost 961,500 – 63 per cent of all pay-TV subscribers now subscribe to digital TV.

The Irish cable TV industry is at the end of a process of consolidation which has left most cable and MMDS franchises in the hands of two companies, NTL and Chorus. In 2005 the US company Liberty Global, already owner of Chorus, acquired NTL Ireland.

There is no digital audio broadcasting available in Ireland, but the regulator of the Broadcasting Commission of Ireland announced in early 2006 that it was studying the feasibility of the provision of digital radio for Ireland.

C. The Internet Media
Main features:

- Disgruntled licence applicants are now 'broadcasting' radio over the Net;
- Traditional media companies dominate;
- The legislative basis for any future developments in convergence is more or less in place.

According to the Irish telecommunications regulator, ComReg, Internet penetration has grown over the last five years, and at the end of June 2005 approximately 50 per cent of Ireland's population had home Internet access. The broadband market continues to grow strongly, to the extent that more than one-third of Internet users were using some form of broadband by the end of March 2006.

Streaming audio over the Internet is provided by some of the legal radio stations as well as by some private individuals. Web radio offers a way of broadcasting which is untouched by regulation and a few disgruntled licence applicants are now 'broadcasting over the Net'.

Of particular interest in the context of this chapter are the two portals of the 'traditional' media companies: *The Irish Times* portal, www.ireland.com, and the one of the public service broadcaster, RTE. Both these portals provide information that goes beyond their remits as a newspaper or a public service broadcaster. However, both portals have been loss-making since their inception.

The legislative basis for any future developments in convergence is more or less in place in that the technical regulations for all communication services are the responsibility of the telecommunications regulator ComReg and the content regulations are in the hands of the Broadcasting Commission of Ireland (BCI). The Broadcasting Act 2001 gives the BCI a range of functions that are usually held by separate state authorities such as the setting of broadcasting standards, the commissioning of research, responsibility for digital broadcasting, the setting of standards with respect to the transmission of information by any electronic means (other than by means of broadcasting) including by means of the Internet, etc.

D. News agencies

As there are no Irish news agencies, Irish media rely on the international news agencies and their own journalists for news-gathering. The public service broadcaster has its own extensive news department. The news on local radio is provided by INN (Independent Network News), a company established in 1997 by seventeen of the local radio stations.

2. State Policies

Main features:

- Even though Irish broadcasting is far more regulated than Irish newspaper publishing, the system of broadcast accountability is not as highly developed as in other countries;
- Broadcasting policy restricted itself to ensuring that Irish broadcasting services were the preferred option for Irish viewers and listeners;
- Concern with the dominance of the Independent Newspaper Group on the Irish market and the alleged below-cost selling of British newspapers in Ireland;
- A framework that includes the operation of digital terrestrial television;
- New Act defines the public service character of the broadcasting services of the RTE Authority.

Over the last few decades Ireland has not had any overall media policy that encompasses all mass media. Cultural and media policies were subsumed under industrial policy in general with its two pillars of attracting foreign investment in Irish industry and the encouragement of Irish exports. Broadcasting policy restricted itself to ensuring that Irish broadcasting services were the preferred option for Irish viewers and listeners.

Although the prime focus of media policy has been and is the broadcasting sector, the current and previous governments have also initiated some developments in the Irish newspaper industry. As mentioned in the previous section most of these are concerned with examining the dominance of the Independent Newspaper Group on the Irish market and the alleged below-cost selling of British newspapers in Ireland. .

The new Freedom of Information Act came into force in April 1998. This has enabled journalists to acquire previously 'secret' government information. Generally the Act's existence seems to have led to a greater openness on the part of state organizations and the civil service. However, that old remnant of Ireland past as a British colony, namely the Official Secrets Act, which designates as a secret any official information, has not been repealed.

With the implementation of the Broadcasting Act 2001 major changes have occurred in the Irish broadcasting sector. The Act is a major piece of legislation and sets out the legal framework for broadcasting in Ireland – a framework that includes the operation of digital terrestrial television (DTT).

The Act makes provisions for the establishment of a Digital Transmission Company which is designated by the Minister to transmit analogue and digital broadcast television services, including those of RTE, TG4 and TV3. This section of the Act has not been implemented. RTE was unable to find a buyer for its transmission network and there seems to have been a lack of financial resources and political will to develop an Irish digital television service. The digital television market is more or less in the hands of BskyB as outlined in a previous section of this paper.

However, today there does seem to be the political will to develop an Irish digital television service akin to BBC's Freeview and there is no shortage of financial resources. In May 2006 the Department of Communications commenced contacting TV stations about their ideas for an Irish digital television service. The Department has apparently issued a number of contracts to put in place the infrastructure for a pilot of a digital terrestrial television service expected to begin towards the end of 2006. One thousand set-top boxes will be distributed in the initial phase of the trial which is expected to last for two years. The plan is to have four multiplexes with each multiplex capable of carrying about eight channels. Commentators believe that this project may materialize because the Government rather than RTE is taking the lead role.

The Act also changes the name of the IRTC to the Broadcasting Commission of Ireland (BCI). The BCI is a new super broadcasting authority that will award the new digital content contracts and that will ultimately determine the content of the digital television channels not yet allocated to anybody. The BCI will draw up and monitor a code of broadcasting standards, when instructed to do so by the Minister. The BCI will also draw up codes or standards with respect to the transmission of information by any electronic means (other than by means of broadcasting) including by means of the Internet.

For the first time in Irish broadcasting law the Act defines the public service character of the broadcasting services of the RTE Authority. The Act increases the amount of money that RTE has to spend on programmes commissioned from the independent production sector and the RTE has had to give increasing justification for its programming spending and is subject to detailed checks by accountancy firms.

The Act establishes a new and separate broadcasting authority, Teilifis na Gaeilge. The Act specifies that this new authority shall establish and maintain a national television broadcasting service (TG4 is not mentioned in the Act) which shall have the character of a public service.

Both RTE and the BCI, the Broadcasting Commission of Ireland, have internal guidelines approved by the relevant government minister. The members of the public can lodge any complaints they may have about broadcast programmes with the Broadcasting Complaints Commission which then adjudicates about the claim. Traditionally the commission had no full-time staff and its powers were quite limited in that it could only enforce the right to reply as set out in the relevant broadcasting laws. This has now changed with the enactment of the Broadcasting Act 2001 as outlined above. The public service broadcaster is ultimately accountable to the Dáil, the Irish Parliament.

Finally all media in Ireland are subject to numerous statutes such as Contempt of Court, Censorship, Copyright, Official Secrets Act, Public Order, etc.

3. Civil Society Organizations
Main features:

■ Numerous employers and employees associations
■ Specialized audience research agencies

The two main employer organizations for the press are the National Newspapers of Ireland (NNI) and the Provincial Newspaper Association of Ireland (PNAI). The main trade unions are the National Union of Journalists (NUJ) for print and broadcast journalists, SIPTU (Services Industrial Professional Technical Union) for technical staff in print and broadcasting. Other professional organizations of note are the Professional Photographers Association of Ireland (PTAI), the Joint National Readership Research (JNRR) – national readership figures for newspapers and magazines as well as for cinema attendances, the Joint National Listenership Research (JNLR) – national listenership figures for radio, AC Nielson for television audience measurement, Audit Bureau of Circulation for newspaper and magazine circulation figures.

The main Advertising association is the Institute of Advertising Practitioners in Ireland (IAPI). The main audience 'group' is RTE's Audience Council.

4. Development Trends
Main features:

- The establishment of a single content regulator for all commercial, community and public service broadcasters
- Introduction of a privacy bill and a defamation bill
- A Press Council is to be set up

In autumn 2006 the Government flagged its intention to introduce a further change in Irish broadcasting law, namely the enactment of a wide-ranging Broadcasting Act with a number of key features. It will establish a single content regulator for all commercial, community and public service broadcasters in Ireland, to be known as the Broadcasting Authority of Ireland, and the public service broadcasters RTE and TG4 will be established as limited companies.

In December 2006 the Government introduced to the Dáil the Broadcasting (Amendment) Bill 2006 which seeks to establish a framework for the introduction of digital terrestrial television to Ireland. Currently, the only digital television in Ireland is that provided by BskyB.

Other measures announced by the Government include the privacy bill and a defamation bill. According to press reports the new privacy Bill will create a specific offence of violating the privacy of the individual. The necessity for this arose from a decision of the European Court of Human Rights, in a case taken by Princess Caroline of Monaco, that all persons are entitled to a personal sphere of privacy.

Only time will tell whether the enactment of this legislation will change the situation in Ireland where some newspapers have appointed internal ombudsmen about whose activities very little is known. The main way of dealing with complaints about the press is to go to court as can be witnessed by several libel actions over the last few years which resulted in the courts awarding substantial damages for libel.

Concerning the press there are traditionally few accountability provisions. This may change over the coming years in the light of the July 2006 announcement by the Government that a Press Council is to be set up. In fact, the Government announced a series of planned legislative changes that are of direct relevance to the Press: the first concerns the establishment of a Press Council which will cover only print and not broadcasting organizations. It is envisaged that the Press Council is an independent one and not set up by the Government. The majority of the council members will be drawn from civic society. The press council will have thirteen directors, seven representing the public interest, five representing the interests of owners and publishers and one representing the interests of journalists. The press council would appoint a press ombudsman to investigate complaints from those affected by breaches of standards. Remedial action where complaints are upheld will include the publication of the ombudsman's decisions, the publication of corrections of inaccurate facts, retractions or any such action as deemed appropriate.

References and Sources for Further Information

A useful source of information on Irish media is the Annual Yearbook of the Institute for Public Administration (IPA). Details of RTE activities can be found in the RTE Annual Reports, details of the private broadcasters in the IRTC/BCI Annual Reports. *The Irish Times* provides fairly detailed coverage of Irish media events. The relevant trade unions also publish material on media matters from time to time, as do RTE and the Independent Radio and Television Commission (IRTC/Broadcasting Commission of Ireland (BCI), the regulatory body for non-RTE broadcasting services. News on Irish films can be found in *Irish Film*, a regular monthly publication, news on Ireland's Broadcasting and Production Industry is detailed in the journal *Inproduction*. *Irish Communications Review*, published by the Dublin Institute of Technology is a more academic publication on media matters.

Extensive information on Ireland's media can be found on the following Irish websites: (links are live at time of writing)

National Newspapers of Ireland: http://www.nni.ie
The Irish Times: http://www.ireland.com/
Independent Newspapers portal: http://www.independent.ie/
Publishers Association of Ireland: http://www.ppa.ie/
Radio Telefis Eireann: http://www.rte.ie/
Irish Film and Television Network: http://www.iftn.ie/
Irish Government: http://www.irlgov.ie/
Broadcasting Commission of Ireland: http://www.irtc.ie/
Irish telecoms regulator: http://www.odtr.ie/
Site for Irish media data: http://www.medialive.ie/
Irish-language television channel: http://www.tg4.ie/
Information Society Commission: http://www.infosocomm.ie (LINK DOESN'T WORK)
radiowaves.fm – http://radiowaves.fm/friday.shtml (LINK DOESN'T WORK)
Advertising Standards Authority of Ireland: http://www.asai.ie/

THE UNITED KINGDOM MEDIA LANDSCAPE

Michael Bromley

The media landscape in the United Kingdom is large, complex and mature, arguably ranking second globally to that of the USA. This status is derived to some extent from the use of English as the primary natural language of production and content. Although none of the major global media conglomerates is based in the UK, a number of media organizations, notably Reuters and the BBC, have international standing in their own right. UK activities also contribute significantly to the operations of global conglomerates, such as NewsCorp, Bertelsmann and Time Warner. A desire to be present in emerging global media markets led to increasing deregulation under both Conservative governments (1979–1997) and the Labour administrations of Tony Blair (1997 to 2007).

The UK media sector is relatively open, with participants from many countries active in almost all aspects – newspapers, television, magazines, radio, film, books, advertising, music and public relations. At the same time, UK media organizations have interests in many parts of the world. Since the late 1990s, successive Labour governments have attempted to elide the distinction between culture and commerce, leading to the adoption of the idea of the 'creative industries'. This has been accompanied by widespread and vociferous concerns about media quality.

It should be remembered that, while, in many respects, the UK media landscape is a single entity, there are distinctive English, Scottish, Irish and Welsh dimensions, reflecting the composition of the state itself, and heightened by devolution in the late 1990s. The UK's adult population numbers 47.5m.

1. The Market

A. The Print Media

Main features:

- The distinctive characteristic is a dominant national press based in London;
- Regional and local newspapers comprise 98 per cent of titles in circulation, however;
- Newspaper sales are generally declining and have been for more than 40 years;
- The magazine sector is large and expanding.

Perhaps the most distinguishing characteristic of the written press is the existence of a large national newspaper sector, comprised of ten daily and ten Sunday titles. Just over 80m such papers are sold every week, which are read by about 70 per cent of the adult population. In February 2006, the total sales of national newspapers were 11.25m daily and 12m on Sundays. These numbers were well below peaks reached in the late 1950s. The last half-century has been one of secular decline in national newspaper sales and readerships. Today no national newspaper sells 4m copies. The *Daily Mirror*, whose circulation peaked at 5.3m, now sells 1.65m. The *Daily Express*, which once sold 4.2m copies, currently circulates just over 800,000. The *News of the World* (8m) has a circulation of 3.6m. Even *The Sun*, the sales of which reached 4.2m as recently as 1988, has subsequently lost 25 per cent of its circulation.

There are considerable disparities in national newspaper circulations, however. Two – *The Sun* and the *News of the World* – have circulations above 3m, while the *Daily Mail* and the *Mail on Sunday* each sells more than 2m. The *Sunday Mirror*, *Sunday Times* and *Daily Mirror* all have sales of more than 1m. At the other end of the scale, the papers with the smallest circulations are *The Independent* (230,000) and *The Independent on Sunday* (211,000).

This press is commonly divided into three sectors – 'quality', 'middle market' and 'red-top tabloid'. For more than twenty years, all the papers in the latter two categories have been tabloid in size. More recently, three of the 'quality' titles abandoned the broadsheet format and adopted either a 'compact' (*The Independent* and *The Times*) or Berliner (*The Guardian*) size. This change stimulated much debate over whether the national press was abandoning 'serious' journalism in pursuit of popularity (see below).

The entire national newspaper press is owned by eight companies, of which the largest two (News International and Daily Mail and General Trust) had 55 per cent of market share in 2005. With Trinity Mirror (16%) and Northern and Shell (14.5%), the top four owners control 85 per cent of the market.

A similar concentration of ownership is evident in the regional and local press. The five largest owners control 72.5 per cent of the market – more than 700 newspapers. Of those, three (Trinity Mirror, Associated and Northcliffe) are also among the top four national newspaper companies. In sum, then, all forms of newspaper ownership are heavily concentrated in three corporations (News International, Trinity Mirror and Daily Mail and General Trust/Northcliffe/Associated), amounting to 360 titles (28 per cent of all newspapers in the UK), some of them the largest circulating in their sectors.

In 1974 there were 187 publishers who controlled only local weekly titles: in 2002, about 60 remained. At the beginning of the 1990s there were 200 recognized publishers of all types of regional and local newspapers. By 2003 the figure had more than halved to 96. Between 1985 and 2003, the number of titles fell by 22.5 per cent. Nevertheless, the sector remained quite diverse. Of the 96 proprietors, half (47) owned just one newspaper: two-thirds (63) controlled five titles or fewer. Only ten organizations owned twenty papers or more.

There are estimated to be 1,286 Sunday, week-day (morning and evening) and weekly (sometime, twice weekly) regional and local titles, further sub-divided between those papers which charge a cover price and those which are distributed for free. In all, around 40m copies of regional and local newspapers circulate and are read by about 84 per cent of the adult population. More than 90 per cent (1,176) circulate once (occasionally, twice) a week. Individual readerships are on the whole small: the largest selling local weekly newspaper (*Kent Messenger*) has a circulation of just over 55,000 copies. The most widely circulated weekly free sheet (*Manchester Metro News*) distributes some 310,000 copies.

The much smaller numbers of regional and local daily (27 morning and 75 evening) and Sunday (21) titles generally have larger circulations. This is the layer at which a distinctive press serving England, particularly London, Scotland, Wales and Northern Ireland exists. The biggest selling regional and local papers are published in Scotland. The partial exception is London where the only daily title, the *Evening Standard*, is the largest selling evening newspaper in the UK.

The regional and local press has suffered long-term decline. In the 1960s evening newspapers were read in nine out of ten households in their circulation areas. In 2006 many commentators believed they would soon cease to exist. Attempts to attract readers with alternative formats began in 1999 when Associated Newspapers (see above) launched the free commuter paper *Metro* in London. By 2003 total distributions of a series of *Metro* titles in British cities totalled 840,000, making it the world's largest free newspaper. In response, some paid-for papers, such as the *Evening Standard* and *Manchester Evening News*, started free 'lite' editions. In September 2006, News International (owned by NewsCorp) launched the free *London Paper* in competition with the *Standard*'s *London Lite*.

The UK magazine sector is also large and has been growing consistently for more than a decade. There are between 8,800 and 10,000 titles (estimates vary). About two-thirds are 'business and professional' titles, and the rest are 'consumer' magazines. The former often have very small, controlled circulations (mostly on subscription), while the 25 best-selling consumer titles have readerships of about one million or more. Neither the very biggest selling titles, nor most of the business and professional periodicals, are normally sold through news-stands. Nevertheless, the consumer magazines which are sold this way are the most visible part of the sector.

News-stand sales of about 300 consumer magazine titles account for around 100m copies each month. Only three magazines sold over the counter, *What's On TV* (1.7m), *Take a Break* and *TV Choice* (each 1.2m) are among the ten with the largest circulations. The others are 'customer' or 'member' magazines, produced for mainly free distribution as marketing tools. The five largest are published for subscribers to Sky Television, customers of the supermarket chain Asda and the pharmacy chain Boots, and members of the National Trust and the trade union Unison. Distributions range from 6.8m (*Sky The Magazine*) to 1.5m (*U*).

Although there are almost 1,000 magazine publishers, as with the newspaper industry, there are also heavy concentrations of ownership. Only 25 are considered to be major players. IPC Media, owned by Time Warner, has claimed that its titles are read by more than 60 per cent of UK adults. However, in a sector where regeneration appears to be endemic, there is more room for smaller publishers, and since the late 1990s the larger companies have been reducing their relative shares of the market. Unlike the newspaper industry, the magazine sector has a number of major European owners, such as H Bauer and Hachette Filipacchi.

Finally, it is worth noting that there are substantial 'minority' and 'alternative' press sectors in the UK. These address a wide range of cultural, ethnic, linguistic, religious, lifestyle, political, environmental and social areas. The press as a whole receives about 52 per cent of advertising revenues. The local and regional press takes 20 per cent; the national press 13 per cent; magazines 12 per cent and directories 7 per cent.

B. The Broadcast Media
Main features:

- The BBC, financed through a universal licence fee, is a major force in both radio and television;
- The public service ethos remains strong;
- Multi-channel and multi-platform delivery and use are widespread;
- Audience fragmentation is commonplace in a 400–500 channel environment;
- Television is leading the 'dash to digital' with 17m homes connected;
- Uptake of digital audio broadcasting in radio is far less widespread;
- Analogue television is due to cease in 2012 and analogue radio in 2014.

The UK's audio-visual media also have a major defining characteristic – the existence of a strong public service broadcaster, the BBC. Supported by a universal compulsory television licensing fee, the BBC emerged from the assault on public service broadcasting in the 1980s and early 1990s arguably in a more, rather than less, commanding position. In part, this has been achieved by the strategic adoption of commercial enterprise, allied to the embrace of digitalization and the opportunities presented by multi-channelling. The BBC has added to its two national terrestrial free-to-air television channels (with national and regional sub-divisions) a range of other channels delivered through cable and digital set-top boxes – a rolling news channel; two children's channels and a number of specialist channels. In all, the BBC operates fourteen television channels. It also has an interactive TV set-up and a datacast operation, Ceefax.

In addition, the BBC operates five national radio stations, four of which were among the five most listened to national stations in the country in 2005; another five digital-only stations; the World Service; regional stations in Scotland, Wales and Northern Ireland (including stations broadcasting in Welsh and Scots), and 30 local stations. The BBC holds one of two national digital multiplex licences. Largely designed to service television and radio, the BBC's news-gathering operation is said to be the largest in the world. The Corporation also has significant arts, current affairs, documentary, education, sport, drama and entertainment departments.

However, the BBC is a quadro-media entity. BBC Worldwide publishes a raft of magazines (see above), and the website bbc.co.uk attracted 22.8m unique British users a month in 2004. Many of these activities are commercial, and there have been concerns about how the nearly £3bn (about €4.5) of public money raised for the BBC through the licence fee has been used in relation to such activities, and their impact on commercial competitors (see below).

All in all, BBC television attracts about a third of the total TV audience. That figure has fallen from 51 per cent in 1981 when the only competition was the commercial television Channel 3 (ITV). In 1990, prior to the introduction of cable and satellite services, the BBC's share was 47 per cent. In 1996, before the introduction of Channel Five, it was 45 per cent. However, the fragmentation of audiences as a result of multi-channelling has impacted on ITV even more. Its share of the national TV audience has fallen over 25 years from 49 per cent to 21.5 per cent.

Partly as a result, ITV (now called ITV 1: ITV 2 and 3 are cable/satellite channels) has undergone fundamental restructure. Originally based on a network of regional stations, it is now largely owned by a single London-based company. Only three regional operators continue to exist. The main problem for ITV 1 has been the dilution of the commercial television audience across multiple channels. The two other terrestrial free-to-air channels, Channel 4 (a hybrid public service-commercial entity created in 1982 to foster innovation and diversity, with a Welsh-language version, S4C) and the commercial Channel Five (created in 1997), have small audience shares of 10 per cent and 6.5 per cent respectively.

The big gains in audience share have been made by a range of channels received in both analogue and digital form through satellite, set-top box, cable and broadband on both free and pay-to-view bases. When audiences for such channels were first measured in 1991, they represented just 4 per cent of viewing: by 2005, that figure had risen to 30 per cent – second only to the BBC's viewerships. Around 70 per cent of UK households have access to multi-channel television.

About 400 channels are available. BSkyB, controlled by NewsCorp, is the major satellite provider with around 8m homes connected. NTL-Telewest provides cable services to about 3m homes. Freeview, a set-top box system jointly owned by the BBC, BSkyB and Crown Castle, reaches 5m homes. Sky operates 26 channels of its own, including nine movie channels and five sports channels. Others available include those from the BBC and ITV (mentioned above) and Channels 4 and Five, plus global offerings such as Cartoon Network, CNN, Discovery, DW-TV, Fox News, MTV, Nickelodeon, TCM and VH1.

Radio is also characterized by a multi-faceted commercial presence alongside that of the BBC, and by fragmentation. Once an issue only of AM and FM, radio services are now provided as well via Freeview (see above), DAB, cable, satellite, mobile telephony and the Internet. About 300 commercial radio stations broadcast across these platforms, the vast majority being local. The major national commercial radio station is Classic FM, reaching more than 6m people (compared to 13m and 10m for BBC Radio 2 and Radio 1). On the other hand, the reach of local commercial radio is about two and a half times that of local BBC services.

Community radio has been traditionally weak in the UK. However, in 2005 the government initiated an attempt to persuade the hundreds of 'pirate' stations which broadcast illegally to convert into legitimate not-for-profit stations by offering five-year licences and start-up money. The difficulty for community radio lies in the commercial interests of mainstream providers. Radio advertising revenues have always been relatively small, and commercial viability has been seen as coming from the conglomeration of stations, some into networks. The sector is dominated by a few large companies which own many local stations.

Independent production has grown significantly in recent years, since the imposition of a minimum quota of 25 per cent of domestic television output. In 2005, the BBC decided that it would increase that to 50 per cent. Independents produce many of the most popular programmes, and some showpieces, such as coverage of Wimbledon and the Olympics. Together, the audio-visual media receive about 31 per cent of total advertising spend – television 26 per cent; radio 4 per cent and the cinema 1 per cent.

Like most mature media landscapes, the UK is beginning to be dominated by digital services. These have been led by television. Since its introduction in 1998, digital television has expanded to 17m homes. This is the point at which most people will confront digital services. Analogue TV signals are due to be switched off from 2008, a process which will see the end of analogue television in 2012. It is being directed by the not-for-profit Digital UK body. A survey published in 2006 found that television was still the most popular medium among all UK people, with the average person watching three hours and 54 minutes a day during the working week – three times the time they spent listening to radio.

As has already been noted, digital radio has expanded, too, since its beginnings in 1999. By the end of 2005 there were estimated to be more than two million digital receivers in use. In addition, listeners access radio through digital television set-top boxes and broadband connections. A projected switch-off for analogue signals has been mooted for 2014.

Alongside television, mobile devices are driving digitalization. 3G mobile telephones, MP3 players and personal digital assistants, offering opportunities for downloading TV and radio programming, as well as music; taking still and moving pictures, and receiving and sending e-mail, are almost ubiquitous. Tapping into this development, media provide both downloadable and 'push' content to mobile phones and facilities for uploading user generated content (ugc). The BBC has taken a lead in these areas, but even local newspapers are hosting facilities for blogging, citizen journalism, Podcasting, video and audio streaming and live forums.

C. The Internet Media
Main features:

■ All significant media have online presences;
■ Two of the world's online media leaders are *The Guardian* and the BBC;
■ In 2005 the UK was the fastest growing market for broadband connections;
■ Government policy is for every home in the UK to have online access by 2010.

All the major UK media have online presences, a trend started in 1994 with the *Electronic Telegraph* followed by *Guardian Unlimited*, whose site has made the paper the most widely read in the world. More than 90 per cent of regional and local newspapers have websites. *BBC Online* is one of the world's most visited sites. The more popular media (the tabloid press and commercial broadcasters) were slower to go online. In many instances, such websites mainly repurpose material.

BBC Online has almost 10m unique users and *Guardian Unlimited* more than a million. Both are clusters of websites: at one time, the BBC ran up to 20,000. Other news sites run by the media and accessed regularly in the UK include sky.com; cnn.com; timesonline. co.uk; ft.com; and thesun.co.uk. Some of these sites have established large global audiences, as evidenced during the invasion of Iraq in 2003, when both *BBC Online* and *Guardian Unlimited* emerged as the news sites of choice among many Americans. The conflict in Iraq also helped popularize blogging through the postings of Salam Pax at blogspot.com. Since then blogging has become a feature of many media websites, from *Guardian Unlimited* to the *Carlisle News and Star*. The BBC is a recognized world leader in facilitating ugc through its web pages.

The mainstream news media share their popularity, however, with other online providers of news, including Yahoo!, Google and Ananova. There is also a number of web-only publishers, such as Handbag.com, MyVillage and Upmystreet.com. Some news media collaborate with non-media organizations in web ventures. These include the *ic* (Trinity Mirror) and *Thisis* (Newsquest) series of locally focused sites.

On a grander scale; having bought the community and networking site *MySpace*, NewsCorp plans to link in one of its UK properties, *The Sun* newspaper, to create a *MySun* online readers' network, while Microsoft's MSN.co.uk is collaborating with the mobile telephone provider 3 to give bloggers access to mobile TV and video sharing, as well as access to *SeeMeTV*, which pays for ugc.

In 2005 the UK was identified as the fastest growing market for broadband services. At the beginning of 2006 13.9m UK households (57%) had Internet access, of which 69 per cent were broadband. Broadband was available through satellite (Sky) and cable (NTL and Telewest) television, as well as both fixed and mobile telephones. In total, there were more than 7m broadband connections – most using telephone lines. A further 10 million connections were using dial-up. Nevertheless, 38 per cent of people do not have Internet access, and on average Britons spend only 48 minutes a day online during the working week. (By comparison, in 2004 they sent 25bn text messages.) It is government policy that every home in the UK will have access to online services by 2010. The Internet as a whole takes about 5 per cent of total media advertising revenues.

C. News agencies

London is a major global communications hub, and many news and picture agencies, working for all media, are located there. It is the world headquarters of Reuters, and a base for a number of other international agencies, including AFX, APTN and Getty Images. Pacemaker, which has an international reputation chiefly for photography, is based in Northern Ireland. Among the international agencies operating London bureaux are Agence France-Presse; Agencia EFE; AP; Bloomberg; Dow Jones; DPA; IRNA; ITAR-Tass; and Xinhua. The national agency is the Press Association (PA), based in London and with offices in Birmingham, Liverpool and Glasgow. There are more than 100 local agencies, supplying mainly the UK media. The National Association of Press Agencies is the industry body. In addition, many journalists work as freelancers.

2. State Policies

Main features:

- The UK identifies the media as part of a wider creative industries sector;
- The future of public service within an increasingly commercialized media is a matter of debate;

- Liberalization of media environments has been accompanied by partial deregulation;
- Voluntary and statutory accountability systems co-exist;
- The general law plays an important role in holding the media to account.

Two government departments – Culture, Media and Sport and Trade and Industry – cover the media. Together they have promoted the idea of the broader creative industries to capture in particular the potential of digital services to provide business opportunities and new forms of employment, especially in small and medium enterprises. However, it can be argued that the major beneficiaries of these media policies so far have been existing large media corporations.

The paradoxical situation is highlighted by the continuing commitment to a large public service broadcaster, the BBC, which has also vigorously pursued a strategy of commercialization and digitalization. While the BBC is the UK's most enthusiastic large-scale media innovator, a significant exporter and a provider of highly popular content and services, it is said by many to distort the market. Questions have also been raised about the separation of publicly funded and commercial activities. At the heart of this debate is the question of what constitutes 'public service' and whether it has a role any longer in the media.

In 2003 a complex system of media regulation and oversight was partially rationalized through the creation of Ofcom to police broadcasting and telecommunications (replacing five separate bodies). This heralded a 'lighter touch' statutory regulation (for example, prohibitions on cross-media ownership were relaxed); however, controls over content were strengthened. This aspect of Ofcom's work also applied for the first time to the BBC. Otherwise, the Corporation is responsible to its own board, and ultimately parliament. The Internet also lies outside the remit of Ofcom.

For the past century the UK has had two main formal accountability systems – voluntary and statutory. Crudely, voluntary regulation occurred in commercial environments (the press) and statutory controls existed where there was a significant public interest dimension (broadcasting). This arrangement reflected the supply side of media: entry into the press market was supposedly open – anyone could start a newspaper without the need for a licence. However, broadcast spectrum was scarce and considered a national asset, and governments authorized radio and television stations. In the 1980s and 1990s many broadcasters complained that statutory regulation was stifling free expression, while others dismissed voluntary regulation of the press as ineffectual. Moreover, convergence and cross-platform media eroded the distinctions between the press and broadcasting, and provided new regulatory challenges.

The press – newspapers and magazines – operate the voluntary Press Complaints Commission. The National Union of Journalists (NUJ) has had a code of ethics since 1936, but its Ethics Council is largely moribund. The Advertising Standards Authority operates a voluntary scheme for the press, but broadcast advertising is overseen by Ofcom.

Behind these forms of regulation lies the law. It is estimated that more than 140 pieces of legislation have direct relevance to the media, and litigation is a favoured method (among those who can afford it) of bringing the media to account. Privacy was not recognized as such in UK law; however, cases could be brought for breaches of confidentiality. Freedom of expression is protected under the 1998 Human Rights Act which enacted into UK law the European Convention on Human Rights, and a Freedom of Information Act came into force in 2005. The 1998 Act also introduced privacy as a statutory right.

3. Civil Society Organizations
Main features:

- The most prominent organizations represent media owners and operators;
- Trade unions and professional bodies represent media workers;
- Many organizations provide specialist services to the media;
- External 'watchdog' bodies are an important element.

There is a plethora of organizations representing every facet of media activity. The most prominent ones represent media owners and operators, including online (British Internet Publishers Alliance, Internet Service Providers Association); radio (Commercial Radio Companies Association); magazines (Periodical Publishers Association); books (Publishers Association); and newspapers (Newspaper Society – regional and local press, Scottish Newspaper Publishers Association, Scottish Print Employers Federation and Scottish Daily Newspaper Society). The Producers' Alliance for Cinema and Television (PACT) represents independent producers.

Media professionals' and employees' groups include trade unions (Broadcasting, Entertainment, Cinematograph and Theatre Union, National Union of Journalists) and specialized bodies (Broadcasting Press Guild, British Academy of Film and Television Arts, British Society of Magazine Editors, Chartered Institute of Journalists, Guild of Editors, Royal Television Society, The Radio Academy, Society of Editors). A number of organizations provide specialist services, including the Audit Bureau of Circulations, Broadcasters' Audience Research Board, Booktrust, British Copyright Council, Joint Industry Committee for Regional Press Readerships, National Readership Surveys and Radio Joint Audience Research.

A number of international media organizations have main offices in the UK – Article XIX, Association for International Broadcasting, Institute for War and Peace Reporting, International Communications Forum, International Federation of the Periodical Press, International Institute of Communications, International Press Institute, International Public Relations Association, InterWorld Radio and Panos London.

Perhaps because of dissatisfaction with, and the uncertainties of, formal accountability systems, there are several informal accountability activities. The trade press (notably, *Press Gazette*) occasionally performs this role: both the NUJ and the Chartered Institute of Journalists publish journals, and there is the *British Journalism Review*. *The Guardian* publishes a weekly 'Media' supplement (on Mondays). Insiders are generally less prominent than outsiders, however. Organizations which seek to explore media issues include the MediaWise Trust (ethics), Campaign for Press and Broadcasting Freedom, Campaign for Freedom of Information, the Runnymede Trust (diversity) and the London International Research Exchange.

4. Development Trends
Main features:

- The UK media are an important global entity;
- Younger audiences are turning away from 'big' media and prefer niche digital services;
- The future of the BBC as a publicly funded, public service is in doubt;
- There is a lively debate about the quality and role of journalism.

As has already been alluded to, the main thrust of policy since the 1980s has been to protect and enhance the UK's position as a significant global media producer. This has meant accepting increasing commercialization and conglomeration; liberalization and de-regulation, and even oligopoly and monopoly. It is argued that these trends are countered by the possibilities of digitalization in multiplying the numbers of services and increasing consumer choice. Investment in 'big' media is threatened, it is argued, by the fragmentation of audiences; but an environment of many 'small' media is not sustainable. Multiple channels and platforms increase risks to investors and encourage user promiscuity. Smaller entities, unable to exploit global markets or to venture in to new areas, are seen as being vulnerable. Thus, recent UK governments have attempted to bolster national media against competition from overseas predators. At the same time, it has been accepted that the biggest media are not national but global and governed primarily by the market. At the same time, while the development of 'new' media has been fostered, digitalization has threatened the considerable historical investment in mainstream analogue media. In particular, the drift of young consumers away from analogue 'big' media is accelerating. Media policies have largely sought to strike a balance between these competing demands.

This approach has been increasingly difficult to maintain, however, as changes in the media became more fundamental, affecting business models and behaviour. Key questions posed by a 'Changing media summit', organized by *Media Guardian* in 2006, were the impact of user-generated media, the demise of the advertising-based revenue model, the role of social media and marketing to 18 to 25 year olds, the so-called Generation Y. Such macro concerns reflected the accelerating shift from analogue, broadcast 'big' media to digital, narrowcast 'grass-roots' media; from one-to-many to peer-to-peer models and from distributed to aggregated audiences. Two aspects of this broader debate had specific resonance for the UK.

The first concerned the future of the BBC. Its Royal charter, which forms the basis of the Corporation's existence, was to be renewed for a further ten years at the end of 2006. The government required 'a step change in the way the BBC is run and held to account'. It laid out terms for the decade up to 2016 which included a new trust to oversee the Corporation and to call it to account; a 'public value test' to be applied to all new services; and assessments of the impact of BBC activities on the wider media market. Most crucially, it seemed that the licence fee might be abolished after 2016. The unanswered question was whether the BBC would then continue as a publicly funded national body or become a commercial media entity.

The second concern was about the quality of journalism. The editor of the *Financial Times Magazine*, John Lloyd, accused journalists of failing to serve the public. Taking up the theme, *The Guardian* solicited and published the views of 50 non-journalists on the inadequacies of journalism. This came at a time when the Hutton inquiry, into the way in which intelligence on Iraq had been reported, had been highly critical of the standards of journalism at the BBC. In 2006 the Reuters Institute donated £5 (about €7.5m) to establish an institute for the study of journalism at Oxford University in an attempt to raise standards. Fears, evident since the 1980s, that the media were 'dumbing down' to try reduce costs and offer new 'lite' content, as their audiences threatened to fragment and migrate to new niche digital formats, and government policy encouraged the transformation from national information-based to global entertainment-focused entities, were augmented by a belief that, far from resisting such trends, many media 'professionals' had colluded in them to serve their own interests. The public, it was said, was no longer getting the media it deserved.

Finally, while these issues questioned the robustness of the 'watchdog' role of the media, this traditional function appeared to be directly challenged by governmental responses to terrorism, especially the Terrorism Act 2006 which followed bombings in London in July 2005. The law prohibits 'terrorist publication' and the 'glorification of terrorism'. The International Press Institute felt this represented 'a noticeable sea change in terms of the balance between…press freedom, and security'. The International Federation of Journalists said the law was 'chilling…the exercise of journalism' and making 'a nonsense of the country's great tradition of free speech'.

References and Sources for Further Information

The hard copy starting point for research is the annual *Media Directory* published by *The Guardian*. There are several publications directed at trade and technical audiences. Historical and contemporary directories are held in the British Library Newspaper Library at Colindale, north London. Accessible journals include: the *British Journal of Photography*, *British Journalism Review*, *Free Press* (published by the Campaign for Press and Broadcasting Freedom); *Press Gazette*; *Broadcasting*; and *Campaign*. *The Guardian* has a weekly media supplement and an associated website, www.mediaguardian.co.uk. All the main media and media organizations maintain websites.

THE NORTHERN EUROPEAN/ DEMOCRATIC CORPORATIST MEDIA MODEL COUNTRIES

INTRODUCTION

Lennart Weibull

Eleven countries here represent what Daniel Hallin and Paolo Mancini (2004:143ff) have proposed as the Democratic Corporatist media model. They are countries of northern and, to some extent, central Europe: the Nordic countries Denmark, Finland, Iceland, Norway and Sweden, Germany, Austria and Switzerland as well as Belgium, Luxembourg and the Netherlands. They are all strongly urbanized and most of them have a long industrial tradition. However, they differ significantly in size – from 90 million inhabitants in Germany to less than half a million in Iceland – and in their cultural and political heritage.

Cultural and Political Heritage
To a large extent the eleven countries are part of a common history and culture. Germanic languages – German, Dutch, Swedish, Danish, Norwegian and Icelandic – are spoken in most of the countries, denoting the common roots. However, Roman languages – French and Italian – coexist in the south as national languages in Belgium and Switzerland. Finnish, the national language of Finland, is part of the Fenno–Ugrian language family with no relation to most other European languages. Moreover, there are a few important language minorities. In all countries, another Germanic language, English, serves as a lingua franca, normally taught from early school years.

The language similarities indicate the intense social contacts between the countries. The Nordic countries for centuries were depending on German culture as the main link to continental Europe. The tradition was broken up after the Second World War and replaced by a strong Anglo-Saxon influence. The close interaction between the countries was reinforced by the fact that they were small and a lot of trade ways crossed the country borders. A typical example is the old Hanseatic League, which in the sixteenth and seventeenth encompassed trading cities in most of the eleven countries of today, e.g. Bergen (Norway), Brügge (Belgium), Lübeck (Germany) and Kalmar (Sweden). Trade also meant a fast dissemination of new ideas and contributing to the establishment of similar political, cultural and legal models. The rise of the first German Reich in the mid-nineteenth century meant the rise of one very strong country, but gradually also the minor nation states gradually increased cooperation, e.g. in the Benelux and the Nordic areas.

Probably the single most important factor in bringing the northern countries together was the Lutheran challenge to the Roman Catholic Church in early-sixteenth-century Germany, followed by other reformers in especially Switzerland. Even though this meant, for more than a century, religious warfare, it gradually changed the perspective on society. Also, in countries where the Roman Catholic Church came back to power, like in Austria, Belgium and southern Germany, the new liberal ideas had an influence on political and cultural life. The authoritarian power structure had been challenged and new bodies had been established, fostering a basic political tolerance. Further, in the countries, where reformation meant that the Bible was translated into the national languages, ability in reading was increasingly regarded as an important factor in the national development.

Of course, the development of coexistence in the north did not take place without conflict. Not only religious wars but also political rivalry characterized the eighteenth and nineteenth centuries. Within the Nordic countries, Denmark and Sweden fought for European influence, where Prussia and Austria were the main combatants. After the Napoleonic wars the patterns of conflict changed, first through the two world wars, later by the openness to Anglo-Saxon culture.

The common northern European tradition can be found not only in a common culture but also in politics and economy. Political democracy was established in the early twentieth century, with the exception of Austria and Germany. Most of the countries are oriented to consensus politics, based on what Hallin and Mancini call a moderate pluralism (Hallin and Mancini 2004: 68), which in practice means a high level of political stability based on strong parties with long tradition. One extreme is Switzerland with an almost permanent coalition government, whereas all other countries have a traditional parliamentary system. In most countries there is a clear left-right dimension in party structure, but even though political majorities may change, large differences in actual politics are less frequent.

Most of the countries have strongly backed the idea of free trade, and even if some of the countries, e.g. Denmark, Norway, Sweden and Switzerland, for political reasons, originally were reluctant to join the European Union, they created the EFTA as free trade association. Today most of the countries have a GNP per capita, which is clearly over the average of Europe. All countries are characterized by a market economy and are traditionally strong welfare states. In most countries there is also a significant involvement of the state in the economy and a large public sector.

The legislative and governmental bodies are generally respected, expressing the strength of the rational-legal authority: The state has normally been regarded as the guardian of freedom and justice as well a guarantor of the welfare state, even though public trust has declined in the latest decades in almost all Democratic Corporatist countries.

Even if the basic principles of the Democratic Corporatist model form the basis of the tradition of the eleven states, it does not mean that they are a totally homogeneous group of states. There are obvious differences within some of the countries, but in most of the areas presented above they represent a common perspective, which makes them different from countries in eastern and southern Europe, but also from the United Kingdom.

Democratic Corporatism in the Northern European Media Systems

The common tradition of the northern European countries in politics, economy and culture is also reflected in their media systems. Daniel Hallin and Paolo Mancini (2004: 144f) point out three so-called coexistences between media and politics, which they regard as distinctive to the Democratic Corporatist countries:

The first is the high degree of political parallelism between the development of the mass press and party political development, meaning that newspaper development has reflected political, cultural and social divisions of society.

The second coexistence is that the political parallelism in media development has coexisted with a high degree of journalistic professionalization, meaning the existence of independent media that report political events according to professional standards.

The third coexistence has to do with relations between the state and the media, which on one hand has meant an early introduction of press freedom (from the state) in most of the countries, but on the other hand means an acceptance of state activities in the media sphere.

The eleven chapters on the media systems of the individual Democratic Corporatist countries shall be read in the light of a theoretical approach. Some of the main tendencies will be summarized under headings, which are taken from the overview by Hallin and Mancini (2004: 67).

The Newspaper Industry

The cradle of the world's newspaper industry stood within the Democratic Corporatist countries. The first papers were published at the central European trade centres of the early seventeenth century, but before the end of the century, also, the first newspapers of the Nordic countries had been established. Also, the roots of the modern mass press can be found in the same area. The mass press developed during the mid-nineteenth and the early years of the twentieth centuries. The first wave of the modern commercial press aimed at industrialists, merchants and intellectuals, who were the main actors of the developing industrial society.

Press freedom was established early, Sweden already in 1766, finalized in 1812, Norway in 1814, the Netherlands in 1815, Belgium in 1831 and Denmark in 1848. In the early twentieth century newspaper readership increased in the working classes, especially in the Nordic countries, with the introduction of cheaper papers.

Today we find most of the countries of the Democratic Corporatist media tradition on the top of the ranking of the most newspaper-buying countries of the world. Norway, Finland and Sweden show the highest figures with between 651 and 489 copies sold per 1000 adults. The other countries of the group range between 300 and 400 copies. Belgium is the sole example, ranks fairly low with only about 170 copies sold, which places it close to the Pluralist Polarized media tradition.

The basic pattern is the same for regular reading, where the percentage of newspaper readers on an average day exceeds 80. In the other countries the figures are around 70 and in Belgium 50 per cent. In the Nordic countries the newspaper market is somewhat stronger in terms of exposure. In spite of the strong tradition of paid newspapers, free dailies have in recent years developed very strongly in most of the countries, especially in Iceland, Sweden and Denmark.

Political Parallelism

The expansion of the daily press coincided in most countries with increased democracy. Especially the liberal press played an important role in pushing political liberties forward. Most newspapers became gradually affiliated to political parties, and in the early twentieth century a strong party press developed, even if conditions differed between the countries. In the Nordic countries a socialist press developed in the first decades of the new century, whereas it was forbidden in Germany because of the authoritarian legislation. In the middle of the century there were national newspapers representing all the major parties as well as other social and religious groups. In Denmark, and partly also in the other Nordic countries, this was true also on the regional and local level. There are reasons to believe that this presence of a broad partisan press, called segmented pluralism by Hallin and Mancini (2004:152f), fostered citizens as newspaper readers, hence, contributing to the high level of Nordic readership in all social groups. In Austria and Germany the Nazi regime took political control of newspapers, but after the Second World War the partisan character of the press was re-established.

The parallelism between political and social groups on one hand and the newspaper industry on the other took different forms both within and between the Democratic Corporatist countries. Generally, conservative and liberal papers were privately owned, whereas socialist and communist papers, at least to a large extent, had party ownership. Editors of most papers also had party political positions or represented the parties in political bodies. During the first half of the twentieth century the traditional political press met competition from popular newspapers starting by a new type of private entrepreneurs. These were more popular in presentation, even though they did not leave out politics and even could have a clear party affiliation.

Characteristic for the political parallelism of the modern press was that in Democratic Corporatist countries it seems to have contributed to the high prestige of the press. Newspapers, even if partisan in coverage, were often regarded as an integrated part of political democracy and reading was a kind of political participation. Even when newspapers changed character in the second half of the twentieth century, and many party political papers had to close down, the tradition was still existent, the most obvious example of this tradition being Luxembourg where a strong party press tradition still characterizes the newspaper market.

The State and the Media
One reason for the general acceptance of the party political press in the Democratic Corporatist countries was to a large extent a general trust in politics and political bodies. The state was not seen as an enemy of the media. In Denmark the prime minister has traditionally been responsible for the press and regarded as the main guardian of free media. Typical is that direct state subsidies to the press exist in all countries with the exception of Germany and Austria. Although they sometimes have been principally debated, there has normally been consensus in practice. The subsidies have mainly contributed to maintain a certain level of pluralism in the newspaper market, even though papers gaining support normally have only a small circulation. The state support is normally given according to neutral rules, based in market economy principles, and does not strongly affect the basic market mechanisms. It is important to add that the state subsidies are not perceived to have any impact on journalism practice.

The important role of the state in the Democratic Corporatist countries is most obvious in the area of radio and television. In all the countries public service television is very strong. As is pointed out by Hallin and Mancini (2004:164), public service radio was developed almost as a parallel to the extension of the welfare state, as *res publica*, almost as an enlightenment programme. In most countries the state dominance, especially from the 1930s when the state replaced local private stations by state-controlled broadcasting, met little criticism. Most of the public service organizations were modelled after the BBC, but the organizational structures differed a lot between the countries. On one hand we have the pillarization of Dutch broadcasting, on the other public service as a government agency, as in Denmark; Finland being a special case, since it was opened up for a commercial company to broadcast in the state television within certain timeframes. The common denominator has been to organize radio and television as an independent organization with internal pluralism, guaranteed by the state – even though the Dutch solution might be more of external pluralism. In most of the governing bodies leading, there are representatives of important political and social groups, but programming is normally left to the professionals of the organizations.

The Broadcast Industry
The use of radio and television has traditionally been lower in the north of Europe than in the south. The Nordic countries have among the lowest figures in Europe on television viewing time compared with the figures for newspaper reading. This seems to

reflect the reading tradition of the Democratic Corporatist countries. Also, the strong profile on news and current affairs in the public service channels, both in radio and television, might reflect the same tradition.

During the 1980s, however, the Democratic Corporatist countries gradually opened up for competition from private broadcasters, mostly both in radio and television. Private radio was originally established mostly on the local level, often as illegal or semi-illegal stations as in Belgium or Sweden, or as community radio as in Norway. When formally accepted they normally created national networks based on the local stations for programming as well as for advertising. Luxembourg differs somewhat because here monopoly was granted a commercial radio company – RTL – on a contractual basis.

The first country, besides Luxembourg, to accept private television was Germany in the mid-1980s, whereas Austria was among the latecomers in 2003 and Switzerland still has no nationwide commercial TV channel; however, in both Austria and Switzerland foreign private channels, broadcasting in the national languages, have an extensive reach, facilitated by cable transmission. Commercial television developed three types of channels: (1) Terrestrial channels by government concessions financed by advertising, (2) Satellite channels financed by advertising and (3) Satellite channels mainly financed by subscription fees. The reach of the latter two was originally depending on the high cable penetration in most of the eleven countries, especially in the Netherlands and Austria. The output of the private channels was mainly popular drama and entertainment shows. In this development Luxembourg media politics played an important role by granting RTL almost exclusivity for its international operations.

The private television sector has gradually expanded in most of the eleven countries. Germany hosts the biggest commercial TV systems with RTL and ProSieben/Sat1. The expansion has meant that public service television has gradually lost market shares. In most countries public service channels together have around 40 per cent of the viewing time or less. The only exception is the SRG/SSR in Switzerland with about two-thirds of the audience, the reason, of course, being that there is no competition from national private television. Since most of the countries have already started or at least decided to introduce digital television it is expected the fragmentation of television will go on. However, this has not changed the general picture in the public attitude to public service television. The public service radio and television has a strong standing among politicians in most of the countries. When it comes to news the audience also prefers public service channels and ranks them high in credibility, using the private channels mostly for entertainment.

Professionalization
The strong press of the Democratic Corporatist countries affected its standing in society. Newspapers and editors formed their own associations across the borders of the party political press. In Norway this development took place already in the late nineteenth century, in most others in the early twentieth century. Approximately in the same period, also, journalists organized themselves in professional organizations.

Most of these organizations became very strong, not least because their high rate of membership. Further, the organizations had close contacts with one another and in some countries there were professional press clubs where both editors and journalists could have membership.

One consequence of the organizational activities was the work on principles of good journalism practice. In most countries this soon developed into formalized systems of self-regulation of the press. Sweden has one of the oldest rules of good journalism practice, originally decided upon in 1916 and extended over the years. Press Councils have been established, normally by the newspaper industry and the journalist associations, to handle readers' complaints against the rules of good practice. The rules and the councils are normally well anchored in the media culture of the Democratic Corporatist countries. There are in most countries also rules for the inner freedom of media organizations, often called editorial statutes. In Norway there is a long tradition of written principles on the national level, whereas internal statutes play an important role also in Germany and the Netherlands.

Taken together these sets of professional organisations and rules form the basis of journalistic autonomy in news reporting, that is often called professionalization. Professionalization here means an independent, not partisan, journalism, where journalists perceive themselves as watchdogs. What might be surprising is that this type of journalistic autonomy has developed in countries with such a strong tradition in terms of party political press and strong public service radio and television. However, it seems to be a part of the Democratic Corporatist media culture to combine strength in the political reporting with active critical reporting.

Development Trends

Even though the political media tradition is very strong in the Democratic Corporatist part of Europe, there are many signs of change, mainly influenced by the Liberal model based in the United Kingdom and the United States. The most important change probably took place in the 1980s, when the monopoly of the public service broadcasting was broken and opened up for new commercial actors. However, it is important to bear in mind the eleven countries grouped as Democratic Corporatist are not homogeneous. For example, the Luxembourgian radio and television almost from its start was part of the Liberal media model. The francophone part of Belgium seems more to be a part of the Polarized Pluralist tradition than the Democratic Corporatist one, illustrating that the character of media systems probably is determined more by cultural traditions than by today's nation states.

However, considering the long-term trends it is obvious that the 1990s meant an increasing media competition, contribution to an increase in market orientation. On the newspaper market, the development of a number of new local newspaper monopolies also changed the character of the press, making it more 'selling' in layout and content. Economic indicators of media performance – market share or profit – became more important than the political influence, if they did not coincide. The market orientation of both press and broadcasting meant an establishment of new media companies, not seen before in most of the eleven countries. Commercially, the Nordic countries gradually developed into one media market, mainly dominated by a few main actors, one of those a US investment company. In media content the role of entertainment is increasing as does the role of the advertising market for the media development.

Another aspect of the commercialization of the media market is an increasing segmentation of the media audience. It is further strengthened by the fast development of Internet, which has especially rapid in the Democratic Corporatist countries, probably reinforced by the strong reading tradition. Internet use, with an enormous potential of sources and increasingly individual choices is a challenge for traditional media. Further, the fragmentation of media audience leaves little room for the political public sphere, traditionally guaranteed by the main newspapers and public service broadcasting. As Hallin and Mancini (2004: 251ff) put it, there is a general tendency of convergence between the different political media models.

However, when interpreting development trends in the Democratic Corporatist part of Europe during the latest decades, two things have to borne in mind. The first observation is that the changes are not only a matter of media development. These trends also reflect changes in politics in the Democratic Corporatist countries, the most important being the decline of traditional corporatism. New values, especially the strengthened individualization, have challenged the legitimacy of the corporate society. The tradition of rational-legal authority is clearly weakened. It is indicated by among other things a decline in public trust in government bodies.

The second observation is that, in spite of these changes, the Democratic Corporatist model must be said to have a strong standing in most of the eleven countries. It is true that newspaper readership is declining, but is still very high. It is also true that public broadcasting has lost substantially in audience shares, but it is equally true that it is strongly trusted among the citizens than other media sources. In some countries, among others the Netherlands the public trust in politics is even increasing. At the same time, Internet penetration has grown very fast. It has opened up for more media sources, which probably will reinforce the impact of the liberal model. But the tradition is strong, and the increased importance of free dailies still points in this direction. Hence, it might be too early to declare the Democratic Corporatist media model dead.

References

Gustafsson, Karl Erik, Weibull, Lennart (1997), Newspaper Readership – Structure and Development. *The European Journal of Communication Research* 3/1997.

Gustafsson, Karl Erik, Weibull, Lennart (2007), *Newspaper Consumption in Europe*. Brussels: European Newspaper Association.

Hallin, Daniel C. & Mancini, Paolo (2004), *Comparing Media Systems. Three Models of Media and Politics*. Cambridge: Cambridge University Press.

Weibull, Lennart (2005), Sverige i tidningsvärlden. In Bergström, A., Wadbring, I., Weibull, L. (eds.) *Nypressat. Ett kvartssekel med svenska dagstidningsläsare*. Göteborg: The Department of Journalism and Mass Communication, Göteborg University.

THE AUSTRIAN MEDIA LANDSCAPE

Josef Trappel

Magnitude and *power* characterize the Austrian media landscape. *Magnitude* relates to the relatively large size of the media compared to the smallish market of some 8.5 million people living in Austria. *Power* relates to the high degree of market concentration providing the dominating media actors with influence not only in their respective media markets but also in the political arena. Media policy in the public interest, therefore, is largely paralysed and vested interests manage remarkably well to define the rules of the game.

Austria is geographically located in the centre of Europe and is part of the German-language area. It shares borders with Germany, Italy, Switzerland, Liechtenstein, Slovenia, Hungary, Czech Republic and Slovak Republic. Austria's only urban area is Vienna with some 2 million people living in and around the capital city. Large parts of western Austria are topographically characterized by mountains. Although there is some medium-sized industry around the provincial towns of Linz and Graz, Austria's economy is mainly based on services.

1. The Market

A. The Print Media
Main features:

- A small number of daily newspaper titles
- A small number of large newspapers and magazines
- A strong orientation towards boulevard newspapers
- A high degree of economic concentration

Daily newspapers are highly popular in Austria. Up to August 2006 more than 2.3 million copies were printed every day for a population of some 8.5 million people. Since early September 2006 another 250,000 copies are printed by a new daily newspaper. These figures do not include the circulation of several free sheets in the capital, Vienna, and in several provinces of the country. The copies sold by these free sheets are not counted officially, but combined they may print another 500,000 copies every working day (no editions on Saturdays and Sundays). Taken all this together, one copy of a daily newspaper is printed for every third person in Austria.

One million copies were printed and 850,000 sold by the *Neue Kronenzeitung* alone in 2005, accounting for some 37 per cent of the whole newspaper market. The remaining 63 per cent are distributed among 15 daily newspapers all over the country. This number includes all local and regional papers, some of which sell less than 10,000 copies every day.

Several waves of press concentration have hit Austria since World War II, leaving the country since 1997 with a rather small number of papers. However, this number has been stable since. A new wave of market restructuring might be the result of the launch of the new daily newspaper *Oesterreich*.

Regional press and national press need to be distinguished. The former is characterized by strong regional newspapers, dominating up to 90 per cent of the regional markets. With only two exceptions, all Austrian provinces (Bundeslaender) are dominated by just one regional publisher who controls one, two or even three newspapers. These secondary papers do not sell more than 10,000 copies each and are hardly profitable, but they help to consolidate the regional market and keep competitors off the ground. In September 2004, for example, the publisher of the daily newspaper *Tiroler Tageszeitung* launched a secondary paper called *Die Neue* in the province of Tyrol. In June 2006, the same publisher started a complementary daily free sheet in the same area. Other regional publishers equally launched their own daily free sheets in 2006 in a tactical move to seal this market segment against national and foreign competitors.

The strong position of the regional publishers is challenged by the regional editions of the *Neue Kronenzeitung*, which competes fiercely with the traditional press in these regional markets. In eight (out of nine) provinces, the *Neue Kronenzeitung* has either taken the lead or is as strong as the respective regional paper. Moreover, the *Neue Kronenzeitung* started its first daily free sheet in Vienna in March 2001 (*U-Express*), but stopped this costly experiment two years later, responding to orders from its major shareholder, the German WAZ Group. Only months later, in September 2004, the daughter-in-law of the *Kronenzeitungs*'s long-standing editor and shareholder launched another, more sophisticated daily free sheet in Vienna (*Heute*), which expanded to other Austrian provinces with regional editions in the following years.

The *national press* consists of seven titles, published in the capital Vienna, including *Oesterreich*, launched in September 2006. Four of the seven titles are tabloid-style papers, while the remaining three titles compete within the quality newspaper market. The resulting competition has amended the quality of these papers significantly. The coverage of economic developments has improved considerably since 1995 when an economic daily (*Wirtschaftsblatt*) was launched, based on the concept of the Swedish *Dagens Industri* and with the strong financial backing of the Swedish Bonnier Group. In 2006, the majority of shares was taken over by an Austrian publisher (*Styria*).

Equally in the tabloid market, competition has forced the papers to renew their concept and layout. The latest market entry in September 2006, the daily *Oesterreich*, is targeting the readership of the largest and second largest national daily newspapers and is oriented towards the market segment of young adults from 18 to 35. The founders and owners of the newspaper, the Fellner brothers, are well-known Austrian publishers who managed to restructure the Austrian magazine market earlier in their careers. They sold their highly profitable magazine group *News* to the German Bertelsmann Group (Gruner+Jahr), investing the revenue in this tabloid newspaper.

German investment capital plays a major role in the Austria newspaper landscape. Without investments from *Axel Springer Verlag, WAZ, Sueddeutsche Zeitung* and *Bertelsmann (Gruner+Jahr)* several newspaper and magazine launches would not have happened in the 1980s and 1990s. Some of these German publishers have pulled out of Austria again, others – in particular *WAZ* (holds 50 per cent each of *Neue Kronenzeitung* and *Kurier*) and *Gruner+Jahr* (controls *News-Group*) hold important shares in the Austrian press.

The Austrian market for news magazines is almost entirely controlled by the *News* Group. It has managed to gain control by acquiring among others the competing news magazine *Profil* in September 2000. This acquisition has established an unprecedented accumulation of media power by assembling practically all news magazines (*News, Profil, Trend, Format*) and some ten other magazines (among them *Woman, tv-media, e-media*) under the same entrepreneurial roof.

The press accounts for the largest share of the advertising market in Austria. Based on Media Focus, the size of the overall advertising market reached 2.8 billion euros in 2005, 79 per cent was spent for media advertising and 21 per cent for direct marketing. Fifty-seven per cent of the media advertising is allocated to the press, 23 per cent to television and 8 per cent to radio. Just 1 per cent each goes to online and cinema advertising, the rest is outdoor (7%) and yellow pages (3%).

B. The Broadcast Media

Main features:

- Strong market position of public service television and radio
- High viewer's market share of foreign television channels
- High degree of cable and satellite households
- Press publishers dominate private radio operations

- Digital switch has not yet happened
- Digital television and radio are tested
- Technical transmission formally separated from ORF

Austrian households are well equipped for the reception of radio and television. Some 87 per cent of all households received their television signal by cable or satellite in 2005, up 20 points within 10 years (1995: 67%). Terrestrial digital television and digital radio have only been tested in Austria, the start of the market roll-out was announced for fall 2006. In contrast, 42 per cent of all satellite households received a digital signal in 2006.

In its infancy, radio and television was the exclusive domain of the public sector, controlling all television and radio networks and operating the entire transmission equipment all over the country. In 2001, the Austrian Broadcasting Corporation (ORF) has changed its legal form and become a Foundation, institutionalized by the Austrian Broadcasting Act. The Foundation's Council is composed of 35 members. Nine of them are nominated by the Federal Government and six by political parties represented in Parliament. Another nine member are nominated by the regional governments, six members are seconded by the Viewers' and Listeners' Council (Publikumsrat) and the remaining five members by the ORF's labour organization. The Foundation Council elects the Director-General for a five-year term, decides on large investments and controls the whole organization. The ORF operates two television channels and four radio channels in line with its legal mission. Its headquarters are located in Vienna. In all other eight provinces the ORF runs a regional studio with the mission to produce regional broadcasting content for radio and television.

In parallel to the re-organization of the ORF, the Austrian Parliament adopted a new law on private television in Austria. Since 2001, private operators are eligible for licences at the national and at the regional and local level. In 2003, the only national terrestrial television frequency for private broadcasters was granted to *ATV plus (*former: *Wien 1)*, a private broadcaster based in Vienna, controlled by several banks in Austria and by the German film trader *Herbert Kloiber*. At the regional and local level, a variety of small broadcasters were granted terrestrial and cable licences.

These Austrian television channels compete with other German-language channels, spilled into the country by satellite and re-distributed by the cable systems. Foreign channels dominate the television viewing market. In 2005, some 54 per cent of all viewing in cable and satellite households was dedicated to foreign programmes. The market share of the two television channels of ORF declined over the last decade from 50 per cent in 1998 to 43 per cent in 2005. The private national channel *ATV plus* reached a market share of 2 per cent in 2005. The most popular foreign television channels were SAT.1 (7%), RTL (6%), ARD and ProSieben (5% each), all from Germany.

With regard to national and regional *radio*, the ORF still dominates all Austrian markets. In 1993, Parliament enacted the first – disputed – legislation to grant licences to private commercial radio operators. It took another five years before the legal basis finally was cleared, and, by April 1998, most of the 53 licensed radio operators were on air. This finally put an end to the period of the national public service monopoly in the radio sector.

In 2001, a new law on regional radios was passed and removed some obstacles for media companies to own and operate radio channels. The initial intention was to restrict ownership of dominant newspaper publishers. However, their interest in this medium and their lobbying was strong enough to succeed in removing most of these ownership barriers. Since 2001, media owners (newspapers, radio, television) are eligible to own even 100 per cent of a radio station, as long as the reach of the radio does not overlap with the reach of its other media. In Vienna (*Kronenzeitung*) as well as in the provinces, publishers made use of these new rules and acquired shares in the local and regional channels. One national terrestrial radio frequency was licensed and granted to *Krone Hit Radio*. By 2006, some 80 private radio operators were granted licences.

In 2005, 80 per cent of the radio listeners market was dominated by the four channels of the ORF and 20 per cent by private radio stations. On average, Austrians listened to radio programmes during 206 minutes every day, with 164 minutes dedicated to the ORF and 42 minutes to its private competitors.

The digital switch-over had not happened by 2006. However, the Federal Law on private television (2001) established the *Digital Platform Austria*, governed by the radio and television regulatory body. This platform has elaborated a multi-annual concept on the management of the digital switch-over.

One strategic key element is the creation of a *Fund for Digitalisation*, financed by parts of the radio and television licence fee revenue. This fund received 7.5 million EUR in 2004 and another 6.75 million annually thereafter to support projects and research in digital television and radio. In 2005, some 500 cabled households were chosen in the provincial capital Linz to participate in a pilot project on digital television. The local cable operator collaborated with the ORF and private broadcasters to learn more about the technical specification and the consumer's needs and interests, e.g. regarding video-on-demand. Each year, several projects are financed by the Fund.

In parallel, the establishment of the technical infrastructure for a national DVB-T network was licensed. In 2005, the technical operations were separated from the ORF's programme activities and relocated to a new company named ORS (100 per cent ORF-owned). The ORS is commissioned to cover 90 per cent of the population with the DVB-T signal by 2008 and 95 per cent by 2010. It started to establish multiplex transmitters in urban areas and roll-out plans were to supply the signal to all province capitals by the end of 2006.

C. The Internet Media
Main features:

- High online market shares for public service ORF and daily press
- Online media dominated by traditional media owners

Austria has a relatively high rate of PC ownership and Internet connection. By 2005, some 58 per cent of all households had a computer (1999: 45%), and equally some 58 per cent of all adult Austrians have access to the Internet at home or in the office (1999: 32%). The number of those qualifying as 'intensive' users surfing the Net daily or several times per week has grown even faster from 17 per cent in 1999 to 50 per cent in 2005.

Among the most frequently visited websites in Austria many Web services from mass media can be found. The ORF with its broad variety of Internet services reached 2.9 million unique clients in July 2006, generating some 171 million page impressions. *News Networld*, the combined Web portal of the *News* Group, the websites of the daily newspapers *Kronenzeitung* and *Der Standard* reached more than 1 million unique clients each in the same month. The highest number of page impressions was measured for *News Networld* (332 million), generated by a high number of slide shows on the website, animating users to click through quickly. Apart from these media websites, Web portals like ebay.at, MSN network, e-mail services like GMX and AON (Austria Telecom) are highly popular.

According to recent research, online media in Austria are in many cases little more than Web extensions of the main medium. However, the ORF, *Der Standard* and the *Kronenzeitung* (krone.at) have established independent online newsrooms and their websites do not – or only partly – correspond with the content of the main medium.

D. News agencies
Main features:

- Market dominated by Austria Presse Agentur (APA)
- Innovative services for different clients

Most Austrian mass media receive their international, national and economic news from the national news agency *Austria Presse Agentur* (APA). It was founded right after World War II in 1946 as a cooperative by almost all Austrian newspapers. In 1959, the *Kronenzeitung* was founded but did not join the APA as a member – and never became a member thereafter. In 1963, however, the ORF, the second largest media conglomerate in Austria, joined the APA and became a few years later the member paying the most important membership fee. Today, APA is far advanced in new information technologies and serves in addition to its members a large number of public and private clients.

2. State Policies
Main features:

- Strong formal regulation, little self-regulation
- High degree of politicization of public service broadcasting
- Direct subsidies for the press
- Communication Senate as complaints organization

Austria's media policy is characterized by strong regulation with little self-regulatory elements. Radio and television are dominated by the strong market player ORF, governed by its Council. Despite the fact that the law restricts full-time politicians to become members of the Council, the ORF became strongly politicized since the new law was enacted in 2001. In 2000, the Federal Government changed and the conservative party took power after the general elections. In 2001, the candidate of the ruling party, Monika Lindner, was elected as new Director General of the ORF. Journalists frequently claimed that the political influence of the Government and attempts to streamline transmissions – in particular in the area of the daily news broadcasts – increased. In 2005, an anchor news moderator publicly announced his frustration caused by direct interventions. The following months some 80,000 Austrians signed a resolution, "SOS ORF", requesting more distance between the political power and the ORF.

In August 2006, the re-election of the Director General failed and the candidate from the opposition social-democrat party, Alexander Wrabetz, was elected new Director General of the ORF.

This episode only illustrates the close relationship between the media and politics in Austria. Another expression of this close relation is the subsidy scheme for the press. Since 1974, the state provides all daily and weekly newspapers with annual direct payments. Subsidies go to all daily papers on their request (smaller amount) and to a few papers who are considered especially important for the diversity of opinions (larger amount). In 2003, the press subsidy scheme was reformed by a new law. The new scheme provides subsidies for the distribution of newspapers, for contributions to regional diversity and for the formation of journalists (school of journalism) and special projects. In 2005, some 12.8 million euros were allocated to the press according to this subsidy scheme with 4.5 million for the distribution scheme, 6.6 million for the diversity scheme and 1.7 for journalism schools and special projects. Ironically, it is irrelevant whether the newspapers are profitable or not, they all receive their share of the subsidy just on request. There is no auditing or reporting obligation.

Another strand of controversial media policy concerns the unprecedented high degree of media ownership concentration in Austria. While the initial legislation on private broadcasting contained some elements to increase the variety of media owners and restrict dominant media organizations at the regional level, most of these barriers have been removed. Actually, the largest newspaper equally owns the only terrestrial national radio channel and in almost all provinces the dominant newspaper publisher also owns the main radio channel and in some cases also the regional television channel. This concentration happened despite the fact that the cartel law in Austria requires the Cartel Court to check whether the merger or acquisition in question would endanger journalistic and media diversity.

Austrian cable networks must carry all national channels, that includes the two channels of the ORF and the relevant local and regional channels. Other than this general rule, cable operators are free to allocate their bandwidth to television, radio or other services. Some large cable networks offer "triple play services", including radio and television as well as telephony and broadband Internet connection. In accordance with European law, all foreign channels can be received in Austria without restrictions.

The reform of the Austrian Broadcasting legislation established a Federal Senate of Communication (Bundeskommunikationssenat). This senate looks into alleged violations of the Broadcasting Act, as well as into individual complaints against radio and television programmes.

3. Civil Society Organizations
Main features:

■ Well-organized sector
■ Strong political influence of employer's and employee's unions
■ Dissolved status of press council

Media employers and journalists have their own organizations in Austria. Journalists have founded their own union (*Sektion Journalisten*) within the National Union Federation of Austria (Österreichischer Gewerkschaftsbund). Their role within the Austrian media landscape is relatively important, as the Federation participates in all relevant deliberations on media policy issues and negotiates collective agreements for all employees. The major print journalist's union has moved within the National Union Federation from the arts and sports section (where radio and television journalists are still members) to the paper and print section in 2001.

Newspaper publishers are organized in the *Verband Österreichischer Presse* (VÖZ). This association has played a key role in all media policy decisions since World War II. It represents the collective will of the large majority of newspaper publishers and became part of all formal and informal deliberations concerning press policy and press subsidies as well as radio and television legislation.

In 2003, private radio and television broadcasters have founded the *Verband Österreichischer Privatsender* (VÖP). By 2006, some 25 private radio stations and eight private television stations were members. One important issue for VÖP is the debate about the definition of the public service remit of the ORF and – in conjunction – the question whether the

ORF makes lawful use of the licence fee revenues or whether the ORF goes beyond its remit. The VÖP filed a lawsuit in this respect.

Violations of personal rights or breach of the journalist's Code of Ethics in the press were followed up by the Press Council (Presserat). Its verdicts were not legally binding and it made recommendations rather than decisions. It was composed of representatives of professional bodies and journalists unions. In 2002, the Presserat was dissolved, following disputes among its members. Up to 2006, no formal institution has replaced the Presserat. Its Code of Ethics still exists, but no organization is watching over its implementation. Subsequently, several individuals (journalists, editors-in-chief, scientists) founded an organization for quality journalism, but it has little formal recognition and, therefore, limited relevance.

4. Development Trends
Main features:

- Ongoing tabloidization of the press
- High degree of media concentration to continue
- Internationalization at the ownership level to continue

Austria's media system underwent a long process of tabloidization with more and more journalistic competitors at this level. Since World War II, the tabloid press represented an important element of the Austrian media landscape. *Kurier* (traditional paper) and *Kronenzeitung* (founded in 1959, took over the popular *Express* in 1970) have prepared the market for many more print titles in this segment. In 1992, a new daily newspaper, *Täglich Alles*, challenged the market leader with short stories, many colours and pictures and tabloid-style journalism, but survived only until 2000. In 1992, a similar concept for younger audiences was introduced to the weekly magazine market. *News* rapidly became the largest selling magazine in Austria. Online journalism, starting in the middle of the 1990s reinforced the trends towards low-cost journalism strongly related to material from news agencies. The subsequent push was exercised by free sheets, launched by domestic newspaper publishers. Again, low-cost journalism dominates these new media outlets.

Since September 2006 the stylish newspaper *Oesterreich* completes this list of popular print media with a mission to reach a mass audience. *Oesterreich* started with high ambitions: 250,000 copies to begin with, some 200 journalists working for the print and online edition in a hyper-modern newsroom in the heart of Vienna. This market entry will claim substantial shares of the print advertising market and might endanger the economic existence of several newspapers in Austria. A new wave of media concentration might be the result.

In general, Austria's media landscape is likely to remain highly concentrated with a low number of powerful media owners. This includes the public service broadcaster who plays a major political role in Austria. This strong position guarantees on the one hand the future of the public service system, as politics depends largely on the ORF. On the other hand, this strong position conflicts with the independence paradigm of public service broadcasting.

Being part of a large language area, international developments might gain importance for the Austrian media landscape. While readership is still low for German newspapers and magazines, large parts of the television audience are already oriented towards German channels with increasing trends.

References & Sources for Further Information

Dörfler, Edith/Pensold, Wolfgang (2001), *Die Macht der Nachricht. Die Geschichte der Nachrichtenagentur in Österreich*. Molden, Wien.

RTR (Rundfunk- und Telekom Regulierungs-GmbH) (2006), *Tätigkeitsbericht des Digitalisierungsfonds*. Wien.

Steinmaurer, Thomas (2004), Das Mediensystem Österreichs. In: Hans-Bredow-Institut (Hg.): *Internationales Handbuch Medien*. Baden-Baden. (Nomos). S. 168–179.

Steinmaurer, Thomas (2002), *Konzentriert und Verflochten. Österreichs Mediensysteme im Überblick*. Studienverlag, Innsbruck.

Trappel, Josef (2004), Austria. In: Kelly, Mary / Mazzoleni, Gianpietro / McQuail, Denis (Hg.): *The Media in Europe. The Euromedia Handbook*. London, Thousand Oaks, New Delhi. (Sage). S. 4–15.

Trappel, Josef (1997), Austria. In: Group, Euromedia Research (Hg.): *The Media in Western Europe. The Euromedia Handbook*. London, Thousand Oaks, New Delhi. (Sage). S. 1 -16.

VÖZ (Verband Österreichischer Zeitungsherausgeber und –verleger) (annually) *Pressehandbuch*. Wien.

Information on Austrian media is scattered over many institutions. The ORF publishes some basic statistics on market shares and programme profiles on its website, (http://www.orf.at). The mass media regulator RTR has some useful information on regulation, law, press subsidies, etc. on its website (http://www.rtr.at). With regard to the press, the Publishers' Association publishes an annual handbook on the press, (*Pressehandbuch*), containing most relevant data on printed media in Austria.

There is a specialized press (e.g. Horizont Austria; on advertising and agencies) and media sections in newspapers (*Der Standard, Die Presse* and their online editions). Furthermore, the Austrian News Agency (APA) publishes a weekly bulletin on media developments. More popular information can be found in the weekly journal *TV Media*, functioning not only as television programme guide but also as a forum for a debate on media policy issues. Finally, a monthly magazine (*Extradienst*) reports on the media business.

THE BELGIAN MEDIA LANDSCAPE

Els de Bens

Introduction

Belgium became a unitary state in 1830. It is a geographically very small country (30,528 sq km) but densely populated with some 10 million inhabitants. It has three officially recognized languages: Dutch (58%), French (31%) and German (11%). The dissensions between Flemings [Dutch-speaking] and Walloons [French-speaking] have had a decisive impact on political life. When Belgium became an independent state, French was the only official language. Under the impulse of the Flemish emancipatory movement, the Flemings gradually acquired equal rights and Belgium became a federal state. This has diminished the power of the central government. Today Belgium has a complicated state structure, with a multitude of institutions and a growing bureaucracy.

Belgium has a multi-party system and there are no clear majority parties. The emergence of a successful extreme right party in Flanders disturbed the traditional political balance but until today the majority of parties have succeeded to keep this extremist party out of government.

Belgium is a highly industrialized country with a high standard of living and an excellent social security system. The population is aging; there are many families without children, the number of single-person households is on the increase and the working population is no more than 35 per cent of all Belgians.

1. The Market

A. *Print Media*
Main features:

- High degree of concentration
- Readership is slowly declining; with 170 readers per thousand, Belgium ranks in comparison with other European countries between high and low newspaper consumption
- Advertising revenues have slightly grown in the last two years
- Free dailies reach a lot of readers, but advertising revenues remain rather disappointing

The process of ownership concentration that started in the 1960s has resulted in a lower number of newspapers and it has also led to a decrease in the number of independent newspapers. Of today's 23 newspapers in Belgium, fourteen are truly autonomous.

In Flanders the market is controlled by three groups: Corelio Media (former VUM Media): *De Standaard*, *Het Nieuwsblad*, *De Gentenaar*, *Het Volk* [VUM changed its name in July 2006 into Corelio Media after they acquired the Walloon newspaper group Medi@ bel (see below)]; De Persgroep: *Het Laatste Nieuws*, *De Nieuwe Gazet*, *De Morgen,De Tijd/ L'Echo*. [In 2006 De Persgroep, together with the group Rossel, publisher of French-speaking newspapers, founded Mediafin (each 50%) in order to obtain the two Belgian financial dailies *De Tijd* and *L'Echo*]; Concentra: *Gazet van Antwerpen*, *Het Belang van Limburg* and the free newspaper *Metro*.

Belgium's French-language press is also dominated by three large groups: The Rossel group (*Le Soir*, *La Meuse*, *La Capital*, *La Nouvelle Gazette*, *La Province*) and *De Tijd/L'Echo* (50%), *Grenz Echo* (50%) and the free newspaper *Metro*; IPM (*La Libre Belgique*, *La Dernière Heure*); Medi@bel (*Vers l'Avenir*, *Le Jour/Le Courrier*, *Le Courrier de l'Escaut*). Medi@bel is now part of the former Flemish VUM media so that the two other media groups, Rossel and IPM, own the remaining French-speaking newspapers.

As a result of mergers the French community has no more left-oriented newspaper. The latest socialist affiliated newspaper, *Le Matin*, disappeared in 2001 so that only centre-oriented papers are published in the French-speaking part of Belgium where the Socialist Party has since long a majority position. In Flanders the remaining socialist affiliated newspaper, *De Morgen*, was bought by De Persgroep and could preserve its editorial autonomy and could survive as a progressive newspaper.

Belgium had traditionally a political opinion press but as a result of mergers the newspapers became more independent from political pressures. Most newspapers still have some affinities with political parties, but the ties with politicians and political parties have weakened.

Initially most newspaper companies were family enterprises, but gradually they came to be controlled by financial holdings and banking institutions. Their ownership structure continues to be Belgian. The only exception was Rossel where the French media tycoon R. Hersant acquired 40 per cent. In 2005 the family Rossel bought Hersant's share. Recently Belgian newspapers acquired a share in foreign newspapers: Rossel 85 per cent in *La Voix du Nord's* and *De Persgroep* obtained 58 per cent of the Dutch newspaper *Het Parool*.

All these newspaper groups have tended to become multimedia enterprises in the last few years. Quite a number of newspapers publish weeklies and free sheets Most Belgian newspapers have also shares in local radio and regional TV as well as in the new commercial television stations.

In 2006 the overall circulation of the Belgian press amounted to 1,790,646, the Flemish press taking 1,171,223 (65.4%), and the French-language press 619,423 (34.6%). Half of the newspapers are distributed as single copies; 55 per cent are subscriptions.

Newspapers are highly dependent on advertising (between 40 and 60%) and as numerous new media players have entered the market, the competition is fierce. Newspapers also lost a lot of classified advertising to the Internet. Recently advertisers spend more money in advertising "below the line", all kinds of direct marketing applications in order to reach the consumer directly using leaflets, websites, samples, etc.

In the last five years circulation figures have been declining slightly. Young people are reading fewer newspapers. Dailies have recently succeeded in increasing their market mainly due to a more popular tabloid strategy. As competition becomes severe in a saturated daily newspaper market, most dailies have tried to develop a 'new' look, have added new columns, new inserts and better distribution systems.

De Standaardgroep (VUM), followed closely by De Persgroep as well as *Le Soir* (Rossel), are the market leaders for both sales and advertising revenues.

B. The Broadcast Media
Main features:

- Belgium has two separate, autonomous public service broadcasting corporations: VRT for the Flemish community and RTBF for the French-speaking community;
- Very competitive TV market;
- Licence fee has been abolished in Flanders; public funding is guaranteed;
- Fragmentation of the television market;
- Total advertising revenue for private TV is declining since 2004 in spite of the new private general and thematic TV stations;
- Highest cable penetration worldwide. Most TV households are connected to cable networks;
- iDTV slower growth than expected (350,000 subscribers).

Belgium is the most densely cabled country in the world (97 per cent of all households with televisions). In the beginning the cable companies only distributed the national programmes, but soon after the programmes of foreign television stations were also distributed (24 to 40 channels).

Initially, only the foreign public service channels were given access to cable, but gradually some commercial stations were admitted as well. The factual monopoly of the PSB was indirectly undermined by the cable networks which were offering an increasing number of television stations. RTBF (PSB French-speaking) was losing viewers to RTL and the French channels, VRT (Dutch-speaking) to the Netherlands and to a certain degree to French, German and UK channels.

Belgium has two public service broadcasting corporations: one for the Flemish community (VRT) and one for the French-speaking community (RTBF). In 1997 a PSB (radio) for the German-speaking community was added. From the 1970s onwards, consecutive reforms will give VRT and RTBF full autonomy and both communities each have different regulations and different broadcast policies.

In Flanders the radio monopoly was broken in 1981 but private radio remained small-scale because their range was limited (no nationwide coverage). In 2001 two new nationwide private stations received a licence (Q Music and 4FM). Public radio until 2001 had a dominant position (85%), a quasi-monopoly and today as a result of competition from the new private radios, the market share was cut to 67.8 per cent.

The Flemish public TV monopoly was broken in 1989: The new commercial broadcaster VTM was very successful from the beginning and obtained the first year a market share of 37 per cent. The success of VTM is inextricable linked to its high ratings, mainly due to a policy of popular programming. Public TV reacted in panic and started imitating the programme strategies of the commercial rival: more entertainment, especially in prime time. In 1994 the market share of public TV had dropped to 29 per cent (VTM got 44%). In 1995 a new decree reformed the public broadcaster.

The PSB received more autonomy, making it independent from political pressures: depoliticization of the management board and of the executive staff. No fewer than 60 executives of the "old guard" were laid off. The new management contract guaranteed substantial funding. The new contract also imposed performance criteria for audience shares. This policy has been criticized because it has triggered a dumbing down, and a tabloidization effect but the market share increased. In 1997 the VRT was transformed in a public limited company that was to be run as an enterprise. In 2002 the licence fee was abolished but the Flemish government guarantees funding. In 2005 VRT had a market share of 30.8 per cent.

VRT TV is not allowed to carry advertising; on public radio advertising is allowed.

In 1994 an unexpected competitor entered the market. The American-Swedish group SBS announced the launch of a new commercial Flemish station, VT4. The new station was located in London so as not to collide with VTM's official eighteen-year monopoly. In 2000 VT4 received a Flemish licence. In order to compete with VT4, VTM launched a second channel Ka2. Meanwhile, other private Flemish stations have been launched: niche stations (lifestyle, financial news, music, etc.).

In the French-speaking part, RTBF (PSB) still suffers from politicization, bureaucracy and shortage of financial means. The competition of the new commercial channel, RTL TVi, was not so fierce as that of VTM in Flanders because RTL had to cope with competition of the French TV stations TF1, A2 and FR3.

The introduction of advertising on RTBF TV did not result in a serious rise of financial needs. A new plan to reform the RTBF was introduced: Horizon 97 intended to balance the budget by 1997. A new decree in July 1997 transformed the PSB into an independent company. This new statute did not change a lot and a new plan, Magellan, was adopted in order to reform once more the RTBF. Meanwhile, the RTBF became an "independent company under contract". The government guarantees funding, but the contract imposes constraints for programming. The contract confirms that the RTBF is allowed to carry advertising. In 2006 the financial situation has improved and the programme strategies have been refocused. The market share of RTBF TV was in 2005 17.7 per cent; RTL has 29.5 per cent.

In Wallonia the private radios received nationwide licences; advertising and networking was also allowed from the beginning. The market share of some of these private radios is higher than that of public radio

With the launch in Belgium of digital TV, fragmentation will increase. In 2006, however, Belgium has no more than 350,000 digital TV subscribers. Growth is slower than predicted.

Pay channels were never very successful in Belgium. The former pay film channel Filmnet that merged with Canal Plus was, in spite of intensive marketing activities (offering football), not very successful and was in Flanders sold to Telenet, the dominant Flemish cable operator in 2005. The name was changed into Prime. Prime is offering film on demand but the number of households with digital decoders is still very small (170,000).

The cable operators have to face the competition of the telecom providers (Belgacom, Vodafone) because they are also offering digital TV. Distribution through satellite is still limited in Belgium, but this situation might change.

The digital terrestrial switch-off is planned for 2008, but very few Belgians receive TV terrestrial so that this will not cause commotion.

C. The Internet Media
Main features:

- Fifty-six per cent of the population uses Internet and 40 per cent is connected to broadband infrastructure;
- All newspapers offer a website on which they present breaking news. Some newspapers have developed a full online version that is constantly updated.

Almost half of the population has access to the Internet: 51 per cent in Brussels, 53 per cent in Flanders and 40 per cent in Wallonia. The penetration of broadband is very high (40%).

All newspapers and most magazines have developed digital activities. Most of their electronic versions complement the "paper" edition and are offered free. Some newspapers publishers offer a complete updated version of their newspaper. The online version of the leading quality newspaper *De Standaard* has 4000 subscribers; the online version is offered free to the subscribers of the paper version. The financial economic newspaper *De Tijd* has been also one of the pioneers. They were the first newspaper in Belgium that has used in the 80s the French videotext technology for their electronic version. Today they are still very active with their online version on the Web. Meanwhile, also, popular newspapers like *Het Laatste Nieuws* have developed a successful electronic version.

Weblogs have become very popular but the credibility and success of the online service of traditional newspapers scores much higher .The online news service of the public broadcast corporation is free and quite successful. Traditional media have "colonized" the information flow on the Internet because Internet users have more confidence in the professionalism of journalists.

On the other hand, online newspapers don't explore the interactive opportunities of this new technology enough. Most online newspapers are understaffed, and journalists work under pressure to update, to cope with the overload of information so that in practice a lot of input is copy/paste, from the main paper daily (the so-called shovel ware).

D. News agencies
Main features:

- Dominant position of the national news agency BELGA

Belga is the national news agency. It has two main functions: it is the prime source for national news and it makes a selection of the news input of the main world news agencies. It has two independent editorial departments: one for the Flemish community and one for the French-speaking community.

Belga is owned by the traditional Belgian mass media institutions: newspapers and broadcasters. There are no other private investors and no governmental participation.

2. State Policies
Main features:

■ Belgium has no specific anti-concentration media law;
■ Broadcast media have specific media regulations, licences, content directives, special advertising regulations. They also have to conform with the EU directives;
■ Belgium has never been at the forefront as far as meaningful media policies are concerned. A lot of media laws have only confirmed situations that were already in existence.

Belgium's constitution guarantees complete freedom of the press. Any form of censorship is prohibited and repressive measures are only allowed if the freedom of speech has been abused of. Offences against the press code (such as privacy, defamation, moral standards, the monarch, etc.) do not fall within the competence of an ordinary court but must be referred to Court d'Assises where judgment is passed by a jury of citizens. This measure protects journalists as public opinion will side with the journalists.

For the last years media policies have been strongly oriented towards neo-liberalism: new private initiatives have been supported. No measures have been taken against the increasing concentration of the media, neither is cross ownership of the media market separately regulated. Competition law regulates all types of mergers.

In order to support the press, Belgium has always adhered to a system of indirect and direct support measures. Indirect support such as reduced postal and telephone rates, zero VAT rate, interest free loans, etc. From 1973 on, the newspapers also received financial support. Socialist newspapers needed mostly this financial aid but the majority of the newspapers were centre oriented. The political compromise was that all newspapers got financial support. This gave rise to criticism because newspapers that were doing well, also received the support. Subsequently, the direct support was made more selective; weak newspapers could get more support but the total amount of money that was allocated kept decreasing so that the direct support wasn't very effective. In 1998 the direct support measures became the responsibility of the Flemish and French communities; indirect support measures remained an issue for the Federal government.

In Flanders the government decided that direct subsidies should disappear in 1999 because all newspapers have become incorporated into the larger press groups. The support measures are now used for special projects such as digital activities, journalistic training and standardized digital archives. Half of the money is spent on actions to promote reading of newspapers.

In the francophone community direct subsidies for newspapers were financed by advertising revenues from public and private broadcast companies. In 2004 it was decided that the government of the French-speaking community will gradually finance the direct support. From 2008 on, all direct support measures will be funded by the government. Newspapers have to apply for direct financial support and they have to submit a file with detailed information about the number of journalists employed, revenue from advertising and sales, etc. In contrast with Flanders, the francophone newspapers can still apply for financial aid.

The Flemish and the French communities are fully autonomous in constructing a regulatory framework for their broadcast system. This explains why they have different regulation frameworks and why they have separate controlling bodies (De Vlaamse Media Regulator, VRM and the Conseil Supérieur de l'Audiovisuel, CSA). In Flanders the Vlaamse Media Regulator and in Wallonia the Conseil Supérieur de l'Audiovisuel give licences for new radio and TV stations. These institutions also control whether the legislation is being observed and eventually they can impose sanctions.

3. Civil Society
Main features:

- Most journalists, publishers and advertisers join their own organization. These organizations take care of social agreements, wages, ethics and the professional statute.

There are three important organizations in Belgium. The Association of Belgian Journalists (AVBB) in Brussels, the Belgian Association of Publishers (BVDU) and Febelma, the association of magazines publishers.

The AVBB has been split up in a Flemish section (VVJ) and a French-speaking section (AJP). In the past the Association of Journalists and the Association of Publishers made collective agreements for the remuneration of journalists and freelancers. In five years these collective agreements have come to an end and now the publishers decide themselves.

The basic deontological code for journalists is the Declaration of Rights and Duties of 1971 (Munchen) as well as a Code of Journalistic Principles (Association of Belgian Journalists). The Belgian Association of Professional Journalists has a Deontological Council. This council considers complaints and gives advice to journalists. After many recent press scandals, Belgian journalists developed a new deontological code that stresses the importance of accountability.

In Flanders a new council for journalistic ethics was founded: De Raad voor Journalistiek. Citizens can complain to this council and they can avoid a lawsuit. This is a self-regulating body but external experts attend the meetings and take part in the decision-making (six journalists, six publishers and six external experts).

Very important was the legalization of the Safeguarding of Sources in April 2006, according to which a journalist cannot be forced to reveal their sources. The law does not only apply to professional journalists but all kinds of information providers (for example, bloggers!).

Advertisers also have a self-regulatory body that takes care of the ethical aspects of advertising (JEP).

4. Development Trends
Main features:

- Newspaper readership is declining;
- The television and radio market become more and more fragmented;
- The fight for readers and audiences stimulates unhealthy competition.

One of the major future problems for print and broadcast media is the declining revenue from advertising. The media market has become very fragmented and the main source of revenues for all the new media players is advertising. The advertising media market is not flexible enough. Advertisers have lost confidence in the 30-second TV spot and in the digital TV market viewers can zap the ads away. The newspapers have lost classified adds to the Internet (cars, real estate, etc.) and to the free dailies. Advertisers seem to be more in favour of advertising below the line (not in media but all kinds of direct marketing).

The neo-liberal policies of the EU and of the European media market have triggered commercialization. Competition has become ruinous and this stimulated a tabloidization effect on content. Public broadcast services, free from economic pressure, become more and more important.

The development of new digital services such as iDTV, mobile TV, UMTS, DVBH, wireless, Internet, etc. have become a hype for politicians and content providers but the question is whether media consumers are ready for these new services and are willing to pay for them.

References and Sources for Further Information
The most useful information sources are the Driemaandelijks Bulletin CIM, an overview of circulation figures, published every three months, CIM News and VRT, Studiedienst, a monthly edition with audience ratings The association of journalists publishes a monthly review, *De Journalist/Le Journalist*.

Both PSBs, RTBF and VRT, publish a report each year with a lot of relevant information.

The Danish Media Landscape

Per Jauert & Henrik Søndergaard

Denmark is by geographical size one of the smaller Nordic countries, covering 43,098 sq km. Denmark is a highly industrialized, knowledge-based society that focuses on education and innovation. Greenland and the Faroe Islands in the Atlantic Ocean are also part of the Danish realm, although they enjoy extensive home rule. Denmark is a member of the EU, whereas Greenland and the Faroe Islands have decided against EU membership.

A figure of 5.4 million people are living in Denmark in 2.5 million households. Although there are many different dialects, all Danes speak the same language – Danish. Approximately 260,000 people – or 5 per cent of the population – are foreign nationals. Approximately 80,000 of them are from the Nordic countries, the EU or North America. The rest come from Eastern Europe, the Middle East or Africa, primarily from Turkey, Pakistan, Iraq, Iran, Somalia or the former Yugoslavia. 1,800,000 people are 65+ years, and approximately 3 million belong to the economically active age group.

1. The Market

A. The Print Media
Main features:

- No competition on local newspaper markets, but increased competition during the last decade on the national market
- There is an overall decrease in the amount of circulation of all three categories of Danish newspapers

■ The readership has for decades steadily declined until the introduction of free newspapers
■ The magazine market accounts for a decline during the last decade

The Danish media landscape has noted a steady decline in the number of newspapers since the Second World War. With an average decrease of more than 25 per cent per decade, today only 31 newspapers remain.

Danish newspapers may be classified in terms of the following categories: large nationally distributed (3), small nationally distributed (4), local and regional papers (22) and tabloids (2) – 30 are published weekdays, eight also on weekends and one just on weekends. The daily press is characterized by the fact that competition no longer exists on some local markets, whereas the large nationally distributed papers have been in a situation of intense competition in the mid-1990s. At present, *Morgenavisen Jyllands-Posten* is Denmark's largest newspaper, with a daily (weekday) circulation of over 150,000. The total circulation of the Danish newspapers has declined by 322,000 over the past ten years, to a daily circulation of all in all 1,293,000. During the same period the three large national newspapers have experienced a decline of 33,000, to a daily circulation in 2004 of 437,000.

The nationally distributed papers with small circulations and narrower target audiences dispersed over the entire country have experienced a minor decline of 3,000 copies to a circulation of 115,000 in spite of the closure of *Det fri Aktuelt* – the oldest Labour Union daily in the world – in 2001. So, in fact, the remaining newspapers in this group have increased the daily circulation with 37,000 copies. Denmark's two tabloids have shrunk, having lost 40 per cent of their combined circulation over the past ten years. Their total daily circulation is currently 204,523.

Among local and regional papers we find a corresponding decline, but also the most comprehensive structural changes that occurred in the branch during the period. Within the local and regional press, where local monopolies have been common for some years now, we note a tendency towards regional monopolies through fusions, concentration of ownership and strategic alliances. The Copenhagen-based *Det Berlingske Officin A/S*, owned by the Norwegian Company Orkla Media, has through mergers and alliances with other newspapers become the most important player in the field as far as direct and indirect control over circulation is concerned. By now its share of the total circulation is 34 per cent, followed by the merged company *JP/Politikens Hus* (*Morgenavisen Jyllands-Posten*, owned by JP and Politiken and the tabloid *Ekstra Bladet*, owned by Politikens Hus A/S), who has a share of 29 per cent.

Since 1985, there has been an overall decrease in the amount of circulation of all three categories of Danish newspapers, among which the two tabloids have faced the biggest loss. The expansion of journalistic input, both quantitative and qualitative, has not resulted in an increase in readership for the traditional newspapers, though. On the contrary, readership steadily declined until the introduction of free newspapers around the turn of the century. In 1993, 74 per cent of the adult population (12+) read one newspaper per day; in 2004 it was 76 per cent.

The competition on advertising has been very intense among the Danish newspapers during the last decade, in some periods of time resulting in price dumping and consequently in considerable loss of income for some newspaper groups. In 1994 the Danish newspapers had a share of 35 per cent (437 million €) of the total advertising market. In 2004 it was reduced to 26 per cent (380 million €). This only adds to the fragile financial situation among all papers losing advertising in favour of electronic media (especially television and the Internet). On average the Danish newspaper industry generated a surplus of 2.8 per cent of the turnover in 2004, the best result in five years with an average of 1.2 per cent.

The distribution of 235 free-of-charge district papers makes those papers a widespread phenomenon in Denmark, with a circulation of approximately 5 million copies per week. This puts Denmark in a league of its own by international comparison. Most of these papers are weeklies, and they are distributed locally in areas defined by the inhabitants' shopping patterns. The district press has increasingly come to assume the role that local newspapers previously played. Surveys have found that as much as 28 per cent of the local population (aged 13 and over) names the district papers as their primary source to local information.

In 2001 a Danish version of the free paper *MetroExpress* was launched in Denmark, followed by similar initiatives from the main newspaper companies in Denmark. The same year Det Berlingske Officin published *Urban*, Nordjyske Medier launched *10 minutter* [*10 Minutes*] in 2002, *Xtra* by Fyens Stiftstidende (2005) and *JP-Aarhus* (2003) by Morgenavisen Jyllands-Posten. In 2004 the three first mentioned had a circulation of 409,000 copies; in 2005 all free papers had 568,000 copies.

According to Dansk Oplagskontrol (Danish Audit Bureau of Circulations) there were fifteen weekly and 31 monthly and quarterly magazines on the Danish market in 2004. In 2004, Danish weeklies had a circulation of 1.5 million copies; monthlies and quarterly magazines a circulation of 900,000. In ten years a decrease for weeklies of 400,000 copies; for monthly and quarterly magazines of 300,000 copies.

B. The Broadcast Media
Main features:

- The Danish Broadcasting Company (DR) is the main actor in the Danish Radio landscape with a market share of 68 per cent;
- DR has served as 'a locomotive' for the roll-out of DAB – Digital Audio Broadcasting;

- The commercial radio market includes approx. 100 local and regional stations, organised in networks or as parts of regional cross-media companies (newspapers, free weeklies, radio and television);
- Nationwide commercial radio was launched in 2003, but still has a weak market position;
- The annual turnover for radio advertisements has never been more than 2 per cent of the total turnover for all commercial media;
- The audience share of the DR and TV 2 public service channels is 69 per cent;
- There has been a proliferation of both public service and commercial channels, leading to an increased competition for audiences and revenues;
- In spite of a fierce competition from the private television companies, TV 2 is a clear market leader with more than a 62 per cent share of the market for television ads;
- Digitalization of the distribution of television is in its initial phase, while DAB so far has been a relative success;
- The role and character of the digital gatekeeper for the commercial digital platforms are still to be decided.

In Denmark people listen to the radio about three hours a day on average (2005). The current (2005) public service radio system in Denmark consists of one independent broadcaster: The Danish Broadcasting Company – DR. DR runs three national FM channels: P1 is a 'serious' talk channel with a daily reach of 10 per cent (2005), P2, a channel focusing on cultural subjects and classical music with a daily reach of 5 per cent and P3, a music and entertainment channel for younger people, with a daily reach of 24 per cent. DR also runs nine regional stations sharing a fourth channel, P4, and on average the regional channels have a daily reach of 37 per cent. Besides, DR runs two AM channels and sixteen DAB channels of which fourteen are produced for DAB whereas the remaining two are parallel distribution of the FM channels P1 and P3.

On the Internet all of these FM and DAB channels (except two of the DAB channels) are distributed along with eleven "pure" Net-radio channels. In total, public service radio in Denmark has a total marked share of 68 per cent of the listeners on the FM- and DAB-net, whereas the use of Internet radio is not yet under independent monitoring.

The commercial radio system in Denmark includes over 100 local and regional stations, an increasing number of which is associated as part of networking agreements (i.e. The Voice (SBS), ANR (Nordjyske Medier) or as parts of regional cross-media companies (newspapers, free weeklies, radio, television). In total, commercial radio in Denmark has a market share of 29 per cent, including both local and nationwide commercial radio, and a daily reach of 33 per cent (2005). Non-commercial local radio (community radio) and foreign stations have a total share of 3 per cent. In November 2003 two new commercial stations were launched, Radio 100FM and Sky Radio.

The new commercial players had initially great expectations to the virgin Danish market for radio advertisements. The share of radio advertising of the total annual turnover for all commercial media in Denmark has never been more than 2 per cent (2% = €37 million in 2005), compared to a European average of 6–7 per cent, and the new players announced a possible increase to reach 4–5 per cent within the eight-year period. These expectations were not met. Instead, the share decreased over the next two years, and with a similar disappointing audience share, the management of Sky Radio decided to close down operations in Denmark November 2005 with a deficit of €40 million – and a debt of €43 million to the Danish state for the remaining part of the licence period. Three main factors are behind the failure of introducing nationwide commercial radio in Denmark: Firstly, the market position of DR is very strong, especially P3 and P4 with updated and popular music formats in combination with popular DJ's; secondly, the buyers of radio commercials showed to be quite sceptical of the efficiency of radio commercials compared to other types of radio. Thirdly, Sky Radio does not seem to have invested sufficient resources in analyzing the specific Danish market situation. The well-known Dutch Sky Radio format (soft, no DJ's, news on the hour) was just imported, but it did not appeal that much to the Danish radio audience.

Television's daily reach in Denmark in 2005 was 71 per cent (with a minimum of five minutes of consecutive television daily), and the accumulated weekly reach was 92 per cent (Gallup 2005). Thus, a smaller cumulative reach, and a significantly lower daily reach. In other words, the Danes are a bit more in contact with radio than with television, and this is true for the time spent using the two media as well. While the Danes listen to the radio for 3 hours on average, the figure for television is 2.5 hours.

In order to understand the way in which Danish television is organized it is important to be aware of the limitations within the terrestrial analogue distribution system. Due to lack of frequencies, according to international regulation, there is capacity only for two terrestrial national channels and a number of local channels. As a consequence the two main public service channels, DR1 and TV 2/Danmark, have a privileged position within the terrestrial system, as all other channels – except the local ones – have to be distributed by cable and satellite, which means that they reach only between 50 and 70 per cent of the population. With the switch to digital television planned to take place in 2009, the structural limitations that DR and TV 2 benefit from today will disappear and the entire balance between the different broadcasters operating in Denmark will change dramatically.

The current Danish television system consists of four major broadcasters. On the one hand the two public service institutions, DR and TV 2, and on the other hand two privately owned transnational commercial companies, Viasat (MTG) and SBS. In most cases the individual broadcasters work independently of one another. However, in reality there is a high degree of interconnection because they compete for the same audience and to some extent for the same economic resources as well.

The two public service broadcasters operate almost independently from each other, but have to fulfil almost the same public service obligations. DR is the former monopoly and is funded by licence fees. DR runs two coordinated channels: DR1, which is distributed on the analogue terrestrial net, and DR2, which is transmitted by satellite. Since spring 2006 both of these channels are distributed on the digital terrestrial net as well. DR1 is the main channel with an audience share of 28 per cent in 2005, whereas DR2 is a kind of minority channel and has a market share of only 5 per cent. Since DR1 and DR2 are public service channels both of them are by legislation "must carry" channels. It means that they have to be included in any cable television "packet" whereby DR achieves a privileged status in terms of distribution.

TV 2's main channel, TV 2/Danmark, is funded by advertising income, which gives it a more 'commercial' or 'popular' profile compared to DR. However, TV 2 is organized as a national channel with eight regional TV 2 stations affiliated, so that part of the TV 2 schedule is regional television. The regional TV 2 stations are funded with a part of the licence fee and have formally independence from TV 2. Moreover, TV 2 only produces news, sports programmes and current affairs, while the rest of its output is based on independent producers. On to that come the TV 2 niche channels, TV 2 Zulu, TV 2 Charlie and TV 2 Film, which are all funded by a mix of advertising income and subscription fees. TV 2/Danmark's audience share amounted to 36 per cent in 2005, which makes it Denmark's most popular channel, whereas TV 2 Zulu still has a very small market share of 3 per cent. In addition to that, TV 2 Charlie delivers a share of 1 per cent, whereas TV 2 film has an almost invisible share of approximately 0.2 per cent. It is worth mentioning that only TV 2/Danmark and its affiliated regional stations are public service channels that enjoys the privilege of a "must carry" status, whereas the new niche channels are regarded as purely commercial enterprises with no such privileges.

Commercial television consists mainly of two companies: Viasat, a satellite station based in England with two channels (TV3 and TV3+) aimed for the Danish market, and SBS, who owns a satellite channel (Kanal 5), broadcasting from England too, and a network of seven local channels forming Kanal 4. Based in England, the commercial television companies can circumvent the restrictions in the Danish media law about the content and placement of advertising. Neither TV3 nor SBS has national reach, but they are nevertheless strong competitors to TV 2, as they attract a substantial part of advertising expenditure. Viasat's main channel (TV3) has a market share of 5 per cent, while TV3+ has 4 per cent. SBS has been relatively successful in the last few years, reaching a market share of 7 per cent in 2000. In 2005, SBS has had a little setback and does now have a share of 6 per cent, as Kanal 4 has a market share of 4 per cent, whereas Kanal 5 has 2 per cent.

Until the late 1990s only three Danish channels were competing for audiences, namely DR, TV 2 and TV3, but from the mid-1990s new developments took place. Due to changes in the regulation of local television a number of local commercial channels established in 1997 a network channel (TvDanmark, which later became Kanal 4) with almost nationwide coverage. At the same time the number of television channels increased. In 1999 DR established a second channel DR2 which was distributed via satellite. The same year Viasat launched its second channel, TV3+, and in 2000 TV 2 established a new satellite channel – TV 2 Zulu – directed at a young audience. Since TV 2 has launched a number of additional channels: TV 2 Charlie addressing an elderly audience was established in 2004, and in 2005 TV 2 introduced a movie channel (TV 2 Film). In 2006, TV 2 will even launch a 24-hour news channel. SBS established an additional channel in 2000, a satellite channel based in the UK, but aimed at a Danish audience, and in 2005 it launched a music video channel called Voice TV.

The proliferation of channels has, of course, led to increased competition for audiences and revenues, but it hasn't really changed the balance between the four main broadcasting companies. The motives behind the launching of new channels vary, but in most cases the broadcasters go for the additional revenues that come from cable and satellite fees.

It is interesting that the expansion within the television market has not really changed the balance between public service broadcasters and their commercial competitors. Actually, the privately owned commercial channels have lost part of their former audiences during the last five years, primarily because DR and, in particular, TV 2 have been able to compete efficiently, but also as a consequence of lack of sufficient commercial funding. Consequently, the commercial broadcasters have found it financially more attractive to run low-budget channels attracting relatively small audiences than to invest in expensive quality programming in order to attract larger audiences. Only DR and TV 2 have the financial resources needed to reach a mass audience and by doing this they are the only ones able to dominate the market.

TV 2 has, after more than ten years with fierce competition from Viasat and SBS, a firm grip on the advertising market and functions as a "market leader" with more than a 62 per cent share of the market for television ads. In 2005 the ad spent on television in Denmark was 300 million € (a share of 19 per cent of the total ad spent). However, the position of TV 2 might change within the next few years, as the government has decided to privatize the company as soon as possible. The privatization was planned to take place in 2003, but due to a number of ongoing trials at the EU Court on matters of state aid the government has to wait until the court has come to a final conclusion.

So far, digitalization has not led to substantial changes within the Danish television system, but there is, nevertheless, a clear tendency to operate television channels in conjunction with other media, be it radio channels, online services or print media. DR in particular has taken steps in order to develop into a multimedia institution, but it is expected that TV 2 and the commercial broadcasters will follow the same route even further.

During the last decade the Parliament has as on several occasions decided to implement digitization of terrestrial broadcasting. For radio, the DAB transmission net is about to be completed at the end of 2006 with a penetration of 95 per cent and for TV digital operations began in early 2006. When completed three digital television platforms will be ready for operation. On the first platform the PSB channels will be placed, and DR and TV 2 will share the function as gatekeeper. Who should be the gatekeeper for the remaining two platforms for commercial services has yet to be decided, but it is a clear statement in the Media Agreement that the gatekeeper has to be selected on the basis of a 'beauty contest' in an open tendering. The switch-over from analogue to digital television in Denmark will be 2009. The switch-over for radio has not yet been decided, but 2015 has been mentioned.

C. The Internet Media
Main features:

■ Denmark has one of the highest Internet penetration figures in the world;
■ The most popular websites belong to the major media companies.

In 2005 Internet penetration in Denmark was 79 per cent. Broadband connections are used in 70 per cent of the households with Internet connection, i.e. 1,225,000 households. In 2005 72 per cent of the population accessed the Internet at least once a week, 57 per cent on a daily basis. Private purposes are mainly search for information and access to online services (73%) and communication (69%).

All newspapers have a regularly updated online version, and the major newspapers have started E-paper versions and/or special sections for subscribers of the printed newspaper.

The most popular websites belong to the major media companies. In 2005, DR and TV 2 were constantly among the top five, DR with an average of 2.9 million unique visitors per month, TV 2 with 2.4 million. Among the top ten were *JP/Politikens hus* (EkstraBladet) with 2.2 and *Det Berlingske Officin* (B.T.) with 1.3 million unique visitors.

D. News Agencies
Main features:

■ In Denmark there is only one news agency, Ritzaus Bureau.

Ritzaus Bureau is an independent Danish news agency, and it has subscribers among most of the printed press and electronic media as well as several ministries and financial institutions. The core product is written news, which is distributed online to Danish subscribers and several media in Scandinavia. Ritzaus Bureau cooperates with the European news agencies and employs special and permanent correspondents in a number of international capitals. Nordic News is an English-language news service, developed and delivered in cooperation between the four leading Nordic news bureaus: STT in Finland, TT in Sweden, NTB in Norway and Ritzaus Bureau in Denmark.

2. State Policies
Main features:

- The national bodies of media are divided into three, the Radio and Television Board having the most comprehensive set of functions;
- The media policy framework for print media is limited to general issues about freedom of expression and constitutional rights in general;
- The media policy framework for broadcast and electronic media is more specified and worked out in detail in Media Agreements running for fours years among parties in the Parliament;
- The Radio and Television Board is in charge of the central supervising functions for the radio and Television Act;
- The cartoon debate about the Muhammad drawings has not influenced the formal bodies in the accountability system in any way.

The national bodies of media are divided in three: The Ministry of Culture is in charge of the electronic media, but the regulatory actions and supervision are placed in an independent regulatory board: the Radio and Television Board. The RTB is the independent regulatory authority in charge of supervising the implementation of the Danish broadcasting legislation. The RTB has the following tasks: to issue licences to private national and local broadcasters, to monitor whether private and public broadcasters are fulfilling their legal obligations, to administer the grants for non-commercial local radio and television. The RTB consists of seven members, appointed by the Minister of Culture, that together represent expertise in legal, financial/administrative, business and media/cultural affairs.

The Media Secretariat, the MS, is an institution under the Danish Ministry of Culture. The MS is the secretariat of the Radio and Television Board and has the following tasks: to carry out the daily administration of the broadcasting regulation, to prepare the RTB decisions and the implementation of RTB decisions, to assist the Ministry of Culture in matters concerning radio and television, to be the national knowledge centre in Denmark within media matters for the benefit of, for example, public authorities, media corporations, science and research and the general public

Operating licences (frequency planning and distribution) is handled by the IT- and Tele Communication Agency within the Ministry of Science, Technology and Innovation. The regulatory framework for print media is handled by The Prime Minister's Department, including press subsidies.

While the media policy framework for print media is limited to general issues about freedom of expression and the press, the broadcast and electronic media sector has its framework described in the Government Programme, according to specific sets of legislation for the broadcast media. This framework and specific actions are specified in a so-called Media Agreement, running normally for four years, the normal election period of the Parliament, entered between the government and those parties from the opposition, which can agree to specific initiatives and general guidelines for later legislation, pointed out in the Media Agreement.

State subsidies to print media are given in the form of exemption from VAT charge and reduced rates on postal distribution, approximately an amount of €160 million per year.

Non-commercial radio and television stations have received subsidies since 1997. In 2006 the grants, which are administered by the Radio and Television Board, totalled €4.3 million. From 2007 the grants will be augmented to €6.6 million, according to the recent Media Agreement.

There is no antitrust legislation on media concentration in Denmark, but the Danish Competition Authority supervises also the public as well as private media in order to prevent any monopoly situation, related to either national legislation, i.e. the legislation about free enterprise and competition, or to supranational legislation, i.e. EU-regulatory framework on state subsidies, for instance, related to public service broadcasting.

The obligation to transmit programmes and services, i.e. the must-carry regulation as part of the Radio and Television Act, ensures that certain channels are also available to those households that have accessed the cable networks. Must-carry provision obliges cable operators to transmit in their networks, without any charging, the programmes of DR and TV 2.

In the Radio and Television Board (RTB) a number of supervising functions are concentrated. RTB monitors the cable operators to see whether the programme delivery is in accordance with the Radio and Television Act, and the same goes for advertising and sponsorship ruling, national networking among commercial radio and television stations, ruling about programme content, related to specific types of broadcasting licences (local/regional/national, commercial or non-commercial stations, harmful content and protection of minors etc.).

According to the Media Liability Act, both the content and the conduct of the mass media must be in conformity with sound press ethics. The act does not give a complete description of sound press ethics. However, "sound press ethics" is interpreted in the light of the Press Ethical Rules of guidance. Thus, the Press Council assesses the circumstances in every single case.

The so-called cartoon debate, following *Morgenavisen Jyllands-Postens* publication in 2005 of a series of Muhammad drawings, caused a severe, global crisis for Denmark, including attacks on Danish embassies in the Middle East, condemnations from the UN General Secretary, former US president Bill Clinton, etc. In Danish media the drawings and their global consequences were subjects of comprehensive public debates. One of the main issues was how the unlimited freedom of expression, stated in the Danish Constitutional Act, should be treated in media products and in public debates. The predominant part of the participants defended the unlimited character of the freedom of expression, but quite a few underlined the responsibility also to consider the context of the matter in question, i.e. the obligation to show respect for religious feelings. This debate was still running through 2007, but so far it has not in any way influenced the formal bodies in the accountability system.

3. Civil Society Organizations
Main features:

- The Press Council is an independent, public tribunal, which deals with complaints about the mass media in general, i.e. printed and broadcast media.

The major media organizations concerning the press, radio and television are Danish Newspaper Publishers' Association. Danske Mediers Forum (Danish Media Forum) is an alliance consisting of seven Danish media organizations and the two broadcasting corporations DR and TV 2/Danmark. The Ministry of Culture (broadcast media), the Prime Minister's Department (print media) the Ministry of Science, Technology and Innovation (Telecommunication), Mediesekretariatet (The Danish Regulatory Board) and Dansk Journalistforbund (The Union of Journalists in Denmark).

The Press Council is established pursuant to the Danish Media Liability Act. The Press Council is an independent, public tribunal, which deals with complaints about the mass media in general, i.e. printed and broadcast media. It can rule in cases relating to whether the publication made is contrary to sound press ethics and whether a mass media shall be under an obligation to publish a reply.

4. Development Trends
Main features:

- Increasing focus on the borderlines between public service and private broadcasting media remits
- Upcoming issues of conflict between national and EU media regulation on public support of public service media

The PSB institutions hold a very strong position in the Danish media landscape. More than 70 per cent of the television viewing is placed on DR or TV 2, and the same goes for the DR radio channels, which holds a market share of approximately 70 per cent, even after the launch of commercial nationwide radio in 2005. Commercial players and liberal-conservative politicians have often argued for restrictions of the PSB obligations, and asked for more precise definitions in the public service agreements of programme content of 'public value', different from programme content that should be left for the commercial operators. In the recent Media Agreement (2007–2010), this ongoing discussion has been met with a clear statement about DR as the main provider of PSB services on all distribution platforms on basis of sufficient economical resources. But, on the other hand, when launching new programme types or services these innovations must pass an internal 'value test' in order to prove their cultural, democratic and social relevance. During that process RTB should be heard, but the final decision will be made by the DR Board.

One of the core aims of the liberal-conservative government is to privatize the public-owned TV 2. Some years ago it was prepared for sale and transformed from an independent institution (similar to DR), but the process has been stopped by the EU because of complaints from MTG, (TV3and TV3+), accusing TV 2 for having received illegal state support through licensee fee involvement in the company surplus of several hundred millions of euros. In the first instance the EU Court has accepted this complaint, and has decided that TV 2 has to pay back an amount of 80 million euro to the Danish state. As long as this question is not settled the sales process is stopped, and it may take several years before trials within the EU system have come to a final conclusion. So instead of more privatization of state-owned radio and television channels, the state ownership has expanded. Recent development is that TV 2 obtained the licence to the main national FM commercial channel when auctioned in August 2006 – the channel formerly run by Sky Radio.

Major media companies operating in Denmark are still mostly in national or Nordic ownership, but the increased competition for market shares and advertising revenue might open up for new international players. During recent years, the Norwegian company Orkla Media, part of The Orkla Group, was the owner of Det Berlingske Officin, but due to unsatisfactory economical outcomes, it was sold in 2006 to a British-owned investment company, Mecom.

Due to the key role of the public service broadcast media, DR and TV 2, this field has not had a major attraction for investments from foreign media companies, with the exception of SBS (Luxembourg), widely engaged in European broadcasting activities, and the Swedish company, MTG (Viasat). New players are the Dutch Talpa Radio (Radio 100 FM) and for a short period of two years also Murdoch's News Corporation through Sky Radio. In general the Danish Media market seems too small and maybe also too regulated to be attractive for foreign investments on a larger scale.

Danish ownership of foreign media is quite limited. The Egmont Group being the largest media company in Denmark is engaged in print publication activities in the UK and the Nordic countries, and also in television programme production and film production. The Egmont Group also owns a third of the Norwegian TV2. The second largest private Danish media company, the Aller Group, owns magazine and other print media companies in Finland, Norway and Sweden.

The main challenge for the media companies operating in Denmark is not of a specific national character, but deals with the main tendencies among consumers of media products in the global media market: more specialized and easy accessible products on demand – from a variety of distribution platforms.

References & Sources for Further Information

Befolkningens brug af Internet 2005 [use of Internet 2005] (2005), København: Statistics Denmark.

Carlsson, Ulla, Harrie, Eva (2001), *Media Trends 2001 in Denmark, Finland, Iceland, Norway and Sweden. Statistics and Analyses*. Göteborg: Nordicom.

Carlsson, Ulla, Harrie, Eva (2006), *Media Trends 2005 in Denmark, Finland, Iceland, Norway and Sweden. Statistics and Analyses*. Göteborg: Nordicom.

Det danske Reklamemarked 2005, [The Danish Advertising Expenditure Survey: English Summary] København: Dansk Oplagskontrol. (Danish Audit Bureau of Circulations).

Danskernes Kultur- og Fritidsaktiviteter 2004 (2005), [The Cultural and Recreational Activities of the Danish People 2004]. København:AKF Forlaget.

Harrie, Eva (2003), *The Nordic Media Market*. Gothenburg: Nordicom.

Ferrell Lowe, Gregory, Hujanen, Taisto (eds.) (2003), *Broadcasting and Convergence: New Articulations of the Public Service Remit*. RIPE@2003. Göteborg: Nordicom.

Ferrell Lowe, Gregory, Jauert, Per (2005) (eds.), *Cultural Dilemmas in Public Service Broadcasting*. RIPE@2005. Göteborg: Nordicom.

Gallup *TV Meter*. 2000–2005.

Index Denmark. Gallup 2004.

Oplagstal og Markedstal (1995), [Circulation Data and Marketing Data]. Dansk Oplagskontrol. (Danish Audit Bureau of Circulations). København.

Oplagstal og Markedstal (2005), [Circulation Data and Marketing Data]. Dansk Oplagskontrol. (Danish Audit Bureau of Circulations). København.

TNS Gallup Radio Index. 2005.

Electronic Sources and Links:

TNS Gallup : http://www2.tns-gallup.dk/

The Ministry of Culture: www.kum.dk

The Media Secretariat: http://www.mediesekretariatet.dk/

Nordicom: http://www.nordicom.gu.se/

Danish Newspaper Publishers' Association: http://www.danskedagblade.dk/

The Danish Union of Journalists: http://www.journalistforbundet.dk/sw921.asp

THE FINNISH MEDIA LANDSCAPE

Jyrki Jyrkiäinen

Finland is an industrially highly developed and technologically advanced, sparsely inhabited country with a population of 5.2 million, including a Swedish-speaking minority of 290,000 people or 5.5 per cent, mostly living along the western and southern coastline. In Lapland lives a Sámi-speaking minority of 1,700 inhabitants. Some 133,000 speak a foreign language as mother language. The area is of 338,000 sq km with a density of 17 persons per sq km. There are 2.4 million households and 80 per cent of people live in urban or semi-urban municipalities. The share of aged population is slightly increasing. Eighty-six per cent of women aged 25–54 are employed outside the home.

The total turnover of mass media makes 2.7 per cent of GDP. On average, a household spends 4 per cent of total expenditures on mass media. Expenditures on telecommunications by households have grown. An average household spends about €1,000 per year on telecommunications charges.

1. The Market

A. The Print Media
Main features:

- More seven-day dailies than in any other Nordic country
- Third in newspaper consumption in the world
- Strength of newspapers in subscriptions and early morning delivery
- Of aged 10 or over, 76 per cent read a newspaper or afternoon paper daily
- Two major publishers account for 56 per cent of the aggregate circulation of the dailies
- Of all 53 dailies, 10 titles appear outside the chain ownership

The newspaper industry has been relatively stable in the last fifty post-war years. In 2006, the number of newspapers is 199 with a total circulation of 3.2 million copies. The aggregate circulation decreased by 0.7 per cent in 2005. In all, 53 dailies are issued from four to seven times a week, with a circulation of 2.3 million copies. Of dailies, 32 appear seven days a week with 1.6 million copies, more than in any other Nordic country. The number of seven-day dailies has increased by five titles since the end of the last century.

Eight dailies appear six times a week in 381,000 copies, nine appear five times a week in 211,000 copies and four papers four times a week with 33,000 copies. In addition, there are 146 non-dailies appearing from one to three times a week with aggregate circulation of 934,000 copies. Of newspaper sales, 88 per cent are based on subscriptions and only 12 per cent on single copy sales. Newspaper readers in Finland rank third in the world, after Norway and Japan, with 522 copies sold per 1,000 inhabitants in 2005. There are some 145 free-of-charge papers.

The readership of newspapers has remained stable. Of all Finns, aged 10 or over, 76 per cent read a newspaper or afternoon paper daily and 52 per cent read a periodical at least once a week. Nearly 70 per cent of households subscribe to a newspaper at home. Eighty-six per cent of Finns read one or more newspapers. At age 12 to 19, some 71 per cent read a newspaper and more than 56 per cent aged 25 to 35 read a newspaper every day. At this age young people read newspapers 19 minutes on workdays, 25 minutes in Saturdays and 29 minutes in Sundays. In the age group from 25 to 35 the most important media is television, the second is newspapers and the third is Internet. In the younger group, from 12 to 20 years, the order is television, Internet, radio and newspaper.

Today, 94 per cent of newspaper titles are unaffiliated and the share of twelve party papers accounts for 2.5 per cent of the aggregate circulation. In 1946, only 34.8 per cent of total circulation was provided by unaffiliated papers. Of party-affiliated papers the Social Democratic Party has seven Finnish-language and a Swedish-language paper, Centre Party three papers and the Left Alliance one paper.

There are eight national dailies. The largest is the politically unaffiliated *Helsingin Sanomat* of SanomaWSOY (431,000), the largest subscription-based daily in the Nordic countries. The other national papers include the country's two six-day afternoon papers, *Ilta-Sanomat* (196,000), founded in 1932 and belonging to SanomaWSOY and *Iltalehti* (130,000), founded in 1980 and belonging to Alma Media. Further national titles are the Swedish-language politically unaffiliated *Hufvudstadsbladet* (51,000), the Social Democratic *Uutispäivä Demari* (17,000), the Centre Party organ, *Suomenmaa* (9,000), and the independent left-wing paper *Kansan Uutiset* (9,000).

Among the provincial dailies, there are two with circulations over one hundred thousand, the second largest seven-day newspaper *Aamulehti* (137,000) in Tampere, and the third largest seven-day newspaper, *Turun Sanomat* (112,000) in Turku. Five newspapers from mid-Finland: *Pohjalainen* in Vaasa, *Ilkka* in Seinäjoki, *Keskisuomalainen* in Jyväskylä, *Savon Sanomat* in Kuopio and *Karjalainen* in Joensuu publish a common Sunday supplement. Through this kind of co-operation the editorial costs can be reduced. The co-operative papers are not under the same ownership.

The financial newspapers *Kauppalehti* (81,000) from Alma Media and *Taloussanomat* (38,000) from SanomaWSOY are competing in the same market of economic and business affairs.

Being officially a bilingual country, Finland has thirteen newspapers published in Swedish. Nine of them are dailies, with a total circulation of 155,000 copies or 4.9 per cent of the aggregate newspaper circulation.

Two major newspaper houses account for 56 per cent of the aggregate circulation of the dailies. SanomaWSOY, the biggest media corporation in the Nordic countries with a turnover of 2.6 billion euro in 2005, has six titles with 760,000 total copies or a 33 per cent share of aggregate circulation of newspapers. SanomaWSOY is a multichannel publisher operating in twenty European countries with a strong presence in the European magazine market in thirteen countries. SanomaWSOY publishes three national and three regional dailies, five local papers and nine free-of-charge papers including online editions and interactive services. The company owns Finland's leading press picture agency, Lehtikuva, and is leading general and education literature publisher. The concern has the largest cable television company, Welho, with 300,000 connections and is a major provider of broadband services. Its newest domestic media outlet are the local radio channel Radio Helsinki and the free-delivery papers, *Metro* and *Uutislehti 100*.

The second largest newspaper house is Alma Media with its ten newspaper titles, it has 511,000 circulation or 23 per cent. In addition, Alma Media publishes thirteen local papers and thirteen free sheets. From the total net sales (counting newspaper sales and advertising sales) of dailies, SanomaWSOY accounts for 35 per cent and Alma Media 22 per cent. The broadcasting operations of Alma Media were transferred to the ownership of the Nordic Broadcasting Company, founded by the Swedish Bonnier and Proventus, in April 2005. After that Alma Media has profiled on publishing newspapers, producing financial information and providing online services.

Major Finnish media houses have been rather active beyond their borders. The most active in Europe has been SanomaWSOY when it acquired the Dutch VNU's magazine publishing business (CIG) in 2001 and grew during 2003 into wider European markets in magazines and media services.

Alma Media's *Kauppalehti* has a business information news bureau, Baltic News Service, operating in Estonia, Lithuania and Latvia. Alma Media has five marketplaces through Internet for domestic and European market consisting of classified services for home-buying, used cars, used equipment, jobs and careers and for real estate in Great Britain, Norway, Poland, Slovenia, Sweden and Ukrainian.

In the ownership structure there is an accelerating trend towards newspaper chains in Finland. In 2006, there were 21 newspaper chains, of which three publish Swedish-language newspapers. Through takeovers and mergers the market share of the biggest media houses has grown. The publishing of dailies has concentrated on five newspaper chains: SanomaWSOY, Alma Media, Keskisuomalainen, Turun Sanomat Group and Ilkka Group, with control over a half of the dailies' total net sales in Finland. Of all 53 dailies, ten titles appear outside the chain ownership.

The second biggest group, by sales volume, after newspapers, are magazines. The share of magazines of media advertising expenditures was 17 per cent in 2005 – like the European average. There are about 2,600 magazines and periodicals, and if publications appearing at least four times a year are counted, the figure is some 5,000 titles. The number of consumer magazines exceeds 284 titles. Of copy sales 86 per cent are based on subscriptions and 14 per cent on single copy sales or some 20.6 million copies. However, the single copy sale of two tabloid newspapers is some fourfold compared to that of magazines. This confirms how strongly the sale of print media is based on subscriptions in Finland.

Yhtyneet Kuvalehdet – United Magazines Group – has in its portfolio 43 general interest magazines and 35 customer magazines. In addition, the company operates fifteen Web services connected to publishing activities. In 2005, the total volume of the company's magazines was over 3.6 million copies. The subsidiary in Estonia since 1998 publishes six periodicals as local versions tailored from the company's domestic titles. The company has a wide archive and agency of ten million photos and images. The country's only general-interest, current news weekly, *Suomen Kuvalehti* (103,000), is by Yhtyneet Kuvalehdet.

Sanoma Magazines of SanomaWSOY publishes 40 titles in Finland and 290 titles in thirteen European countries. It is a leading magazine publisher in Belgium, Bulgaria, Czech Republic, Hungary Netherlands, Russia and Slovakia. The two biggest publishers, Yhtyneet Kuvalehdet and Sanoma Magazines, make over 60 per cent of magazine market. A-Lehdet publishes eighteen titles.

B. *The Broadcast Media*
Main features:

- Two public service and two commercial generalist channels for nationwide TV
- Oldest private TV channel passed into Swedish ownership in 2005
- Biggest commercial radio companies in foreign ownership
- Switched over to digital television in the beginning of September 2007
- Amount of commercial digital channels in increase
- New digital pay-TV channels will be launched

Finland has traditionally had a dual system of public and commercial television broadcasters. In nationwide TV operation, there are three players and four generalist channels. In 2005, Finns watched television for 2 hours 41 minutes a day. Of those aged 10 or over, 77 per cent watch TV daily, 71 per cent listen to the radio daily.

The public service Finnish Broadcasting Company (YLE) transmits via YLE TV1 and YLE TV2. YLE's television output was over 20,000 hours in 2005. In ten years, the television output has tripled. YLE TV1 broadcasts of 55 hours of news in Sámi language in co-operation with Norwegian and Swedish broadcasting companies. Regional television news broadcasts in eight different areas cover the whole country and can be seen nationwide via the digital YLE Extra news channel.

The largest commercial channel is MTV3, owned by the Nordic Broadcasting Company (Bonnier, Sweden) which also owns the only national commercial radio network Radio Nova.

The second commercial national television network, Channel Four Finland (Nelonen), started broadcasting in 1997. Nelonen broke MTV3's monopoly of national TV advertising as well. In 2005, television had a 20 per cent share of media advertising.

Nelonenr belongs to SanomaWSOY. By 2006, Nelonen had reached a share of 31 per cent of television advertising expenditures. Both YLE and MTV3 have lost out equally in terms of viewers since Nelonen began. The biggest cable-television operator is Welho, owned by the SanomaWSOY, operating in Helsinki area with 300,000 cable connections and providing broadband services.

The public service company YLE broadcasts radio signals on three nationwide channels in Finnish: YLE Radio 1, Radio Suomi and YLEX and two channels in Swedish: YLE Radio Vega and YLE Radio Extrem. YLE operates twenty regional windows in Finnish and five in Swedish in the coastal area. An interesting difference in regional broadcasts is that the share of music in Swedish stations is 40 per cent but in Finnish-language stations 58 per cent. This might indicate the greater role of radio in community interaction among the Swedish-speaking population.

According to the law on the Finnish Broadcasting Company, YLE Sámi Radio broadcasts programmes for the listeners in Northern Lapland six newscasts in Sámi language on weekdays. Sámi Radio is a co-producer of the Nordic Sámi TV News. The newscast lasts for fifteen minutes and can be seen in all of Sweden and Norway with Swedish/Norwegian subtitles. In Finland, the newscast can be seen throughout Finland on the digital channel YLE Extra with Finnish subtitles.

YLE broadcasts news in Latin on the national FM network YLE Radio 1. *Nuntii Latini* is a weekly review of world news in classical Latin – the only international broadcast of its kind in the world. *Nuntii Latini* is heard around the world on short or medium wave and via satellite on Radio Finland and also on the Internet.

The first licences for commercial radio stations were issued in 1985. In 2006, there were 77 commercial radio stations. The share of local radio stations has remained at 4 per cent in recent years. The biggest commercial radio companies are in foreign ownership. In 1997, the first – and until now the only – nationwide commercial radio station, *Radio Nova*, started operation. These moves of 1985 and 1997 largely broke the radio monopoly of the public service YLE and increased the number of channels available on radio. The ownership of *Radio Nova* transferred to Nordic Broadcasting Company (Bonnier, Sweden) in 2005.

In addition to local stations, there are nine semi-national networks. SBS Broadcasting Group (Luxembourg) owns three semi-national networks, *Kiss FM*, *Iskelmäradio* and *Radio City*, and four city radios, *Radio Sata* in Turku, *Radio 957* in Tampere, *Radio Jyväskylä* in Jyväskylä and *Radio Mega* in Oulu. Other semi-national networks are *NRJ Energy* (France), *Metroradio* (Communicorp Group, Ireland) which owns *Radio SuomiPOP*, *Metro FM*, *Groove FM* and *Classic Radio*, and special radio channels are *Radio Dei* (Christian) and *Sputnik* (Russian). The market for commercial local radio operation is highly saturated. In May 2006, some new licences were granted for 2007–2011 – aimed at more diverse and local programming.

The national public service radio channels still dominate the market accounting for 51 per cent of all listening time, the figures for private radio being 49 per cent – 12 per cent for *Radio Nova* and 37 per cent for other private stations – in 2005. The daily listening time stood at 3 hours 17 minutes a day among listeners aged over nine.

Finland switched over to digital TV on 1st September 2007. The digital channels are gathered into four-channel packages called multiplexes. YLE has a multiplex for its five TV channels and five radio channels. Another multiplex is for the commercial channels (MTV3, MTV3 MAX, Subtv, Subtv Junior/Subtv Film, Nelonen and JIM). These two multiplexes cover 99.9 per cent of the population and the other two multiplexes cover from 78 to 90 per cent of the population. In all, there are fourteen free-on-air digital channels and fifteen pay-TV channels. Three commercial channels are, in addition, available by mobile receivers. In September 2007, over 84 per cent, or 1.9 million of Finnish households, had a digital terminal or an integrated digital TV set.

The public service company YLE's core services for digital terrestrial broadcasting will be the generalist channels TV1 and TV2. In addition, it has three nationwide specialist digital channels: YLE Teema (culture, education and science), YLE Extra and FST5 (YLE's Swedish-language channel). Much of their content comprise of simulcasts or rebroadcasts of programmes shown on TV1 and TV2. The digital satellite channel TV Finland shows a selection of YLE and MTV3 programmes for receivers in Europe, totalling 5,600 hours in 2005.

The commercial nationwide digital channels are MTV3 and Subtv (entertainment and fiction), both owned by MTV3 and Nelonen Plus (Channel Four), owned by

SanomaWSOY, and digital sport channel Urheilukanava, owned by SWelcom, SanomaWSOY's electronic media division. MTV3 has announced to launch four new pay channels in November 2006.

In addition, there are special free-of-charge channels, The Voice TV (music service with trailers), Digiviihde (entertainment) and Harju ja Pöntinen (entertainment). The digital pay-TV channels include Canal+ Finland, Canal+ Film1, Canal+ Film2, Canal+ Sport and Disney Channel.

Furthermore, there is a range of digital multimedia services including subscription-on-demand, video-on-demand, 3G mobile services and live Web-streaming provided by TV companies and teleoperators. The network services for television are provided by the company Digita Oy that is part of the international TDF Group.

The transition from analogue to digital television broadcasting brings new services, from which the newest for-fee-only and tightening competition for fragmented audience. The commercial broadcasters are challenging the print media for media advertisements.

C. *The Internet Media*
Main features:

- Internet penetration approaching that of newspapers
- 366 Internet connections per 1,000 inhabitants
- Five media-owned websites among the top-ten visited portals

In Finland, Internet penetration was 70 per cent in 2006. The number of Internet connections was 1.9 million at the beginning of 2005 or 366 per 1,000 inhabitants. Broadband connections are used in 36 per cent or 860,000 households. In January 2007, the broadband coverage was at 26 per cent per 100 inhabitants. There were about 1.5 million broadband subscriptions (DSL, cable modem, WLAN, PLC) in Finland on 30 June 2007. Of the DSL subscriptions provided, 78 per cent were in domestic use and 22 per cent in business use.

In sparsely populated rural areas where the population is ageing, South Karelia leads the field in Finland in broadband use: in the South Karelia village broadband project, more than 40 per cent of households in the villages involved subscribed to broadband, and in the most active villages more than 65 per cent of households have a broadband connection.

The number of weekly Internet users at home, work and place of study aged from 15 to 79 is 2.6 million. In 2006, about 67 per cent of all public services were available online in such a manner that it was possible to carry out an entire transaction without leaving the Internet. Although the growth figures for Internet advertising have been impressive, the share is still relatively modest, about 4 per cent of total media advertising, like that of local radios.

In September 2006, Elisa had a market share of 35 per cent of all broadband connections, TeliaSonera 29 per cent and Finnet Group, a consortium of regional phone companies, 24 per cent. Other telecom operators together accounted for 12 per cent; for over 82 per cent of all broadband connections are DSL connections.

Most newspapers have a regularly updated online version and 50 papers have launched PDF versions that are complete online copies of printed papers. In most cases, the front page of PDF versions is free while wider contents and archives are for fee only. Sixty per cent of the Internet users read online newspapers.

In October 2007, the most popular websites was MSN.fi (Microsoft network, 1.5 million weekly users). The most popular media-owned sites were MTV3 (Nordic Broadcasting Company, 1.3 million), *Iltalehti* (Alma Media, 1.1 million), *Ilta-Sanomat* (SanomaWSOY, 1.1 million, YLE (public service broadcasting, 930,000) and *Helsingin Sanomat* (SanomaWSOY, 841,000) that all ranked among the top-ten most popular portals.

D. News Agencies
Main features:

■ Practically one national news provider, owned by newspaper houses

The Finnish News Agency (STT) is an independent and an 'official', national news provider. STT produces a real-time and comprehensive news service and number of other services for media as well as communications services for leading companies and other organizations. STT is bilingual: most news is covered in Finnish as well as in Swedish.

The major owners of STT are media companies Alma Media, SanomaWSOY and TS-Group (Turun Sanomat), along with some other 50 media companies. The combined circulation of the newspapers that publish STT news is practically that of all newspapers. In 2006, the Finnish Broadcasting Company YLE discontinued the subscription of STT's news service. YLE intensifies national and regional news-gathering of its own.

A minor agency, UP-Uutispalvelu (UP-News service) provides news on politics, labour market and economy for 30 newspapers and 60 publications of trade unions.

2. State Policies
Main features:

■ Ministerial agency promotes development of information society
■ Media policy is aimed at improving productivity and competitiveness
■ New constitutional law regulates all media regardless its technology
■ No antitrust legislation on media concentration

- Public service broadcasting operates under an act of its own
- Private radio and television operation are regulated by separate legislation

The general frame for the communication policy is stated in the Government Programme (2003) under the heading 'The policy in information society and communications'. The policy is aimed at improving productivity and competitiveness and promoting social and regional equity.

The Act on the Exercise of Freedom of Expression in Mass Media (2004) regulates all media regardless its technology covering the responsibilities of editors, corrections in publications and rights to anonymity of sources of publishers.

The relevant national bodies for electronic communication policy are the Ministry of Transport and Communications, the Finnish Communications Regulatory Authority (Ficora) and the Ministry of Education. The Government grants operating licences for radio and television operation. The EU regulatory framework for all electronic communications is implemented in Finnish legislation.

The Ministry of Transport and Communications is responsible for matters concerning state subsidies given to newspaper publishing. The Government's budget includes an annual allocation towards political party newspapers and information provision for the province Åland Islands and, also, for discretionary press subsidies. The discretionary subsidies are granted in order to reduce newspaper delivery, distribution and other costs. The Ministry of Education grants subsidies for cultural periodicals.

The Press Subsidies Committee assists the Ministry in making amendments to the subsidy-granting criteria and application guidelines. The composition of the Board is based on the political make-up of the prevailing government.

There is no antitrust legislation on media concentration in Finland. According to the Communications Market Act (2003), telecom operators' obligations mainly concern operators with significant market power. The percentage of transmission time to be reserved for programmes produced by independent production companies accounts for 15 per cent.

'Must carry' provision obliges cable television companies to transmit in their network without charge the programmes of the Finnish Broadcasting Company (YLE), other national channels and services related to all these channels.

The Finnish Communications Regulatory Authority (Ficora) supervises the use of radio frequencies. Ficora supervises advertising and sponsorship in radio and television operation, collects the television fees and performs a market analysis of relevant wholesale and retail markets. Customers can turn to Ficora with complaints relating to the Act on Television and Radio Operations. The decision of Ficora can be appealed to the Supreme Administrative Court.

The Finnish Broadcasting Company (YLE) operates under the Act (2005). In the YLE the highest decision-making body is the Administrative Council, elected by Parliament.

YLE is a limited company owned almost wholly by the state. The company is governed by legislation on limited companies, such as the Companies Act and the Bookkeeping Act. The Act on YLE prohibits radio and television advertising in YLE's channels. Sponsored programmes are banned from YLE.

The only separate accounting arrangement concerns the separate limited company Digita Oy that provides the terrestrial distribution network for radio and television broadcasting.

The Act on the Exercise of Freedom of Expression in Mass Media (2004) applies to publishing and programme-making. Communication via information networks is subject to the legislation on the mass media.

3. Civil Society Organizations
Main features:

- Employers' associations formed a federation
- Union of Journalists negotiates collective agreements
- Renewed version of 'Guidelines for good journalistic practise' adopted in 2005
- Council for mass media cultivates responsible freedom in mass media

The central employers' organization is the Federation of the Finnish Media Industry. The major lobby-associations dealing with press publishing, commercial radio and television are the Finnish Newspapers Association, Finnish Periodical Publishers' Association, Association of Finnish Broadcasters and Association of Television in Finland.

The major journalist organization is the Union of Journalists in Finland (14,000 members). The Union negotiates with the employers' associations on collective agreement in the media field. The largest associations of the Union are the Finnish Association of Radio and Television Journalists (4,700) and the Finnish Association of Magazine Journalists (3,000). In 2005, the Union of Journalists has adopted a renewed version of 'Guidelines for good journalistic practise' and this code of conduct is recognized by all relevant media houses. The code consists of 35 paragraphs and is the basis for the adjudications of the Council for Mass Media in Finland.

The Council for Mass Media in Finland was set up in 1968 by publishers, journalists and their associations to act as a self-regulatory body for mass media content. Its function is to interpret the code of conduct 'Guidelines for good journalistic practise' (2005) which cover all journalistic work in the press, television and radio and on the Internet. The decisions of the Council are published by the professional magazines of the contracting associations. The public service YLE has 'Programme Regulations' that set guidelines for all its radio and television programmes.

Supervision with respect to the ethical principles of advertising, tele-shopping and the protection of children is carried out by the Consumer Ombudsman.

YLE, MTV3 and Channel Four have together agreed (2004) on adjusting and staggering the TV watershed timings and on examining the entire programming content when considering suitability for children. The restrictions for different age groups are shown before each classified programme.

The monitoring of harmful Internet content is currently undertaken by the Council for Mass Media in Finland, the Finnish Information Processing Association's Ethics Advisory Committee, the Council on Ethics in Advertising, the Consumer Agency and the Consumer Ombudsman.

4. Development Trends
Main features:

- Amount of media outlets has increased in electronic media
- Newspapers are developing their presence in the Web
- Newspapers have launched more 'lifestyle' and entertainment supplements in magazine format
- Of local newspapers 93 per cent are issued in tabloid format, from seven-day dailies only 16 per cent are tabloids
- Commercial radio stations have developed towards tight scheduled formats with very thin journalistic content

High readership for printed media continues, but not at the previous rate especially among the younger generation. The amount of media outlets has especially increased in radio channels, TV channels and in the area of new digital online media.

The share of foreign ownership has risen in Finnish electronic media when the Nordic Broadcasting Company (Bonnier/Proventus, Sweden) acquired the biggest private television (MTV3) and radio operation (Nova), and a semi-national radio (Sävelradio) from the Alma Media in 2005.

The newspaper companies especially are developing their presence in the Web. Major newspaper houses have intensified their internationalization to the Baltic countries, Russia and wider Europe.

The newspaper markets are nearly saturated and new market niches are hard to find. Major newspaper companies are still mostly in national ownership. The newspapers have launched more 'lifestyle' and entertainment supplements in magazine format.

Major newspaper companies in bigger cities have entered into the market free-of-charge papers. The aim is to compete with local and classified advertising expenditures. The biggest media company in Finland, SanomaWSOY, has recently bought the local edition of the free-delivery paper *Metro* that is delivered in eighteen cities.

The newspaper companies have increased the co-operation between their chain papers in news-gathering to face the increasing production costs.

Especially, the small and middle size non-daily newspapers have changed their format to tabloid. Of newspapers published from one to three times a week, 93 per cent are issued in tabloid format; of those published four to seven times a week, 42 per cent. However, from seven-day dailies the great majority are broadsheet papers, only 16 per cent or five of those 31 papers are tabloids.

In the entertainment industry, the competition has increased when the console and game industry has challenged the recording industry and cinema admissions. The television companies are worried about their audience rates when younger people use prime time more for playing on the Internet than watching television programmes and advertisements.

The spreading of broadband will obviously accelerate the shift of prime-time use, especially among the younger audience segments.

The commercial local radio stations have developed towards tight scheduled formats with robotized playlists but with very thin journalistic content. However, the local channels have built some new modes to be in interaction with the help of Internet pages, mobile phones and SMS messages.

One reason for the decrease in the circulation figures of the newspapers might be the increased popularity of online versions of the titles. Non-subscribers are moving to journalistic Web publications or PDF versions. The share of those readers who read only Web publications has grown, and typically among the younger readers. The other reason is that the number of single-person households has increased, particularly in larger cities and it is less probable that these households subscribe to or buy a newspaper than family households.

References & Sources for Further Information

Books and Articles
Aslama, Minna, Hellman, Heikki, and Sauri, Tuomo (2004), Digitalizing Diversity: Public Service Strategies and Television Program Supply in Finland in 2002. *The International Journal on Media Management*, 6: 3&4, pp. 152–161.
Aslama, Minna, Sonck, Fredrik, and Wallenius, Jaana (2006), *Finnish Television Programming 2005*. Publications of the Ministry of Transport and Communications, 40/2006 (English summary).

Brown, Allan (2005), Finland: Uncertain Digital Future in a Small Market. In: Allan Brown & Robert G. Picard (ed.), *Digital Terrestrial Television in Europe*. Mahwah, N.J.: Lawrence Erlabaum, pp. 223–243.

Heinonen, Ari and Kinnunen, Terhi (2005), Finland – Cautious Online Strategies. In: Richard van der Wurff & Edmund Lauf (eds.), *Print and Online Newspapers in Europe. A comparative analysis in 16 countries*. Amsterdam: Het Spinhuis, pp. 117–130.

Hujanen, Jaana (2003), From consuming printed news to making online journalism? Young Finns' newspaper reading at the Millennium. *Nordicom Review 2*, pp. 61–70.

Finnish Mass Media 2004, (English summary). Official Statistics of Finland, Culture and the media 2004:2. Helsinki: Statistics Finland [in Finnish].

Picard, Robert, G. (2003), Media Economics, Content, and Diversity: Primary Results from a Finnish Study. In: Hovi-Wasastjerna, P. (ed.), *Media Culture Research Programme*. Helsinki: Academy of Finland, Ilmari Publications, University of Arts and Design, pp. 107–120.

Picard, Robert G., Grönlund, Mikko (2003), Development and Effects of Finnish Press Subsidies. *Journalism Studies*, vol. 4, number 1, pp. 105–119.

Salokangas, Raimo (1999), From Political to National, Regional and Local. The Newspaper Structure in Finland. *Nordicom Review* 1, pp. 77–105.

Sauri, Tuomo (2001), Mass Media in Finland: Structure and Economy (English summary). *Culture and the Media 2001:1*. Helsinki: Statistics Finland [in Finnish].

Electronic Sources and Links

Jyrkiäinen, Jyrki, 2004, *Finnish Media: Outlets increase, audiences diversify*. The Ministry for Foreign Affairs of Finland, August 2004.

http://virtual.finland.fi/netcomm/news/showarticle.asp?intNWSAID=27113

http://www.finnpanel.fi (Television and Radio Audience Measurement)

http://www.finlex.fi/en/ (The database of Finnish acts and decrees and legislation)

http://tilastokeskus.fi/til/jvie/index_en.html (Media statistics Finland)

http://www.sanomalehdet.fi/ (Finnish newspapers: facts, statistics and links to online newspapers)

http://www.aikakaus.fi/index.asp?site=english (Statistics on magazines in Finland)

http://www.radioliitto.fi/asp/system/empty.asp?P=130&VID=default&SID=819276750720767& S=0&C=24716 (Information on commercial radio stations in Finland)

http://www.uta.fi/viesverk/fmcs/ (Overview on Finnish Media System)

http://www.jsn.fi/english/ (Council for Mass Media in Finland)

http://www.mintc.fi/ (Ministry of Transport and Communications/Communications)

http://www.mintc.fi/oliver/upl615-LVM11_2007.pdf (National broadband strategy. Final report. Publications of the Ministry of Transport and Communications 11/2007)

NORDICOM – Nordic Information Centre for Media and Communication Research http://www.nordicom.gu.se/?portal=mt&main=nat_stat_publ.php&me=5

THE GERMAN MEDIA LANDSCAPE

Hans J. Kleinsteuber & Barbara Thomass

Germany is the country in the "heart of Europe", located very much in the centre of the continent. In terms of population and economic strength it is the largest state west of Russia on the continent. About 82.5 million people live (2005) in Germany in 33 million households of which 98 per cent have at least one TV set. About 10 per cent of the population are foreign or have roots outside of Germany. The language is German and, together with Austria and the German-speaking part of Switzerland, about 100 million people make up a German-language space, constituting a rather large market.

Germany looks back at a long history of mass media. Some of the first newspapers started here roughly 400 years ago. During the years of the Nazis the mass media had become a tool of the dictatorship. In 1945 the media experienced an "hour zero" and started nearly completely anew. The post-war media system was based on the principle of press freedom as stipulated in the Basic Law of 1949. Until 1990 Germany was a divided country. The media system of the former GDR was highly centralized and worked under the control of the Communist Party. It disappeared during the process of unification, but patterns of media usage still differ between East and West. Today the major media production centres are located in the "old" West, newspapers of the former GDR are usually controlled by western companies.

1. The Market

A. The Print Media
Main features:

- A large number of titles
- A strong local and regional newspaper market
- A small number of national newspapers
- A large number of magazines
- A dependency on advertising income
- A high degree of economic concentration

In 2006 the number of 'independent editorial units' (meaning full publishing entities that produce all parts of a newspaper) for daily newspapers in Germany was 137 and the number of newspapers 353. If local editions of all papers are included, there are 1,529 different newspapers. Since the early 1990s, the number and circulation of newspapers in Germany have shown signs of decline. The penetration of daily newspapers has fallen from 74.8 per cent to 73.7 per cent in 2006.

Circulation figures show that the local and regional press is very important in Germany. A total of 95 per cent of the subscription press claim to be local, which is a circulation of 15.90 million. On first view, the German press appears to be highly diversified and local, but, in fact, much of the content of the newspaper is produced by central offices. The 'Heimatpresse' (local press) is in many cases only legally independent. Because of concentration processes and for financial reasons, these papers work closely together with larger newspapers or other local and regional newspapers.

There are only a few national papers in Germany: *BILD*, *Süddeutsche Zeitung* (*SZ*), *Frankfurter Allgemeine Zeitung* (*FAZ*), *Welt*, *Frankfurter Rundschau* (*FR*), *Tageszeitung* (*taz*). They claim to be independent and 'above parties', but most cover a liberal and conservative spectrum. *Die Welt*, controlled by Springer, is definitely on the conservative side, *Frankfurter Allgemeine Zeitung* is moderately conservative, *Frankfurter Rundschau* close to the Socialdemocratic Party, *Süddeutsche Zeitung* tends to the moderate left. The small left-wing newspaper *Die Tageszeitung* began in 1979 and has a rather un-traditional approach: It is published on a co-operative basis and has several thousand owners. There are two dailies with a clearly economic format, the *Handelsblatt* and *Financial Times Deutschland*. Among the 8 per cent of ethnic minorities who are living in Germany, the people from Turkey are the biggest group and they have some supply of their own, *Hürriyet* and *Milliyet* being the most important newspapers.

In terms of circulation figures, German national newspapers account for 1.65 million. Another 5.04 million papers are sold on the street. The tabloid press in Germany is often referred to as 'boulevard press'. The top-selling German tabloid paper is *BILD Zeitung*, with a circulation of 3.55 million. *BILD* is printed in tabloid format, has various regional editions, often questionable reporting standards and traditionally exerts a right-wing political orientation.

The German market for daily newspapers is dominated by a small number of publishers. The largest market share is controlled by the Axel Springer Group with around 22.5 per cent of the market (*BILD, Welt, Hamburger Abendblatt, Berliner Morgenpost*, etc.) The second position is taken by the WAZ Group (*Westdeutsche Allgemeine Zeitung*, etc.), which is more a regional publisher with nearly 5.6 per cent of the market. The third place is taken by Verlagsgruppe Stuttgarter Zeitung (5.2 per cent) and the fourth by the Ippen Gruppe with 4.1 per cent. DuMont Schauberg form Cologne takes the fifth place with 3.9 per cent. The ten largest publishers of dailies together control 41.3 per cent of the market. They include further on the Holtzbrinck Group with a 3.7 per cent market share, *FAZ* (3.0 per cent), *SZ* (2.6 per cent), Madsack (2.5 per cent) and DDVG, controlled by the Socialdemocratic Party (with 2.2 per cent).

With the takeover of the Berlin publishing house Morgenpost by the British media manager Montgomery, the first takeover of a foreign investor in a German newspaper took place.

The German magazine sector is extremely buoyant with some 873 general magazines and 1,081 specialized periodicals currently on the market. A weekly news magazine, modelled after the American *Time Magazine* and for long time with a virtual monopoly in its market is *Der Spiegel*. With its investigative style of journalism, it represents the most influential political publication in Germany. It competes directly with the magazine *Focus*, which is more colourful, more flashy and more conservative.

The market for general interest magazines is still quite lively. It participates in the whole advertising market with a share of 23.3 per cent. *Der Stern* by Gruner + Jahr (Bertelsmann) is the best known with its liberal and investigative format, although its circulation is on the decline.

The four largest publishers of general magazines which are Bauer Verlagsgruppe (20.7%), Axel Springer AG (16.1%), Hurbert Burda Media (15.5%) and Gruner+Jahr (10.6%) enjoy a market share of about 62.9 per cent together (2006).

Gruner + Jahr increased their portfolio since 2004 at about 100 per cent with acquisitions, e.g. Gruner + Jahr took over Motorpresse Stuttgart.
Burda increased their portfolio at about 10 per cent by the takeover of the Verlagsgruppe Milchstraße.

Another type of publication, which became popular after 1945, is the weekly newspaper. It presents less actual news and more analysis and background information. The most successful and important is *Die Zeit*, a liberal and independent paper. Free sheets just started and might be an important segment of the market in the future.

B. *The Broadcast Media*

Main features:

- A 'dual system' of both public and commercial broadcasting
- Federalism and a strong role for the Länder in public broadcasting
- An important role for supervisory councils in both the public and private sector
- An above-average percentage of cable households
- Two groups controlling commercial TV and a strong position for Deutsche Telekom
- An ongoing digitization of the terrestrial TV
- An active governmental policy of developing infrastructures for digital services
- A lack of innovative services and programmes
- An active role of PSBs to develop digital services

Germans use audio-visual media during 8 hours and 55 minutes per day (use of PC included). Three hours and 41 minutes of this duration is dedicated to radio use, 3 hours and 40 minutes to TV consumption. Broadcasting media have a 50 per cent share of the advertising pie.

The German Federal Constitution stipulates that the sole responsibility for broadcasting rests with the states (Länder) of the Federal Republic as part of their 'cultural sovereignty'. Exceptions are only those radio corporations whose main function it is to provide foreign countries with information and which therefore are based on federal legislation: the Cologne-based Deutschlandfunk (DLF) and Deutsche Welle (DW). The organizational and legal structure of all other broadcasting corporations is defined in Länder laws and, if more than one state is involved, in agreements between several or all Länder (e.g. ZDF). Because of this, the public service broadcasters are a creation of the Länder.

The traditional public service broadcaster consists of an independent and non-commercial organization, financed primarily by licence fees. The public service broadcasting organization (Anstalt) in Germany resembles to some extent the BBC system. The typical Anstalt provides a region, usually a Land, with public service radio and television (such as WDR in Northrhine-Westphalia or BR in Bavaria). NDR is the joint corporation for the Northern Länder (Schleswig Holstein, Hamburg, Lower Saxony, Mecklenburg-Vorpommern). All regional corporations together founded the ARD (Arbeitsgemeinschaft der Rundfunkanstalten Deutschlands) and contribute according to their size to the first TV channel. In addition they independently organize a regional programme that offers regional news and more culturally and educationally oriented programming.

The second German Television, ZDF (Zweites Deutsches Fernsehen), is based on an agreement of all Länder (ZDF-Staatsvertrag) and is located in Mainz. ZDF offers one national television service, but maintains offices in the different parts of the country.

All Länder broadcasters offer between three and five different radio channels in their respective region, some of them regionalized or localized. Usually one channel offers a popular music format with advertisements, while the other channels focus on more conservative programming with classical music, etc.

All broadcasting corporations are governed by an independent Broadcasting Council (Rundfunkrat), whose representatives are supposed to reflect the "socially relevant groups" of society, according to a Federal Constitutional Court's ruling. These delegates are either elected in parliament or they are selected and sent from the various groups, including parties, business and labour organizations, churches, farmers, sports, women's, cultural organizations, etc. While in theory only a few or none have been sent directly from the major political parties, the Councils are heavily influenced by party interests.

The public broadcasters ARD and ZDF also offer a channel in cooperation, the former started as a minor cable channel and now broadcasted via satellite and DVB-T,[1] called 3Sat (together with ORF and SRG), showing mainly cultural programming and reruns from the main channels. In 1992 ARTE, a joint German-French project for cultural programming, began transmission. On the German side the responsibility rests with ARD and ZDF and is based in Baden Baden, also the home of SWR. In Germany ARTE is only available on cable, DVB-T and satellite. Furthermore ARD started a channel specialized in information and documentaries (Phoenix) and another for children's programmes (Kinderkanal).

Digital Video Broadcasting – Terrestrial.

Both ARD and ZDF are active in digital television. The ARD offers a whole range of freely accessible digital channels. They are also involved in different projects to test and develop distribution via the Internet. The activities of public broadcasters in the new media technology field are and will be one of the most heavily discussed media topics of the future.

In the mid-1980s commercial competition started to challenge the public system, resulting in a 'dual system'. Two commercial television channels started operation, one out of Luxembourg (RTL), the other around a cable pilot project in Ludwigshafen (Sat.1). Both proved successful and soon more programmes were available.

Today German commercial television is controlled by two media groups calling themselves 'sender families'. One, formerly led by Leo Kirch, is called ProSiebenSAT.1 Media AG and consists of Sat.1, Pro 7, N24, Kabel 1 and 9live; the other, called RTL Group, is headed by Bertelsmann and the Luxembourg-based CLT, including RTL, RTL II, Super RTL, VOX and n-tv. N24 and n-tv are new channels. Many more specialized programmes were offered in 2007, among them viva and viva 2, two music channels, since 2005 both a part of Viacom together with MTV. Other channels concentrate on sports, movies, erotica, etc.; some are open, others have to be subscribed to. In large cities such as Berlin, Hamburg, etc., regional commercial TV has been established.

The market share of all public service broadcasters in television is at 44.6 per cent, of which ARD has a market share of 14.3 per cent, ZDF 13.6 per cent, the third channels 13.4 per cent, 3sat 1 per cent, Phoenix 0.6 per cent, Arte 0.5 per cent and Kinderkanal 1.2 per cent. Among the private channels RTL (12.8%), SAT1 (9.9%) and ProSieben (6.6%) have the biggest audience shares. The television advertising market is participating in the whole advertising market with 40.2 per cent, the radio advertising share is at 3.6 per cent.

Radio in Germany is a very scattered market. According to the different broadcasting laws of the Länder, which stipulate plurality and diversity as a common norm, some Länder prefer a model according to which many radio stations should cater for plurality (external plurality), while others prescribe the representation of different shareholders within few radio stations (internal plurality) in order to guarantee a broad supply. Thus, the number of (terrestrial) radio stations differs a lot from Land to Land, having, i.e., 66 in Bavaria and only five in Schleswig-Holstein.

With the advent of cable and satellite all Länder drafted media laws in the 1980s. These laws specifically regulate the electronic media outside the conventional public corporations, mainly by handing out commercial radio and TV licences and deciding what programmes may be fed into cable systems. For this purpose new supervisory bodies (Landesmedienanstalten) were created, each with a council, resembling those of the public broadcasters. A national framework of regulations is laid down in agreement between all Länder (Medienstaatsvertrag). Starting in 1990, this federal structure was also introduced in the newly established Länder in the East, thereby marking the end of the old GDR's centralized TV broadcaster. The final structure was laid down in a Medienstaatsvertrag of 1991, last updated in 2007.

In comparison with other European countries with large populations, Germany has the highest number of cabled households, (53.5 per cent of 36.18 million households). Another 46.5 per cent of households receive their programming via ASTRA satellites and via DVB-T and terrestial direct broadcasting. Kirch was the first to start with digitally packaged television, offering Digitales Fernsehen DF 1 since 1996. Subscription is rather low and did not go up as expected due to fierce competition between DF 1 and Premiere, both controlled by the KirchGroup, which merged in October 1999 under the name of Premiere World, renamed again Premiere in 2002. Premiere, since the insolvency of the KirchGroup (KirchMedia) in 2002, was mostly held by the Permira Investment Group until the initial public offering in 2005.

The German Telecom (Deutsche Telekom AG) is a purely federal institution, based on federal law and administered as a privatized company. It is supervised by a body for the regulation of telecommunication (Regulierungsbehörde). From 2000 to 2001 the German Telecom sold the cable systems on a regional basis, in accordance with the territory of the Länder. Every regional system was sold to another company or investor, except Hesse and Baden-Wuerttemberg, they were sold to Kabel BW. Later on, several regional companies merged to one group, called Kabel Deutschland. Today, the major cable provider is Kabel Deutschland (represented in thirteen Ländern), furthermore there is Unitymedia, covering Hesse and North Rhine-Westphalia and Kabel BW in Baden-Wuerttemberg. These companies are mostly owned by American-British investors.

Digital radio and television are well established in the country. Much of the development of Digital Audio Broadcasting (DAB), the digital follow-up specification of FM radio, was pushed in the country. Regular service started in 1999 and a transmitter network has been built, covering 90 per cent of the country. But innovative programmes are rare and use of receivers is still disappointingly low. The future of AM will be with Digital Radio Mondiale (DRM), again some of the development took place in the country (mostly supported by the international broadcaster Deutsche Welle). Pilot projects have also started with terrestrial DVB-T radio.

Digital television started in 1996 when programme packages were introduced by the leading pay-TV company, Premiere. Transmission was later extended to cable and satellite. Public broadcasters offer about ten specialized free digital programmes, based on their huge programme library and time-shifting. Beginning in 2003 DVB-T (terrestrial digital TV) started in German urban centres: Berlin was the first place worldwide, where after the introduction of digital TV all analogue TV was switched off. Other cities followed. Digital terrestrial TV makes between 20 and 30 programmes in city agglomerations available, but introduction in the less populated countryside seems impossible. In 2005 about 20 per cent of all households had access to digital TV.

C. The Internet Media
Main features:

- T-Online and AOL being the most successful websites
- A predominance of news online media generated by the traditional media

In 2006 about 59.5 per cent of all Germans were using online services. The most successful websites (in terms of page impressions) were provided by T-Online (of Deutsche Telekom) and by AOL. Among the portals that carried the name of media companies, rtl.de is on top, followed by spiegel.de, prosieben.de, focus.msn and stern.de. Some publishers maintain a separate news office with online journalists – Spiegel is leading here – others mostly use material that has been produced by their journalists and is additionally presented on their website. Some newspapers take over online material of news agencies – dpa is leading here – and offer it under their name. Important news services of the public sector are tagesschau.de, provided jointly by the ARD-TV corporations and dw-world.de, the portal of Deutsche Welle, leading in international news.

There is nearly no popular news websites which are not the ones of the traditional media, netzeitung.de being one of them and according to their claim the first news service which is distributed only online. They started as well a readers-edition.de, which gets its content only from readers. golem.de is a news website on current issues around computing and telecommunications. indymedia.org, which has a German branch is a news portal which is edited by professional journalists and claims to create sort of a counter public sphere.

Online is an established medium and is especially popular among young people; 96.1 per cent of those in the age range of 14 to 19 use it regularly. Among all Internet users about one-half report that they use the Net for up-to-date information.

D. News Agencies
Main features:

- One dominating, internationally active agency (dpa)
- A variety of small specialized agencies

In Germany competition between the news agencies is fiercer than anywhere. Often seconds count to decide which is the fastest agency. Nevertheless, the principle of agency journalism is "Get it first, but get it right". Eight agencies are on the market, which have certain relevance. The leading agency is dpa (Deutsche Presseagentur, www.dpa.de), which is as well very strong in the international market. dpa has a co-operative structure; approximately 200 newspapers, magazines and broadcasting stations are participating. Within the old Länder the infrastructure of dpa is not comparable to any other of the competitors. Worldwide, dpa has 46 offices which is an extremely high-ranking density of correspondents. As nearly all newspapers are subscribers of dpa, it can be regarded as the primary source, whereas the other news agencies are complementary sources. There are as well more than twenty newspapers which subscribe only to dpa. It is not only the source with the highest amount of subscribers, but as well with the widest range of specialized thematic services. There are critics concerning dpa; that it is too close to government and prefers official statements to any other sources. This might be explained with the fact that financial support is granted to the news agency from the federation and the Länder. The German news agencies get subsidies from the state, and dpa receives the highest amount with 60 per cent.

Other players in the global news market are active in Germany as well. The US-American AP (Associated Press, www.ap-online.de), the German Reuters (rtr, www.reuters.de) which is a complete subsidiary company of the British Reuters and Agence France Presse (AFP, www.afp.de) are ranking second, third and fourth place in the German market.

The second largest news agency of German origin is ddp (Deutscher Depeschendienst, www.ddp.de). ddp was founded in 1971 after the end of the German branch of UPI, but it went bankrupt in 1983, although the name was held by a German publisher. After reunification he bought the Eastern German ADN and unified both agencies, although it still offered two services. It was retransformed to ddp and made a limited company. This agency is mostly active in German national and regional policies, and by its former GDR heritage it has a strong representation of correspondents in the new Länder.

Beside those, two confessional news agencies are in the market: the Protestant Evangelischer Pressedienst (epd, www.epd.de) and the Catholic Katholische Nachrichten-Agentur (KNA, www.kna.de). They are held both by the two main organized religions in Germany. Furthermore, thematic agencies offer their services on the German market. This is a sports service (sid, Sport-Informations-Dienst, www.sid.de), a business service (vwd, Vereinigte Wirtschaftsdienste, www.vwd.de) and Kid (Kinderinformationsdienst, www.kidweb.de), a news service which specializes on news presentation adequate for children. The news agencies of the German-speaking neighbours Austria and Switzerland, APA (Austria Presse Agentur) and SDA (Schweizerische Depeschenagentur), are not important within the borders of Germany.

2. State Policies
Main features:

- A variety of actors on different levels, due to the strong federalism of Germany
- A tentative and compromise-orientated style of policies
- An ongoing dispute on the high degree of media concentration
- An ongoing dispute on the role and the rights of public service broadcasting

Media freedom and freedom of expression are guaranteed in Germany within the constitution (Grundgesetz, Art.5). Within the international rankings on press freedom, Germany is listed on rank 23 within the 168 countries comprising a list of the NGO Reporters without Borders, and on rank 17 of 194 listed countries within the Global Press Freedom Rankings of the US-American NGO Freedom House.

The central actors in the German audio-visual media policy are the political parties, especially the Länder organizations of the two large parties, the conservative CDU and the social democratic SPD which control much of the public broadcasting sector. During the 1980s they initiated new broadcasting laws for the commercial sector and made sure to occupy the central positions in the newly founded supervising bodies. The Federal Government generally exerts little influence; its main tool before privatization was the Deutsche Telekom. Most of the large media conglomerates (Springer, Bauer, Burda) tend towards the CDU, the Bertelsmann company acts in close association with the SPD.

During the 1980s the central issue had been the question of commercialization, the CDU being in favour, the SPD defending the public service sector. After years of strong polarization, media policy is now again based on a broad consensus between the Länder. In an agreement between all Länder, the basics of a 'dual system' of broadcasting have been put in place. It includes regulation for media concentration, stating that one programmer cannot control more than 30 per cent of all TV ratings. The high degree of media concentration, especially the two 'sender families', are causing concern. This was especially highlighted with the threat of a merger of Springer with one of the two families, the Pro7Sat1 media group, which finally did not take place.

The update of the Länder agreement of the Rundfunkstaatsvertrag includes the provisions of the EU television directive, especially the provision stating that important events, such as the Olympic Games, should be broadcast for free.

Future topics of media politics are participation of public service broadcasters in the new media technologies and their existence in general. There are repeated efforts to submit scenarios of a changed media landscape which offers public service broadcasting a complementary 'niche' existence. Questions of convergence of telecommunication, information technology and television will be strongly influenced by the interests of the big 'sender families' in dominating the developing pay-television market.

The hitherto state independent procedure of fixing the augmentation of the licence fee was damaged with the last round, and the PSB's plan to complain before the constitutional court, because of this political intervention. In recent times, debates about the future of German public service broadcasting are more and more influenced by decisions and challenges of the EU, as, for example, the complaint of the EU Commission about behaviour of German PSB concerning licence fees transparency. On the grounds of the German legislation, they are not regarded as a state subsidy.

State subsidies do not exist within the print sector, although special aids as a reduced valued added tax rate and reduced prices for distributing print products via mail serve as a state-generated support for the press.

3. Civil Society Organizations
Main features:

- A clear organizational structure of journalists' and employers' organizations
- An absence of strong media-related NGO's
- A vast variety of media research institutions
- An important position of the German Press Council
- A weak position of the public within the organizations of media accountability
- A growing concern of journalists' organizations about quality of journalism

On the journalists side there are two major organizations. The German Journalists Association (Deutscher Journalisten Verband, DJV), calling itself a 'trade union' but being, in fact, a professional organization. The other one is the German Journalists Union (Deutsche Journalisten Union, DJU), part of Verdi, a service workers and clerks trade union, that is in turn a member of the German Trade Federation (Deutscher Gewerkschaftsbund, DGB).

On the employers' side, the owners of the daily press are organized in the Bundesverband Deutscher Zeitungsverleger (BDZV) and the magazine press is represented by the Verband Deutscher Zeitschriftenverleger (VDZ). The commercial radio and television industry co-operates in the Verband Privater Rundfunk und Telekommunikation (VPRT).

The advertising industry is represented within the ZAW (Zentralverband der Deutschen Werbewirtschaft), which includes 41 organizations concerned with advertising.

There is not a strong tradition of media-related NGO's. Media issues are dealt with within the political foundations of the parties (SPD: Friedrich-Ebert-Stiftung, CDU: Konrad-Adenauer-Stiftung, Greens: Heinrich-Böll-Stiftung, FDP: Friedrich-Naumann-Stiftung, PDS: Rosa-Luxemburg-Stiftung). Consumer associations like the Verbraucherzentrale (a consumers' association) deal as well with media issues, although only very rarely.

Media research is hosted in Germany in very many different institutions, beginning with the university-based institutes and university-related institutions, like the Hans-Bredow-Institut which is dedicated to many fields of media politics, media law and audience research. All public service broadcasters as well as many commercial broadcasters have media research divisions, mostly dedicated to audience and programme research. Important independent research institutes are the Formatt-Institute, dealing with press concentration issues, the Adolf-Grimme-Institut, which focuses on monitoring, evaluation and analyses of TV programsme, and the newly founded Institut für Medien- und Kommunikationspolitik.

There is no ombudsman in Germany. In 1956 the German Press Council (Deutscher Presserat) was established, consisting of an equal number of representatives from the journalists' organizations and the publisher organizations (twenty in total). Members of the general public may appeal directly to the Council. If the Council supports the complaint, the respective newspaper is expected to publish the Council's ruling. The decisions are taken on the basis of a Press Codex which is regularly renewed according to the recent journalism developments. The effect of this self-regulation is limited, especially in relation to the practices of the 'boulevard' press. A discussion emerged on how the German Press Council can work more overtly with the participation of the public sphere.

A similar organization is the German Advertisement Council (Deutscher Werberat), consisting of approximately ten to twelve representatives from the advertising industry, the media and the advertisement agencies, which are co-operating in their trade organization ZAW. They publish their decisions on complaints in a handbook. The Council, made up entirely of industry representatives and excluding consumers, is not known for strong criticism.

Complaints against the public service broadcasting may be brought to the members of the Broadcast Councils. In the commercial broadcasting media some of the large television programmers employ a Commissioner for Youth Protection (Jugendschutzbeauftragter) that reports only to the company. The new Staatsvertrag proposes to establish informal Councils of Advisors to the licensed programmers.

A developing, but weak part of media accountability systems is the fact that some media, especially newspapers, have special media sections, which contribute to more transparency for the audiences, but which are not strong in media criticism. Journalists' organizations as Netzwerk Recherche (Network for investigative journalism) are trying to improve quality of journalism.

4. Development Trends
Main features:

- The announcement of sale of ProSiebenSat.1
- The announcement of encryption of digital programs

The most debated event of 2005/6 was the public announcement that the Springer company, largest printing house of Europe, intended to buy the leading commercial broadcaster, ProSiebenSat.1. The merger was opposed by the Federal Cartel Office, responsible for defending market principles, on account of cross-media concentration. Also the KEK, another commission for the monitoring of concentration, objected to the move. Without waiting for the decision of the Economic Minister, who has the final say, Springer decided to withdraw from the merger. There were other investors prepared to take over the lucrative ProSiebenSat.1 company, the Turkish media mogul Dogan, being one of the most powerful. The developments have prompted discussions about the introduction of new concentration limits. In December 2006 the Private Equity companies Permira and KKR took over the ProSiebenSat.1.

In 2006 leading media actors Astra (for satellites), RTL and ProSiebenSat.1 made public that they intend to introduce basic encryption of their digital programmes by 2007. This forces all viewers to invest in a digital decoder and buy a smart card (for a few euros so far). This specification allows for additional programming, pay-TV and new interactive features. Smaller media actors claim that the alliance already dominates commercial TV markets and intends to discriminate against them. The Federal Cartel Office has looked into the matter. The public sector announced to remain freely accessible (ARD, ZDF).

References & Prime Sources for Further Information
Altendorfer, Otto: Das Mediensystem der Bundesrepublik Deutschland. 2 Vol. Wiesbaden: VS 2001/2004.
Arbeitsgemeinschaft der Landesmedienanstalten (ALM): Privater Rundfunk in Deutschland. Berlin: vistas, published annually.

Arbeitsgemeinschaft der Rundfunkanstalten Deutschlands (ARD): ARD-Jahrbuch. Hamburg: Hans-Bredow-Institut, published annually.

Bundesverband Deutscher Zeitungsverleger (BDZV): Jahrbuch Zeitungen. Berlin: ZV, published annually.

Dreier, Hardy: Das Mediensystem der Bundesrepublik Deutschland. In: Hans-Bredow-Institut, ed.: Internationales Handbuch Medien 2004/2005. Baden-Baden: Nomos 2004, pp. 245–268.

Kleinsteuber, Hans J.: Germany. In: Mary Kelly/Gianpietro Mazzoleni/Denis McQuail, eds.: *The Media in Europe*. London : Sage, pp. 78–90.

Media Perspektiven, Basisdaten. Daten zur Mediensituation in Deutschland (annually).

Meyn, Hermann: Massenmedien in Deutschland. Konstanz: UVK 2004.

Home pages with English information: www.ard.de (ARD), www.zdf.de (ZDF), www.bdzv.de (newspaper editors association), www.vdz.de (magazine editors association), www.kek.de (commission on concentration in the media).

THE ICELANDIC MEDIA LANDSCAPE

Rúnar Pálmason

In order to get some sense of proportion it is necessary to keep in mind some statistics about this small island nation. Although Iceland is three times the size of the Netherlands the population is only 300,000, living in just over 100,000 households. Iceland is heavily urbanized, around 80 per cent of the population live in urban areas and 60 per cent live in the capital, Reykjavík, and surrounding localities.

1. The Market

A. The Print Media
Main features:

- Three national daily newspapers with a combined circulation of more than 250,000 copies
- Two newspapers are distributed to homes, free of charge
- The newspaper market has gone through significant transformation in recent years, mainly as a result of the advent of the first free newspaper
- The number of magazines has doubled in the past two decades

Icelanders are devoted newspaper readers. In a 2004 Gallup poll about 80 per cent of the population (12–80 years) claimed to read a newspaper daily and 96 per cent to read a newspaper every week. All the newspapers are tabloid in format and there is no tradition for broadsheets.

There are three national daily newspapers, *Blaðið*, *Fréttablaðið* and *Morgunblaðið*. *Fréttablaðið* is owned by 365-Miðlar, by far the largest and most diversified multimedia and entertainment corporation in Iceland. *Morgunblaðið* is published by Árvakur which is almost wholly concerned with newspaper publishing and online news service. In December 2005 Árvakur bought a 50 per cent share in *Blaðið*. At the time of the deal, *Blaðið* had been published for about seven months.

Fréttablaðið and *Blaðið* are free of charge while *Morgunblaðið* relies mainly on subscriptions. *Fréttablaðið* is distributed to households in Reykjavík and surroundings as well as in most other major population centres and is considered to have almost nationwide reach. *Blaðið* is distributed throughout the greater Reykjavík area and also to subscribers of *Morgunblaðið* elsewhere in the country. The fourth newspaper is *DV*. Until April 2006 it was published six times a week, but because of fast shrinking sales and advertising revenue, following one particularly controversial story the paper ran, it is now only published on Saturdays. Like *Fréttablaðið*, 365-Miðlar owns *DV*.

In February 2006 Fréttablaðið had an average daily circulation of a little over 100,000, of which 93,000 were delivered to homes. At the same time *Morgunblaðið* sold just over 50,000 copies daily. A Gallup poll, taken in January 2006, revealed that the average readership of *Fréttablaðið* was 63 per cent while 50 per cent read *Morgunblaðið*. The circulation of *Blaðið* is about 100,000. In a Gallup poll in January 2006 the readership had reached 32.4 per cent. When the poll was taken, readers received *Blaðið* in the afternoon but since September 2006 it has been distributed in the mornings, which generally is considered to have given the readership a boost. Since *DV* was changed from a daily to a weekly, new circulation figures have not been published.

Two newspapers of special interest are published weekly, *Fiskifréttir*, which reports on the fishing industry, and *Viðskiptablaðið*, a business newspaper. *Fiskifréttir* and *Viðskiptablaðið* have a combined weekly circulation of about 6,000. In addition over twenty local and regional papers are published weekly; some sold, but the majority is free of charge. In 2004 their combined average weekly circulation was 49,000.

The arrival of *Fréttablaðið* in 2001 marked a watershed in the Icelandic newspaper market. Although free of charge it is distinctly different from the free "metro" newspapers on the European continent. It does not rely on news agencies but has its own editorial staff and is much richer in content. More importantly it is delivered to homes, reflecting the fact that the overwhelming majority of Icelanders commute by car and not by public transport.

The newspaper market has gone through significant transformation in recent years. This is in stark contrast to how the market developed for the better part of the twentieth century when changes were slow and incremental. There were several national newspapers, usually five or six, which all had formal or informal ties to political parties, and readership was, to a large extent, based on political affiliation. Those ties gradually faltered forcing the papers to find a new base for their sales, a move that proved difficult for most. In one decade, from 1990 to 2000, the number of national newspapers plummeted from six to two, with *Morgunblaðið* and *DV* as the only survivors. *Morgunblaðið*, which for decades had been the most powerful and influential newspaper, now dominated the market and *DV* was a distant, non-threatening second. At the turn of the century, the situation changed when *Morgunblaðið* had to face its toughest rival to date, *Fréttablaðið*.

At first *Fréttablaðið* wavered and one year after its inception it had to file for bankruptcy. The paper's demise did not last. Following a few days lull it was announced that a group of investors, led by Baugur Group, had bought the publishing rights and publication was promptly resumed. *Fréttablaðið* was now a much more formidable competitor.

Morgunblaðið has responded to increasing competition by changes in editorial content and layout. Furthermore, in January 2002, it started publishing seven days a week, ending several decades' old tradition of not publishing on Mondays. The readership and circulation of *Morgunblaðið* has remained roughly the same, but the paper has experienced a significant drop in advertisement revenue, in part because advertisers that belong to Baugur Group have largely turned to 365-Miðlar.

The advent of *Fréttablaðið* resulted in an aggregated increase in newspaper circulation, rising from 90,000 in 2000 to 156,000 in 2003 (distributed papers) and to around 250,000 in 2006. The circulation of paid-for newspapers has declined by about 20,000 (between 2000 and 2003).

Fréttablaðið was deemed so successful by the majority owners of 365-Miðlar that they decided to try a similar business model in Denmark, where Baugur Group, the biggest shareholder in 365-Miðlar, has significant business interests. Thus, the idea of *Nyhedsavisen*, a free newspaper distributed to homes in Denmark, was born. When plans of the publication were made public in February 2006, two Danish publishing houses responded by announcing that they would also publish and distribute free newspapers. *Fréttablaðið* therefore has not only had an impact on the Icelandic media landscape.

In contrast to the declining number of newspapers, the number of magazines has doubled in the past two decades. In 2004 there were around 850 magazines and periodicals published at least annually. Most of them had miniscule circulation. In 2000 only ten magazines had a circulation of 5,700 copies or more per issue, seven of which were published by Fróði. Fróði has since gone bankrupt and a new media house, Íslendingasögurnar, has bought the publishing rights to Fróði's entire magazine. The flagship of the publication is *Mannlíf*, a traditional mixture of news-related articles and interviews, fashion and lifestyle. In the fall of 2006 it was announced that a former editor of *Mannlíf* was launching a new magazine, *Ísafold*, seemingly in direct competition with *Mannlíf*. Through a subsidiary, Baugur Group has a majority share in the new magazine.

The most popular magazine in Iceland is *Séð og heyrt*, which can best be described as a mild-gossip magazine. It is published by Íslendingasögurnar, formerly by Fróði. 365-Miðlar publishes a similar magazine, *Heyrt og séð*, but it has not reached the same level of popularity.

In 2004 the print media (newspapers and weekly magazines) enjoyed a little under 60 per cent of the total advertising revenue, according to Statistics Iceland.

B. *The Broadcast media*
Main features:

- Ten domestic television channels
- High degree of consolidation in television
- The state-owned broadcasting corporation still the most powerful broadcaster
- Content mainly of American and British origin
- Limited interactive service
- According to a government plan, almost the whole population will have access to digital television by 2007

Nine out of ten Icelanders watch television daily, making it the most widely used medium. The average viewing time is around 2½ hours (age 12–80), measured by participants keeping a diary (2004 figures). Such measurements, however, have a tendency to show a greater viewing time than Electronic Peoples Meters.

In 2004 Icelanders could choose from ten domestic television channels. Out of those ten, four channels broadcasted to all regions of the island and could be considered to have a nationwide reach as they could be received by at least 90 per cent of the population. In addition some 50 foreign channels were available, either by cable or by continuous relay. There are around twenty radio stations, four of which broadcast nationally.

Just as in the newspaper and magazine markets, the broadcasting sector is characterized by a high degree of consolidation.

The Icelandic National Broadcasting Service, RÚV, is the still the biggest broadcaster, although only by a thin margin. It operates a television station, two national radio stations and four regional radio stations. The regional stations are broadcasted off-the-network.

RÚV has been broadcasting since 1930 when RÚV-Radio was launched. For more than half a century, from 1934–1986, RÚV was ensured a broadcasting monopoly in Iceland by law. In effect however, the monopoly was broken in 1951 when the American military forces, stationed on a NATO base some 60 kilometres from Reykjavík, launched their own radio station. To the delightful surprise of most, but horror of others, the transmission could be picked up by more than half of the Icelandic population. When the Americans started a television station a few years later, and especially when its transmission signal was increased in 1960, the scene was set for a furious dispute about the perceived dangers of foreign (i.e. American) cultural influence. That debate increased pressure for an Icelandic television station, which was launched by RÚV in 1966. By then Yankee TV, as the American TV station was generally known, had switched to cable, thus eliminating the potential threat from its broadcasts.

By 1983 pressure for a more diverse programming sparked RÚV to launch a second radio channel, Rás tvö. The same year RÚV´s television channel, Sjónvarpið, also faced up to mounting pressure by starting to broadcast in July, but until then there had been no broadcasts during July. In 1987, following the loss of its monopoly and competition from Stöð 2, a private TV channel, RÚV finally started television broadcasts on Thursdays. In 2004 Sjónvarpið had about 43 per cent market share.

RÚV is funded by a licence fee, which is levied on all households with TV or radio and from revenues from commercials and sponsorships. Commercial earnings account for about a quarter of RÚV´s television revenue and as much as half of its revenue from radio.

The governing board of RÚV is appointed by the parliament, Alþingi. The term of the board corresponds to that of Alþingi with the result that its composition closely reflects the balance of power between the political parties. The minister of culture appoints RÚV´s director-general for a five-year period.

By far the largest private broadcasting firm is 365-Miðlar with five television stations and about half of the dozen private radio stations. Measured by their share of viewers/listeners, the company has 37 per cent of the market in television and 44 per cent in radio (2004 figures).

The most important part of 365-Miðlar interests is Stöð 2, the oldest and largest private television station, established in 1986. Stöð 2 is based on subscription and is estimated to have around 40,000 to 50,000 subscribers, roughly half of the households in the country. From its introduction in 1987, the flagship of Stöð 2 has been its free news service.

Other television stations owned by 365-Miðlar are Sýn, a sports station, Stöð 2-Bíó, a movie station and, finally, Popp tíví and Sirkus. The two latter are free of charge and mostly broadcast American TV programmes and music videos.

The only serious competitor to 365-Miðlar in television is Skjár einn. It is a free-for-all channel, offering mostly entertainment, predominantly from the United States of America. Skjár einn has around 20 per cent market share, measured by the number of viewers. Síminn, the largest communication firm in Iceland, owns Skjár einn. Síminn also owns Enski boltinn, a subscription TV channel centred on football games in England.

Other television stations are much smaller and only broadcast regionally, some only for a few hours a day.

In addition, Icelanders can subscribe to numerous foreign television channels. Around 35 per cent of households reach those transmissions by cable and 65–70 per cent by antenna.

Television programmes in Iceland are predominantly of foreign origin. The public television station, RÚV, has the highest share of domestic material or 41 per cent (2004 figures). As much as 37 per cent originates in the USA and the United Kingdom. Only 2 per cent is from the other Nordic countries. The share of foreign material at the three biggest private stations ranges from 70 to 75 per cent, mostly from the USA and the UK.

RÚV's two radio channels dominate the airwaves, with around 52 per cent of listeners tuning into them daily, according to a March 2004 survey. Rás eitt offers the widest range of programmes as half of its programming time is devoted to what can be termed information and culture. Bylgjan is by far the most popular private station with 24 per cent of listeners. 365-Miðlar owns Bylgjan. Other radio stations have a much smaller share and mostly concern themselves with playing music.

In 2004 television had about 28 per cent of the total advertising revenue and radio had about 12 per cent, according to Statistics Iceland.

Skjár einn operates a digital and interactive television service (Video on demand), with about 25,000 subscribers, distributed via broadband. In the spring of 2005, RÚV launched an experimental digital radio station, Rondo, which broadcasts classical music and jazz.

The Icelandic minister of transport is working on a plan to make digital and interactive radio and television available to 99.9 per cent of the population by 2007. According to the plan, digital television broadcasts are set to completely replace the analogue system by 2010.

C. The Internet Media
Main features:

■ Very high accessibility to Internet
■ Three popular news websites

Icelanders have warmly embraced the Internet and in 2002 more than 80 per cent had access, either at home or at work. The biggest media website, whether in terms of visitors or page impressions, is www.mbl.is, run by Árvakur, publisher of *Morgunblaðið*. It has its own editorial staff and also publishes stories from *Morgunblaðið*. The second largest media website is www.visir.is, owned by 365-Miðlar. RÚV also has a website, www. ruv.is, which, among other things, offers recordings of RÚV's broadcasts, mainly news or news-related programmes, as well as text versions of the news.

D. *News agencies*
There are no news agencies in Iceland and the different media, instead, relies on its own editorial staff and on foreign news agencies for news from abroad.

2. State Policies
Main features:

- No specific law for media, but new laws are in the pipelines which will put limits on ownership of media corporations;
- The press is subjected to assorted general legislation.

Freedom of expression is guaranteed in the Icelandic Constitution which prohibits all kinds of censorship. Iceland is also a signatory to the European Convention of Human Rights.

Newspaper publishers are private enterprises and do not receive subsidies from the government. Newspapers and magazines are subjected to VAT, albeit at reduced rates of 14 per cent instead of the standard 24.5 per cent.

As is the case with most public broadcasters, RÚV must meet certain obligations, cultural and functional. Among those obligations is to offer impartial news services, cultural programmes and cater to all age groups. Its transmission must reach throughout the country and RÚV is obliged to maintain a short-wave service.

Apart from being obliged to provide translation for foreign programmes, delivered by subtitles, and honour democratic principles, few obligations are put on private broadcasters. The Broadcasting Rights Committee that hands out concessions has chosen to interfere as little as possible. Concessions for radio can be given for a maximum period of five years and for seven years for television.

With the exception of RÚV the media has largely been left to its own devices. However, in face of increasing media concentration in the hands of 365-Miðlar, the government appointed a committee to evaluate the need for specific legislation dealing with media ownership. The committee concluded that the Icelandic media market was characterized by a "high degree" of consolidation and made some suggestions on how to ensure adequate diversity in the media, which could serve as a basis for a political debate. As soon as the committee delivered its report in early 2004, the government put forward its bill for a new media legislation, which led many to criticize the government for not allowing the necessary political discourse to take place (see developments and trends section).

The media is subject to assorted general legislation, such as anti-defamation laws, copyright laws, etc. According to the Printing Act of 1956 authors are responsible for their published material. If they are not identified by name, the responsibility falls on the publisher. Broadcasters and publishers are required by law to publish corrections. If they fail to do so, they can be forced to by a court ruling.

3. Civil Society Organisations

Main features:

- Two organizations for journalists and reporters
- No organization of media proprietors
- The Union of Icelandic Journalists has an Ethics Council that deals with complaints

The Icelandic Union of Journalists has over 500 members. Most journalists at RÚV belong to the Reporters Association, an in-house organization. Its members usually number 50–60. The great majority of journalists belong to either organization.

There is no organization of media proprietors. Árvakur and 365-Media are members of The Confederation of Icelandic employers. The seven largest advertising agencies and two publishing houses form the Society of Icelandic Advertising Agencies.

The Union of Icelandic Journalists has an Ethics Council that deals with complaints from the public. It accepts cases even if the journalist concerned is not a member of the Union. The five-member Council delivers rulings of whether or not the journalist or publication involved was in breach of the Union's Code of Ethics but its rulings have no binding effect. All rulings are published on the website of the Union of Journalists, www.press.is, as well as in its journal. Complaints against RÚV can be brought up in RÚV's governing board as well.

4. Development Trends

Main features:

- High degree of consolidation has provoked fierce debate and political turmoil;
- A bill put forward by the government in 2004 put strict conditions on ownership;
- Parliament approved by a thin margin but the president refused to sign the bill, thus preventing it from becoming law;
- Laws regarding the national broadcaster are set to change.

Increased concentration of ownership, and a proposed new legislation designed to counter it, has to a large extent overshadowed current discussions about the Icelandic media. After one of the longest and fiercest political debates in living memory a highly controversial government-backed media bill was passed by parliament in 2004. The controversy heightened when the president of Iceland, Ólafur Ragnar Grímsson, refused to confirm the legislation, an unparalleled decision since Iceland became a republic in 1944. His refusal meant that in order for the media bill to become law, a national referendum had to be called. All was set for a late-summer referendum when the government decided to cut its losses and withdrew the bill.

The centrepiece of the 2004 media bill were the four new conditions required to get a broadcasting licence, all of which put strict limits on ownership. A company could not receive a broadcasting licence if:

- Its main business interests were not in the field of media;
- More than five per cent of its shares belonged to a company or business-bloc that had a dominant market position in another business domain. This did not apply if the company or business-bloc had an annual turnover of less than 22.8 million euro;
- Another company owned more than 35 per cent of its shares. This also applied if companies in the same business-bloc owned a combined share of more than 35 per cent;
- It owned a newspaper publisher, or had shares in a newspaper publisher, or was owned, in part or in whole, by a newspaper publisher.

The 2004 media bill was also designed to change the composition of the Broadcasting Rights Committee. From now on the minister for culture would appoint three members, two of whom the Supreme Court would nominate and one which the minister appoints without nomination. Currently, the Committee has seven members, all appointed by Parliament.

All of the new conditions applied to Norðurljós (later 365-Miðlar) and, if passed, the company would have been drastically affected. Not only did it run two newspapers and numerous TV and radio stations, but a company (Baugur Group) that had "dominant market position in another business domain" owned a controlling share in the Norðurljós, about 30 per cent at the time. Companies, which in one way or another are connected to Baugur, also had substantial shares.

Baugur Group was and still dominates Icelandic retailing. In 2000 it had 70 per cent market share in food retailing in Reykjavík and surroundings and just less than 50 per cent nationwide as well having vested interest in various other domains, domestically and abroad. Together with a few other companies, Baugur Group forms one of the most powerful corporate blocs in Iceland.

The media bill was heavily criticized. Not just because of its content, but, also, and even to a greater degree, because of the methods used by the government when drafting and getting the bill approved in Parliament. The Union of Icelandic Journalists protested against the bill, as did Árvakur, Norðurljós and several other companies and associations.

During the debate the Norðurljós media, Stöð 2, *Fréttablaðið* and *DV* drew heavy political fire, mainly from the leadership of the conservative Independence Party, the senior partner in the two-party government coalition. The leadership of the Independence Party criticized Norðurljós for what it considered a sustained underhanded effort to oust the party from government, especially directed against its then leader, Mr Davíð Oddsson. The Norðurljós media denied all such claims and retorted by saying that the Independence Party was trying to stifle democratic debate. During the debates it was also pointed out that *Morgunblaðið* tended to support the views of the Independence Party, with which the paper has historical ties and that the media bill was custom-tailored to hurt Norðurljós and Baugur Group.

Once the media bill had been withdrawn another committee was formed, this time with representatives from all political parties. A reasonable consensus emerged and, in April 2006, a new bill was introduced in Parliament. The limit to ownership is not nearly as restraining in the new bill; now any one company or individuals cannot own more than 25 per cent in a media company that has more than 33 per cent market share. The new bill is also supposed to ensure more transparency, for example, by requiring media companies to state without delay any change in ownership.

The makeup of RÚV is also set to be changed. In a separate bill, introduced in the spring of 2006 by the Icelandic minister of culture, the laws regarding RÚV and its regulatory framework will be significantly altered. Among the most important changes is that the licensing fee will be abolished and RÚV, instead, funded by a poll tax, RÚV will be made an incorporated company, although 100 per cent state-owned. The proposed law will severely curb the power of the governing board and more power instead given to RÚV's commissioner. There seems to be less consensus on the RÚV bill than the general media legislation, mostly because the opposition parties fear that by making RÚV into an incorporated company, the government is taking the first steps towards privatization. The government fervently denies this claim and points out that the in the new bill it is stipulated that RÚV cannot be sold, partly or as a whole.

References and Sources for Further Information

By far the most comprehensive source of information in English is *Media in Iceland*, written by Þorbjörn Broddason and Ragnar Karlsson in 2003 for the Internationales Handbuch Medien 2004/2005.

Statistic Iceland has an English version of its website, www.hagstofan.is.

The Union of Icelandic Journalists publishes a journal in Icelandic. The association has a website, www.press.is, which regularly publishes stories concerning media developments.

THE LUXEMBOURGIAN MEDIA LANDSCAPE

Mario Hirsch

Luxembourg is with its size of only 2,500 square kilometres and a resident population of 464, 000 (2006), out of which only about 240,000 hold citizenship, the smallest Member State of the European Union, except Malta.

The country is a founding member of the European Communities and hosts important EU institutions such as the European Court of Justice, the European Court of Auditors and the European Investment Bank. It enjoys the highest per capita income worldwide with a thriving economy based mainly on services such as banking and insurance. The economy is oversized thanks to the presence of the headquarters of major global players such as Arcelor-Mittal, the world's largest steel producer; RTL Group, Europe's largest private broadcaster and SES Global, the world's leading satellite operator. The working population of 310,000 reflects this. It includes some 130,000 commuters from neighbouring countries. Altogether, 67 per cent of the working population are foreigners, either immigrants primarily from Portugal, Italy and Spain or commuters.

Three official languages are being used: Luxembourgish, French and German plus, of course, the languages of the most important immigrant groups. The linguistic diversity is also present in the media. The country enjoys a remarkable political stability. The main political party is the Christian-Social CSV with about one-third of the vote. It forms coalition governments alternating with the Social-Democratic LSAP or the Liberal DP as partners. The integration of the large foreign part of the resident population doesn't create too many difficulties thanks to the fact that over 90 per cent of the immigrants come from EU countries.

1. The Market

A. The Print Media
Main features:

- The written press distinguishes itself with a great diversity and strong readership;
- The main reasons for this atypical situation have to do with the support from political parties and generous public subsidies;
- Competition from other media as far as advertising markets is limited since press revenues are protected and free press sheets have not yet materialized.

Interests closely linked to political parties control the press or trade unions as far as ownership and editorial policy are concerned. These partisan links explain to a large extent the surprisingly high number of newspapers (six altogether) for such a small country. The other explanation for the vitality of the press is the generous public aide scheme provided by the government, both direct and indirect. Ten publications (the six dailies plus four weeklies) benefit from this scheme. It amounts to over 10 million euro per year, one-third is evenly divided between the ten beneficiaries and two-thirds of the public subsidies are proportional to the volume of printed pages carrying original content, the so-called "pages rédactionnelles". Circulation figures for the press and audience shares for radio and TV are not very reliable since no independent auditing is available, except for the two main daily newspapers, *d'Wort* and *Tageblatt*, whose circulation is controlled by the Belgian CIM. The figures we give are based on indications from the publishers and broadcasters. The necessary adjustments and corrections have been made under the author's sole responsibility. Notwithstanding this remark, newspaper readership is doing quite well and on the increase according to most statistics. Because of the partisan orientation of the daily press, many Luxembourgers subscribe to or read more than one publication.

The largest daily newspaper, *Luxemburger Wort* (circulation ca. 79,000), belongs to the Catholic Archbishop of Luxembourg and has close links with the dominant political party, the Christian Social Party (CSV). The *Imprimerie Saint-Paul*, the country's largest printing outfit, publishes *d' Wort*. The paper has published since 2005 in the tabloid format and has adopted a new title. The parent company Groupe Saint-Paul controls as editor also the largest weekly, *Télécran* (ca. 37,000), a magazine focused on TV programmes, the commercial radio stations *DNR* and *Radio Latina* (indirect participation, see below) a number of other publications and extensive book publishing activities. It also edits a weekly, *Contacto*, in Portuguese (ca. 10,000). Since 2001 the pages which provided a résumé in French of the *Wort* predominantly written in German, were incorporated into an autonomous daily, *La Voix du Luxembourg* (ca. 6,000), entirely written in French, which shares, however, commercial advertisements and family-related announcements ("petites annonces" or "annonces classées") with the *Wort*. Groupe Saint-Paul had a 16 per cent stake in Medi@Bel, the second largest publishing group in Wallonia, for ten years, which it gave up in 2003 when it was confronted with economic difficulties of its own.

The second largest newspaper, *Tageblatt* (ca. 26,000), belongs to socialist trade unions and it has close links with the Socialist Party (LSAP). It publishes also a weekly, *Le Jeudi*, in French (ca. 6,000) as well as a weekly, *Correio*, in Portuguese (ca. 8,000). The *Républicain Lorrain* (ca. 10,000) was a local edition of the Metz-based French regional newspaper of the same name. The Luxembourg local edition was stopped in 2001 and replaced by *Le Quotidien* (ca. 6,000), a common venture between the publisher of the Lorraine newspaper and Editpress, the parent company of *Tageblatt*, which has also bought in 2001 the weekly magazine *Revue* (ca. 27,000). This publication, which has a 60-year-old tradition as family magazine, has today the same approach as *Télécran*, providing an overview of TV programmes and dealing with "people issues" such as events related to the Grand-Ducal family. Editpress holds also a stake in the commercial radio Eldoradio.

The *Lëtzebuerger Journal* (ca. 4,000) is owned by the Liberal Party (DP). The *Zeitung vum Lëtzebuerger Vollek* (ca. 2,000) is owned by the Communist Party (KPL).

The influential weekly *d'Lëtzebuerger Land* (ca. 6,500) is the only truly independent publication together with the satirical weekly *Den Neie Feierkrop* (ca. 12,000). Both of these publications lack the party or interest group affiliation typical for the other press products in Luxembourg. The weekly *Woxx*, the former *Grënge Spoun* (ca. 3,000), rebranded and renamed in 2002, has close affiliations with the Green Party, Déi Gréng.

In the magazine sector, the publications of the independent publisher Mike Koedinger Editions (mke), especially the two monthly ones, *Nico* (a city magazine) and the business magazine *paperJam*, play with circulations of around 25,000 each, an increasingly influential role, and they have a growing share of the advertising revenues pie which allows them in turn to be distributed largely for free. Two publications in English of the independent publisher Pol Wirtz, the weekly *352 Luxembourg News* and the monthly *Business Review*, function along the same lines with a readership of around 8,000 each.

In 2005, the advertising market in Luxembourg was estimated to be worth around 90 million euro. The market share of the press, although declining, following the broadcasting liberalization of the early 90s, is still at around 70 per cent despite the multiplication of commercial radio and TV stations. The reason for this high share has to do with the slow start of the new commercial radio stations and limitations on RTL's advertising revenues in Luxembourg. The multinational broadcasting group has been observing a kind of self-restraint as far as advertising revenues of its Luxembourg programming activities are concerned. Another reason can be seen, of course, in the limited TV and radio outlets RTL, still the country's main broadcaster, offers to the resident population. Even though programme activities have been considerably increased, there still is no around-the-clock radio and television service dedicated to local audiences. The media law of 1991 has, however, led to a doubling of the direct state aid to the press in order to compensate for possible loss of advertising revenues following the liberalization of the radio landscape. The law also contains a provision that calls for periodic review of the level of press subsidies (in 2006 direct and indirect subsidies such as preferential postal tariffs and reduced VAT rates amount to nearly 10 million euro).

In October 2007 the two main newspaper publishers launched free sheets in French targeted at the 150,000 or so commuters coming to work everyday in Luxembourg. Editpress teamed up with the Swiss publisher Tamedia, editor of the Zürich-based *Tages-Anzeiger* and of the most successful free sheets in Switzerland and launched *L'Essentiel*. Groupe Saint-Paul, who was initially opposed to this idea, had to follow suit a few weeks later with *Point 24*, its own product.

B. The Broadcast Media
Main features:

- Audio-visual media used to be dominated by the local radio and TV programmes produced by RTL;
- The liberalization introduced in the early 90s produced a certain diversification, especially as far as radio goes;
- Full-fledged programmes for local audiences suffer from the smallness of the country and the strong demand for foreign programmes, which is being fostered by the near-complete coverage of the country by cable television and satellite reception.

The media law of 1991 (see below) formally abolished the monopoly RTL enjoyed on a contractual basis since 1930. Broadcasting franchises were allocated in 1992 to four consortia involving the written press to some extent. Eldoradio, the most successful of the new radio stations, with an estimated audience share of 15 per cent, is indirectly controlled by RTL. Other shareholders are newspaper publishers such as Editpress, the *Lëtzebuerger Journal* and the *d'Lëtzebuerger Land*. Eldoradio is a typical music radio, targeting the younger audiences. Den Neie Radio (DNR), with an estimated audience share of 7 per cent, has amongst its shareholders the Groupe Saint-Paul, Luxembourg's leading press group, some Catholic associations and some business interests. This radio aims at competing with RTL Radio Lëtzebuerg as far as news and current affairs coverage is concerned. Radio Latina, with an estimated audience share of 10 per cent, addresses itself primarily to the foreigners residing in Luxembourg (39 per cent of the country's total population). Its shareholders are immigrants' associations, the Christian trade union LCGB and Régie Saint-Paul, the advertising outlet of Groupe Saint-Paul. Radio Ara (estimated audience share is 4 per cent) is owned by organizations belonging to the so-called associative movement. It is the only radio station that tries alternative programming, taking into consideration the needs and desires of all kinds of marginal groups and English-speaking foreigners living in Luxembourg.

The law identified a third category of radio stations, the so-called local radio. In theory, some 40 locations are possible, but in 2006 only fifteen were in operation, most of them broadcasting only for a few hours a day or week. These local radios have to respect strict technical limitations (power of 100 watt, radius of 5 kilometres) and they are subject to tight restrictions as far as advertisement financing is concerned.

The law enables the government to grant TV franchises besides those held by RTL. This provision has, however, not been used until 2002 for the obvious reason that advertising revenues were thought to be too limited to support a second national TV programme. Two franchises have been granted to regional initiatives carried on cable networks in parts of the country a few hours a month (Uelzechtkanal, a non-profit undertaking and Nordliicht, a commercial operation with limited ambitions). In 2002, a licence was granted to Tango TV, a national commercial programme operated by Tele 2, the cellular phone operator, which belongs to the Swedish Kinnevik Group. Tango TV, or TTV as it was called, stopped broadcasting in February 2007. Its owners came to the conclusion that there was not enough room for a second TV channel in Luxembourg. In 2004, an Open Channel, called DOK ("Den openen Kanal"), started broadcasting on cable networks. It is used by some associations and individuals, but has no ongoing programming. Since 2000, the Luxembourgish Parliament broadcasts live plenary sessions and background information about legislative activities via Chamber TV.

Despite these timid attempts at liberalization, RTL continues to dominate the Luxembourg audio-visual landscape. Its radio programme, *RTL Radio Lëtzebuerg*, remains the most popular with an audience share of above 50 per cent. Its local television programme, *RTL Télé Lëtzebuerg*, has no real challenger and enjoys an audience share above 40 per cent for its daily one-hour broadcasts. This programme is being rebroadcasted on regular intervals, including a version with an audio channel in French and carried, also, via an Astra satellite thanks to government subsidies.

In 1993, the government established a public radio station called RSC ('établissement public de radio socio-culturelle') or 100.7, which refers to the frequency it uses. RSC, which initially had to share its national FM frequency with RTL, started with broadcasts limited to only a few hours per day. Since 1998 it transmits a 24-hour programme and has the exclusive use of its frequencies. It still relies, however, on transmission infrastructure owned by RTL. This radio station, which benefits from substantial public funding (around 4 million euro in 2005) and which pursues an ambitious, rather elitist, programming policy, has not been a great success so far. Its audience share still does not exceed 2 per cent, a fact that in the eyes of its critics proves the point that it is superfluous in a liberalized environment.

C. The Internet Media

Online media are slowly taking off. Most media operators have their websites, and the content of newspapers is available online but most of the time restricted and not free of charge. Except for the *d'Wort*, which employs four Internet journalists, there are no separate newsrooms for online offerings. The most popular sites are those operated by *d'Wort*, *paperJam* and *RTL*, *www.wort.lu*, *www.paperjam.lu and www.RTL.lu*, respectively. These sites attract most of the advertisement on the Net, which represents less than 4 per cent of the advertising pie. Luxembourg has a very high Internet penetration with over 60 per cent of households connected, out of which some 20 per cent have high-speed connections of the DSL kind.

D. News agencies

Owing to the smallness of the place, there is no news agency permanently represented in Luxembourg and the country is not very well covered by correspondents from foreign news agencies, except for Reuters with a Financial Monitor unit and the French AFP, which has a permanent stringer. Other news agencies cover Luxembourg including European affairs taking place in the country via their Brussels offices. The government's communication department, the "Service Information et Presse" (SIP), which is attached to the Prime Minister's office, compensates in a very efficient way the absence of regular coverage of Luxembourg affairs by news agencies or correspondents from foreign papers.

2. State Policies

Main features:

- Media developments in Luxembourg have been the affair almost exclusively of private initiative;
- The government has encouraged through subsidies and some regulation, some developments, especially in the field of print media;
- Content regulation and ownership rules have been for most of the time non–existent and it is only with the advent of a regulatory framework at the European level that some measures have been taken.

Media activities have always been almost exclusively the domain of private initiatives. With the exception of videotext and satellite developments (SES, the Luxembourg-based operating company of the ASTRA satellite system), the public sector never had any real stake in media developments, notwithstanding the 'oddity' of RSC. The government has, however, been instrumental in providing a 'liberal' environment for entrepreneurial developments in the field, encouraging Luxembourg's role as a platform for international operators. This was the main concern of Luxembourg's media policy until 1991 when a new broadcasting law was passed with the intention to diversify the audio-visual offer beyond RTL's de facto monopoly.

The RTL strategy to become a major player in European broadcasting, highlighted by its merger with Bertelsmann in early 1997, inevitably has led to a dislocation of its programming activities away from Luxembourg. Only the group headquarters remain in Luxembourg. The growing internationalization of RTL and the dislocation it entailed led the government to realize that something had to be done to improve the broadcasting offer for the resident population. The considerable success of pirate radios since the early 80s clearly indicated that there was a demand for local broadcasts not fulfilled by the minimalist programmes RTL proposed.

The government was, and is, however, keen to keep some links between Luxembourg and RTL Group (as the company is called since Bertelsmann became its owner in 2001). To that effect the new franchise agreement signed in April 1995 between the government and RTL Group (called at that time CLT-UFA) establishes a contractual relationship for the next fifteen years. All the existing radio and TV licences are prolonged for that period. RTL continues to enjoy a certain commercial exclusivity for its international operations out of Luxembourg. The government pledges to grant licences to third parties only if they do not compete with RTL activities. RTL succeeded in being freed of most of its public service obligations, including the requirement to maintain a symphony orchestra, as well as franchise fees. In return for these favours RTL has pledged to keep some activities in Luxembourg and to offer TV and radio programmes for local audiences (the cost of these local programmes, which result in loss-making activities, has been estimated at 120 million euro for the duration of the franchise agreement).

Luxembourg's media remain only loosely regulated, despite some attempts (notably the 1991 law) to introduce elements of supervision.

Press legislation is rudimentary. The constitution mentions freedom of the press with hardly any limitations. An antiquated law of 1869 deals with infractions committed by the press and regulates the right of reply in a not very satisfactory way. A new Press law of 2004 has brought some progress on these matters but most trials that involve the press are based on damage suits along the lines of civil liability (articles 1382 and 1383 of the 'Code civil').

A 1976 law introduced the already mentioned direct subsidies to the press in order to safeguard diversity. There are no ownership rules or limitations except for cross-media ownership. The 1991 law on electronic media has limited to 25 per cent the stake one single shareholder can have in one of the commercial radios. There is some pressure coming from RTL to get rid of this limitation in order to increase its stake in Eldoradio. No particular content rules are applicable except for offending comments dealt with by the 1869 law and now the 2004 law, which are governed for all practical purposes by the general rules pertaining to civil liability. In the absence of specific legal provisions, the press is subjected to general legislation and litigation before ordinary courts remains the preferred means to call the media to account.

After long-drawn preparations a new Press law has finally been adopted by Parliament in 2004. It redefines the right of reply and it introduces the right for journalists to protect their sources among its main provisions.

3. Civil Society Organizations
Main features:

- Content regulation of the media is not very well developed;
- Self-regulation is supposed to deal with contentious issues;
- Regulatory matters are hampered by the government's policy to promote the country as host to international media developments and vested interests of local media.

The main employers' organization is the "Association Luxembourgeoise des éditeurs de journaux", which regroups the publishers of the daily newspapers, a very efficient lobby in matters of concern to its vested interests (its share of the advertising pie and the level of public subsidies).

Journalists are organized in three separate associations, the largest and oldest being the "Association luxembourgeoise des journalistes", regrouping some 150 professional journalists. The "Union luxembourgeoise des journalistes" is the platform of journalists working for the media controlled by Groupe Saint-Paul (some 60 affiliates). Altogether there are more than 400 professional journalists, i.e. holders of a press card. About two-thirds of them work for print media. One-third of all journalists are foreigners living in Luxembourg or neighbouring regions and one-third women.

For the last 150 years the issue of the responsibility of the media for their deeds was dealt with according to common law principles. The 2004 Press law introduced some interesting innovations but encouraged the media to go for self-regulation. Journalists' unions have their code of conduct, albeit vague, and a Press Council ("Conseil de Presse"), composed at par by editors and journalists, is supposed to police the profession. It is guided by a "Code de déontologie" and has a complaints' commission chaired by a magistrate. Its main activity consists, however, in delivering press cards.

The 1991 law established supervisory or regulatory bodies such as the Independent Broadcasting Commission ("Commission indépendante de la radiodiffusion") in charge of granting broadcasting authorizations and controlling applications, an advisory Programme Commission ("Conseil national des programmes") and a consultative Media Commission.

Only the Programme Commission has taken up issues of accountability, but it is not empowered with sufficient authority to have any real impact. All it can do is to attract the attention of the government or public opinion to offences in the media. It has, nevertheless, been very active in its attempts to police the media and especially RTL radio and TV programmes. But its attempts to extend its competence to the latter's programming activities abroad, at least those programmes that sail under the Luxembourg flag to bypass national prescriptions in the target countries (Belgium, the Netherlands and Poland among others), have failed for lack of human resources. The Programme Commission was also instrumental to bring about a Code of Ethics ("Code de déontologie") adopted in 2006 by the Press Council. It is expected that this instrument will enable this body to increase the self-regulation of the profession.

4. Development Trends
Main features:

- ■ Despite a remarkably lively media landscape, Luxembourg's media will have to take on sooner or later the market test of their viability;

■ Luxembourg has been for decades at the forefront of media liberalization in Europe (RTL and the ASTRA satellite system). It could become a victim of developments it has initiated so successfully for so long.

Over the last years, Luxembourg has experienced significant changes in its media organization. The abolition of RTL's monopoly status in 1991 was certainly overdue, but so far it has not led to dynamic media activities alongside RTL's domestic activities. The radio liberalization that started in 1992 was too ambitious and a concentration process is likely to take place, particularly as the government has pledged to abolish the ownership ceilings in radio activities. It has also announced that it is going to lift the limitations on advertising revenues imposed on RTL's local radio and TV activities.

The Luxembourg press is, of course, a special case. Its amazing diversity can be attributed to the generous public subsidies but also to the more than obvious links between political parties and newspapers. Provided these two requisites stay in place, Luxembourg will continue to enjoy pluralism in the printed press, which is unusual in the European context and a remarkable endeavour by itself.

The audio-visual media are rapidly switching from analogue to digital modes of transmission. This should be achieved by early 2007, even though analogue transmission will go on for some time. This eagerness for an all-digital environment is related to ambitious plans by the government to push broadband developments by setting up LuxConnect, a competing company to the incumbent telecoms operator, the "Entreprise des Postes et Télécommunications", which is 100 per cent state-owned. It has also to be seen in relation with SES Global's plans to force the pace of digital developments in particular in Germany.

As far as its traditional role as home for international activities in the broadcasting field is concerned, Luxembourg certainly suffered some serious setbacks. RTL has outgrown its Luxembourg origins, especially after its absorption by Bertelsmann. The main reason why broadcasting as one of Luxembourg's preferred export articles has declined in importance has, of course, to do with the fact that commercial broadcasting has become a common feature in Europe. Consequently, the detour via Luxembourg is no longer necessary.

References and Sources for Further Information
Hilgert, R. (2004), "*Les journaux au Luxembourg 1704–2004*", Service Information et Presse, Luxembourg.

On the media landscape and, in particular, audio-visual media, see the chapters on Luxembourg written by Mario Hirsch in the *Internationales Handbuch für Rundfunk und Fernsehen*, Hans-Bredow-Institut, Nomos, and Baden-Baden 2001 and in *The Media in Europe: The Euromedia Handbook*, Sage, London 2004.

THE DUTCH MEDIA LANDSCAPE

Piet Bakker & Peter Vasterman

The Netherlands is a densely populated country; 16.5 million people live on 34,000 square kilometres. Three big parties dominated the political arena for the last decades: the socialists (PvdA), the Christian party (CDA) and the liberals (VVD); in different combinations they have formed coalitions.

In 2002 the popular politician Pim Fortuyn was murdered just before the general elections, this shook the Dutch political system as it was the first political murder after the Second World War. Fortuyn focused in his campaign on social issues like the integration of foreigners, rising crime and the welfare state and was about to cause a landslide in the Dutch political system. His party, however, proved to be without direction after his death. The murder also led to discussions about the role of the media, which were accused of being indifferent to problems of 'common' people.

At the same time many media felt economic pressures. Print media, in particular paid newspapers, saw circulation decline, the TV landscape showed signs of fragmentation and rising commercialism while new media were luring away users from traditional media, although, in many cases without making real online profits.

1. The Market

A. *The Print Media*
Main features:

- High readership but decline in paid circulation
- Concentrated newspaper market, growing foreign ownership, one-paper-cities predominant
- Growing market share of free dailies
- Newspapers innovations: tabloids, Sunday edition, Web editions, multimedia, new sections, magazines, convergence
- Traditional magazines lose readers
- Magazine publishing heavily concentrated
- Print has high but, also, declining share of advertising

The Netherlands has a relatively high readership of newspapers and magazines, together with Scandinavia, German-speaking countries, the UK, Canada and Japan. There is no longer any party press, unlike in a lot of European countries while it is also unlikely that a newspaper endorses a political party or specific candidates. Also, there are no sports papers like in Italy or Spain and no 'tabloid' press like in the UK (*The Sun*) or Germany (*Bild*). Quite a few papers, however, have adopted the compact tabloid format or are preparing for a format change.

Print media are very concentrated; three publishers control 90 per cent of the paid-newspaper circulation. PCM, publisher of four national dailies (*de Volkskrant, NRC Handelsblad, AD* and *Trouw*) is owned by UK-investor APAX; the Amsterdam local paper *Het Parool* is owned by the Belgian Persgroep while two papers in Limburg are owned, since 2006, by UK-investor Mecom (David Montgomery). Apart from paid papers there are two free daily newspapers. Two newspapers introduced a Sunday edition in 2004.

Newspaper readership in the Netherlands is going down, but still high compared to other countries. For every 100 households, 55 copies of paid daily newspapers are distributed in 2005. Twenty years ago, however, there were 75 copies for every 100 households. For 2005 this means that there is a daily circulation of 3.8 million copies. Readership is also relatively high, in 2004 and 2005 65 per cent of the Dutch read a paid newspaper on a daily basis, when free papers are included this rises to 71 per cent. To attract more – and younger – readers, most papers have tried to innovate their products by switching to tabloid, introducing new sections and design and experimenting with multimedia features and joint ventures with other media. Results so far have been disappointing.

Almost half of the total circulation of paid newspapers can be attributed to the national daily press. There are seven national daily newspapers. Circulation of paid dailies is going down by 2 to 4 per cent every year for the last five years *De Telegraaf* is still the paper with the highest paid circulation in the Netherlands (650,000 copies), the new *Algemeen Dagblad*, that merged with several regional titles, has a circulation of 460,000.

The five biggest national dailies are based in Amsterdam (*De Telegraaf*, *de Volkskrant*, *Trouw*) and Rotterdam (*Algemeen Dagblad*, *NRC Handelsblad*). *De Telegraaf* and *Algemeen Dagblad* (*AD*) are considered 'popular' newspapers while the others are called (by their own readers) 'quality papers'. Popular papers use more colour, bigger headlines than the so-called quality papers and devote more space to crime and show business, but they have little in common with papers like *Bild Zeitung* or *The Sun*. *De Telegraaf* and *AD* can be considered as (political) to the right, *NRC Handelsblad* is a liberal-conservative paper (the only evening newspaper of the big five) while *Volkskrant* and *Trouw* are more to the left. *Nederlands Dagblad* and *Reformatorisch Dagblad* are conservative Christian newspapers. Numbers 2 to 5 belong to the same company: PCM. Subscription is high: 91 per cent of the total circulation. There are two free dailies in the Netherlands: *Spits* (by *De Telegraaf*) and *Metro* (Metro International), both distribute ±450.000 copies through public transport, restaurants, universities, shopping centres and other crowded places. Both papers started in 1999.

Four specialized newspapers exist: *Het Financieele Dagblad* (business, circulation 50,000), *het Agrarisch Dagblad* (agriculture, circulation 11,000), *Cobouw* (construction, circulation 13,000) and *Nederlandse Staatscourant* (government, circulation 6,000).

Nine regional newspapers have a circulation of more than 100,000 in 2005 with *Dagblad de Limburger* (circulation 174.000) as the biggest. One-paper-cities are common in the Netherlands because of heavy concentration in the daily regional press. The last major operation was the merger of national daily *Algemeen Dagblad* with seven regional papers. Only seven independent publishers remain (in 1970 there were 35 independent publishers, in 1980 there were 24). Three firms control 90 per cent of the total circulation with Wegener as the biggest free local weeklies, financed only by advertising, are available in every Dutch household. On average between two and three free weeklies are delivered to every home. Total circulation is estimated to be between 15 and 18 million. The majority of the circulation is controlled by publishers of regional newspapers.

There are at least 8,000 different magazine titles available for Dutch readers. These can be divided in different categories. First, there are small but very profitable scientific journals (often in English) and many professional magazines. Important publishers are Elsevier (part of Reed Elsevier) and Wolters Kluwer in these markets. Also, Sanoma (Finnish) publishes some professional magazines although their focus is more on magazines for the general audience.

Magazines for the general public have really a wide reach. Woman's magazines have a combined circulation of 1.3 million every week. *Libbele* and *Margriet* have a joint circulation of 900,000, while also 540,000 gossip magazines are sold, TV guides reach almost every household (4.2 million in 2005) and lots of other magazines (girls, boys, lifestyle, etc.) are read. But at the same time circulation of many 'traditional' magazines is going down. Publishers, therefore, are launching new titles that might interest readers. More than half of the circulation of general interest magazines are published by Finnish publisher Sanoma.

B. The Broadcast Media
Main features:

- Signs of fragmentation with a rising amount of commercial broadcasters, high share of foreign ownership
- Unique system of public broadcasting through private organizations
- High cable penetration, analogue switch-off end 2006, fast introduction of digital TV
- TV viewing-time still rising
- Advertising revenues rising

The Dutch Media system is dominated by commercial channels on the one hand and a strong public broadcasting system on the other, although there are no national government-owned television or radio stations. Cable penetration is one of the highest in Europe: ±95 per cent. In December 2006 the analogue signal will be shut down – digital TV is available in every part of the country.

In the Dutch media landscape the broadcast media are hard to explain to foreigners. The unique system was created around 1925. Radio was broadcast by different organizations (socialist, Catholic, Protestant, liberal) that rented radio time. This system survived World War II and was also introduced for television around 1955. It is not government broadcasting. Organizations are independent, the government cannot interfere with programming.

Throughout the years, there have been commercial initiatives but until 1989 without any success, except for commercial pirate stations in the 60s. In 1989 a commercial television station (RTL Veronique, later renamed RTL4) started with television programmes from Luxembourg, which were also shown by cable networks in the Netherlands and later also by satellite. It was a Dutch programme made in the Netherlands but transmitted from Luxembourg. Soon a second programme followed: RTL5. In the 90s the law changed so legal commercial broadcasting was made possible for Dutch and foreign companies.

Now a Dutch television viewer can receive three public national channels, two 'foreign channels' (Luxembourg-based) and five commercial Dutch channels. A average cable network contains apart from the ten national Dutch-language channels at least one regional or local channel, two Belgian Dutch-language channels, Dutch MTV and one or two other Dutch music channels, Dutch-spoken or Dutch subtitled special interest channels (Discovery, Eurosports, National Geographic), BBC 1 and BBC 2, German channels and a choice from TV5 (France), RAI Uno (Italy), TVE (Spain), TRT (Turley), CNN, etc. – 25 to 30 channels is normal. And there is an average of 40 radio stations available, five of them Dutch national public channels.

Television viewing is growing. In 1988 the average Dutch viewer spent 124 minutes in front of his TV set, while this has risen to 195 minutes in 2005. The (Luxembourg) commercial station RTL4 and public channel Nederland 2 were the most popular stations in 2005 (both 16 per cent market share); commercial broadcasters together have seen their market share rise to 50 per cent in 2005; the three public channels lost viewers and now have a market share of 35 per cent.

The Dutch listen to the radio for more than three hours daily. It is divided between public broadcasting (44 per cent market share) and commercial stations (49 per cent market share). The rest goes to small commercial broadcasters, local and foreign stations.

In 2005 Dutch advertisers spend about 4.3 billion euro on advertising, an increase of 1.5 per cent compared to 2004. The print media (newspapers, magazines and professional journals) may have a much larger share than the electronic media (51 versus 24 per cent), but this is declining since TV commercials were introduced in public broadcasting (1966). The introduction in 1989 of commercial television accelerated this loss of advertising revenues for print media. Compared to 1995 the print media lost about 10 per cent of its share of the advertising pie to television (plus 28 per cent). Daily newspapers had a market share of 37 per cent in 1975; in 2005 this was 20 per cent. Television had 9.6 per cent in 1975, and now 18 per cent. Advertising on the Internet is rising sharply with an almost 50 per cent growth in 2005 to a total of 97 million euro, a share of 2.25 per cent of total advertising spending in 2005.

In the first half of 2006 advertising expenditure increased with 4.6 per cent, showing a recovery after years of slow economy. Of the print media the daily newspapers still face a decline in advertising revenues in 2006.

From December 2006 all TV signals are broadcast in digital format only. Most households will not experience any change because most areas have a heavy cable penetration which means that the switch is handled by the cable operator. For people in remote areas, or with mobile devices, digital signals can be received via satellite of digitenne, an in-house antenna capable of receiving digital TV signals. Apart from that many cable operators and Inter Service Providors are offering digital TV, often including more options (more channels, electronic programme guides, interactive possibilities) and often, also, telephone and Internet connection. Dutch public broadcasters offer all their own productions online via the website "uitzendinggemist.nl".

C. The Internet Media
Main features:

- High penetration of Internet and broadband
- High and diverse Internet use

Internet use is high in the Netherlands, 10 million Dutch use the Internet on a regular basis which amounts to almost 70 per cent of the population over 6 years old. Many people connect to the Internet through broadband, 60 per cent of the Dutch homes have a cable or ADSL connection; only Iceland has a higher broadband penetration in Europe. The amount of Internet hosts is almost 7 million in the Netherlands.

News is barely visible if we scan the twenty most visited sites in 2005 (table 4). In fact, news seems to become less popular. In 2000, six sites, with or mainly devoted to news, were in the top twenty (names in bold), *De Telegraaf*, the only newspaper in the top twenty then dropped from the list in 2005, new is nu.nl, a news site without connections to a traditional news organization. Also, omroep.nl (national broadcaster) and teletekst.nl (text TV service) left the top twenty. The Dutch use the Internet mainly for seeking information, buying online, banking and communication, like chat and mailing (MSN).

D. News Agencies
Main features:

- Near-monopoly by ANP
- Rising competition because of new media outlets

In the Netherlands only few news agencies are active on the market. Traditionally, the most important news agency is ANP (Algemeen Nederlands Persbureau), which was founded by the Association of the Dutch Daily Press (De Nederlandse Dagbladpers, NDP) in 1934. In 2000, ANP became an independent company and in 2003 an investment company (NPM Capital NV) acquired the majority of the shares, leaving the rest in the hands of the newspapers publishers. Almost all Dutch news media subscribe to the news feeds of ANP. The press agency also sells news to online news sites like Nu.nl. ANP has offices in The Hague, Amsterdam, Rotterdam and Brussels. ANP represents foreign news agencies like AFP, EFE, DPA, and Belga in the Netherlands.

For a long time ANP had no serious competitor but a new player, Novum Nieuws, was founded in 1999. Main customers are local commercial radio stations, regional TV stations, online news sites and a few newspapers. Novum's position might become more important by the planned cooperation with the GPD (Geassocieerde Pers Diensten), a joint news service run by twenty regional newspapers.

2. State Policies

Main features:

- Constitutional press freedom (excluding advertising)
- Media law defines (open) broadcasting system
- Commission for the Media supervises implementation
- Stronger anti-cartel legislation enforced by Netherlands Competition Authority
- Diversity in the media supported by Dutch Press Fund

The fundament for Dutch media policy is article 7 of the constitution: "Nobody needs permission in advance to make thoughts or feelings public use of the press, except everybody's responsibility according to the law." The latter phrase refers to slander, libel, insult and wrongful act. Advertising is excluded from this freedom of speech: there are laws prohibiting or limiting advertising, for instance, for tobacco, alcohol and medicines.

The Media Law regulates radio and TV, but there is no state supervision (censorship) in advance regarding the content of broadcasted programmes. Media policy in the Netherlands is mainly broadcasting policy, defining the organization of the public broadcasting system. Regarding print media the government's policy is focused on preventing disruptions of the free market due to vertical and horizontal media concentration.

The Commission for the Media supervises the implementation of the media law regarding public, as well as commercial television and cable operators. The Commission allocates broadcasting time to national, regional and local public media and gives licences to commercial stations. Broadcasting organizations have to meet two criteria to get into the public broadcasting system: they need at least 300,000 supporters and they have to carry out the requirements of the media law to broadcast a prescribed amount of programmes in categories like information, culture and education. Public broadcasting organizations also have to produce a certain share of domestic programmes. The Commission also monitors the financial situation of public broadcasting and is authorized to fine the broadcasting organizations for clandestine advertising, illegal sponsoring or commercial sidelines.

The Netherlands Competition Authority (NMa, established in 1998) investigates and sanctions cartels and misuse of economic power in all sectors, not only in the media, and assesses mergers and acquisitions. The NMa ended the tradition of price arrangements in the newspaper business. On several occasions the NMa took action against mergers of newspapers and ordered to maintain the independence of the newspaper that was taken over. The government is planning to limit concentration in the newspaper market to a maximum share of 35 per cent. It was also announced that cross-ownership in newspaper and television will have fewer restrictions in the future.

Another important goal of Dutch media policy is to stimulate media diversity. The Dutch Press Fund plays an important role in that respect: It is an independent authority that supports newspapers, magazines and websites with loans or subsidies. The Press Fund also supports research projects and joint efforts to improve minorities' access to the media.

Dutch media policy in regard to the EU has always been quite defensive, successive administrations tried to prevent commercial competitors to enter the TV market. But EU policy made it possible for Dutch-based commercial stations to broadcast from outside the country. The 'Television Without Frontiers' EU Directive has now been implemented in Dutch legislation. The Netherlands also participates in the Media Plus (2001–2006) programme, supporting the development of European audio-visual productions.

3. Civil Society Organizations
Main features:

- Journalists highly organized
- Publishers united in Dutch Publishers Association
- Professionals in AV-industry: Professional Association of Film- and Television Workers
- Several funds support special journalistic, television and documentary projects
- Advertisers are organized in the Association of Dutch Advertisers
- Dutch press relies on self-regulation through Journalism Council
- Courts decide on an unlawful acts like slander, libel, insult, etc.
- Dutch journalism uses codes
- No national press ombudsman, but newspapers employ their own
- Advertising Code Commission deals with complaints about advertisements
- The Dutch Watchguide advises parents on violence in media

In Dutch journalism the most important organization is the Dutch Association of Journalists (Nederlandse Vereniging van Journalisten, NVJ), which is a combination of a trade union and a professional organization. The Amsterdam-based NVJ has about 9,000 members and deals with issues of press freedom as well as collective labour agreements and freelance fees. Reporters covering parliament in The Hague can join the Parliamentary Press Association (Parlementaire Pers Vereniging, PVV). Foreign correspondents can become a member of the Foreign Press Association of the Netherlands (Buitenlandse Persvereniging in Nederland, BPV). An important role in Dutch journalism is played by the Dutch Society of Chief Editors (Nederlands Genootschap van Hoofdredacteuren). This society issued a journalistic code in 1995 and functions as an important platform for debate.

The Dutch publishers are organized in the Dutch Publishers Association (Nederlands Uitgeversverbond), which organizes publishers of daily newspapers, as well as magazines, professional and scientific journals and books (general and educational). The Dutch Association of local newspapers (Nederlandse Nieuwsbladpers, NNP) organizes publishers of weekly and bi-weekly newspapers and cable news.

Professionals working in the film and television industry are represented by the Professional Association of Film- and Television Workers (Beroepsvereniging van Film- en Televisiemakers, NBF). The production companies in this area are organized in the Dutch Trade Association of Independent Television Producers (OTP, Onafhankelijke Televisie Producenten). Local and regional media have united in the Dutch Federation of Local Public Broadcasters (Organisatie van Lokale Omroepen in Nederland, Olon).

Apart from the professional organizations and unions two other foundations are important, because they subsidize media projects. The Dutch Cultural Broadcasting Fund (Het Stimuleringsfonds Nederlandse Culturele Omroepproducties) provides grants to encourage the development and production of cultural radio and television programmes.

The Foundation for Special Journalistic Projects (Fonds Bijzondere Journalistieke Projecten) supports journalists who want to realize special research projects.

Advertisers are organized in the Association of Dutch Advertisers (BVA, Bond van adverteerders), while advertising agencies are united in the union of communication consultancy agencies (VEA, Vereniging van Communicatie-adviesbureaus).

The Joint Industry Committee , in which advertisers, advertising agencies as well as the media work together, supervises media research like the National Research Multimedia (NOM), the Foundation for Viewer Research (SKO, Stichting Kijkonderzoek), or the Circulation Figures Institute (Het Oplage Instituut, HOI).

Nielsen Media Research is the leading company in the area of advertising spending. The Central Agency for Newspaper Publicity (Centraal Bureau voor Courantenpubliciteit, Cebuco) supports the marketing of the Dutch newspapers.

For people with complaints about the press, two options – apart from complaining to the medium itself – are available: the court or the Journalism Council (Raad voor de Journalistiek). Filing a suit is possible in the case of an unlawful act like slander, libel, insult, etc., all other complaints can be brought before the independent Journalism Council, established in 1960 by the Dutch Association of Journalists (NVJ). In Dutch journalism several professional codes have been formulated over the years, which are used by the Council to evaluate complaints. The Councils' verdicts and arguments in turn generate jurisprudence for the codes. Because of freedom of speech this Council is not able to force anyone to render account over his/her publications or to impose any sanctions (like rectifications). Not all Dutch media support the Journalism Council, but the majority does, as well as the Dutch Public broadcasting organization NOS. Verdicts by the Council are published in the bi-weekly magazine of the Dutch Association of Journalists and on the website of the Council.

The Dutch press does not has a national press ombudsman like Sweden, but several national and regional newspapers employ their own ombudsman who investigates complaints of readers and who writes critically about the newspapers' policy.

Complaints regarding advertising can be filed at the Advertising Code Commission (Reclame Code Commissie). The Dutch Advertising Code states that advertising should not be deceptive, (unnecessary) hurtful or in conflict with good taste and decency. The Advertising Code is based on self-regulation so only the supporting media organizations will accept the verdicts of the Commission. The Commission also monitors advertising messages on its own initiative.

Pressures for self-regulation within the audio-visual industry resulted in the Kijkwijzer (Watchguide), aimed at protecting young viewers against possible harmful effects. This Watchguide, established in 1997, classifies films, TV programmes, videos and games, to give advice to parents. By using pictograms the public is warned for content with violence, fear, sex, bad language, alcohol and drug abuse or discrimination.

4. Development Trends
Main features:

- ■ Relaxing of cross-ownership rules expected
- ■ High investments in online media
- ■ Innovation by newspapers publishers

New media law is not expected very soon. In May 2007 the government introduced a new, although temporary, law on media concentration, relaxing the cross-ownership rules. If there will be changes, the relaxing of cross-ownership rules is expected.

The major technological change was the analogue switch-off in December 2006. Digital signals are offered by commercial cable and telephone companies, but also through satellite and 'digitenne', a technique with small in-home receivers.

One of the most pressing challenges for broadcasting in general and public broadcasting in particular is the rising competition and growing importance of the Internet. Although TV-viewing time is growing, there also seems to be a trend for younger people to watch less television. All broadcasters, therefore, invest in multimedia solutions to reach this disappearing part of the audience.

Print media still face declines in circulation. It is not very likely that this trend will be reversed soon. Magazines publishers will try to fight this trend by launching new titles. Newspaper publishers will speed up innovation. A substantial part of the existing titles will move to a compact (tabloid) format while all publishers will invest in digital media. At least three publishers and two entrepreneurs are thinking about launching free dailies in the Netherlands, which will stimulate fragmentation even more.

References and Sources for Further Information

Books

Bakker, P. & Scholten, O. (2005), *Communicatiekaart van Nederland; Overzicht van media en communicatie* (5th edition). Alphen a/d Rijn: Kluwer. [A reference book on the Dutch media with many tables and other data that is updated every two years.]

Websites – some of them with information in English

www.mediafacts.nl – Online version of monthly magazine with focus on publishing and media companies.
www.bedrijfsfondspers.nl – Official Dutch Press Fund. Research, publications and subsidies for media and researchers.
www.broadcastmagazine.nl – Website of leading magazine on Dutch broadcast situation.
www.cebuco.nl – Marketing organization of Dutch newspapers: circulation data, facts on addresses, campaigns and advertising.
www.cvdm.nl – Controlling body for all Dutch broadcasters.
www.denieuwereporter.com – Weblog and discussions on current affairs in journalism.
www.handboeknederlandsepers.nl – Facts on all printed titles (magazines and newspapers).
www.hoi-online.nl – Official auditing organization for all Dutch print publications. All data available after free registration.
www.kijkonderzoek.nl – Recent and historical data on TV viewing, ratings, market shares.
www.kijkwijzer.nl – Self-governing body for broadcasters, rating TV programmes, games and videos/DVDs for content not suitable for children.
www.mediaonderzoek.nl – Weblog on media research.
www.nmanet.nl – The Netherlands Competition Authority.
www.nuv.nl – Organization of newspaper and magazine publishers.
www.persmediamonitor.nl – Data on circulation of newspapers, paid weeklies, magazines and market shares of radio and TV channels.
www.rvdj.nl – The Press Council in the Netherlands – complaints about journalists and newspapers.
www.tijdsbesteding.nl – Statistics on how the Dutch spend their time, including time on media, from 1975 until 2005.
www.vea.nl – Association of communication agencies active for the advertising industry.
www.villamedia.nl – Daily news on media and journalism.

THE NORWEGIAN MEDIA LANDSCAPE

Helge Østbye

The Norwegian media landscape has some very stable, institutional elements. The dominant newspapers and magazine and book publishing houses were established 75 to 150 years ago, and they still play an important role. The most important changes in these sectors are related to ownership of the companies. The major public service broadcasting company is approaching 75 years of age, and despite dramatic changes in the broadcasting sector, Norsk rikskringkasting (NRK) has been able to maintain its position as the supplier of the most popular radio and television channels. But the non-commercial public service sector is now competing heavily with a lively commercial sector for the attention of the audience.

All these media activities take place in a country located in the European border with the North Atlantic Ocean and the Arctic Sea, with a population of only 4.6 million people. The most densely populated in the areas are in the south-eastern parts of the country, surrounding the capital (Oslo), but all regions in the country have cities with administrative functions, which also function as centres for regional and local newspapers and radio and television production.

1. The Market

A. The Print Media

Main features:

- Newspaper circulation reached its peak in the mid-1990s. Since then there has been a minor drop in circulation;

- Revenues from advertising are still high;
- The number of newspaper titles is very high, but there is a considerable concentration of newspaper ownership;
- Most newspapers in Norway are sold by means of subscription. Only two popular newspapers are sold mainly by single copies;
- Free newspapers so far play a minor role in the Norwegian newspaper market;
- Newspaper readership is very high, and all segments of the society are regular newspaper readers.

In two ways, the newspapers in Norway have a very strong position. There is a high number of newspaper titles (approximately 215 papers) and the newspaper readership is the highest in the world (550–600 copies are sold per 1000 inhabitants).

These two characteristics are linked: one reason for this high level of newspaper readership is the diverse structure of the Norwegian newspaper industry. There are 63 newspapers with six or seven editions per week. Another fifteen have four or five editions. If we include all papers with at least one edition per week, we find 217 newspapers (2001 figure). Most of the papers have a circulation of less than 10,000, with a very limited geographic distribution. But the local and regional daily newspapers account for more than 75 per cent of the total circulation. Five regional newspapers (*Aftenposten*, 252,000; *Bergens Tidende*, 88,000; *Adresseavisen*, 79,000; *Stavanger Aftenblad*, 68,000 and *Faedrelandsvennen*, 43,000) account for 20 per cent of total newspaper sales. The national press is dominated by two national popular newspapers, *VG* (344,000) and *Dagbladet* (162,000). Subscription is the dominant form of selling newspapers in Norway, but the two popular papers are sold exclusively in single copies. In addition there are six medium-sized to small national political or ideological papers (5 per cent of total national circulation). Almost all segments of the population – geographically and socially – are regular newspaper readers. Both quality papers and popular newspapers are read in all segments of the society.

General legislation on working conditions in 1919 stopped the production of Sunday newspapers, but such papers were reintroduced in 1990. There has been a gradual increase in the number of Sunday editions, but still there are only thirteen papers with Sunday editions, and newspaper sale on Sundays is only one-third as compared to weekdays.

Since the early 1950s, the number of newspaper titles has remained stable, but the structure has changed. A system where most cities and towns had three or four newspapers representing different political parties has been replaced by local monopoly newspapers without formal links to political parties. In the same period new newspapers have been established in smaller towns and villages that did not previously have their own paper. These two trends have led to a monopolization of the local newspaper markets. Local competition exists in only fifteen places, compared with 54 in 1952. In the same period, the two national, popular newspapers have increased their sales outside the Oslo area from 60,000 copies to more than 400,000, increasing the competition between local and national newspapers. Nevertheless, the situation for the local newspapers is quite healthy.

The total circulation of the Norwegian newspapers increased gradually until the early 1990s. Since 1994 there has been a decrease, mainly due to reduced sales for the two popular tabloid newspapers, but recently the decrease has also hit the regional newspapers. Of more concern is the reduction in the newspapers' share of total advertising revenue, and perhaps a reduction in the volume of newspaper advertisements. But still the newspaper sector provide their owners with a substantial profit.

There is a strong concentration of ownership. For the last fifteen years, three major newspaper owners account for 55–60 per cent of circulation: Schibsted, Orkla and A-pressen. All these three companies are Norwegian.

Two of these companies have a strong position on national newspaper markets outside Norway. Schibsted controls two of Sweden's largest newspapers, *Aftonbladet* and *Svenska Dagbladet*, and is a major newspaper owner in Estonia. The free newspaper concept «20 minutes» was established by Schibsted in 1999. Some of the papers have been sold, but Schibsted is still involved in free newspapers in twelve European cities (six in Spain, six in France). When the Polish newspaper market was re-established after Communist rule, Orkla invested heavily, and is now one of the major newspaper owners in the country. In 2000 Orkla also bought the Danish newspaper group Berlingske (national, regional and local newspapers).

In 2006, Orkla's 38 local Norwegian newspapers (in addition to Orkla's Polish and Danish papers) were sold to the British newspaper group Mecom. (More about regulation of media ownership in sections below.)

Weekly family magazines used to have a strong position. This was the first media sector where foreign ownership of Norwegian media was an important factor. Two Danish magazines, *Hjemmet* and *Allers*, were pioneers in this media sector, and they still exist, both as family magazines and as publishing houses (Egmont and Aller) with a variety of periodic publications. The third important publishing house, Ernst G. Mortensens Forlag, is Norwegian (now owned by Orkla). Probably as a result of increased competition from other mass media, and partly as a consequence of a specialization, family magazines have been in a decline. But the publishing houses have increased the number of hobby and other special-interest magazines. The most successful is the picture magazine *Se og Hør*, with its focus on royalty and the rich and famous. In 1992 Egmont and Orkla merged their magazine divisions to Hjemmet-Mortensen. In addition to Aller and Hjemmet-Mortensen, the Swedish publisher Bonnier plays an important role in the Norwegian magazine market. Like other print media, the magazine sector has lost readers during the last fifteen to twenty years.

Before the introduction of national, commercial television (1992–93) newspapers were the dominant advertising media, followed by magazines. In 2005 the newspapers' share of total estimated advertising revenue is still close to 50 per cent (Nielsen; via MedieNorge).

B. *The Broadcast Media*
Main features:

- Advertising was banned in Norwegian television until 1992 (in radio until 1988);
- A public service broadcasting company was established in 1933. This company maintained a monopoly status until 1981;
- Between 1981 and 1992 local radio and television was established. In 1992 a national, commercial television channel was opened. This was Norway's second national television channel with terrestrial distribution;
- Private, national radio and television channels also have some public service obligations;
- Although television viewing has increased since the early 1990s, Norwegians still watch television much less than most other European countries;
- Digital radio services have been available fore more than ten years, but by the end of 2006 few people have invested in digital receivers;
- Digital television will be introduced gradually from 2007;
- There are plans to close down the analogue networks when the digital services have been in full operation for a few years.

Broadcasting in Norway was, for almost 50 years from 1933, identical to NRK (Norsk Rikskringkasting), a state-owned public service monopoly in the West European tradition. The NRK was, and is, financed mainly by a licence fee. Norway was among the last countries in Western Europe to introduce television: Following some years of test transmissions, Norwegian television was officially opened by NRK in 1960. In reality, NRK's monopoly was broken in 1981, when independent local radio and television were introduced. Local radio became a success, but local television never took off. Gradually during the 1980s, satellite television reached a substantial part of the population through cable networks and satellite dishes. The first satellite channels were in English language (Sky Channel, Superchannel, etc.), but in 1988 the first two channels transmitting in Norwegian language (TVNorge and the pan-Nordic conglomerate TV3) were launched. In 1992, the first, commercial, terrestrial television channel was introduced, owned by the private company TV 2. Other terrestrial channels are NRK2 and TVNorge (part of the country).

This means that at the moment, there are now two terrestrial television channels with full national coverage: NRK1 and TV 2. NRK2 and TVNorge combine terrestrial transmission with satellite distribution (cable and dishes), and reach somewhere between 60 and 80 per cent. In 2005, NRK1 had a market share of approximately 40 per cent; NRK2 had 4 per cent; TV 2, 29 per cent; TVNorge, 11 per cent; TV3, 6 per cent and other channels together (Swedish public service channels, CNN, Eurosport, etc.), 10 per cent.

NRK's monopoly on national radio broadcasting lasted until 1993, when the private, commercial radio company P4 was established. At the same time NRK increased its number of channels from two to three (P1, P2 and P3). In 2005 a second private channel was established, called Kanal24. The two private channels have a similar profile, where AC music (Adult Contemporary) is dominant. The three NRK channels each have a distinct profile, and this has resulted in a clear segmentation of the listeners: P1 is the most general of the four channels, but the channel's heaviest supporters are found among the adults and elderly people.

P2 is labelled as the 'culture channel', also with in-depth news. P3 is aimed at teenagers and younger adults and has become a success in this segment, which had for a period been lost for the NRK. P4 and Kanal24 created its programme profiles in order to attract an audience with spending power (the age group between 25 and 45). In addition to these national channels, there are a lot of local channels. Two chains compete for the audience in the major cities: Radio1 and Radio NRJ.

The Norwegian radio and television is divided into a privately owned, commercial sector, and a state-owned public service broadcasting sector. NRK (three radio channels and two television channels) is owned by the Norwegian State. An interesting actor in the Norwegian media market is Telenor – the old state-owned telecommunications monopoly. It has been partly privatized, but the state owns more than 50 per cent of the shares. Telenor owns one of the two large cable television operators and a payment system for satellite channels.

Three media groups, all with heavy interests in print media (Schibsted, A-pressen and the Danish company Egmont), each own one-third of TV 2. TV 2 is a dominant owner of the radio channel Kanal24. For some years TV 2 also controlled 49 per cent of the shares in TVNorge and was managing this channel, but their shares in the television channel was sold back to the majority owner: the American group Scandinavian Broadcasting System (SBS). SBS also controls the Radio1 local radio chain and a system of pay-TV channels for movies and sports (Canal+ Norway). The Swedish company Kinnevik controls 90 per cent of the shares in P4, in addition to the TV channel TV3.

A recent development is two crossovers between the private – public divide. TV 2 and Telenor joined forces in a successful, but expensive, bid for the rights to transmit the Norwegian football series. TV 2 and Telenor together own a satellite-TV channel called Zebra with reruns of TV series from TV 2 and sports (mainly Norwegian football). TV 2/Telenor's main rival in the bid for the football rights was a coalition between NRK and Kinnevik. The two companies now jointly operate a satellite sports channel called SportN.

Norwegians used to watch less television than most other Europeans (1 hour 40 minutes in the early 1980s, increasing to 2 hours in 1990). With an increasing supply of television channels, the consumption has also increased. TNS Gallup estimates an average viewing time of 2 hours 40 minutes in 2005. This figure has been stable during the last 5 to 6 years. Radio listening is more difficult to assess. Different sources give different figures, varying from 1½ hours (SSB) to 2½ hours (TNS Gallup).

Approximately one-third of the estimated total national advertising revenue comes from television. Radio's share is approximately 6 per cent. Since the turn of the millennium the print media have increased their share at the expense of the audio-visual media.

Digital television already reaches many households via satellite and cable (see above). As some cable systems are old, it is difficult to give exact figures as to how many are receiving the signals in a digital form. Approximately one-third of the population have their own satellite dish. This reception is digital.

Digital television via terrestrial transmission has been discussed for the long time. In 2006 Norges Television (NTV) was granted permission to establish and operate a digital network. NTV is owned jointly by Telenor, NRK and TV 2. The network will be gradually expanded from the autumn of 2007 until the end of 2008, when the whole country will be covered. According to the present plans the analogue network will be closed down between one and two years after the opening of the digital transmissions.

Norway has chosen the DAB system for digital radio. At the end of 2005 some 70 per cent of the population lived in areas covered by digital radio, but very few had invested in digital radio receivers. The national channels are transmitted in digital form as well as in ordinary FM. One national channel – Radio 2 Digital – is transmitted in the digital system only. Some specialized NRK channels (news, classical music, folk music, etc.) are available in the digital system (in addition to FM in some areas).

Podcast radio exists, but is limited due to copyright problems. WAP radio via mobile phones has been available for several years.

C. The Internet Media
Main features:

- Internet services are popular, and a lot of people spend a lot of time consuming national and international services;
- The old media are the main providers of news and other information services.

Almost three out of four Norwegians have access to the Internet at home. In addition there are those with access at work or at school. According to an annual survey, more than half the population used the Internet on an average day in 2005.

Information providers in the old system (radio, television, print media) are also providing information on the Internet. All major newspapers, radio and television channels have websites with news and other material, and these are the most frequently used sources of news and other kinds of general information. Instead of introducing new actors along with the new technology, the Internet has increased the concentration of ownership. One of the major newspapers, *Dagbladet*, has more readers on the Internet than on paper. Internet reading is free, and the papers blame the Net for the reduction of readership of the paper edition.

The major regional newspapers (*Aftenposten, Bergens Tidende, Adresseavisen, Stavanger Aftenblad* and *Fædrelandsvennen*) have traditionally dominated the market for classified advertisements. Since the year 2000 these papers cooperate on the Internet and have been able to maintain their dominant position in this important market. On an average day, 200,000 advertisements for jobs, real estate, travel, cars, boats and other items are available at finn.no, which has become an important source of income for the papers.

D. News Agencies
Main feature:

■ There is uncertainty about the future of the old, national news agency, as its services are being undermined by agencies belonging to the major newspaper chains are expanding.

Norsk Telegrambyrå (NTB) was established in 1867. For a long period, NTB's position was unchallenged. The social democratic press (now: A-pressen) established their own news agency (now called Avisnenes Nyhetsbyrå – ANB) in 1912, but in the post-war period, the larger newspapers in this group also subscribed to NTB's services. ANB was reorganized in 1990 and newspapers outside the A-pressen group have also subscribed to these services. In recent years, the newspapers in the Orkla group have also established a news and article service. Increased competition has reduced NTB's dominant position, bur it is still the dominant Norwegian news agency.

2. State Policies
Main features:

■ Freedom of expression is secured by the Constitution and the European Convention for the Protection of Human Rights and Fundamental Freedoms;
■ Advance censorship in prohibited (with the exception of cinema films intended for children);
■ Newspapers and books are exempted from VAT. There is a continuous discussion about a similar exemption for magazines and journals;
■ The state-owned public service broadcasting company is regarded as an important contribution to the diversity of the Norwegian media system;
■ In order to maintain local competition and national diversity, there is a system for newspaper subsidies.

The Norwegian Constitution was written in 1814. The clause on freedom of printing made it easy for the parliament to pass legislation that made exemptions from the general rules of freedom of expression. Court cases where Norwegian media had been sentenced for libel, ended in the European Court of Human Rights, where the media were freed. In 1996 the government appointed a commission to look into legislation relation to freedom of expression, and especially the Constitution. In 2004, the parliament changed the Constitution in a way that gave better protection for freedom of expression and instructed the government to promote diversity in the media and public debate.

There is specific legislation for broadcasting, film and cinema, but no press law and very little legislation specific for the Internet, etc.

In 1935 a general purchase tax was introduced in Norway. The newspapers were among the few commodities that were exempted, and when the purchase tax in 1969 and 1970 was replaced by a value added tax, VAT, the newspapers maintained their privileged position. In addition to newspapers, only books benefit from the same exemption. Direct newspaper subsidies were introduced in 1969. In 2005 the direct subsidies added to 300 million NOK (approximately 40 million euros) and account for some 3 per cent of the newspapers' total revenue. The subsidies are distributed according to specific criteria in order to reach national ideological and political newspapers, the 'number 2' newspapers in areas with local competition and the smallest local newspapers. The system of subsidies slowed down the process of local monopolization, but the amounts were not big enough to halt the process. It has also made it easier to establish small, local newspapers in rural areas.

Norway maintained a 'classic' West European public service system for the broadcasting media (state-owned monopoly, financed by a licence fee) until 1981. A conservative government introduced local radio and television in 1981, and allowed the distribution of satellite television channels via cable networks. In 1991 the parliament decided to introduce a private sector for national radio and television, financed by commercials, but with some public service obligations.

In the post-war period, there was a concentration of ownership as a result of competition. Some book and magazine publishers had to close down, others merged with larger companies. To some extent the same processes led to local monopolization of the press, but until the early 1980s, most newspapers had separate owners (one major group existed, Schibsted, which controlled three of the four largest newspapers in Norway). Since then, two newspaper chains have emerged: A-pressen, based on the old social democratic newspapers, and Orkla, which is an old industrial conglomerate. Orkla's newspapers were sold to the British company Mecom in 2006.

The break-up of the state monopoly in broadcasting led in the first instance to the entry of new actors, but well-established media actors soon took over both local and national commercial radio and television. This way multimedia corporations were established.

Major actors in the newspaper (Schibsted and A-pressen) and magazine business (Egmont) were the major owners of the commercial television channel. With a few exceptions, the Norwegian media are owned by Norwegian (the State, Schibsted, A-pressen, Orkla), Swedish (Kinnevik, Bonnier) and Danish (Aller, Egmont) multimedia companies. The major exception is SBS (TVNorge, Radio1 and Canal+ Norway).

In 1998, the Norwegian parliament passed new legislation to prevent ownership concentration. A new administration was established in 1999 in order to enforce the new law. Details in this regulation have changed. So far there is no indication that regulation in this area will be able to reverse the process of multimedia ownership concentration, but the system has prevented the Schibsted group from taking control of regional newspapers outside Oslo and a possible merger between A-pressen and Orkla Media.

Through different means, the state has promoted diversity in the media sector. Newspapers, radio, television and the book industry are the main areas for this effort. Books and newspapers are exempted form VAT. The system of newspaper subsidies (see section 2 above) and the regulation of ownership concentration are also parts of this effort. In the broadcasting sector, state support has made it possible for the old public service broadcasting company to maintain a strong position, despite strong competition from commercial companies. And the privately owned, national radio and television channels operate under some public service obligations.

The accountability system can be divided into two parts: One is based on formal legislation, and breaches are handled by government bodies or courts of law. The other are rules and practises within the media, and breaches are handled either informally or by committees or councils with representation for the media.

Freedom of expression is now well protected by the Constitution and the European Convention for the Protection of Human Rights and Fundamental Freedoms (Council of Europe 1950). Exemptions are made for pornography, blasphemy, revelation of state secrets, etc.

The Constitution from 1814 abandoned advance censorship for print media. In 1913 film censorship was introduced. The new freedom of expression clause in the Constitution abandoned advance censorship in all media, but made an exemption for moving pictures for children.

Most other regulation of media content is done within the media themselves.

3. Civil Society Organizations
Main features:

■ There is one organization for journalists, one for editors and one for most of the media firms;

- A separate organization within the media sector is responsible for media ethics;
- The Press Council is responsible for the monitoring of media ethics, not only limited to the press;
- Some media have their own ethical rules and ways of handling complaints.

There are a lot of organizations in the media field in Norway, but four are important across different media.

Norsk Journalistlag (NJ – Norwegian Union of Journalists) organizes journalists from all sectors of media. The organization takes care of salary negotiations with the employers and is involved in the promotion of professional standards, etc.

Mediebedriftenes landsforening (MBL – Norwegian Media Businesses' Association) started as an organization for newspapers, but it has extended its membership to other sectors in the media industry. This organization is the journalists' opposite party in the negotiations on salaries, working conditions, etc., but the two organizations often work together in order to promote the media in the public debate.

Norsk Redaktørforening (NR – Association of Norwegian Editors) organizes editors from several media. An agreement with MBL — "The rights and duties of editors" — protects the independence of the editors vis-à-vis the Board and the owners.

Norsk Presseforbund (NP – the Norwegian Press Association) is an agency where media and media organizations are members. The founding members were NJ, the forerunner of MBL and NR. At the moment organizations representing radio, television, magazines, etc. are also members. NP focuses on media ethics. NP is responsible for the preservation and development of the "Codes of Ethics for the Norwegian Press" (which is also applicable for other media).

All these organizations are members of international associations in their respective areas.

The press has laid down ethical rules that have gradually been adopted by other news media. Radio and television channels may lose their transmission rights if they break regulations.

The most general system for accountability in the media is the Pressens Faglige Utvalg (PFU – the Press Council), which was founded in order to improve the ethical standards of the press. In 1936 a set of ethical rules were adopted: "Code of Ethics of the Norwegian Press". This code has been changed several times, and the present rules are from 2005. Debates and decisions in the Press Council can be initiated by complaints or from the secretariat of the Council. All news media are covered by the code and the Press Council.

NRK's Director of Broadcasting is responsible for the content of the organization's radio and television programmes. Members of The Broadcasting Council are appointed by the Parliament and the Government. The Council discusses programmes based on complaints from the public or on its own initiative. The Council can give recommendations, but not decide in matters concerning programmes or programming policy.

Some newspapers have an ombudsman for the readers.

Medietilsynet (The Norwegian Media Authority) is a branch of the public administration, subordinate to the Ministry of Culture. It performs administrative duties for radio and television (licensing of local stations, etc.), the press (press subsidies), film and cinema (film censorship) and the ownership regulations (radio, television and the press).

4. Development Trends
Main features:

- Compared to most European countries, the press plays a more important role in Norway;
- In most media there are trends towards commercialization of the production of content. There is also a strong tendency towards segmentation of the audiences in several media.

One important feature of the Norwegian media system is the continuous importance of the press. So far, there has only been a small reduction in newspaper circulation, and local and regional newspapers have maintained a strong position on the market. Economically, the newspapers are still doing fairly well, but the introduction of commercial radio and television has challenged the newspapers' position as the dominant media for advertising. The newspaper owners (Schibsted and A-pressen) have extended their interests into the electronic and interactive media, thereby, maintaining their strong position in the media.

Another important feature is that public service broadcasting has maintained a strong position. In both radio and television NRK channels are the most popular. NRK's position as a state-owned institution financed mainly by a licence fee is under continuous discussion, but not really threatened. And the dominant privately owned channels also operate according to at least some public service obligations.

Concentration of ownership has become the most important issue in media policy. The owners have mainly been Norwegian or Danish and Swedish companies. This tendency has changed. SBS and Mecom are important actors in the Norwegian media field. The main fear is that non-Nordic owners will change the modes of operations in the Norwegian media for the worse.

Tendencies towards homogenization, as well as specialization can be observed. For the media with a broad approach, aiming at the mass market (commercial radio and television channels, some magazines and popular newspapers), there is a trend towards homogenization of content, both within and between the media. At the same time, however, there is a distinct trend towards specialization in the magazine, radio and television markets. In the television market, specialized movie and sports channels are operating in the Norwegian language (films subtitled in Norwegian, transmission of international sports events with Norwegian commentaries). These channels, and international news and music channels, are available on cable networks and directly from the satellites.

A majority of the population are frequent users of the Internet. This gives access to a wide variety of sources and can provide diversity. But the most frequently used Internet sites in Norway are controlled by media that are already important actors on the Norwegian media market.

Experiments with digital radio and television on terrestrial transmitters have been in operation for some years. Already some radio channels are only available in digital form in terrestrial distribution (and on the Internet). Permanent services will make it technologically possible to increase the number of national and local radio and television channels. This will mean a big challenge for the established operators in this market. Some new actors may appear on the scene, e.g., a network of Christian radio and television. But the odds are that the old actors will still dominate the field, but with the possibility of more international dominance.

Although Norway is not a member of the European Union, most of the EU regulations are implemented. But the most important European influence on the Norwegian media regulations has not come from the European Union, but from the Council of Europe and the European Court of Human Rights (changes in the Constitution, see sections 6 and 7 above). So far, anti-terror legislation has not affected Norwegian media.

References and Sources for Further Information

Nordic Media Trends 4: Nordic Baltic Media Statistics 1998, Gothenburg: Nordicom 1999, see also Internet: http://www.nordicom.gu.se/. Updated information is available at Nordicom: http://www.ij.no/omij/aboutij.htm, which also provide information on available literature, media legislation, professional organizations, etc.

MedieNorge provide statistical information about important aspects of Norwegian media. From 2006 the most important information is available in English: http://www.nordicom.gu.se. Updated information is available at Nordicom: http://www.ij.no/omij/aboutij.htm.

See also information from Statistics Norway: http://www.ssb.no/english/subjects/, in particular Subject 07.

THE SWEDISH MEDIA LANDSCAPE

Lennart Weibull & Anna Maria Jönsson

Sweden is situated in the north of Europe. It is the largest of the Nordic countries with 9 million inhabitants. The national language is Swedish. The country is socially and culturally homogeneous, but gradually changing because of immigration, mostly in metropolitan areas. Sweden is characterized by its strong welfare system. In the 1990s there was an economic recession with increasing unemployment, but the beginning of the twenty-first century has meant economic recovery and a strong growth.

Typical for Swedish politics is strong political parties and organizations. There is a clear left-right dimension in political preferences of the Swedish electorate, but government politics is generally middle-of-the-road. The social democrats have been the leading party since the 1930s, but gradually losing ground. After the 2006 election a non-socialist government was formed.

1. The Market

A. The Print Media
Main features:

- The newspaper market is very strong and readership is high in most social groups;
- The role of free dailies is gradually increasing, mainly in the metropolitan areas;
- There is a slow decline in circulation of paid newspapers;
- The newspaper business has generally a good economy, even though it has lost in shares of the advertising market to television;
- The magazine market is strong especially in the area of specialized magazines.

The Swedish newspaper market has traditionally been very strong. More than 80 per cent of the adult population read a newspaper on an average day. There are about 160 papers in Sweden. Of those, however, about 50 are published only once or twice a week and have a very low circulation. The newspaper market is characterized by five main features. First, newspapers are mainly locally or regionally based, in fact, only two tabloid newspapers and one business paper can be regarded as having a national readership and, secondly, almost 100 per cent of the morning newspapers are sold by subscription, with early morning home delivery. A third feature is the fact that almost all social groups read newspapers. A fourth point is the state press subsidy system, which, however, nowadays plays a minor role for the newspaper structure in general. A final feature is the strong presence of free dailies, mainly distributed in metropolitan areas.

The total audit circulation figures of dailies, published at least four days a week, in 2005 was about 3.6 million, equivalent to roughly 420 copies per 1,000 inhabitants, and the circulation also includes the non-dailies amounts, 4 million. If we only consider the adult population the penetration of dailies is 590 copies per 1,000 persons. In addition the circulation of the free dailies was estimated at 0.9 million copies in 2005.

The Swedish newspaper market is traditionally divided into five main segments:

The metropolitan morning papers: dailies published in the three main cities Stockholm, Göteborg and Malmö, like *Dagens Nyheter* in Stockholm, *Göteborgs-Posten* in Göteborg and *Sydsvenskan* in Malmö. These are quality papers published seven days a week. The group represents about 25 per cent of total newspaper circulation.

The metropolitan single-copy sale papers: two tabloid dailies published in Stockholm, *Aftonbladet* and *Expressen*, including local editions in Göteborg (*GT*) and Malmö (*Kvällsposten*), all published seven days a week focus on entertainment and sports. The group represents about 20 per cent of total newspaper circulation.

The regional and local papers: all other papers published at least three times a week, the biggest being *Helsingborgs Dagblad*, Helsingborg; *Dalarnas Tidningar*, Falun; and *Nerikes Allehanda*, Örebro. Most papers in the group are published six days a week and sold almost exclusively on subscription. The average circulation amounts to about 35,000 copies. They represent about 45 per cent of the total circulation.

The low-frequency papers: comprising all general newspapers published once or twice a week, both local papers in the metropolitan areas and small regional papers, all of them with small circulation and mostly in tabloid size. The group represents less than 10 per cent of the total newspaper circulation.

The free dailies form a group of their own, since their circulation is calculated differently from paid newspapers. The biggest paper is *Metro*, six days a week, with editions in

Stockholm, Göteborg and Malmö, and *Stockholm City*, five days a week, in Stockholm and, from 2006, also in Göteborg and Malmö.

In addition there are metropolitan niche papers – e.g. the business daily *Dagens Industri* and the small Christian daily *Dagen*. Almost all dailies are published on the Internet.

The Swedish newspaper market has been relatively stable over the past three decades. However, since the mid-1980s there has been a gradual circulation decline. In the first phase it was a decline mostly within the group of single-copy newspapers, but during the 1990s a gradual decline in circulation started for subscribed mornings, especially for the metropolitan papers. Also the local newspapers, which for a long time were more successful in attracting readers, have begun losing readership.

The total revenues of the newspaper market were in 2004 about 17 billion Swedish Crowns (approximately 2 billion euros). The metropolitan morning papers, with a share of around one-third, and the regional and local papers, with almost about half of the total revenues, are the two dominating groups. The relatively higher shares of those two groups are explained by their high share of advertising revenues: they have mainly between 55 and 60 per cent of their income from advertising, in comparison with about 25 per cent of the single-copy sale tabloids.

In general the Swedish newspaper industry during the late 1990s has been a profitable business. The net margin increased in the late 1990s after a period of decline due to a period of economic recession. In the early twenty-first century it is also increasing – in 2004 about 7 per cent, mainly because of the expanding advertising market. It is true that the newspaper share of the media advertising volume has gradually declined, but is still more than 50 per cent (2005). Further, newspapers have a declining share of the total advertising volume in Sweden – in 2005, 31 per cent to be compared with 35 per cent in 2000. The main competitor here, however, is not other media but direct mail, which has increased dramatically in the last decade.

Local newspapers have applied different strategies to cope with the development. One important measure has been to develop their editorial content, especially by including more of what can be called instrumental contents, such as consumer pages as well as more news on entertainment and music. Another measure has been to change the size of the paper from broadsheet to tabloid. It has developed gradually in the local press but in 2004 it became very visible, when all the main metropolitan papers changed to tabloid size.

The dominating actor on the newspaper market is the Bonnier Group (among others *Dagens Nyheter*, *Expressen*, *Sydsvenskan*, *Dagens Industri* and the free daily *City*), with over a quarter of the total newspaper circulation. Second biggest is the Stampen Group (*Göteborgs-Posten* and a lot of local papers). A typical feature of the Swedish newspaper market is regionally based chains, e.g. the Ander Group in Karlstad and the Herenco

Group in Jönköping. The Bonnier Group also owns several newspapers abroad, mostly in the Baltic area, including Poland.

There is a huge number of other periodical publications in Sweden. The total market is estimated at more than 4,000. However, the general popular magazines are only 25 and have, like in most other countries, a declining circulation; in 2003 an annual sale of a little more 100 million copies. The decline has mainly affected family and women's magazines, some of them having changed frequency to bi-monthly or monthly. However, the specialized magazines – devoted to food, sports, computers, science, etc. – have expanded rapidly. In the late 1990s, also, an expansion of lifestyle magazines took place. Hence, Swedes' exposure to magazines has increased during the last decade. Sweden never had any strong political magazines, probably because of its strong daily press with extensive political coverage. Within the magazine industry, the main publishers, such as the Bonnier (mostly specialized magazines) and the Aller Group (mostly popular magazines), have survived and even increased in importance. The magazine market is characterized by a quite large degree of concentration.

The organizational press, i.e. magazines published by all kinds of associations and businesses, plays a very important role in Sweden. Many of these publications have developed into sort of specialized magazines, the biggest of all being *Buffet* (1.9 million copies) and *IKEA Family Live* (0.9) published by two main shop chains in Sweden as customer magazines. The Association for Tenants publishes the third biggest magazine, called *Hem&hyra* (*Home and Rent*) with about 0.6 million copies. In the latest decades papers published by the trade unions for their members with a monthly circulation of roughly 4 million copies have modernized their journalistic form.

B. *The Broadcast Media*
Main features:

- The public service is strong both in radio and television, but it is gradually losing the youth audience;
- The development of commercial radio and television was relatively late;
- There is an increasing fragmentation of both radio and television audiences, reinforced by the ongoing digitalization process;
- The television industry has generally a good economy, whereas the commercial radio has not been an economic success.

Radio started in 1925 as a private company under strong public control granted a monopoly of broadcasting. In 1956 television was introduced as an extension of the radio company, which was then renamed the Swedish Broadcasting Corporation. Advertising was banned from radio and television from the start. Voluntary organizations were given the right to develop so-called neighbourhood radio in 1978. In 1987 the first Swedish satellite channel (TV3) began broadcasting from the United Kingdom. In 1992 public service radio and television was divided into two companies, one for radio and one for television. Furthermore, there is one public service company for production of educational programmes. The same year a commercial terrestrial TV channel (TV4) was permitted and in 1993 commercial local radio was introduced.

In 2005 radio reached 74 per cent of the Swedes and television 86 per cent. Listening time to radio in Sweden was 105 minutes on the average, while among those who listened it was 141 minutes. Radio listening has gradually decreased in the latter years in Sweden, probably because of the expansion of MP3 players, which in 2005 had a reach of 10 per cent. Viewing time for television on an average day was 96 minutes, among those who watched television it was 112 minutes. It is somewhat increasing, but only slowly. In a European comparison the time spent on television is low in Sweden.

In the radio market the public service company Sveriges Radio (Swedish Radio) is the dominant actor. It has about 60 per cent of the radio audience market. It offers three national channels, P1 (news, culture and public affairs), P2 (classical music) and P3 (youth) and one regional channel, P4, which offers news and current affairs programming in 25 regions. P4 also contains some national programming, especially news and sports. It is targeted for an age group of 40 plus and is the individual Swedish radio channel with the highest ratings (about 37 per cent in 2005).

Formally commercial radio only consists of local stations. However, since the introduction of commercial radio, four Swedish networks with national ambitions gradually developed: Energy/NRJ, Mix Megapol and Rix FM. Based on local stations they offer to a large extent national programming. Energy/NRJ has a clear youth format, and the others have targeted listeners aged between 20 and 40. The private radio market has from its start been under economic pressure. The stations have not attracted as large an audience as expected and their percentage of the media advertising has been only 3 per cent (2005), less than the half of the European average. Most stations have been making substantial losses, with the exception of some stations with a strong local profile. One consequence is an increasing concentration in the private radio market. In 2005 two companies – the MTG and the SBS, both strong also in television – controlled most of the stations.

The so-called neighbourhood radio is very local. The transmissions normally have a radius of only 10 kilometres. The right to broadcast is only open to voluntary associations and the fee for using the frequencies is low. In 2003 more than 1,250 associations had the right to broadcast neighbourhood radio, covering about 170 municipalities.

Public service television is organized by Sveriges Television (SVT; Swedish Television). It has traditionally been the main actor in the television area. It had monopoly on terrestrial television until 1992. It broadcast in three channels: SVT1, SVT2 and SVT24. SVT1 is the more popular and broader channel, whereas SVT2 is profiled as more specialized. Moreover, the SVT24 is a 24-hours news and current affairs channel. Further, SVT distributes a digital children's channel. The television market share for SVT1+SVT2 was, in 2005, 38.5 per cent.

Privately owned television channels financed by advertising were introduced in Sweden in the second half on the 1980s, mainly as a spin-off from the liberal cable legislation enacted in Sweden in 1986. Since cable penetration was quite high it offered an interesting market for satellite channels. In 1987, TV3 started its transmissions and, after some years, the Nordic Channel, later Kanal 5, both transmitting from abroad, and TV4. After the tender based on the decision in 1991 to permit a Swedish terrestrial TV channel based on advertising, TV4 was given the licence and moved from satellite to terrestrial transmissions. Today the main commercial broadcaster is TV4 (23.2 per cent of the TV market in 2005), competing with five Swedish satellite channels, where the biggest are TV3 (10.5) and Kanal 5 (9.2) and the smaller ZTV, TV6 and TV8, with audience shares of some 1 per cent.

TV4 holds the licence for terrestrial commercial television until the year 2008. Only news and some public affairs programming are produced within TV4. It has sixteen local windows, broadcasting about one hour each weekday. TV4 has expanded into satellite television and digital terrestrial television by offering among others a lifestyle and sports channel. It is owned mainly by three major groups: Bonnier and the Swedish investment company Proventus.

TV3 was originally intended as an all-Scandinavian channel but in 1990 it was divided into three separate channels with national profiles. The Swedish TV3 is dominated by entertainment programming with US origin. It is owned by the Modern Times Group (MTG) as part of its satellite platform Viasat Broadcasting. MTG later has launched other satellite channels – ZTV as a Swedish youth channel with a similar concept as MTV, TV6 as an adventure channel and TV8 with economic news. Kanal 5 was launched by a Swedish industrialist in 1989, but later bought by the Scandinavian Broadcasting System (SBS). The channel broadcasts mainly US entertainment but also has tried to include Swedish talk shows.

Of course, many non-Swedish satellite channels can be received in Sweden. Of the foreign channels, however, only Discovery (1.9 per cent in 2005) and Eurosport (1.6 per cent) have more than 1 per cent of the television market.

Until 2005 digital television has been dominated by the private satellite platforms with a penetration of about 45 per cent of the Swedish households. The two leading actors are Canal Digital, owned by the Norwegian Telenor, and Viasat, owned by MTG. Also, cable has gradually been digitalized, but does not yet exceed 10 per cent of Swedish households. The main cable actors have been Com Hem and UPC, which merged in 2006.

By decision of Parliament, terrestrial digital television was gradually introduced, starting in September 2005. In 2008 the analogue transmissions will be switched off. The experience so far is that the public has adapted to the new situation without severe problems. It has also meant an increasing market share for the main actor in terrestrial digital television, Boxer, which has the state as the majority owner, but where the market will be opened for competition. Experiments with digital radio have been carried out since the late 1990s, but no decisions on future actions have been taken.

C. *The Internet Media*
Main features:

■ Early adaptation and widespread use of the Internet
■ Newspapers have a very strong presence on the Net
■ Information-seeking and newspaper reading are important among Internet users

In 2005 about three-fourths of the population between 15 and 85 lived in households with Internet access. About 50 per cent of the Swedes use the Internet regularly and the number is expanding because of the increasing access to broadband (in 2005 around 40 per cent). Thus, the daily Internet reach is predicted to exceed 65 per cent in 2006. The use is much lower among persons over the age of 65.

A lot of newspapers started Web versions of the print paper already in the mid-1990s or soon after that. In the early twenty-first century almost all Swedish newspapers have developed online versions, trying to find a format completing the print version, e.g. by news updates or special services. The most popular online medium by far is *Aftonbladet. se*, founded by the newspaper with the same name in 1995 with almost 3 million unique visitors per week, meaning a national reach of 33 per cent. The visitors of the Web of the five big metropolitan morning papers amount to 2 million. In most regions local papers offer the dominating online service. The reach of the two main television websites, *SVT. se* and *TV4.se*, is significantly lower than those of the national papers.

There have been initiatives to develop online media with no counterpart in print or broadcasting. So far all of them have failed. One obvious reason has been the problem to attract advertising to the Net media. It also means that most papers still lose money on their online services. However, the online service has been regarded as important as a complement to print or broadcasting and an investment in knowledge for the future.

D. *News Agencies*
Main features:

■ One strong national news agency, owned by the leading newspapers
■ Increasing importance of centrally produced pages

Sweden has one national news agency, Tidningarnas Telegrambyrå (TT), founded in 1921 by a merger of two competing agencies. It was organized as a cooperative agency owned by the Swedish newspapers. After a period of economic problems in the 1990s, TT was re-organized. Its ownership model was replaced by a company formed by the three biggest newspaper groups – Bonniers, Schibsted and Stampen bought TT. FLT could not compete and closed down its news wire in 2001.

TT has developed its services. Through its subsidiary TT-Spectra, originally a news agency for the social-democratic press, it offers readymade newspaper pages. It also produces a radio wire for the private local radio. The main telephoto service is offered by Scanpix, a Nordic company owned by the Bonnier and Schibsted groups.

There are also some minor agencies, mainly specialized in feature material on economic and cultural affairs.

2. State Policies
Main features:

- Long tradition of media freedom and basic laws for the press as well as for radio, television and other media including access to public documents
- Some content regulations for radio and television specified in contractual agreements and supervised by public agencies
- Controversies concerning regulation of media ownership

Media legislation is based on a strong tradition of press freedom. It is regulated in a basic law originally from 1766. Freedom is granted also for the content of radio and television by a parallel basic law, the Freedom of Expression Act. Additional laws regulate organizational and technical conditions. Internet is generally treated like the press, meaning a freedom to establish sites and no restriction on contents. The basic laws on press freedom also grant citizens' access to public documents.

Press freedom means both the right to publish and to inform with very few restrictions. In terms of active state policy there are state subsidies to economically weak newspapers introduced in the early 1970s. The subsidy system at first created intense controversy, but the criticism gradually decreased. Today state subsidies represent only about 3 per cent of the total revenues of the Swedish press, but can be very important for individual papers. The supports are based on general rules and are not subject for political decisions in individual cases. There are also some indirect benefits for all newspapers, e.g. a reduced VAT (6 per cent instead of the general one of 25 per cent) and a distribution subsidy.

The general principles of broadcasting are presented in the Freedom of Expression Act. Details are set out in the Radio and Television Act. There is a licence for terrestrial broadcasting of television and for public service radio. It is issued by the government on the basis of a contractual agreement, normally for a period of five years. For the contractual period certain specifications are presented, concerning, for example, news organization, children's programming and amount of Swedish productions, but also in terms of fairness and bias. A fee decided by Parliament finances public service; for 2006 it is 1996 SEK (about 215 euro). The licences for private radio stations, normally for ten years, were originally given away after a public auction. They are nowadays granted by the Radio and Television Authority (Radio-och TV-verket) and based on an agreement concerning the volume of local programming – but there is no other requirement of the content. All radio and television programmes, with the exception of satellite channels from abroad, are formally supervised by a government agency, the Broadcasting Commission (Granskningsnämnden för radio och TV).

Radio and television policy has often created political controversy. The main issue has been the organization and character of public service. The current policy lined out by the social democrats, stresses a broad public service with no advertising but acceptance for sponsored programming, like sports events.

Another media policy area that has meant strong controversy is media concentration. Since the early 1980s there have been proposals of potential measures to restrict ownership dominance, the latest delivered by a government commission in 1999. Its majority recommended a change in the Freedom of Press Act to facilitate measurements against media monopolies. However, the proposal was widely criticized and has not been implemented.

3. Civil Society Organizations
Main features:

- Strong media organizations both for employers and journalists
- Long tradition with a code of conduct for media content (1900) and a Press Council (1916)
- Strong anchoring of the accountability systems among both publishers and journalists
- No consumer organizations, but some smaller watch groups observe the media development

The Swedish media world is characterized by a small number of very powerful organizations. Tidningsutgivarna (TU; The Association of Newspaper Publishers) is both an interest group and an organization for labour negotiations. Almost all Swedish newspapers are members of this organization. TU is considered as one of the most central media organizations in Sweden. There is no comparable association for the radio and television industry. The organization of magazine publishers (Sveriges Tidskrifter) is fairly strong.

Also Svenska Journalistförbundet (SJF; The Union of Swedish Journalists) has about 18,000 members and is considered to be very strong. The level of organization of Swedish journalists is almost 100 per cent and the SJF is the only professional organization. It is also responsible for labour negotiations.

A third organization, Publicistklubben (PK; The Publicists' Club), is an organization of publishers and journalists, interested in the ethical conduct of Swedish mass media.

Together with the TU and the SJF it formed the Swedish accountability system by setting up the first Press Council.

The Swedish accountability system has a long tradition. The first rules, decided by the so-called Publicists' Club (PK) – an organization of people working in the newspaper trade, later, also, other media, both editors, journalists and writers – in 1900, concerned fairness in publishing. Gradually the rules were extended, especially in the 1950s and 1960s, when a Press Ombudsman (PO) was established by the press organizations. In 1968 the Association of Swedish Journalists (SJF) decided on a professional code of conduct. The Press Council was established in 1916, originally as a 'Court of Honour' for editors and journalists.

Today there are three sets of rules, which form the basis of the media accountability system in Sweden:

The publicity rules (the rules of good journalistic practice): these rules regulate the fairness of reporting, respect of privacy, the rights of interviewees, the right to reply and the treatment of pictures and so forth. These rules are the oldest part of the code of conduct.

The rules of professional journalism: these rules deal chiefly with the journalist's professional conduct and concern the integrity of journalists, humiliating assignments, acquisition of material, relations with news sources and so forth. These rules are the code of conduct of the SJF.

The guidelines of editorial advertising: these former rules cover the relationship between advertising and editorial content. They state that news should be judged by news value, not by advertising value. Advertising must not look like editorial pages. These rules were initiated by the TU (The Association of Newspaper Publishers) in 1970.

All the rules are voluntary, initiated by independent organizations, in order to prevent legislation. The rules of good journalistic practice, which are regarded as the most central, are supervised by the Press Council and the Press Ombudsman and the rules of professional journalism by a special committee appointed by the board of SJF. There is also a special council for co-operation in the field of media accountability.

Since 2005 the rules of editorial advertising have no supervising body, because TU withdrew its support meaning that the rules were too strict and are mainly regarded as guidelines for the responsible editors. Further, both the leading newspapers and the national TV channels have their own ombudsmen handling complaints from the public.

No consumer organizations are active in observing the media development. However, there are some smaller activist groups following media content and contributing to media debate, especially in the field of immigration.

4. Development Trends
Main features:

- Stability in the general media development
- Increasing role of the Internet for all media
- Swedish media companies expand abroad
- Age segregation in the use of media, which might lead to a shift in media preferences in the next generations

The transition of the Swedish media landscape has been very rapid in the latest years, making it difficult to determine which the most important trends are as we enter the twenty-first century. Another factor, especially affecting media policy issues, is the change in government in the fall of 2006.

In terms of legislation there are few changes to expect. The new government might reduce the press subsidies somewhat especially for metropolitan papers, but probably not change the system. Also, for radio and television, small changes are expected at least in the short run.

Digitalization of television is under way and the analogue transmission will be switched off in 2008. So far the changes have met little opposition and the schedule is expected to be held. Digitalization means an increase in the number of TV channels, including both channels now only available through satellite and cable and new channels. How this will affect the television market is so far difficult to tell. On the other hand the digitalization of radio will probably not be an issue during the next years.

Internet will continue to expand as a media arena because of increasing broadband access. Both newspapers and public service media have already a very strong presence on the Net. So far it seems that this had little effect on print and broadcasting. The importance of the Net as a distribution form of news is gradually increasing. However, media based only on Net publication are few. Thus, traditional media companies probably will continue their control of the Net media. In this perspective it is to expect that the newspaper companies can compensate the decline of print with the Internet versions of the papers.

Media concentration is gradually increasing but only slowly. On the local markets a number of mergers between local newspaper companies have created a debate on pluralism. On the national level the leading Bonnier Group has met competition from the Swedish expansion of the Norwegian Schibsted Group, in the newspaper field by both the MTG and the Stampen groups and in radio from SBS, which has taken over some of its activities. The most interesting development in the later year is the increasing presence of foreign media companies in Sweden. Swedish companies also expand abroad; Bonnier has about half of its revenues from media activities in other countries, mostly newspapers, magazines and books. MTG is the second biggest in foreign investments, most through the free daily *Metro* but also in radio, television and telecom.

The main problem for public service radio and TV is that they are gradually losing the young public to the commercial channels, a tendency that is reinforced by the digitalization, as the satellite channels will be available to a larger audience. Both public service companies have in 2006 presented plans to recapture the youth. Almost all the plans, meaning among other things to put priority to drams to news and current affairs, have met strong opposition. It is very probable that this controversy will lead to a new debate on the role of public service in the Swedish media system.

The development of the radio and television audience is a good illustration of the fragmentation of the Swedish media system of the early twenty-first century. All existing channels lose audience shares when new channels are introduced. A survey of the total media market defined by the gross average daily time devoted to media use – about six hours – shows that the biggest channel is the national public service radio channel P4 with about 8 per cent. Second are SVT1 and TV4 with about 7 per cent each. More interesting, however, is the audience fragmentation in Sweden has meant a strong age segregation, where traditional newspapers and public service are preferred by the elderly and the new commercial media, including the free dailies, by the youth.

References & Sources for Further Information

Statistics on the newspaper market are found in *TS-boken*, the annual publication concerning the audit circulation figures (www.ts.se).

The Nordicom, the information centre on media and media research at Göteborg University, regularly publishes analyses of media developments in Sweden (www.nordicom.gu.se). It also carries out an annual study of media use, called *Mediebarometern* (the Media Barometer). Current media statistics is also available from the homepage of Nordicom.

Every second year, *MediaSverige* ('Media Sweden') is published by the Nordicom, presenting all basic statistics and covering the development of most media. There is also an English version called *Media Trends* covering all the Nordic countries, which is published on a non-regular basis.

Dagspresskollegiet, at the Göteborg University, regularly presents data on readership development, most of them available on the Internet (www.jmg.gu.se).

The SOM Institute, also at the Göteborg University, annually publishes *Swedish Trends*, presenting data on media and public opinion in Sweden based on surveys (www.som.gu.se).

Radio-och TV-verket (the government agency for radio and television publishes a yearbook presenting statistics and current trends for the broadcasting area, including satellite and cable (www.rtvv.se).

The textbook *Massmedier* by Stig Hadenius and Lennart Weibull, published by Albert Bonniers Förlag and updated regularly (latest edition 2005), offers a general introduction to the Swedish media system.

The Swiss Media Landscape

Werner A. Meier

Switzerland is a small, landlocked country in the heart of Europe. Neighbours of Switzerland are Germany, Austria, Liechtenstein, Italy and France. Switzerland has a strategic location at the crossroads of central Europe and covers 41,290 sq km for 7,476,000 inhabitants. One key feature of Switzerland is its cultural diversity. There are as many as four different official languages – German, spoken by 64 per cent of the population, French (19 per cent), Italian (8 per cent) and Romansh (<1 per cent) – which more or less define four different mentalities. The remaining 8 per cent can be attributed to the languages spoken by immigrants. Foreigners account for some 20 per cent of the population.

The Swiss political system is highly differentiated and complex. The principle of direct democracy applies to three different levels: federal, regional and local. Switzerland consists of 26 "cantons", i.e. states. Each canton is divided into districts. Each district consists of a number of municipalities. All in all, there are 2,929 municipalities in Switzerland. The municipalities are in charge of, for instance, community services, electricity, water, fire brigade, police, local roads, schools and taxes.

This multilevel system is the result of Switzerland's sociocultural and sociopolitical diversity. This structure, on the one hand, creates opportunities for political articulation but, on the other hand, is also responsible for a variety of tensions among interest groups on these three levels.

The Swiss political party scene is exceptionally stable. For more than 50 years, the centre/right-wing parties (Democratic Union of the Centre SVP, Liberal Democratic

Party FDP and Christian Democratic Party CVP) have received 60 to 65 per cent of the vote, while the left-wing (socialist and green) parties have drawn support from 25 to 30 per cent of the voters.

Switzerland is one of the last remaining European countries that are not a member of the European Union. In May 2000, the Swiss people accepted far-reaching bilateral contracts with the EU but Switzerland's currency remains the Swiss franc. In March 2002, Swiss voters narrowly accepted a popular initiative making Switzerland a full member of the United Nations.

1. The Market

A. The Print Media
Main features:

- A large number of regional titles, but no national newspapers
- A regional newspaper market that remains strong but is highly dependent on advertising income
- An increase in economic concentration
- A free-of-charge press with a large share of readership and increasing commercial success
- A newspaper readership, which has not varied substantially in the last decade and remains on a very high level compared to most of EU countries

All daily newspapers in Switzerland featuring a circulation over 100,000 copies are owned by multimedia companies. Ringier, the largest publishing company, owns the tabloid newspaper *Blick* and *Sonntagsblick*, the leading Sunday newspaper. Ringier also publishes the weekly magazine *Schweizer Illustrierte*. Tamedia AG publishes *Tages-Anzeiger* and *SonntagsZeitung*, a Sunday newspaper and the news magazine *Facts*, and has a minority share of 49 per cent in the leading newspaper in Berne, the *Berner Zeitung* owned by the publishing company Espace Media Groupe. Tamedia AG also publishes the daily newspaper *20 Minuten*, a Monday to Friday daily for commuters, which is free of charge. Both Ringier and Tamedia are based in Zurich and are owned by one single family each, although *Tamedia* went public six years ago offering 20 per cent of their shares.

The AG für die Neue Zürcher Zeitung, also situated in Zurich, is the publisher of *Neue Zürcher Zeitung*, *St. Galler Tagblatt* and *Neue Luzerner Zeitung*. It also publishes the third Sunday newspaper in the greater region of Zurich, *NZZ am Sonntag*. The leading publishing house in the French-speaking part of Switzerland is Edipresse which controls two-thirds of the newspaper circulation with its four large dailies and the Sunday paper *Le Matin Dimanche*. The eight most important daily newspapers, i.e. those with a circulation of over 120,000 copies, are read by as many people as the combined readership of the remaining 105 newspapers in Switzerland. More and more small and medium-size newspapers have been forced out of the market or have been taken over by large publishing companies. In 2005 only about 30 fully staffed daily newspapers remained. Furthermore, hardly any new dailies are being launched (1959 the tabloid *Blick*, 1989 *Le Nouveau Quotidien* – relaunched in 2000 as *Le Temps*). A new phenomenon greatly influencing the newspaper market is the launch of the free-of-charge paper *20 Minuten* in 1999.

Advertising provides around 75 per cent of revenues. The profitability of newspapers increasingly depends on the advertising industry as circulation is falling. Therefore, all common forms of press concentration – publisher concentration (a declining number of publishing houses), journalistic concentration (a declining number of fully staffed papers) and a concentration of circulation can be observed in Switzerland. This tendency towards concentration also leads to increasing co-operation between publishing houses in logistics and printing.

B. The Broadcast Media
Main features:

- A strong position of the public broadcaster SRG SSR idée suisse
- A strong role for the linguistic regions in public broadcasting
- A very high degree of cable households
- An ongoing digitization of the terrestrial TV
- Convergence: Digital Audio Broadcasting (DAB), Internet radio and Digital Video Broadcasting (DVB-T)

SRG SSR idée suisse plays a special role since it has the legal right to issue licences to broadcasting operators and to provide them with funding from licence fee resources for the production of radio (fully funded) and television (partially funded) programmes. Public service and the licence fee are, thus, inseparable. In return, SRG SSR idée suisse is entrusted with a special mandate to provide all linguistic regions with programmes of equal quality on a public service basis. SRG SSR idée suisse has to reflect the realities of Swiss life in all its facets, including politics, the arts, society, the economy, sports and entertainment. Its programmes are designed to help viewers and listeners find their way in the complex realities of life in Switzerland. In particular, its programmes have to promote mutual understanding and exchange between the various parties, linguistic communities and cultures that exist in the country. Apart from the licence fee revenue, Swiss broadcasting is co-financed by advertising.

In 2005, SRG SSR idée suisse received 700 million euros through licence fees, while advertising (only on TV – ads on national radio are prohibited) generated a revenue of 219 million euro. Annually, a private user pays 104 euro licence fee for radio reception and another 173 euro for TV reception. Since the Federal Council has the final say as far as the actual amount of the licence fee is concerned, there is an element of dependence in the relationship between the SRG SSR and the state.

The SRG SSR idée suisse structure reflects the fact that Switzerland is multilingual as well as multicultural, and production facilities are distributed all over the language regions. Six radio studios (Zurich, Berne, Basle, Geneva, Lausanne and Lugano) and four regional studios (Aarau, Chur, Lucerne, St. Gall) providing regional news produce sixteen channels, totalling 120,745 hours of radio broadcasting annually (2005). Three television studios in Geneva, Lugano and Zurich produce six independent programmes – two for each linguistic region – as well as special programmes in the Romansch language. In addition, *SF info* repeats the German-language news and information programmes. In total, SRG SSR idée suisse employs 5,800 people, 43 per cent of whom are women (2005).

Its programming charter reads as follows: serving the public, freedom and responsibility, integrity, committed to truthful and impartial reporting, transparency, fairness, consideration for the audience, accountability and conducting remarks.

Regarding programme categories, in 2005 SRG radio allocated 68 per cent of all airtime to music, 10 per cent to news and current affairs, 12 per cent to spoken-word entertainment, 6 per cent to spoken-word culture shows and 2 per cent to sports.

For the distribution of funds, there is a system of financial compensation in place which transfers money from the largest linguistic region to the two smaller ones. In order to enable the French- and the Italian-language regions to produce and receive programmes that are of an equally high quality as in German-speaking Switzerland, they receive an over-proportional amount of the funding. Although the licence fee revenues from the German-speaking population add up to 71 per cent of the of licence fee revenues in total, the programme producers in that region only receive around 44 per cent of that total amount. Without cross-subsidies – as a sort of contribution to national solidarity – it would be nearly impossible to set up and maintain a full television programme in all linguistic parts of Switzerland.

In the television sector, competition is more or less limited to the SRG SSR and the foreign television channels, while in the radio sector, national public radio competes heavily with regional commercial radio. There are also commercial TV stations, but only in the German-speaking part of Switzerland, namely STAR TV, U1 und 3+. In addition, there are regional commercial TV broadcasters in all three language regions. In the German-speaking part: Schaffhauser Fernsehen, TeleBärn, Telebasel, Tele Bielingue, Tele M1, TeleTell, Tele Ostschweiz, Tele Südostschweiz, TeleTop, TeleZüri; in Suisse romande: Canal 9, Canal Alpha, Canal Nord, Vaudois ICI, TV Léman Bleu, TV Région Lausannoise and in Svizzera italiana: TeleTicino.

Eighty per cent of all households have access to cable TV and receive over 40 channels. Ten per cent of all Swiss households have access to a satellite dish. Twenty-four per cent share of the whole advertising market goes to TV, and 57 per cent of the whole advertising market is absorbed by print media. Radio has a share of merely 4 per cent.

SRG SSR idée suisse is about to extend digital terrestrial reception for radio and TV. Digital Audio Broadcasting (DAB) is the medium-term, digital extension to the FM system. Terrestrial digital radio solves the problem of the shortage of frequencies in the existing FM system and significantly improves the quality of mobile radio reception. More importantly, it is a convergent system that permits the transmission of radio, text, pictures and data-only files of all types. Digital Video Broadcasting-Terrestrial (DVB-T) allows the transmission of digital added-value services via the conventional television aerial (terrestrial broadcasting). It is the current standard for broadcasting digital television to households, which do not have cable, and to mobile receivers. Digital service is a long-term project. At the time being, about half of Switzerland is covered with digital signals. Complete nationwide coverage should be achieved by 2008 for television and by 2009 for radio. Moreover, many radio stations offer Internet radio.

C. The Internet Media
Main features:

- An increase of Internet usage from 7 (1997) to 57 per cent (2005)
- Strong digital divide
- Differences in usage depending on income and other demographic characteristics

Representative surveys provide information on the use of the Internet since 1997. The number of people using the Internet on a daily or nearly daily basis has grown from 7 per cent in 1997 to 57 per cent in 2005. The typical Swiss user of the Internet is well educated, well off, young and male – digital divides are obvious and resistant. Sixty-six per cent of men use the Internet daily or nearly daily while only 49 per cent of women do so. Eighty-four per cent of the daily users have higher education, while users with basic education are daily users in only 56 per cent of all cases. Thirty-four per cent of people over 50 are daily users, while 77 per cent of the people between 14 and 29 use the Internet daily. Income accounts for the biggest gap: 84 per cent of the people with a monthly income over CHF 10,000 use the Internet daily, while only 24 per cent of those earning less than 4,000 CHF a month use the Internet on a daily basis. In fact, over the years, some gaps have even widened – especially with regard to age, income and education while the differences between the sexes have remained constant over the past years.

Another finding is that the Internet is used differently by different socio-demographic groups: highly educated people use the Internet in a rather instrumental way, while less educated people seem to use the Internet almost exclusively for entertainment purposes. The most common purposes for Internet use are (in order of priority): e-mails, search engines, current news, timetables, reading articles from newspapers and magazines, Internet banking, downloading programmes, information about job vacancies, information about stock exchange and online games.

The most frequently visited news websites are All News & Information, telsearch. ch, Bluewin news Directories, Blick online, SF DRS, MeteoSchweiz, NZZ Online,

SWISS TXT, tagesanzeiger.ch, google News, 20min.ch, espace.ch, gate 24, MIGROS Magazin.

D. News Agencies
Main features:

■ Two main news agencies (SDA, AP)
■ SDA providing information for all linguistic regions

There are two main news agencies, SDA (Schweizerische Depeschenagentur) and an AP affiliate (Associated Press). SDA, situated in Berne, is the only Swiss national agency that generates information in German, French and Italian. SDA is a publicly listed corporation owned by the Swiss publishers but in principal a non-profit organization. It is a classic news service, providing information about politics, economics, culture, social issues and miscellaneous from at home and abroad.

2. State Policies
Main features:

■ Freedom of the Press and freedom of trade guaranteed
■ Mandate of the Swiss National Television and Radio Stations to provide a programme reflecting and maintaining the linguistic and cultural diversity of the country
■ Mandate of the Swiss National Television and Radio Stations for the adequate supply of all regions
■ Four interest groups influencing, defining and enforcing the standards, norms and values of the Swiss Media Landscape
■ UVEK and Bakom supervising the performance of Swiss radio and television broadcasting
■ Institutionalized programme-controlling and quality-ensuring authorities (UBI, Ombudsman)

Freedom of the press, radio and television is guaranteed in the Swiss Federal Constitution (Art. 16). Furthermore, Article 93/4 of the Constitution, which regulates radio and television, explicitly calls for the protection of the written press. There is, however, no legal obligation for the Swiss press to fulfil a public service mandate. Newspapers – as private enterprises – are only subject to free entrepreneurial decisions and, of course, the market.

Switzerland's linguistic and cultural diversity is a challenge to the public and commercial broadcasters. SRG SSR idée suisse, i.e. the Swiss Broadcasting Corporation, has the mandate to produce and disseminate radio and television programmes in the four official languages of the country. The institutionalization and organization of radio and television is based on Article 93 of the new Swiss Federal Constitution. The act specifies information, education and entertainment – in this order – as the main tasks of Swiss radio and television. In addition, the act set up an independent complaints authority (UBI). The Federal Radio and Television Law (RTVG) dates from 1991 and has been revised in 2006 by the Federal Council and the Federal Assembly. The new law has entered into force in April 2007. According to the law, the electronic media – especially the public service – must:

1. Contribute to the unrestricted formation of opinion, to the provision of general, wide-ranging and accurate information for listeners and viewers for their education and entertainment, and communicate knowledge on citizens' rights and obligations in the democratic decision-making processes.
2. Take into account the diversity of the country and its inhabitants, reflect this diversity, and promote mutual understanding.
3. Promote Swiss cultural creativity and stimulate listeners and viewers to participate in cultural life.
4. Facilitate contact with Swiss nationals living abroad and promote the presence of Switzerland and understanding of its interests abroad.
5. Focus attention on Swiss audiovisual productions, especially films, and broadcast as many European productions as possible.
6. The programmes dealing in a specific area must not favour specific political parties, interests or ideologies.
7. The different parts of the country must be adequately provided with radio and television programmes.

Within this system, at least four interest groups influence the definition and enforcement of standards, norms, values and regulations in the Swiss media landscape:

Transnational actors: Among them the council of Europe is of particular importance for Swiss broadcasting policy, since Switzerland is not a member of the EU. The Swiss Government and Parliament have given their approval to the European Convention on transfrontier television, although the traditional liberal ideal of the free flow of information does not account for the structural handicaps of small, multicultural states.

National authorities: Mainly the Federal Government, the Federal Transportation, Communication and Energy Department (UVEK), the Parliament, the Federal Office for Communication in Bienne (Bakom) and the Independent Authority for Programme Complaints (UBI) contribute to the definition, protection and enforcement of norms, standards, values and regulatory activities.

Political parties: The political parties react – if at all – in the media sector according to their traditional platforms. The liberal and conservative parties in general favour the privatization and deregulation of the media system; the social democrats prefer the mass media to be as independent as possible from commercial pressure and support a viable public broadcasting system.

Media organizations: As powerful multipliers, on which politicians depend to a certain degree, media organizations can challenge or even obstruct government strategies, regulations and values they judge unfavourable to their interests. Especially the privately owned media companies are usually only willing to comply with special social, cultural or political obligations as long as the market rewards such activities. The fact that the willingness to oblige with these obligations vary across the commercial media landscape makes it difficult to implement a coherent media policy.

The regulation of the Swiss broadcasting system is moving in two directions: Offering access to private broadcasters while at the same time securing the structures of a productive system of public broadcasting, mainly for political and cultural reasons.

Bakom and UVEK are in charge of supervising the performance of Swiss radio and television broadcasting. Since 1984 the Independent Authority for Programme Complaints (UBI) has been evaluating complaints about programming. The eleven-member committee judges individual programmes according to professional norms and social values. In practice, the procedure works as follows: Within twenty days of the initial transmission of a certain programme, anyone can lodge a complaint about a certain programme before the conciliation body of the broadcaster that has aired the programme (Ombudsman's Office). The Ombudsman will then investigate the matter and try to mediate between the parties. If the person lodging the complaint is still not satisfied with the Ombudsman's findings, he or she can complain to the UBI. The complaint must be counter-signed by at least twenty people. UBI's final decision can be challenged in the Federal Court. The UBI complaint procedure was originally designed to secure certain reporting standards. However, the number of complaints being filed through lawyers is growing and some proceedings thus take on a 'legal' dimension.

The Ombudsman's Office and the UBI have to balance freedom of speech of producers and viewers, and the responsibility of electronic media to inform citizens in a reliable way. The institutionalization of 'programme-controlling' authorities is an interesting, but also problematic way to secure the quality of programmes and the interests of viewers.

In 2005, the number of complaints submitted at the Ombudsman's Office stood at 150. Forty-three per cent of all complaints were being considered as legitimate. Seven per cent (11 cases) could not be settled and reached the level of the UBI. In the past years, most complaints have been filed in the television sector, while the number of complaints against radio is negligible.

3. Civil Society Organizations
Main features:

- Several organizations, syndicates and associations for employers, journalists and media organizations
- Viewers are given the opportunity to complain about programming

The main employers' organization is the Swiss Association of Newspapers and Magazine Publishers (Swiss Press). The commercial TV Channels cooperates in Telesuisse, while commercial radio stations are associated in the Association of Swiss Private Radios. The main professional groups are the Swiss Association of Journalists (SVJ), the Swiss Journalist's Union (Comedia) and the Swiss Syndicate of Media Professionals (SSM).

Print Media – apart from publishers, who are not part of the Press Council – have set up directives relating to the Declaration of the Duties and Rights of the Journalist. These directives summarize the practice of the Press Council since 1977 and interpret the rules of the Declaration.

4. Development Trends
Main features:

- All forms of press concentration in Switzerland
- No private television stations on a national level but several stations on a regional level with a small audience and only little commercial success
- Intense competition in the press market due to the launch of several free papers

As mentioned before, all common forms of press concentration can be observed in Switzerland. The trend seems to be heading towards a two-tier newspaper landscape. Only a few high-circulation papers will serve the economic centres and the suburbs, meanwhile many small newspapers will have to fill the gaps, taking advantage of narrow local advertising and readership markets. In addition, cross-media concentration is also a fact. Big publishing houses have entered other media markets. Just to name one example, Tamedia has expanded its radio and television business in recent years and acquired commercial regional radios and a regional TV channel.

The attempt to start a private television programme on a national level, however, has never succeeded. At the end of the twentieth century some private channels tried to establish national programmes, but without great success. Programme windows have proved commercially viable. Examples are *SAT 1*, a German channel which offers some Swiss programming, and the public broadcaster SF Schweizer Fernsehen (SF zwei) lending airtime to "Press TV". One example of Press TV is NZZ format, the one-hour programme of *Neue Zürcher Zeitung*. Its documentaries are dedicated to topics from science, technology, medicine and social life. They provide background information and address an up-market audience.

The status and public service remit of the Swiss Broadcasting Corporation (SRG SSR idée suisse) are unchallenged. Its services are viewed as reliable and professional, and SRG SSR radio and TV stations are considered to be leaders in their fields.

Private TV programmes were able to assert themselves on the regional level, albeit with a small audience and little commercial success. They produce only a modest programme of a maximum three hours per day and fill the remaining hours with reruns. The revised Federal Radio and Television Law (RTVG) awards local TV stations 4 per cent of SRG SSR licence-fee revenues on the condition of a regional public service remit.

The most dramatic change on the newspaper market happened in 1999. Two free-of-charge sheets were launched, at the time both were owned by foreign publishing houses and targeted commuters in the greater area of Zurich. *20 Minuten* and *Metropol* intensified the competition among the newspapers in this area but also fought against each other. Eventually, in 2002, *20 Minuten* prevailed and subsequently expanded to other urban regions all over the German-speaking part of Switzerland. At present, specific editions are made for the regions of Zurich, Berne, Lucerne, Basle and St. Gall. Since 2004, *20 Minuten* is the most widely read daily newspaper in Switzerland, even surpassing the (former market leader) tabloid *Blick*. Since 2005, *20 Minuten* is owned by Tamedia. In the first quarter of 2006, *20 Minuten* managed to obtain a readership of over 1 million people which means a scope of almost 25 per cent of the total readership in Switzerland. Furthermore, *20 Minuten* has also entered the French-speaking part of Switzerland: *Tamedia* launched its French counterpart, *20 minutes*, in March 2006. In the greater area of Geneva and Lausanne, it competes with the free sheet *Le Matin Bleu* from Edipresse.

References & Sources for Further Information

Meier, Werner A. (2004), Switzerland. In: M. Kelly, G. Mazzoleni, D. McQuail (eds.) *The Media in Europe. The Euromedia Handbook*. London 2004. S. 249–261.

Meier, Werner A. (2004), *Das Mediensystem der Schweiz. In: Internationales Handbuch für Hörfunk und Fernsehen 2004/2005*. Baden-Baden/Hamburg, S. 594–605.

SRG SSR *Profile of SRG SSR idéesuisse 2005*, Berne 2005.

SRG SSR *Geschäftsbericht 2005*, Berne 2006.

SRG SSR *Facts and Figures 2006*, Berne 2006.

THE MEDITERRANEAN/POLARIZED PLURALIST MEDIA MODEL COUNTRIES

INTRODUCTION

Stylianos Papathanassopoulos

The Mediterranean Media Model

The media systems of Spain, Italy, France, Greece, Portugal, Turkey, Malta and Cyprus represent what Daniel Hallin and Paolo Mancini propose as the Mediterranean or Polarized Pluralistic model. This is because the media systems in southern Europe share a number of characteristics which distinguish them from the rest of the central, western and northern Europe. According to Hallin and Mancini (2004: 89), the mass media in the southern European countries were intimately involved in the political conflicts that mark the history of this region, and there is a strong tradition of regarding them as means of ideological expression and political mobilization. The location of France with the Mediterranean model is recognized as problematic, according to several key dimensions (p. 90). At the same time, the development of commercial media markets was relatively weak, leaving the media often dependent on the state, political parties, the Church, or wealthy private patrons, and inhibiting professionalization and the development of the media as autonomous institutions.

Cultural and Political Heritage

Political, social and economic conditions, population and cultural traits, physical and geographical characteristics usually influence the development of the media in specific countries, and give their particular characteristics (Gallimore 1983: 53–62; Hiebert, Ungurait and Bohn 1982: 33–55). An additional factor, which may need to be considered for a better understanding of media structures, is that of media consumption and the size of a market. Across Europe there are some significant differences between countries when it comes to the penetration and consumption of the traditional media, such as the press and television. Although some other factors may play a part, it seems that economic conditions, religion, political freedom and culture are the conditions that mainly influence the development and the structure of most media systems.

Industrialism and the market were developed rather late in most southern European countries, while cultural life was dominated by religion and its institutions. As Hallin and Mancini (2004: 128) note "the late, uneven and conflictual development of liberal institutions in Southern Europe is fundamental to understanding the development of the media in this region".

Moreover, the lack of market development in relation to the counter-Enlightenment tradition discouraged the development of literacy, which affected the development of mass circulation press. On the other hand, most countries have witnessed a political instability and repression in their history.

Another characteristic which these seven countries obviously have in common is a late transition to democracy. Liberal institutions were only consolidated in Italy after World War II, in Greece, Spain and Portugal from about 1975–1985, while Turkey has witnessed three military coups (1960, 1971, 1980). This is of profound importance to understanding the media systems in the region. The transition to democracy is of course a complex process. It involves the transformation of many political institutions – including the mass media – and of the relationships among political, social and economic institutions. These transformations are often slow and uneven and for that reason knowledge of political history is crucial to understanding current institutions. It is not a coincidence that the development of the media in the region has been deeply affected by the political patterns of Polarized Pluralism, and they have historically served and participated in this process of bargaining. Even though the media operate in a market framework, they offer information, analysis and comments produced by a few elite groups, which address other political, cultural and economic elites in order to send messages and start up negotiations. This pattern has been most characteristic of Italy and Greece, but is seems to apply to the other Mediterranean countries too. Last but not least, since the state due to the atrophied civil society has played a central role in most aspects of social and economic aspects of society, it has also affected the development of the printed and electronic media, either through heavy subsidies (in the case of the press) or through tight control and heavy interference (in the case of public/state electronic media).

The Main Characteristics

According to Hallin and Mancini (2004) and Hallin and Papathanassopoulos (2000), the media in southern Europe share some major characteristics: low levels of newspaper circulation, a tradition of advocacy reporting, instrumentalization of privately owned media, politicization of public broadcasting and broadcast regulation and limited development of journalism as an autonomous profession.

Low Levels of Newspaper Circulation

The most obvious distinction between the media of the eight Mediterranean countries and those of the rest of Western Europe is their low level of newspaper circulation (and a corresponding importance of electronic media). Mass circulation newspapers did not develop in any of the countries of southern Europe. In effect, as Hallin and Mancini (2004: 91) note "a true mass circulation press never fully emerged in any of the Mediterranean countries". On the other hand, the church has played a significant role in development of the media, while tabloid or sensationalist popular newspapers have never really development in the region. The only true mass media of southern Europe are electronic media, and their importance for the formation of mass public opinion is, therefore, particularly great. A recent development is the advent of several free newspapers in Spain, Portugal, Italy and Greece posing a new problem for the conventional newspapers.

Political Parallelism

As Hallin and Mancini point out,

> the media in the Southern European countries are relatively strongly politicized, and political parallelism is relatively high. The style of journalism tends to give substantial emphasis to commentary. Newspapers tend to represent distinct political tendencies, and this is reflected in the differing political attitudes of their readerships; at times they play an activist role, mobilizing those readers to support political causes. Public broadcasting tends to be party-politicized. Both journalists and media owners often have political ties or alliances (2004: 98).

In effect, most of the countries covered have traditions of advocacy journalism. In contrast with the Anglo-American model of professional neutrality, journalism in Southern Europe tends to emphasize commentary from a distinct political perspective. There is some variation in this characteristic. It is stronger in Greece and in Italy, for example, where strong and highly polarized political parties have existed for all or much of the post-World War II period, than in countries like Spain, Portugal, where long periods of dictatorship suppressed the development of political parties.

Advocacy traditions have been modified both by diffusion of the Anglo-American model of journalism and by traditions of passive reporting that developed during periods of dictatorship. But, in general, journalism in these countries tends to emphasize opinion and commentary and newspapers to represent distinct political tendencies. This characteristic, however, is not distinct to southern Europe, but is also characteristic of most of continental Europe, though over the last decade or so the movement away from advocacy journalism has probably been faster in northern than southern Europe.

On the other hand, the paternalism of the state in most Mediterranean European countries has remained one of the most important features of the state electronic media. Public broadcasting systems in the Mediterranean countries present a symbiotic relationship with the political controversies of their countries. Both radio and television have been regarded as "arms of the state" and in many cases the debate about the electronic state media was focused on governmental control and interference in television TV, principally news, programmes. This condition became part of post-war ritualized politics in France during the De Gaulle administrations as well as in Greece, Portugal and Spain after the restoration of their democracies. The case of RAI's *lottizazzione* by the Italian leading political parties is another manifestation of the heavy use of the media by the political parties. In Turkey, TRT has heavily been used by the military and the government of the day.

Instrumentalization of Media

There is a strong tendency in all countries for media to be controlled by private interests with political alliances and ambitions who seek to use their media properties for political ends. In Italy, for example, the old media companies such as Mondadori, Rizzoli and Rusconi are now controlled by non-media businesses, such as Berlusconi (soccer, insurance, commercial television) and Fiat (automobile). Carlo DeBenedetti of Olivetti controls *La Repubblica* and *L'Espresso*; Agnelli family of Fiat controls *La Stampa* and, though RCS, with Benetton (apparel) and Dealla Valle (shoes), the largest Italian daily, *Corriere della Sera*; the Caltagirone Group (construction) daily, *Il Messaggero*; while *Il Ciornale* is owned by Paolo Berlusconi, bother of Silvio Berlusconi, and the Italian Manufacturers' Association (Confindustria) publishes the best-selling financial newspaper, *Il Sole 24 Ore*. Private television, meanwhile, is dominated by Silvio Berlusconi, who is also a party leader and former prime minister.

In Turkey, all the major media groups, Doğan, Merkez, Çukurova, İhlas, Doğuş, etc., are large conglomerates and their activities expand to other sectors of the economy (tourism, finance, car industry, construction and banking). And it seems that they use their media outlets to protect their interests in the other sectors of the economy, while there seems to be no efficient way to control the concentration of the media ownership.

In Greece industrialists with interests in shipping, travel, construction, telecommunication and oil industries dominate media ownership, and a long tradition of using media as a means of pressure on politicians continues. In Spain the media are increasingly dominated, not by industrialists with their primary interests outside the media but, by two broad multimedia conglomerates which, however, do have strong political alliances. For many years the dominant company was PRISA, whose interests include *El País*, SER radio and cable and satellite television, and whose owner was close to socialist President Felipe González. A rival media empire is now emerging around the former state telecommunications monopoly, Telefónica de España, which was privatized under the conservative Partido Popular government. This conglomerate includes the private television company Antena 3, the newspaper *El Mundo*, which made its name breaking the news of a number of major scandals involving the PSOE government, the radio network Onda Zero and a satellite television platform. The two media empires have become intense rivals, as much in the political as in the commercial world. The conservative newspaper *ABC* and the Catholic Church's radio network, COPE, were also aligned with Telefónica in this conflict. Major banks also have ties to these conglomerates, and Spanish journalists and media analysts often describe them as major powers behind the scenes, though their role is very difficult to document.

In Portugal the transition to democracy began with a two-year period of revolutionary upheaval during which the media were, for the most part, taken over by radicalized journalists who conceived them as instruments of class struggle. Ownership of much of the media passed to the state when the banks were nationalized, and by the early 80s, effective control had, to a significant extent, passed to the political parties. In the late 80s state-owned media were privatized. One of the principal media conglomerates, Impresa, is owned by F. Pinto Balsamão, a former prime minister and leader of the (conservative) Social Democratic Party, though instrumentalization of the media in Portugal is perhaps less intense today than in the other countries of southern Europe.

Politicization of Public Broadcasting and Broadcast Regulation

All public broadcasting systems are to some degree subject to political influence and manipulation, and disputes over the independence of public broadcasting are common to the history of European media. Most countries in Western Europe, however, have succeeded in developing institutions which separate public broadcasting from the direct control of the political majority. The countries of southern Europe, however, have not moved as far in this direction. Italy has moved the furthest. The Italian public broadcasting company RAI was essentially under the control of the ruling Christian Democratic Party in the 1950s and 60s, but in the 70s, when a broader coalition was formed and the "historic compromise" allowed the Partido Comunista to share in the *lottizzazione* – the division of political power and benefits – control of RAI was divided among the parties, with the Christian Democrats retaining control of one channel, the "secular parties" the second and the Communists the third. In recent years the board of directors of RAI has been reduced in size, making proportional representation impossible, a move which is likely to require a degree of depoliticization of appointments to the board. In Malta, the state, the political parties, the Church and the university own radio and TV stations. TRT in Turkey has been always under tight state control, and its audience fell dramatically after the advent of private channels.

Spain and Greece, meanwhile, are the two countries remaining in Western Europe in which the ruling party directly controls public broadcasting. In both countries the management of the news divisions of public television changes with a change in government, and the news is at important moments mobilized to support the government politically. In Greece, news and editorial judgments are expected to be in close agreement with, if not identical to, government announcements across a whole range of policies and decisions. It should be noted that Spain and Greece are essentially majoritarian systems, unlike Italy which is a consensus system. A governing board appointed by parliament according to proportional representation therefore results in government control in the former, while it results in power-sharing in the latter. Portugal similarly has had a public broadcasting system in which the government majority had effective control.

In most countries politicization of regulatory bodies coexists with relatively weak regulation of private broadcasters in the sense that few public service obligations and few restrictions on commercialism are imposed, and many regulations are laxly enforced.

"Savage Deregulation"

Across Europe, broadcasting has been in ferment, as governments of every political persuasion try to cope with the stress and upheavals caused by the deregulation. However, in Mediterranean countries, broadcasting and politics seem to form an inextricable relationship. The imminent deregulation of broadcasting in most southern European countries has been associated with politics and eventually led by a haphazard reaction of the politics of the time, rather than a coherent plan. In short, the deregulation of southern European broadcasting systems has led to an unregulated environment as market logic has in recent years been allowed to develop essentially unchecked. The dominance of private television as well as the downgrading of public broadcasters has increasingly forced politicians to have good relations with the media owners. In Italy commercial television monopolies were allowed to develop without government intervention. In Greece, meanwhile, licence applications are not adjudicated and large numbers of radio and TV stations continue for years in legal limbo. In Spain, as in Greece and Portugal, it could be said that public service broadcasting in the full sense of the word never really existed. As Hallin and Mancini (2004: 126) note, "It is probably significant that democracy was restored in Spain, Portugal and Greece at a time when the welfare state was on the defensive in Europe, and global forces of neoliberalism were strong; these countries missed the historical period when social democracy was at its strongest".

Limited Professionalization

The instrumentalization of the news media by oligarchs, industrialists, parties or the state implies that journalistic autonomy will be limited. Journalists will at times have to defer to their political masters. As Hallin and Mancini (2004: 110) note, "journalism originated in the Southern European countries as an extension of the worlds of literature and politics". However, as they argue, "this history of journalistic professionalisation is closely parallel to what occurred in the Liberal and Democratic Corporatist countries" (p. 111). The process did not develop as strongly in the Mediterranean countries, however, as in the north. The political and literary roots of journalism were deeper, and the political connections persisted much longer. Limited development of media markets meant that newspapers were smaller and less likely to be self-sustaining. And state intervention, particularly in periods of dictatorship, interrupted the development of journalism as a profession. The level of professionalization thus "remains lower in the Mediterranean countries, though it increased in important ways in the last couple of decades of the twentieth century".

This, however, does not mean that the level of professionalization is lower. For example, journalists in the Mediterranean countries are not less educated than elsewhere – in Italy and Greece, for example, famous writers and intellectuals have often been journalists. On the other hand, the close connection of journalism with the political and literary worlds and the orientation of newspapers to educated elites have meant that journalism has in some sense been a more elite occupation in southern Europe than in other regions. Limited professionalization is also manifested in a limited development of institutions of journalistic self-regulation, like the press councils which exist in much of northern Europe (Hallin and Mancini 2004: 112).

The Media and the State

The interplay between the state and the media has largely arisen from the tensions in most southern European societies. These tensions, combined with the absence of a strong civil society, have made the state an autonomous and dominant factor. The over-extended character of the state has coincided, as noted above, with the underdevelopment of capitalism. This makes the southern European systems less self-regulatory than developed capitalist systems such as in Liberal model. The lack of self-regulation is also noticeable at the level of politico-ideological superstructure, because with a weak civil society, even the economically dominant classes do not manage to form well-organized and cohesive pressure groups. As Hallin and Mancini (2004//) note: "the state's grasp often exceeds its reach: the capacity of the state to intervene effectively is often limited by lack of resources, lack of political consensus, and clientelist relationships which diminish the capacity of the state for unified action".

In the case of the media, the state's intervention can be seen in various aspects (Hallin and Mancini 2004: 119–121). First, the state has played the role of censor. The direct authoritarian control of the years of dictatorship is presumably a thing of the past, but some remnants have carried over into the democratic period. Second, the state has also played an important role as an owner of media enterprises. The electronic media have traditionally been under the total and tight control of the state, but apart from the state-owned electronic media, the state has also had significant ownership in commercial media in the Mediterranean countries, including in the print press (for example, the Franco regime in Spain often had state-owned newspapers) and, of course, in news agencies (Agence France Presse, the Italian Agency AGI, EFE in Spain, ANA in Greece, Anadolu Ajansi in Turkey, Agência Lusa in Portugal). Publicly funded news agencies function both to maintain the presence of the national press on the world scene and as a subsidy to domestic news media which use the service. Thirdly, in a more indirect but more effective way, the state acts to support its policies on ownership as well as to enforce the unwritten rules of power politics by using a wide range of means of intervention which are at its disposal. These means include sizable financial aid to the press, on which individual enterprises become dependent because they cannot cover their production costs. For example, as Hallin and Mancini (2004: 121) note, extensive indirect subsidies have been provided to the press as a whole in the form of tax breaks, reduced utility rates and the like. For example, in France direct subsidies in 2005 amounted to 249,2 millions euro, while the non-direct subsidies were far higher.

By and large, state subsidies to the media, especially the press take the form of "soft" loans, subsidies both overt and covert, and state jobs and other subsidies offered to many journalists. Finally, the central role of the state in Mediterranean media systems has no doubt limited the tendency of the media to play the "watchdog" role so widely valued in the prevailing liberal media theory. The financial dependence of media on the state and the persistence of restrictive rules on privacy and the publication of official information have combined with the intertwining of media and political elites and – especially in the French case – with a highly centralized state not prone to the kind of "leaks" of information that characterize the American system, to produce a journalistic culture which has historically been cautious about reporting information which would be embarrassing to state officials.

Clientelism and Rational/Legal Authority

Clientelism refers to a pattern of social organization in which access to social resources is controlled by patrons and delivered to clients in exchange for deference and various kinds of support. It is a particularistic and asymmetrical form of social organization and is typically contrasted with forms of citizenship in which access to resources is based on universalistic criteria and formal equality before the law. Clientelistic relationships have been central to the social and political organization in most southern European countries (Hallin & Papathanassopoulos 2000). The greater prevalence of clientelism in southern than northern Europe is intimately connected with the late development of democracy. Both are rooted historically in the fact that autocratic, patrimonial institutions were strongest in the south. The emergence of clientelism represented not simply a persistence of traditional hierarchical social structures, but a response to their breakdown, in a social context in which individuals were isolated, without independent access to the political and economic centre, e.g. through markets, representative political institutions or a universalistic legal system, and in which "social capital" was lacking (see also Eisenstadt and Roniger 1984; Gellner and Waterbury 1977; Kourvetaris and Dobratz 1999; Mouzelis 1980; Roniger and Günes–Ayata 1994; Putnam 1993; Katzenstein 1985). Clientelism affects the development of the news media in many ways.

First, it encourages the instrumentalization of the news media. The politicization of business is a result not only of the important role the state plays in the economy, but of the nature of the political process. In northern Europe clientelist relationships have been displaced to a large extent by rational-legal forms of authority and, especially in the smaller continental European countries, by democratic corporatist politics, both of which decrease the need for economic elites to exert particularistic pressures and form partisan alliances. In countries with a history of clientelism, rational-legal authority is less strongly developed. The judiciary and administrative apparatus are more party-politicized and there is often a tradition of evasion of the law. The persistence of a culture in which evasion of the law is relatively common means that opportunities for particularistic pressures also are common: governments can exercise pressure by enforcing the law selectively, and news media can do so by threatening selectively to expose wrongdoing. Legal proceedings against media owners are fairly common in many southern European countries.

Second, it makes the media systems less self-regulatory and the regulatory bodies less independent compared to their counterparts in liberal countries like the US and Britain and in democratic corporatist countries. In southern Europe, the regulatory institutions tend to be more party-politicized and weaker in their ability to enforce regulations.

Third, clientelism has also affected the content of the media, especially newspapers, as means of negotiation among conflicting elites rather than means for the information of the public and, therefore, mass circulation. It forces the logic of journalism to merge with other social logics – of party politics and family privilege, for instance. And it breaks down the horizontal solidarity of journalists as it does of other social groups. Thus, the journalistic culture of the northern, corporatist countries which is manifested both in relatively strong journalistic autonomy and in highly developed systems of ethical self-regulation is absent in countries with a stronger history of clientelism because of the overriding importance of political interests. A sense of a public interest transcending particular interests has been more difficult to achieve in societies where political clientelism is historically strong, and this contributes to the difficulty of developing a culture of journalistic professionalism.

Development Trends

In the eight countries covered in this section, significant social forces have undermined the development of the media similar to North America or Western Europe. Although the developments in the media sector may not entirely respond to the needs of their industry, yet, their media systems have been surprisingly adaptable and flexible in the face of new developments. To understand this, one must remember that most of the media systems of southern Europe have worked under western democratic rule for only 30 years now, and this has had suddenly to face all the upheavals that other western media systems have taken years to deal with.

The commercialization of their media systems may have led to a de-politicization of their content, the political affiliation of the media, especially newspapers, is always manifest in periods of intense political contention. This is also due to the fact that political parties still play an important role in most southern European countries. It is, therefore, as Hallin and Mancini (2004: 140) note: "not surprising either that parties would have considerable influence on the media, nor that the media should focus to a significant degree on their activities".

However, the logic of media markets may under certain circumstances undermine these relationships. It can make media organizations less dependent on political subsidies, substitute marketing for political criteria in the making of news decisions and discourage identification with particular political positions. It may also make media enterprises too expensive for most politicians to afford or even for most industrialists to buy purely for political motives.

Finally "globalization" may under certain circumstances undermine the close relationship between media and the political world. One particularly obvious instance is the effect of the common legal framework of the European Union. The "Europeanization" of the EU countries could be seen as an incremental process that re-orientates the direction and shape of politics to the degree that EU political and economic dynamics become part of the organizational logic of domestic politics and policymaking (Harcourt 2002; Radaelli

1997). The EU "Europeanization" process will certainly affect their media systems as well. At present, however, we believe that in order to understand the complexities and particularities of media systems in southern Europe, the concept of Hallin and Mancini's model remains crucial.

References

Eisenstadt, S. N. and Roniger, L. (1984), *Patrons, Clients and Friends: Interpersonal Relations and the Structure of Trust in Society*. Cambridge: Cambridge University Press.

Gallimore, T. (1983), "Barriers to Media Development. In Merril, J. C. (ed.) *Global Journalism*, White Plains, New York: Longman Publishers, 1983.

Gellner, E. and Waterbury, J. (1977) (eds.), *Patrons and Clients in Mediterranean Societies*, London: Gerald Duckworth and Co.

Hallin, C. D and Mancini, P. (2004), *Comparing Media Systems; Three Models of Media and Politics*. Cambridge: Cambridge University Press.

Hallin, D. and Papathanassopoulos, S. (2000), "Political Clientelism and the Media: Southern Europe and Latin America in Comparative Perspective", *Media, Culture & Society*, vol 24, no. 2: 175–195.

Harcourt. A. (2002), "Engineering Europeanization: the role of the European institutions in shaping national media regulation", *Journal of European Public Policy*, vol 9, no. 5: 736–755.

Hiebert, R. E., Ungurait, D. F. and Bohn, T. W. (1982), *Mass Media III*, London: Longman.

Katzenstein, P. J. (1985), *Small States in World Markets: Industrial Policy in Europe*. Ithaca, NY: Cornell University Press.

Kourvetaris, G. and Dobratz, B. A. (1999), "Political Clientelism in Athens, Greece: A Three Paradigm Approach", pp. 237–262. In G. Kourvetaris (ed.) *Studies on Modern Greek Society and Politics*. Boulder, CO: East European Monographs.

Mouzelis, N. (1980), "Capitalism and the Development of the Greek State". In R. Scase, ed. *The State in Western Europe*. London: Croom Helm.

Putnam, R. D. (1993), *Making Democracy Work: Civic Traditions in Modern Italy*. Princeton: Princeton University Press.

Radaelli, C. (1997), 'How does Europeanization produce domestic policy change?', *Comparative Political Studies*, vol. 30, no. 5: 553–75.

Roniger, Luis and Günes-Ayata, A. (1994) (eds.), *Democracy, Clientelism and Civil Society*. Boulder, CO: Lynne Rienner.

The Cypriot Media Landscape

Myria Vassiliadou

The Republic of Cyprus is a well-known regional holiday resort, a services centre (mainly banking and shipping) and telecommunications node. It is also in the middle of a difficult political situation which has been the centre of a lot of media attention throughout Europe recently.

The Cypriot political system is based on Republic Presidential Democracy and it has two official languages, Greek and Turkish, although English is widely spoken. The majority of the population is Greek Orthodox [78%] but there are also an estimated 18 per cent Muslims, while Maronite, Armenian Apostolic and others represent an overall 4 per cent of the population. The population was estimated at 784,301 in July 2006 in the non-occupied territories and around 200,000 in the north.

Cyprus has been geographically and ethnically divided since 1974 when Turkey moved into more than a third of the island in response to a coup inspired by the military junta in Greece, and after decades of inter-communal tensions and violence. In 1983, the area under Turkish military control declared itself independent and proclaimed a republic called "Turkish Republic of Northern Cyprus" [TRNC], which, to this day, has not been recognized by any country except Turkey and is considered as illegal by the international community.

UN-lead negotiations together with the possibility of a settlement through the island's accession in the European Union have dominated the political discourse. The last peace plan proposed by the UN in 2002 before EU accession led to a deadlock. Despite this, the Republic of Cyprus joined the European Union in May 2004. With the rejection of the reunification 'Annan Plan' in 2004, special measures were adopted by the EU regulating its relations with the occupied territory, starting with the policing of the Green line that separates it and extending to trade, funding and official representation.

Every effort has been made in this chapter to address both parts of the island. However, unless otherwise stated, the following report is based on international and national information available concerning the non-occupied part of the Republic of Cyprus.

1. The Market

A. The Print Media
Main features:

- Very high concentration of newspapers and periodical titles per capita, especially in the occupied territories
- Close ties between many newspapers/periodicals and political parties
- Partisan newspapers have decreased in circulation, while there is a multiplication of specialized publications

The first newspaper was published in 1878, the year of Cyprus' transition from the Ottoman occupation to the British colonial administration. Since then, more than 400 newspapers and periodicals have been published mainly in Greek, but also in Turkish, Armenian and English, for [and by] the respective communities and minorities. Keeping in mind the political situation on the island, the development the Cypriot media has shown great progress, with all newspapers having switched to computerization and adopting up-to-date printing techniques. However, the small size of the population defines some of the barriers imposed on all the aspects of organizational structure and outcomes of the press.

According to the UNESCO Institute for Statistics of 2004, the newspaper circulation ratio was 124.7 per 1000 people. No readily available information is available at all times, since the amendment of the 1989 Press Law makes the accessibility to information on newspaper circulation non-obligatory by the distribution agencies. Partisan newspapers have decreased in circulation, while there is a multiplication of specialized publications. The market of weekly newspapers suffered a major blow in the 1980s when dailies decided to appear seven days a week, and the only afternoon daily ceased publication after about thirty years of wide circulation.

Most of the daily newspapers are linked to various political parties which both reflect private and/or pluralistic political opinions and at the same time limit in part expression of opinion. (There are actually no restrictions for political parties and organizations in relation to media ownership – political parties are considered as legal persons and follow relevant provisions in the existing legislation). There exists an impressive number of eight dailies (seven in Greek, one in English) available in the Republic of Cyprus: *Politis* (4.500

circulation in 2004) and *Phileleftheros* (25,000 copies daily, most widely read, considered not to be party affiliated), *Haravgi* (4,500 copies mouthpiece of the Communist Party AKEL) *Alithia* (5,000 copies), *Machi* (1,200 copies), and *Simerini* (6,500 copies, right-wing, linked to right-wing party DESY), *XPress Economiki* (financial newspaper) and *The Cyprus Mail* (in English, 3,600 circulation).

There are no media ownership restrictions in relation to the print media. *Simerini* newspaper is controlled by the DIAS Publishing House, the biggest media owner on the island, who also controls the very popular *Sigma TV* and *Radio Proto*, widely read magazines *Madame Figaro, To Periodiko, Time Out, Star, Exclusive* and *Harpers Bazaar*.

The largest in circulation newspaper, *Phileleftheros*, belongs to the same group which is the owner or is associated with the publishers of eleven special interests magazines. The group recently signed an agreement of cooperation with the Publishing Group Lambrakis in Greece.

In the Republic of Cyprus, there are 27 weekly newspapers and other periodicals which reflect the diversity and often the ownership of the media. Corporate and trade union publications are increasingly very popular. The most popular weekly is the *Cyprus Weekly*. There are also *Tharros, Antilogos,* the *Financial Mirror, Egatiki Foni* ['Worker's voice' in Greek, mouthpiece of SEK, the right-wing labour union The Cyprus Workers' Confederation] and *Ergatiko Vima* [Worker's Tribune' in Greek, mouthpiece of left labour union PEO- The Cyprus Labour Federation], *Demosios Ypallilos* (Civil Servant/ Fortnightly published by the Cyprus Civil Servants Association Nicosia (PASYDY), *Chrimatistiriaka Nea* (Stock Exchange News), *Athlitiko Vima* (Sports Tribune), *Trifylli* (twice a week, sports) and *Athlitiki tis Kyriakis* (Sunday Sports News).

The five registered weekly magazines include *Periodiko, Selides, TV Mania, Star* and *Super Kid*. There are further 47 registered periodicals/magazines published every two weeks, month or two months, which cover areas such as lifestyle, fashion, football, hunting, sport, health, design, political parties and more. There are further more 33 registered magazines and periodicals which are published every three months or occasionally and which cover areas such as architecture, hunting, hairdressing, cooking, nursing, culture, chess and more.

It is estimated that the overall advertising expenditure for 2004 was around 70 million euro of which the print media account for approximately 18 per cent.

In the Turkish-occupied area there is a choice over eight daily papers, representing one of the highest concentrations of newspaper titles per capita anywhere in the world. However, mainland Turkish papers sell best on the island. Conservative Turkish dailies *Sabah* and *Hurriyet* have a daily circulation of 13,000 between them, while sales of the most popular Turkish Cypriot paper, *Kibris*, never exceed 10,000 copies a day. There are further five weeklies and three periodicals. It is important to note here that the newspapers are sold to the army by default and, thus, any circulation statistics may be skewed.

The local daily newspapers, strongly linked to political parties, are *Afrika*, *Kibris*, *Gunes*, *Halkin Sesi*, *Kibrisli*, *Vatan*, *Volkan and Yeni Duzen* and the *Cyprus Today* in English. The weeklies are the *Cyprus Post* in English, *Yenicag*, *Ortam*, *Yeni Cag*, *Ekonomi* and *Cumbez* as well as *Baris Gasette* and *Gasette Spor*.

There are also a number of magazines such as the *Alem*, *Aktuel*, *The Cypriot Cicada*, *Kiprisli*, *Fotograf*, *Aksiyon*, *Barometre*, *Magazine Fiore*, *Yeni Akrep*, *New Scorpion* and *Beauty Forum*.

B. The Broadcast Media
Main features:

- Very high concentration of broadcast stations per capita
- TV channels linked to Greece and Turkey

The Cyprus Broadcasting Service was established in 1956 under British colonial rule, and later on the Cyprus Broadcasting Corporation [CyBC] was established with the country's 1960 independence. CyBC used to operate as a semi-governmental organization in conditions of monopoly until 1990, when private radio and television were introduced. Today, there are two state and six private Greek Cypriot channels with an island-wide coverage and two in the occupied north. Further, relays of Greek and Turkish stations are available across the island with a number of channels from Turkey, and one from Greece beams (ERT, the Greek public service broadcaster) directly to Cyprus while satellite television is becoming increasingly widespread.

The island-wide TV stations operating in Cyprus are the state-owned Cyprus Broadcasting Corporation CyBC and the private Mega TV, Antenna TV, Lumiere TV, Sigma TV, Alpha TV, Astra TV and CNCPlus. A second channel of CyBC was established in 1992 to face the competition from commercial TV stations. It is more entertainment oriented and broadcasts news bulletins in English and Turkish and a magazine in both Turkish and Greek. In 2004, it signed an agreement with channel Alpha in Greece. Euronews is broadcast in the early morning hours from CyBC2. LTV (Lumiere TV) is a pay-TV channel with coded signal and belongs to a company and concentrates on movies and sports.

The state channel has lost the lead in the numbers of viewers and listeners to private channels and all the private channels belong to multimedia conglomerates. Most specifically, Mega TV, Antenna TV and Alpha TV are closely affiliated to the channels with the same name in Greece who transmit their productions to the Cypriot branches respectively. Interestingly, though, local, Greek Cypriot sitcom productions are by far more popular than Greek productions.

The share of Sigma TV in 2004 in prime time was about 30 per cent, MEGA had 15.9 per cent (with the main news bulletin counting for 13.4 per cent – 25.6 per cent of the viewers or around 5–8.5 per cent population), Antenna TV had 20.3 per cent, CyBC1 12.5 per cent and CyBC2 6.9 per cent.

On the other hand, people in the Turkish Cypriot community receive and generally prefer to watch Turkish TV channels. The local Turkish-speaking TV channels are Bayrak (B.R.T.K.) [controlled by the authorities], Akdeniz TV, Kanal T, Kibris TV, Genc TV and Avrasya TV.

There are ten radio stations transmitting island-wide in Greek. These are Cyprus Broadcasting Corporation (CyBC): [four programmes], Radio Athina, Radio Proto, Logos [popular and owned by the Church of Cyprus] Radio Astra [owned by AKEL, the Communist Party] Radio Ant1 FM, Radio Super FM Radio Sfaira, Kanali Exi and Energy 107.6 FM. There are also about 40 local radio and TV stations.

The Turkish-speaking Bayrak transmits in three programmes, and there are also Akdeniz Fm, First Fm, Sim Fm, Kibris Fm, Radyo Vatan, Güneş Fm, Dance Fm, As Fm, Cool Fm, Uluslararasi Kibris Üniversitesi, Ydü Fm, Radyo Daü, Gaü Fm, Laü Fm, Kuzey Fm, Radyo T, Radyo Güven, Açik Radyo and Avrasya FM.

The advertising expenditure on broadcasting media in 2004 was around 24,250,000 Cyprus pounds for television and 3,100,000 CYP for radio.

There are three other types of television currently emerging in the Republic of Cyprus; namely, satellite television (Athina), cable and digital television (Cablenet). Athina Satellite offers free installation and a monthly payment, subject to a two-year contract. Cablenet has signed a deal with the Cyprus Electricity Board (EAC) and has a set installation price and a monthly fee. There is further a very recent deal of the Cyprus Telecommunications Authority (CyTA) with MiVision with a fixed installation price and, finally, Novacyprus, a satellite service with a deal with LTV/ALPHA.

C. The Internet Media
Main feature:

■ Sharp increase of Internet users and Internet hosts

Most of the important media outlets have their own websites as the Internet becomes ever more important in the media market. According to the CIA Factbook, in 2005 in the Republic of Cyprus there were 298,000 Internet users and 46,863 Internet hosts. By 2006, the Internet hosts went up to 67,589. Popular information and news websites include http://www.cyprus-news.com, http://kypros.org/, http://www.go2.com.cy, http://www.ikypros.com, www.typos.com.cy, http://grhomeboy.wordpress.com and The Cyprus International Press Service, http://www.cips.com.cy.

Popular Turkish Cypriot news sites include Kibris Portasi, http://www.kibrispostasi. com/, Yerel Information, http://www.yerel.info, Hamamboculeri http://www. hamamboculeri.org and Kuzey Kibris Haber, http://www.haber.net.kk.tc/.

The private telecom operators Primte Tel could potentially present a challenge to the state-owned CyTA (Cyprus Telecommunications Authority) in fixed telephony and ADSL-linked home entertainment. Triple Play combines a package of fixed telephony, fast and continuous access to the Internet and home entertainment services like TV, movies and video-on-demand through one single connection. It is expected to be launched soon and has already signed an agreement for the use of CyTA's access to local cable network. For the right to also use the Cyprus Electricity Authority's network, PrimeTel pays an annual rent of £300,000. It is 93 per cent owned by Teledev East, the Cypriot telecom multinational active in Russia, which so far has invested £10 million in the Cyprus project and plans to invest more in the future once fully operational. Its international calls are slated to be 30 per cent cheaper than CyTA's. The company faced delaying tactics from the state monopoly's reluctance to open its network and allow private operators to hire and place their equipment at the sub-loops. It has also faced other challenges from governmental and local authorities by not allowing it to lay its fibre-optic cables underground. CyTA currently controls 97 per cent of the fixed telephony market, 93 per cent of the mobile telephony, 94 per cent of the Internet market and 100 per cent control of the broadband service market.

D. News Agencies
Main features:

- The Cyprus News Agency (CNA) is an independent and autonomous corporation functioning within the framework of the Cyprus Press Law;
- High concentration of international news agencies who use Cyprus as a regional base for the Middle East.

The Cyprus News Agency (CNA) is an independent and autonomous corporation functioning within the framework of the Cyprus Press Law. The agency is governed by a seven-member Board composed mainly of journalists representing the Union of Journalists, the Publishers' Association, the Cyprus Broadcasting Corporation and the Press and Information Office. The law which established the agency expressly provides that CNA cannot promote the interests of any political party or economic group. In addition to the Greek language, CNA offers news in the Turkish language, which it distributes to Turkish Cypriot news media and political parties, as well as to the news media of Turkey. Further, CNA news in English is distributed to international news agencies.

The Associated Press (AP), Reuters, UPI, Agence France Press, TASS, XINHUA, ANSA, the Athens News Agency, EFE (Spanish News Agency), DPA (German Press Agency), Itar-Tass and RIA Novosti are other news agencies which use Cyprus as a regional base in the Middle East. The BBC, ABC and NBC also maintain news-gathering units and television crews in Cyprus. Since 1975 the island has grown into a major centre for the publication of numerous Arab and Russian magazines and newspapers.

The Turkish News Agency Cyprus (TAK) [since 1973], Akdeniz News Agency (ANA), Lefkosia News Agency (LNA), Uludag News Agency, Foto Arca News Agency and Famagusta News Agency operate in the Turkish-occupied area.

2. State Policies
Main features:

- The state policies ensure freedom of expression and freedom of the press in the Republic of Cyprus;
- There is a distinct lack of policies relating to the freedom of the Press in the occupied north;
- Formal ownership restrictions.

Article 19 of the Constitution of the Republic of Cyprus provides that every person has the right to freedom of speech and expression in any form, that this right includes freedom to hold opinions and receive and impart information and ideas without interference by any public authority and regardless of frontiers. It further states that seizure of newspapers or other printed matter is not allowed without the written permission of the Attorney-General of the Republic, which must be confirmed by the decision of a competent court within a period not exceeding seventy-two hours, failing which the seizure shall be lifted. It reiterates that nothing shall prevent the Republic from requiring the licensing of sound and vision broadcasting or cinema enterprises.

The 1989 Press Law aimed at setting guidelines and a professional code of ethics and at stimulating greater competition by allowing private radio stations. This law safeguards the freedom of the press, the unhindered circulation of newspapers, and free access to state sources of information. The law provides for freedom of speech and of the press, and the authorities generally respect these rights in practice; however, in some cases journalists have been obstructed in their reporting, fined, and threatened with more serious charges. The State Department's Report on Human Rights for 2006 indicates indeed that "Individuals can and do publicly criticize the authorities without reprisal. There were no reports of the authorities attempting to impede criticism"

The Cyprus Radio – Television Authority was established as an independent regulatory body under the Radio and Television Stations Law. It is a member of the European Platform of Regulatory Authorities (EPRA) and of the Mediterranean Network of Media Regulatory Authorities. The Authority is not concerned with the state–owned Cyprus Broadcasting Authority but rather with private radio and television stations broadcasting in Cyprus. It is composed of the Chairperson, Vice-Chairperson and five members, appointed by the Council of Ministers for a six-year term. The Authority is "responsible for appointing the Radio-Television Advisory Committee which is a consulting body and which reflects public opinion, the views of government services and various interested organisations and associations, and the positions of private radio and television broadcasters".

The responsibilities of the Authority include the issuing and renewing broadcasting licences for radio and television; monitoring media ownership; monitoring media content; safeguarding editorial independence; ensuring the equal treatment of political parties; monitoring international developments in the media; examining complaints about the content of radio and television programmes and commercials; examining breaches of the law and regulations and of the code of conduct and imposing sanctions; and issuing circulars and directives regarding observance of the code of journalistic conduct. The Authority also has the responsibility for the implementation of clauses of the European Convention on Transfrontier Television with regard to the content of the private broadcasters' programmes.

The law opposes concentration of ownership (although in practice this does not appear to be the case, as indicated in previous sections). Owners of regional and national television are allowed to hold only one licence and there are restrictions to cross-media ownership, as well as a 5 per cent limit for non-EU ownership.

The Union of Cyprus Journalists is pointing to the need for provisions to be incorporated in order to eliminate tendencies of monopolization in the media and to safeguard editorial independence and journalists' rights. The Union urges the state to give the print media (and predominantly the economically weak opinion newspapers) every possible support and assistance in order to ensure pluralism and freedom of the press, the right to information and freedom of expression as well as contribute to effectively deal with intense competition by the electronic media.

The law secures the protection of minors and of private life and human rights, respect for the personality, dignity and private lives of persons, and the right of individuals to reply or redress in the event that reports affecting them or their activities are inaccurate or misleading. It further incorporates the prevention of commercializing information and the regulation of advertising in accordance with rules adopted by the European Union and the Council of Europe. The contents of all broadcasted programs are subject to various rules aiming at securing the respect towards any person on the screen (or the voice of whom is broadcasted). The public may submit a complaint to the Cyprus Authority of Radio-television for unjust treatment by radio/TV stations in informative/recreational programmes; for the violation of their personal life by broadcasting information about them in such programmes; for the broadcasting of scenes of sex or violence which are in contrast to the relevant laws and regulations. The Cyprus Authority of Radio-television has the right to examine possible violations of laws and regulations by a station, even if no complaint has been filed.

All journalists have the right not to reveal their source of information and to refuse to give testimony without being liable to prosecution for doing so. The only exception is in instances where a journalist publishes information regarding a criminal offence. S/he may then be obliged by the Court examining the case or the coroner to reveal his source, provided that the Court or the coroner is satisfied that the information is clearly related to the criminal offence, that the information cannot be obtained otherwise and the reasons of superior and imperative public interest require that the information be revealed.

The public broadcasting service (Cyprus Broadcasting Corporation) is operating under a completely separate law and a separate board appointed by the Council of Ministers. There is no TV licence fee for viewers. Its income derives from advertising, subsidy by the state and duty paid by electricity consumers. The CyBC is currently facing serious financial problems due to fierce competition by private broadcasters. The Government and the Parliament are pressing for extensive cuts in the CyBC expenses and for reduction of its staff, thus promoting its co-existence rather than dominance over the private media sector.

No specific law in relation to the media can be found in the occupied north. Journalists can be arrested, put on trial and sentenced under chapter 154 of 7th paragraph of the so-called 'Criminal Code', concerning "Unjust actions", "The Courts" and "Military Adjudication" covering 84 items, all remnants of legislation from the British colonial times and still in use. Based on 'possibilities', these laws require no need to have a 'complete action' in order to be arrested, put on trial or imprisoned. A more recent legislation, from the 1980s, namely covering 'Military crimes and punishments' covers 'crimes' and 'punishments' within the military forces based in the northern part of Cyprus. Even though this law relates to the military, journalists are also put on trial under military courts.

3. Civil Society Organizations
Main features:

- Lack of readily available information on the limited number of media associations
- Increasingly formalized accountability systems although lacking in implementation

The Union of Cyprus Journalists in the Republic of Cyprus has around 400 members. It is a member of the International Federation of Journalists and the European Federation of Journalists. The Union is represented in the Radio-Television Advisory Committee and the Administrative Council of the Cyprus News Agency and in various cases it is invited to parliamentary committees to express its views when matters that concern the media are discussed.

There are also the Association of Newspapers and Periodicals Publishers and the Association of Owners of Private Electronic Media on which little public information is available. Together with the Union of Journalists, they bare the operational expenses and other relevant expenses of the Press Ethics Committee which is charged with monitoring and implementing the Journalists Code of Practice – available on the Press and Information Office website.

In the occupied north, the Union of Press Workers (Basin-Sen) is also a member of the International Federation of Journalists.

The accountability systems in Cyprus seem in principle to be in place. The establishment of an Ombudsman's Office since 1991 appears to have had a positive impact in accountability systems. Having said that, it could be asserted that to a large extent, the various committees set up in order to provide for better accountability standards are not publicly regarded as very active towards that effect and do not seem to be consistently implementing their own objectives and regulations.

The independent press council 'Cyprus Media Complaints Commission' (CMCC) was established in May 1997 by the Association of Newspapers and Periodicals Publishers, the owners of private Electronic Media and the Cyprus Union of Journalists, responsible for the self-regulation of the news written and electronic media. The Cyprus Broadcasting Corporation (it is a self-governing organization operating under public law) later acceded to the regulations governing the operation of the CMCC and the Code of Media Ethics.

The CMCC asserts itself to be "free from government interference or judicial supervision, ensuring that through self-regulation freedom of the press is maintained, standards of conduct are raised and the members of the public are given the opportunity to lodge their grievances against the media when they feel they have been offended." Its panel accepts complaints submitted within 30 days of the offending publication first appearing or becoming known to the offended party or even a third party. The right to examine publications on its own initiative also exists.

As mentioned above, the Union of Journalists together with Association of Newspapers and Periodicals Publishers and the Association of Owners of Private Electronic Media bare the operational expenses and other relevant expenses of the *Press Ethics Committee* which is charged with monitoring and implementing the Journalists Code of Practice. In the absence of a Press Council to deal with complaints or non-compliance with journalistic standards, journalists are expected to be self-regulating and to adhere to their own Code of Practice which applies to all media (print and electronic, semi-state or private) and all those working for them and defines the duties and rights of journalists and covers the following topics: accuracy, right of reply, private life, hospitals, mourning-grief, obtaining of information, copyright, bribery-receiving gifts, presumption of innocence, sexual crimes, children, discrimination, economic benefits, journalistic confidentiality and public interest. The agreement was effectively signed by all on 21 May 1997. Six months later, the public service broadcaster CyBC signed also the code and agreed to subject itself to the authority of the Commission. Following the adoption of the broadcasting law of 1998, the journalistic Code of conduct was incorporated as an appendix in the Regulations on radio and television stations, adopted in 2000.

The Press Ethics Committee consists of thirteen members who are "individuals of high moral standard and established high reputation" appointed by the Union of Journalists, the Association of Publishers and the Owners of Electronic Media. The Committee receives, deals with and decides upon complaints about alleged violations of this Code by a journalist and/or the media. It also issues, within the spirit of this Code guidance notes for interpretation purposes, but it is not entitled to impose any penalty or to adjudicate compensation or to deal with a complaint which is the subject matter of a procedure before a Court or other organ having jurisdiction under law.

4. Development Trends
Main features:

■ Evidence of increasing self-censorship (and censorship) in the Republic of Cyprus in the last three years, whereas that was not the case in the past
■ In the occupied north, evidence of violation of the freedom of the press exists
■ Cable Net and new broadcasting channels in the Republic of Cyprus

The Worldwide Press Freedom Index 2005 of the Reporters without Frontiers places Cyprus 25th in its record together with Namibia and Benin. In its 2006 Annual Report, the Reporters without Frontiers say that "Press freedom improved in 2005 but obstacles to the free flow of news between the northern and southern parts of the island still weigh heavily on journalists and their work". It further stated that "On the territory under control of the Government of Republic of Cyprus, there were only a few cases in 2005 where the rights of journalists were violated. In the northern part of Cyprus, freedom of the press and the right to free expression continue to be violated in 2005"

Recent examples of violation of the freedom of the press in the occupied north in 2006 include the decision of the Turkish government to sue the Turkish Cypriot journalist Serhat Incirli for criticizing Turkey, explaining that this was the first time Turkey tried to "sue a Turkish Cypriot journalist for insulting the Turkish nation". In June 2006 Turkish-Cypriot police arrested and detained for several hours three Greek Cypriot journalists of the public station CyBC while covering a non-political event that is a beach festival in Famagusta. In November 2006, the European Federation of Journalists condemned the arrest of two French TV journalists by Turkish Cypriot police, saying the arrests overshadowed plans by the Turkish Cypriot authorities to reform press freedom laws. The journalists were fined approximately 600 euro each (the Turkish Cypriot journalists' organization Basin-Sen paid the fine) and in December eight Turkish Cypriot journalists were arrested while filming a house fire next to the military zone on the Green line in Nicosia. The journalists were held for a few hours and subsequently released without charge.

There exists anecdotal and documented evidence of increasing censorship and self-censorship in the Republic of Cyprus in the last three years, whereas this did not appear to be the case in the past. In terms of censorship, one example was the refusal of the Republic of Cyprus to allow journalists working in the occupied north who wanted to cover a football match in the south. Further, in its January – June 2004 Report on "Europe and Central Asia – Summary of Amnesty International's Concerns in the Region", Amnesty International expressed concern that during April, following the president of the Republic's endorsement of a 'no' vote in the referenda to support the plan proposed on 31 March by the UN Secretary General for a comprehensive settlement to the Cyprus problem [see above in introduction the 'Annan Plan'], the government and state authorities had failed to act in a way that showed due diligence in carrying out its duty to respect, protect and defend the right to freedom of expression.

Further, as a reaction to what was perceived as direct media influence in relation to the result of the 'Annan Plan' referendum, a leading journalist produces a highly critical documentary titled "The Construction of Reality and the mass Media – The case of the "Ambient Atmosphere" [available to download at http://www.makarios.ws/cgibin/hweb?-A=980&-V=perireousa] which was not aired by any of the TV channels in Cyprus. An intense media campaign towards the 'yes' in the north and the 'no' in the south took place prior to the referenda – a campaign which has been highly criticized in various circles for its censorships and propaganda which was understood to be led by the governments of both sides.

References & Sources for Further Information

Detailed information on the owners and publishers of all media in Cyprus can be found on the website of the Press and Information Office of the Republic of Cyprus.

Further, information and links on all media-related firms can be found at the vertical portal Cyprus Media http://www.cyprusmedia.com/, which includes all major television and radio stations, newspapers and magazines, as well as companies that offer media-related services.

Journalists Code of Practice http://www.mmc2000.net/docs/leggi/CYPRUS.pdf.

Other online sources

http://ec.europa.eu/comm/competition/publications/studies/media/2005/cyprus.pdf
http://www.cyprus-mail.com/news/main.php?id=25250&cat_id=1
http://www.cyprus-mail.com/news/main.php?id=18668&cat_id=5

Finally, The Mediterranean Institute of Gender Studies based in Cyprus published in 2005 a manual for training journalists titled "The Gender and Media Handbook: Promoting Equality, Diversity & Empowerment" available online at http://www.medinstgenderstudies.org/Downloads/Handbook_final.pdf, where it provides a critical account of how the media portrays issues of gender and equality in both the Turkish Cypriot and Greek Cypriot communities.

THE FRENCH MEDIA LANDSCAPE

Bernard Lamizet & Jean-François Tétu

France has a population of 60 million. French colonial past is a major contributing factor in the presence of a multicultural population. Due to colonization, there is a large Muslim population and that explains the high audience ratings of Arab satellite channels. The country's area is 547,030 sq km with a density of 114 persons per sq km.

The number of elderly people is increasing, even though the birth rate (11.99 for 1,000 people) is one of the highest in Western Europe. In 2006, 25.1 per cent of the population was in the age group 0 to 20, and 20.7 per cent were over 60. Life expectancy is 75.2 years for men and 82.1 for women.

France has a high unemployment rate and a weak economic growth. The retirement age is one of the lowest in Europe (about 58), and the 35 weekly working hours give people plenty of leisure time. Ninety-six per cent of French households possess a television set. All these facts shape the configuration of the contemporary media system.

1. The Market

A. Print media
Main features:

- Circulation decline for paid newspapers
- Increase of titles and circulation of free newspapers
- Advertising revenues are increasing
- Unprecedented concentration and 'invasion' of foreign companies

■ One of the highest readerships of magazines in the world
■ Increase of titles, circulation and revenues of magazines
■ Increase of free arts and culture town newspapers

The national daily newspaper circulation is 1.18 million copies and the daily newspaper readership is 8.25 million, which means that there is a low number of buyers (140 per thousand). A regular decline of readership of daily national papers can be observed. The popular national press has been collapsing in the last 35 years. *France-Soir*, for instance, which used to sell over 1 million copies in 1961, is now running into severe financial problems (circulation was about 50,000 a day in 2005).

A regular decline of the number of daily regional newspapers can also be observed, although they are still in good health and their circulation is increasing. Magazine readership increased until 2002 (1,200 per thousand people) but has been decreasing since then. The circulation of professional and technical press though is still strong. As in other countries, the number of free sheets is strongly increasing in France too.

The number of papers have strongly increased [+ 217 new titles (+ 5 %) in 2004], but that has little impact upon general turnover. Since 1990 up to 2005, general circulation has been declining by 15 per cent, receipts by 14 per cent, and turnover by 30 per cent.

Roughly speaking, with some variation from one year to another, advertising revenues are increasing and sales are declining, but this increase is mostly for free sheets. For instance, in 2003 and 2004, the print media advertising revenues were 80 million euro for free sheets, 65 million for newspapers, and, in 2004 and 2005, the growth of advertisement income as a whole (60 million euros) was for free sheets. The sale of daily issues remains the most important of the written press circulation (46.7%), while subscription is the second one (29%), and it increased from 1990 until 2005.

Concentration of ownership is high, according to turnover data. The twenty first titles represent 27 per cent of the share of the newspaper market. The national press is far more concentrated (95.6 % of the turnover for the twenty first titles). The local press comes is less concentrated (69.6 % for the twenty first titles). Magazines (general or professional) are even less concentrated (31.1% and 29.1%).

The top ten daily newspapers according to World Association of Newspapers, [Word Press Trends 2005] are *Ouest France* 783,000; *Le Monde* 381,000; *L'Equipe* 369,000; *Le Parisien* 353,000; *Le Figaro* 346,000; *Sud Ouest* 326,000; *La Voix du Nord* 307,000; *Nice Matin* 258,000; *Le Dauphiné Libéré* 256,000; *Le Progrès* 249,000.

Among the national newspapers, *La Croix* speaks for the Catholic Church and *L'Humanité* for the French Communist Party. All other national dailies carry a political identity, such as the conservative-leaning *Le Figaro*, the leftist *Libération* and the center-left *Le Monde*.

Compared to its British counterparts, the French tabloid press – la presse indiscrète – is relatively mild. Weeklies such as *France Dimanche* (575.000), *Voici* (575.000), *Ici Paris* (442.000), *Gala* (304.000) and *Entrevue* (308.000) live their finest moments during the summer holidays.

The most significant change is the introduction of the free newspapers. There are, in France, three free sheets networks. The first one, *Métro*, belongs to the Swedish Metro press group and TF1, a French television company. The second one, *20 minutes*, is owned by the Norwegian press group Shibsted and by the French regional press group *Ouest France*. Third, there is a number of free sheets edited mostly in towns, which belong to a set of press groups: Socpresse (Hersant group), Hachette group and *Sud-Ouest* group.

Cultural information takes more and more place in regional and local mass media; there are, nowadays, many regional and local cultural papers, often free, and, last, since culture is very important in urban policies, cultural mass media are quite important in the information about towns.

In the twentieth century, they were roughly speaking of three kinds of print media owners: a) Regional publishing groups, often built by 'old' families, as Hutin (*Ouest –France*), the far most important one, Lignac (*L'Est Républicain*), Brémond-Lignel (*Le Progrès*, Lyon), Lemoine (*Sud-Ouest*, Bordeaux), Baylet (*La Dépêche du Midi*, Toulouse), Varenne (*La Montagne*, Clermont-Ferrand), etc.; b) national press, generally independent or owned by specialized publishing groups, such as the Hersant group; c) magazines, often owned by big companies (e.g. Lagardère, Prouvost or Béghin).

But, due to constant difficulties of French print media since 1945, the situation has changed over the last 30 years, and has led to an unprecedented concentration and to the 'invasion' of foreign companies in French mass media (e.g. Roussel from Belgium, Bertelsmann from Germany, EMAP from Great Britain, Mondadori from Italy, etc.). The most important of these groups is Lagardère, a weapons company, who owns Hachette publishing house, present in all kinds of mass media. Hachette's subsidiary company, *Hachette Filipacchi Médias*, is a leader magazine; another subsidiary, *Hachette Livre*, is the main publishing group in France, and the other subsidiary, *Lagardère active*, is in the dominant position in audio-visual and multimedia matters.

Dassault, who is also a high-tech weapons company, recently bought Socpresse company (who belonged to Hersant group), but sold, later on, a big part of Hersant group's titles, particularly those in the north of France (*La Voix du Nord* and *Nord Eclair*) to the Belgian company Roussel, the major title, *L'Express- l'Expansion*, and also *Lire, L'Entreprise, l'Etudiant, Point de vue* to Roularta, a Belgian company, who has become a major publishing group in France. Dassault has also sold a group of papers in the south-east of France (*Le Progrès* (Lyon), *Le Dauphiné Libéré* (Grenoble), *Le Bien Public* (Dijon), etc.) to the press group, *L'Est républicain*, who, nowadays, is a leader of all mass media in eastern France and in the major part of southern France.

If the French read relatively few daily newspapers, they are among the biggest readers of magazines and periodicals in the world. The French magazine sector (copies free of charge excluded) has a circulation of nearly 3 billion copies a year. Contrary to the daily newspaper market, the magazine market in France flourishes with 590 weeklies and biweeklies, 1,350 monthlies and bimonthlies and 1570 quarterlies.

Leading weekly magazines of general interest are *Paris Match* (707,000), situated on the centre-right, *Marianne* (118,000), with a slightly nationalistic bias that borrows from the right as from the left, and *Le Nouvel Observateur* (544,000), *L'Express* (554,000) and *Le Point* (358,000), all situated on the centre/centre-left of the political spectrum. All five carry the format of *Time* magazine and *Newsweek* and are, despite illustrious pasts, quite colourful and polished nowadays, both in their appearance as in their opinions. Steadily increasing its circulation is the *Courrier International* (180,000), which offers a weekly survey in French of the international press.

Worth mentioning is the existence of a range of periodicals dedicated to marginal political causes, reflecting France's erstwhile politicized and divided society, such as on the extreme right: *L'Action française* (30,000) and *Royaliste* (10,000) and on the extreme left: *La Nouvelle Vie Ouvrière* (120,000), *Lutte Ouvrière* (15,400) and *Informations Ouvrières* (20,000).

Periodicals concerning matters of religious interest are the Catholic *Pèlerin Magazine* (302,000), *La Vie* (176 000), *Témoignage chrétien* (20,000) and *France Catholique* (18,000), the Protestant *La Voix Protestante* (6,000) and the Jewish *L'Arche* (20,000) and *Actualité Juive* (17.500).

In accordance with the French intellectual tradition there exists a wide range of periodicals dedicated to the world of ideas and reflection. Addressing a general public are *Le Monde Diplomatique* (240,000), *Etudes* (140,000) and *Passages* (35,000). *Le Monde Diplomatique* is owned by the Monde group, but has an autonomous, radical-left editorial staff. French intellectuals flock together in such highbrow magazines as *Esprit* (10,000), *Commentaire* (5,500), *Les Temps Modernes* (5,000) and *Le Débat* (5,000).

The most notorious of all French periodicals, however, is the satirical and investigative weekly *Le Canard Enchaîné* (430,000). *Le Canard* is known for its independence; it does not publish any advertisements and its owners are not tied to any political or economic group. *Le Canard* is notable because of its focus on scandals in the governmental, juridical, administrative and business circles of France. Most major French newspapers are reluctant to challenge government corruption, or pursue embarrassing scandals, except *Le Canard Enchaîné*. Each Wednesday, its 70 well-paid editors (all male) deliver eight pages "insider knowledge" on politicians and "leaks" from administration officials, along with satirical cartoons and jokes. In general *Le Canard* is well informed on what goes on within the French political world, whereas its international coverage is spotty and relies mostly on the French government and the other media. *Le Canard* has a left-wing political bias, but is known for publishing incriminating stories and criticizing all political parties with no preference. It is also fairly anti-clerical.

Finally, although advertising investment in France is increasing (the whole market was 31.8 billion euro in 2005), the share of media advertising expenditure is decreasing (35.5%), while non-media advertising is increasing (64.5%). Advertising expenditures are distributed as follows: press is 41.8 per cent, TV 35 per cent, street posters 13.6 per cent, radio 8.5 per cent and, last, cinema (1.1%). There are huge disparities in this evolution: in 2005, for instance, the increase of the percentage share of the press in media advertising (+ 60 million euro) is only due to free sheets. National daily press is losing commercial advertisements and even classified advertisements (jobs, flats, etc.) have switched to Internet. Local advertisers are more increasing than national ones, particularly in 2005, and the same evolution is expected in 2006: + 1 per cent for national advertisers, and + 4 per cent for local ones.

B. *The Broadcast Media*
Main features:

- Dual system with strong financial support for public broadcasters
- Very low cable penetration
- Impressive number of new digital channels

The public service broadcaster, France Télévisions, operates the channels France 2 (20.5% audience share), France 3 (15.2%) and La Cinquième/France 5 (3%). France 5 shares the terrestrial frequency with the Franco-German cultural channel Arte (2%). The main commercial broadcasters are TF 1 S.A., operating channel TF1 (31.8%); Métropole Télévision operating channel M6 (12.5%); while The Group Canal+ has a total of about 8.4 million subscribers (3.8%).

The number of the French TV channels has considerably increased over the last decades, particularly due to the end of state monopoly and to the multiplication of thematic or local channels in cable or satellite networks. So, beside the seven terrestrial channels, there are, today, more than 200 thematic channels (while there were only three TV channels in 1980).

The state policy is to provide public channels in order to offer a large choice of programmes and services for the largest audience possible, and to be regarded as a reference point in information, audio-visual creation and cultural diversity. The public sector TV group France Télévisions was set up by a law of 1st August 2000. This holding company, which includes the three national public TV programme companies (France 2, France 3, La Cinquième), defines these channels' strategy, coordinates their program policies and leads their development strategies. The law also defines the public missions of public channels. France Télévisions must sign a contract (aims and means) every three or five years.

Public TV is mainly financed by audio-visual licence fee, paid by the consumers. More than 76 per cent of public audio-visual sector is financed by the state including the licence fee. It is also financed by advertisement. In order for France 2 and France 3 programmes to be more independent, the law reduced advertisement time and the income decline has been entirely compensated by the state budget.

Because of the new distribution systems (satellite, cable, the Internet, digital TV service); new programmes have appeared, particularly in local television and new services, particularly interactive ones. But nearly 25 years after the great Cable Plan was inaugurated in 1982, there are only 3 million cable subscribers, although the amount of investment has been 30 billion euro. The major cable operators, such as Caisse des Dépôts et Consignations, have not been able to offer attractive programmes, when private channels such as Canal Plus, which needs a decoder, have won great market shares in sport and cinema. Therefore, cable TV looks like a failure, in France, although one may receive more than 100 channels. Altogether, cable TV seems now to be more used for high output Internet.

Digital terrestrial television, called T.N.T., in French, "Télévision numérique terrestre", was launched in 2005. Its major aim is to offer TV programmes to two-thirds of French people who depend on analogic means to get TV. With analogic means they can only receive six national channels. For the first time since 1986, because of T.N.T., there are new free TV programmes: fourteen free-to-air channels can be received since March 2005, and an additional eighteen new ones since November 2005. TNT offers also eleven pay-TV channels. It will also, later on, potentially allow for high-definition subscription services.

In the radio sector, the end of the state monopoly in 1982 brought a big increase in the number of radio stations, resulting in a more pluralistic and decentralized broadcasting system. Besides public radio stations (Radio France and the France Bleu network of local stations), there are great generalist national private stations and a number of thematic stations, mostly musical.

There are today about 1200 radio stations in France, including more than 600 associative radio stations. Eighty-one per cent of French people aged more than 15 listen to the radio, for about three hours a day (60% at home, 20% in car and 18% at work). The audience shares are split between general interest ones: 39 per cent, including 15.5 per cent for public stations (France Inter, France Bleu), and 22.7 per cent for private stations, including RTL (11.5 %) and Europe 1 (8%), and specialized channels: 61 per cent including musical channels: 39 per cent (NRJ, Nostalgie, Europe 2, Fun radio, Sky rock, etc.); thematic channels: 7.6 per cent (including Radio France network: France Cultures, France Musiques, France Info and private channels, as Radio Classique); local channels: 11.3 per cent (public stations as Le Mouv', or private sector of associative radios); other channels: 3.1 per cent.

C. *The Internet Media*
Main features:

■ User variation based on socio–economic status
■ Traditional off-line media dominate the online world

Internet penetration is very variable according to social classes: so, in 2004, 58.2 per cent of managers use the Internet, instead of 86.3 per cent among high executive and people with high levels of education. Eighty-five per cent of home Internet users have broadband (usually ADSL).

Almost all French newspapers have online editions, which can be found today on the Internet, but they have a long experience of online, because of the Minitel. Radios and TV channels are in the same situation, and offer the same services and programmes: daily news (usually free), thematic files and records, chats and blogs and various services depending on the papers.

All institutions, public services, research institutes, etc. and all the companies which delivered off-line information (on paper or CD-ROM) are nowadays online. There are only few start-ups in this field, except in the information technology field (*01net.com*). On top of the ratings list is the Skyrock group, which is well known for its free blogs. As, for the press, *Le Monde* is the first one (there are five times more users than for *Le Nouvel Observateur* or *Libération*).

D. *News Agencies*
Main features:

■ Home of one of the three biggest news agencies in the world
■ A number of specialized agencies exists
■ Home of some of the best photo agencies in the world

The Agence France Presse (AFP), a national press agency, is one of the greatest news agencies in the world (with Associated Press and Reuters). It was founded in 1944, but its contemporary status has been fixed by a law of 10 January 1957, which defines it as an independent worldwide news agency. Nowadays, the AFP faces increasing needs of modernization and strategy renewal. The AFP is ruled by civil law, but is not a private company. Although it does not have any shareholders, nor capital, it depends only on its business resources.

AFP's turnover (250 million euro in 2003) is as follows: state (40%), press and foreign sales (about 35%), photo sales (10%). There are 2,200 full-time employees who work in 165 countries, in 6 languages. About 2,000 mass media are AFP's customers. It is now trying to develop video activities.

There also are many highly specialized news agencies (health, city planning, etc.), which deliver news to regular subscribers.

France was the world leader of photo agencies in the 1960s and 70s. The digital photography has led to the end of that supremacy, since digitization required very high investments. The other world agencies, such as Reuters or the Associated Press, since their job was quicker, have dominated the news photographic market. None of the four great world agencies is independent any longer: SYGMA has been bought by Corbis (Bill Gates), RAPHO and GAMMA have been bought by Hachette and the last one, SIPA, has been bought by Sud Communication (held by a pharmaceutical group). Some quite small agencies are still operating, but they mostly work with independent photo reporters (e.g. Editing).

2. State Policies
Main features:

- Freedom of expression is protected since 1881
- Home of Reporters Without Boarders
- High volume of subsidies
- Many regulations regarding ownership

Freedom of expression is, in France, protected for every kind of press by law of 1881, in the audio-visual field by a law of 1982, and by a great number of other rules. A great association, "Reporters sans frontières", informs about all the breaches of freedom of expression in France and all over the world.

State subsidies are quite high for all types of media. For print media in 2005 there was a total amount of direct subsidies of 249.2 million euros, including financial help to modernization (38 million) and state subscriptions to A.F.P. (French national press agency) (105.7 million). But the non-direct subsidies were far higher with postal aid reaching 743 million euros.

The state helps particularly associative radios, for installation, equipment and running costs through the "Fonds de soutien à l'expression radiophonique" (FSER), which is a public fund for "radio" expression. Since 1984, when this fund was created, nearly 600 associative radios whose trade benefits were less than 20 cent of their total turnover have been able to benefit from such help. The Foreign Office also helps Radio France Internationale (international public radio channel), owing to abroad audio-visual action. The state gives public TV channels a compensation for their low advertisement time, in order to assure their programmes to be independent. The government's part of public TV budget was, in 2005, 2.66 billion euros.

The most important piece for legislation for the 'must carry' obligations of broadcasters is the EU Television without Frontiers Directive. The provisions of the directive allowed France to establish stricter rules about the way French and European cultural programmes should be transmitted, and these rules were extended to radio in 1994, which was not provided for in the 1997 directive. As for advertising, in France, private channels are limited to twelve minutes per hour (i.e. 20 %) of advertisement, but there are stricter rules for public channels. Since a law of 1 August 2000, this loss of revenue has been compensated by some aid from the State.

The Conseil Supérieur de l'Audiovisuel (C.S.A.), i.e. the Higher Audiovisual Council, an independent administrative authority, was established in 1989, and controls audio-visual activities. This authority, in particular, appoints the directors of public TV and radio channels, allocates frequencies, TV and radio franchises. But also negotiates contracts with private sector channels and makes sure the rules of the broadcasting field are observed, especially the respect of programmes obligations, pluralism of opinions, protection of authors' rights and deontological matters. C.S.A. also makes industrial and political concentration to be limited and looks after freedom in audio-visual matters.

Television ownership is subject to three limits based on: Capital share, number of licence (together with audience share), participation in more companies in the same sector. No physical or legal person can own more than 49 per cent (national TV) and 33 per cent (local TV) of the capital or voting rights in a station whose average annual audience exceeds 2.5 per cent of the total audience. If a person holds two stations s/he cannot hold more than 15 per cent in the second, while if a person owns three stations he cannot hold more than 5 per cent in the third. For terrestrial TV, s/he can not own more than one (analogue) or seven (digital) stations, while for satellite TV one cannot have more than two licences.

At the same time, companies are not allowed to acquire a new newspaper if the acquisition boosts their total daily circulation to over 30 per cent nationally. And for cross-media ownership, an operator may not be involved in more than two of the following situations: TV audience of 4 million; radio audience of 30 million; cable audience of 6 million; 20 per cent share of national daily newspaper.

Finally, non–EU investment is limited to a share of 20 per cent of a capital of a daily newspaper or of a terrestrial broadcasting in French language and there are no restrictions for political parties and organizations to own media.

Furthermore, a law of 1935 protects the independence of journalists (particularly the so-called "clause de conscience" ("individual conscience clause")), which enables a journalist to leave a newspaper whose owner has changed.

Advertisers are ruled by Bureau de Vérification de la Publicité (B.V.P.), i.e. Avertisement Control Board, and all TV advertisements are controlled by the Higher Audiovisual Council.

3. Civil Society Organizations
Main features:

- Large number of associations with large membership
- Active participation of citizens groups
- Widespread use of the ombudsman institution
- Recent revisions of codes of ethics

In press matters, professional syndicates look after regulations. Those are the Syndicat National de la Presse Quotidienne Régionale, the Union Syndicale de la Presse Régionale (for regional daily papers) and Syndicat National de la Presse Nationale (for national daily papers).

The most important journalists' trade unions publish their own paper. SNJ (Syndicat National des Journalistes, independent) publishes *Le journaliste*, the Union Syndicale des Journalistes (CFDT) publishes *Journalistes CFDT*, the Syndicat Général des Journalistes (independent) publishes *La Morasse*, and the Syndicat National des Journalistes (which belongs to CGT, the other important trade union federation) publishes *Témoins*.

The most important employers associations are Fédération Nationale de la Presse Française (FNPF), the association of audio-visual public sector employers and the national union of press agencies.

The main advertising associations are Information, Presse et Communication, which is an association of people who work in communication and public relations services, the national trade union of press attachés and the national union of companies papers and journalists. There are national and regional associations for every communication job.

Apart from consumers' associations, which are very active in some areas related to media, there are some very active associations against advertising (*Casseurs de pub*, i.e. advert rioters) or against the low quality of TV programmes (*Les pieds dans le paf*) and of mass media news (*Acrimed*).

For the last twenty years, the Médiateur de la République (Republic's Ombudsman), who is an independent administrative authority, deals with conflicts between people and administrations about communication and there are such médiateurs (Ombudsmen) in all the big mass media.

Journalists have had to abide by a code of conduct for quite a long time (S.N.J. adopted one in 1918). Since 1990, the directors of newspapers and audio-visual companies have prepared and imposed new codes to their journalists, mostly to avoid legal proceedings, and sometimes for ethical considerations. The most remarkable of these has been enacted by the regional western paper, *Ouest-France*, which has inspired many other codes of this kind.

4. Development Trends

Main features:

- The end of financially independent newspapers
- Free newspapers changed the print media landscape of the country
- Digital television is changing dramatically the TV landscape of the country
- The youth is turning to Internet media and away from print
- Widespread surge of broadband use

In the print media, with *Libération* accepting the offer of Baron Edouard de Rothschild to come to her rescue and selling him 37 per cent of her shares in January 2005, the era of financially independent newspapers in France came virtually to an end.

In the past five years according to the AFP, "*Metro, 20 Minutes*, and the other free papers that followed have transformed French media and their audience". This is a recap on free sheets' path and how paid-for papers are still seeking countermeasures. *20 Minutes* is the third most read national daily, trailing behind *L'Equipe* and *Aujourd'hui en France*, while *Metro* is fifth, just behind *Le Monde*. Renowned political figures regularly give interviews to *Metro* and *20 Minutes*, showing how credible these have become.

In response to this competition and success of the free papers, five regional papers have launched their own free daily, all associated under the group Ville Plus. Le Monde and the Bolloré group just launched their own, *Matin Plus*. *Le Monde, Le Figaro, L'Humanité, La Croix* and *La Tribune* all launched new formulas, either by launching their own free paper, or emphasizing online services or diversifying their activities.

Still, despite national paid-for newspapers' new ventures, these lost 1.1 per cent of their readers in 2005 and 2006, while free sheets gained 9.8 per cent. Still, free papers' business model isn't perfected. Only *Metro* is profitable so far.

Digital television technology will revolutionize television in France, since, in most cases, a single digital receiver is enough to allow access to a big variety of free channels. In 2006 the equipment penetration rate was already 14 per cent in the areas covered, with more than 1.7 million TNT reception terminals.

In 1999, 13 per cent of the French population older that 11 years had access to the World Wide Web. Since then, this percentage has augmented to 51 per cent (November 2004). And 50 per cent of this group lives in cities with over 100.000 inhabitants. Especially among the younger generation, the Internet is rapidly replacing traditional media. To the question – posed in January 2005 to 302 average Internet users at the age of 15 to 25, which medium they would choose when then could only name two – 61 per cent answered the Internet, 49 per cent television, 35 per cent the cinema, 29 per cent the radio, 17 per cent a daily newspaper and 9 per cent a magazine.

France recorded one of the strongest broadband markets in Europe in 2005, largely on the back of surging demand and pro-competitive action from the regulator. The country had the highest number of broadband subscribers in the EU by mid-year, dominated by DSL lines but with a growing cable footprint.

The chapter has been translated by Claude Arnaud, also professor at the Institut d'Etudes Politiques, Lyon.

Also, the chapter makes extensive use of extracts of the previous EJC media landscape version written by Pieter van den Blink, Paris-based correspondent for *Trouw* and Radio 1, Netherlands.

References & Sources for Further Information
Direction of Mass Media Development (Prime Minister's Office).

O.J.D. (Office de Justification de la Diffusion) is a mass media independent association, whose job is to measure mass media audience.

INA (Institut National de l'Audiovisuel) is a public institute for recording audio-visual activities and for new uses of audio-visual media.

Commission Nationale de l'Informatique et des Libertés.

Circulation Justification Office.

Superior Press Distributing Board.

http://www.editorsweblog.org/print_newspapers/2007/02/france_how_free_press_transformed_the_me.php.

http://www.huenga.com/european_media/france/index.htm.

THE GREEK MEDIA LANDSCAPE

Maria Kontochristou & Georgios Terzis

Greece, officially called Hellenic Republic, is a country situated in southern Europe, on the Mediterranean, in the southern part of Balkans. Greece's official language is Greek (99%), though a considerable percentage of the Greek population is fluent in English, German and French. Its religion is Christian Orthodox (98% of population). Its population is estimated 10,688,058 people.

The literacy level is considerably high considering that 98.6 per cent of the population can read and write. In 1981 Greece joined the EC and it became the twelfth member of the Eurozone in 2001. Greece has a capitalist economy with the public sector accounting for about 40 per cent of GDP and with per capita at least 75 per cent of the leading Eurozone economies.

1. The Market

A. The Print Media
Main features:

- During the last years there is an increase in sales of newspapers;
- Sunday newspapers take the lead in circulation;
- The press is highly concentrated in the hands of a few publishers;
- The magazine market is in good shape and segmented;
- Specialized magazines (e.g. astrology, cooking, etc.) take the lead in sales.

In Greece today there are a total of 87 newspapers which are national in circulation. Of these 14 are morning, 14 evening, 24 Sunday and 19 weekly newspapers. In the category of specialized newspapers there are 6 financial papers and 10 sport newspapers. Moreover, in Greece they circulate around 1.450 newspapers, which are local/regional. In particular, the regional press (all prefectures included apart from Attica) counts for the 51.9 per cent of the national press.

In terms of circulation, Sunday newspapers seem to take the lead with 51.1 per cent of the sales for 2005, followed by evening newspapers (14.1%), sports (15.4 %), weekly (16.5%), morning (2.7%) and financial (0.1%) newspapers. Among the morning daily newspapers, the market leaders are *Kathimerini* and *To Vima*. There is a wide range of evening daily newspapers. The most important of them are *Ta Nea*, *Eleftherotypia* and *Ethnos*. The same newspapers mentioned above also dominate the Sunday market (*To Vima tis Kyriakis*, *Kyriakatiki Eleftherotypia*, *Proto Thema*).

Total newspaper sale figures show a continued decline from the late 1980s to the beginning of the 1990s. The advent of private television in 1989 has generated a decline in circulation. In particular, from 1989 to 1992 as print and electronic media competition peaked, national newspapers lost approximately 28 per cent of their circulation and fell from a daily average of 2.597.056 copies in 1989 to 1.867.001 in 1992. Over the same period, due to severe competition, many newspapers were forced to close down. The mid-1990s found the majority of the Greek print media in a difficult financial situation.

By the end of the 1990s, the press was on a sounder financial basis, with some increases in circulation, albeit tied to partisan tradition and aligned towards political parties, but also more pluralistic and critical. In particular, Sunday newspapers produced "quality" editions, which provided the public with in–depth analysis of events, as well as entertainment and education. These papers also introduced special sections on the arts, science, etc., a trend that continues today. The years that followed found the press in a good situation in terms of readership and in particular circulation since, from 2000 to 2005, there was an increase in sales of approximately 26 per cent.

Today, the press is the second most important source of information for Greeks (after television), and it is highly concentrated in the hands of few publishers (e.g. *Lambrakis Publishing Group*, *Bobolas Publishing Group*, *Tegopoulos Publishing Group*, *Alafouzos Publishing Group*, *Press Institution Apogevmatini Publishing Group*).

There is a trend towards intense segmentation in the magazine sector. There are titles in print for every conceivable need and interest, while competition between the different types of magazines is strong. Glossy publications now have to compete with free supplements provided in newspapers, which have proved very popular. In January 2006, magazines accounted for 42 per cent of total advertising expenditure, up by 2 per cent from 40 per cent in 2003. In particular, specialized magazines (e.g. astrology, cooking, etc.) took the lead in sales (25.0%), followed by TV magazines (22.9%), women's magazines (14.6%), various content magazines (8.4%), children's magazines (8.1%), recreation & leisure magazines (6.5%), car magazines (6.1%), new technology magazines (3.9%), men's magazines (3.1%) and sports & fitness magazines (1.4%).

B. The Broadcast media
Main features:

- Private television assumes a dominant position, in terms of advertising revenues and size of audiences, in comparison with the public one;
- Both the public and the private operators maintain satellite channels targeting at the Greeks abroad;
- Pay-TV has been expanded in Greece in contrast with the cable television that has not been developed as an important distribution system due to poor infrastructure and high cost;
- Radio is an important source of information and entertainment in Greece;
- The digital television in Greece is regulated by the Law 2644/1998;
- There are two digital television providers: one private, NOVA, and one public, ERT.

Today, television is a well-established feature of contemporary Greek society, having assumed a dominant role in people's lives. It has become the major source of information, entertainment and culture for the mass public. Nowadays, there are four public channels and nearly 150–160 private channels (most of these are regional/local).

The public operators in Greece are ERT (Hellenic Radio and Television S.A.) and the newly established Vouli TV (national network with programming produced by the Hellenic Parliament). ERT is composed of three terrestrial channels (ET-1, NET, ET-3) that have national coverage, one satellite channel, ERT-World (worldwide satellite service, broadcasting free-to-air in Europe, Asia, Africa, Australia and via subscription in North America), ERT Digital, six national radio stations, two world service radio stations, and nineteen regional radio stations. Moreover, ERT's terrestrial frequencies also rebroadcast satellite channels, for free, such as CNN International, Euronews, Eurosport, TV5 Monde, Cyprus Sat/RIK 1, RAIUNO, and SAT.1. ERT's income comes from licence fees, which are imposed as a surcharge on all consumer electricity bills, regardless of whether they own a television set. Furthermore, the state subsidizes part of the expenses of ERT.

The vast majority of private channels operate with no broadcasting licence. Of these, only eleven private channels have permission to broadcast at a national level (902 Aristera sta FM, Alpha, Alter, Ant1, Mega, T/S SKAI, Star, Macedonia TV) or local/regional level (TELE ASTY, TV Cosmopolis, Municipal Television Salonica TV).

Private television assumes a dominant position, in terms of advertising revenues, size of audiences and prestige. The dominant players in the media landscape are the two private channels, Ant1 and Mega, which monopolized audience shares and advertisement revenues. They are followed by Alpha, Star Channel and Alter, ERT, (share ET-1 4.2%, share NET 9.1%, share ET-3 2.1% and NET+ET-1 3.6% advertising expenditure). As it is indicated above the public channels enjoy little mass appeal in comparison with the private ones. Mega, Ant1, Alpha, Star and Alter like ERT, have their own satellite programmes (Mega Cosmos, Antenna Satellite, Pacific and Music, Alpha International and Star International, Alter Globe respectively), which broadcast abroad and aim at the Greek Diaspora.

On average, daily TV viewing is on the increase. In 2003 average daily viewing time was 233 minutes and in 2004 was 244 minutes a figure that was increased to 245 minutes in 2005.

Concerning Pay-TV, since 1994, Multichoice Hellas has been providing three satellite TV services to Greek viewers, namely: Filmnet (films), Supersport (sports) and Fox Kids/K-TV (now named Jetix), (for children). In 2006, ERT launched ERT Digital, which is a pay-TV channel (for details on both providers and their services, see below: Digital Television).

Cable television has not developed as an important distribution system due to poor infrastructure. Until recently in Greece, it was forbidden by law for private operators to lay and operate cable infrastructure for telecommunications and/or broadcasting purposes. Only the public broadcaster ERT and national telecom operator OTE could develop cable TV networks, set up subsidiary companies and undertake contracts with private and local government organizations for providing cable TV services. Law 2644/1998, "on the provision of subscription radio and television services and related regulations", rescinded this restriction. However, this provision has not encouraged the development of cable television since it is considered to be very costly. Cable TV network household penetration is below 1 per cent. In general, Greece has the lowest development not only of cable, but also of satellite television in the EU. Their combined penetration is merely 8.9 per cent.

Finally, it is worth noticing the existence of the Hellas Sat. Hellas Sat is the owner and a wholesaler of capacity and services of the Greek "Hellas-Sat 2" satellite, an Astrium Eurostar E2000+. Hellas Sat has developed a network of strategically located teleport partners with DVB platforms, carrying over 100 television channels, and IP-based services through its two fixed beams over Europe and two steerable beams over the Middle East and South Africa. It offers high-power, direct-to-home transmissions as well as occasional video feeds and Internet access services.

Radio is another important source of information and entertainment in Greece. Currently, around 1,156 radio stations broadcast regularly in Greece. The vast majority of radio stations are private (24 are public), and transmit locally or regionally. Most private stations operate without a licence; only 35 of them have permission to operate while 138 have been considered as eligible to be awarded a licence.

In terms of programme content, most radio stations broadcast news and music programmes. Radio's advertising revenue counts for the 3.6 per cent of the overall news media advertising share. According to the results presented by the IOM, in 2004 the 91.6 per cent of the commercials was aired by the private radio stations, followed by the public (5.10%) and local ones (3.3%). Finally, the number of people who listen to the radio has increased during the last year, reaching in Athens 56 per cent and in Thessaloniki 53.8 per cent of the average daily listening.

Today there are two operators providing digital services, ERT and NOVA. NOVA was the first digital platform in Greece and started providing officially digital satellite services in 1999. Nova platform's offering includes: domestic football and basketball (particular games in exclusivity) and a pay-per-view service called Nova Cinema. Basic channels include international services like Discovery Channel, Eurosport, Animal Planet, National Geographic, the History channels, Jetix, cartoon network, etc. Its rival Alpha Digital Synthesis platform, which was established in 2001, went bankrupt and closed in September 2002.

The public operator ERT started recently providing digital services through ERT Digital. ERT Digital is a new terrestrial digital television service, formed by three state-owned national digital television networks, i.e. cine plus (broadcasting an entertainment programme, with films, documentaries and selected shows from ERT's substantial archive), sport plus (focuses mainly on sports) and prisma plus (includes entertainment and informative programmes, specially designed also for handicapped and those with special needs).

C. The Internet Media

Main features:

- The majority of the mainstream newspapers, magazines and TV channels have online publications, quite well developed, which are free of charge for their readers;
- Greece during the last few years has shown progress towards developing online services and promoting the information society;
- Despite the progress made in promoting the information society the rate of Internet use is comparatively low to the EU average.

Another important trend is the investment in new technologies, in particular the Internet. Almost all mainstream newspapers have an online version free of charge for their readers, and there are many electronic magazines and TV websites, while many radio stations provide for online access (345 radio stations have their own website and 112 of them broadcast live).

In general, Greece proceeded with considerable regulatory reforms concerning online services and has launched itself on the road to market liberalization. The Ministry of Development, in line with its target to create an information society in Greece and under the auspices of the operational programme *Information Society and Competitiveness*, funded by the 3rd community support framework in the EU, has adopted a number of initiatives that aim at: promoting competitiveness, improving business support networks for companies, providing for the delivery of government services online, installing computers linked to the Internet in schools, universities and equipping students with basic skill in computers, increasing Internet penetration, encouraging start-ups, enhancing e-commerce, providing access to finance.

It is quite early to say whether or not the aforementioned goals have been realized and to what extent. However, looking at the figures it can be argued that online services have gradually assumed a significant role in people's lives and in everyday communication. In particular, user growth of the Internet has estimated about 280.0 per cent over the period that spans from 2000 to 2006. Today the Internet adaptation is 3.8 million, representing a penetration of 33.7 per cent, while the EU average is 51.9 per cent.

D. News Agencies
Main features:

- The leading national news agency is the Athens News Agency (ANA);
- There are many smaller and specialized news agency, most of them regional.

The Athens News Agency (ANA) which was founded in 1895 and the Macedonian News Agency (MPA) which was founded in 1991 in Thessaloniki by the state were merged in 2006. The aim behind this union was the creation of a powerful national news agency. The agency has approximately 250 employees of whom 180 are journalists. It has offices in Brussels, Istanbul, Nicosia and Berlin and correspondents all around the world (Washington, New York, Montreal, Melbourne, London, Paris, Vienna, Rome, Belgrade, Skopje, etc.). In addition, collaborates with a number of leading international news agencies (e.g. Reuters, AFP, DPA, ITAR-TASS), other national news agencies (e.g. Cretan News Agency) as well as the EPA photograph agency. All the agency's services are online in Greek, English and French.

Moreover, there are many other news agencies which are regionally situated (e.g. Cretan News Agency, Aegean News) or cover a specific thematic area and interest: sports (e.g. Sport idea, Action image), religion (e.g. The Religious News Network), agriculture (Agrnonews Agency), Greek Diaspora (Hellenic World, Greek American news agency, Diaspora news agency, etc.) and photography (Inke photography agency).

2. State Policies
Main features:

- The Greek Constitution guarantees freedom of expression and declares the independence of the press from the State. However, the Constitution does not mention the independence of the broadcast media from the State;

- The public and private broadcast media are regulated by a number of provisions covering various aspects, set in specific laws;
- The Greek broadcast media are supervised by an independent authority, the National Council for Radio and Television (NCRTV);
- There are several provisions in audio–visual and consumer law, as well as the general criminal law, which regulate the online services in Greece and comply with the EU regulations.

Freedom of expression is guaranteed by the Greek Constitution. Article 14 states that every person may express and propagate his thoughts orally, in writing and through the press in compliance with the laws of the State. Furthermore, the article states that the press is free, and censorship, as well as all other preventive measures, including the seizure of newspapers and other publications before or after circulation, is prohibited.

The right to reply to inaccuracies published or broadcast by the media is also guaranteed by Article 14 of the Constitution.

The constitutional basis of media ownership derives from paragraph 9 of the same Article. This paragraph outlines the obligation for media outlets to register ownership status and information regarding the financing of the outlet. The paragraph also directly prohibits the concentration of ownership.

Finally, Article 15 of the Greek Constitution states that the

protective provisions for the press are not applicable to films, sound recordings, radio, television or any other similar medium for the transmission of speech or images. Radio and television shall be under the direct control of the State. The control and imposition of administrative sanctions are under the exclusive competence of the NCRTV, which is an independent authority, as specified by law

The law [1092/1938] proceeds to provide for a number of privileges for the press such as discount on telephone and postal tariffs, as well as for a number of obligations for the press, such as the respect of the personality and privacy of an individual, the respect for the truth and against forging or concealing the content of the publication to ensure that information and news can be easily distinguished from comment. In cases where there has been a publication of untrue or wrong facts, there is an obligation to publish a correction.

According to the same law, the press has to respect different opinions and it has obligations concerning the forming of public opinion and the publication of information in such a manner that no unnecessary panic is caused to the public. In cases of violations, the accountability is due to a third party (if involved), but is the responsibility of the author, editor, manager and the owner of the newspaper.

The mission of ERT S.A., as stated in the law [1730/1987], is the organization, the exploitation and the development of state radio and TV, the contribution of those means for public education and entertainment, as well the presentation of the activities of the Greek Parliament. The Law further provides that state TV and radio should reach as many social groups as possible and cover a wide range of fields, since its purpose is not the increase of profit, but the satisfaction of public interest.

In 1989, Law 1866 gave birth to the commercial radio and TV sectors and was the first step to the abolition of the state monopoly, which was completed later with Law 2328/1995. According to this law, the National Council for Radio and Television [NCRTV] grants licences for commercial TV and radio stations for Radio and Television, only when it would serve public interest. The commercial stations are obliged to provide high-quality programmes, objective information and news reports and promote cultural development. The Law gives the power to the NCRTV to request information from the radio and television stations regarding their organization and financing.

The same law also defines limits for the concentration of media ownership. In printed media, the law provides that a physical or legal person and his/her relatives up to the fourth degree may be holders of or participate in only:

■ Maximum of two daily political newspapers (a morning and an afternoon one) issued in Athens, Piraeus or Thessaloniki
■ One daily financial paper and one daily sports paper issued in Athens, Piraeus or Thessaloniki
■ Two non-daily provincial newspapers issued in different regions
■ And one Sunday publication

Concentration is also restricted in the broadcast industry. According to this law a joint stock company can have only one licence for a television station and/or one licence for a radio station. More specifically, ownership of more than one electronic information medium of the same type is prohibited, and every physical or legal person can participate in only one company and with only up to 25 per cent of its capital and up to 40 per cent for the pay-per-view broadcasting media. The same rules apply to relatives of physical persons of up to the fourth degree.

Regarding cross-media ownership, a 'two out of three' rule exists. A single company or individual cannot participate in more than two media categories (television, radio and newspapers). The participation of foreigners (outside of the European Union) in the shareholding of limited companies with a licence to broadcast free-to-air television or limited companies with a licence to broadcast free-to-air radio should not exceed 25 per cent of the total capital.

Law 2644/1998 regulates the provision of subscription-based radio and television services through analogue or digital transmission, either terrestrially or via cable or satellite. A competitive licensing procedure exists only for terrestrial transmission, due to the scarcity of the specific frequencies. At the same time, those applying for a satellite transmission licence should submit the appropriate application to the NCRTV. Licences are only granted to limited companies (S.A.), the shares of which should be registered. The Law sets limits to the holding of licences in order to secure pluralism and to avoid the creation of dominant market positions. For example, an interested party may only participate in one company providing subscription-based services using the same means of distribution, and in one additional company which uses different means of distribution. At the same time, the state broadcaster ERT S.A. is authorized to establish an affiliated company providing subscription-based services, but it is excluded from the licence holding requirements as they have been defined by law for the commercial companies.

Regarding EU legislation, Greece has adopted the amended TWF directive 97/36/EC with the Presidential Decree 100/2000. Finally, Greece participates actively to the European initiatives for combating illegal and harmful content on the Internet (child pornography, content which incites hatred on grounds of race, sex, religion, nationality or ethnic origin). There are also several provisions in audio-visual and consumer law, as well as the general criminal law that can be applied for protecting citizens from harmful content. Furthermore, for issues related to Internet crime (hacking, libel or slander) the Criminal Code is applied.

The NCRTV was established by law to oversee the operations of both state and private broadcasting. According to law, the Council is an independent authority and its members are officially independent in the execution of their tasks. The Council has the power to impose penalties for violations of the relevant state laws and for copyright and intellectual property infringements or violations of professional codes. In some cases, depending on the gravity of the violation the Council may even suspend or cancel licences. However, it has no real regulatory powers. The Ministry of Transport and Communications, and until the elections in 2004, the Ministry of Press and Information are the ones that grant the licences with only the consultation of the NCRTV. It is worth noticing that the NCRTV is supported by the National Committee of Electronic Means of Communication (EEHME), which monitors the quality of public and private services and reports about that to the NCRTV.

3. Civil Society Organizations
Main features:

- There is a considerable number of public and private media unions and associations in Greece, which are affiliated with other European and International media networks;
- There are several journalists unions in Greece, with a long history and strong trade action;
- However, the majority of the Greek journalists, 52.1 per cent, does not belong to any journalists union;

- There are codes of Ethics, Conduct and Advertising, which provide for a self-regulating framework of the Greek media;
- There is an independent self-funded decision-making body, which supervises the telecommunications, a National Committee which monitors the quality of public and private services, a consultative body on media content and advertising and, finally, a non-profit, self-regulating body for the Internet, which mainly aims at protecting Internet users.

There are several journalists unions according to geographical regions. The Union of Journalists of Daily Newspapers of Athens, the Union of Journalists of Daily Newspapers of Macedonia-Thrace, the Union of Journalists of Daily Newspapers of Peloponnesus, Epirus and Islands and the Union of Journalists of Daily Newspapers of Thessaly, Sterea Ellada, Evia. Finally, there is the Union of Journalists of Periodical [magazine] Press and the Pan Hellenic Confederation of Associations of ERT's personnel represents the employees of the public broadcasting sector.

Furthermore, there are a number of employers' associations such as: The Association of Athens Daily Newspaper Publishers, Association of Daily Provincial Newspaper Publishers and the Union of Owners of Athenian Private Radio Stations. Moreover, The Association of Regional TV Channels, which represents the major regional private TV channels, and the Union of Owners of Athenian Private Radio Stations, which represents the majority of the private radio stations of the greater Athens area, are among the most significant associations of the private broadcasting sector.

Other major industry organizations include: The Union of Hellenic Advertisers, Hellenic Advertising Agencies, The Association of Hellenic Market and Opinion Research Companies, comprising the major market and opinion research companies, and The Hellenic Audiovisual Institute, a scientific body that is supervised by the Ministry of Press and the Mass Media.

An important consulting role is played also by the Assembly of Viewers and Listeners (ASKE), which exercises control over programmes and advertising.

Regarding self-regulation of the Greek media, the Code of Ethics of Greek journalists, which was agreed in 1988 by the five major journalists unions declares journalism's freedom and objectivity. In addition to the above code, a Code of Conduct for News and Other Political Programs for journalists working for broadcast media was ratified by a Presidential Decree in 2003. The code was developed by the NCRTV in consultation with the National Federation of the Reporters' Associations, with advertising agencies and public and private broadcasters. The code applies to all radio and television broadcasts, both free-to-air and subscription services, and is intended to protect individuals' rights and respect for public order, pluralism and democracy within the framework of the Greek constitution.

The Hellenic Advertising Code contains the rules agreed by the advertising industry, the major advertisers and the main media. Issues that might arise out of the self-regulatory process are addressed by two committees: a first-degree Committee for the Control of Advertisements and a second-degree Joint Committee for the Control of Advertisements. Furthermore, the TV Audience Research Control Committee (TV A.R.C.C.) is composed of representatives from the Union of Hellenic Advertisers, the Union of Hellenic Advertising Agencies, the public broadcaster (ERT), the major commercial broadcasters and the Association of Hellenic Market and Opinion Research Companies, which controls and audits the television audience measurement system.

Finally, a non-profit organization, known as the Greek self-regulating organization for Internet content, namely Safenet, was founded and supported by several Greek organizations such as the three largest Greek ISPs, the Greek national research network, the Greek association of Internet users and a large Greek consumers association (Ekpizo). Safenet's aim is to promote self-regulation arrangements for safer use of the Internet through combating illegal and offensive content on the Internet. An additional objective is to raise awareness of issues regarding illegal and harmful content.

4. Development Trends
Main features:

- Expansion of the media industry in the Balkans and Eastern Europe
- Changes regarding the media concentration, ownership and media competition are under way due to adjustments in Greek legislative framework
- Digital television poses questions regarding the reallocation of audience shares and profit among the media players
- The role and the significance of regulatory bodies in the media industry is under discussion

There is an ongoing discussion about the expansion of the Greek media abroad. Many media companies in Greece envisage a future in which they and companies from other sectors will benefit greatly from expansion into the Balkans and Eastern Europe, either on their own or through strategic alliances with international business groups.

The recent digitalization of terrestrial television along with the already existence of satellite digital TV presents a challenge for the future of Greek broadcasting, in particular, in terms of market shares, profit and reallocation of power among media players. Digital television, in general, has given more quality and choices, nonetheless, has raised questions about the cost and sustainability of such a development.

Greek broadcasting faces soon another challenge. Greece has to adopt a new framework for broadcasting services in order to comply with the EU competition rules (Directive 2002/2/77/EC). According to the European Commission, Greece must complete the long over-due transposition of the Directive on competition in the markets for electronic communications networks, which aims at ensuring that competitive market conditions prevail across Europe. Greece has to extent the principle of full market liberalization to all electronic communication services, included broadcasting services, which were explicitly excluded from the scope of the Greek Law. New competitors must be free to offer broadcasting transmission services and, in particular, digital terrestrial broadcasting.

Changes regarding the media concentration and ownership are also under way. The new revised version of the Law, widely known as the 'Law for the basic shareholder' is due to be published. It is anticipated when this law comes into force to bring significant changes in the media landscape in terms of the distribution of media pie and ownership stakes. One of the main concerns of the Greek Government regarding the 'basic shareholder Law' is how to be complied with the Greek constitution and aligned with the fight against corruption, without, however, confronting the EU regulations on media concentration.

Furthermore, there is a discussion for the role and purpose of regulatory bodies as well as the need for the establishment of new ones. There is an ongoing discussion about the role of the NCRTV, as a body that supervises the media sector and, more specifically, the enhancement of its role as a decision–making body. Finally, currently there is not a regulatory body which will supervise and regulate the Internet as well as no code of conduct has been drawn up by the ISPs (Internet service providers). Any development in this regard is anticipated to put into question the power of media operators and to influence the media's content and profile.

References & Sources for Further Information

The European Institute for the Media (2004), Final Report of the study on: 'The information of the citizen in the EU: Obligations for the media and the Institutions concerning the citizen's right to by fully and objectively informed', Düsseldorf: Paris, p. 90.

For more on the regulatory and legal reforms regarding online services, see: Iosifidis, P, (2005), Media System of Greece, Study commissioned by the European Commission, Directorate Information Society, available at: www.hans-bredow-institut.de/forschung/recht/co-reg/reports/1/Greece.pdf.

Kanellos, Leonidas (2000), Internet law in Greece, available at: http://droit-internet-2000.univ-paris1.fr/di2000_16.htm.

More information on the operational programme Information Society and Competitiveness, 3rd community support framework is available at: http://www.ypan.gr and http://www.antagonistikotita.gr/epan/site/Home/t_section.

Emmanoul N. (2004), 'Greece-Legal Situation', in South East Europe Media Handbook 2003/2004, Vienna: SEEMO, pp. 90.

For more on the period on the liberalization of Greek media, see: Dimitras P. (1992), "Greece", in Ostergaard, B. S. (ed.), *The Media in Western Europe*, London: Sage.

Dimitras P. & Doulkeri T. (1986), "Greece" in Kleinstenber, H. (et al.) (eds.), *Electronic Media and Politics in Western Europe*, New York: Campus Verlag.

Katsoudas D. (1985), "Greece: A Politically Controlled State Monopoly Broadcasting System" in Kuhn, R. (ed.), *West European Politics: Special Issues on Broadcasting and Politics in Western Europe*, London: Cass.

Katsoudas D. (1987), "The Media: The State Broadcasting", in Featherstone, K and Katsoudas, K. (eds.), *Political Change in Greece: Before and After the Colonels*, London: Croom Helm.

Daremas G. & Terzis G. (2000), "Televisualisation of Politics in Greece", *Gazette*, 62.2, pp. 117–132.

For more on the Greek television programming in the 1990s, see: Tsaliki L. (1995), The Role of Greek Television in the Construction of National Identity Since Broadcast Deregulation, unpublished Ph.D. thesis, Sussex: University of Sussex.

Kontochristou M. (2004), 'The role of public and private media in constructing a European identity', Review of Public Administration, Athens: Papazisis, pp. 219–244 (in Greek).

Paschalides G. (2005), 'The Greel Television', in Vernikos (et.al.) (eds.), *Cultural Industries: Processes, Services and Goods* (in Greek), Athens: Kritiki.

Furthermore, for the early days of the Greek programming, see Manthoulis R. (1981), *The State of Television* (in Greek), Athens: Themelio.

For more information regarding the code of ethics, see the ESIEA, the biggest journalist union in Greece (http://www. esiea.gr/gr/index.html).

For more regarding the audio-visual sector in Greece, visit the Hellenic Audiovisual Institute (IOM) at http://www.iom.gr as well as the Secretariat General of Communication, available at: http://www. minpress.gr.

For statistical information on the Greek media, see National Statistical Service of Greece (http://www.statistics.gr); Athens Daily Newspaper Publishing Association (A.A.D.N.P), available at: http://www.eihea.gr; Secretariat General of Communication, available at http://www.minpress.gr; the Greek Statistical and Economic Data Service (http://www.hellastat.gr).

The trade press includes the magazines *Advertising Week*, *Contemporary Advertising*, *Ad Business*, *Media Weekly* and *Marketing Age*.

Detailed annual media guides are published by the company Infopublica (Publicity Guide) and by the audience rating company AGB.

Finally, the Association of Athens Daily Newspaper Publishers and the National Statistical Service of Greece provide statistical information about the media in Greece.

THE ITALIAN MEDIA LANDSCAPE

Fabrizio Tonello

Located in the European south, on the Mediterranean Sea, Italy is a founding member of the European Union. The territory is about 300,000 square kilometres and the population is 58 million inhabitants, according to the last census. Its GDP is higher than the average of the 25 EU countries, but its growth was rather slow during the last years.

The structure of the country is a parliamentary republic, with a Chamber of Deputies and a Senate. It is divided in 21 regions, five of them with large autonomous powers. Its official language is Italian, although in some of its communities near the Alpine border other minority languages have an official status as well.

Between 2001 and 2006, media tycoon Silvio Berlusconi was at the same time the prime minister of Italy and the owner of Mediaset, the group controlling the three most important commercial TV networks. In 2007, the Italian media landscape will go through significant shifts, as a result of the defeat of the governing centre-right coalition at the general elections of April 9–10, 2006. The new Prodi cabinet has already proposed media legislation (not yet discussed by Parliament at this writing) in order to put some limits to media ownership, now regulated by a 2004 law conceived to protect Mediaset's interests.

1. The Market

A. *The Print Media*
Main features:

- The newspaper readership remains very low compared to most of EU countries and has not varied substantially in the last decade;
- The free press is reaching large audiences but not yet gaining real commercial strength;
- The main newspapers seem not able to increase their circulation but maintain important revenues thanks to product distribution (books, etc.);
- The magazine market is growing, with an important segment of "gossip" magazines.

In Italy, the newspaper circulation (less than 6 million daily copies sold) is very low by European standards: only Greece and Portugal are below Italy in ranking. One reason may be the low level of formal schooling still existing today, and the fact that TV was introduced when important parts of the population still were illiterate. Another fact often mentioned by journalism historians is the lack of a popular press: Italy, still today, only has "quality" papers, and sport papers cover the niche which is occupied by tabloids elsewhere.

A rather recent development is the birth of several free dailies, on the example of Swedish *Metro*. In Milan, Rome and some other medium cities, people can find *Leggo*, *City* and a chain of free local newspapers created by maverick publisher Nicky Grauso (each one take the name of the city where it is produced, like *Il Firenze* in Florence). So far, the Italian free press can boast 2 million readers per day.

There are about 150 daily newspapers in Italy, the most important of them owned by publishing trusts:

- Editoriale *L'Espresso* owns *La Repubblica*, and about 20 local newspapers. The group key shareholder, and chairman, is financier Carlo De Benedetti;
- RCS, controlled by an alliance of Fiat, a car manufacturer, Benetton (apparel), Della Valle (shoes) and others, owns the largest Italian daily, *Corriere della Sera*, the most important sport daily, *Gazzetta dello Sport*, and several weekly and monthly magazines;
- The Italian Manufacturers' Association (Confindustria) publishes the best-selling financial newspaper, *Il Sole 24 Ore*. Local branches of the Association often control city newspapers, for example, *L'Arena* in Verona;
- The Fiat Group owns *La Stampa*;
- The Monti-Riffeser family (Poligrafici Editoriale) publishes *Il Resto del Carlino*, *La Nazione* and *Il Giorno*;
- The Caltagirone Group (construction) owns Rome's daily, *Il Messaggero*, Naples' *Il Mattino* and Venice's *Il Gazzettino*;
- *Il Giornale* belongs to Paolo Berlusconi (brother of Silvio Berlusconi).

Some minor groups publish other dailies, like *Libero* and *Il riformista* owned by the Angelucci group (main business: health care) or Baldini Castoldi Dalai, now controlling *l'Unità*, formerly the daily of the Italian Communist Party. Bishops control some newspapers, like *L'Avvenire* and *L'eco di Bergamo*, while the Catholic Church has its own house organ, *L'osservatore romano*. More important are local Catholic weeklies, present almost everywhere in Italy, and often politically influential (*La difesa del popolo* in Verona, for example). Padua has a publishing giant called *Il Messaggero di S. Antonio*, a monthly magazine published in several languages that reaches millions of readers all over the world. Journalists control some minor newspapers, like *il manifesto*.

Italy does not have tabloid daily newspapers, the popular dailies are the sport papers like *La Gazzetta dello Sport*, whose circulation on Mondays exceeds that of all newspapers but *Corriere della sera* and *Repubblica*. Boosted by the good performances of Italian team at the Football World Championship, *La Gazzetta* sold a record 2.2 million copies in the days after the victory of the "Azzurri".

Corriere della sera and *Repubblica* compete for the top spot, leaving competitors rather far in the ranking by paid circulation. *Corriere della sera* was founded in the late nineteenth century in Milan and quickly became the voice of Lombardy bourgeoisie. A conservative newspaper, it always tried to keep on its payroll the best reporters, editors and writers. High-profile reporters, like Indro Montanelli, and Nobel Prize winners (1975), like Eugenio Montale, belonged to the *Corriere* family.

Repubblica is a far more recent enterprise. A spin-off from progressive weekly magazine *L'Espresso*, it was born in 1976 and led by talented editor Eugenio Scalfari until recently. While *Corriere* still is a broadsheet, *Repubblica* adopted from the beginning the so-called "berliner" format, a larger than usual tabloid.

Close to the the Left opposition, and more militant than *Corriere*, *Repubblica* was also host to a number of fine journalists like Mario Pirani, Miriam Mafai and Bernardo Valli. A thick paper already in the 1980s, *Repubblica* expanded its coverage to culture, science and travel in order to offer to its readers a large menu of news and features. It was the first Italian newspaper to create a weekly supplement, becoming competitive in the rich advertising market of periodicals. *Corriere della sera* and most medium-size newspapers followed.

Now, *Corriere* and *Repubblica* publish their own weekly magazines (*Corriere della sera-magazine* and *Il Venerdì di Repubblica*), together with magazines for women on Saturdays (*Io donna* and *D*, respectively). *La Stampa* publishes *Lo specchio della Stampa*. These magazines often outsell general interest weeklies like *L'Espresso* and *Panorama*. They severely damaged the niche of fashion magazines like *Amica*, *Anna* and *Grazia*.

For decades, magazines were best-sellers in Italy. The three most important markets were the so-called "family magazines", the "fashion magazines", and "general interest magazines". The first ones were born in the 1950s: independent publishers like Angelo Rizzoli and Edilio Rusconi created a successful formula mixing royal families gossip; reportages from exotic lands and quality pictures. Their products (*Oggi* and *Gente*) are best-sellers to this day.

Arnoldo Mondadori was another independent publisher who specialized in books and magazines. His main successes were *Sorrisi e canzoni tv* (a guide to TV programmes during the week) and *Panorama*, a general interest weekly that imitated the American *Newsweek*. After the death of the founder, his family sold the majority of the group to Mr Berlusconi, after a confusing legal battle against financier Carlo De Benedetti, publisher of *Repubblica* and *L'Espresso*. This epic business war may still resurface in the future because Mr Berlusconi's lawyer, Cesare Previti, was recently convicted of corrupting the judge in charge of the proceedings.

Mondadori profited enormously of its association with Mr Berlusconi's TV empire (see below) and now the group is rich in cash and ready for expanding abroad. In June 2006, it bought Emap France (a subsidiary of British publishing group Emap) entering the French market. Now it controls 44 magazines there, with best-sellers like *Télé Star*, *Biba*, *Max*, *Science et Vie*. Mondadori paid 545 million euro for this acquisition.

The market of the gossip press covering the star-system gossip expanded enormously in the last years, and now the oldest magazines, like *Novella 2000* (Rizzoli) must compete with new entries with a very large circulation: *Chi* (Mondadori) and *Di più* (Cairo).

The old families that made their money out of their printing and publishing activities (Mondadori, Rizzoli, Rusconi) are now controlled by non-publishing businesses, such as Berlusconi (soccer, insurance, commercial television) and Fiat (automobile). Rusconi is now controlled by French group Hachette Filipacchi. Other non-publishing businesses that recently bought newspapers are Caltagirone and Angelucci. The main reasons for their inroads into the media business are both financial and political (in the attempt to influence public opinion and the political arena). Dailies remain politically influent, and corporate interests use them to put pressure on the political parties, which are traditionally responsive to communication.

Italy has an important sector of small-circulation political dailies. *Il manifesto*, *l'Unità* and *Europa* on the Left compete with flip-flopping *il riformista* and hard-right *Il foglio* and *Libero*. This abundant choice was made possible by generous subsidies disbursed by the state since the 1970s.

One reason of the long-term weakness of the daily press is its meagre share of advertising revenues: in Italy the advertising market is dominated by TV, and the print media command only a third of it. Specifically, the daily press obtains about 20 per cent of the investment, 1 billion euros in the first seven months of 2006 (up 2.4% on the same period of 2005). Magazines' advertising revenues in the same period were 716 million euros, up 8 per cent.

B. *The Broadcast media*
Main features:

- Italian TV market is oligopolistic: two players, Rai and Mediaset, control 85 per cent of the audience and 90 per cent of advertising revenues;
- The public service, RAI, has three channels, similar to commercial channels;
- Mediaset commercial stations tilt towards entertainment and advertising, but its evening news are competitive with those of RAI;
- Rupert Murdoch is the only owner of a pay-TV channel, SKY;
- Digital broadcasting is still underdeveloped, it should cover completely the country only by year 2011;
- Radio is growing, with more listeners and advertising revenues (now a 5% share of the global advertising market).

Italians can choose from eight national TV free channels: RAI1, RAI2, RAI3, Canale Cinque, Rete Quattro, Italia Uno, La Sette and MTV. There are about 800 local TV channels. Two groups control 85 per cent of the audience and 90 per cent of advertising revenues: Rai and Mediaset.

Rai, a public company, started broadcasting in 1954 and quickly became immensely popular. While a strict preserve of the Italian government's main political party, the Christian democrats, it allowed many leading left-oriented intellectuals to work there at one moment or another: authors Umberto Eco and Andrea Camilleri, journalists Furio Colombo and Enzo Biagi.

Since 1975, RAI has three channels, now not much different from commercial channels. They offer large doses of fiction, infotainment, talk shows, reality shows and quizzes. The menu of news is also important, with several different editions of "telegiornale" on all the three channels, 24 hours a day.

Mediaset now has the three other channels and about half of advertising revenues. It grew in the 1970s and the 1980s, first as a network of local stations, then as a national channel. Mr Berlusconi was extremely skilful in understanding the need of gathering large audiences to lure advertising contracts to Mediaset. He bought at low price large libraries of American films and soap operas, convinced popular entertainers to join his enterprise, and quickly put competition out of business.

Compared to the variety of the programming on the public channels, Mediaset commercial stations tilt towards entertainment and advertising, but the three evening news (Tg5, Tg4 and Studio Aperto) are competitive with the public television information.

Political protection, first by socialist leader Bettino Craxi, and later by Mr. Berlusconi himself, was instrumental in the development of Mediaset (see section 6 below). Mediaset also tried to expand in France (La Cinq) with no success, while its Spanish affiliate, Telecinco, is an important player there.

Two smaller networks are La Sette, owned by telecommunication leader Telecom Italia (see below, section 8), and Italian MTV, which commands a growing following among youngsters.

In Italy, pay TV was introduced by two organizations: TELEpiù, owned by Canal Plus-Vivendi, and STREAM, formerly owned by Telecom Italia and Rupert Murdoch. The merging between the two of them gave birth to SKY, which has now established a monopolistic position, supported by the rich market of football matches. Telecom Italia sold its part, and Rupert Murdoch is now the only owner. However, it is not clear whether this situation could last and which shape pay TV may take in Italy in the coming years. The merging of TELEpiù and STREAM was authorized by antitrust authorities because of the catastrophic losses of the two companies. Now, this monopolistic position will be strictly scrutinized.

A pillar of law n. 112/2004 (see below, section 6) was the support to digital broadcasting that should be complete by the year 2011, like in France. Mr Berlusconi's cabinet promoted the introduction of decoders that allow old TV sets to receive digital broadcasting, offering €250 million of subsidies to families buying the decoders. Nevertheless, digital broadcasting reaches today only 3.8 million Italian families.

As of yet, there is a modest amount of digital broadcasting. RAI has a few channels, the most important of which is RAI-sport, and Mediaset has its own. Italian passion for football notwithstanding, penetration of the decoders needed to receive digital services remains, nevertheless, slow. Much depends on the policies adopted by Mr Prodi's government, that will decide soon whether to continuing support for the switch from analogical to digital broadcasting or not.

In Italy there is no stagnation of radio: listeners are up, and advertising revenues grow even faster: 10.6 per cent more in the first seven months of 2006, reaching for the first time a 5 per cent share of the global advertising market.

The Italian radio is led by two public stations, the divisions of RAI, RADIO UNO and RADIO DUE (first and third in the ranking of most-listened stations), but the larger share of the audience belongs to the private networks. Among these ones, the clear leader is Radio Deejay that belongs to *L'Espresso* group (5.8 million listeners on the average day), followed by RDS (4.8 million) and RTL (4.2 million). All these are "music" radios, while three "talk" radio with culture and information are Radio Capital (*L'Espresso* group) with 2 million listeners, RADIOTRE (RAI) with 1.9 million and RADIO24 (*Il Sole-24 ore* group) with 1.7 million. In addition to these networks, there is a great number of local radio stations in FM.

C. The Internet Media
Italians have been slow in embracing the Internet, even if 60 per cent of families are now online. The most visited websites are those created by *Repubblica* and *Corriere*, which

are rather traditional in their design and contents. Both are stuffed with offers of travel, merchandising and the like.

Real online newspapers have been scarcely successful, so far. However, some blogs like the one proposed by former TV entertainer Beppe Grillo are enormously successful.

D. News Agencies
Italian leader in this field is ANSA, a cooperative among Italian newspapers born in 1946. It used to be important in Latin America, but in the last years it lost its rank as a medium-size world news agency. Smaller outlets are Radiocor that specializes in economic news, Adn-Kronos, and ASCA.

ANSA is constantly losing money, even if it tries to enter the rich business of providing contents to various media, from free press to cellphones, and it is heavily subsidized by the government.

2. State Policies
Main features:

- Italy never had a comprehensive plan to shape the broadcast media;
- The laws approved in 1997 and 2004 didn't include any meaningful antitrust provisions;
- After the fall of the Berlusconi cabinet, the new centre-left government is working on new media legislation, which will try to put some limits to media ownership, liberalizing the TV sector while guaranteeing access, pluralism and competition among the operators;
- There is an independent authority to look over the communications sector. Its political origins, however, make a rather timid and ineffectual regulator of it.

In the 1980s and 1990s, Italy's media landscape has been shaped by a number of laws, and Corte Costituzionale (Italy's Supreme Court) decisions that reflected a discontinuous approach, partisan considerations and private interests. There has never been a bipartisan plan to shape the Italian electronic media vis-à-vis the challenges of globalization. The turbulence in the political system, the lack of government clear-cut programmes, the strong lobbying by major operators and a general short-sightedness of the Italian political parties in this field are the reasons of the present state of uncertainty and fogginess in the media landscape.

The law n. 249/1997 reformed the audio-visual and telecommunications system, creating a broadcasting frequencies blueprint. It divided broadcasting frequencies between three public channels (RAI1, RAI2, RAI3) and eight national commercial networks including the most important three: Canale 5, Italia 1, Rete 4, all by Mediaset. There were about 800 small to medium-size independent private local television stations, too.

The 1997 law incorporated some antitrust provisions. No one was allowed to own more than 20 per cent of the free television channels or more than 30 per cent of the whole financial resources of the broadcasting market (licence fees, advertising, merchandising, etc.). Cable and satellite were not included in this market. No operator could own more than one pay TV network. The Italian Parliament, however, failed to approve a law regulating the conflicts of interests of businessmen elected to political positions, as it happens in the United States.

In 2001, following the victory of the centre-right coalition led by Mr Berlusconi (who was the owner of the major commercial TV group Mediaset), this problem became a major source of political turmoil. Any decision regarding either state-controlled RAI (such as appointing its board of governors and management), or changes in the existing media policies, fell under the suspicion of promoting the prime minister's political and corporate interests. Mr Berlusconi's conflict of interests was never solved between 2001 and 2006 because his cabinet had large majorities in both chambers of Parliament.

The 1997 law, never really implemented, was changed in 2004 after violent Parliament clashes. The centre-right majority approved a new law (n. 112/2004, also known as "Legge Gasparri", from the name of the cabinet minister who proposed it). This regulation had to tackle the difficult issue of the Mediaset dominant position in the domestic television market (three channels out of the main six). Gasparri's solution was to introduce the concept of "Integrated system of communication", where revenues produced by TV advertising, written press, movies, books and many other things are calculated together. The law forbids a single operator to collect more than 20 per cent of this basket. Otherwise, he can have as many TV channels or newspapers as he wants.

The law made RAI a public-owned company, governed by a board of nine members appointed by a Parliamentary Committee ("Commissione di vigilanza"). It enjoys the financial privilege of getting about half of its income from a tax paid by owners of a TV set (currently €99.60 per year) and the rest from advertising and other activities. Besides broadcasting, RAI undertakes a series of related activities: publishing, programmes sales, recording industry. While the commercial channels are heavy importers of foreign programmes, RAI traditionally is a strong producer in its own right, particularly of European fictions (to which it must reserve 20 per cent of its tax revenues).

There is no doubt that law n. 112/2004 was conceived to protect Berlusconi's broadcasting empire, grown in the last twenty years defying any attempt of regulating it. Mediaset, together with RAI, controls more than 80 per cent of the audience and 90 per cent of advertising revenues, leaving to local TV companies only crumbs. A small channel, "La Sette" (owned by telephone giant Telecom Italia), and music channel MTV have a niche in the national market.

As a result of the victory of the centre-left coalition at the general elections of 9–10 April 2006, a new cabinet, led by Mr. Prodi, was sworn in. In October 2006, the communication minister, Mr Paolo Gentiloni, has put forward new media legislation, which will try to put some limits to media ownership, liberalizing the TV sector while guaranteeing access, pluralism and competition between more operators, in tune with EU guidelines. The first step was an analysis of the broadcasting frequencies allocation, which is under way; the second step (should the parliament approve) would be the switching to digital-only broadcasting of one RAI network and one Mediaset network.

The new bill will abandon the concept of "Integrated system of communication", and will limit media ownership of analogue channels to two, partially implementing a long-forgotten decision of Italian Constitutional Court that ordered Mediaset's Rete Quattro to be broadcasted only by satellite. The transition to purely digital broadcasting will take longer than 2011, but no date has been set so far.

The main obstacle to reform Italian communication system is RAI, a public company overstaffed, too big, and not too different from a commercial firm. In the past, many observers have proposed splitting it in small pieces; for example, selling the most popular channel (RAI 1), keeping RAI 2 as it is and making RAI 3 a cultural network financed only by taxes, without advertising. Another possible solution would be to split RAI in two: one company will keep the hardware, and another company will produce news, fiction and entertainment.

It appears that RAI will remain one company because there is no agreement inside the Prodi government about the possibility of a partial privatization. The ownership of it, however, may be transferred to an independent foundation, in order to sever the links with the government. Many dream of an Italian BBC, but this still is a vague possibility only.

This would require a complete overhaul of the Italian media landscape, where another stumbling block is present: Mediaset. This company now controls half of the Italian Parliament (like CBS presiding over one of the two main parties in the US) and will remain vocal in defending its own corporate interests. Mr Gentiloni has trouble in putting pressure on Mediaset, because Mr Berlusconi (still the leader of the opposition) claims that it is a political vendetta against him. With a parliamentary majority of only three seats, Mr Prodi's government has not much room to manoeuvre.

The law n. 249/1997 created an independent authority to look over the communications sector ("Autorità per le Garanzie nelle Comunicazioni"). This is a collegial body with a president (appointed by the government), a council of eight members (elected by Parliament) and two committees (one for networks and infrastructures, another for services and products). This authority extends its control over the telecommunications sector, the electronic media and the publishing industry.

Its political origins, however, made it a rather timid and ineffectual regulator. It holds important control powers over the telephone market, but it has shown little capacity to effectively regulate the TV system.

There is a Parliamentary Board to supervise RAI, too. It was introduced in 1975, and it is a political authority, made up of 41 MPs from all parties. This body has only jurisdiction over the activity of the public broadcasting company, RAI, but it was given the important role of electing its president by the 2004 law.

3. Civil Society Organizations
Main features:

- Journalists must be members of a professional corporation;
- The Ordine dei giornalisti should be an ethical watchdog, but it has not been efficient in this activity.

The most relevant professional organizations in Italy are the Italian Publishers' Association (FIEG) and the Federation of Television Broadcasters, both powerful lobbies. There is also UPA, the association of advertisers, and there is a large journalists' union, Federazione della Stampa Italiana (FNSI).

Journalists must be members of a professional corporation ("Ordine dei giornalisti"), established in 1963, to which one is admitted by showing that he works as a full-time employee in a newspaper, radio or TV, and after an admission examination. There are also several schools of journalism that allow access to the corporation. The existence of the Ordine dei giornalisti is threatened by the wave of deregulation in the area of professional corporations promoted by Mr Prodi's government, but no immediate changes are forecast.

The Ordine dei giornalisti claims for itself a role of ethical watchdog over its members, but it has been particularly inefficient in this activity. Periodically, scandals created by reporters' conflicts of interest surface: in 2006, some RAI journalists were named as accomplices in a sport furore over Juventus football club's manipulation of referees. More headlines were created by the cooperation between the deputy editor of *Libero*, Renato Farina, and Italian intelligence in a dubious operation of political skulduggery against the then opposition leader, Romano Prodi.

4. Development Trends
Main features:

- Italy has a rich telephone market, with mobile phones outnumbering house phones;
- Only one company has begun to offer services using UMTS standard;
- TV services on cellphones is considered an important area of possible development for TV in the near future.

News and games available on your mobile phone: this seems to be the future of Italian media. The reason is the exceptional penetration of cellphones in the Italian market, where owners of mobile phones outnumber citizens with house phones. Italians elected the cellphone as their favourite medium already many years ago, almost taking over from Finland the world record.

The process started with the liberalization of the telephone market in 1998 that changed dramatically the domestic telecommunication system. Former public operator Telecom Italia was privatized, and, in 1999, it was taken over by Olivetti. Since 2001, the control is in the hands of Pirelli, led by financier Marco Tronchetti Provera. Residential, long-distance and mobile telephone services are now offered by several competing operators, all offering Internet access, too. The main service providers are the following: Telecom Italia, Vodafone (formerly Infostrada), Wind (owned by Egyptian financier Naguib Sawiris), Fastweb, Albacom (owned by British Telecom), Tele2 (Swedish group Tele2 AB), Tiscali (Italian industrialist, and now politician Renato Soru).

In October 2000, the Italian Government organized an auction to assign five UMTS licences. The only company that has begun to offer services using this standard is "3" controlled by the Chinese group Hutchison Whampoa Limited, also present in the UMTS telephone service of several European countries. In 2006, "3" has introduced TV services on its cellphones, and this is considered an important area of development for TV, where RAI, Mediaset and new operators will compete in the future.

New and important developments concerning an interest of Mr Murdoch for Telecom Italia surfaced in July 2006. Media speculation had the Australian tycoon acquiring a majority of Telecom Italia that suffers from increasing competition by new operators, and by a high debt created by a previous takeover. Supposedly, Telecom Italia and SKY could merge, making available on new-generation mobile phones a large menu of premium TV contents. However, during the summer this plan collapsed, and CEO Tronchetti Provera put forward an alternative plan: the sale of Telecom Italia's mobile phones unit (TIM) in order to reduce the staggering debt that is strangling the company (about 42 million euro). This project faced great difficulties with the Italian government, and this precipitated the resignation of Mr Tronchetti Provera, who remains, nevertheless, the biggest shareholder. There is talk of a strong interest by Mediaset (that has plenty of cash from the sale of a 17 per cent of its shares in the spring 2006) in taking over Telecom Italia, but political opposition in this case would be even stronger than in the previous hypothesis of a takeover by Mr Murdoch.

References & Sources for Further Information

Figures and statistics about audiences and circulation figures can be found at the Internet sites of Auditel, which is a Joint Industry Committee created by advertisers and broadcasters (www. auditel.it). The equivalent sources for the press and radio are Audipress (www.audipress.it) and Audiradio (www.audiradio.it). Information about the legal framework of the communication sector can be found at the Internet site of the Authority for Communications (www.agcom.it).

There are a number of trade publications. A comprehensive one is the annual report "L'industria della Comunicazione in Italia", published by the Istituto di Economia dei Media of Milan (www. fondazionerosselli.it). About the written press, a useful report is "Il grande Libro della stampa italiana", published by "Prima Comunicazione", a monthly trade magazine (www.primaonline. com).

Finally, each broadcasting and publishing organization has its annual report (see, for example, www.rai.it, www.mediaset.it, www.mondadori.it, www.feltrinelli.it, www.rcs.it).

THE MALTESE MEDIA LANDSCAPE

Joseph Borg

The Mediterranean islands of Malta with a surface area of 316 sq km and a population of just over 400,000 are some of the smallest but most densely populated countries. The country is made of the main island, Malta, and a secondary island, Gozo.

It became a member of the European Union on 1 May 2004. The two political parties represented in Parliament are the Nationalist Party (currently in government) and the Malta Labour Party. A third very small party is the Green Party. The main religion of Malta is Catholicism almost all the Maltese are baptised in that religion.

Malta's economy is dependent on foreign trade, tourism and the IT industries with the financial services sector increasing in its importance. The country ranks as the 32nd country in the Human Development Index of the United Nations as it has a very advanced system of education and health, among others. The currency is the Maltese lira which is equivalent to 0.43 euros.

Malta was a British colony for over 160 years until it achieved independence in 1964. An important remnant of this colonial period is bilingualism. While the national language is Maltese the official languages are English and Maltese. The national language is a synthesis of the Semitic and Romance families of languages.

1. The Market

A. *The Print Media*
Main features:

- A strong presence of the institutions though it is not as strong as in the broadcast media
- Bilingualism: half are published in English and the other half in Maltese
- A decrease in their importance as preferred source of news
- High number of daily or weekly newspapers. There is one paper for every 28,000 people
- Dependence on advertising or subsidies from owners

Newspapers are not as popular as radio and TV. Research shows that 66 per cent say that they watch TV every day; only 21.6 per cent say that they read a newspaper every day (Media Warehouse 2006). In addition newspapers are definitively losing out to radio and television (and radio is losing to television) as the preferred source of news.

The presence of the institutions – the Church, political parties, unions – in the print media is not as large as their presence in the broadcasting media; moreover, they are absent from the ownership of the newspapers published in English.

The most widely read, and financially the strongest newspapers, are published by Allied Newspapers Ltd., mainly *The Times* (27%) and *The Sunday Times* (51.6%). These papers have been in existence since the 1920 and the 1930s, respectively.

In the beginning of the 1990s a group of business people decided to set up Standard Publications Ltd to compete for the advertising monies accrued by Allied Newspapers. *The Malta Independent on Sunday* (8.9%), the daily, *The Malta Independent* (3.9%), and the mid-weekly, *The Malta Business Weekly* (0.3%), are their products. The group did not make inroads in the readership and advertising market of the papers published by the Allied Newspapers Ltd.

Media Today, another commercial enterprise, is now publishing a Sunday tabloid called *Malta Today* (4.4%) and a mid-week paper called *Business Today* (0.3%). Since November 2006 it started publishing *Il-lum* (*Today*) a Sunday paper in Maltese. This is the only paper in Maltese which is not run by an institution. It is too early to predict what kind of reception the paper will receive.

The focus of these three groups is different. The papers published by Allied Publications Ltd are the most credible. They defend, more than the others, the world-view and value system that have traditionally shaped Maltese culture and history and legitimized Maltese society. The Media Today papers are the most sensational and non-conformist. Standard Publication papers are somewhere in between these two groups. Generally the papers of these three groups, in different degrees, defend middle-class values and the free market.

The market leaders among the newspapers published in Maltese are those published by the General Workers Union. Malta's biggest union publishes the daily *L-Orizzont* (*The Horizon*) (11%) and the weekly *It-Torca* (*The Torch*) (16%). The former was published in the beginning of the 1960s. The GWU papers support the policies of the General Workers Union and also those of the Malta Labour Party, with which the Union is closely connected.

The Malta Labour Party publishes a Sunday tabloid called *KullHadd* (*every Sunday*) (7.8%). The party also publishes a Web-based paper called *Maltastar.com*.

The Partit Nazzjonalista publishes the daily *In-Nazzjon* (*The Nation*) (6.5%) and the Sunday *Il-Mument* (*The Moment*) (11%). They sell fewer copies than the GWU papers. They have their own Web-based news site called *maltarightnow.com*.

Though the Catholic Church is the largest institution in Malta, the market penetration of its two weeklies is the smallest of all institutions. *Il-Gensillum* (*The people today*) (0.7%) has been published by the Media Centre of the Archdiocese of Malta since 1988. *Lehen is-Sewwa* (*The Voice of Truth*) (2.3%) is published by the Catholic Action, an association of Catholic laity. Besides covering religious topics, it gives importance to political, economic and social developments. *Lehen is-Sewwa* has been in circulation since the beginning of the 1930s. Almost all of its content is religious in nature.

Hundreds of magazine titles are published. These cover all sorts of topics including religion, sports, fashion, hobbies, TV programmes and several special interest topics. The presence of commercial interests and civil society is very strong in the sector of magazine publication. Several magazines are published together with newspapers. These are generally chic magazines printed in full colour and on glossy art paper. The newspapers publish some of these magazines, while others have different commercial publishers. These prefer to piggyback on the circulation of the newspaper and make their money by selling space while distributing the magazine for free.

Advertising, sales and subsidies are the three main methods of financing newspapers and magazines. Sources very close to the industry informed the author that during 2002 it is estimated that 13.65 million euro were spent on newspaper advertising while almost four million euros were spent on magazine advertising. The advertising budget spent on the print media is higher than that of the broadcast media. Sources close to the industry say that *The Times* and *The Sunday Times* take more than 50 per cent of all advertising monies spent on newspapers. Most of the papers and magazines tied to institutions are subsidized by the same institutions.

B. The Broadcast Media
Main features:

- A strong presence of the institutions, especially the political parties
- A dual system of public and commercial media
- A very high presence of radio stations
- A high percentage of cable households
- A rapid increase in the use of broadband.
- Two TV organizations broadcast digitally
- Digital radio transmissions start in 2007

Rediffusion Ltd started radio broadcasts in the 1930s and TV broadcasts in September 1962. Five years earlier the Maltese started receiving television signals from Italy after RAI set up a booster in Sicily on Mount Camarata. Italian television was always very popular. In 1995 – the first year of pluralism – the Maltese spent 51 per cent of their TV viewing time following Italian channels, mainly the Berlusconi ones (Broadcasting Authority 1995). Maltese stations made inroads in that high figure and are today watched by 72 per cent while 22 per cent watch the Mediaset and the RAI stations (Ernst & Young 2006).

There are twelve national radio stations, 26 community radio stations broadcasting with a permanent licence, 26 community stations broadcasting with a temporary licence and five TV stations. In all there are 69 stations which translate into a station for every 5800 persons! Ninety-nine per cent of houses have at least one TV set. This means that there are more houses with TV sets than with washing machines or fridge freezers (NSO 60/2003).

The state, the political parties, the Church and the University of Malta own radio and/or television stations. Together they dominate the broadcasting media. Eight out of the twelve national radio stations are tied to institutions. Two-thirds of Maltese listeners tune in to these stations. The TV scenario is an example of market failure. Four out of five TV stations are run by the institutions. The only commercial TV station attracts an audience of 2 per cent.

The two main political parties own a radio station and a television station. Super One Radio, owned by the Malta Labour Party, is the largest station with a following of 9 per cent but is neck and neck with a revamped Radio Calypso. The MLP also owns Super One TV, which shares the second place with Net TV (18%), the station run by the government party, the Nationalist Party. Its radio station, Radio 101, has 4 per cent of the audience share.

There is a lot of station loyalty in the case of listening of political stations, while there is a lot of programme loyalty in the case of TV-watching. Political parties increasingly target the party faithful who use radio to satisfy their needs as party supporters more than any other need (Borg 2002).

TV stations owned by political parties tended to be more soft sell except in times of enhanced political controversy. The reasons are mainly financial; they need a large audience to attract advertising. The most popular programmes on Maltese political stations can easily be shown on the competing station, as their content tends to be non-political.

The Catholic Church has three different presences in the radio sector. RTK is owned by the hierarchy. Radju Maria is run by an organization which is part of the World Family of Radio Maria. Besides these stations broadcasting on a national frequency, there are several Church community radio stations, most are run by Gozitan parishes.

RTK has been broadcasting since 1992 with the express aim of commenting on all human experience from a Christian perspective. This is structurally translated into a generalist radio station featuring a full format schedule but with a significant percentage of religious content.

Radju Maria has been broadcasting on a national frequency since mid-2004 after transmitting on a community frequency since 1995. Radju Maria and the community stations are purely religious stations that consider broadcasting as an extension of the pulpit. The community stations are almost a literal extension of the parish and several are physically wired to a church.

RTK had established itself as the second largest station. However, since 2000 the increase in the audience of Radju Malta was made, to some extent, at the expense of RTK, who also lost several of those who considered it as their favourite station (Vassallo 2000b; Vassallo 2003b). Radju Maria (5%) also affected negatively RTK audience. RTK (6%) is now in the fourth position.

A radically revamped Radio Calypso has in the past months established itself as one of the leading stations. It has by far outstripped Bay Radio which was for several years the most popular commercial station. The success of Calypso is generally attributed to the number of popular presenters it managed to attract. The other commercial radio stations have very small audiences.

Smash TV, the only commercial station, has an audience close to 2 per cent (Vassallo 2002b; Ernst & Young 2006). For a long time it was strong on video music and films, including adult movies. Now it sells its airtime to any buyer. TV-based healing services, the retransmission of God TV and talk shows feature prominently.

PBS Ltd is the main public service broadcaster. Two other stations with the same ethos are Channel 22 (a TV station run by the Ministry of Education) and Campus FM (a radio station run by the University) which only have an audience of around 1 per cent each.

The audiences of PBS Ltd were negatively impacted as a result of the advent of pluralism in 1991. Up to 2000, Radju Malta oscillated between fifth and seventh position (Vassallo 1999a and Vassallo 2002b).

A restructuring exercise mainly of the radio sector was started in September 2000. This strengthened the radio sector. Radju Malta now consistently occupies the third or second position (Vassallo 2003b; Broadcasting Authority 2004; Ernst & Young 2006). TVM has once more established itself as the largest TV station in Malta with a viewership of 34 per cent.

A radical restructuring of PBS Ltd from the content and structural point of view was initiated in the middle of 2004 by the Minister of Investment and Information Technology. The National Broadcasting Policy laid down the new structures of public broadcasting (National Broadcasting Policy 2004). Now PBS owns TVM and two radio stations: Radju Malta (a generalist station) and (since October 2006) Magic (a music station addressing younger audiences).

Cable, terrestrial and satellite reception are all available, though the cable service run by Melita Cable since 1992 is the most diffused. Melita rebroadcasts all Maltese stations referred to above as well as several Italian stations, a number of stations originating from other countries and satellite stations. It also broadcasts a film and sports channel originated by itself and Malta's first teleshopping station that started broadcasting in October 2006. Cable subscriptions rose from 90,000 in December 2001 to almost 124,000 in February 2006 reaching about 80 per cent of Maltese households (NSO Press Release 67/2006). Other households use an aerial to receive several terrestrial stations broadcasting from Italy. Satellite receivers are on the increase.

The rapid development of broadband use and the introduction of digital transmissions offer many possibilities. From December 2004 till February 2006 broadband subscribers increased from 39 per cent to 47 per cent of all Internet users (NSO Press Release 67/2006). The diffusion of broadband compares very well with its diffusion in other states of the European Union.

While the final date for the change over to digital TV has been set to 2012 by the EU Commission, the Malta Communications Authority set the end of 2010 as the changeover date for Malta. Two organizations – Melita Cable and Multiplus – have been given a licence and started broadcasting digitally. The former is using its cable network for its digital transmissions, while the latter is providing the service terrestrially. Maltacom – up till now the only fixed-line telephone company – is expected to follow suit. Though digital transmission has just been introduced, there was already a 28 per cent increase in subscriptions between January and February 2006 (NSO Press Release 67/2006). Melita Cable is, though, the dominant player in the market.

The Government is expected to publish a consultation document on general interest objective stations. The consultation will help government adopt a policy so that when in 2010 Malta turns to digital everyone will be guaranteed reception of a number of stations independently of financial means.

No date has been set for the changeover from analogue to digital radio. The Malta Communications authority has already given the go-ahead to Digi-b Network. It is expected to start its transmissions during 2007.

C. *The Internet Media*
Main features:

- A very rapid increase of Internet subscriptions
- Presence of print and broadcasting media on the Web
- Strong presence of e-government services

Internet subscriptions increased from 34,400 in December (NSO Press Release 081/2002) to over 89,000 in February 2006 (NSO Press Release 67/2006). Almost 50 per cent of private homes have access to the Internet. All secondary schools and 85 per cent of primary schools are connected to the Internet (NSO 2005). Government is committed to popularize as much as possible the use of the Internet and to beat the digital divide.

Almost all the broadcasting and print media are present on the Web through their own sites which present selected news stories and feature articles. Some also update their news service throughout the day. A number of radio and TV stations stream their programmes via the Internet. This service is appreciated by the large number of Maltese migrants.

There are also a number of media organizations that exist only as Web-based media. Recent research data shows that di-ve.com, gov.mt and searchmalta.com are the most popular (Media Warehouse 2005).

Terranet, a subsidiary of Maltacom PLC, runs di-ve.com which also provides updated news, streamed Maltese radio and TV stations and archived programmes on demand. Terranet also runs SearchMalta, which provides search facilities to information about Malta.

The Government portal is increasing its popularity not only for the information it provides but also for the great number of services that are now available online. Malta is in fact considered as one of the best countries for e-government services.

D. *News Agencies*
There are no Maltese news agencies. For the coverage of international news the media depends on foreign news agencies; mainly Reuters followed by A.P.

2. State Policies

Main features:

- The Constitutions establishes the right to freedom of expression;
- The National Broadcasting Policy sets the new structures for PBS;
- PBS has a policy in favour of outsourcing most of its programmes;
- One of the main financing features is the sale of airtime to independent producers;
- The Broadcasting Authority regulates the content of the broadcasting sector;
- The Malta Communications Authority regulates the networks and services of the broadcasting and Web-based media.

Section 41 of the Constitution includes the right to receive and communicate ideas and information without interference as part of the right to freedom of expression. Freedom of the press is guaranteed; however, Malta does not have Freedom of Information law. The Press Act also guarantees the right of journalists to protect their sources and the right of qualified privilege, i.e. when they quote public sources, the source and not the paper is held responsible for the content of the quote.

The broadcasting sector is mainly regulated by the Broadcasting Act (1991) which also provided the legislative framework for the introduction of pluralism in 1991. A National Broadcasting Plan (appended to the Broadcasting Act, 1991) laid down the general policies on which the pluralized broadcasting structure was to be based. In 1993 the Broadcasting Act was amended so that one organization could own both a radio and a television frequency. This amendment was made mainly to enable political parties to own both a radio and a television station.

In 2000 the Broadcasting Act was emended to bring it in line with the TV Without Frontiers Directive of the European Union. Changes affected, among other things, advertising and sponsorship, the protection of minors and the setting up of a new complaints system.

In 2004 the National Broadcasting Policy was published outlining new structures and objectives for PBS Ltd. It regulates PBS's relationship with government through a Public Service Obligation contract which is up for renewal in 2009. Government gives an annual grant for programmes of extended public service obligation. An Editorial Board was set up alongside the Board of Directors. It is responsible for the content of the news and the schedules of the station. The Board of Directors can overrule the Editorial Board if financial matters are involved.

PBS has a policy in favour of outsourcing most of its programmes. The percentage of outsourced programmes is, thus, by far larger than that mandated by the TV Without Frontiers Directive. This policy of PBS gave a considerable boost to the audio-visual industry, and today the number of independent producers has greatly increased.

The main sources of income of broadcasting stations – even PBS stations – and the print media is advertising. Another sizeable source of income of all TV stations is the sale of airtime to independent producers. This would include the time they need for their programme and the time allotted to advertising which, in turn, they sold to finance their programme. The institutions, i.e. Church, unions, political parties, have a policy of subsidizing, where necessary, their media.

The Broadcasting Authority is a constitutional body independent from government. Among other things it ensures the preservation of due impartiality in matters of political or industrial controversy or relating to current public policy. It also monitors radio and TV stations and regulates their performance in terms of their legal and licence obligations. The Broadcasting Authority also published a number of guidelines and legal notices – e.g. news coverage, participation of vulnerable people – which the stations are obliged to follow.

The Malta Communications Authority, which was established on January, 2001 regulates the networks and services but not the content of the broadcasting and Web-based media. The primary role of the Authority is to enable choices and value for money for consumers. The Authority also grants licences, resolves disputes relating to communications and, in general, ensures the well-being of the communications markets.

3. Civil Society Organizations
Main feature:

■ Few in number and not strong

As a result of the relatively small size of the industry and the intense competition between its different sectors there are few active media organizations. The Malta Institute of Journalists has been established for a number of years. Recently a Journalist Committee was set up in competition. There is also a Malta Printers Association and the International Advertising Association Malta Chapter.

Self-regulation characterizes the print media. There is no need for a licence to start publishing a newspaper; one only needs to register with the Press Registrar. The Malta Institute of Journalists has its own Code of Ethics monitored by a committee headed by a retired chief judge. But there are also laws covering libel and readers have, in certain cases, a legal right of reply.

4. Development Trends
Main features:

■ The future of public service broadcasting following the restructuring of PBS
■ The new possibilities following the rapid development of broadband use and the introduction of digital transmissions

While observers from overseas and most Maltese have been saying for a long time that the airwaves are saturated, developments show that there are those who beg to differ. In fact, over the last decade the number of broadcasting organizations has increased, not decreased. It can increase more since the Broadcasting Authority has seven expressions of interest pending for a television channel, ten new requests for a community radio station; nineteen new requests for a nationwide radio station.

Two areas of development would be of future interest are (i) the future of public service broadcasting following the restructuring of PBS and (ii) the new possibilities following the rapid development of broadband use and the introduction of digital transmissions.

The Annual Report of the Editorial Board (September 2005) warned that the ethos of public service broadcasting is under pressure since the commercial aspects of the company are being given prominence over its public service obligation. Own productions by PBS have almost disappeared. The main method of outsourcing used by PBS is the selling of airtime to independent producers. The Acting Chairman of the Editorial Board this year echoed the same sentiments, highlighting the danger that the commercial interests are taking over the public service interests. Even the Minister responsible for Government's investments in PBS was quoted as saying that he is "a bit concerned" with the programming that PBS is broadcasting!

Will the new technologies of broadband and digital transmission be used mainly for the broadcast of "traditional" TV stations or will they carry interactive stations which can provide the viewers with many services from the comfort of their homes? Malta has still to clear jurisdiction questions with neighbouring countries to have enough frequencies to serve all local needs. The conclusion of such negotiations as well as the level of creativity of local producers will bear on the future of the service.

The possibilities of the new technologies combined with the more traditional ones are expected to keep changing the Maltese media landscape and the media usage patterns of the Maltese. Past experience has shown that though several technological innovations were introduced in Malta, some time after their introduction in other countries, once they are introduced their diffusion is very fast, and existing patterns and scenarios are changed in a relatively short period of time.

The future lies interestingly wide open.

References & Sources for Further Information

Bord Editorjali (2005), *L-ethos tax-xandir pubbliku that pressjoni*. Rapport Annwali. Jannar–Settembru 2005.

Borg, J. (2002), "The Democratisation of the Airwaves. Reflection on some cultural and institutional effects of the introduction of radio pluralism". Paper presented at the *9th Meeting of European Conference of Christian Radios* held in Malta 14–17 November 2002.

Broadcasting Act, Act nos. XII, 1991. Retrieved 10 December 2002 from www.ba-malta.org.

Broadcasting Authority (1994), *Annual Report*. Malta: Broadcasting Authority

Broadcasting Authority (1995), *Annual Report*. Malta: Broadcasting Authority.

Broadcasting Authority (2004), *Radio and TV Audiences in Malta*. June–December 2004.

Ernst & Young (2006), *Audience Survey March 2006*. Malta: Ernst & Young.

Media Warehouse *Audience Survey October 2005*. Malta: Informa Consultants.

Media Warehouse *Audience Survey April 2006*. Malta: Informa Consultants.

National Broadcasting Policy (2004), Malta: Ministry for Tourism and Culture; Ministry for Investments and Information Technology.

National Statistics Organisation (29 April 2003), *Dwelling and Household possessions*. Press release 60/2003.

National Statistics Organisation (26 January 2005), *Information Society Statistics*. Press release 081/2002.

National Statistics Organisation (3 April 2006) *Information Society Statistics*. Press release 67/2006.

National Statistics Organisation (2005), *Survey on Information Communication Technology in Schools*. Malta: National Statistics Organisation.

Vassallo, M. (1999a), *A Report and A Study of TV and Radio Audiences in Malta*. April 1999 Malta: Broadcasting Authority.

Vassallo, M. (2000b), *A Report and A Study of TV and Radio Audiences in Malta*. November 2000. Malta: Broadcasting Authority.

Vassallo, M. (2002b), *A Report and A Study of TV and Radio Audiences in Malta*. November 2002. Malta: Broadcasting Authority.

Vassallo, M. (2003b), *A Report and A Study of TV and Radio Audiences in Malta*. November 2002. Malta: Broadcasting Authority.

White Paper. Broadcasting: A Commitment to Pluralism (1990), Malta: Department of Information.

THE PORTUGUESE MEDIA LANDSCAPE

Fernando Correia & Carla Martins

The mainland part of Portugal is located at the extreme south-western tip of the Iberian Peninsula and covers an area of 91,985 square kilometres. It is bounded to the North and East by Spain and to the west and south by the Atlantic Ocean. Portugal also includes the Azores and Madeira archipelagos.

At the end of 2004 Portugal had a population of 10.536 thousand inhabitants, of whom 9.8 million live on the mainland. Population density is 112 inhabitants per square kilometre. Portugal has one of the youngest populations in the European Union: about 16.7 per cent are less than 15 years old. Lisbon is the nation's capital and has 1.8 million inhabitants, including those in the greater metropolitan area.

By the mid-1920s the country's economic and financial situation was very serious – something that led to the so-called "New State", which was marked by corporatism, authoritarianism and the suppression of democratic liberties, like it happened with national-socialism in Deutschland and with fascism in Italy. Following a military coup in April 1974, Portugal returned to a democratic regime. Since 2005 the Political Parties represented in the Parliament are Socialist Party, Social-Democratic Party, Portuguese Communist Party, Popular Party, Left Block and the Ecologist Party "Os Verdes".

Of Latin origin, *Portuguese* is the third most widely spoken European language in the world and is the mother tongue for about 200 million people. Countries in which Portuguese is the official language are Angola, Cape Verde, Guinea-Bissau, Mozambique, São Tomé and Príncipe (Africa), Brazil (South America) and East Timor in Asia.

1. The Market

A. The Print Media
Main features:

- Press circulation numbers tend to diminish in the future;
- Free press tends to increase in importance;
- Four main media groups control media property;
- The Catholic Church has, directly or indirectly, a strong presence in local and regional press.

Portugal has one of the lowest average circulations of daily newspapers across Europe: only 83 numbers for one thousand inhabitants. Television captures the main slice of advertising market (47.5% in 2004, which corresponds to 1.332 millions of euro), followed by press (27.2% of ad market, which corresponds to 763 millions of euro). Half of advertising investment in press is allocated to general information publications; on the other hand, 21 per cent of advertising investment in press is allocated to women's, society and television magazines.

In a scenery characterized by the fall of general newspaper circulation, contrasting with the "explosion" and the growing predominance of free press, the leadership, in terms of paid daily general papers, is occupied (all the editions indicated refer to the average circulation in 2005) by *Correio da Manhã* (118,254 copies), followed by *Jornal de Notícias* (95.231), both with more "popular" characteristics. Next in list are *Público* (50,701) and *Diário de Notícias* (37,992), both qualified as "quality" papers. Another "popular" daily, the tabloid *24 Horas*, has an average circulation similar to *Público*'s.

There are three daily sport papers (predominantly dedicated to football): *Record* (84,303), *O Jogo* (42,854) and *A Bola*, which is not audited by APCT, but which circulation is similar to *Record*.

The weekly generalist papers are dominated by *Expresso* (126,480), followed by *Tal & Qual* (16,067). The weekly paper *O Independente* ended its life cycle of eighteen years in 2006, due to serious economic debts. Also in the newsmagazines' area there's an isolated leader, *Visão* (97,000), which is followed by *Sábado* (48,737) and *Focus* (16,685).

The economic press embraces ten newspapers and magazines, including two dailies. The sector is dominated by the magazine *Exame*, with an average circulation of about 26,000 copies.

The women's, society and TV magazines continue, like in the past years, to be publications of great circulation. The leadership is occupied by the weekly magazine *Maria*, created in 1978, with a paid average circulation of 255.894, followed by *TV Sete Dias* (180.834), *Nova Gente* (146.896), *Telenovelas* (114.020) and *Caras* (100.175).

Readers of all the newspapers and magazines above mentioned are mainly concentrated in Lisbon and in the south part of the country, except for *Jornal de Notícias* and *O Jogo*, which readers concentrate in Oporto and in the north of the country.

Regarding free press, it appeared in Portugal in 1996, with *Jornal da Região*, from the group Impresa, with a single edition for the Cascais, Sintra and Oeiras, in Lisbon periphery. It adapted, later on, a strategy of different editions for each region, reaching fourteen editions, ten of them in Lisbon periphery and three in the Porto region, which totalized seven in 2005, with a combined circulation of about 210,000 copies. It lost importance with the conversion of *Destak* into a daily newspaper and the launching of Portuguese edition of *Metro*, with a circulation in 2005 of 129,603 and 121,000 copies, respectively.

There are in Portugal about 600 local and regional newspapers, mainly with a weekly periodicity; the number of daily local and regional newspapers is not very significant, neither their circulation (usually circulation doesn't exceed ten thousand numbers). The Catholic Church is, directly or indirectly, the main owner of regional and local press. Advertising revenues in local and regional newspapers come predominantly from local institutions and enterprises.

Almost all of the great expansion media are integrated in large economic groups (large at a Portuguese level, but with small significance at a European level). In the middle 80s the propriety of the main newspapers began to leave the hands of traditional families to large groups. This was due to two main reasons: media internal reasons, like the rising of the production costs, the need to considerable investments, the open possibilities of offer enlargement and the advantages offered by the scale economics and group synergies; general reasons, like the integration of Portugal in the European Common Market, the re-privatization of companies, which had been nationalized after the April Revolution of 1974, and the Governmental policies favouring the capital concentration.

Media concentration results from the attempt of some great economic groups to expand its interests to media sector and from the enlargement of companies already implemented in the sector. It's based, in the case of main groups, in a plurimedia strategy, including, after the year 2000, an emergent participation in Internet and new media; it obeys, mainly, to objectives of economic nature but also taking into account political and social motivations; it's supported by a significant participation of foreign capital.

The four leader groups dominate almost everything related to press and audio-visual, with exception to what belongs to the state and to the Catholic Church. They are

- Impresa, property of the former Prime Minister Francisco Balsemão – In press, it holds: *Expresso, Visão, Jornal de Letras, Exame, Telenovelas, Caras* and half a dozen of specialized magazines; in television, the generalist channel SIC and also SIC Notícias, SIC Radical, SIC Mulher, SIC Comédia and SIC Internacional;

- Media Capital – Besides numerous specialized magazines, has its most important power in the audio-visual, with TVI and the radio stations Rádio Comercial, Rádio Clube Português, Cidade FM, among others;
- Cofina – Great influence on the press, with the dailies *Correio da Manhã, Jornal de Negócios* and *Record*, the free newspaper *Destak* and the magazines *Sábado* (newsmagazine), *TV Guia* and more than ten specialized magazines;
- Controlinveste – The only of the four main groups with presence in all sectors: *Jornal de Notícias, Diário de Notícias, 24 Horas, O Jogo, National Geographic* and several other specialized magazines and newspapers; TSF (informational radio) and Sport TV (cable).

Only one of the groups, Media Capital, is owned by a non-Portuguese group, the Spanish Prisa, but in all of them there's a small or large participation of foreign capital.

Besides these groups, there are two other important media owners, the state and the Catholic Church. To the public sector belongs, in addition to Lusa (see point 5), two generalist television channels, RTP1 and 2, RTP Açores, RTP Madeira, RTP Internacional and RTP África and, in cable, RTPN (news) and RTP Memória (historical archive); and seven radio stations, Antena 1 (generalist), Antena 2 (classical music), Antena 3 (younger publics), RDP Madeira, RDP Açores, RDP África and RDP Internacional.

Regarding the Catholic Church, it detains the radio station, which controls audiences, with three channels: Rádio Renascença, RFM and Mega FM. It also owns, directly or indirectly, dozens of radio stations and local and regional newspapers, including, in the north of the country, *Diário do Minho*.

In 2005, and for the first time, free daily press achieved larger circulation figures than traditional press. *Destak, Metro* and *Jornal da Região* achieved together, by daily edition, an average of 450,000 copies, overcoming, by far distance, traditional daily press (both quality and popular press). *Destak*, the major free daily newspaper, increased its average circulation in 70 per cent between 2004 and 2005. Preliminary figures referred to 2006 show that this tendency persists.

Circulation of every generalist daily newspapers and sport newspapers falls between 2004 and 2005, in some situations more than 10 per cent, which didn't happen since the mid-90s. This phenomenon is related to free press phenomenon itself. On the other hand, when we analyse factors which contribute for traditional press decline, we must add the influence of economic crisis which affects Portugal and the persistence of structural reasons such as illiteracy and low numbers of press readers. We must also reflect on the lack of press innovation and its difficulty in keep pace with social and mental transformations, namely, resulting from new information and communication technologies impact.

Only press specialized in economics increased circulation, at 10 per cent – and, in spite of all main daily newspapers, include editorial sections and special supplements on this subject. *Exame* magazine, which leads this segment, grew 30.5 per cent. Also women's, social and television magazines increased circulation.

The shutdown of *A Capital* – an afternoon daily newspaper converted into a morning newspaper in its last phase – reinforced the end of afternoon daily press in Portugal (three afternoon newspapers were still published in Portugal in the beginning of the 90s). Apparently, it constitutes an irreversible tendency.

Enterprises use now more often marketing strategies in order to enlarge reader basis, namely, selling products such as books and DVDs and also domestic objects, tools, etc. Every indicators point out that this strategy doesn't increase the number of readers, but only contributes to prevent an even more dramatic loss in newspaper circulation.

General information weekly newspapers tend to lose favouritism of readers against news magazines, broadly with larger circulation than the former.

B. The Broadcast Media
Main features:

- Television continues to concentrate the major slice of advertising revenues (47.5% in 2004), followed by press and radio (7.2%);
- Each Portuguese sees, in average, 3 hours and 30 minutes of television per day;
- Television commercial channels SIC and TVI, the last one with more popular characteristics, continue to dispute audience share leadership;
- Programming choices for the two commercial operators increased; namely, in the so-called reality shows;
- Portuguese fiction, sports, in particular football games, and information are the television genres which gather public preference;
- TV Cabo was the first television cable platform launched in Portugal and, in spite of the emergence of other competitors, holds a market share of around 80 per cent. TV Cabo is the only Portuguese provider of television satellite service;
- In 2005, cable television service was subscribed by 1.4 million customers, which represent 13.3 per cent of the Portuguese population;
- The satellite television service was subscribed in 2005 by 394 thousand customers, which represent 3.7 per cent of the Portuguese population;
- In the first trimester of 2006, RFM and Rádio Renascença were the most listened radio stations in Portugal, followed by Rádio Comercial and Antena 1;
- The introduction in Portugal of digital terrestrial radio and television has been rather slower than expected;
- RDP owned the contest for management of national digital network of radio broadcasting.

In the hertz space coexist, in strong competition, three national generalist television operators: the public service operator RTP (channels RTP1 and 2) and SIC and TVI, both commercial stations created in the beginning of the 90s.

Public radio and television services have suffered a tremendous organizational transformation, which started during the Government of José Manuel Durão Barroso (2002–2004), with the purpose to solve financial problems of this set of companies. A new holding, Rádio e Televisão de Portugal, was created in 2003, gathering RTP, RDP (radio) and RTP Meios de Produção (television production). The development of this company model had its most important impact with the end of the holding Portugal Global, which included news agency Lusa as well. Lusa is now under the State's direct administration. On the other hand, public service channels are submitted to a contract of obligations signed with the State.

The possible selling of the second public television channel, which created an intense social debate, was never fulfilled; instead, channel 2 was opened to institutions of "civil society", which participate through production and exhibition of programmes. Public service second channel, with a share of around 5 per cent, is focused towards more demanding and segmented groups and, in terms of programming, emphasizes culture, education, social activities, sports, religious confessions, independent production, Portuguese cinema, audio-visual environment and experimentalism.

Created in 1992, SIC is owned by Impresa, one of the main Portuguese multimedia groups; launched in 1993, TVI is owned by Media Capital, also a main national multimedia group. In 2006, SIC and TVI saw their licences to operate for the next fifteen years renewed by the media regulator.

According to Instituto Nacional de Estatística (National Institute of Statistics), television continues to concentrate the major slice of advertising revenues (47.5% in 2004), followed by press, which represented 27.2 per cent in the same year. RTP1 has a mixed funding model based on advertising and public subsidies. In 2003 the government applied a new "contribution for the audiovisual", which is collected every month with the electricity bill. This tax, which was established in 2006 in 1.1 euro/month, is the main funding source of public radio and channel 2 (in both cases, commercial advertising is forbidden).

Between 2000 and 2005, the time of television consumption didn't change in Portugal. According to Marktest (see point 10), in the first trimester of 2006 each Portuguese saw, in average, 3 hours and 36 minutes of television per day. The major consumers live in the Interior region, belong to social classes C2 and D, are women and have more than 64 years old. Adults (more than 14 years) see in average more 40 minutes of television per day than children (4 to 14 years).

The two hertz channels of public service television had, in 2005, a combined share of 28.6 per cent (RTP1, 23.6% and 2.5%). Commercial stations had the biggest television audience shares: SIC, 27.2 per cent; TVI, 30 per cent.

In the last years programming choices for the two commercial operators increased, namely, in Portuguese fiction and the so-called reality shows. Sports, in particular football games, and information are the other two television genres which gather public preference and where competition is more visible between channels.

Television commercial channels SIC and TVI, the last one with more popular characteristics, continue to dispute audience-share leadership. In the years that followed the birth of private televisions, RTP1 tried to fight back the loss of viewers competing directly with commercial channels, using similar programme and information formulas. In the last two years, programmatic and editorial philosophy of public service channels distinguished itself from other commercial channels. It's a fact that RTP1 managed recently to reinforce audience share, which in a way constitutes a prize for dismissing a direct competition strategy.

All in all, opening channel 2 to civil society has been a positive experience. The new direction will probably keep this strategy for the public service channel and continue to ensure quality of programmes resulting from partnerships with social institutions.

RTP and SIC transmit international emissions, dedicated to Portuguese communities around the world or to Portuguese-speaking countries (RTP International, RTP Africa, SIC International) and, more recently, with a partnership with TV Cabo, have launched thematic channels (RTPN, RTP Memória, SIC Notícias, SIC Mulher, SIC Comédia, SIC Radical).

Cable television services were launched in Portugal in 1994. Combined with the licensing of commercial channels, this new distribution platform had a major impact in the Portuguese audio-visual landscape. TV Cabo (integrated in the holding PT Multimédia, Portugal Telecom group) was the first television cable platform launched in Portugal and, in spite of the emergence of other competitors, holds a market share of around 80 per cent. TV Cabo is the only Portuguese company which provides television satellite service (DHT_Direct to Home).

In 2005, cable television service was subscribed by 1.4 million customers, which represent 13.3 per cent of the Portuguese population. Lisbon region concentrates half of the total number of subscribers (50.6%), followed by North (23.4%), Centre (12%), Algarve (3.6%) and Alentejo (2.7%). Madeira gathered 4.7 per cent of subscribers and Azores 2.9 per cent. In the same year, the satellite television service was subscribed by 394,000 customers, which represent 3.7 per cent of the Portuguese population.

Cable service subscription and subscription of codified channels (cinema, erotic, kids, etc.), allowing a more diverse and segmented television offer, will most probably continue to increase. However, it is interesting to observe that traditional channels (RTP, SIC and TVI) are still the most popular of cable service programme offer. Twenty-four hours a day information channels such as SIC Notícias and RTPN are also successful.

In terms of advertising revenues, radio holds a share of only 7.2 per cent, after television, print media and outdoor advertising.

National and regional stations' ownership is concentrated in the hands of the state and Portuguese media groups. Public service radio company, RDP, includes Antena 1 (generalist), Antena 2 (cultural), Antena 3 (dedicated to music for a younger public) and RDP Africa.

However, Catholic Renascença Group – which holds Rádio Renascença, RFM and Mega FM – continues to lead the radio segment in Portugal. In the last few years, Media Capital, through its affiliate Media Capital Rádios, reinforced its presence in the radio sector. Media Capital Rádios *portfolio* includes Rádio Comercial, Rádio Clube Português, Rádio Cidade, Best Rock FM and the website Cotonete. On the other hand, TSF, created in 1988, is the main thematic Portuguese station specialized in news. In 2005, the company which owns TSF, Lusomundo Media, was bought by Controlinveste.

According to Marktest, in the first trimester of 2006, RFM and Rádio Renascença were the most listened radio stations in Portugal, followed by Rádio Comercial and Antena 1. Great Lisbon, Littoral North and Interior were the regions which register the high levels of radio listening. Great Oporto and South are, by contrast, the Portuguese regions with less degree of radio consumption. Generally speaking, men hear radio more often than women (a proportion of 55% to 44%). Radio is mainly consumed by individuals between 18 and 44 years old.

In the last years, as worldwide, radio sector registered a diversification of distribution platforms and equipments, which alters the listening experience. Such platforms and equipments include Internet, cable network, cellphone or *podcast*.

Data gathered by OBERCOM indicates the existence of approximately 400 local stations in Portugal.

Although there's some optimism around new technologies and the process of migration to digital, the introduction in Portugal of digital terrestrial radio and television has been rather slower than expected. The licence ascribed in 2001 to a consortium to operate a platform of Digital Terrestrial Television ended up being revoked. Now it's expected the launch of a new licence opening contest.

RDP owned the contest for management of national digital network of radio broadcasting – in which it invested significantly over the last years, having adopted the DAB system – Digital Audio Broadcasting. In Portugal digital radio emissions can be heard since 1998, but massive utilization of this technology will only take place by large-scale distribution of equipment to cars as well as to homes.

C. The Internet Media
Main features:

- In the end of 2005, there were in Portugal 1.4 million Internet users and 11.1 million subscribers of mobile phone service;
- The majority of national and regional media, including press, radio and television, holds an Internet website.

ANACOM statistics indicate that, in the end of 2005, there were in Portugal 1.2 million customers of broadband Internet, which already represent 82 per cent of the total customers who have access to Internet (1.4 million customers).

The ADSL technology and cable are, in this order, the main options of access to broadband Internet.

The mobile phone service represents another domain that combine the traditional voice services with data transmission, Internet access and multimedia services. By the end of September 2005, there were in Portugal 11.1 million subscribers of mobile phone service, corresponding to a penetration rate of 105.8 per cent.

The first online media projects were created in the second half of the 90s. Setúbal na Rede, a regional newspaper brand, was the first media project created on the Web in 1998. General information national dailies *Jornal de Notícias, Público* and *Diário de Notícias* were the first to update their respective electronic editions. Enterprises quickly looked forward to launch innovative electronic projects (for example, Diário Digital, Portugal Diário, Cotonete). Cotonete, an innovator project created in 2001, consists of a website which allows individuals to personalize their own radio station ("personal radio") according to their own music preferences.

Today, the majority of national and regional media, including press, radio and television, holds an Internet website.

The sustainability of Internet projects is, however, the major concern of media companies, confronted with the question of knowing if gratuitousness of access to products and services will hold. Means like *Expresso* or *Público* give electronic access to printed editions by means of payment.

Like in the other countries, the question if online journalism constitutes a fourth type of journalism is still unanswered.

D. News Agencies
Main features:

■ At national level there is only one news agency, Agência Lusa, which shareholder structure combines public and private stakeholders.

Lusa, Agência de Notícias de Portugal (www.lusa.pt), is a society with a majority of the State's capital, but where some of the main mediatic national companies participate as well. It has a workforce of 200 journalists.

Lusa makes available contents in text format, photography and television and covers the following news services: national, economics, sports, international and Africa.

Among its clients we found all Portuguese national media, as well as a great number of regional and local newspapers and radio stations. One of its specific characteristics is the privileged connection which maintains with African Portuguese–speaking countries.

As a way of making the company more profitable, Lusa has expanded also to services production, namely, in economic field, designed for companies with no media liaison.

2. State Policies
Main features:

■ Cavaco Silva Governments (1985–1995) brought a media policy characterized by privatization and liberalization;
■ After Antonio Guterres's six-year socialist governments (1995–2001), XV Constitutional Government Program, conducted by José Manuel Durão Barroso (2002–2004), defined again more liberal policies for media sector;
■ Government headed by José Sócrates (since 2005) proposed for media sector the creation of a new media regulator; new legislation to regulate ownership concentration and abuse of dominant position; the promotion of transition to digital platforms;
■ The reform of regulatory framework in 2006 caused the extinction of Alta Autoridade para a Comunicação Social (AACS – Media High Council) and the creation of Entidade Reguladora para a Comunicação Social (ERC – Regulatory Entity for Media).

Media regulation, sector legislative reviews, local and regional media public grants, media concentration are major concerns of political representatives in the last two decades, expressed in public policies applied to media sector.

Cavaco Silva's Cabinets decided, between 1985 and 1995, to open television sector to private initiative and to legalize hundreds of local radios which spread all over the country since the 1980s. The same liberal policies, which meant the progressive withdraw of state from media sector, were applied to press market (for instance, *Diário de Notícias* and *Jornal de Notícias* were privatized).

In 2005, the XVII Constitutional Government Program, headed by José Sócrates, proposed for the media sector the following major measures: the creation of a new media regulator; a more relevant state participation in media enterprises besides RTP, RDP and Lusa; new legislation to control property concentration and abuse of dominant position; the definition limits to horizontal, vertical and multimedia concentration; the promotion of transition to digital platforms.

The reform of regulatory framework implied the extinction of Alta Autoridade para a Comunicação Social (AACS – Media High Council) and Instituto da Comunicação Social (ICS – Institute for the Media), which will evolve to a new institutional configuration: Gabinete para os Media e Novos Serviços de Comunicação (Media and Communication New Services Office).

ERC pursues the assurance of following mainly principles: pluralism and diversity; freedom of speech and information; protection of more sensitive publics and audiences, such as children; accuracy and reliable nature of information. To avoid an excessive media property concentration affecting principles such as pluralism and diversity is one of ERC'S main tasks; the media regulator must also be alert to media independency towards political and economic powers. In addition, ERC should promote co-regulation and encourage self-regulation mechanisms.

3. Civil Society Organizations
Main features:

■ Journalists and media owners have the most powerful organizations within media organizations.

There are about 7,000 journalists in Portugal, accredited with professional licence, although not all are actually working. About 5,000 are organized in the National Journalists Union (Sindicato Nacional dos Jornalistas), a European Federation of Journalists (FEJ) and International Federation of Journalists (IFJ) member.

Besides the Union, there are many others and diverse journalistic organizations, which act in cultural, training and health assistance fields. Clube de Jornalistas – Press Club publishes a magazine every three months, *Jornalismo e Jornalistas* (*Journalism and Journalists*); broadcasts weekly a TV programme on channel 2, (RTP), where media and journalistic issues are debated; it also has a website (www.clubedejornalistas.pt) and every year awards journalists with Prémios Gazeta (Gazeta Prizes), the most prestigious awards in the journalistic field (endorsed by the President of Portuguese Republic). Casa da Imprensa (Press House) is a mutual association, founded on 24 April 1905.

Confederação Portuguesa de Meios de Comunicação Social (Portuguese Media Confederation) is the largest entrepreneurs association in media sector, direct or indirectly representing more than 600 media enterprises. Some of the Confederation reference members are Associação Portuguesa de Imprensa (Portuguese Press Association), which represents 450 newspapers and magazines; Associação Portuguesa de Radiodifusão (Portuguese Radio Association), which represents more than 200 national and local radio stations and, furthermore, RTP, SIC, TVI and Agência Lusa (national news agency). Within its members we also must indicate Associação de Imprensa de Inspiração Cristã (Christian Press Association) and Associação de Rádios de Inspiração Cristã (Christian Radio Association), the last one with 70 members.

CENJOR, Centro Protocolar de Formação Profissional para Jornalistas (Journalistic Professional Training Centre), founded in 1986, associates official professional training institutions, the journalists union and entrepreneur associations. CENJOR's financing programme is assured by public funding: state and European Social Fund. The nature of CENJOR training is mainly practical, supplementing the kind of teaching offered by more than 30 undergraduate and graduate media and journalism courses in Portugal.

Government proposed a new legal framework for journalists ("Estatuto do Jornalista"); a professional ethics commission is intended to be created within Comissão da Carteira Profissional do Jornalista, an organization headed by a judge and where journalists and entrepreneurs are represented. This putative commission will enforce compliance with professional ethics principles, admonishing or punishing journalists in case of misconduct.

In turn, Union Journalists Professional Ethics Council addresses recommendations based on Ethic Journalist Code principles, a document approved by journalists in May 1993.

Created for the first time in Portugal in 1997, an ombudsman exists nowadays in *Record*, *Diário de Notícias*, *Público* and *Jornal de Notícias* daily newspapers. In April 2006 there were vested television and radio ombudsmen, which will deal with audiences' commentaries addressed to RTP and RDP.

4. Development Trends
Main features:

- Main media conglomerates reinforce their positions and don't hide their wish to grow even further, in the country and abroad, which raise questions about the future of pluralism and employment of journalists and other professionals;
- In 2005, and for the first time, free daily press achieved larger circulation figures than traditional press. Free press tends to grow even further in the future.

The shutdown of *A Capital* – an afternoon daily newspaper converted into a morning newspaper in its last phase – reinforced the end of the afternoon daily press in Portugal. Apparently, it constitutes an irreversible tendency. It also aggravated the professional fragility and identity crisis of journalists, tied up between contradictory demands:

the respect for professional and ethic rules and the corporate interest for information essentially turned to audiences and commercialization.

As a consequence of progressive development of convergence processes, stimulated by growing implementation of new technologies, the decrease of journalism specific prestige and its dilution within a content industry controlled by telecommunications, information technologies and audio-visual is notorious.

One single corporate, PT, concentrates main telecommunication networks: copper, terrestrial television and cable. If SONAE, property of Belmiro de Azevedo, manages to buy PT, then it's very likely that cable network will be alienated.

Transition to digital radio and television and *switch-off* will take longer than previously foreseen due to the uncertainty about the future and quick technological changes.

Digital journalism is incognito in the near future. Until 2000 enterprises showed much enthusiasm for multimedia projects and for trainings of future multimedia journalists. After 2000, however, many projects were terminated or downsized, which led to the unemployment of thousands of journalists. Yet, new technologies are changing journalistic practices and the nature of reception of news.

Finally, the convergence of technologies, networks, services and enterprises will most probably stimulate an approximation between media and telecommunication regulators.

References & Sources for Further Information

Reliable data related to media activities and results is provided by the following institutions: Observatório da Comunicação (OBERCOM – Communication Observatoy www.obercom.pt), Entidade Reguladora para a Comunicação Social (www.erc.pt), Instituto da Comunicação Social (www.ics.pt), Autoridade Nacional das Comunicações (ANACOM – telecommunication regulator www.anacom.pt), Associação Portuguesa para o Controlo de Tiragens e Circulação (APCT – Portuguese Association for Press Circulation Control www.apct.pt), Marktest, audience studies enterprise (www.marktest.pt) and Instituto Nacional de Estatística (INE – Statistics National Institute (www.ine.pt).

Several universities (in Lisboa, Minho, Porto, Beira Interior) have research and investigative centres in media and communication studies. Two national institutions congregate professors, investigators and professionals: Associação Portuguesa de Ciências da Comunicação (SOPCOM – Portuguese Association of Communication Studies (www.sopcom.pt) and Centro de Investigação Media e Jornalismo (CIMJ – Media and Journalism Investigative Centre (www.cimj.org)), the last one turned specifically to the study of the journalistic field.

Finally, there are several magazines and journals concerned with media studies: *Jornalismo e Jornalistas* (every three month), edited by Clube de Jornalistas; *Media XXI* (every two month), which also focuses on publicity, marketing and managerial activities; and, in academics field, *Media & Jornalismo* (two numbers a year), published by CIMJ; *Revista de Comunicação e Linguagens* (two numbers a year), published by Centro de Estudos de Comunicação e Linguagens; *Trajectos* (two numbers a year), published by ISCTE; *Comunicação e Sociedade* (two numbers a year), published by Centro de Estudos de Comunicação e Sociedade.

THE SPANISH MEDIA LANDSCAPE

Ramón Salaverría

Located in the European southwest, Spain is a vast and very populated country of the European Union, thanks to its more than half a million square kilometres and its 44.1 million inhabitants, according to the census of 2005. Its GDP is at the average level of the 25 EU countries: 19,637 euro per capita in 2004. The administrative structure of the country is divided in 17 autonomous communities, distributed in 52 provinces. Its official language is Spanish, although in some of its autonomous communities other minority languages have an official status as well: Catalan and Valencian (spoken by 17% of the population), Galician (7%) and the Basque (2%), respectively.

Since the end of Franco's dictatorship in 1975, Spain is governed by a parliamentary political system under a regime of constitutional monarchy. The country joined the European Union in 1986 and, since then, it has obtained an important and sustained economic growth that placed it as the tenth most powerful economy of the world in 2005. Such economic wealth, together with the tourist resources of the country, have attracted a growing number of immigrants that have established their residence in Spain in the latest years and have become a relevant target for the media companies; in 2005, 9 per cent of the population were foreigners.

1. The Market

A. *The Print Media*
Main features:

- The newspaper readership has not varied substantially in the last decade, but remains very low comparing to most of EU countries;
- The free press is reaching great audiences and is gaining remarkable commercial strength;
- The newspapers, with their circulation stagnated; maintain their income rates thanks to product distribution;
- The business press circulation is declining;
- The magazine market, also stagnated, is led by women's magazines.

The landscape of the press in Spain presents similar characteristics to those of other developed countries, except for an important peculiarity: the percentage of newspaper readers is remarkably lower than that of other European countries.

According to Estudio General de Medios (EGM) – the main audience survey of printed, audio-visual and online media in Spain, based on thousands of interviews to citizens – 41.1 per cent of the Spaniards used to read newspapers in 2005. By the same time, the percentage of magazine readers was of 53.8 per cent, and that of supplements 27.7 per cent. Regarding the social-demographic profile of newspaper readers, nearly two out of three newspaper readers are men, with an average age over 43, of middle class, with residence in big cities (Madrid and Barcelona) or, mainly, in the northern regions of the country.

These low percentages of reading compared to other European countries of similar economic wealth and cultural development are not due to a fast decline during the latest years. In fact, they have remained quite stable during the last decade. According to EGM, in 1995, newspaper readers were 38 per cent of the population, those of magazines 54.5 per cent, and those of supplements 33.8 per cent. However, this maintenance or, in the case of newspapers, slight rise in the numbers of readers, is not even due to an increase in the sales. As in other countries, newspaper and magazines sales have declined in Spain, especially during the last years. The percentage of reading population has remained more or less the same primarily thanks to the emergence of free newspapers.

At the beginning of 2005, according to data of the Oficina de Justificación de la Difusión (OJD), main auditor organization of the circulation of printed and online press, Spain counted with 135 pay newspapers. On the other hand, this same organization controlled the circulation of 576 magazines and 19 supplements. In contrast to these numbers, by those same dates it is calculated that in Spain there were more than 7,000 free publications, among newspapers and, mainly, magazines.

As it is evident, free press is hegemonic and not only in terms of number of publications. In December of 2005, the year in which the added diffusion of Spanish pay newspapers fell a weighed 2.13 per cent, an historical fact took place as well. For the first time, the most read newspaper of general information in Spain was not a pay one, but a free one. Until that date and since more than two decades, the leadership of the general information press in Spain corresponded to *El País*; nevertheless, since that moment the most read newspaper in Spain is *20 Minutos*, a free newspaper of national scope launched on 3 February 2000. The increasing leadership of the free press is clearly seen in the following top ten of general information newspaper audiences, according to EGM of December of 2005: 1st *20 Minutos* (free; with an average of 2,298,000 daily readers); 2nd *El País* (traditional newspaper; 2,048,000); 3rd *Qué!* (free; 1,923,000); 4th *Metro* (free; 1,904,000); 5th *El Mundo* (traditional; 1,342,000); 6th *El Periódico* (traditional; 854,000); 7th *ABC* (traditional; 840,000); 8th *La Vanguardia* (traditional; 649,000); 9th *El Correo* (traditional; 592,000); 10th *La Voz de Galicia* (traditional; 572,000).

Another example of the increasing force of free publications may be found in business press. In 2006, Spain counts on four business newspapers of national circulation: *Expansión* (47,577 copies of daily average circulation in 2005), *El Economista* (launched on 28 February 2006, without any circulation data registered yet), *Cinco Días* (30,425) and *La Gaceta de los Negocios* (27,802). Only the first two remain as strictly traditional newspapers; the other two, on the contrary, have a mixed-circulation model since the end of 2004, in which 20 per cent of the circulation is sold and the remaining 80 per cent is given for free.

The fall of newspapers and magazines sales have not entailed their economic decline, at least up to the moment. On the contrary, according to data of Infoadex, the main auditor of advertising expenditure figures, the Spanish newspapers enjoyed a good economic situation in 2005 since, in addition to its circulation income, they obtained 1,666 million euro through advertising, 5.2 per cent more than in 2004. The advertising income was the second best result of the last decade. Magazines, on the other hand, raised 674.5 million euro through advertising in 2005, hardly a 1.5 per cent more than the previous year.

Considering the registered circulation instead of the estimated audience, the data of the daily press in Spain presents other peculiar characteristics as well. The 91 titles controlled by OJD came to an average of 3.95 million newspapers sold daily in 2005. At the same period, nine out of the fifteen leading newspapers saw how their sales decreased, including the two main pay newspapers, *El País* and *Marca*, in spite of the intense promotional activity unfolded by all the sector. According to OJD, in 2005 only eight pay newspapers of general information had a circulation above 100,000 copies daily. The leader was *El País* (national newspaper owned by Prisa group and published in Madrid), with a daily circulation average of 453,602 copies. It was followed by *El Mundo* (national, Unedisa, Madrid), 314,591; *ABC* (national, Vocento group, Madrid), 278,166; *La Vanguardia* (national-regional, Godó group, Barcelona), 208,139; *El Periódico de Catalunya* (regional, Zeta group, Barcelona), 170,181; *La Razón* (national, Planeta group, Madrid), 140,088; *El Correo* (regional, Vocento group, Bilbao), 124,843 and *La Voz de Galicia* (regional, Voz group, A Coruña), 102,978. On the other hand, there were four sports information newspapers with figures over 100,000 copies: *Marca* (owned by Recoletos group and published in Madrid), 328,761; *As* (Prisa group, Madrid) 209,585; *Sport* (Zeta group, Barcelona), 114,682 and *Mundo Deportivo* (Godó group, Barcelona), 103,004.

Regarding the magazine market, this was clearly led by women's magazines. According to OJD, the top ten in 2005 included the following publications: *Pronto* (weekly, women's), 1,000,580; *¡Hola!* (weekly, women's), 553,042; *Diez Minutos* (weekly, women's), 287,681; *Glamour* (monthly, women's), 276,220; *Lecturas* (weekly, women's), 266,484; *Muy Interesante* (monthly, scientific spread), 258,297; *Semana* (weekly, women's), 237,297; *Qué me dices!* (weekly, women's), 232,567; *Cosmopolitan* (monthly, women's), 225,477 and *FHM* (monthly, life style), 210,373.

Finally, it should be mentioned that some Spanish media companies lived during the last decade a process of internationalization. For instance, Prisa group bought newspapers, magazines and radio networks in Latin America. In 2005, it also bought the 15 per cent of the French newspaper *Le Monde*, as well as some magazines in Portugal. Another media group that owns newspapers abroad is Vocento, which shares the ownership of some newspapers in Argentina.

On the other hand, some foreign media companies have installed in Spain during the last few years. This foreign presence is especially noticeable in the free press market. Schibsted, a Norwegian press group, owns the 80 per cent of *20 Minutos* since 2001. Another Swedish group, Metro International, publishes *Metro* in most of the Spanish cities. Considering the traditional press, the most significant case of foreign ownership is that of *El Mundo*, which belongs to the Italian group RCS (Rizzoli).

B. The Broadcast Media
Main features:

- There is an increasing fragmentation of television markets;
- The audience leadership belongs to private companies, both in radio and in television;
- There is a significant decline of the national public broadcasting company, RTVE;
- The penetration of cable television is very low comparing to other analogical and digital television formulas;
- So far, the DAB radio broadcasting technology has totally failed.

Among all the media, television rules in Spain. Everyday it is seen by almost nine out of ten Spaniards. In addition, it is the medium to which citizens dedicate more time: 244 minutes per person daily in January 2006. Therefore, it is not surprising to find that it is also the medium that attracts more advertising investment: 2,876.6 million euro in 2005.

This amount means the 21 per cent of total advertising expenditure in mass media and other platforms, which reached to 13,709.6 million euro in 2005.

Nevertheless, according to EGM, since 2003 the television consumption has begun a slow decline. That year the penetration of this medium reached to 90.7 per cent of the Spaniards, but in 2004 went down to 89.6 per cent, and descended to 88.9 per cent in 2005, the latest data available at the moment of writing this report. The reasons of this slight decline still are not clear, but the experts suggest mainly two factors. First of all, the success of Internet and other interactive devices are causing a tenuous substitution effect between the television and the computer, especially among the young public. The second factor, much more evident so far, is the increasing fragmentation of the television market and the development of alternative forms of audio-visual consumption, such as the DVD.

The Spanish market of television is going through times of increasing fragmentation. In 2006, the television in Spain includes the following offers:

1. *Analogical television*. It is still the main way of watching television in Spain. There is a public entity of radio and television, RTVE, which broadcasts through two analogical channels of national scope: La Primera and La 2. In addition, other twelve similar public bodies, which correspond to a like number of autonomous communities, are grouped around the Federación de Organismos de Radio y Televisión Autonómicos (Federation of Autonomous Bodies of Radio and Television; FORTA). Each one of these regional public broadcasters have one or two analogical television channels. Regarding the analogical offer of private television companies, it consists of the networks Antena 3 (whose biggest shareholder is Grupo Planeta), Telecinco (owned by Mediaset, as main shareholder, and Vocento), Cuatro (Sogecable's channel, launched on 4 November 2005, as an analogical substitute of Canal+) and La Sexta (inaugurated on 27 March 2006, and owned by the Mexican company Televisa in partnership with a group of Spanish audio-visual producers). With regard to local television stations, there are not any precise data as those of the case of written press, since the map of local television and radio companies in Spain is very fragmentary. However, there is a census, published in October of 2002 by the AIMC, which counted 897 local analogical televisions distributed among 606 localities all over the country. According to the law, the transition from the analogical television to the digital system – so-called "analogical blackout" – will have to conclude in April of 2010, five years before the deadline established by the European Broadcasting Union (EBU). From that moment, the emissions of television in Spain would only be received by those citizens who have a decoder or an integrated digital television set (TVDI).

2. *Digital Terrestrial Television (DTT)*. The history of this type of television in Spain started in 1998, when the Government approved the first National Technical Plan of DTT. In 1999, the Government granted the first licence to Quiero TV, a platform which had a pay-TV business model and whose emissions began in May of 2000. Thus, Spain

became one of the first countries in Europe in setting up the DTT. Nevertheless, in June of 2002, Quiero TV had to close after a bankruptcy. As a result of this, the transition towards the digital television in Spain stagnated. In the meantime, in 2001 a second public set of concessions of DTT licences was awarded. These new licences went to TVE, Antena 3, Telecinco, Canal+ (owned by Sogecable, whose biggest shareholder is Prisa group) and to two new television companies: Veo TV (ruled by Unedisa and Recoletos media groups) and Net TV (Vocento). In 2005, the Spanish legislation gave a new impulse to the DTT distributing among these companies fourteen channels which were available after the closing of Quiero TV. After this distribution, from 30 November 2005, the Spanish households equipped with a decoder may receive twenty channels of DTT: five of RTVE, three of Antena 3, three of Telecinco, three of Sogecable, two of Veo TV, two of Net TV and two of La Sexta. The market of the DTT in Spain is completed with several autonomic and local channels, whose concession of licences is in process. At the end of 2005, it was estimated that there were some 850,000 decoders of DTT in Spain.

3. *Satellite television*. The satellite television in Spain appeared in 1997. In January of that year began the emissions of Canal Satélite Digital (CSD), platform of Sogecable. A few months later, those of Vía Digital, the platform owned by Telefónica, began as well. Both television platforms offered a set of contents based on several dozens of thematic channels of cinema, sports, news, documentaries, music and international channels, which were available for a monthly fee, plus a pay-per-view system for certain special contents, such as movies and football matches. After a harsh commercial struggle to catch subscribers during several years, in 2002 CSD was undoubtedly the leader of the market with 1.1 million users, whereas Vía Digital had some 700,000 users and was suffering important financial problems. This struggle concluded the 21 July 2003, with the takeover of Vía Digital by Sogecable, and the renaming of the new platform as Digital+. This platform had almost 2 million subscribers at the end of 2005.

4. *Cable television*. At the beginning of this decade, the landscape of cable in Spain included two national operators, Ono and Auna, as well as many small operators at a regional level. These companies were offering from the late 1990s integrated services of telephony, television and broadband connection to the Internet. Meanwhile, Telefónica, the most powerful and spread telecommunications company, discarded the cable and opted for the ADSL technology to provide its services of broadband connection to Internet and, more recently, television services. In order to face the difficulties due to their small market penetration, a process of concentration among the regional cable operators began in 2003. At the same time, Ono and Auna started a struggle to reach the monopoly on a national scale. This competition ended in 2005 with the takeover of Auna by Ono. This company also acquired most of the small regional operators. After this process, Ono has become in 2006 the unique cable operator in most of the Spanish regions, with the exception of Asturias (Telecable), Basque Country (Euskaltel) and Galicia (R).

As for the radio, it is a medium that lives a good economic moment in Spain. Nevertheless, this financial bonanza coincides with slight audience stagnation and with an exhaustion in radio formulas and programmes. In many cases, these formulas have not been reviewed since more than a decade ago.

According to the annual report *Guía de la Radio en España 2005*, there were 4,877 active radio stations at the end of 2004. Out of this total number 2,655 were legal radio stations, including both private and public, and another 1,803 stations – 45.5 per cent – were transmitting without a legal licence.

In 2005, the advertising investment in radio was of 609.9 million euro, a 12.9 per cent more than in 2004, and a 21.5 per cent more than in 2000. However, as stated above, such advertising improvement occurred simultaneously with slight audience stagnation. According to EGM, in 2005 the percentage of daily radio listeners was 55.5 of the population, whereas in 2004 it was of 56.8 per cent. In spite of this stagnation, the radio –specially, the AM – still has in Spain a very significant journalistic influence.

The Spanish radio market is clearly led by the private networks, although there is a broad public national network owned by Radio Nacional de España (National Radio of Spain; RNE), a division of RTVE. Furthermore, the regional public bodies of radio and television also have a great number of radio frequencies, mainly in FM. In addition to these networks, there is a great number of local radio stations in FM.

Considering the private radio networks, the clear leader is Cadena SER, owned by Prisa group. It is the one which counts with more radio stations (230). According to EGM of December 2005, Cadena SER had 4,996,000 daily listeners, a much bigger audience than the other three big private radio networks considered as a whole: COPE (a network which belongs to the Episcopal Conference; 2,316,000 daily listeners and 166 stations), Onda Cero (a network sold in 2003 by Telefónica to Grupo Planeta; 1,872,000 listeners and 164 stations) and Punto Radio (a network set up by Vocento in fall 2004; 523,000 listeners and 74 stations). There are many commercial radio networks devoted to music. The most successful one is Los 40, a pop music network, which also belongs to Prisa group.

On the other hand, there is a significant amount of public radio networks, mainly devoted to general information and cultural contents, which are offered by the national as well as the autonomous broadcast public companies. The most popular public channel, with 1,403,000 daily listeners in December of 2005, is Radio 1, an advertising free channel that belongs to RNE. RNE, which also has music and non-stop news channels, had 897 frequencies of FM and AM in 2005.

Digital radio (DAB), on the other hand, has been a great failure so far. On 10 March 2000, the Spanish government conceded ten licences of digital radio. This concession established that the emissions would begin when the operators covered at least the 20 per cent of national population, and these would have to happen in any case before the 30 June 2001. Moreover, the operators were urged to cover 50 per cent of the population by June of 2002, and 80 per cent in 2006. Nevertheless, these plans have been frustrated by a commercial failure of the digital radio. Very few people have bought digital radio devices and, considering this lack of audience, the broadcasters have done very little investment in that technology. Meanwhile, the cheaper Internet radio and, more recently, the *podcasting*, have gained great popularity as new digital alternatives for the analogical broadcasting in Spain.

C. The Internet Media
Main features:

- The rate of Internet use is low compared to the EU average;
- There is a great number of online publications, but only few of them are well developed, both in editorial and business terms;
- The online market leadership belongs to *Elmundo.es*, which is the second among the pay newspapers.

When many online publications have already reached their first decade of life, the penetration of Internet in Spain remains one of the lowest in Europe: only 34.4 per cent of the Spaniards were Internet users at the end of 2005, according to EGM. Since the 90s, different national governments have tried to improve these rates of use, but the results of these policies have been modest so far. Nevertheless, Internet continues its slow growth in Spain and, in fact, it was the only mass medium whose consumption grew in 2005. According to EGM, the written press, the radio and the television reduced to a greater or smaller extent their penetration that year, whereas Internet enjoyed a growth of 3.8 per cent compared to year 2004.

In spite of these modest numbers of penetration of Internet, the online media landscape in Spain is notably developed. According to a national online media census made by a research team of several universities, in January 2005 there were 1,274 active online publications. This meant approximately one online publication per 10,000 Internet users.

The most reliable audience study of Internet corresponds to the interactive division of OJD. According to this source, at the end of 2005 the leader was *Elmundo.es*, on line edition of the newspaper *El Mundo*, with 7.4 million unique users monthly. Far behind there were *Marca.com* (2nd), *As.com* (3rd) and a little further back *Sport.com* (7th), which are sport portals linked to other so many homonymous newspapers. Among the most popular online media there was also *Abc.es* (4th), the online edition of *ABC* newspaper. It is also worth mentioning the high audiences of *20Minutos.es* (5th), the online edition of the biggest circulation free newspaper, and *Libertad Digital* (6th), an online-only medium.

The lack of interest for the cable by Telefónica explained above resulted in, in 2004, only 6.1 per cent of the Spanish households having this type of technology. At the end of that year, according to the report *eEspaña 2005*, the country had 500,000 domestic cable users whereas the ADSL users were 2,583,000. Telefónica has continued with its strategy to promote the ADSL technology not only offering Internet connection, but also interactive television services. After testing the system since 2003, Telefónica started to offer for the whole country a new service of television by ADSL in 2005, called Imagenio. Since the beginning of 2006 other ADSL operators have also begun to offer similar services, such as Jazztelia TV by Jazztel telecommunications company.

D. News Agencies
Main features:

- The leadership belongs to the public news agency, EFE;
- There are many smaller and specialized news agencies, most of them regional.

Leaving aside the international agencies, the market of news agencies in Spain is led by Agencia EFE. This agency, founded in 1939 and nowadays present in more than 100 countries, is the worldwide leader in Spanish language, with a staff of 1,175 people in 2004. Just like RTVE, Agencia EFE is a public company owned by the State.

In addition to EFE, there are another 50 agencies of diverse characteristics. Some of them, such as Europa Press, the second biggest news agency, are of national scope and offer general services of text and audio-visual contents for all type of media. Other many agencies – in fact, most of them – work in a regional level or they are specialized in specific subjects or news formats.

2. State Policies
Main features:

- The Spanish Constitution protects as basic rights the freedom of expression, the clause of conscience and the professional secret;
- The broadcast media have specific laws for their contents and schedules of emission, inspired in the European regulations;
- The content providing through Internet is regulated by one specific law since 2002.

The Spanish Constitution, passed in 1978, recognizes and protects in its 20th article the freedom of expression as a fundamental right of all Spaniards. It also protects the right to the clause of conscience and the professional secret and forbids all kind of previous censorship. The freedom of expression is only limited, according to the Constitution, by the right to the honour, the privacy, the self-image and the protection of youth and childhood.

The Spanish legislative system does not have specific laws for printed media. However, the audio-visual media works under a regulatory system of administrative licences, granted by the national or the regional authorities, who are the owners of the spectrum. Recently, the Internet media have begun to be the object of specific legal norms as well.

The newspapers and magazines do not receive subsidies, except in the case of some publications written in minority languages. The VAT of publications is 16 per cent, like any other consumer product.

Broadcast media and, more particularly, television have a specific legislation that regulates their contents and schedules of emission, inspired in the European laws. These regulations also restrict the ownership of radio and television stations by foreign companies. Since 1st January 2006, digital televisions have a reduced VAT of 7 per cent.

3. Civil Society Organizations
Main features:

- Although there is a significant amount of media-related professional associations, the Spanish journalists have low rates of associationism;
- There are three big associations of media publishers: AEDE for newspapers, UTECA for commercial television, and AERC for commercial radio;
- There are not professional councils with authority to control media or journalists' mistakes, except two Audiovisual Councils on a regional level;
- Five newspapers have an ombudsman.

Associationism is little extended among the Spanish journalists. There are, however, 40 regional and local press associations and a handful of professional colleges, integrated altogether by more than 10,000 journalists. The press associations are grouped around the Federación de Asociaciones de la Prensa de España (Federation of Press Associations of Spain; FAPE), the main organ of representation, coordination and defence of the journalistic profession in Spain.

Along with these professional associations and colleges, there are half a dozen trade unions of journalists, of regional scope, which defend the improvement of the working conditions of journalists. These organizations are grouped in the Federación de Sindicatos de Periodistas (Federation of Journalist Trade Unions; FeSP) which, at the beginning of 2004, counted with more than 2,000 affiliated.

Publishers have also their own organizations. The most important are the following ones:

1. Asociación de Editores de Diarios Españoles (Spanish Newspaper Publisher Association; AEDE): an association founded in 1978 that is formed in 2006 by 82

associates, which altogether represent the 90 per cent of total newspaper circulation in the country.

2. Unión de Televisiones Comerciales Asociadas (Associated Commercial Television Union; UTECA): organization founded in 1998 to defend and to represent the common interests of the private televisions.

3. Asociación Española de Radiodifusión Comercial (Spanish Association of Commercial Radio Broadcasting; AERC). An organization that gathers 1,150 private radio stations that broadcast with legal licences.

There are no professional councils with authority to punish bad practices or abuses made by journalists. These cases are solved by conventional courts of justice. However, in the latest years two regional Audiovisual Councils have been created, in Catalonia (2000) and Navarre (2001), to look after the contents of the audio-visual sector and their respect to the laws. The Government also announces the creation of a new national Audiovisual Council before 2008. On the other hand, some newspapers have their own newsroom statutes, which work like deontological norms that only apply to those publications.

Five newspapers (*El País*, *La Vanguardia*, *La Voz de Galicia*, *El Correo Gallego* and *El Punt*) and one magazine (*PC Actual*) have an ombudsman. In addition, a news weekly magazine (*Tiempo*) has a council of readers.

There are also dozens of organizations of radio and television users, which are especially active in regional and local levels, but not so much at a national scale. Most of these associations are grouped around the Federación Ibérica de Asociaciones de Telespectadores y Radioyentes (Iberic Federation of Television and Radio Users; FIATYR).

Regarding the audience measurement systems, there are diverse companies that audit the circulation of printed, audio-visual and online media. These are the main ones:

1. Información y Control de Publicaciones (Information and Control of Publications; Introl): it is the main controller of the press circulation, both printed and online. Up until 2004, it was named Oficina de Justificación de la Difusión (Office of Circulation Justification; OJD).

2. Asociación para la Investigación de Medios de Comunicación (Association for the Mass Media Research; AIMC): it is an organization which gathers most of the advertising and communication companies. It publishes the EGM every quarter of the year, which is the main market study of media audiences in Spain.

3. Taylor Nelson Sofres (TNS): it measures the television audience rates daily.

4. Development Trends

Looking into the future of Spanish media, two deeply controversial questions arise in 2006: the legislative proceeding of a Statute of the Professional Journalist and the plans for the industrial rationalization of RTVE.

Regarding the Statute, the process began in April 2004, when Izquierda Unida, a leftist political party, presented to the Parliament a law proposal to regulate the journalistic profession in Spain. According to its defenders – mainly trade unions and professional colleges – such Statute proposal ensures more stable work conditions for the journalists. However, in accordance to its detractors – particularly media publishers and press associations – the Statute erodes the independence of journalists, since it reinforces the regulatory ability of the political powers. The opposition to the Statute has been more powerful so far, and as a consequence, since 2006, the Parliamentary proceeding of the Statute has been stopped.

On the other hand, the problem of RTVE is economic. It is a public entity, which belongs to the Sociedad Estatal de Participaciones Industriales (State Society of Industrial Participations, SEPI), with a staff of 9,369 people, according to data of 2004. Its income sources are the National Budget and advertising (around 260,000 spots per year). This company had a debt of more than 7,000 million euro at the end of 2005. Due to this economically unsustainable situation, the Government announced an industrial rationalization of the company, which included harsh measures such as to reduce the number of workers to 4,855 in the forthcoming years.

Apart from these two specific questions, the main problems that the Spanish media companies will have to face in the near future are more or less the same of the rest of Europe: the circulation decline of newspapers and magazines, the growing competence and diversification on radio and television markets and, above all, the impact of the digital technology on the media organizations.

References & Sources for Further Information

AEDE (2006), *Libro blanco de la prensa diaria 2007. Madrid: AEDE.*

Fundación Auna (2005), *eEspaña 2005. Informe anual sobre el desarrollo de la Sociedad de la Información en España*. Madrid: Fundación Auna.

Salaverría, R. (coord) (2005), *Cibermedios. El impacto de internet en los medios de comunicación en España*. Sevilla: Comunicación Social Ediciones y Publicaciones.

Segarra, L. (2005), *Guía de la radio en España 2005*. Barcelona: Guiadelaradio.com.

Telefónica (2005), *La Sociedad de la Información en España 2005*. Madrid: Telefónica I+D.

WAN (2004), *World Press Trends. 2004*. Paris: World Association of Newspapers (WAN).

Online resources

Agenda de la Comunicación (Communication Yearbook) <www.la-moncloa.es/ServiciosdePrensa/Agendadelacomunicacion/>.

Asociación para la Investigación de Medios de Comunicación (Association for the Mass Media Research; AIMC) <www.aimc.es>.

Infoadex <www.infoadex.es>.

Guía de la radio (Radio Guide) <www.guiadelaradio.com>.

Información y Control de Publicaciones (Information and Control of Publications; Introl) <www.introl.es>.

Instituto Nacional de Estadística (National Institute of Statistics; INE) <www.ine.es>.

THE TURKISH MEDIA LANDSCAPE

Ruken Barış

Turkey geographically bridges Europe and Asia with a territory of 773,473 sq km. Its population is around 74 million and the population density is 97 persons per sq km. Forty-seven per cent of the population is under the age of twenty-five.

There are many religious and ethnic groups in Turkey. Of these Kurds constitute the largest. The others are the Laz people, Arabs, Circassians, Bosnians, Roma people and ethnic Bulgarians. Armenian and Greek Orthodox Christians and Jews are officially recognized non-Muslim minorities. However, there are also Syrian Orthodox Christians and Yazidis. Alevi identity too is defined in cultural/religious terms as a distinctive form of Islam and permeates across ethnicities.

1. The Market

A. The Print Media
Main features:

- Dominancy of the national media and weak local media
- Monopolization of the media
- Nationalist rhetoric

Compared to its population the total number of readers (of any kind of newspaper & periodical), is considered to be low. On the other hand Turkey has a quite young reader population. The majority of readers are between 16 and 34.

The total number of newspapers currently circulating in Turkey is estimated to be 2,124. Forty of these are national, 23 regional and 2,061 local. Istanbul and Ankara, where the headquarters of all the national newspapers and broadcasting companies are placed, are the main media centres of Turkey. Among the national dailies (with their average daily sales) *Posta* (644.413), *Hürriyet* (522.880), *Zaman* (509.667), *Sabah* (445.679) and *Milliyet* (263.538) are the major ones.

Turkey's media is heavily dominated by large multimedia and multisectoral groups such as Doğan Group, Merkez Group, Çukurova Group, İhlas Group, Doğuş Group and Feza Group. All the major commercial channels and newspapers belong to these multimedia groups. Moreover, the distribution of the print media, too, is monopolized by Doğan Group's Yay-Sat and Merkez Group's MDP. Indeed, these large conglomerates are also active in many other sectors.

The Doğan Group, the largest and the most prominent of the media giants, owns a substantial part of the media in Turkey: The mainstream (indeed nationalist leaning) major dailies *Hürriyet* and *Milliyet*, "the biggest selling" boulevard daily *Posta*, the quality paper *Radikal* (40,665), which also has a Sunday supplement with in-depth political and cultural analysis, the sports daily *Fanatik* (260.650), the business daily *Referans* (8,906) and the English daily *Turkish Daily News* are all owned by the Doğan Group. (There are two more English dailies: *The New Anatolian* which is founded by the initial owner of the *Turkish Daily News* and very recently *Todays Zaman* which seem to follow the line of *Zaman*).

The other major player in the media business, the Merkez Group, too has a quite large share in the media market. The mainstream *Sabah* which competes with *Hürriyet*, the boulevard paper *Takvim* (288,018), the sports daily *Pas-Fotomaç* (221,558) and the most prominent regional newspaper, *Yeni Asır* (43,921), do belong to the Merkez Group. Some national dailies publish regional pages and/or supplements and this is claimed to be one of the reasons to undermine the independent regional press. In this sense, *Yeni Asır* is the only regional paper which can compete with the national press.

A smaller multimedia group Feza (allegedly directed by the Gülen movement) owns the liberal Islamic daily *Zaman*, which also has regional editions in Australia, the United States, Azerbaijan, Bulgaria, Germany, Romania, Kazakhstan, Kyrghizistan, Macedonia, and Turkmenistan. The Çukurova Group owns the daily *Akşam* (219,877), another daily *H.O Tercüman* (37,724) and the boulevard paper *Güneş* (136,449). Finally, the İhlas Group owns the nationalist and pro-state Islamic daily *Türkiye* (212,547).

Indeed, relatively new daily *Birgün* (12,826) was established by a group of journalists with the motto of *"for independent and unbiased journalism, a newspaper without boss"* as a reaction against this ownership patterns. The daily *Vatan* (244,598) is not owned by any multimedia group either and sporadically publishes articles and interviews about controversial issues of Turkey.

The liberal Islamic *Yeni Şafak* (108,605) is known for its more balanced journalism while the Islamic *A. Vakit* (67,688) is radical and sensationalist in content and has been prosecuted several times. *Milli Gazete* (38,021) is another Islamic daily known to be the voice of "Milli Görüş" which has been the ideology of a certain Islamic political tradition in Turkey aiming at substantial restructuring of the state in compliance with the maxims of Islam. This vision has been promoted by the group led by Necmettin Erbakan and entered into the politics with National Salvation Party in the 1970s and with Welfare Party during the 1990s. "Milli Görüş" is considered to be well organized in Europe.

Interestingly, the heavy reliance on subscription-based sales seems to be a common feature of liberal Islamic and pro-Islamic newspapers: approximately 92 per cent of *Zaman*, 94 per cent of *Türkiye*, 89 per cent of *Milli Gazete* sales is due to subscription. Remarkably, liberal Islamic press (*Yeni Şafak* and *Zaman*) employs liberal and left-wing columnists, thus, offers a broader perspective especially about the controversial issues.

D.B. Tercüman (98,505) is a nationalist daily which was in the past popular among the nationalist right-wingers. *Cumhuriyet* (58,735) which is not entirely owned by any multimedia group and once seen as the newspaper of the left-wing in Turkey is now considered as the voice of the staunch Kemalists and nationalist leaning pro-status quo groups. *Özgür Gündem* (9,126) is a distinct paper which has been considered (or accused) to be the voice of the Kurdish population of Turkey and subjected to harsh prosecutions.

The interest for the magazines and periodicals in Turkey is also low compared to the size of the population. However, the magazines (which are also owned by multimedia groups) succeeded in increasing their sales tenfold from around 10 thousand up to 100 thousand due largely to the substantial reduction in their prices. The biggest selling ones are the weekly "colourful and light" news magazines *Yeni Aktüel* and *Tempo* with approximately 100 thousand sales. The other periodical, *Haftalık*, has the average circulation of 75 thousand and finally the liberal Islamic *Aksiyon* has a quite steady rate of 20 thousand. Weekly economy magazines *Tek Borsa* and *Ekonomist* have around 10 thousand sales. The celebrity magazines have a total weekly circulation of 110 thousand copies while the automobile magazines circulate over 20 thousand.

There are also newspapers of the officially recognized minorities. IHO and Apoyevmatini are published by Greeks; Agos, Jamanak and Nor Marmara by Armenians and Şalom by the Jewish community. These newspapers are struggling to maintain their existence.

B. The Broadcast Media
Main features:

- Average time spent viewing TV is very high
- Monolithic content despite large number of TV channels
- Small advertising market

■ The monopolization of the media
■ The digitalization process to be completed in 2009

Indeed, the television is the main information and entertainment source in Turkey. Radio Television Supreme Council's (RTÜK) first ever TV viewing survey (covering two weeks' time) shows that average daily time spent watching television (per person) is 5.09 hours in the weekdays and 5.15 hours in the weekends.

The first broadcasting company in Turkey, *Turkish Radio and Television Corporation (TRT)*, was established in 1964 by the state and it had enjoyed the monopoly in broadcasting (granted by law which prohibited private TV and radio channels) as the public (i.e. state owned) broadcaster for more than twenty years. However, in 1990 the first private commercial TV channel, *STAR 1*, began broadcasting via satellite from Germany (thus, in theory, not breaching the law which banned broadcasting *from* Turkey by private agents). This has paved the way for some 100 local commercial TV channels and 500 local radio channels which began operating subsequently without licences. Consequently, the broadcasting scene faced radical changes due to this quasi–illegal, but *de facto*, situation. Finally, on August 1993, the parliament lifted the monopoly on TV and radio broadcasting by amending the related article of the Constitution. Now there are 24 national, 16 regional and 215 local television stations.

The public broadcaster TRT has four national television channels: *TRT 1* (general), *TRT 2* (culture and art), *TRT 3* (youth channel with sports and music programmes and broadcasts live from the Turkish National Grand Assembly at specific hours) and *TRT 4* (education). *TRT* has also a regional channel, *TRT-GAP*, for the south–eastern region of Turkey and two international channels: *TRT-INT* for Europe, USA and Australia and *TRT-AVRASYA* for Middle Asia and Caucasus.

The multimedia groups again are the main actors in the private broadcasting market: Doğan Group owns *Kanal D*, *Star TV* and *CNN-Türk*; *Merkez* Group owns *ATV*; Çukurova Group owns *Show TV* and *Sky-Türk*; Doğuş Group owns *NTV* and Feza Group owns *Samanyolu TV*. İhlas group owns TGRT (but in September 2006 News Netherlands Company owned by Rupert Murdoch bought 51 per cent share of this channel).

The most popular private television channels (*ATV*, *Kanal D*, *Show TV*, *Star TV* and *TGRT*) and, to a certain degree, *TRT 1* offer a quite similar content comprising entertainment, news, football and locally made dramas and sitcoms. *Samanyolu* and *Kanal 7*, the channels with liberal Islamic orientation, too, attract considerable attention. *TV 8* distinguishes itself with more quality programmes comprising unusual political debates, music and news. *Roj TV*, which broadcasts in Kurdish from abroad via satellite, is quite popular among the Kurdish populated areas despite the official resentment. There are also thematic TV channels in Turkey: the *NTV*, *CNN-Türk* (a joint venture with CNN International), *Habertürk*, *Sky Türk* and *TGRT Haber* are 24–hour news channels. *Kral*

TV and *Number One TV* are music channels which broadcast, rank and promote music clips and in this way, to a certain extent, manipulate the music market in Turkey.

On cable there are approximately 60 TV channels including *BBC World*, *BBC Prime*, *CNN*, *TV5*, *RTL*, *MTV*, *Eurosport*, *National Geography* and *Discovery*. However, after the completion of the digitalization process the number of TV channels available on cable is expected to reach 300.

Most of the TV channels quickly imitate each other's programmes which proved to attract viewers' attention and create quite a monolithic understanding of television broadcasting. Consequently the apparent lack of diversity and creativity in programme-making undermines the quality of the audio-visual media. On the other hand the recent expansion of the demand for locally made productions created a market for independent production companies with a high degree of technical sophistication.

The number of private radio channels currently broadcasting in Turkey is around 1,100 and 100 of them are also available on cable. Of these 36 are national, 102 are regional and 950 are local radio stations. *TRT* has four national radio channels: *Radyo 1* (general), *Radyo 2* (*TRT-FM*) (native classical, folk and pop music), *Radyo 3* (primarily classical music and also jazz, polyphonic and western pop music, broadcasts news in English, French and German) and *Radyo 4* (pop music). *TRT*'s international radio service *Türkiye'nin Sesi/The Voice of Turkey* broadcasts in 26 languages. *TRT* also has ten regional radio stations. Besides the radio stations owned by the multimedia groups there are also many independent radio stations. Private radio stations mostly offer music programmes. The most popular ones are *Kral FM* (Turkish pop music), *Süper FM* (western pop music), *Metro FM* (western pop music), *Power Türk* (Turkish pop music) and *Best FM* (Turkish pop music).

Television's share in the advertising market (of around 1 billion dollars) is expanding. In 2005 it reached to 56 per cent of the market while written press (36%) and radio (3%) saw the decline in their revenues. However, the advertising market in Turkey is considered to be relatively small compared to the number of actors in the broadcasting scene and that makes it difficult for small entrepreneurs to enter the broadcasting market or to survive. The fact that most of the commercial broadcasters function under media conglomerates (which have stakes in other sectors) renders the media independency rather dubious. Characteristically, the major media groups also get the largest share from the advertising revenues.

According to RTÜK's action plan the switch-over from analogue to digital in terrestrial broadcasting will begin in 2007 and it is planned to be completed at the end of 2009. The trial services have already been launched by TRT in Ankara, Istanbul and Izmir in February 2006. RTÜK officials mention that the switch-over will be gradual because of the lack of free frequency spectrums to launch digital broadcasts. The analogue broadcasting will continue together with digital broadcasting till the digital penetration reaches over 80 per cent. The switch-over in satellite has been completed and the process on cable is still ongoing. Since the major channels are also available terrestrially, the penetration of satellite and cable TV is low. The Digiturk is the main digital platform provider (on satellite) and it has a subscriber base of over 1 million.

C. The Internet Media
Main features:

- Internet penetration is low, but increasing steadily
- Large numbers of online news portals and magazines but yet lack of alternative news-making

The Internet penetration in Turkey is relatively low, but the number of the Internet users has increased to 16 million as of September 2006 showing a penetration of 21.4 per cent which was only 7.5 per cent in 2004 and 13.9 per cent in 2005. By the end of 2008 the rate is expected to reach 29 per cent. Turk Telekom is the leading ADSL provider in Turkey. (After its privatization in 2005, 55 per cent of its shares were sold to Oger Telecoms.) The number of ADSL subscribers is around 3 million as of March 2007. The average age of Internet users is 28 and 83 per cent of them is male. The vast majority of the users (80%) do have university education. The access to Internet is mostly common at Internet cafés and workplaces.

All the national newspapers and TV channels have Web editions updated throughout the day, some of these are also in English. There are numerous news portals and Internet magazines. Despite the low Internet penetration the interest in online media is considered to be high. Yet it is hard to talk about alternative news-making. Due to the heavy costs of having correspondents, most of the news is almost "copy-pasted" from the news agencies and the traditional media. Only few of the online media employ journalists.

D. News Agencies
Main feature:

- The major news agencies belong to the multimedia groups;
- Anadolu Ajansı (AA), Doğan Haber Ajansı (DHA), İhlas Haber Ajansı (İHA), Cihan Haber Ajansı (CİHA) and ANKA are the most prominent news agencies in Turkey;
- DHA, İHA and CİHA have high-technical facilities due to their belonging to affluent multimedia groups.

AA (Anadolu Ajansı) is the primary source for the press in Turkey. It was founded by Mustafa Kemal Atatürk in 1920 to promote the independence war of the Turkish Republic. It is the 'official' news agency of Turkey (48 per cent of its shares belong to the treasury). AA has 28 offices in Turkey and 22 offices abroad and provides approximately 800 news and 200 photos to its subscribers each day.

Independent news agency ANKA, founded in 1972, too, has daily news and photograph services: it provides a daily economic bulletin in Turkish and a weekly one in English.

DHA is owned by Doğan Group and primarily provides news services for the newspapers, TV and radio stations which belong to the Doğan Group.

Ihlas Group's news agency İHA has 145 offices in Turkey and abroad. It also covers Europe, Middle East, Arabian Peninsula and Central Asia and provides news services to European, American and Arabic TV channels. İHA services in English and Arabic too.

CİHA belongs to the Feza Group and it is well organized on a local level in Turkey. CİHAN has offices in 31 countries including Gaza, Baghdad, Erbil and Kabul and gives service to 22 foreign media organizations in Arabic language.

Another independent agency, Dicle Haber Ajansı (DIHA), which was established in 2002, provides services in Turkish, English and Kurdish. Other than these native agencies, there are also foreign news agencies operating in Turkey, like Reuters.

2. State Policies
Main features:

■ Problematic allocation of frequencies and granting broadcasting licences
■ Restrictive and vague broadcasting law and its harsh implementation

After the termination of the state monopoly over broadcasting in August 1993, Radio Television Supreme Council (RTÜK) was established by the Radio and Television Law (law 3984) in April 1994 in order to regulate the private broadcasting and to control the compliance of the broadcasts with the legal framework. RTÜK was made responsible for assigning frequencies and issuing broadcasting permits and licences to private companies, and all television and radio broadcasters were placed under its supervision.

RTÜK is granted with the authority of giving penalties (for breaching the legal framework) to the broadcasters, which may range from warning to the suspension of the TV and radio channels. However the RTÜK does not have the authority on *TRT* because the public broadcaster is subject to a separate law (no 2954).

To speed up the process of allocating the frequencies and to end the chaos in an unregulated broadcasting market, the Communications High Council HYK (founded in 1983 to approve communication policies) and Telecommunication Authority TK (established in 2000 to regulate and control the telecommunication sector) have been rendered the partners of RTÜK in 2002. The duty of frequency planning is transferred to the TK. However, the process of auctioning the frequencies by RTÜK has been unsuccessful mainly due to discordance among these regulatory bodies and the pressure of the media conglomerates. Governments did not try to hasten the process in fear of retaliation by the media giants. Another reason preventing the commencement of frequency auctions was the intervention of the MGK (National Security Council) to oblige broadcasters to acquire a national security clearance document which would supposedly prevent establishment of religious TV channels. Consequently, acquiring a national security document has become mandatory for all the TV channels. Today the frequency distribution continues to be a problem and all the terrestrial radio and television stations still operate without licences.

RTÜK's decisions of penalizing the broadcasters so as to implement the Radio and Television law have been criticized domestically and internationally. Though broadcasting law was softened by an amendment in May 2002 so that in case of violation of broadcasting standards which are listed in the Radio and Television Law, RTÜK would suspend the programme instead of suspending the entire TV or radio channel. These compulsory broadcasting standards are regarded to be too comprehensive and yet very vague including statements such as "not violating the national and moral values of the community and the Turkish family structure", "not undermining the state and its independence and the undisputable unity of the country with its people" and "not undermining the ideals and reforms of Atatürk". The broadcasters also complain that the Council's interpretation of the law has been extremely severe and subjective, and the sanctions implied by RTÜK have been anti-democratic and disproportional. Moreover, the composition of the Council (i.e. the political position of the appointed members) is another controversial issue which is considered to be profoundly influenced by the political considerations of governments and, thus, substantially undermining the Council's claim of impartiality.

In 2004 and 2005, "having negative effect on children" has been the most common reason for RTÜK to issue penalties to media companies. In 2005, twenty national television channels were asked defence statements, 33 received warnings, programmes in nine television channels were suspended and four were fined. In the same period RTÜK forced Adana Radyo Dünya off the air for 30 days for "disseminating separatist propaganda" and "inciting hatred and enmity" by promoting a book. RTÜK also suspended two local television channels in Malatya and Diyarbakır for violating article 4 of the RTÜK Law 3984: "undermining the state and its independence".

Commercial TV channels are also obliged by the law to devote 15 per cent of their weekly broadcasting time to education- and culture-related programmes.

On the other hand the public broadcaster TRT has always been criticized for not being objective and impartial because of its permanent endorsement of the official position of the state and/or government in almost any subject. This attitude has created a broadcasting policy which is marked by careful avoidance from any engagement with the controversial issues. The disturbance of democracy by three military coups in Turkey (1960, 1971 and 1980) has radically affected the structure and the functions of TRT. After the first coup d'état in 1960, TRT was established and given autonomy in compliance with the expectations of more democracy. After the second coup d'état in 1971, TRT's autonomy was largely lifted. Finally, the new notorious constitution prepared during the military government of the third coup d'état paved the way for a new law in which TRT's autonomy was curtailed further. Although in 1993 its autonomy was to a certain extent restored, TRT is still considered to be not capable of fulfilling the function of a public broadcaster, for it fails (or chose not) to reflect the diversity of thought in the country. Moreover, TRT's staff, as public employees, has to act in accordance with the mandate of protecting the priorities of the state as mentioned in the article 9 of the Radio and Television Law.

The audience of TRT fell dramatically after the establishment of the private channels. Consequently it has lost most of its share in the advertising market and, thus, begun to rely increasingly on the state expenditure.

3. Civil Society Organizations
Main features:

- A weak trade union undermined by the pressure of the media owners and journalists' fear of dismissal
- There are many associations but the unionization of the media sector is very low
- The interests of the multisectoral media groups jeopardizing the impartiality of the media
- Voluntary ombudsman mechanism

Most of the media employees are working under harsh conditions without having job security and social security as they are forced to work outside the legislation regulating the rights of journalists (known as the law 212) and without permanent contracts. Consequentially, during the economic crisis in 2001, approximately 5,000 media workers have lost their jobs. Media workers who are not provided a contract under the law 212 cannot obtain a press card and cannot become a member of Turkish Journalists Union (Türkiye Gazeteciler Sendikası, TGS) which is the only trade union that has the authority to negotiate collective agreements for journalists. The influence of TGS has diminished considerably at the beginning of 1990s due to the pressure of the media owners. Most of the media workers are cautious about the union membership due to fear of employer retaliation which may cause dismissal.

Although the unionization level is very low there are many journalist associations all around the country. Some of the important journalist associations in Turkey are as follows: Türkiye Gazeteciler Cemiyeti (Journalists Association of Turkey), Türkiye Gazeteciler Federasyonu (Federation of Journalists), Çağdaş Gazeteciler Derneği (Progressive Journalists Association), Ekonomi Muhabirleri Derneği (Association of Economy Reporters), Foto Muhabirleri Derneği (Association of Photo Reporters) and Parlamento Muhabirleri Derneği (Association of Parliamentary Reporters).

According to the statistics of the Ministry of Labour and Social Security (Labour Statistics 17.01. 2006 *Resmi Gazete/The Official Journal of the Republic of Turkey*): There are 14,439 persons registered as journalists with permanent contracts. Of these, 3,847 are affiliated with Türkiye Gazeteciler Sendikası (TGS) and 370 are members of the other union MEDYA-SEN. Due to the threshold conditions, only Türkiye Gazeteciler Sendikası is granted with the right to bargain collectively.

Some other media associations are Televizyon Yayıncıları Derneği (Association of Television Broadcasters), Anadolu Gazete Radyo ve Televizyon Yayıncıları Birliği (Union of Anatolian Newspaper, Radio and Television Publishers and Broadcasters), Televizyon Yayıncıları Birliği (Union of Television Broadcasters), Yayıncılar Birliği (Turkish Publishers' Association).

There are also associations in the advertising sector: Turkish Association of Advertising Agencies (TAAA) (Reklamcılar Derneği), Association of Advertisers (Reklamverenler Derneği) and IAA Turkey (International Advertising Association).

The characteristic feature of the heavily monopolized media landscape of Turkey is the prominence of countrywide print and audio-visual media with highly nationalistic rhetoric and weak regional/local media suffering severely from financial problems. Accordingly, addressing certain issues (such as the position of the Army, Cyprus, Kurdish and Armenian issues) without complying with the official position of the state is considered almost to be tantamount to a kind of heresy across the media.

According to a recent survey done by AC Nielsen the media in its entirety is the least trusted institution in the country. Indeed, the monopolization of the media "business" as depicted by the ownership patterns, inevitably raises doubts as to the objectivity and independence of the journalists and the quality of journalism in Turkey. All the multimedia groups are, in fact, large conglomerates and their activities expand to other sectors beyond media, including tourism, finance, automotive industry, construction and banking. It is not unusual to hear the claims that certain news was deliberately ignored or inflated for sake of protecting or furthering multimedia groups' interests in other sectors. Although RTÜK, in theory, may enforce media groups to sell their shares in order to prevent monopolization, under current conditions (in which the legal definition of media monopoly remains highly ambiguous and all the media companies operate without licences) there is no efficient way to alter the increasing concentration of media in few hands by using any legal means.

In this environment journalism ethics are tried to be promoted by two documents: the "Declaration of Rights and Responsibilities" by Journalists Association of Turkey (1998) and the "Code of Professional Ethics of the Press" by the Press Council (1989).

In September 2006 a voluntary ombudsman mechanism has been introduced by RTÜK. Accordingly, TV channels may have this self-monitoring mechanism by establishing ombudsman branches but they are not legally obliged. The ombudsman should be an individual with a university degree and with a minimum seven years of working experience in the media. S/he will evaluate the calls, e-mails and letters from the viewers and prepare a monthly report. The television ombudsman mechanism will first start in the national TV stations then will also be established in the local media. Some dailies like, *Milliyet*, *Sabah*, *Hürriyet*, *Vatan*, *Yeni Şafak*, *Akşam* and *Zaman* also have an ombudsman. However, this self-regulatory mechanism is still very controversial since ombudsmen are not independent but employees of these media institutions some with high-ranking positions.

Another development is BİA, a project initiated in 2003 and funded mainly by the European Union's Initiative for Democracy and Human Rights. The purpose of the project is establishing a countrywide network in Turkey for monitoring and covering media freedom and independent journalism. BİA monitors and reports violations of freedom of expression, monitors the newspapers' coverage about human rights, women's and children's rights issues and the functioning of the media in terms of media ethics. Within the framework of the project legal assistance is given to the local media and the findings of the monitoring are published six monthly and annual reports of "Violations against Local Media". The project connects more than 130 local media to promote co-operation. Its news and information network, Bianet (www.bianet.org), provides daily coverage of the issues that are ignored in the mainstream media especially about human rights, gender rights, minority rights and children's rights issues. Bianet has also an English version.

In the advertising sector Advertising Self-Regulatory Board (Reklam Özdenetim Kurulu) established by the members of Advertisers Association, TAAA and the media institutions in order to monitor the advertising practices.

TİAK (Television Audience Research Committee), BİAK (Press Research Committee) and RİAK (Radio Audience Research Committee) are established to organize and monitor the research about the broadcasting and the print media.

4. Development Trends
Main features:

- EU pressure for further democratization
- Prosecution of journalists
- Broadcasting in minority languages

Turkey's candidacy to the EU is the main driving force behind the recent democratization process in Turkey which also means more freedom for the media. As a part of the policy of fulfilling the EU membership requirements the legal reforms were carried out in Turkey: Prison sentences for journalism-related offences were replaced with heavy fines. Penalties of banning newspapers and the distribution of the newspapers and shutting down the media outlets were repealed.

However, despite these improvements, 157 journalists, publishers and human rights activists were prosecuted in 2005 for expressing their ideas. Twenty-nine of them were charged with "insulting the Turkish identity, the Republic and the institutions of the State" while seventeen journalists commenting on the human rights issues were accused of "influencing the court decision" and "attempting to influence the fair trial". Twelve journalist-writers were charged with "disseminating terrorist propaganda" based on the TCK (Turkish Penal Code) or the anti-Terrorism Law. Fifteen journalists/human rights activists were charged with "inciting hatred and enmity or humiliation" based on TCK. In 2006, the editor of the Armenian weekly Agos, Hrant Dink, was sentenced to a six-month suspended imprisonment while five journalists from pro-Kurdish media were arrested for reporting about the release of a soldier by PKK. The total fine on media in 2005 has amounted to 1,120,000 US dollars.

Indeed the new penal code enacted on June 2005 introduced additional constraints on media. According to the article 305, endangering 'basic national interests' will be subject to imprisonment from three to ten years. Similarly, article 301 envisages imprisonment from six months to three years for those who "insult Turkishness". Although the EU has increased its pressure for the abolishment or amendment of the article 301 of the penal code which is quite often invoked to prosecute journalists, activists and authors, the rising tide of aggressive nationalism in Turkey renders any radical change in this law unlikely. In fact, the assassination of Hrant Dink, the chief editor of the Armenian newspaper Agos in January 2007, has been the result of his prosecution from the article 301. Despite large-scale protests after the assassination against the article 301, politicians (both in "left" and right wing) revealed their unwillingness to repeal this article in fear of losing nationalist votes in upcoming elections.

Broadcasting in languages other than Turkish was another requirement of the EU to be fulfilled by Turkey before the commencement of the membership negotiations. Initially the task of broadcasting in Arabic, Bosnian, Circassian and in Kurdish dialects of Kirmançi and Zaza was given to the public broadcaster *TRT* and, after long debates on the issue, the broadcast of TRT started in June 2004. The programmes in native languages would be broadcasted within strict time restraints: they would not exceed a total of 4 hours per week and 45 minutes per day while radio broadcasts are allowed for 5 hours per week and 60 minutes per day. On 23 March 2006, two private TV channels, *Gün TV* and *Söz TV*, in Diyarbakır, and a radio channel, *Şanlıurfa Medya FM*, in Şanlıurfa, began broadcasting in Kurdish after a long-awaited RTÜK permission.

References & Sources for Further Information

Minority Rights Group International, July2004: "Minorities in Turkey".

2005 – Zenith Optimedia: "Medya ve Reklam Dünyasına Genel Bakış".

RTÜK 2006: "Televizyon İzleme Eğilimleri Araştırması".

Open Society Institute 2005 & EUMAP & NMP: "Television across Europe: regulation, policy and independence – Turkey".

IDC-Turkey/A&G Research.

Internet world stats.

www.byegm.gov.tr/TURKBASINI/turkishpress.htm.

Ministry of Labour and Social Security (Labour Statistics).

Resmi Gazete/The Official Journal of the Republic of Turkey).

"The Call to Media Owners "by Türkiye Gazeteciler Sendikası (TGS):
www.tgs.com.tr or www.ifj.org/docs/Turkey03062004.doc.

The RTÜK law (no 3984).

BIA (The Countrywide Network for Monitoring and Covering Media Freedom and Independent Journalism in Turkey) Media Monitoring Desk: report 2005.

Reporters Without Borders: Turkey – 2005, 2006 Annual reports.

TRT website: www.trt.net.tr/wwwtrt/tarihce.aspx.

AC Nielsen, July 2006: "Medya Güven Araştırması".

L. Doğan Tılıç, "2000'ler Türkiye'sinde Gazetecilik ve Medyayı Anlamak" (2001).

Ayşe Buğra, "State and Business in Modern Turkey: A Comparative Study" (1994).

Media Ownership Structure in Turkey by L. Doğan Tılıç.

Çağdaş Gazeteciler Derneği; www.cgd.org.tr.

Note: Detailed references used in the text can be requested from the author.

THE EASTERN EUROPEAN/POST-COMMUNIST MEDIA MODEL COUNTRIES

INTRODUCTION

Karol Jakubowicz

The collapse of the communist system led to a debate among media policy-makers and scholars as to the direction and expected final outcome of that process. Some assumed straight transplantation of generalized 'Western' models. Others argued that media change was an open-ended process and that the "idealized Western European model" had either vanished or become inaccessible (Sukosd and Bajomi-Lazar 2003; Mungiu-Pippidi 2003).

Had Hallin and Mancini's (2004) book come out earlier, it would have been clearer that though the process may be open-ended, the range of options is not limitless. Hallin and Mancini confirm that media systems are shaped by the socio-political and cultural features of their countries, including notably the degree of democratic consolidation and the level of actual or potential societal conflict. In other words, they display a high degree of what we may call "systemic parallelism". We will take this as our point of departure in the following analysis. The goal is to see whether Central and Eastern European media systems can be compared to any of Hallin and Mancini's systems.

The term "post-communist countries" covers nations in the following regions: Central Europe (Poland, the Czech Republic, Slovakia, Hungary, Slovenia and the Baltic States – Estonia, Lithuania and Latvia); eastern Balkans (Romania, Bulgaria); western Balkans (Croatia, Bosnia-Herzegovina, Serbia, Montenegro, Macedonia and Albania); European CIS countries: Russia, Ukraine, Belarus, Moldova); south Caucasus countries: (Armenia, Azerbaijan, Georgia); Central Asia (Kazakhstan, Kyrgyzstan, Tajikistan, Turkmenistan and Uzbekistan) and Mongolia. They differ widely in many respects (history, culture, religion, level of development) and practically the only thing many of them have in common is the legacy of the communist system.

Some of these countries have few prospects of progress towards a democratic system (see Carothers 2002; Krastev 2006). However, there are also examples of relatively encouraging post-communist democratization, though what has been achieved so far are hybrid forms of democracy, including formal democracy; elite democracy; partitocrazia; or a system of a tyrannical majority (Cichosz 2006). In these cases, parallels with systems identified by Hallin and Mancini may, perhaps, be sought given that they identify precisely political system development as the main factor affecting the shape of the media system, including especially the fact of early or late democratization (and by the same token the degree of consolidation of democracy achieved in a particular country).

Sitter (2005) discusses two approaches to comparative analysis of political systems in Western and Eastern Europe:

- Looking at similarities with earlier developments in Western Europe. Perhaps the most obvious comparison, says Sitter, is to the Mediterranean transitions to democracy in the 1970s, or even post-war democratisation in Germany and Italy;
- East European exceptionalism.

We would agree with Sitter that developments in the region since 1989 have been less 'exceptional' than is sometimes argued. Also with Dryzek and Holmes (2002: 256) who state that "differences between at least the more democratized CEE states and the West look to be of degree rather than kind" (see also Sukosd and Bajomi-Lazar 2003).

Sitter's suggestion that comparison of the situation in post-communist countries with the Mediterranean ones is potentially most fruitful seems to be supported by Splichal's (1994, 2004) use of the phrase "Italianization of the media" to describe the process of media change in post-communist countries.

Like the countries with the "Mediterranean" media system, post-communist countries are characterized by late democratization and incomplete, or (in some cases) little advanced, modernization and weak rational-legal authority combined in many cases with a *dirigiste* state (for analyses of the situation in Mediterranean countries, also in terms of their media systems, see, e.g., Statham 1996; Marletti and Roncaloro 2000; Papatheodorou, Machin 2003; Mancini 2000; Hallin, Papathanassopoulos 2002). Like their southern European counterparts, they also display features of "state paternalism" or indeed "political clientelism", as well as *panpoliticismo*, i.e. a situation when politics pervades and influences many social systems, economics, the judicial system and, indeed, the media; the development of liberal institutions is delayed; and there is a political culture favouring a strong role of the state and control of the media by political elites.

Another shared feature is highly tumultuous political life. Discontinuous social change (rapid change, broad in scale) generally has pathological consequences, generating especially intense conflicts (Eckstein 2001). This cannot but affect the media system.

Theorists of post-communist transformation often call it an "imitative" or "mimetic" process. It can be seen to contain two forms of imitation:

- Deliberate copying of Western European arrangements
- Natural repetition or replication of the same processes in comparable circumstances, when more or less the same factors and forces impact on the situation as in other countries

Where post-communist countries sought to approximate western arrangements, many policy or legislative measures in the media field represented the first form of imitation. Later, as the new political systems and market forces began to affect media systems, imitation increasingly began to take the second form.

The Newspaper Industry
Change in the print media after 1989 involved three main process: the increase in the number of titles, growth in the number of companies and the emergence of new market segments (Gulyás 1999). In most post-communist countries, demonopolization of the media was followed by a veritable flood of new print media, many of them published by new political parties. Demand for party newspapers proved to be non-existent, however, and soon this category began to disappear.

With time, consolidation of the market, much of it foreign controlled in many post-communist countries, went hand in hand with its segmentation, especially the appearance of segments which had previously been underdeveloped or non-existent, such as tabloid newspapers, hobby magazines, women's and fashion magazines and so on. At the same time, democratization of the market also meant that local and community newspapers, NGO publications and minority newspapers made their appearance.

Chorazki (1999) has identified the following sequence of events with reference to local and sub-local dailies and periodicals in Poland:

- 1988–1991 – a heroic period of civic and public service involved in spearheading the process of change;
- 1992–1993 – a period of party political involvement, as the media scene is politicized and new political parties win control of many media;
- From 1994 onward – a period of market-driven changes and consolidation (with two main trends observable since 1997: on the one hand, the influx of foreign capital into the local and sub-local media market, and on the other – the consolidation of strong Polish publishers of regional chains of dailies and periodicals of this nature).

Similar processes have taken place in the newspaper industries in all the countries under consideration in this volume. Tabloidization, falling circulations and the survival of only limited numbers of quality newspaper now appear to be the norm in all of them.

Political Parallelism

Immature democracies produce either "politics-over-broadcasting" or "politics-in-broadcasting" systems. This is very much the case in post-communist countries. Political parallelism is high in their media systems, especially in public service broadcasting. This is reflected first of all in the manner of appointing members of broadcasting regulatory authorities. Two methods are most prevalent:

- Appointment by legislative: "the Central European model" (Slovenia, Slovakia, Bulgaria, Czech Republic, Estonia)
- Appointment by both executive and legislative: "the French model," adopted in Poland, Romania, Bulgaria and the Ukraine

In both cases, care is usually taken to ensure direct reflection of the balance of political forces in Parliament in the composition of the regulatory body.

Another area where political parallelism is evident is the composition of governing bodies of public service broadcasters. Irrespective of the method of their appointment, these bodies are usually an extension of the ruling party or coalition of the day. True, in Poland there have been examples of "cohabitation" between governments and leaderships of public service television of different political persuasions, but the change of the broadcasting law in 2005 – eliminating staggered terms for members of the National Broadcasting Council (the regulatory body) – will seriously reduce the likelihood of this happening again. It is the Council which appoints the Supervisory Councils of the nineteen public service broadcasters that in their turn appoint Boards of Management. In 2006, this ensured direct political parallelism between the composition of Parliament, the National Broadcasting Council and supervisory and governing bodies of public service broadcasters, setting in train changes in managerial positions according to the same principle.

Croatia and Slovenia provide other examples of regression into political parallelism from legal and institutional solutions which were originally designed to counteract it. In Croatia, the 2001 law on Croatian Radio-Television, the public service broadcasting (which provided for its Broadcasting Council to be made up mostly of people designated directly by civil society organizations) was replaced with a new law in 2003 in which the Broadcasting Council is appointed directly by Parliament. In 2004, Croatian public television HRT selected new television leadership from among politically unaffiliated professionals. This is good news, but the possibility of reversion to political appointments always remains. The Slovenian broadcasting law was amended in 2005, so that the Programme Council of Radio-Television Slovenia would be appointed by Parliament and would have the power to appoint all top and middle-level managers, down to the heads of editorial departments.

Surprisingly, Estonia – where the authorities have refrained from interfering with the media – is reported here to be proceeding with a similar change of the broadcasting law.

In Hungary, the Presidential Bodies of the Boards of Trustees of public service broadcasters are to have an equal number of members from both the ruling coalition and the opposition, so as to prevent any political party from exercising control. However, opposition parties have often declined to fill "their" seats, leaving public service radio and television in the hands of the ruling majority – as it is the Boards of Trustees which appoint the Directors General of the two broadcasters.

As reported in this volume, political partisanship extends also to commercial media, both broadcast and print, both caused by profound divisions and high political tension within Hungarian society and tending to exacerbate those divisions.

Another example of this situation is Poland, where highly divisive policies of the post-2005 government have encouraged many media outlets to take a stand either for or against them and to join the political fray as players rather than observers.

Media partisanship also seems to prevail in Latvia.

The State and the Media

Leaving aside the autocratic post-communist regimes, the state's presence in the media has usually taken the form of:

1. Gaining indirect control of the media through proxies (e.g., oligarchs known to be friendly to the government, as in Russia or Ukraine)
2. Privatization strategies designed to prevent media outlets falling into foreign hands
3. Attempts to promote the emergence of politically friendly media, sometimes with the use of state companies or funds
4. Attempts to delay transformation of state broadcasters into public service ones, and later heavy involvement in the appointment of their governing and managerial bodies
5. Operation of subsidies for the media

Estonia is one of very few countries where state interference into the media is reportedly not a real issue.

In Slovenia, a strategy of press privatization was designed to prevent the Hungarian experience of an almost immediate takeover of the press by foreign publishers. As a result, the incumbent newspapers and magazines evolved, with a few exceptions, into (limited) stock companies owned by (a) their many current and former employees (typically holding more than 50 per cent of the stock), (b) two state-controlled funds, holding each 10 per cent (the Retribution Fund and the Pension Fund) and (c) various investment companies that managed the citizens' "ownership certificates". Very seldom did the media companies capitalize by selling their stock on the market.

As reported in the present volume, this can have direct political effects as when after the change of the government after the parliamentary elections in November 2004, the editors-in-chief and managers at three daily newspapers (*Delo*, *Primorske novice* and *Večer*) were replaced with people chosen by the new government.

In Slovenia, but also in Hungary and Poland, (mostly right-wing) governments have tried, using public funds or through the intermediary of state enterprises, to promote the establishment of "politically friendly" media outlets, whether newspapers, or – as in Poland in the late 1990s – a television station into which state companies were encouraged to invest. In Hungary, this was officially sanctioned as an effort to create a "Media Equilibrium" as a way of countering what the Fidesz government of the late 1990s perceived as "hegemony of the leftist-liberal press". The Fidesz government also introduced the concept of "loyal journalism". The job of the loyal journalist was described as reporting events from the government's perspective, protecting its position and promoting the government's interests.

As reported in the present volume, the Croatian government controls approximately 40 per cent of radio stations. In particular through local politicians, it influences both their editors and the editorial policies.

It is also common practice for governments and the power elite in general to support friendly media by discriminating in their favour in placing (sometimes quite unnecessary) advertisements in them, while denying this source of income to opposition or independent media.

Assistance and support schemes are in operation in various countries to promote greater diversity of content by subsidising cultural, youth, children, minority and scientific media outlets. They are sometimes used to assist media that are friendly to the government of the day.

The Broadcast Industry
Two main trends have been the demonopolization of broadcasting and licensing of private (mostly commercial) stations and the transformation of state into public service broadcasting. One exception is Bulgaria where, as reported in the present volume, licensing of new commercial broadcasters has been suspended for years. Of late, introduction of digital technologies has spurred the development of new platforms and new television services using them.

The imitative orientation of media policy, combined with considerable pressure exerted on particular governments by the European Union, the Council of Europe and other international organizations, has led to widespread introduction of what is described as PSB in the region. As already noted, however, where modernization and consolidation of democracy are incomplete, only hybrid political systems can emerge. As a consequence, also PSB stations in the more advanced post-communist democracies are in reality hybrid constructs, combining disparate (public service; political elite mouthpiece; political battlefield; commercial) elements within one organization. That is not a feature of post-communist countries alone: many PSB organizations in older democracies are also hybrid constructs, combining these and/or other elements in various degrees.

In general, public service broadcasting is so far generally seen as failing to deliver on its promise of independence and political impartiality, as well as of serving as a mainstay of the public sphere and of delivering diverse and pluralistic content of high quality. Many of the stations are heavily in debt and their audience share is falling, especially in countries where national commercial radio and television stations have been licensed. Many are facing enormous managerial, financial and programming challenges. These outward manifestations of crisis are accompanied by problems of a far more fundamental nature: lack of social embeddedness of the idea of public service broadcasting and lack of a social constituency willing and able to support public service broadcasters and buttress its autonomy and independence.

As noted above, political parallelism is rife in PSB systems in post-communist countries.

In some countries (Bulgaria, Croatia, Poland) public service television still has the largest following. Elsewhere (Czech Republic, Estonia, Latvia, Romania, etc.) it has fallen behind commercial competitors.

Public service radio has almost universally lost the ratings battle to national commercial stations.

The more advanced countries are seeing the development of many thematic and niche satellite channels, extending the range of content. With digital technologies spreading, digital satellite platforms abound everywhere, and the most advanced countries are witness to the emergence of IPTV and other services (Czech Republic, Estonia, Hungary, Lithuania, Slovakia, Slovenia) (see Screen Digest Ltd, CMS Hasche Sigle, Goldmedia Gmbh, Rightscom Ltd, 2006)

Plans to introduce digital terrestrial broadcasting are being developed everywhere, but the process is largely in disarray and is often approached from a telecommunications, rather than a broadcasting, perspective.

Professionalization
There are different ways of classifying media and journalistic roles. One speaks of three types of journalists: watchdogs, lapdogs and hunting dogs (the last case applying mainly to tabloid journalism, see Lauk, Harro 2003). Another view names three models of media: market, trustee or advocacy (Schudson 2003, cited in McQuail 2006). McQuail (2006) lists the following roles of journalism:

- Monitorial: finding, processing and publishing objective and reliable news accounts; setting an agenda;
- Facilitative: aiding democratic activity in the wider public sphere of civil society;
- Collaborative: the wider needs of a society take precedence over profit or journalistic purpose and require cooperation of the media with other external agencies, sometime even the government;
- Radical or critical: an adversarial stance in relation to authority, on clearly motivated normative grounds. Often there is a fundamental challenge to the society and its economic and power structure.

Professionalization of broadcasters and journalists in general has been seen as an important element of the process of media change. Journalists, it was assumed, must rid themselves of the role of propaganda tools and adopt a different professional identity, generally summed up under the concept of the watchdog of the powerful. The trustee model as well as monitorial and facilitative roles would probably best describe what was expected of journalists in the new situation.

At the same time, as we have seen, the authorities in many countries expected them to adopt a collaborative role.

In reality, journalists often originally appeared either as lapdogs of the powerful, or have applied the advocacy model. By throwing themselves with relish into what had previously been strictly forbidden, i.e. often merciless criticism (whether justified or not) of their new governments and political elites, they turned the establishment against themselves, with disastrous consequences for government-media relations.

This not to say there has not been a great deal of fine journalism in post-communist countries and that the monitorial function has been neglected. However, journalists have found it very difficult to aspire to the classical ideal of impartiality and aloof professionalism.

There are deep-seated reasons why the watchdog role was originally often rejected. Hungarian writer Janos Horvath points out that the traditions of Central and Eastern European journalism have led media practitioners to seek leadership and, perhaps, also hegemony roles:

Common in Europe is the concept of the active or participant journalist, the journalist who sees himself as someone who wants to influence politics and audiences according to his political beliefs. This sense is even stronger in Eastern Europe, where journalists are closer to artists and writers, and many poets and writers contribute regularly to daily publications. Together with the journalists, they feel a sort of messianic vocation. They want to become a mouthpiece for the people (Janos Horvat, "The East European Journalist", cited in Gross 1996, p. 111)

By subordinating their work to promoting social and political change, journalists must necessarily opt for a partisan, advocacy-oriented and campaigning style of writing, bordering at times on propaganda. In addition to any paternalism inherent in the traditional Central and Eastern European role of the intelligentsia, this is sometimes sincerely meant as a sense of responsibility for one's country and a way of executing what journalists felt was their "civic responsibility" (Żakowski 1996).

Another set of reasons for inadequate journalistic performance has had to do with the fact that media practitioners – who still have vivid and painful memories of censorship and what used to be called "manual steering" of the media by the authorities, and who are today under considerable pressure from politicians and public authorities – usually reject any talk of responsibility out of hand. "Professionalism" took on the form of a defensive occupational ideology based on rejection of anybody's claim to influence the performance of journalists.

Two processes have affected this initial state of affairs. One is the growing foreign control of many media outlets and the other is the related process of their tabloidization. Many (though not all) foreign owners tend to steer away from direct involvement of their media outlets in political confrontations, imposing on them some degree of impartiality (one exception is Axel Springer which established *Dziennik*, a quality daily in Poland, which promptly became a mouthpiece of centre-right forces). Tabloidization (a very powerful trend, as evidenced by many reports from Central and Eastern Europe in this volume) produces sensationalism, a concentration on exposing the real or imagined crimes or transgressions of the mighty. In fact, as Lauk and Harro (2003: 157) point out in relation to Estonia: "at the end of the 1990s, when capital has become the main force influencing the media, a tendency to hunt down scandals and public figures in order to gain more attention for a publication or channels tends to fend off serious investigative journalism".

Systems of professional journalistic accountability exist in many Central and Eastern European countries, including codes of conduct, or ethical codes, journalistic courts, etc. Nevertheless, the fact that journalistic unions are weak and divided, as well as the general disintegration of value systems due to fast social change and the incomplete institutionalization of new socio-political regimes with their corresponding cultural and axiological systems means that these efforts are less effective than they should be.

Development Trends
Hallin and Mancini (2004: 305) believe that "the Democratic Corporatist model, we suspect, will have particularly strong relevance for the analysis of those parts of Eastern and Central Europe that share much of the same historical development, like Poland, Hungary, the Czech Republic, and the Baltic States". At the same time, they suspect that scholars working in Eastern Europe will find much that is relevant in their analysis of southern Europe, including the role of clientelism, the strong role of the state, the role of the media as an instrument of political struggle, with limited development of the mass circulation press, and the relative weakness of common professional norms.

How to reconcile these statements? Probably they should be taken to mean that had the countries listed by Hallin and Mancini been able to develop and consolidate their democracies, they would now have a Democratic Corporatist media system, instead of the "Mediterranean" one. Should this be taken as prediction that with time and with successful consolidation of democracy, they will move in that direction?

It is this potential dynamic aspect of the media system typology developed by Hallin and Mancini (which otherwise appears quite static) that interests scholars from Eastern Europe most, as they try to discern what is ahead for their media systems. These systems are affected by all the same processes of change as their Western European counterparts, including strong neo-liberal tendencies. Given all the political and cultural baggage, any thought of leapfrogging into the Liberal system should be seen as pure fantasy. "Advancement" into the Democratic Corporatist model is more of a realistic proposition, but can hardly be expected any time soon.

References

Carothers, Thomas (2002), The End of the Transition Paradigm. *Journal of Democracy*, 13(1): 5–21.

Chorazki. W. (1999), Polskie media lokalne i sublokalne 1989–1999. *Zeszyty Prasoznawcze*, XLII(1–2), 59–82.

Cichosz, Marzena (2006), "Transformacja demokratyczna – przyczyny, przebieg i efekty procesu" (in:) Andrzej Antoszewski (ed.) *Systemy polityczne Europy Środkowej i Wschodniej. Perspektywa porównawcza*. Wrocław: Wydawnictwo Uniwersytetu Wrocławskiego, pp. 35–66.

Dryzek, John, Z., Leslie Holmes (2002), *Post-Communist Democratization. Political Discourses across Thirteen Countries*. Cambridge: Cambridge University Press.

Eckstein, Harry (2001), Lessons for the "Third Wave" from the First: An Essay on Democratization. http://www.democ.uci.edu/publications/papersseriespre2001/lessons.htm.

Gross, Peter (1996), *Mass Media in Revolution and National Development. The Romanian Laboratory*. Ames: Iowa State University Press.

Gulyás, Agnes (1999), Structural Changes and Organisations in the Print Media Markets of Post-Communist East Central Europe, *Javnost/The Public*, VI(2), 61–74.

Hallin Daniel C., Paolo Mancini (2004), *Comparing Media Systems: Three Models of Media and Politics*. Cambridge: Cambridge University Press.

Hallin, Daniel C., Stylianos Papathanassopoulos (2002), "Political clientelism and the media: Southern Europe and Latin America in comparative perspective". *Media, Culture and Society*, 24(2): 175–196.

Jakubowicz, Karol (2007), *Rude Awakening: Social and Media Change in Central and Eastern Europe*. Cresskill, N.J.: Hampton Press, Inc.

Krastev, Ivan (2006), Democracy's "Doubles". *Journal of Democracy*, 17(2): 52–62

Lauk, Epp, and Harro, Haliki (2003), The Estonian Media and Society in the Process of Change. In D. Paletz, and K. Jakubowicz (eds.). Business as Usual. Continuity and Change in Central and Eastern European Media (pp. 147–178). Cresskill, N.J.: Hampton Press.

Mancini, Paolo (2000), Political complexity and alternative models of journalism: The Italian case (in:) James Curran, and Myung-Jin Park (eds.) *De-Westernizing Media Studies*. London and New York: Routledge, pp. 265–279.

Marletti, Carlo, Franca Roncarolo (2000), Media Influence in the Italian Transition from a Consensual to a Majoritarian Democracy (in:) Richard Gunther, Anthony Mugham, (eds.). *Democracy and the Media. A Comparative Perspective*. Cambridge: Cambridge University Press, pp. 195–240.

McQuail, Denis (2006), "Media roles in society" (in:) Nico Carpentier, Pille Pruulmann-Vengerfeldt, Kaarle Nordenstreng, Maren Hartmann, Peeter Vihalemm, Bart Cammaerts (eds.) Researching Media, Democracy and Participation. The Intellectual Work of the 2006 European Media and Communication Doctoral Summer School. Tartu: Tartu University Press, http://young.meso.ee/files/teaching_series_1ok.pdf.

Mungiu-Pippidi, Alina (2003), From State to Public Service: The Failed Reform of State TV in Central Eastern Europe. (In:) Miklos Sukosd, Peter Bajomi-Lazar (eds.) *Reinventing Media. Media Policy Reform in East-Central Europe*. Budapest: CEU Press, pp. 31–84.

Papatheodorou, Fotini, David Machin (2003), "The Umbilical Cord That Was Never Cut: The Post-Dictatorial Intimacy between the Political Elite and the Mass Media in Greece and Spain". *European Journal of Communication*. 18(1): 31–54.

Screen Digest Ltd, CMS Hasche Sigle, Goldmedia Gmbh, Rightscom Ltd (2006), *Interactive content and convergence: Implications for the information society*. A Study for the European Commission (DG Information Society and Media). London: Screen Digest

Sitter, Nick (2005), *Finlandisation or The Danish Model? Party Competition and Euroscepticism in East Central Europe*. Paper presented at a One-Day Workshop *Enlargement and Civil Society* University of Nottingham. http://www.bi.no/FellesFiles/Nottingham-paper.pdf.

Splichal, Slavko (1994), *Media Beyond Socialism: Theory and Practice in East-Central Europe*. Boulder: Westview Press.

Splichal, Slavko (2004), Privatization: The Cost of Media Democratization in East and Central Europe? (In:) Pradip N. Thoas, Zaharom Nain (eds.) *Who Owns the Media. Global Trends and Local Resistances*. Penang: Southbound.

Statham, Paul (1996), "Television News and the Public Sphere in Italy. Conflicts at the Media/Politics Interface". *European Journal of Communication*, 11(4): 511–556.

Schudson, Michael (2003), The Sociology of News. New York: Norton.

Sukosd, Miklos, Peter Bajomi-Lazar (2003), The Second Wave of Media Reform in East-Central Europe. (In:) Miklos Sukosd, Peter Bajomi-Lazar (eds.) *Reinventing Media. Media Policy Reform in East-Central Europe*. Budapest: CEU Press, pp. 13–30.

World Bank (2002), *Transition. The First Ten Years. Analysis and Lessons for Eastern Europe and the Former Soviet Union*. Washington.

Żakowski, Jacek (1996), Etyka mediow. In G. G. Kopper, I. Rutkiewicz, K. Schliep (eds.). Media i dziennikarstwo w Polsce (pp. 202–211). Krakow: OBP.

THE BULGARIAN MEDIA LANDSCAPE

Vessela Tabakova

Bulgaria is an industrial country with a population of 7.9 million, including a Turkish minority of 746,664 people or 9.4 per cent, a Roma minority of 370, 908 people or 4.7 per cent and small minorities of Russians, Armenians and Jews. Almost 83 per cent of the population are East Orthodox Christians.

The share of the aged population is increasing – 9 per cent is in the age group from 0 to 10 years, 13.4 per cent from 11 to 19, 14.7 per cent from 20 to 29, 41.8 per cent from 30 to 59 and 22.7 per cent are over 60 years old. Sixty-nine per cent of the population live in urban or semi-urban municipalities. The area of the country is of 111,000 km. Bulgaria is a member of NATO and on 1 January 2007 it became a member of the European Union.

From the outset democratic changes in Bulgarian society after 1989 had considerable influence on the development of the media. Market liberalization and free competition entered the field of the media very quickly. Market development in the media preceded the development of private enterprise in other economic spheres. The process of change and transformation is very dynamic. It transformed the media landscape in the country radically.

1. The Market

A. The Print Media
Main features:

- It is currently estimated that there are over 900 print media outlets in the country;
- The dominant type of newspaper is defined as "hybrid tabloids": it combines and integrates elements of both tabloids and quality press;
- The biggest owner on the Bulgarian newspaper market is the German media group: Westdeutsche Algemeine Zeitung (WAZ);
- The tendency towards reduction of the circulation of print media is seriously affecting Bulgarian dailies.

The first major changes after 1989 took place in the press. Until 1989, Bulgaria had seven national dailies. After 1990, the market was flooded with new titles. About 103 newspapers were launched in 1991, 147 in 1992 and 174 in 1993. At the same time, many of the newly launched papers failed to survive: in 1992 and 1993 alone, 160 newspapers closed down. New publications continue to emerge on the market while others totally disappear.

There is no law governing the press in Bulgaria and newspaper publishing is entirely liberal and unregulated. This is why it is not possible to establish the exact number of publications currently coming out. It is currently estimated that there are over 900 print media titles in the country.

One distinctive feature of the development of the Bulgarian written press after 1989 is the domination of both daily and weekly tabloids. The most typical cases are the best-selling dailies: *Trud* and *24 chasa*. This type of newspaper is defined by Bulgarian media researchers as: "hybrid tabloids". They combine and integrate elements of both tabloids and quality press, of serious and popular reporting. Both of these newspapers regularly define themselves as "serious" newspapers.

One of the explanations of the convergence of the two types of press – quality and tabloid – is based on the fact that several attempts at creating a quality press in Bulgaria have failed. None of the quality newspapers initiated in the 90s survived. They couldn't find a stable market niche. This situation enabled the developing popular dailies to expand into the territory of the quality press accepting some of its functions.

The only quality daily, for the time being, is *Dnevnik* which was established in 2001. *Dnevnik*, the only broadsheet daily when it first appeared, switched to tabloid format after conducting an opinion poll among its readership. It seems that the broadsheet format cannot establish lasting positions on the Bulgarian market.

Most existing dailies are addressed to the broad readership audience. There are many dailies in Bulgaria. According to some statistics there are 25, including the regional dailies. There were fifteen national dailies as of 15 October 2006. Some of them (except the above mentioned *Trud*, *24 Chasa* and *Dnevnik*) are *Standart*, *Telegraph*, *Novinar*, *Sega*, *Monitor*, *Zemya* and *Pari*. The only afternoon daily that succeeded in keeping a relatively steady market position is *Noshten Trud*, which is closer to the typical western tabloid. In recent years, "boulevard" weeklies have emerged that totally disregard ethical journalistic standards.

In 2006, there are four national weekly newspapers of relatively substantial circulation. Two of them, namely, *Capital* and *Banker*, largely business-oriented, can be described as quality press. The other two, *168 Chasa* and *Politika*, address to the masses. There is one more specialized quality weekly with limited circulation, namely, *Kultura*. The latter is the successor to a well-known dissident publication (before 1989) called *Narodna Kultura*.

During recent years, the regional and local newspapers have flourished. Most regional and local newspapers are published twice or three times per week or weekly, except the dailies, which are issued in the bigger regional centres like: Plovdiv, Varna, Burgas and Russe. The readership audience of the newspapers and magazines is lower in the small towns and villages.

The successful launching of the *Tema* magazine should be singled out among the efforts to establish a quality weekly social and political magazine. It has secured steady market positions and won prestige. One more social and political weekly magazine, *Lider*, established in 2005, is also developing successfully. There are magazines with specific profiles targeting women, lifestyle, etc. The magazine media market, however, continues to be dominated by magazines dealing exclusively with domestic and foreign gossip, celebrities and sex.

The biggest owner on the Bulgarian newspaper market is the German media group Westdeutsche Algemeine Zeitung (WAZ). It owns the two above-mentioned dailies with the biggest circulation in Bulgaria: *Trud* (which is the only title of a newspaper that survived the changes in 1989) and *24 Chasa* (which was the first private paper in Bulgaria). WAZ invaded the Bulgarian newspaper market in 1996, declaring its intention: "to promote the development of the Bulgarian press by uniting the commercial activity of the publishers without affecting editorial policy". The print media situation after 1996 is characterized as a period totally dominated by WAZ-owned newspapers. The latter made serious (and successful) efforts to target the regional market and succeeded in launching local editions or supplements. Local editions of WAZ have put many local newspapers out of business.

WAZ's share of the market amounted to 41.7 per cent in 1997. Their monopoly led to legal procedures under the Protection of Competition law. After a series of ownership transfers, WAZ emerged as a winner and has carried on further developing its advertising policy which guarantees it the position of market leader, with the highest annual revenue in the whole media industry: about 48 million euro in 2001.

The 'small miracle' of the advertising policy of WAZ is due to the parallel publishing of the same advertisements, paid messages and short announcements, arranged in the same manner, on the same pages, in both dailies (*Trud* and *24 Chasa*). The price of this common offer was higher than that of a separate advertisement in any of the two newspapers, but lower than the aggregate price of two separate advertisements in both newspapers. This advertising policy has secured the monopoly of WAZ on the Bulgarian print media market.

One of the characteristics of the print media market is that the newspapers that used to be openly dependent on political parties are gradually disappearing. In 2002, the daily of the Union of Democratic Forces, *Demokratsiya*, disappeared putting an end to the era of party papers. The paper of the Bulgarian Socialist Party (BSP), *Duma*, disappeared twice. Both times the BSP found a way to bring it back to the news-stands when businessmen, affiliated with the party, took over its funding. *Duma* still exists as a left-oriented daily newspaper with limited circulation and weak advertising. One notable exception to this trend was the establishment of the *Ataka* daily, in 2005, as a newspaper fully dependent on the right nationalist party Ataka. (The appearance of the Ataka nationalist party itself is a 'media phenomenon' as it is closely related to the Ataka television programme on one of the national cable television networks. The same year, Ataka was elected to parliament gaining more electoral support (9%) than the entire audience share of the cable TV.

The tendency towards reduction of the circulation of print media is seriously affecting Bulgarian dailies. The overall circulation of daily papers has considerably dropped in recent years. There are no statistics with precise data about papers' circulation, but it is estimated that the current single daily circulation of the six biggest circulated dailies is no more than 400,000. (By comparison, in 2003, the figure for *Trud*, the daily with the highest circulation alone, was 320,000). There is an office for the independent audit of circulation, but it is not fully functional or reliable. Exact figures are unavailable both for newspapers and for magazines. The new practice to sell DVDs, at very reasonable prices, along with newspapers is a symptom of the reduced circulation and proof of changes in the market behaviour of the national dailies.

B. *The Broadcast Media*
Main features:

■ There are currently three national terrestrial televisions: two private and one public service;
■ The former state radio was transformed successfully into a public service broadcaster and still has the largest audience;

- There are 184 registered cable operators in the country (at the national, regional and local levels) broadcasting their programmes;
- Efficient market-driven activities of the Bulgarian electronic media are compromised by the lack of reliable ratings.

Since the political changes in 1989, the development of the electronic media has been characterized by one paradoxical peculiarity: the state monopoly was kept at national level, while a liberal environment for the establishment of regional and local radio and television stations was introduced.

In the last six years the situation has changed. There are currently three national terrestrial television channels in Bulgaria: the Bulgarian National Television (BNT, which is the former state television, defined in the broadcasting law as a public service TV) and two private television channels: Murdoch's Balkan News Corporation owned by bTV (licensed in October 2000) and the Greek Antenna Group owned by Nova Televisia (licensed in 2002). All three television channels broadcast round the clock and compete for larger shares of the advertising market.

BNT still has a large audience, although recent surveys show that bTV currently has the largest audience. The surveys show an increasing preference for the programmes of Nova Televisia. Since 2005 there has been considerable interest in "reality shows" like *Big Brother* and *Vip Brother* on Nova TV which have had substantial commercial results.

There has been occasional tension, conflict and controversy at BNT, mostly due to attempts to control it on the part of the incumbents or corporate structures. The transition from state to responsible public service media has been difficult, particularly, within BNT.

Data from 2002 show that the average duration of TV-viewing is 246 minutes daily, while the average radio programmes listening time is 213 minutes daily. The inhabitants of the small towns and villages spend more time watching TV.

BNT and the Bulgarian National Radio (BNR) are funded through the national budget. The law envisages that the duration of advertising may not exceed fifteen minutes per 24 hours, four minutes per hour for BNT and six minutes per hour for BNR. The accumulation of a national fund of consumer fees has not yet begun given that a mechanism for their collection has not been found and it can be said that there is no commitment to this end.

As a whole, the situation of the audio-visual media has thoroughly changed. The first national private radio, Darik Radio, was launched following a licensing competition in 2000. Before that, Darik had established a comprehensive radio network and had been broadcasting in fourteen (of a total of 28) regions throughout the country. However,

BNR and its *Horizont Programme*, in particular, continually have the highest number of listeners. The former state radio was transformed into a public service broadcaster, much more successfully than BNT. The main radio programme kept its audience mostly striving towards political independence and the presentation of different opinions and points of view and with the citizens' access to expression.

According to the Council of Electronic Media Register of licensed operators, 111 private terrestrial regional and local radio outlets are currently operational. In the capital (Sofia) alone, with a population of 1.5 million, there are 32 FM radio stations. Purchase of radio stations by bigger networks has begun in the radio sector. Several big radio networks, such as FM Plus, BG Radio, Inforadio have established themselves in the country.

According to the latest data there are 184 registered cable operators in the country (at the national, regional and local levels). The cable network has been developing comparatively quickly and most recent data show that 55 per cent of households in the country are cable-operator subscribers. According to Bulgarian Radio and Television Law, only terrestrial media outlets need to be licensed. Licensing requirements for cable operators were replaced by a simple registration procedure in 2001.

Licensing was stopped in 2001, when the parliament passed amendments to the Radio and Television Law requiring the adoption of a strategy for the development of broadcasting before any new licences could be issued. Because of this particular situation, more than 110 radio outlets are operating with temporary permits and many are outspoken pirates.

Efficient market-driven activities of the Bulgarian electronic media are compromised by the lack of reliable ratings. The only people meter group, TNS, functions in partnership with a local business. The objectivity of the people meter system is widely questioned because its owners have stakes in media outlets and advertising agencies. A new company, the consortium GFK – Austria, has announced intentions to run a people meter system, but these are still at the planning face.

Digital services are emerging. All programmes currently broadcast by satellite are digitally coded. There are two companies offering digitalized transmission of foreign programmes. According to estimates of telecommunications experts, terrestrial TV will be fully digitalized by 2015 at the latest. As far as cable TV is concerned, experts are aiming at 2012 for digitalization.

C. The Internet Media
Main features:

- The number of online media is continually increasing;
- Almost all mainstream newspapers have online versions.

In Bulgaria, Internet penetration is 28.5 per cent in 2006. The user growth in the period 2000 to 2006 is an estimated 411.6 per cent.

A large number of news portals, electronic media and agencies have emerged in recent years. Their information is uncontrolled and unregulated, but they have been establishing themselves ever more firmly as news-making sources. It is practically impossible to find reliable data on the number of Web-based news sources. It is clear, however, that their number is continually increasing.

The Web-based media www.Mediapool.bg enjoys considerable prestige among the educated audience with its high quality and professionalism.

Almost all mainstream newspapers have online versions with readers' fora. The lack of Internet versions has proved an inefficient instrument in the efforts to maintain higher rates of circulation.

D. News Agencies
Main features:

- One strong news agency operating for over one hundred years
- Web-based private news agencies are very active as an information source for the newspapers

The Bulgarian News Agency (BTA) continues to be the most reliable and professional news agency in the country, operating for over one hundred years.

At present, BTA employs several hundred journalists and translators. The agency also possesses a network of correspondents throughout the country. Due to financial difficulties, BTA has almost no full-time correspondents abroad. It has, however, a well-developed network of stringers in the Balkans and Western Europe.

BTA has a considerable number of subscribers in Bulgaria and abroad: about 230 subscribers in the country and some 90 abroad. Practically, all larger media in the country are BTA subscribers. Institutions of public administration and other large departments also subscribe to the agency's services. Apart from large numbers of information products (newsletters, review articles, photos, etc.), the agency publishes two weekly magazines.

BTA is a self-financing structure with revenues from subscription fees. Funding under the national budget covers only 10 to 15 per cent of its budget and can be disbursed only on technical equipment and other similar needs.

Along with BTA, Web-based private news agencies like *BGnes* (www.bgnes.com) and *Focus news* (www.focus.bg) as well as Internet news portals like *SEEnews* (www.SEEnews.

com) and *novinite.com* (www.novinite.com) are very active. They are available through standard subscription and increasingly, through value-added services via websites and mobile telephony providers. Web-based agencies are often an information source for newspapers.

2. State Policies
Main feature:

■ There are shortcomings of the existing legal framework for the electronic media, but political will for changes is lacking.

Article 39 of the Bulgarian Constitution guarantees freedom of expression. It states that "everyone is entitled to express an opinion or to make it public through words, written or oral, sound or image, or in any other way." Article 40.1 guarantees freedom of the press and other mass media and bars censorship. Article 40.2 of the Constitution imposes a ban on the spreading of hate speech and incitement to hatred and violence.

In compliance with its functions, set by the Radio and Television Law, the regulatory body (previously the National Council for Radio and Television and now the CEM) monitors compliance with statutory requirements on advertising, sponsorship, copyright, protection of youth and minors. CEM considers cases of violations established by its experts and complaints by citizens and organizations.

There are no special statutory regulations of printed media. Texts from other laws, such as, for example, laws about slander and libel (under the Penal Code), can be applied both to printed and electronic media.

Following a series of events and pressure by various civil organizations, the Penal Code texts on slander and libel were amended in 2000. These changes limited possibilities for prosecution of journalists. Imprisonment was revoked and the maximum penalty is a fine of 15,000 Leva (about 7,500 EUR).

After the adoption of the Radio and Television Law in 1998, a number of amendments to the Act were passed. Shortcomings of the existing legal framework include: a lack of sufficient guarantees about independence of the regulatory body; inadequate expert knowledge and professionalism on the part of members of the regulatory body; legally restricted competence of the regulatory body regarding licensing; gaps and lack of clarity in licensing procedures; lack of clarity in regulation of the management and financing of BNT and BNR. There has been an active debate regarding the need for change, but political will to change is lacking. Changes would guarantee more independence of the regulatory body and in the regulation of management of public service broadcasting, for example. The proposals concerning the election of a civil quota in the regulatory body had no consequences.

Quick-fix" changes in the Bulgarian media, the emergence of numerous papers and the exceptionally high number of radio and television outlets compared to the size of the population have inevitably been accompanied by shortcomings and weaknesses. Lack of adherence to professional standards (particularly in regional and local media), and excessive focus on sensation, crime and violence, are continuously criticized both by the audience and from within the professional community.

3. Civil Society Organizations

Main features:

- The Bulgarian Media coalition is the joint body of different non-governmental organizations;
- Associations representing the interests of media owners are very active;
- An ethical code of Bulgarian media was approved in 2004;
- Separate self-regulatory bodies: Ethics Committee for the Print Media and Ethics Committee for the Electronic Media started their work in 2006.

Non-governmental agencies supporting development of independent media and professionalization of the media (the Access to Information Programme, the Free Speech Civic Forum, the Centre for Independent Journalism, the Association of Investigative Journalists – among many others) have maintained their stable and continuous position and active public advocacy roles.

The joint body of the media organizations, the Bulgarian Media Coalition (BMC), was established in 1999 to unite intellectual, professional, media and organizational potential of various non-profit organizations. Specific interests of the media organizations in the BMC cover all aspects, problems and activities related to media practice and theory. These include ethical standards and professional norms in journalism, protection of the constitutional right to freedom of speech and expression, professional education and the very media industry. BMC has maintained considerable public authority, for years, as well as a good record of media assistance and effective public actions. It has alerted the public when attempts to violate the freedoms of national and regional media took place. BMC has influenced public policy and the process of decision-making in the media.

Associations representing the interests of media owners are very active in the media sector. In 2005, the Union of National Media emerged bringing together associations of media owners in print (Union of Publishers) and broadcasting (Association of Bulgarian Broadcasters). It was actively involved in addressing the problems of the media community discussing and presenting statements on current media development and putting important issues of media legislation on the public agenda.

In 2004, under an EU-funded Phare project on technical assistance for improving professional standards of journalism, an Ethical Code of Bulgarian Media was drafted with the participation of EU experts. It was approved by various organizations and media. After debates regarding the mechanisms of the establishment of committees on ethics and possibilities for the existence of separate self-regulatory bodies for the electronic and print media, the establishment of an Ethics Committee for the Print Media and Ethics Committee for the Electronic Media in the end of 2005 – through a procedure of nomination and election – is considered as a success. Both committees adopted working rules and in June 2006, their activities started. There are grounds to believe that self-regulation (that has been debated by professionals for years) will be tough to develop due to contradictions among partners. The positive process has nevertheless started.

4. Development Trends
Main features:

- A strategy for the development of the audio-visual media was adopted in 2005;
- In the next few years, the most important goal of national media policy will be digitalization.

The excessive fragmentation of the audio-visual market prompted the need for a strategy to develop radio and television. Its declared purpose was to formulate national priorities and public interests in licensing with a view to more efficient usage of free frequencies.

As was mentioned above licensing had been stopped in 2001 when the parliament passed amendments in the Radio and Television Law requiring the adoption of a strategy for the development of broadcasting before any new licences were issued. In 2005, the strategy was finally adopted, opening the way for renewed licensing.

The total absence of licensing over the past few years has placed legitimate licensees at a disadvantage to outlets that broadcast without undertaking official licensing procedures. Most of the temporary permits have long since expired but, because no new licences are being awarded, the permits are still considered valid. The result is a type of licensing that circumvents legal provisions instead of adhering to them. The existing situation is expected to generate a lot of tension and contradictions in the process of renewed licensing.

As announced by the CEM and the Committee for Regulation of Telecommunications, there are 87 free frequencies for new terrestrial regional televisions and 96 for radio outlets. For the time being, there are 195 applicants for the licensing competition launched on 12 May 2006 and the licensing procedures have started.

In the next few years, the most important goal of national media policy will undoubtedly be digitalization. Its development depends largely on technical and economic development and on the interests of broadcasters and customers. Bulgarian society is still not aware of the new opportunities of digitalization and as a result there is currently a lack of public interest.

Transition to digital broadcasting requires significant investment by current operators. It will be particularly difficult to arrange for such investment in a small market like the one in Bulgaria.

Regarding the consumers, experts highlight the tension related mostly to considerable costs for digital equipment, smart cards or different smart cards. For many Bulgarian customers, the lack of Bulgarian language in the EPG of new digital receivers will be a problem at the outset.

There are grounds to believe that the digitalization process will develop considerably faster than initially estimated.

References & Sources for Further Information
Financial difficulties of printed publications, dealing with professional analysis and self-reflection in the field of journalism and the media led to the disappearance of the quarterly journalism and media magazine, *Chetvartata vlast* (The Fourth Estate), published by the Free Speech Civic Forum. The monthly magazine *MediaMarketing* also disappeared from the market. The only magazine, *MediaSviat*, existing in the beginning of 2006 disappeared in June 2006.

The *Capital* weekly has a media section, publishing analyses of phenomena and tendencies in media development paying particular attention to business and management aspects of the media industries. Dailies also devote articles to media although they lack analyses, and issues related to the media appear mostly in connection with possible scandals.

The BMC website, www.bmc.bulmedia.bg, as well as other organizations' sites, such as www.media-cij.org, the Access to Information Programme: www.aip.org, etc. provide other sources of news and analyses about professional discussions related to media legislation; compliance with professional standards; and accountability, as well as regarding a series of other problems, relevant to the development of media in Bulgaria.

THE CROATIAN MEDIA LANDSCAPE

Nada Buric

Croatia is a presidential, multi-party parliamentary democracy located in south-eastern Europe. The country's population is 4.4 million with an annual GDP of approximately €6,900 per capita.

The major language is Croatian and major religion Christianity. Nearly one-third of citizens live in the greater area of the capital, Zagreb. The country area of 56,594 square kilometres swings in a horseshoe shape from a thousand islands and the east coast of the Adriatic Sea across hilly central Croatia to the continental Pannonian Plains in the east.

Once a state within Yugoslavia, Croatia held its first multi-party elections since World War II in 1990. A 1991–1995 war broke out after it declared independence. The war ruined the economy, notably tourism, and left one-third of the territory's property destroyed and over ten thousand casualties. In the post-war era, the country was under a rather autocratic regime, which ended by opposition victory in 2000 elections. The new government introduced democratic changes that also brought about the freedom of the media.

Croatia is hoping to become a member of the European Union by 2010. In terms of the EU, the population is about 1.2 per cent and economy about 0.26 per cent of GDP. The EU accounts for more than half of both exports and imports, with Italy, Germany and Austria being the most prominent partners.

1. The Market

A. The Print Media
Main features:

- There are no official figures in Croatia that would accurately describe the media landscape;
- There is a steady decline in production of newspapers;
- Newspapers are sold mainly at news-stands;
- Newspapers are becoming more tabloid-like;
- The magazine market is led by women's magazines.

The media struggle for more ads reflects in more commercial and more tabloid-like media, and a decreasing quality of professionalism. In addition, fifteen years of a post-socialist period were harsh for the press: five years of war and another five years of conservative government have left its toll in that independent and accurate reporting is still not a predominant quality of the media.

Despite laws ordering publishers to publish their circulation figures, the lack of penalties for disregard is misused by all: besides public opinion surveys, there are no official figures that would accurately indicate the readership. An official database by the Chamber of Commerce on quantities of newsprint used in production of print media shows steady decline. Regardless, publishers announce they would fight for the market and its more than €175 million worth of advertising revenue in print media (2005).[1] On an average day, an estimated 530,000 copies of daily newspapers are printed.

An increasing advertising revenue in print media from 23 per cent in 2000 to 35 per cent in 2004 dropped to 32 per cent in 2005, mainly due to improved television production. In 2005, fourteen daily newspapers had a 14.3 per cent share in total advertising revenue, and 55 weekly magazines 6.1 per cent.

Four largest daily newspapers, *Jutarnji List*, *Večernji List*, *24 Sata* and *Slobodna Dalmacija*, struggle for readership – and advertising – with sensational news stories and photos and promotional prizes. The pressure to be more 'commercial' discourages good investigative reporting and turns the newspapers into full-colour layout filled with photographs and ads. In his editorial about pressure from advertisers, a deputy editor-in-chief of *Jutarnji List* wrote in spring 2006 that an advertiser blackmailed the paper with annulment of their rich advertising contract after having disliked a news report.

Jutarnji List (or *Morning Paper*) was launched in 1997 by a local publisher, EuropaPress Holding (or EPH), which sold 50 per cent of its ownership to German publisher WAZ in 1998. Today EPH is the market leader with more than a dozen publications, including two daily newspapers, weeklies *Globus* and *Arena* and Croatian editions of *Playboy* and *Cosmopolitan*.

Once the leading state-owned daily, *Večernji List* (or *Evening Paper*) was bought by Austrian publisher Styria in 2000. The new owners kept its traditional A3 format but adapted its layout to look more similar to Styria's Austrian tabloid. Each newspaper, the *Jutarnji* and *Večernji*, had about 16 per cent of average daily readership in 2005, or an estimated hundred thousand copies sold on an average day.

In the first quarter of 2006 a new tabloid, *24 Sata* (or *24 Hours*), took the second position from *Večernji List*. It was launched in 2005 following plans of its publisher Styria to become the market leader through, what Styria called, a 'battle for Croatia'. The paper is aimed at younger generations, it is abundant with photographs and it features short stories.

The fourth best-selling national newspaper with seven per cent of average daily readership is *Slobodna Dalmacija*. It owes its position to its regional dominance in Dalmatia where it had 49 per cent of the readership in 2005. Among local media struggling to gain profit in this small market, a rather respected regional daily, *Novi List*, scored fifth in the country with four per cent of readership in 2005, but first in the Rijeka region with 52.9 per cent.

Among weekly magazines, the leaders are women's magazines *Gloria* and *Story* with 10 and 6.5 per cent[2] of average readership in 2005 through the first quarter of 2006, and the top ten weeklies include six women's magazines. Political magazines scored third and fourth: the average readership of *Globus* and *Nacional* is just above 5 per cent.[3] Both won their position among political magazines through investigative reporting but, also, at times sensationalist stories and controversial interviews.

Prior to the country's democratization in the 1990s, all major newspapers were published by a state-owned company, *Vjesnik*. Still public, this publisher issues only one newspaper, the daily *Vjesnik*. With six decades of being the leading newspaper in former Yugoslavia, *Vjesnik* is the only daily newspaper regarded as pursuing objective and professional reports. However, the state ownership apparently prevents it from acquiring an audience above only 1 per cent of average issue readership (2005), which could roughly translate to five thousand copies.

In an attempt to boost their sales, daily newspapers offered in 2004 various books along newspaper copies. In 2005 and 2006, the gifts became attractive prizes such as cars, motorbikes, personal computers. However, the research into readership showed no particular gains, except for the new daily newspaper *24 Sata*, launched in mid-2005. Its release brought the publisher Styria a leadership in the market of daily newspapers: *Večernji List* and *24 Sata* on aggregate had nearly 30 per cent of average readership in spring 2006,[4] which Styria claimed equalled almost 45 per cent of sold daily newspaper publications. Publishers continue to insert various glossy magazines free of charge in daily newspapers.

Three foreign publishers entered a joint venture with Adria Magazines in May 2006. With seventeen titles, Adria Magazines expects to gain a 25–30 per cent share in the growing magazines market.

In Croatia, daily newspapers are sold at news-stands and in grocery stores and supermarkets.

B. The Broadcast Media
Main features:

- Television is a predominant source of information;
- The audience leadership belongs to the public television;
- Two private music-only stations are leaders among radio audience;
- The penetration of cable and digital television is low compared to analogical receivers;
- National Telecom Agency plans to increase digital television coverage to 90 per cent in 2007.

Among some 150 radio stations and fifteen TV channels that broadcast in Croatia, only six radio stations and four TV channels are licensed for national coverage. The state-owned television is the leader by audience on the national level. In the radio market, as many as five state-owned radio stations are among top ten stations ranked by audience. But they cannot take the lead from private music-only broadcasters.

Television is a predominant source of information. Nearly all households have a colour television set, while half of the population do not read any newspapers and listen to any radio. The competition of four national TV channels sheds some new light onto the reporting arena.

The largest and the most influential Croatian television belongs to the chain of the state-owned HRT (Hrvatska Radio-Televizija or Croatian Radio-Television). The television company operates two channels: HTV1 and HTV2, with an aggregate audience share of 54 per cent in 2005, according to a regular AGB Nielsen audience monitoring. The television company was founded 50 years ago and it was one of the largest television centres in former Yugoslavia. In the past, HRT was subjected to political control, particularly until the 2000 government was elected. Under influence of international and domestic watchdog organizations, it has been steadily pursuing a path of becoming an independent public service broadcaster. Public polls show its relentlessly influential position among citizens: its main headline news is the most prominent source of public information. Along with TV commercials, above 50 per cent of its revenues are still paid by a monthly subscription levied from households with a television set – and nearly all households have one.

Founded in 2000 by Central European Media Enterprises (or CME), Nova TV was the first commercial television with national coverage, while German TV channel

RTL launched its Croatian outlet in April 2004. Their more relaxed approach, with movies, soaps, fun games and other entertainment, has been increasingly matched by the public broadcaster HTV. Under new directors appointed in 2004, HTV affirmed its pole position among television broadcasters, having increased entertainment-orientated content to match its new competitors while at the same time increasing news content. In return, Nova TV and RTL have extended their news departments and increased the length and number of informative programmes in 2005 and 2006. Having HTV as a role model for audience interest, they also introduced political talk shows and employed experienced reporters from print media but also from the national broadcaster.

Besides these four national TV channels, another thirteen private channels broadcast on a regional level. They are constantly faced with financial problems.

After a steady decline from 76 per cent in 2000 to 64 per cent in 2004, the share of advertisement revenues increased for television to 68.2 per cent or 365 million euro in 2005, matching the increasing entertaining content of four national broadcasters and their struggle to gain more audience. In 2004, public television took 37.29 per cent of the advertising revenues and increased it to 39.51 per cent in 2005. Nova TV and RTL on aggregate had 62.71 per cent in 2004 and 60.48 per cent in 2005.

Since 2003, the Croatian Telecommunications Agency has been developing plans for digital switch-over and 90 per cent coverage in 2007. Broadcasting experimentally, nine transmitters had 65 per cent coverage in 2006. The multiplex signal included all four national television broadcasters – HTV 1 and 2, Nova TV and RTL. Considering an overwhelming number of terrestrial receivers, initially the Agency plans to air only DVB-T signal for terrestrial reception of television programmes.

After a decade of satellite dishes popping up on Croatian roofs in the 1990s, a dozen of cable operators have moved into the television market since 2000, having penetrated some 160,000 households by mid-2006. Their coverage is fragmentary, mostly owing to high costs of cable installation and concession licences. Besides all available terrestrial programmes, the cable operators broadcast dozens of international satellite television stations. Along with television, some cable operators also provide Internet cable access.

A novelty in the Internet television market is MAXtv launched in autumn of 2006 by telecommunications company HT, which covers more than 90 per cent of DSL subscribers. In the first two months, it had more than five thousand subscribers. The service provides also video-on-demand.

In competition with public radio stations, private stations took a commercial attitude: steady market leaders are two national broadcasters which air only music, the Narodni (or People's) radio airing only domestic music and Otvoreni (or Open) radio, a regular MEDIApuls study showed. They scored 11 and 7 per cent, respectively, of 2005 average daily reach among population.

The government controls approximately 40 per cent of radio stations. In particular through local politicians, it influences both their editors and the editorial policies. Regional journalists also struggle with financial problems, both in public and private radio stations.

C. The Internet Media
Main features:

- The broadband access rate is much below the EU's average;
- The rate of Internet use is around 35 per cent;
- Major newspapers are among the top twenty websites;
- Leading websites provide entertainment, job ads, health issues and lifestyle stories.

The country's economic post-war recovery became evident also in the computer and Internet market that reached a steady annual growth of 10 per cent by 2004. But it was halted in 2005 around 35 per cent among populations older than 15, or about 1.5 million users, primarily due to a lack of access options, a lacking infrastructure competition and undeveloped broadband market.[6] Half of Croatian households had a computer in the end of 2005, and three in four surfers accessed the Internet at least once a week.[5] In its 2006 Strategy, the Government laid out plans to increase penetration of broadband access to at least 12 per cent, or 500,000 users, by 2008. In the end of 2005, this rate was under 4 per cent compared to the EU's average of nearly 12 per cent. The Strategy envisaged an annual growth rate of 4 per cent, the EU level.

Nearly 70 per cent of Internet surfing is usually done from home and 20 per cent from the workplace. As regards the Web content, 66 per cent of Internet connections are made to check e-mail, 59 per cent to read the news, 47 per cent to seek information about literature, 26 per cent for games and MP3 downloads, while 15 percent of surfers pay their bills over the Internet.[6] The top ten Croatian websites contain scarce news compared to lots of entertainment, job ads, health issues and lifestyle stories. Reading the news on the internet dropped from 75 per cent to 69 per cent in 2005.[6] Regardless, nearly all major newspapers had a website in 2005 and immediately entered the top twenty Croatian sites. Except for the *Novi list*, all other newspaper sites are free of charge.

The leading websites in early 2006 were the sites of two major Internet providers, T-portal by HT and net.hr by Iskon, offering mainly entertainment, but also news by the public news agency HINA. Among the leading ten sites were also sites of two leading daily newspapers, *Jutarnji list* and *Večernji list*.

HT, by far the leading national telephone operator and Internet provider, bought in autumn 2006 Iskon, its major competitor, having thus affirmed its monopoly in providing Internet access. The buyout followed promises of the Agency for Telecommunications that it would use all means to prevent the buyout in an attempt to liberalize the market.

D. News Agencies
Main features:

■ The leadership belongs to the public news agency HINA;
■ Several international radio stations provide news feed in local language.

The most prominent among three Croatian news agencies is HINA, the state-owned Hrvatska izvještajna novinska agencija or Croatian Reporting News Agency, and it reaches out to literally all media. Founded in 1991, it grew into a full-service agency, which provides 200–300 news dailies, including politics, sports, science, business and entertainment.

The other two news agencies are IKA and STINA. Owned by Croatian Episcopal Conference, IKA – or Informative Catholic Agency – is the primary source for journalists covering the Catholic Church. STINA is a regional private agency, specialized in diversity and minority reporting.

International news agencies that operate in Croatia are the Associated Press, Reuters and AFP, which sell their services to about a dozen major media. The AP and Reuters also sell their TV feeds.

Economic difficulties that prevent radio stations from employing news reporters have been a fertile ground for a number of Croatian news outlets of international radio stations, such as BBC, VOA (Voice of America) and Deutsche Welle. They provide their news broadcasts in Croatian language to smaller private radio stations.

2. State Policies
Main features:

■ The Croatian Constitution guarantees the freedom of expression and the freedom of the press;
■ As an EU candidate member, Croatia is in process of transposing European laws into its legislation, including the media laws.

The Croatian Constitution guarantees the freedom of expression and the freedom of the press. It bans censorship, and journalists are entitled to report and to access information. The Constitution also guarantees the right for correction if legal rights are violated by published news.

Croatian media are governed by the Law on Media, the Law on Electronic Media, the Law on Croatian Radio-Television and the Law on the Right to Access Information. In the past several years, they have been harmonized with European standards and underwent the EU screening in July 2006, as part of membership negotiations. The Law on Electronic Media and the Law on Media have transposed a number of provisions from the EU's Television

Without Frontiers Directive, but some issues still need to be addressed regarding advertising, the majority rule of European works and independent works, freedom of reception and judicial appeal.[7] Amendments are expected to the Law on Croatian Radio-Television in order to ensure political independence of the Programme Council. The removal of political influence is also expected in election of the Council for Electronic Media governed by the Law on Electronic Media. The Council is a regulatory body for broadcasting media that grants concessions to broadcasters and supervises the implementation of programme principles under which broadcasters obtain such concessions.

Indirectly, the media are also governed by the Criminal Code and Civil Code through provisions about defamation and libel. The 2005 amendments to the Criminal Code on libel have shifted the burden of proof to prosecutor, thus making the most favourable Croatian libel laws. International watchdog organizations have continued advising the government to regulate libel through means other than the criminal law, in particular through use of civil procedures. Provisions for crime against reputation and honour, prosecuted privately, still include libel. Despite the UN and OSCE recommendations that press offences should not be punished by prison terms, four journalists were convicted to suspended prison sentences for libel in 2005.

As regards restrictions to capital concentration in the media, the Law on Media establishes an upper ceiling for ownership in general information dailies or weeklies at 40 per cent of the total market sales. The Law on Electronic Media allows cross-media ownership of national electronic media if the ownership at any other regional, county and city level does not exceed 25 per cent. National broadcasting licence excludes ownership in any daily newspapers with circulation above 3,000, or ownership of more than 10 per cent in any news agency and vice versa. National and regional licences prevent licensees from having more than 30 per cent share in similar media or in local daily newspapers in the broadcasting area. Broadcasting licences are issued by the Council for Electronic Media, and publishers must report all changes in ownership structures to the Council and to the Agency for Protection of Market Competition. A publisher can have either a radio or a television broadcast.

Telecommunications Users Council was established in 2005 within the national Agency for Telecommunications as a mediation body in the out-of-court disputes between users and providers of telecommunications services, and as an Agency's advisory body on protection of consumer rights.

The state-owned media – newspapers, various magazines or radio and TV stations – receive state funds. The daily newspaper *Vjesnik* received 33.5 million Kuna (an equivalent to €4.5 million) in 2005, which was its eleventh such financial support since 1990. The compulsory subscription fee for television funds only the public broadcaster.

The Law on the Media entitles all whose rights or interests have been violated by information in the media to publish correction. Editors-in-chief are liable for all information published and to civil proceedings if correction's publication is denied.

3. Civil Society Organizations
Main features:

- Nearly all journalists are members of Croatian Journalists Association;
- Two organizations of publishers cover about 80 per cent of all media employees;
- The Code of Ethics of the Croatian Journalists' Association, limited to moral condemnation, is the only institute that oversees mistakes of journalists;
- One newspaper has bylaws regulating autonomy of reporters.

Nearly all Croatian journalists are members of Hrvatsko novinarsko društvo or Croatian Journalists' Association (CJA). The organization is an active participant in democratization of media laws, it services some social aspects of its members and issues its regular paper distributed among members free of charge. It was founded in 1910 and it is one of the oldest professional associations in Croatia. It became a member to the International Federation of Journalists in 1992. Among more than 3,000 members, nearly 60 per cent work in Zagreb, the country's capital. The Association works closely with the Trade Union of Croatian Journalists, mostly in protection of journalists' labour and social rights.

In 1998, in co-operation with the Zagreb Faculty of Journalism, CJA founded the International Centre for Education of Journalists, aimed at improving journalists' professional skills. Its seminars and round-table discussions are held by foreign and domestic lecturers as well as public and political figures.

Hrvatska udruga radija i novina *or* HURIN (Croatian Association of Radio Stations and Newspapers) is an organization of 156 mainly smaller electronic media and newspapers. The sixteen largest publishers are members of Udruga novinskih izdavača (Association of Newspaper Publishers), which operates as part of Croatian Employers' Association. Together with HURIN it covers about 80 per cent of employees in Croatian media.

Influential in the arena of media freedom is the Media Council of the Croatian Helsinki Committee (HHO).

In absence of official figures, only private research agencies monitor regularly the circulation of printed media and measure the audience of broadcast media: AGB Nielsen, GfK, Media Metar, Mediana Fides and Puls.

The Code of Ethics of the Croatian Journalists' Association is limited to moral condemnation. The Association's Ethical Council decides on cases of Code's violation, but its judgment is limited to making the judgment public. According to laws, autonomy of reporters should be covered by bylaws of individual media; however, only one newspaper (*Jutrnji list*) adopted such rules.

4. Development Trends

Main features:

- Public media expected to face open-market issues once Croatia enters the EU
- First free newspaper launched, hit the top four dailies in six months of distribution
- Television market competition forces public broadcaster to modernize in order to keep its leading position
- National agencies plan to reach 90 per cent coverage of digital terrestrial television signal for 2007 and 12 per cent penetration of broadband Internet access for 2008

Being an EU candidate country, Croatia is expected to amend its media laws in order to meet more transparency and effectiveness, to remove political influence from the media and to liberalize the telecommunications market. Attention has been steadily focused on independence of the public television HRT and the public news agency HINA. Both appear to encounter problems in implementing standards of professional journalism while protecting themselves from possible political influence. The national television is expected to face open-market issues once Croatia enters the EU. International experts encourage a revision of professional and ethical evaluation systems of the national broadcaster.

The first free newspaper in Croatia, a daily *Metro Express*, became the fourth leading daily newspaper in the end of 2006 after just six months of its distribution, having reached some 10 per cent of the readership. It is published by EPH, which plans to increase its circulation from 250,000 in the end of 2006 to 350,000 copies in 2007. The newspaper did not affect the readership shares of other daily newspapers.

In a successful move to secure the leading position on the national TV scene, public television HRT selected new television leadership among politically unaffiliated professionals in early 2004. Unprecedented, the top two positions went to two women, and the changes they have been introducing have not been just cosmetic. They sharpened the edge of news reporting, gave more space to professionally anchored political talk shows and introduced new shows that address public interest. New strategy also includes local production of largely viewed soaps, regular daily political talk shows on controversial topics, richly produced musical shows.

The national Agency for Telecommunications plans to reach 90 per cent coverage of digital terrestrial television signal in 2007. In experimental broadcasting, it reached 65 per cent coverage in 2006.

National strategy for broadband Internet access plans to increase access penetration by 9 percentage points by 2008, to the current European level of 12 per cent.

Notes

1. AGB Nielsen Media Research.
2. MediaPULS research.

3. AGB Nielsen television audience measurement.
4. GfK research, March 2006.
5. AGB Nielsen Media Research.
6. Source: Overview of Telecom Indicators 2002–2005, Croatian Telecommunications Agency.
7. EU's Croatia 2006 Progress Report.

References & Sources for Further Information

Despite legal provisions about the public right to information on publishers, polls are the only source of information on media readership and audience. The leading research agency that regularly surveys the media is Puls with its MEDIApuls project, which is used by advertising agencies that cover some 90 per cent of the advertising revenue of the media other than television. Other agencies that survey the media are GfK, Media Metar and Mediana Fides. The Puls daughter company, AGB Nielsen, is the only researcher of television audiences. Puls and AGB Nielsen also provide data on media advertising.

Online resources

Hrvatsko novinarsko društvo (Croatian Journalists' Association) <www.hnd.hr>. Directory of Croatian media regularly updated.

Državni zavod za statistiku (National Agency of Statistics) <www.dzs.hr>. Croatian national agency in charge of official statistics.

The Czech Media Landscape

Milan Šmíd

The return of freedom of expression to the Czech society and the fast introduction of the market economy were two main elements that influenced media development after the political change in November 1989.

The rejection of the former totalitarian political system by Czech society was profound, and led to the long-lasting support for the concept of political and economic reform, in which the role of the state is to be as small as possible, and where free market forces are to govern society as a whole, including the mass media. That was the political climate in which the privatization of entire industries, including the media, took place.

The separation of the former federal state of Czechoslovakia into two independent states, the Czech Republic and the Slovak Republic, in 1993, had no major impact on the media, which were organized in the both parts of the federation already before the split. The state federal media Czechoslovak Radio and Czechoslovak Television were dissolved on 31 December 1992.

The Czech Republic has a size of a medium European state with the area of 78,886 sq km and with the population of 10.2 million people. Besides the Czech capital, Prague, with 1.2 million inhabitants, there are only four towns with populations exceeding 100 thousand people. The largest of them, Brno, has 370,000 inhabitants.

National minorities (Slovak, German, Polish, Roma) are rather small, their media does not play any significant role at the Czech media landscape. Besides, the largest minority, Slovaks, understand Czech language, which is similar to Slovak language. Slovaks living in the Czech Republic usually consume either the Czech media or the Slovak media imported into the Czech Republic from Slovakia.

1. The Market

A. *The Print Media*
Main features:

- Nine national dailies make two-thirds of the newspaper market;
- Sold circulation of newspapers is declining, only the boulevard press grows;
- The regional press is nearly completely controlled by a single publisher – VLP;
- Both, newspaper and magazine, publishers are mostly foreign owned.

The number of national daily newspapers is – with regard to the size of the Czech media market – rather high. The nine national dailies make up two-thirds of the newspaper market. The share of local and regional dailies is about 30 per cent. Nearly all of the daily press, with the exception of the leftist daily *Právo* and communist daily *Haló noviny*, are foreign owned. From the point of view of ownership, no publisher occupies any monopoly or dominant position in the national daily press.

The boulevard daily *Blesk* (Flash) ranks first (average circulation in 2006: 480,000 copies). The *Blesk* was launched by the Swiss company Ringier in 1992, and modelled on Swiss tabloid *Blick* or German *Bild*. *Blesk* is a cornerstone of Ringier's publishing business in the Czech Republic, which encompasses another national daily, *Sport* (66,000 copies), the weekly *Nedělní Blesk* (*Blesk on Sunday* – 300,000 copies, and several magazines (see below).

The second most sold newspaper is *MF Dnes* (*MF Today* – 300,000 copies), a descendant of the former socialist youth organization daily *Mladá Fronta*, which perished in 1990. The publisher of the paper is Mafra a.s., owned by Rheinisch-Bergische Verlagsgesellschaft (RBVG). The same German investor publishes another Czech national daily, *Lidové noviny* (*The People's Daily* – 70,000 copies).

The third place at the circulation chart occupies *Právo* (*The Right* – 165,000 copies), a descendant of the former communist party daily *Rudé právo* (*The Red Right*), which severed all ties with its former publisher in December 1990. The *Pravo*'s publishing company, Borgis a.s., was originally owned by editors and reporters of the paper. Later on, the editor-in-chief, Zdeněk Porybný, acquired the majority.

Unlike all the other Czech newspapers, which are distributed by newsagents, the daily *Hospodářské noviny* (*The Economic Daily* – 63,000 copies) relies mainly on subscriptions. Its publisher, Economia a.s., is owned by publishing group Verlagsgruppe Handelsblatt, represented by the HB-DJ-Investment B.V., which is connected to the Dow Jones Group.

In the situation in which the sold circulation of newspapers has been declining, and only the boulevard press has tendency to grow, two extra national boulevard dailies were launched in 2005–2006: *Šíp* (*The Arrow* – 60,000 copies) and *Aha!* (80,000 copies). Life expectancy of these projects is uncertain.

Besides national daily papers, about 80 regional and local papers are published in the Czech Republic, most of them by the publisher Vltava-Labe-Press (VLP), owned by the German publishing house Verlagsgruppe Passau and its company POL-Print Medien GmbH. In 2000, the VGP consolidated several of its Czech companies, including the publishers Vltava and Labe, into one big company, Vltava-Labe-Press. The next year VLP took control over all regional press in the Czech Republic thanks to an arrangement with other German publishers. In September 2006, VLP unified different headers of the regional newspapers. All of them contain the word "Deník" (The Daily) with regional adjectives, eg. Pražský deník, Brněnský deník, etc. The local identity represents a section inside the paper with local news.

Verlagsgruppe Passau was one of the three German publishing groups which invested into the Czech newspaper industry after 1989. The other two were Rheinisch-Bergische Verlagsgesellschaft (RBVG) and Mittlerhein Verlag (MRV). All of them took part in both the national and regional newspaper business. After several years of competition, the German investors reached a mutual agreement about division of interest and on the future of Czech regional press. The RBVG and MRV passed their regional dailies to the Passauer VGP group, which became a monopolist in the Czech regional press. MRV pulled out of the publishing industry in the Czech Republic and remains active only in the Czech printing industry. As a result of this arrangement, RVBG became a minority (20%) owner of the POL-Print Medien GmbH.

The first free Czech daily, *Metro*, published by Swedish MTG and distributed in Prague since July 1997, has been facing new competitors since 2005. Ringier, publisher of the tabloid *Blesk*, entered the free paper market with the free daily *24 hodin* (*24 hours*) in November 2005. Mafra, publisher of the daily *MF Dnes*, launched another free paper, *Metropolitní Expres* (*Metropolitan Express*), in April 2006.

The major part of the Czech magazine market is controlled by foreigners as well. Foreign publishers seized the opportunity to bring to the Czech magazine market clones of their home products (e.g. *Burda, Bravo, Tina, Reader's Digest, Chip, Autotip,* etc.) after 1989. However, some of the elder Czech magazines have survived the challenging market economy environment, and several new projects emerged after 1989 as well.

While there is a plenty of lifestyle magazines for women, girls, family or home, only three or four magazines, launched after the Velvet Revolution (*Respekt, Reflex, Týden*), have some ambition to be more than a lifestyle and an entertainment media.

Respekt is the successor of an opposition samizdat paper from 1989, whose readership consists mainly of intellectuals (16,000 copies). *Reflex* (55,000) stands on the borderline between a current affairs periodical and a "society" glossy. *Týden* (*The Week* – 52,000) tries to be a newsmagazine of western style. Czech business weeklies are represented by the periodicals *Ekonom* (*The Economist* – 22,000), *Euro* (24,000) and *Profit* (14,500).

The Czech magazine market is a rather stable one; the spheres of influence have been divided already in the 90s. Finnish Sanoma Magazines International (SMI) has a strong position in women's and lifestyle magazines. The publishing house Ringier ČR is active not only in the daily press (*Blesk*, *Sunday's Blesk*, *Sport*), but also in the magazine market. Besides the above-mentioned weekly *Reflex*, Ringier prints several TV guides, and a bi-weekly for young readers. Bauer Verlag's company Europress has a dominant position in societal and lifestyle cheap weeklies. Axel Springer Verlag publishes teenager monthlies, the auto-moto magazines and a computer magazine. Bertelsmann, which is active mainly in Czech book publishing, teamed together with the Verlagsgruppe Passau in a join venture, Astrosat. Astrosat publishes weekly magazines, which serve as supplements of VLP regional dailies. Another joint venture of foreign publishers, the company Vogel Burda Communications, specializes in technical and computer magazines.

Only 34.5 per cent of the total advertising revenue flows into the print media, while the television media enjoys 50 per cent share of disposable advertising revenue (about 18 billion crowns; 630 million euro).

2. The Broadcast Media
Main features:

- The four terrestrial channels, two public, two private, enjoy 90 per cent of TV audience
- The TV public service broadcaster operates four channels (two digital) with 30 per cent audience share
- Both dominant private TV networks Nova and Prima have foreign owners
- The penetration of cable and satellite television is low
- Two digital satellite services operate in the Czech Republic – UPC Direct and Digi TV
- Digital terrestrial TV broadcasting was launched on a regular basis only by the public broadcaster Czech Television in October 2005
- The other digital terrestrial TV broadcasts are supposed to be launched in 2007 after the quarrels about digital licensing will be cleared;
- Experiments with digital radio broadcasting DAB was halted in 2005.

Czech Republic introduced a full-fledged dual public-private system in both the radio and the television broadcasting in the years 1991 to 1994.

There are four terrestrial nationwide television channels available: two public service channels, CT1 and CT2, and two private commercial channels, TV Nova and TV Prima. Besides, twelve local TV stations in the regions operate mainly as a local "window" programme, sharing frequencies with the overall frame of the TV Prima broadcast system.

The four nationwide channels enjoy more than 90 per cent of the total television audience. The market leader is the TV Nova with 41 per cent audience share. Another private channel, Prima, got the attention of 23 per cent of viewers, both channels of public service television CT1 and CT2 attracted 30 per cent audience share in 2005. It means that only 6 per cent of the TV audience were allocated to the cable and satellite channels.

This situation stems from low penetration of cable and satellite in Czech households, and from a rather short supply of Czech TV programming services on cable and on satellite, where most of the channels are the foreign ones (Eurosport, HBO, Discovery, Animal Planet, MTV, etc.). Since the major part of the Czech population lives in smaller towns, up to ten thousand inhabitants, building of cable networks was not profitable, and availability of cable TV is restricted to the densely populated area of the larger towns.

With the perspective of digital broadcasting, several new cable and satellite Czech channels emerged since 2002. Among them are two public service channels: the news channel CT24 (2005) and the sport channel CT4 Sport (2006), and private television channels Ocko (music – 2002), Top TV (teleshopping – 2005), Galaxie Sport (sport – 2002) and others.

The strong position of TV Nova has historical roots because the channel, when launched in February 1994, received the frequencies of the former Czechoslovak federal channel F1 with 100 per cent coverage. TV Prima, the very first Czech private commercial TV, which started in June 1993 as a small Prague local station, TV Premiera, later, after 1995, evolved into the nationwide channel.

The owner of TV Nova is the American company Central European Media Enterprises (CME), which operates several other television stations in Central and Eastern Europe (Slovakia, Romania, Slovenia, Croatia, Ukraine). The Prima TV Holding company, which operates the TV Prima channel, is controlled by 50/50 partnership of the Czech investment group GES Holding and Scandinavian Modern Times Group (MTG).

The public service broadcaster Czech Television (CT), established by the Act 483/91 as an independent public service corporation, is a descendant of the former state Czechoslovak Television, whose record of regular broadcasting commenced in 1953. The Czech Television separated from the Czechoslovak Television in January 1992. After the split of Czechoslovakia in January 1993, CT became the sole public broadcaster in the country.

CT is funded by a TV licence fee, which is levied on every household with a TV set. The additional revenues come from commercials and sponsorship. The advertising time in CT broadcast has been limited for 1 per cent of total broadcasting time so far. An amendment of the Czech Television Act of 2005 determined that the amount of commercials in CT shall be gradually decreased, and since January 2008 the advertising in the public service channels CT1 and CT2 shall wholly disappear.

Unlike the other European public service broadcasters, the Czech Television and the public broadcaster Czech Radio are not associated in one organization; they are separate and detached bodies. The history of Czech Radio is similar to the Czech Television's. Like the Czech Television, the Czech Radio is funded by a radio licence fee together with commercials and sponsorship and other commercial activities, which together make about 15 per cent of the total income.

Czech Radio operates networks of seven stations, from which three have fully nationwide coverage. CRo1 Radiozurnal is a 24-hour news and current affairs station. CRo2 Praha is a family station. CRo3 Vltava is a culture station. CRo4 Radio Wave targets to teenagers. CRo5 Regina encompasses the regional stations. CRo6 is an AM current affairs station with broadcasting time limited to the afternoon and evening hours. CRo7 is a short-wave international broadcasting station.

Apart from radio programmes broadcasted by the public service broadcaster Český rozhlas (Czech Radio) there are 77 other radio stations, among them two – *Frekvence 1* and *Impuls* – with nationwide coverage.

Among the Czech private radio broadcasters there is no dominant station with a position comparable to that of television Nova in the television market. The three stations with the largest audience share are Čro1 Radiožurnál, operated by the public service Czech Radio, and two commercial nationwide radio stations, *Frekvence 1* and *Radio Impuls*. All of them have nearly the same share of the listening public, between 10 to 12 per cent. The rest of the audience share is dispersed among 70 other private local stations, some of which are interconnected into co-operating mini-networks (e.g. Evropa 2, Radio Hey).

From the point of view of the ownership, the most powerful position in the radio market is occupied by a group of French investors, Lagardere Active Radio International SA, which consists of a nationwide station, *Frekvence 1*, a set of the stations, Evropa 2, and a media sales agency, Radio Regie Music (RRM). The second largest private broadcaster, the nation-wide station *Radio Impuls*, is controlled by a joint venture of radio broadcasters from Eastern Germany, the investment consortium Eurocast Rundfunk Beteiligungs GmbH.

About 70 per cent of households receive television broadcasting terrestrially only. The cable companies claim that about 1.2 million households could be connected; however, only 700,000 of them, i.e. 20 per cent, have subscribed. The satellite penetration varies between 9 and 15 per cent of households. The cable market is controlled by two companies, UPC Czech and Karneval, which are going to merge on condition that the Czech Office for the Protection of Competition will endorse it. Karneval currently has 310,000 subscribers, of whom 57,000 have broadband Internet access, while UPC has 420,000 subscribers for its cable and satellite services, with around 100,000 receiving broadband Internet access.

The digital satellite service *UPC Direct*, launched in September 2000 offers to its clients more than thirty TV channels in Czech language, apart from dozens of foreign channel not localized in Czech. Number of subscribers in 2006: 120,000 households. New digital satellite service Digi TV, based in Romania with services in Hungary and Slovakia, entered the Czech market in autumn 2006. Number of channels supplied by the service is smaller; however the subscription fee is considerably lower.

Since 2000 the digital terrestrial broadcasting has been tested locally in Prague. In July 2004 the Czech Telecommunication Office (CTU) has granted a set of permits for operation of three DVB-T networks/multiplexes, "A", "B", "C", to the Czech Radiocommunications (CRa), the Czech Digital Group (CDG) and to the Cesky Telecom (today's Telefónica O2).

The regular DVB-T started in October 2005 on the multiplex "A" in Prague only. The multiplex "A" was assigned to public service channels CT1, CT2, CT24, CT4 Sport), whose licences are based on the Czech Television Act. The initial broadcasting in Prague was extended to other towns Brno and Ostrava in February 2006.

The other multiplexes operate still on the experimental temporary basis, due to the unclear situation as to their licensed programming services.

The Council for Radio and Television Broadcasting (RRTV) has allocated six new digital licences to commercial broadcasters in April 2006. Because courts allowed the appeals of failed licence applicants, among them TV Nova, the licensing process has to start from the very beginning again. When the new digital channels will go on the air is not clear today.

Experiments with digital radio broadcasting DAB have been halted after several years of testing by the Czech Radio Communications company. The digital radio broadcasting is going to be incorporated as a part of the DVB-T traffic.

C. *The Internet Media*
Main features:

■ The rate of Internet use is low compared to the EU average;
■ Czechs are using Internet more at their workplace than in their homes;

■ All the traditional media has its online versions, the number one webpage operated by a traditional media publisher is *idnes.cz*;
■ The most visited Internet portal is *Seznam.cz*.

About one-third of the Czech population regularly use the Internet. In comparison with the more developed countries like Finland, Germany, United States, Czechs are using Internet more at their workplaces than in their homes. The Czech Republic ranks in the OECD Broadband Statistics at the 24th place with 650,000 total broadband subscribers, i.e. six people out of a hundred have access to high-speed Internet.

Since 1995, when the first private Internet providers broke monopoly of the state telecoms, plenty of informative websites have emerged. Some of them turned later into the full-fledged Internet portals, which either co-operates with, or are directly operated by, the big media organizations.

The website www.seznam.cz is the most visited Internet portal, whose news sections, www.novinky.cz and www.super.cz, are supplied by the daily *Pravo* and by the local tabloid *SuperSpy*. The second most visited portal, www.centrum.cz, launched its own online daily, www.aktualne.cz, in October 2005. The third most visited portal, www.atlas.cz, is connected to the news service of the Czech wire agency CTK.

The publishing house Mafra runs its own news website, www.idnes.cz. Also, the other media launched websites with services, in which its range depended on the size and on the scope of activities of their publishers. Among them are www.lidovky.cz (*Lidové noviny*), www.ihned.cz (*Hospodářské noviny*), www.blesk.cz (tabloid *Blesk*), www.denik.cz (*Vltava-Labe-Press*), www.ct24.cz (Czech Television), www.cro.cz (Czech Radio), www.ceskenoviny.cz (CTK) and others.

D. News Agencies
Main features:

■ There is only one full service news agency, CTK;
■ CTK offers text, picture, video and audio news, infographics and other services.

The Czech News Agency (CTK) is the only Czech full service information agency in the Czech Republic. CTK supply the Czech media with the text, audio, and, since March 2006, some video news content. CTK is an independent and economically self-supporting public service company, controlled by the CTK Council, appointed by the parliament.

Neris, the subsidiary completely owned by the Czech News Agency, runs three news websites, www.ceskenoviny.cz (general news), www.sportovni noviny.cz (sport news) and www.financninoviny.cz (finance), and offers its clients specialized informational services based on text and audio and photo news services from CTK.

2. State Policies

Main features:

- There are no state media in the Czech Republic;
- Its freedom is guaranteed by the Constitution and by the Charter of Fundamental Rights and Freedoms;
- There are no limits for foreign ownership in both print and broadcast media;
- Czech legislation is compatible with EU Directives;
- Publishers are responsible for observing general legal norms (Constitution, Civil Code, Penal Code, etc.);
- The public broadcasters' activities are surveyed by the Czech Television and the Czech Radio Councils appointed by the parliament.

All the Czech media are now in private hands. The only exceptions are the public broadcasting organizations Český rozhlas (Czech Radio), Česká televize (Czech television) and the news agency CTK (Czech Press Agency), which are established by law, have a status of independent public corporations and are controlled by the parliament.

Print media are not subject of any specific regulation. The Press Act stipulates that a publisher of media can be either any natural or any legal person possessing either Czech or foreign citizenship, who registers the periodical at the Ministry of Culture. The Press Act defines the rights and duties of the publishers (e.g. right to reply, obligatory copies, etc.) but does not mention any provision regarding ownership or content of the media.

Broadcast media are regulated by the Broadcasting Act on radio and television broadcasting. The Act set up the Council for Radio and Television Broadcasting (www. rrtv.cz), which is responsible for the licensing of private broadcasters and for supervising both private and public broadcasters as to their adherence to the provisions of the Broadcasting Act.

The Czech Radio and the Czech Television have been established by a special Act, which stipulates the special rules and principles for their public mission and for public control of their activities. Both public service broadcasters are funded by the licence fee, whose rate is determined by a special Act approved by the Parliament.

The Czech legislation is in accordance with the basic principles of the EU legislation, namely with the "Television Without Frontiers" Directive.

Freedom of expression is guaranteed by the Charter of Fundamental Rights and Freedoms. The Czech Republic is a signatory to the European Convention of Human Rights.

The journalists shall observe the Constitution and general legal norms, in particular the Civil Code and the Penal Code in respect of defamation. According to the Press Act and the Broadcasting Act, publishers and broadcasters are responsible for their published material.

The accountability of public service media shall be preserved by the Councils of the media (Czech Television Council, Czech Radio Council, CTK Council), whose members, appointed by the parliament, represent various societal groups.

The Czech Television Code adopted by the Chamber of Deputies of the Czech Parliament "set out and establish the principles for the operation of public service television and thus become an effective instrument for ensuring that the objectives of public service television are fulfilled." The Code also establishes an Ethics Panel of the Czech Television, the members of which will be appointed by the Director General of Czech Television.

3. Civil Society Organizations
Main features:

- Two most important associations are UVDT for newspapers, APSV for commercial radio;
- Public and commercial television operators are members of the ATO association, which organizes the audience research for all of them;
- Only minor part of working journalists are members of the only professional association: The Union of Journalists;
- The Ethical Commission of the Union of Journalists handles complaints from the public;
- The advertising agencies, media and advertisers set up a self-regulation body: the Council for Advertising.

The Czech media companies are associated in different associations in accordance with their branches of activity. Most of the print media publishers are members of the Czech Publishers Association (www.uvdt.cz), which use the audit services of the Audit Bureau of Circulation Czech Republic (www.abccr.cz).

Czech private radio broadcasters established the Association of Private Radio Broadcasters (www.apsv.cz). Czech television broadcasters joined together in the Association of Television Organizations (www.ato.cz) for the purpose of financing the people meter–audience research operated by Mediaresearch company (www.mediaresearch.cz).

The only working organization of journalists is the Union of the Czech Journalists. However, only a minority of active journalists are members of the association.

The Union of Czech Journalists, the professional association of Czech journalists, set up the Ethical commission as an independent professional body of eleven members in 1998. The members of the Ethical commission are volunteers from the media and university world approved by the Union board. The general meeting of the Union approved the Code of journalists' ethics, which is applicable for the Union members.

An initiative of Czech advertising agencies, media and advertisers, led to the foundation of the Council for Advertising in 1994 as a non-profit organization by the association of advertisers, advertising agencies and media and became the first self-regulatory association from Central and Eastern Europe.

4. Development Trends
Main features:

- The transition from analogue to digital terrestrial broadcasting is the main issue of Czech media development;
- Four digital multiplexes are to be operational in 2008, however, their coverage and their content is not yet decided;
- The growing consumption of online media stands behind ongoing decrease of consumption of traditional media;
- Television takes still the largest share of the advertising pie; the Internet's advertising money is growing.

Nowadays the main issue of the Czech media policy is the transition from analogue to digital terrestrial broadcasting, which is marked by a lack of co-ordination between legislators and two regulators: the Council for Radio and Television Broadcasting and the Czech Telecommunication Office.

A Law assigned the responsibility for transition to the CTU, which is working on the binding document "Technical Plan for Transition from Analogue to Digital Terrestrial Television Broadcasting" (TPP). The conflicts between incumbent private terrestrial broadcasters (TV Nova, TV Prima) and newly licensed channels have paralyzed the transition for the time being. The incumbent's interest is to maintain their audiences as big as possible for as long as possible; therefore, they are trying to block the early switch-off date by way of court actions against the licensing body RRTV. However, the CTU is still determined to end analogue broadcasting as soon as possible, at the latest in the year 2012.

According to the TPP, the frequencies for four multiplexes networks, numbered 1–4, shall be available in 2008. The maximal coverage shall be given to the multiplex No. 1, reserved for the public service Czech Television. The current multiplexes, "A", "B", "C", shall be transformed into networks No. 2–4, but there is still no decision about programming services to be allocated there.

The recent merger between UPC and Karneval (see above) would on the one hand create a virtual monopoly in the Czech cable industry but on the other hand it should reduce the dominance of the incumbent telecommunication company Telefónica O2 in the provision of voice and Internet services. When launching the IPTV service in September 2006, Telefónica O2 entered the audio-visual media field.

The newspapers are facing a small but permanent decrease in the circulation numbers, which is caused by growing consumption of online media and by emergence of free papers in the market. However, there is still the growth capacity in the advertising income. Despite declining sales, the print media publishers still have been increasing their turnovers.

The ratio of the advertising expenditures is still in favour of television, which takes the largest share of advertising money available. The share of the Internet in the advertising pie is lagging behind the outdoor and radio ads spending, however, the gap is getting smaller.

Due to the current political instability in the Czech Republic, caused by election results without any winner in 2006, there is no perspective of any radical change in media legislation. That does not rule out a possibility that the process of media digitalization may bring about some necessary amendments in the existing media law.

References & Sources for Further Information

Annual Reports of Publishers Union (in Czech) http://www.uvdt.cz.

Annual Reports of the Council for Radio and Television Broadcasting (in English) <http://www.rrtv.cz/en/>.

Collection of Laws of the Czech Republic (in Czech) <http://www.mvcr.cz>.

Czech Parliament – documents, stenos <http://www.psp.cz/cgi-bin/eng/ >.

Czech Media and Marketing Useful Sources – fekar.cz <http://fekar.webpark.cz/media-en.htm>.

Czech Republic, In: Television Across Europe – regulation, policy and independence. Open Society Institute, Budapest 2005. ISBN: 1-891385-35-6 <http://www.eumap.org>.

Šmíd, Milan: Czech Republic. In: Media Ownership and Its Impact on Media Independence and Pluralism Peace Institute, Institute for Contemporary Social and Political Studies, Ljubljana 2004. ISBN: 961-6455-26-5 <http://www.mirovni-institut.si/media_ownership/czech.htm>.

Kroupa Vladimír, Šmíd Milan: Media System of the Czech Republic.

http://www.hans-bredow-institut.de/forschung/recht/co-reg/reports/1/Czech-Republic.pdf.

Šmíd, Milan: Medien in der Tschechischen Republik. In: Internationales Handbuch fuer Rundfunk und Fernsehen 2004/2005. Hans-Bredow Institut, Hamburg. Nomos Verlagsgesellschaft 2004, ISBN 3-8329-0603-7, p. 661–670, ISSN 0946-3348.

THE ESTONIAN MEDIA LANDSCAPE

Urmas Loit

Estonia is a small country – 45,000 sq km – at the Baltic Sea, which during the past twenty years has gone through comprehensive transition from a colonial territory within the USSR into an independent democracy, which became a Member State of the EU in 2004. The population of 1.36 million is made up by two relatively detached communities – ethnic Estonians (927,000) and Russian-speaking community. These two communities are characterized by distinct media consumption patterns. Traditionally, Estonians have been avid readers, listeners and viewers.

Media consumption is an important feature of people's everyday life in Estonia. 74.5 per cent of the population (Estonians: 82.1%, Russian-speakers: 59.7%) read newspapers regularly; 69.7 per cent (E: 77.8, R: 54.0) read magazines regularly. Still only 32 per cent turn to newspapers for news daily. 68 per cent of the population watches TV daily for news, 55 per cent listens to radio daily for news. The average inhabitant of Estonia listens daily to radio for 4 hours and 52 min and watches TV for 4 hours and 4 min per day. 46.6 per cent of the population has used Internet during the past six months (Source: TNS EMOR, Eurobarometer; 2003). Television and radio are notably more trusted media types than newspapers. According to Eurobarometer (2004) 75 per cent trust or generally trust radio and television, compared to 52 percent for newspapers. Public radio and television are by about one third more trusted than private radio and television (Source: University of Tartu 2003). The trust rating for Internet news portals is as low as 20 per cent.

1. The Market

A. The Print Media
Main features:

■ The newspaper sector, like the rest of media, is characterized by heavy concentration;
■ The market has stabilized since major mergers in 1998;
■ The newspaper sector maintains its majority share in the total advertising expenditure, although gradually ceding it to television sector;
■ The magazine market is led by family, home and lifestyle magazines.

The press has fully moved away from being under the state control and is now an independently run sector. The government holds a stake only in a few cultural and educational publications, which still enjoy full editorial independence from the authorities. The transformation of the press from being a tool of official communist ideology and part of the state-run system into a privately run sector took place in an evolutionary manner from the end of the 1980s to 1994. Contrary to predictions, this transformation did not result in massive closures of titles or other major structural changes, although the market contracted and sales went down.

The first new privately operated newspapers, set up at the end of the 1980s, introduced a new style of reporting – more probing, bold, and a presentation that took their cue from the tabloid press.

Newspaper privatisation took place at the beginning of the 1990s, on a case-by-case basis, with the government agreeing that it should no longer be involved in newspaper publishing. In most cases, newspapers were privatised by management and/or staff buyout. A few years after that, however, most of these original shareholders sold out to core owners, either from among the local publishers or from abroad. Thus, by the end of the 1990s, the number of journalists as shareholders in their own newspapers had been reduced considerably.

The first newspaper to be privatized (in 1991/92) was the *Postimees* daily. Currently, this paper is the nation's top-selling title, with a daily circulation over 60,000.

Newspapers in Estonia claim complete editorial independence from political parties and the government, and in an overwhelming majority of the cases it is true. A few parties have tried to publish their own papers but only that of the Centrist Party (*Keskerakond*) has endured as a regular general-interest weekly publication.

There is a growing tendency towards concentration of ownership in the media sector. Publishing companies owning just one newspaper or magazine have been forced to sell themselves to bigger publishing concerns or go out of business. In 1994, for example, there were eleven national dailies in Estonia. In 2006, the number is six.

The main newspaper figures in the second quarter of 2006 were as follows (members of the Estonian Newspaper Association):

- Six national dailies (four in Estonian, two in Russian)
- Ten weeklies (six in Estonian, four in Russian)
- Twenty-four regional papers (nineteen in Estonian, five in Russian)

As a result of the concentration, the national market is being dominated by two major publishing groups: Postimees Group (formally known as Eesti Meedia) and Ekspress Group, both of which are involved in the publication of newspapers and magazines. 1998 saw major developments towards foreign ownership of the Estonian press. Until that time, foreign owners were almost absent from the Estonian market, with the exception of Sweden's Bonnier Group, which had been publishing the business daily *Äripäev* already since 1989.

In 1998, however, two Scandinavian media companies, Sweden's Marieberg and Norway's Schibsted, made important acquisitions in Estonia. Marieberg became part owner in the second biggest daily, *Eesti Päevaleht*, while Schibsted obtained control over the biggest daily, *Postimees*. The two papers had held a consumptive circulation war for several years. In 2001 the Estonian businessmen re-acquitted the stakes of Ekspress Group they had sold in 1998.

Schibsted's acquisitions first led to the disappearance of *Sõnumileht* from the crowded quality market: *Sõnumileht* was converted from a quality daily into a tabloid by the recent Norwegian owners in 1998. In 2000, furthermore, the two competing tabloids were merged into a joint venture of two rival media groups under the title *SL Õhtuleht*. The new publication was based on the underlay inherited mainly from the other party of the merger – *Õhtuleht* – including the basic part of the title and the staff, although the ownership share was divided equally between two companies.

Similar merging happened to the variety of competing magazines, which are now also operated by a joint venture. Only recently new competitors to the joint magazines have started to pop up with new titles.

The powerful entry into the Estonian market of the two Scandinavian companies has further strengthened media concentration. Schibsted, for example, also has a 100 per cent stake in the commercial TV broadcaster Kanal 2. Besides, Schibsted has stakes (from 42 up to 100 per cent) in five local newspapers.

In 1998, the publishing company Eesti Päevaleht daily made a major entry by developing the family of free regional weekly advertising papers. In 2006, the city papers have reached a circulation from 15,000 in Pärnu to 36,800 in the capital city, Tallinn, where also the Russian version is being published (20,600).

The print media continues to enjoy a 0 per cent value added tax for subscriptions although the single copy sales are taxed with the regular rate of 18 per cent. The 0 per cent VAT has been under the question by the government for several times, but the Newspaper Association has maintained the remission.

The circulations of the papers have seen a dramatic decrease. The biggest circulations at the end of the 1980s exceeded 200,000 per title (in a population of 1.5 million where Estonians were under a million). The top circulations in 2005 were up to 67,000 which means the actuarial readership of approximately 256,000.

The combined daily circulation of all the member papers of the Estonian Newspaper Association in 1992 was 831,400. In 2005, it was 543,600. *SL Õhtuleht* (daily tabloid; 65,600), *Postimees* (general interest daily; 64,000), *Eesti Päevaleht* (general interest daily; 31,000), *Eesti Ekspress* (general interest weekly; 48,900) and *Maaleht* (rural weekly; 43,400) are among the titles with the highest circulation standing at September 2006. The highest circulations among Russian-language titles were held by *Vesti Nedeli Den za Dnem* (among weeklies; 19,000) and *Vesti Dnya* (among dailies; 12,000).

Local newspapers, which are published in every county (region; *maakond*) along with many municipalities, are regularly read by 57 per cent of the population. Despite the drop of the circulation during the fifteen years of Estonia's independence, the local papers have maintained their position in the community and their readership and economic situation have been improving during the past years. The circulations range from 15,700 (*Pärnu Postimees*) to 1,500 (some town papers).

The print media have been successfully defending their large share of the advertising market, in competition with the electronic media. According to TNS EMOR, the newspapers' share of the total advertising expenditure is still the largest, although gradually shrinking – from 55 per cent in 1995 to 45 per cent in 2005. The share of TV is concurrently rising – from 23 per cent in 1995 to 27 per cent in 2005. Magazines held the share of 12 per cent in 2005, radio – 8 per cent and Internet – 3 per cent.

The number of magazines, despite above mentioned total mergers in 1998 reaches 211 titles among the general interest magazines. The specialised magazines number to 969 titles (data of 2003). The circulations vary from 44,600 (*Kroonika* – a magazine about social life and celebrities) to 1500 (e.g. *Teater. Muusika. Kino* – a cultural magazine) or even 300 (some scientific publications, e.g. *Oil Shale*). The family, home and lifestyle magazines are among the most popular ones. Slightly less influential are magazines for women, about health and crossword magazines. In general, the number of soft-topic publications among the general interest magazines is notable, while the political analysis magazine from among the general interest magazines has been missing since 2001, when *Luup* ceased to appear. The magazines have national coverage, no regional magazines are published. Most of magazines appear monthly.

B. The Broadcast Media
Main features:

- According to law amendments of 2001 there is no advertising in public broadcasting and the number of nationwide terrestrial channels is limited to two;
- The television sector is being operated by Scandinavian players;
- Estonian population is avid viewer and listener. Estonians prefer domestic programmes, Russian-speakers prefer those broadcasted from Russia;
- Most of urban areas have been covered by cable television networks, which are being remodelled into digital networks within broadband data communication service packages;
- Digital radio has not been implemented.

Deregulation in the field of broadcasting has brought radical change when compared to 1990. The first private radio station went on the air in 1991. The first licences for private broadcasters were issued in 1992. The Broadcasting Act was adopted in 1994.
A major change on the TV scene took place in 1993 as Estonia stopped the retransmission of broadcasts of the two central TV channels from Moscow and one from St Petersburg. The three channels along with the local ETV used to be part of the state-controlled daily viewing diet of people in Estonia during the Soviet period.

Today, the public channel Eesti Televisioon (ETV), where the bulk of the programming is in Estonian, also includes a daily newscast and some feature programmes in Russian. Besides ETV, Estonian viewers can watch two private TV channels: Kanal 2 and TV3. The third – TV1 – went bankrupt in 2001.

Channels from the Russian Federation (as well as other pan-European satellite channels) can now be watched on cable TV. Finnish TV can be watched via terrestrial broadcast in the northern part of Estonia, while cable networks include it to the package all across the country.

TV3 has enjoyed for some time the highest ratings among the most watched TV channels. For example, in 2003 TV3's share was 24.4 per cent compared to 20.0 per cent for Kanal 2 and 16.8 percent for ETV. By fall 2006 Kanal 2 took over the leader position, achieving 23 per cent share compared to 19 per cent for TV3. Analysts say that the efforts of Kanal 2 in improving its programming may have far-reaching impact on television market. In re advertising market, TV3 still is the best selling company, controlling slightly over 50 per cent of the total television advertising turnover.

Estonians prefer local television channels, while the Russian-speaking population watch predominantly programming from Russia via cable. The audience share of all Estonian television channels combined among the Russian-speaking population has been less than 10 per cent since 2001/2002 and has been falling constantly. Around one-third of the Russian-speaking audience does not watch Estonian television channels at all or does it less than once a month.

The national commercial TV channels are owned by foreigners (Norway's Schibsted owns Kanal 2 and Sweden's MTG Group owns TV3).

The public service radio organization Eesti Raadio broadcasts on four different channels (general information channel targeted to age group 40+; the programme for young listeners to age group 15–35; the classics channel and the Russian channel).

There are 25 private radio stations operating. Two largest radio companies, Trio LSL and Sky Media (First Media), are building up nationwide coverage, while others are predominantly local or regional. Still, according to the statute by the Broadcasting Act the radio licences can be either local or regional – the latter includes both local coverage with two low-radiation antennas and nearby-national coverage. Trio LSL (with six different radio stations) is owned by the Metromedia Inc. and Schibsted (32 per cent of stakes), while Sky Media (also running six radio stations) is owned by Estonian capital.

The data about radio stations' audience shares do not provide explicit comparability, as the programmes of the public radio are granted quality nationwide coverage areas by law, while private stations are limited to coverage areas provided by 'regional' licences. None of them actually has nationwide coverage comparable with those of the public radio, even though regional licence does not directly exclude the possibility for it. The most influential Russian-language radio station is that of the public radio. The radio advertising market is dominated by two large radio companies – Trio LSL (with 67 percent ownership by Metromedia Inc.) and Sky Media (First Media, Estonian capital) – each of them holding a third of the total market. The rest is being divided among all other players.

Since July 2002 public television does not carry advertising. Private television stations pay a fee for their licences to the state. Under these terms the number of television channels with national or international coverage is limited to two. Since January 2005 the same non-advertising regulation applies to the public radio broadcasters. Private radio broadcasters still do not pay any fee in return for these statutory provisions. The non-advertising policy for the public broadcasters not only stabilizes the tight advertising market but also assures non-commercial quality programming. Although financed from the state budget, government interference has not been an issue for the public broadcasting since 1990.

The number of cable television operators amounts to 42. However, only five of them produce their own programming. Three cable operators operate nationwide: Starman, STV and Esdata (Elion). The latter provides, as of 2006, digital cable services associated to its data communication services. Also Starman and STV are in the stage of implementing cable services digitally.

In re terrestrial digital broadcasting – television – it is the stage of testing. The government has renewed the deadline for final transition from analogue to digital, which is December 2012. In radio – the digital standard has not been implemented.

C. *The Internet Media*
Main features:

- The rate of computerization and Internet penetration in Estonia is comparatively high;
- The Estonian media landscape is characterized by scarcity of new media outlets.

The rate of computerization and Internet penetration in Estonia is comparatively high. Forty per cent of households and 90 per cent of offices have Internet connection. Some 58 per cent of the population aged 15 to 74 use the Internet, while 52 per cent do it at least once a week. 75 per cent of the Internet users visit Internet banking facilities, 62 per cent read Estonian online media publications, 35 per cent listen to radio and 20 per cent watch TV programmes via Internet (sources: TNS EMOR, Eurostat 2006).

In 1999 new media outlets started to appear. Among all, *Delfi.ee* has proved to be the most vital news portal. Also a unique and innovative comment centre has been supplemented to all news items – any reader can add his comment to the issue. Other independent portals have had less success in providing online news, e.g., *Everyday.com* and *Mega.ee* winded up their activities as a *Delfi.ee*-like newsroom. Still there is a number of other news portals (*Minut.ee*, *Teadus.ee*, *Greengate.ee*, *Materialist.netikuller.ee*, etc.), which rather act as alternative to the mainstream media or a specialized portal than an independent business. Often the traditional news criteria do not apply to the materials publicized on these websites.

The first traditional paper to work seriously with an online version was the economic daily *Äripäev* – which currently charges for visiting its online site. Soon also other newspapers introduced their online versions, enduringly providing fresh news. In 2005, also, the public television created an online news portal – *ETV 24* – which along with the newspapers' online versions often serve as news agencies for radio newsrooms. A variety of TV programmes can be retrieved from Internet archives (e.g. tv.ee), public radio and some private talk radios (e.g. Kuku) provide audio archives.

Also the first Podcast sites have emerged (*www.superkinod.ee/podcast/*). Most of the terrestrial radio programmes of Estonia can be listened to online. Blog journalism has also instituted itself. However, the experts evaluate that the Estonian media landscape is rather characterized by scarcity of new media outlets. The smallness of the market has not left much room for other commercial undertakings besides big ones – *Delfi.ee*, *Postimees Online* and *EPL Online*.

D. *News Agencies*

There is one news agency operating in Estonia – the Baltic News Service (BNS), which is a regional news agency covering Estonia, Latvia and Lithuania. BNS is fully owned by Finnish Alma Media. The domestic Estonian News Agency (Eesti Teadete Agentuur, ETA) was privatized to a Latvian news agency in 2000 and went into bankruptcy three years later.

2. State Policies

Main features:

- Estonia offers a liberal environment for the media;
- No specific print media law exists; print media issues are covered by general laws, sometimes leaving unregulated areas;
- Broadcasting and advertising are predominantly regulated by statutory rules, written press relays on self-regulation and good practices;
- Broadcasting is regulated in line with EU directives;
- State policy about digitalization leaves the question about financing unanswered.

Freedom of expression is granted by the Constitution. From the legislative point of view, Estonia offers a liberal environment for the media. Some experts consider it to be too liberal and therefore lacking enough social responsibility. There is no general press law although attempts have been made to write one in the early 1990s. Among other things, the lack of the law has created a legal situation where it is not clear whom should one sue in case of violating his/her rights: would it be the publisher, chief editor, journalist or somebody else.

There are three authorities in total supervising directly the broadcasting issues, while there are no state enforcement authorities for the written press and new media. Internet has been regulated only from the technical point of view.

Under the 1994 Broadcasting Act, the activities of the public service broadcasting is supervised by the Broadcasting Council, a parliament-appointed body. Five members of the total nine of it come from among the MPs, the rest of them are appointed from among experts. In fall 2006 the new version of the Broadcasting Act (concerning the public broadcasting) is being proceeded by the Government and the Parliament, according to which all members of the Broadcasting Council ought be politicians. The Legal Chancellor has drawn the MPs' attention to the fact that politicized supervision of the public broadcasting inhibits the functioning of it. However, the MPs often refer to the public broadcasters as 'state' broadcasters.

An expert commission drawn up under the law on the protection of minors from pornography and violence has been created by the Ministry of Culture. The commission's task is not to issue licences but give expert opinion on works provided to them by law enforcement bodies or importers. This commission also provides opinion about programmes publicly broadcasted, usually when there has been a filed complaint.

Advertising is regulated by the Advertising Act as of 1997. According to experts it has been a 'dormant' law, often disregarded in many accounts. The Parliament has been proceeding with a new version of it in 2006. So far the industry has failed to introduce overall self-regulation in the field of advertising, despite some recent actions advocated by the European Advertising Standards Alliance.

For print media, Estonia does not require any licence, permit or registration to set up a newspaper. The same applies for using the services of a printing plant or distributing the publication.

Broadcasting is governed by the Broadcasting Act, passed in 1994. The law provides for the allocation of licences for private broadcasters as well as setting the foundations of the public service TV and radio and defines the general terms for broadcasting. The law has been brought in line with EU directives, which was mandatory for EU accession.

As of 2005 the Act on Electronic Communication entered into power, replacing the Cable Act valid heretofore. This law prescribes, in combination with the Broadcasting Act, the competencies between the Ministry of Culture, issuing the broadcasting licences (for content), and the Estonian National Communication Board, issuing the technical licences. Those kinds of licences are required from every broadcaster, including cable broadcasters.

The "must carry" regulation is stricter towards television than radio, deriving from the EU TWF directive. In addition to the obligations set by the Directive, the television stations need to broadcast their 'own production', and half of it should be broadcasted during prime time. Both radio and television should broadcast news for at least 5 per cent of their daily output with the exception of Sundays and national holidays.

Cases regarding libel are covered primarily by the Law of Obligations Act. In libel, the burden of proof rests with the media. The media in Estonia is also affected by the Copyright Act, Competition Act, Language Act, Advertising Act, State Secrets Act, and the Public Information Act. Libel has been excluded from the Penal Code where it was incorporated until 2002 as remains of the Soviet jurisprudence. The law courts have been relatively dormant in sentencing the recompense for non-patrimonial damage (libel), although in several cases the media organization has been found guilty for violating individuals' personal rights.

There is no fixed state subsidy system for the press in Estonia. Every year, however, the parliament earmarks a certain sum for the postal authority *Eesti Post* to subsidize the delivery of periodicals to the countryside. Private broadcasters receive no subsidies from the state, while public broadcasting receives the bulk of its financing from the state budget.

Policies for digital television have been envisaged in concepts adopted by the government. According to the document, Digital Video Broadcasting Terrestrial (DVB-T) and Handheld (DVB-H) are considered the most promising standards. Digital satellite broadcasting (DVB-S) has been defined as a standard with no big future, as the country's territory is compact. Still, *Viasat* does rebroadcast the terrestrial programmes of TV3 and ETV also via satellite. The government has also adopted a Concept for broadband standards. But both Concepts lack vision regarding financing, thus, they have not had much impact on actual developments in the field of digitalization.

3. Civil Society Organizations
Main features:

- Due to dissentions towards principles of self-regulation two press councils exist;
- Public involvement in discussion about media quality is poor.

The main media organizations are the Newspaper Association (defining itself as a multi-task organization for the newspaper publishers, editors and journalists) and the Association of Broadcasters (representing the interests of commercial broadcasters). The Journalists' Union executes the role of a trade union as well as that of a professional guild. Media educators have formed the Society Media Educators. Independent producers in the audio-visual sector have also a representation body as well as the advertising agencies do have theirs.

Media research is carried out by TNS EMOR (former Baltic Media Facts), as well as by some other Gallup organizations.

In December 1997, the Estonian Newspaper Association passed a Code of Press Ethics, the first of its kind in post-independence Estonia. The Association of Broadcasters joined in by approving it, and as of 1998, the Code has served as a source document for the Press Council, a non-statutory self-regulatory body set up to handle complaints about the media. The business daily *Äripäev* has an individual code of ethics for itself, along with the national code. Also the Broadcasting Council has set principles for good conduct, inter alia referring to the national code.

The Press Council (Avaliku Sõna Nõukogu) was set up by the Newspaper Association in 1991, but was put on a wider footing in 1998, when it was reconstituted into a independent organization with member organizations as the Society of Media Educators, the Journalists' Union and the Union of Consumer Protection, the Council of Churches, to name some.

In 2002 the chief editors of major newspapers posed a demarche against the then chairman accusing him in mismanagement. The talks of the Newspaper Association with other member organizations failed (others did not sustain the accusations) and the Newspaper Association founded a new Press Council of their own (Pressinõukogu). By 2006 the Internet portals and public broadcasters have joined the self-regulatory system of the Newspaper Association. The original Press Council keeps operating as well, supported by the Journalists' Union, media educators and some other non-media civic organizations. It predominantly acts in a quality of a think tank.

The non-media NGOs have been keeping a low profile in publicly discussing the media quality. They usually lack appropriate professional competency, but also, as the above described press council's experience indicates, the media itself is not much willing to accept criticism originating from outside the professional circle itself.

4. Development Trends

Main features:

- Further media concentration
- New PSB law

The future will probably bring further media concentration, as the state's media policy will remain quite liberal towards this issue as well as towards the media issues in general. The tensions provoked by the revision of provisions in reference to the organization of the PSB will probably end up with a new law merging public radio and television into one, as expected, while the efforts to intensify the political control over the public broadcasting will die away like in several earlier cases when the political interference was feared.

The newspaper titles and broadcast stations currently existing have shown perseverance, which most likely will help them economically to survive also during the future periods. The market has stabilized, still for some market players remaining shaky, hindering the improvement of quality. Also the commercial television stations keep making profits. Even the loss-making titles and stations tend not to remain as in Estonia the media is largely considered rather a cultural than economical phenomenon.

References & Sources for Further Information

Online resources

Web page of the State Information System (in English), *www.riso.ee*, incl. "Use of Internet among individuals and enterprises", Eurostat 2006, <*http://www.riso.ee/et/files/Statistika_Eurostat_ 2006.pdf*>.
Web page of the marketing research and consulting company TNS EMOR <*www.emor.ee*>. Data about media market research.

<*http://ec.europa.eu/public_opinion/index_en.htm*>. Eurobarometer information.
Web page of the Estonian Newspaper Association <*www.eall.ee*>. Data about circulations and their
Press Council.
Web page of the original Press Council <*www.asn.org.ee*>.
Web page of the Legal Language Center of Estonia <*www.legaltext.ee*>. Translations of legal texts,
incl. laws, into English.
EJC's "Estonian landscape" by Tarmu Tammerk http://www.ejc.nl/jr/emland/estonia.html.

Bibliography

Bærug, R. (ed.) (2005), *The Baltic Media World*. Riga.

Kalmus, V. et al. (ed.) (2004), *Eesti elavik 21. sajandi algul. Ülevaade uurimuse Mina. Maailm. Meedia tulemustest, (Estonian habitation at the beginning of the 21st century. Overview of the research project Me. World. Media)*, Tartu: TÜ Kirjastus.

Harro-Loit, H., and Lauk, E. (2003), "Self-Regulation: watchdog's collar or shelter for the guild?", in N. Malmelin (ed.), *Writings on International and National Communication*, in *Viestinnän julkaisuja*, 8, Department of Communication, Helsinki: University of Helsinki, pp. 98–108.

Loit, U. (2005), Estonia chapter, in *Television across Europe: regulation, policy and independence*. Monitoring Reports. Budapest: Open Society Institute, volume I, pp. 555–621.

Paju, T. (2004), Estonia chapter, in B. Perković (ed.), *Media Ownership and its Impact on Media Independence and Pluralism*, Ljubljana: Peace Institute and SEENPM.

Šein, H. (2005), *Suur teleraamat, (Big TV-book)*, Tallinn: TEA.

Vihalemm, P. (ed.) (2002), *Baltic Media in Transition*, Tartu: TÜ Kirjastus.

Vihalemm, P. (ed.) (2004), *Meediasüsteem ja meediakasutus Eestis 1965–2004, (Media system and media usage in Estonia in 1965–2004)*, Tartu: TÜ Kirjastus.

THE HUNGARIAN MEDIA LANDSCAPE

Ildikó Kaposi

Hungary is a landlocked Central European country with a population of around 10 million. The main language of the country is Hungarian. Culturally, the country is comprised of a colourful mix of majority Hungarians (Magyars) and Roma, Jewish, German, Croat, Serb, Croat, Romanian, Slovak, Bulgarian minorities.

Under Soviet occupation after World War II, the country was part of the communist bloc until the peaceful, negotiated political transition in 1990. Since the first free elections in 1990, Hungarian democracy has been stable, with all governments serving their full four-year terms and the economy picking up after the restructuring along market principles. Hungary's accession to the European Union in 2004 confirmed the process of democratization. At the same time, civil society, like in post-communist countries elsewhere, is recognized to be weak. Citizen participation remains relatively low, with average turnout at the last two elections 64.4 per cent, and membership in political, professional and voluntary organizations lower than in the EU. The processing of the historical heritage of wars, dictatorships and revolutions that caused severe disruptions in the country's development during the twentieth century is far from complete.

As in all post-communist countries, the media in Hungary is defined by the heritage of decades of communist rule and the influence of market mechanisms introduced in the country after 1990. The ownership structure of the media was radically transformed from the communist times when all media were state-controlled. The media's role in society was also reconceptualized according to democratic norms. Yet the historical heritage of the communist regime continues to create points of tension to this day by serving as a reference point in much of the political, economic and ethical debates centred on the media. Hungary with its population of 10 million is a small market, where the diversity of media cannot be ensured through market mechanisms exclusively. Consequently, the country's media landscape is characterized by a duality of market principles and different forms of state intervention.

1. The Market

A. The Print Media
Main features:

- Newspaper readership remains in the middle tier of European countries;
- Foreign ownership in the press dominates;
- Tabloid and magazine segments are growing, quality dailies are in slow decline;
- Local newspapers have monopoly positions in the counties, national quality dailies are strongly partisan.

Hungarians read fewer newspapers than in Nordic countries and more than in southern Europe. In 1998, 167 papers per 1,000 inhabitants were sold in Hungary, and the country continues to belong to the lower third of the middle tier of newspaper consumption in Europe. On the other hand, Hungary is in the top tier for publishing journals, monthly or quarterly publications on culture, literature, the arts, sciences, or a combination of these, with 76 per cent of the population reporting to occasionally read such journals.

According to the Hungarian Publishers' Association, there are several problems the publishing industry in Hungary is struggling with. The VAT on newspapers and magazines is 15 per cent, making it one of the highest in Europe. The price of newspapers is relatively low (the equivalent of around 0.3 euros), half of which sum is spent on distribution. The advertising market favours television and the competition between commercial channels is driving prices down, lowering advertising revenues in publishing too. Some segments of Hungary's written press like tabloid newspapers and magazines are growing and expanding, others, like political broadsheets, are stagnating or constricting. Despite the problems, however, in 2004 Hungarian publishers boasted a 44.56 per cent increase in advertising revenue over five years.

Hungary has ten national and 24 local dailies. All of these newspapers are privately owned, by foreign owners in the majority of cases. When the newspapers came to the market, there was not enough Hungarian capital or interest in acquiring them, and no Hungarian government proposed restrictions on foreign ownership in the press. As a result, six of the ten national dailies and all of the local dailies are owned by western investors.

In terms of circulation, the most popular national newspaper is *Metro*. Owned by the Swedish Modern Times Group, the Budapest edition of *Metro* was launched in 1998 with 160,000 copies. Circulation soon went up, and in 2000 the paper went national, having its free copies distributed not only in Budapest but also in major cities across the country. Currently *Metro* has 340,000 free copies distributed daily in Hungary.

The local dailies enjoy virtual monopolies in the counties where they are published. Of the 24 local newspapers, Axel Springer owns ten; Westdeutsche Allgemeine Zeitung owns five; Vorarlberger Medienhouse owns three and Daily Mail Group Trust owns three. Although there were several attempts to launch rival local newspapers, these mostly failed due to the undercapitalization of the new papers and the inflexibility of local markets, where subscribing to the family newspaper-style county daily is a tradition going back decades. In some cases, a county has two dailies, but both ended up being owned by the same company.

On the national newspaper market, the situation is somewhat different. Among political quality dailies, the old communist party newspaper, *Népszabadság*, managed to preserve its market leader position among quality dailies with a circulation of just under 160,000 in 2005. The Swiss company Ringier is the majority owner of *Népszabadság*. Ringier bought its share in the newspaper from the German Bertelsmann group who were forced to sell because they also have an interest in Hungary's commercial terrestrial television channel RTL Klub and Hungary's media law prohibits such cross-ownership. A further 26.7 per cent of the paper is owned by a foundation of the Hungarian Socialist Party (MSZP), while the employees also retain a small share. The employees are also granted the special privilege of nominating their editor-in-chief, a legacy of the negotiations around the original privatization of the newspaper.

The second largest quality daily, *Magyar Nemzet*, has a circulation of around 73,000. *Magyar Nemzet* is Hungarian-owned and its editor-in-chief is also the owner of the newspaper. He acquired control of the paper under a right-of-centre government in 2000, the same year when *Magyar Nemzet* was merged with another, small right-wing newspaper. The merging left *Magyar Nemzet* the only right-of-centre national broadsheet, boosting circulation figures and readership.

It is generally believed that among national broadsheets, *Népszabadság* and *Magyar Nemzet* are the only ones with large enough market shares to enable profitable operation. Yet two more national political newspapers exist: *Magyar Hírlap* and *Népszava*. *Magyar Hírlap* had a circulation of 29,000 in 2004 when its owner, Ringier decided to close it down. The paper was eventually bought by a Hungarian entrepreneur and continues to be published as a liberal-centrist daily. First published in 1877, *Népszava* was the newspaper of Hungary's social democrats until the communist takeover. After the collapse of communism the paper was privatized and sold to a Hungarian entrepreneur, but after the entrepreneur was assassinated no single owner was willing to finance the loss-making publication for long. Since 2001, *Népszava* has had a string of owners, usually smaller Hungarian companies with ties to MSZP. The paper has been losing readers, currently its circulation is around 28,000.

All of the broadsheet titles existed before 1989, and no new quality political daily managed to survive in the market after the regime change. Except for successful tabloids and *Magyar Nemzet*, the circulation of all titles kept going down throughout the 1990s, and Hungarian newspapers further reported a -9.48 per cent loss in total circulation from 2000 to 2004.

The market for tabloid journalism was created and began to flourish only with the advent of democracy. This is probably the most volatile segment of the national newspaper market, and competition for readers' attention is severe. The leading title among tabloids is *Blikk*. It is owned by Ringier and has a circulation of around 245,000. The other tabloids, *Színes Bulvár Lap* and *Napi Ász*, have circulations of around 62,000 and 26,000 and are owned by the US firm Elliot Associates and a Greek businessman, respectively.

Among national dailies, Hungarians can further choose between two financial dailies, one of them owned by a Hungarian group of investors, the other by Axel Springer (audited circulation figures are unavailable for either newspaper). Finally, the old sports daily managed to survive as *Nemzeti Sport*, the only newspaper dedicated to sports exclusively. It too is owned by Ringier and has a circulation of around 83,000.

Another segment of the print press that got a boost from the collapse of communism is the magazine market. Lifestyle and fashion glossy magazines (including Hungarian editions of *Cosmopolitan* and *Elle*), erotic magazines like *Playboy*, as well as celebrity gossip weeklies (e.g. *Story*) were started in the 1990s and continue to appear on the news-stands. The two largest publishers on the magazine market are the Finnish company Sanoma and Axel Springer. Sanoma's publications include the weekly gossip magazines *Story* (circulation 367,000) and *Best* (circulation 178,000), the women's weekly *Nők Lapja* (circulation 302,000) that dates back to communist times, women's magazines *Cosmopolitan* (circulation 40,000) and *Maxima* (circulation 68,000), as well as the prestigious economic weekly *Figyelő* (circulation 15,000). Axel Springer's magazines include *Popcorn* (circulation 53,000) and *Glamour* (circulation 52,000), as well as weekly women's magazines *Kiskegyed* (circulation 206,000), *Hölgyvilág* (circulation 52,000) and *Gyöngy* (circulation 33,000).

The press is the second most-favoured choice of advertisers after television, getting a roughly 40 per cent share of the advertising market. The lack of transparency in advertising rates, however, makes it difficult to know how much actual revenue the press gets from advertising. In 2003, it was estimated that HUF 55.7billion was spent on advertising in the press.

B. The Broadcast Media
Main features:

- Hungarians are avid television watchers;
- The two terrestrial commercial channels have come to dominate the television scene since their 1997 launching;

- The television market is multi-channel, fragmentation of audiences is occurring;
- Public broadcaster MTV is threatened by the loss of its audience, bankruptcy and political pressure;
- Competition in radio markets is severe;
- Digital television is in an experimental phase;
- A 2005 government decree outlines broadly the frame of digital switch-over, but making the necessary changes in the media law is hindered by political disagreement.

Ninety-eight per cent of Hungarian households have a television set. According to a 2006 poll, three out of ten Hungarians claim their lives would not be complete without television. This sentiment grows stronger with age as television perhaps becomes the only everyday companion for the elderly. On the other hand, the same poll reports that only 15 per cent of respondents think that television provides good programmes relatively frequently.

Despite the critical reflections, Hungarians are avid television watchers. The average time people spend watching television has been growing steadily since the 1990s, and by 2004 people on average spent over 33 hours per week in front of the small screen.

This can in part be attributed to the growth in Hungary's television market. Through the 1990s, Hungary's television environment has proliferated into a multi-channel market where a multitude of terrestrial, cable and satellite channels continue to vie for viewers' attention.

Before the collapse of communism, commercial broadcasting did not exist, and the state-controlled Magyar Televízió (MTV – Hungarian Television) enjoyed a monopoly. A decisive step in transforming MTV from a state-controlled monolith to a public service channel was the 1996 Media Law, which opened the way for creating a dual broadcasting system, modelled after Western European traditions. Currently there are three terrestrial television channels: MTV, the public service channel; TV2, whose majority owner is Scandinavian Broadcasting System (SBS); and RTL Klub which is owned by a consortium of CLT, Bertelsmann, Pearson, and the Hungarian national telecom company Matáv.

MTV is financed by a fee each citizen who owns a television set must pay, but it is also allowed to carry advertising. Until recently, the fee was included on the tax sheet of citizens, but in 2002 the government allocated funding from the budget to pay for it.

The situation of MTV is characterised by recurring threats of bankruptcy and political pressure, as each government so far has treated the channel as an important terrain of extending its political influence. The 2002 modification of the Media Law, which harmonized Hungarian legislation with EU television directives, failed to effect changes in this area because the modifications hardly concerned public service broadcasting. Similar to other European countries, the entry of commercial broadcasters also proved a major challenge to public service broadcasting. Public service television in Hungary has suffered even more losses than in many other countries. By 2000, the market share of commercial channels was around 70 per cent, while public service broadcasters hovered under 20 per cent. The two terrestrial commercial broadcasters also manage to attract the majority of advertising revenues. By 1999, around 85 per cent of all television advertising went to them, and they still attract nearly three quarters of advertising spending in television.

The formerly terrestrial second MTV channel is now available through cable or satellite. A third public service channel, Duna TV, was launched as a satellite channel in 1992, with the primary mission of broadcasting to Hungarian minorities living outside the country. In many ways, Duna TV is the channel that continues to perform the tasks of public service, broadcasting documentaries, European and art films and other non-commercial programmes. In 1999, it won the UNESCO prize for best cultural television of the world.

The crisis of MTV in Hungary coincides with the Europe-wide crisis of public service broadcasting. So far, MTV reacted with more political bargaining and attempts to revamp its image and programming in a commercial style. It remains to be seen how successful this strategy can be.

Although TV2 and RTL Klub are safe from competition from the public service broadcasters, their market shares are increasingly challenged by DVD-viewing on the one hand and smaller, specialized commercial channels that are accessible via cable or satellite on the other. In 2005, around 66 per cent of Hungarian households had access to satellite channels and cable television. The number of Hungarian language channels available through cable networks grew from 17 in 1998 to 38 in 2002 and keeps growing, promising further fragmentation of audiences. The largest non-terrestrial commercial television, Viasat3, had a mere 2.4 per cent market share in 2003, but the share of the MTG-owned channel is growing thanks to their programming which includes the most popular US series (e.g. *Sex and the City*, *CSI*) and European football matches (including Champions League games) that are magnets to the audience.

New cable channels are typically thematic, their areas of specialization including music (e.g. Viva), sports (e.g. Sport1), news (e.g. Hír TV), children's programmes (e.g. Minimax), lifestyle (e.g. Vital TV), documentary (e.g. Spektrum TV), film (e.g. Film+ TV), entertainment (e.g. Story TV), etc.

The radio scene is similar to that of television. There are three national public service stations (Kossuth, Petőfi, Bartók), and two major national commercial stations, Danubius and Sláger. The owner of Danubius is Advent International, while Sláger's main owners are the US company Emmis Broadcasting International Broadcasting Corporation and Credit Suisse First Boston Radio Operating BV.

National radios compete for audiences with numerous local stations, ranging from commercial to public service, non-profit and community radios. Age is a characteristic division line in radio audiences, with people under 49 preferring to listen to commercial stations and people over 50 more typically listening to public stations. The market share of the two major national commercial radios is about the same, with both Danubius and Sláger listened to by about 25 per cent of 15+ audiences. Competition for audiences and advertising revenue among radios can be extremely strong, especially in a crowded market like Budapest where two commercial music radios were forced to close down recently.

As with magazines and thematic cable channels, commercial radios also raise the question of the limits to which the Hungarian market can support the proliferation of niche media outlets.

Television has dominated the advertising market, and commercial channels have been the market leaders, but no audited data are available about the exact figures. In 2006, the main radios and televisions decided to supply information on their actual revenues. Based on the data supplied by the companies, Ernst & Young summarized the net revenues of the Hungarian television market for 2005 to have been HUF 60.447 billion, while those for the radio market were HUF 7.789 billion.

The introduction of digital television promises to reshape the television landscape. Currently, in its experimental phase, digital television service is available on one multiplex to customers in Budapest. It is planned to be launched in densely populated areas of Hungary in 2007, and switch-over is to be completed by 2012 in sync with EU efforts.

One of the obstacles of the diffusion of digital television is the lack of clear regulation. The 1996 Media Law does not include provisions for digital terrestrial services, and the lack of adequate regulation hinders the process even though the government accepted the digital switch-over strategy in 2005. The terrestrial commercial television channels are also dragging their feet about digital services. As current market leaders, it would not be in their best interest to switch to digital where smaller channels can better compete with them for viewers. In 2005, TV2 and RTL Klub lobbied the government and the media regulatory authorities successfully for a five-year renewal of their terrestrial licence a year before it expired. In spring 2006, TV2 sued DigiTV, a Transylvanian-based small satellite broadcasting service provider, because the company failed to get the channel's consent before including them in the low-priced subscription packages they offer. The director of TV2 said that the market success of DigiTV's cut-price service would speed up the diffusion of multi-channel digital platforms, which would be against the channel's interests.

The move was interpreted as the start of the digital television war. It remains to be seen precisely how and at what pace digital television will evolve, but it is going to thoroughly reshape the television landscape.

C. The Internet Media

Main features:

- Internet use is low compared to the EU average, but growing slowly;
- Offline media have established online versions.

Among online-only news media, the market leader is owned by the national telecom firm, while the second position is taken by the portal that was the first of its kind in Hungary.

The percent of Hungarians with access to the Internet has been growing steadily if not fast in recent years, but the country still ranks below the EU average, gaining the 29th place among 37 European countries in 2005. There are different survey data available on Internet use. According to some surveys, 15 per cent of households had Internet access in 2005, with 67 per cent of those households subscribing to broadband. According to others, the number of households with Internet access is slightly higher, around 18 per cent. Another indicator says that just over 30 per cent of the population has Internet access.

Most of Hungary's newspapers, weeklies and magazines have online editions, and a selection of Hungarian radios can also be listened to online. In addition to the content of the print editions, newspaper websites also offer services like discussion forums or newspaper archives, but the content of the sites is not significantly different from the print version. There are some exceptions to this trend, however, with, e.g. the economic weekly *Figyelő* launching *FigyelőNet*, a daily version of the publication that also offers additional news content and services.

Of the Internet-only portals that offer news and other services, two major ones emerged as market leaders within the segment. One is *Origo*, owned by the former national telecom monopoly Matáv, the other (*Index*) is owned by Hungarian entrepreneurs and enjoys the benefits of having been the first such initiative. Apart from specialized websites like *Portfolio*, which focuses on financial information, most of the other online-only news service initiatives failed to become successful, and interest in them as targets of investment by and large waned after the international dotcom crash.

Television channels seem to follow a clear strategy with their online presence. All three national terrestrial channels have their portals, and they use their online presence to build on and strengthen their on-the-air brand identities. MTV focuses on news and its archives to showcase its public service history, while the commercial channels TV2 and RTL Klub focus heavily on entertainment and promoting the stars of their most popular programmes online. Reality shows or the Hungarian version of *Pop Idol* have also been the first programmes that allowed the functioning of a new, hybrid television model where it became possible to charge Internet users for television-produced content online (e.g. downloading videos of performances by *Pop Idol* contestants, or viewing reality show participants online in real time). The websites can also serve for building communities of faithful audiences through features like chat, discussion forum or blogging, and the commercial channels have been building on these possibilities.

Online media have been claiming a growing share of the advertising market. In the nine months of 2006, Hungarian Online Advertising Index (MOHI), which incorporates the main online media outlets, managed to attract HUF 3.313 billion advertising revenue, a 63 per cent increase from the same period in 2005.

D. *News Agencies*
Main features:

■ The most prominent news agency is the state-owned national wire service;
■ Other, smaller news agencies provide specialized news nationally.

The oldest, and previously monopoly, national news agency, Magyar Távirati Iroda (MTI), continues to dominate the market of news agencies. It is a state-owned company, managed by a board of trustees which is set up from delegates of the political parties in Parliament.

The only challenge so far to the virtual monopoly of MTI as the national supplier of news came from Reuters, which opened its Hungarian-language branch but closed it down due to difficulties in the parent company. Reuters continues to be present in Hungary, but not in the Hungarian-language market.

Other, alternative news agency services continue to be provided by Axel Springer-affiliated Europress photo agency and Havaria Press which was set up by Hungarian journalists and specializes in stories of crime, fire and accidents. Apart from these, there is also the Roma Press Centre, a small, non-profit news agency dedicated to covering the Roma minority.

2. State Policies
Main features:

■ Legal guarantees are in place for the freedom of speech, expression and the press;
■ Broadcasting is regulated separately in the media law;
■ The press and online media do not have separate supervisory organizations;
■ Broadcasting content and ownership in electronic media are regulated by the media law.

Access to public interest data is guaranteed by the 2005 Electronic Freedom of Information Law. Declarations of freedom of the press are included in the Constitution, the 1986

Press Law, and the 1996 Media Law. Freedom of the press includes the freedom to launch media outlets, editorial freedom and the prohibition of censorship.

Freedom of expression is limited by restrictions on the dissemination of harmful content. Hate speech is regulated in the Penal Code, and the Media Law includes passages about it, thus, the National Radio and Television Board (ORTT) can sanction it. There is no law regulating content harmful for children across all media, but the Media Law guarantees protection for minors in relation to electronic media programmes.

Freedom of information as a guarantee of transparency in the public sector is supported by the rights of citizens to learn about public interest data. In 2005, Parliament also passed a law on electronic freedom of information, which obliges government bodies and organizations to make relevant information about their work, including the outcomes of legislative and judicial procedures, publicly accessible on the Internet.

There is no separate supervisory organization for the press or new media in Hungary. If someone has a complaint against what was published in the press, the person can take the case to court, citing relevant legislation (libel, slander, etc.).

In the case of broadcasting, the main supervisory body overseeing the industry is ORTT which was created by the 1996 Media Law. It allocates frequencies and supervises the observation of the media law, including the amount of time taken up by advertising, or the appropriateness of the content of programmes. It also has a commission for dealing with complaints from viewers. The supervisory body has the authority to fine broadcasters, or even to suspend broadcasting (it usually does so for a short while only). The members of ORTT are selected from nominees of the parliamentary parties, its president is jointly nominated by the president and the prime minister of Hungary. The Board reports to Parliament, and its members cannot be called back. These provisions of the Media Law were aimed at insulating the Board from political pressures.

The Media Law also imposes restrictions on ownership, but only for audio–visual media, not the press. Concentration issues in the press are dealt with by the Competition Council (GVH).

3. Civil Society Organizations

Main features:

- The dominant association of journalists is MÚOSZ;
- Publishers, commercial broadcasters, online content providers have separate associations, along with smaller organizations uniting different segments of the media.

The main professional organization for journalists is MÚOSZ, the national association of journalists. Other, smaller associations were founded as alternatives to MÚOSZ by

Catholic journalists (MAKÚSZ) and conservative journalists (MÚK), as well as sports reporters (MSÚSZ).

Newspaper publishers, including proprietors and employers, form the Association of Hungarian Newspaper Publishers (MLE). Online media set up the Association of Hungarian Content Providers (MTE), a body for self-regulation in 2001. The Association of Hungarian Electronic Broadcasters (MEME) incorporates the largest radios and televisions.

Apart from these professional associations, many other actors in the media industry have their own organizations, including the National Association of Local Radios (HEROE), the National Association of Local Televisions (HTOE), the Association of Hungarian Cable Televisions and Communication (MKKSZ) and the Hungarian Federation of Free Radios (SzaRáMaSzer) for community radios, while the umbrella organisation for companies and individuals active in marketing communication is the Hungarian Advertising Association (MRSZ). These organizations function to coordinate their members' activities and represent the interests of particular segments of the media.

4. Development Trends

Main features:

- The lack of independence for public broadcaster MTV continues to be an issue;
- Partisanship is the norm in the media.

The issue of the independence of public service broadcasting has been a central one in Hungarian media since 1990. Each successive government has applied financial and political pressure on Hungarian Radio and Hungarian Television to secure favourable coverage, which, coupled with weak ethical norms among journalists, has prevented the development of objective, independent news and current affairs programming. Most recently, the president of the European Broadcasting Union called MTV "one of the worst" public television systems in Europe and criticized the government for its practices of putting MTV under political pressure. In a letter addressed to Hungary's prime minister in summer 2006, the EBU president also repeated allegations that the funding of programmes is decided on a basis of political cronyism, and some of those funds trickle back to political parties.

Partisanship is also the norm of commercially operated media outlets, the majority of which have clear left- or right-wing profiles. In the absence of a strong, shared professional ethos among journalists, party political news management tends to drive the agendas and interpretations offered in the media. This contributes to the increasingly pervasive sense of deep divisions and splits in Hungarian society along political lines. With the eventual introduction of digital television and the growth of online media, the further erosion of a shared, common understanding of public affairs is likely to occur. Analysts are already beginning to discuss the emergence of a 'new partisanship' in Hungary's media.

References & Sources for Further Information

www.hullamvadasz.hu (in Hungarian) A comprehensive media portal with databases, information, and news concerning the media.

www.ittk.hu The website of the Information Society and trend Research Institute; this is a good source of reports and analyses on new media developments in Hungary (in English and Hungarian).

www.emasa.hu (in Hungarian) The online source about Hungarian media for and about journalists, content on this site is produced by MÚOSZ, the national association of journalists.

www.mediainfo.hu (in Hungarian and English) and www.kreativ.hu (in Hungarian) Trade and industry websites for media professionals.

http://www.akti.hu/ Website for the Institute for Applied Communication Research, a research body set up to support the work of the radio and television board (ORTT).

http://www.mediakutato.hu/ (in Hungarian) Academic journal dedicated to media studies.

THE LATVIAN MEDIA LANDSCAPE

Ilze Šulmane

Latvia is one of the three Baltic States and has a territory of 64.6 thousand square kilometres. The ethnic structure of the 2.3 million population is diverse – 59 per cent Latvians, 29 per cent Russians, 3.8 per cent Belo-Russians and several other ethnic groups. The last decade of the twentieth century and the first years of the twenty-first are of dramatic change for Latvia – it regained independence from the Soviet Union and joined NATO and the EU.

The transformation of the Latvian media system that started with the glasnost at the end of the 80s came to its end alongside with the consolidation of the democratic political regime (1996–2001), which manifested itself by stabilizing the mass communication market, professionalization of journalism and media management.

The media system is divided into two subsystems, the Latvian- and Russian-language media. The Russian-language media in Latvia do not fulfil the functions of typical minority media outlets. The Russian press represent not just the citizens of a certain minority, with specific interests and needs, but also non-citizens, who see newspapers as a resource in accessing the public sphere and as a bastion during times of change.

In general, the media market in Latvia is quite diverse. However, since it is split into two parts (two languages); it is difficult to get one and the same information product to both target groups simultaneously. The division of the small media market influences the advertising revenue. The market size and other economic conditions do not promote specialization and the development of qualitative journalism.

1. The Market

A. The Print Media
Main features:

- Transformation of press system after regaining Latvia's independence
- Division of the comparatively small press market in two languages
- Sharp competition among daily newspapers
- Success of the newcomer – free daily in Latvian and Russian
- Different reading habits of Latvian and Russian audiences
- Diverse magazine market, especially in the area of specialized and women's magazines

According to 2006 statistics, one out of 294 press editions during last six days was read by 96 per cent inhabitants of Latvia (age 15–74). A single inhabitant of Latvia reads the average of 0.8 issues of daily papers a day, while a single subscriber of daily papers reads the average of 1.2 issues of daily papers. There are 201.9 daily newspaper copies per thousand Latvia inhabitants.

The readership of daily newspapers is close to that of weekly newspapers (48 and 50%) and is slightly higher than the readership of weekly magazines (44%) and monthlies (43%).

The top publishing companies are AS Diena and AS Preses Nams. AS Diena is a joint stock company, 49 per cent belong to the Swedish shareholders – the Bonnier group, 51 per cent to the local private shareholders. The company has its own printing plant and independent delivery system. Petit and Fenster are the biggest publishers of the Russian-language press in Latvia.

Among the national daily newspapers there are three Latvian-language dailies issued six days a week. *Diena* tends to be a prestigious quality paper. It is the first western type newspaper [started after 1991] that tried to separate facts from opinions and trained its journalists in-house. *Diena* has changed its outlook several times; the last changes show the wish to maximize its audience and becoming slightly more popular. *Diena's* circulation is about 55,000. *Diena* has openly expressed its political sympathies towards right-wing and centre parties, but the pre-election strategy has been to give an equal share of attention to all main political players and to present different viewpoints. *Diena* gradually became involved in the local newspaper business in the mid-1990s. It now owns nine local papers.

Rīta Laikraksts Latvijai Neatkarīgā (*Independent Morning Paper*) is printed in Preses Nams (Press House), owned by Ventspils transit and oil business. Its history goes as far as the beginning of the twentieth century; during the Soviet regime it was the organ of the communist party, during the transformation time it changed from *Cīņa* (Struggle) to *Neatkarīgā Cīņa* (Independent Struggle) and then became *Independent Morning Paper*. Political sympathies of the paper are more to the centre and left (social democrats) than *Diena*.

Latvijas Avīze (previously a paper for the countryside) has high subscription figures and its circulation is 59,000. It has several supplements for education, health, beauty care, housekeeping and on Fridays – a TV programme and a magazine. It is a popular nationalistic and conservative newspaper.

Russian-speaking audiences in Latvia also have several dailies competing for their audiences. The popular mass newspaper *Vesti segodnja* (*Today's News*), has the largest circulation among them – about 35,000. It focuses on the interests of Russian society of Latvia and demands of the marketplace.

The daily *Chas* (*Hour*) with a circulation of 16,000–22,000 has the highest subscription rates among Russian dailies (about 13,000). It is printed in the Publishing House Petit, which also publishes a popular weekly, TV programme and several advertising papers.

The Russian daily *Telegraf* also tends to be a western-style newspaper; at the beginning it was the thickest Russian-language newspaper with a comparably high circulation. Its publisher has admitted the financial losses; the paper has lost page numbers as well as subscribers. Recently it has changed its format from broadsheet to tabloid.

The Russian-language press represents the diverse sub-system of the media system in Latvia, particularly when compared to the minority media in other Baltic States. There are only a few areas in which Russian publications lack an analogue to Latvian-language publications. At the same time, readership levels of Russian-language newspapers are far lower than those of their Latvian counterparts.

Russian-language press market is less stable than the Latvian one. Several dailies have ceased their publication or changed their title (*Panorama Latviji, Respublika*). The ownership of the national Russian dailies is mostly local and has no investors from western countries, like *Diena* has. Russian-language newspapers are less expensive than their Latvian counterparts. That is not just because Russian newspapers have fewer pages and a smaller audience, but also because some of them engage in price dumping. There was some stabilization in subscription prices in 2005, and this can indirectly be seen as stabilization in the Russian press market, too.

Another evening paper, *Rīgas Balss* (*Voice of Riga*), is a paper for the inhabitants of the capital city. It was published in both the languages but, like *Diena,* it ceased publishing its Russian version, which was commercially unsuccessful. So we can see that bilingual newspapers (and there have been four different attempts) have not been able to meet their different audience needs.

Reading habits of Latvians and non-Latvians are different: non-Latvians prefer weekly newspapers, Latvians – weekly magazines, regional press and monthly magazines. The free of charge advertising papers together with TV programme papers are especially popular with the Russian-speaking audiences.

Appearance of *5 min* (*5 minutes*) in 2005 – a free-of-charge daily newspaper in Latvian and Russian has caused the increase of the readership of daily newspapers. It is distributed at the bus stops and in the public transport (like *The Metro* in Sweden) and is viewed by media experts as an integrating factor of Latvian- and Russian-speaking audiences.

There are many regional and local newspapers in Latvia; only some of them face local competition – a second newspaper in a town or region. Low-income people quite often prefer local papers to national ones, and the local papers are the only source of information (besides TV and radio) for them. The problem for regional and local newspapers is their close link to the local governments (except for papers which are partly owned by their own journalists).

Developmental tendencies of Latvia's diverse magazine market are similar to that of other countries at the end of the 90s – audience fragmentation, development of niche and business journals. The number of magazines increases for about fifteen a year; and recently there are about 190 magazines in Latvia offered for subscription.

Audience increase of magazine readers has changed the press readership structure – number of daily press readership gradually decreases. It has also caused increases in the magazine-advertising market since 2000.

The year 2002 marks the beginning of the process of internationalization in Latvia's magazine market: the first adapted magazine belonging to an international publisher is *Cosmopolitan*, then came music business journal *FHM* and *Shape*.

Women's magazines – monthlies and weeklies in Latvian and Russian – represent the largest share of the magazine market in Latvia. *Ieva,* the most popular weekly magazine in Latvian with circulation of 73,000 competes with circulations of national daily papers.

The increase of leisure hours and improvement of living standards has caused the popularity of magazines for specific interest areas and hobbies, as well as lifestyle magazines: celebrity weeklies in Latvian and Russian; lifestyle magazines, special interest magazines for music and entertainment fans, sports magazines and a popular journal of science.

Magazines about housekeeping and gardening are also quite popular in Latvia. There are several monthly health magazines and monthlies for parents and family. Another group of magazines is for professionals and specialists in different businesses, like magazines for doctors, businessmen and environmentalists.

There are several publications for young people: children and young teenagers (7–to 13-year-old boys and girls). The Publishing House Egmont Latvija (company of Scandinavian media group) also offers several magazines for these audiences.

Almost half of the readers of the most popular monthly magazines are subscribers; among weeklies the subscription rate is 10–30 per cent. For Latvia it is typical that the largest amount of subscribers is countryside inhabitants at the age 45 and more.

B. The Broadcast Media
Main features:

- Two public service TV channels gradually lose audience, the market leaders are commercial channels
- Latvia's Russian-speaking audiences prefer TV programmes from Russia and watch cable TV
- Commercial TV channels are more successful competing for Russian-speaking audiences
- Public radio still quite popular among Latvian audiences
- Public TV and radio have financial problems as the introduction of subscription fees has not received support
- The transition to digital TV is planned to be finished only by 2011, as the government contract with foreign investor was announced invalid

Households of Latvia are well equipped with television sets, the ownership of which reaches almost 100 per cent. The TV-viewing time of an average inhabitant of Latvia has increased to more than 3 hours a day.

There are two public service channels, LTV1 and LTV7, both covering the whole country. LTV1 is a Latvian-language channel. The share of information programmes has grown, especially those of local news. The programmes on public affairs and topical political issues are produced not only by LTV1 journalists, but also by independent producers. Culture, feature films and entertainment programmes created by Latvia's producers are also offered by this channel.

LTV7 produces sports programmes, educational shows, entertainment and programmes for various social groups and minorities, including a daily news programme in Russian. The public TV is state funded, and additional revenue is gained from advertising and sponsored programmes. During the last few years public TV has improved the quality of self-advertising. Nevertheless, public TV has lost a part of its audience (e.g. from 22% in 1997 to 11% in 2006), and the market leaders are two commercial stations.

LNT (Latvian Independent TV) is the first and the biggest commercial TV station in Latvia, started in 1992. It broadcasts news and sports, films and original or adapted programmes. Its news programme competes with *Panorama* (LTV1) – a popular and traditional news programme for the Latvian audience. At the end of the 90s, LNT successfully took over the Russian TV audience after stopping of broadcasting Russian Public TV (KST) on the third national network.

TV3 started its operation in 1998 and has won over a part of the LNT audience. Most of the programming consist of films, entertainment programmes and locally produced entertainment shows. In September of 2006 the LNT audience share is 20.7 per cent; TV3 takes the second place – 17.7 per cent, LTV1 ranks the third, but LTV7 – only 4.6 per cent.

Quite popular, especially for the Russian-speaking audiences is PBK (Pervij Baltijskij kanal – The first Baltic channel) with a share of 10.4 per cent. It mostly retransmits programmes from Russia; however, it also airs local evening news in Russian. Latvia commercial channels are more successful than the second public channel when competing with Russia TV channels for the local Russian audience.

There are also seven regional and seventeen local TV channels in Latvia. The local TV stations broadcast only a few hours a day.

Eighty-five per cent of the inhabitants of Latvia have listened to radio at least once a week, 67 per cent – once a day. The total average amount of listening to radio is 275 minutes a day. There are seven national, nine Riga and twenty local/regional radio stations in Latvia.

Public radio is still quite popular among Latvian audiences: LR 2 – Latvian popular music channel (30% total week's audience in the summer 2006) has the largest audience, LR1 – national news and talk channel (16%); news, music and talk programmes for Russian speakers – Channel 4 (10%) and a channel for classical music fans – Klasika. Thanks to the four programmes of the public radio and its wide coverage, it still takes quite a big share, though the audience is becoming older.

As the funding from the state budget is diminishing, LR has to operate also in the commercial radio market. LR has captured one-fifth of the radio advertising market, thus causing protests of the commercial channels and putting its public mission under question.

Commercial radio stations have kept appearing in Latvia since 1991. Radio SWH (adult contemporary format) is among the most popular stations (weekly reach – 17 per cent). Radio SWH+ broadcasts in Russian, the private channel Radio PIK (in Russian) has been used as a propaganda channel for promoting one political party during the local elections.

The LTV and LR are forced to get involved in commercial activities to secure additional income from commercials. The long-discussed issue of the introduction of subscription fees still has not received support from the government.

Private radio stations – regional and local – have been developing very quickly, several have been granted the right to broadcast across Latvia.

The government of Latvia has made the first steps to introduce digital TV but, as the contract with the foreign investor about financing the project was announced invalid, the introduction was postponed.

Since 2002 the signal of digital TV has been receivable for 50 km around Riga. Several TV and radio channels are aired in the test regime. LLC "Baltcom TV" has started transmitting programmes in digital format (DVB – standard).

In 2004 the National Radio and Television Council developed a new strategic plan for digitalization. According to the concept of development of digital TV the transition from analogue to digital TV is planned to be finished by 2011.

C. The Internet Media
Main features:

- Considerable growth of intensity of Internet users after liberalization of fixed telecommunications
- Most active Internet users among Riga inhabitants and youth
- Diversity of audience of Internet portals (by language) in comparison with press audience and their growing role in creating a common information space

The number of Internet subscriptions in Latvia is one of the lowest in the EU. The high subscription fees hindered the spread of Internet subscriptions among households. Only after the liberalization of fixed telecommunications in 2003 Internet use started to grow – from 24.7 per cent of the population in 2004 to 32 per cent in 2005 and 40 per cent in 2006. Riga inhabitants (43%) are the most active Internet users, whereas only 18 per cent of people who live in Latgale, the least developed region in Latvia, use the Internet. There are no differences in Internet usage by gender, but age and education play a role: the most active age group is 15- to 19-year-old users (71%) and users with higher education (62%). Advertising on the Internet has grown from 0.9 per cent in 2001 to 3 per cent in 2005.

Several dailies have their Internet versions, e.g. *Diena*, *Latvijas Avīze*, *Telegraf* and others. There are only a few magazines that have their Internet versions and that can be read on the Internet for a smaller subscription fee. Majority of other magazines offer only information about the magazine in their home pages or answer to their readers' questions and promote subscription.

The audience of Internet portals is more diverse than that of the press. Although the proportion of non-citizen audience of the Latvian-language portals is comparable to that of newspapers (5–9%), when the division by languages is examined one should say that these Latvian-language portals – *delfi.lv, apollo.lv, tvnet.lv* – have the largest share of the non-Latvian audience.

The most popular Internet pages are inbox, google, delfi.lv, draugiem.lv (for friends). Delfi.lv and delfi.ru publications quite often cause vivid and sharp discussions and sometimes quite intolerant commentaries.

On the whole Internet journalism can be evaluated as rather underdeveloped. The main content of the most popular portals is filled up with information of news agencies. Publication of newspaper and magazine articles with following commentaries is a reasonable way to make the content more diverse.

There is a portal for social and political information, analysis and online publication of recent research results *politika.lv*. The aim of the portal *dialogi.lv*, which has translations of articles and commentaries in the Latvian and in the Russian languages, is to create a common information space.

D. News Agencies
Main feature:

■ Coexistence of national news agency LETA and the biggest agency in the Baltic countries, BNS

The private agency BNS (Baltic News Service) is the biggest agency in the Baltic countries. It started its work in 1991, with bureaus in Estonia, Latvia and Lithuania. Since 2001 the agency has been incorporated in the Finnish Media group Alma Media.

The national news agency LETA is a full-service information agency supplying news, social and political, as well as business information to media and other organizations in Latvia.

2. State Policies
Main features:

■ The Constitution, the Press, and the Radio and Television Laws guarantee freedom of speech;
■ The concentration of the mass media has not reached a level that would threaten the information diversity;
■ The lack of access to information about media ownership does not ensure media ownership transparency;

■ Newspapers that are financed by western investors support editorial autonomy and are more likely to support the integration of society;

■ There are no government subsidies in the newspaper market in Latvia;

■ A need to improve laws in the area of the electronic media and to formulate more precisely the tasks of the public broadcast media and the criteria when applying for a frequency.

The Constitution of Latvia guarantees freedom of speech and prohibits censorship. The 1990 Press Law and the 1995 Radio and Television Law prohibit censorship and interference in the work of mass media.

The Press and the Radio and Television Laws also prohibit the monopolization of the mass media. However, the documents do not define the monopolization criteria. The Competition Law speaks about the dominant position, which occurs when the market share of one or more market participants is at least 40 per cent of this market, and they have the capacity to significantly hinder, restrict or distort competition. However, it does not specify precisely if this condition applies to the dominating position in the media market as well.

The concentration of the mass media has not reached a level that would threaten the information diversity yet. The biggest problems are created by the lack of access to information about the media owners, because the laws in Latvia do not ensure media ownership transparency. The information on the true owners of various media companies is not publicly accessible.

A study on journalists in Latvia showed that the structure of ownership has a serious influence on editorial autonomy. Newspapers that are financed by western investors support editorial autonomy and are more likely to support the integration of society.

There are no government subsidies in the newspaper market in Latvia, but publications for children and culture magazines regularly apply for some funding to Kultūrkapitāla fonds (Foundation of Cultural Capital) or seek for other sponsors.

The National Radio and Television Council is responsible for supervising the implementation of the Radio and Television Law.

The Radio and Television Law does not strictly formulate journalistic standards, it only demands editorial political neutrality. Neither public nor commercial TV has any in-house documents where professional standards would be formulated, except LTV's Ethical Code for News Service.

The National Remit Contract defines the task of the Latvian public broadcast media: to create balanced and diverse programmes for all society groups, including a certain amount of programmes that comply with the public interest, dedicated to minority groups. Media experts do think that the national remit, as well as the demands to be met when applying for a frequency, are too vaguely defined.

The two new draft laws in the area of the electronic media – the Law on Public Broadcasting Organizations and the Radio and Television Law are postponed waiting for the newly elected Parliament to adopt it.

3. Civil Society Organizations

Main features:

- Strong media organizations for employers
- A weak and non-prestigious professional organization for journalists
- Formally operating code of ethics
- Lack of press ombudsman
- The National Broadcasting Council regulates both public and commercial broadcasting

The Latvian Journalist Union acts neither as a trade union, nor as an authoritative, self-regulating professional association. It has low prestige in the eyes of Latvian journalists and its membership is decreasing.

There have been attempts to organize new associations or media clubs but with no real success.

The lack of self-regulating professional or public institution induces a desire to regulate and control journalists from outside. In 2003, the Deputy Prime Minister suggested that the Council of Mass Media Ethics should be created. Although the media experts themselves fervently denied this idea, it has not stimulated a counter-reaction – a creation of an authoritative self-regulating organization of journalists.

The aim of Latvia Association of Press Publishers (LPIA) is to work on the developmental policy of print media and to defend the principles of press freedom.
Latvia's Advertising Association now consists of 54 members. Their activities are aimed at improving the quality of advertisements and advertising market and acting as a self-regulating agent.

The code of ethics for Latvian journalists was adopted by the Latvian Journalists Union in 1992. Some of the newspapers have their own in-house codes or some ethical principles or obligations as a constitutive part of the employment contract. In 2001 the editorial staff of seven newspapers and the Radio KNZ signed a new code of ethics.

An attempt to organize the Council of Ethics did not succeed; neither did it stimulate journalists themselves to organize a self-regulating institution. There is no press ombudsman in Latvia or an institution that would investigate the potential violation of individual journalist's rights before court interferes.

The National Broadcasting Council of Latvia until now regulates both public and commercial broadcasting. It also monitors TV content and can punish TV channels for broadcasting violence, pornography and national hatred.

The public benefit organization Centre for Public Policy "Providus", among other activities, investigates possible hidden advertising in print and broadcast media during preelection campaigns.

4. Development Trends

Main features:

- Market pressures have resulted in a simplified media content and commercialization of media in Latvia;
- The politicization of the media companies and their ties to political economic groups cause the political engagement of journalism;
- Partisanship is less manifested in TV than in press;
- Qualitative press and investigative journalism is underdeveloped in Latvia.

The calculations of scholars prove that the amount of resources invested in political advertising by Latvian political parties exceeds the amounts spent in other western countries. As the result the Parliament of Latvia has adopted a law that limits pre-election advertising in quite a drastic way. Though monitoring has partly diminished the practice of merging the political advertisements with the editorial material, the limitations have caused new sophisticated ways of dealing with them during Parliament elections of 2006, like advertising of so-called third parties – NGO's that are closely linked to and financed by parties they advertise.

The lack of investigative journalism decreases the effectiveness of the media operation. The group of independent journalists – NIP – has ceased to exist. The investigative broadcasts made by a journalist of public radio LR1 have revealed to the public violations of the law, but the follow-up activities of the civic society and the government institutions have been with little effect.

Media experts also point out the lack of diversity of genres in the press and, due to the poor financing, the decline of TV documentaries.

The electronic media represent the diverse composition of the society to a greater extent than it can be observed in the daily press, and partisanship is less manifested in TV than in press.

A paper on the National Concept for development of electronic media (20062008), as well as the above-mentioned draft laws, try to diminish the impact of state funding and advertising in public broadcasting on freedom and independence and stresses the role of the public broadcasting media in the development of democracy and foster debates among different cultures.

The politicization of the media companies and their ties to political economic groups cause the political engagement of journalism. The pronounced support of specific political forces by the daily press, together with the low purchasing capacity of the people – the incapacity to use multiple information sources – does not promote tolerance, dialogue and the coexistence and desirability of diverse opinions within the society in Latvia.

References & Sources for Further Information

Brikše, I, Skudra, O., Tjarve, R. (2002), Development of the media in Latvia in the 1990s. In: Baltic Media in Transition (ed. by P. Vihalemm). Tartu: Tartu University Press.

Dimants, A. (2005), Editorial Censorship in the Baltic and Norwegian Newspapers. In: The Baltic Media World /ed. by R. Berug. – Rīga: Flēra Printing House.

Dupuis, I. (2003), Journalism in Latvia: a profession in transition. – Berlin: Nordeuropa-Institut der Humboldt-Universitat zu Berlin.

Kruks, S, Šulmane, I. (2005), The Media in a Democratic Society. In: How Democratic is Latvia. Audit of Democracy. Scient. ed. J. Rozenvalds. Rīga: LU Akadēmiskais apgāds.

Kruks, S. (2005), Radiožurnālistika. Rīga: Valters un Rapa .

Nagla, I., Kehre, A. (2004), Latvia. In: Media ownership and its impact on media independence and pluralism. Ed. by B. Petkovic. Ljubljana: Peace Institute, p. 262.

Rožukalne, A. (2005), Latvijas žurnālu tirgus attīstības tendences: 1991–1995. (Development trends in Latvia's magazine market) Komunikācija. Acta Universitatis Latviensis. Vol. 683

Riga: The University of Latvia Press.

Šulmane I. (2006), Russian Media in Latvia. In: Latvian-Russian Relations: Domestic and International Dimensions. Ed. by N.Muižnieks. – Rīga: LU Akadēmiskais Apgāds.

Šulmane I., Kruks S. (2006), Neiecietības izpausmes un iecietības veicināšana Latvijas presē 2004. gadā. Laikrakstu publikāciju analīze. – Rīga: ĪUMSIL.

Sulmane I., Kruks S. (2002), Ethnic and political stereotypes in Latvian and Russian press in Latvia" In: Humanities and Social Sciences. Latvia. Riga: University of Latvia, 1(34).

Television across Europe: regulation, policy and independence. Latvia. (2005), (S. Kruks) OSI, Riga: Nordik p. 179–236.

TNS Latvia.

Veinberga, S. (2005) Masmediji: prese, radio un televīzija/ Rīga: Zvaigzne ABC .

www.tns.lv

www.lpia.lv

www.bns.lv

www.leta.lv

www.nrtp.lv

The Lithuanian Media Landscape

Audronė Nugaraitė

Situated on the eastern shore of the Baltic Sea, Lithuania is the southernmost and largest of the three Baltic countries in terms of the population, territory and economy.

Lithuania shares borders with Belarus, Latvia, Poland and Russia (Kaliningrad). Its territory is 65,300 sq. km. The country has a predominantly urban population of 3.389,9 million (2006) of which over 80 per cent is of Lithuanian origin, 6.7 per cent Polish, 6.3 per cent Russians, and 3.5 per cent of other nationalities.

The state language is Lithuanian, which is closely related to the old Sanskrit and belongs to the Baltic family of Indo-European languages. The major religion is Roman Catholicism and there are small communities of Lutherans and Russian Orthodox believers.

On 11 March 1990, Lithuania declared the re-establishment of its independence. In 2004 Lithuania became a full member of the EU, also a member of the World Atlantic Treaty Organization (NATO).

Political developments since the mid-80s have led to changes in the media landscape of Lithuania. During 1989 and 1996 Lithuania's mass media and the context it operates was reshaped from dependent to free mass media model. The majority of the country's media enterprises were privatized and new were established, and an independent structure of printing and distribution was created. The old media system was replaced by a market-oriented system. Advertising has become the main source of income of the mass media.

The arrival of the new technology (Internet) has urged the majority of mass media companies to rethink and reshape their organizational structure.

1. The Market

A. The Print Media
Main features:

- The press market development operates in a highly competitive environment at local, national and international levels;
- The amount of specialized magazines increased;
- The percentage of newspaper readers is remarkably lower than TV viewers;
- In 2006 a free newspaper was launched which currently has the highest readership;
- The title with the highest circulation figures are tabloid;
- The magazine market attracted quite a lot of foreign investors from Scandinavia, Estonia;
- Fragmentation process in the magazine market dealing with concentration and diversification taking place concurrently.

The national press market consists of a limited number of newspaper and magazine titles. The years 1988 to 2006 brought out inconsistent change in the number of titles of publications and their circulations. During this period, the number of titles of newspapers increased three times, or from 140 in 1987 to 334 in 2006, while their circulations contracted nearly tenfold. Daily circulation amounts to 2,576,000 copies in total. Yearly circulation of newspapers is 258.3 million copies. All newspapers are private.

Newspapers and magazines are mainly published in the Lithuanian language (307 newspapers and 397 magazines), in the Russian language (19 newspapers and 3 magazines), in the English language (2 newspapers and 40 magazines), as well as in the German, Yiddish and other languages.

There are fourteen dailies published in Lithuania. Many of them are in the capital Vilnius. The competition is very strong for new arrivals. Multiple sections were introduced and these newspapers took over the expanding volume of advertising. Newspapers issue a lot of the supplements devoted to television programmes, lifestyles or sports. The advent of new information technology strongly influenced the press market. Two-thirds of the newspapers introduced their Internet versions.

According to the National Readership Survey data carried out by TNS Gallup (2007), the top five dailies by readership are tabloid *Vakaro žinios* (*Evening News*) – 21.5 per cent, *Lietuvos Rytas* (*Lithuanian Morning*) – 18.0 per cent. A free daily, *15 minučių* (*15 minutes*), is at the third position – 15.2 per cent. At the fourth position is *Respublika* – 7.2 per cent. At the fifth position is daily *Kauno Diena* (*Kaunas Day*) – 5.9 per cent.

Lietuvos Rytas can be regarded as a media corporation because the distribution service, the printing house, regional newspapers, magazines and Lietuvos Ryto Televizija (Lithuanian Morning TV) making broadcasts belong to it.

Newspapers are encouraged to specialize by advertisers who seek target audiences. In 2005 the structure of specialized newspapers was as follows (data from 1988 in parentheses): leisure newspapers made up the largest percentage, or 33 per cent (5%); newspapers of political parties, unions, nongovernmental organizations and societies were 21 per cent (2%); advertising newspapers were 12 per cent (4%); professional newspapers made up 9 per cent (9%), and newspapers of organizations and one-time newspapers accounted for 25 per cent (80%) of the total. The rise in the number of leisure and advertising newspapers was related with the commercialization of the contents of newspapers.

The regional press, two-thirds of which are newspapers that were funded in the Soviet period and have changed their titles and become private companies, are most popular with residents of the regions as compared to the national dailies. They are published two to three times a week.

Regulation which introduced market rules gave official approval to private ownership in the print media market. An important characteristic of ownership changes was internationalization. Foreign capital entered the print media sector.

The first newspaper privatized by a foreign company was the daily *Kauno Diena*, published in the second largest city of Lithuania. In 1998, the Norwegian concern Orkla bought a 100 per cent stake. In 2007 *Kuano Diena* was sold to local industry company Hermis Capital. In 2005, a Scandinavian interest group, Schibsted, acquired an interest in the tabloid *Ekstra žinios* (*Extra news*) published by Lietuvos Rytas. Since the spring of 2006, it has been published under the title *L.T.* (*Newspaper for You*). Schibsted also purchased (99.99 %) the free daily *15 Minutes*.

The Lithuanian magazine sector has been growing considerably for the past decade. Since 1989 the number of titles has increased by about 50 per cent. The main trend is toward more specialized monthly or bimonthly periodicals aimed at groups with particular interest in leisure activities, sports and hobbies. Their readership has increased markedly during recent years. There are currently 543 magazines and other periodicals. Yearly circulation is 59.2 million copies.

For the past few years, the weeklies writing about television and celebrities have enjoyed the greatest popularity. These include *TV Antena* (*TV Antenna*), *TV Publika* (*TV Audience*) and *Žmonės* (*People*).

TV guides remain the most widely read among weeklies (editions that are published one to three times a week). The most read monthlies remain the women's magazines. Since

1990 ownership of magazines was more related to local capital. Industrial concerns (Alga, Achemos group) are acquired, profitable journals.

During last two years a new tendency was observed: foreign capital came to the market of magazines. The Estonian media group Ekspress Grupp has already purchased and publishes such popular magazines in Lithuania as *Panelė* (*Girl*), *Moteris* (*Lady*), *Antra Pusė* and *Namai Pagal Mus* (*Home According Us*) and *Aha*, *Naminukas*.

Private limited liability company *Žurnalų leidybos grupė* managed by the Norwegian *Schibsted*, which also owns such other popular women's magazines as *Laima, Edita* and *Ji*, is a serious competitor to the Ekspress Grupp in the Lithuanian magazine publishing market.

Over the past five years, the volume of advertisements in newspapers has shrunk, while that in magazines, in particular in specialized ones, has expanded. On average, Lithuanian newspapers derive more than 70 per cent of their revenues from advertisement. TNS Gallup announced that the country's media advertising market grew up by 8.6 per cent last year. In 2005, LTL 363.6 million in total was allocated to advertising in Lithuania, including the media channel volume and other concessions: Television – 42.63 per cent ; Newspapers – 29.15 per cent; Magazines – 12.10 per cent; Radio – 7.01 per cent; Outdoor – 6.88 per cent; Internet – 2.20 per cent; Cinema – 0.03 per cent.

B. The Broadcast Media
Main features:

- Analogical television is still the main way of watching television in Lithuania;
- The advertising market of both TV and radio is growing every year;
- National broadcaster Lithuanian Radio and Television are financed from the state budget and advertising;
- There is an increasing fragmentation of the television market;
- Most TV companies rent the facilities from the State;
- Public Radio is the most popular;
- The number of Lithuanians able to watch multi-channel TV (cable or satellite) programmes has been gradually growing in the past five years;
- Digital television GALA is the beginning of digitalization of the Lithuanian TV market;
- Digital terrestrial TV development is greatly dependent on the state policy.

On 31 December 1989, the first private commercial radio station *M-1* that broadcast its programmes on the air of Soviet Lithuania at that time utterly destroyed the state monopoly of the audio-visual market. This marked the beginning of private enterprise in the electronic media of Lithuania.

The distribution network consists of 48 radio stations in Lithuania. Among them there are 11 national, 7 regional and 30 local radio broadcasters. Radio programmes are being broadcast by 47 commercial stations and 1 public radio station – Lithuanian radio, broadcasting three nationwide radio programmes: LR1, LR2 and LR3.

Public radio LR1 ranks as the most popular in the scale of ratings. Most radio stations broadcast in Lithuanian language. Regional radio stations are very popular and some are heard in the largest cities of Lithuania.

There are 31 television stations in Lithuania, 30 of them are commercial and one public – Lithuanian Television, broadcasting two national television programmes, LTV1 and LTV2. The ownership of the Lithuanian major players in the television sector falls into the following major groups: *LTV1, LTV2* (public/state funded, advertising allowed), LNK, TV1 (UAB MG Baltic Media – 80 per cent, Amber Trust S.C.A. – 20 per cent). TV3, Tango TV (MTG Broadcasting AB), BTV (UAB Achema).

The share of four national TV channels (LNK, TV3, LTV1, BTV) accounts for about 7) per cent of the entire watching time, and the daily reach of these TV channels is 66.6 per cent of the Lithuanian population over 4 years of age. The most popular are LNK and TV3, the main competitors on the scale of ratings in television market in Lithuania.

In a total number of 1,000,440 households, the number of households with TV is 980,431, cable 295,500, households with MMDS is 34,800 and the number of households with satellite is approximately 75,000.

The number of Lithuanians able to watch multi-channel TV (cable or satellite) programmes has been gradually growing in the past five years – since 2002 the number of such people has grown by 5.9 percentage points, and in 2005 it reached 43.7 per cent.

In Lithuania privatization and concentration of the audio-visual market differed from the print media market. With the exception of the national broadcaster, all other radio stations and television channels are commercial institutions that have been established in the route of sixteen years of independence. The television market began to develop after foreign capital (from the USA, Great Britain and Scandinavian countries) poured into Lithuania.

Changes of the recent years lead to a conclusion about the active penetration of different local business groups into the media market. In 2004, the Lithuanian Industrial Concern *MG Baltic Investment* purchased LNK from the Swedish concern Bonnier (100 per cent). The industrial concern Achemos grupė purchased the TV channel Baltijos televizija, which later was renamed BTV. The industry concern Senukai, which specializes in the sale of building materials, has purchased the radio station Žinių radijas (news radio). The financial industrial group RUBICON has acquired 100 per cent of the shares of

Vilnius and Kaunas televisions and renamed them as TV5, making a new entity one of Lithuania's largest regional televisions.

In 2004 the Government of Lithuania approved the model of digital television implementation in Lithuania. According to this, programme broadcasting through digital terrestrial TV networks in the five largest cities of Lithuania should start by the end of 2007, and by the beginning of 2009 at least one digital terrestrial TV network should cover at least 95 per cent of Lithuania's territory, and in 2012 gradual switch-off of analogue TV would start. So in the nearest future the TV market will face rapid changes.

This Resolution did not only approve the model of introduction of digital television in Lithuania but it also established that by the second quarter of 2008 a plan of measures encouraging the use of digital terrestrial television should be devised. In 2005, the Communications Regulatory Authority of Lithuania issued authorizations to use radio frequencies (channels) in digital terrestrial television networks to two private companies: AB Teo LT and AB Lietuvos radijo ir televizijos centras. Telecoms operator *Teo LT* plans to invest about LTL 20 million (around 5.7 euro) into the Internet digital television services. Teo provides these services under the name of GALA, offering more than 50 different channels to the clients.

GALA television is beginning a new period in the area of television – digital video and audio quality and state-of-the-art technologies for managing the contents of television will give completely new opportunities to the viewer. GALA will allow checking one's e-mail on the screen, select thematic channels, review films and shows from yesterday and rent films with the help of a remote control unit. In the long run, these GALA functions are expected to influence changes in TV viewer habits. GALA television will cover almost the whole of Lithuania and will reach the clients' homes through the same line that brings TEO's voice telephony and Internet services. Viewers cannot yet watch digital television, as they are not supplied with MPEG-4 type add-ons for their TV sets.

Lithuanian TV market with a conditionally low multi-channel TV penetration has potential for digital terrestrial TV penetration. However, it must be pointed out that the lowest multi-channel TV penetration is in rural areas and small towns, where relatively poorer citizens reside. So the digital terrestrial TV penetration will greatly depend on what policy is pursued in this field, how much set-top boxes will cost and whether they will be subsidised by the State.

So the Lithuanian TV market just sees the start of those changes that are under way in the TV markets of Western European countries. On the other hand, it must be pointed out that digitalization of the Lithuanian TV market is still not due to changes of the TV market proper and any internal need but due to the active government policy.

C. The Internet Media

Main features:

- The number of Internet users has been gradually increasing in the past three years;
- Young people are the one of the most active groups of Internet users.

The total number of Internet subscribers in Lithuania is 38.9 per cent of the population (2007). In 2005, as compared to the end of 2004, this number increased by as much as 2.1 times. And 21.7 per cent of this number used broadband communications technologies for the Internet access. In spite of this the rate of Internet use is low compared to the EU average.

It is evident, that Internet as a new communications medium has matured into a commodity available at least to one-third of the population in Lithuania. In the wake of the reduced digital isolation of the Lithuanian population and the increased use of computers, young people are becoming one of the most active groups of media users.

According to the figures of TNS Gallup for winter 2006, the most popular portal in Lithuania were www.google.com, www.delfi.lt and www.one.lt. Delfi has been the leader since the date of its founding.

Since the beginning of 2001, the development the online media and penetration of the Internet into other spheres of life increased. Telecommunications companies do invest in their own Internet portals – www.omni.lt, www.takas.lt, verslo.banga.lt (in Lithuania). At that time Delfi and Omni were turned into poly-media enterprises integrating online news and mobile telecommunications services.

Another sort of easily accessible source of information are supplements in specialized portals. Real estate Internet portals usually have specific parts dedicated to the latest news, provide segmented packets of information, for example, – www.aruodas.lt.

The past five years, dailies *Verslo zinios* and *Lietuvos rytas* turned their own portals into news portals.

Business groups have begun more active penetration into the Internet media market. The summer of 2006 saw the launch of one more multi-purpose portal, Alfa.lt, financed by the conglomerate MG Baltic, which controls the television company LNK. In autumn 2006, the Norwegian media group Schibsted ASA, through its subsidiary Schibsted Baltics, acquired a 51 per cent stake in UAB Plius (in Lithuania, Schibsted is a majority shareholder of the country's biggest magazine publishing enterprise, *Žurnalų leidybos grupė*, which issues the Baltics' largest magazine, *Žmonės*, as well as the magazines *Laima*, *Edita*, *Ji* and others. Schibsted Baltics holds a 51 per cent interest in the tabloid newspaper *L.T.* and owns 70 per cent of the free newspaper *15 minučių*. UAB Plius operates the auto website www.autoplius.lt, issues the weekly magazine *Autoplius* and runs the real estate website www.domoplius.lt.

In addition to running their websites, television and radio companies also create their own mini portals. For example, the portal LRT.lt of Lithuania's national broadcaster both announces its shows and provides domestic and foreign news.

Autumn 2006 saw the launch of a digital magazine, *Sveikas LT*, devoted to medicine. Such changes indicate a trend towards the development of specialized Internet media. The growing influence of the Internet is associated with the falling circulations of print periodicals, especially those of national dailies.

D. *News Agencies*
Main features:

- There are two news agencies in Lithuania;
- The leadership belongs to BNS, the first private news agency in Lithuania.

The monopolist position of the state-owned Lithuanian Telegraph Agency ELTA was broken by new private News Agency Baltic News Service (BNS). In April 1990, a group of students from the Baltic States established a news agency in Moscow, which became the major source of Baltic news within several months. In 1991, its office was also founded in Lithuania, which was registered as an independent company a year later. Since 2001, the owner of the BNS has been the Finnish media group Alma Media.

Lietuvos telegramų agentūra (ELTA) was established in 1920 and in the Soviet times it was part of the unified system of information services of the USSR – TASS (Telegraph Agency of the Soviet Union), which from 1940 to 1990 received foreign news from Moscow. In 1996, ELTA changed its status from a state-owned agency to an independent national news agency. At present, ELTA is a private company whose shares belong to three owners: 39.51 per cent is owned by the State, 18.43 per cent belongs to the media company Žinių partneriai, which is controlled by the owner of the daily *Respublika*, Vitas Tomkus, and 39.5 per cent belong to the media group Respublikos investicija.

2. State Policies
Main features:

- Censorship of mass media is prohibited by the Constitution;
- The state is subsidizing cultural and educational media;
- The Internet is regulated by the Law on Electronic Communications.

The Constitution of the Republic of Lithuania guarantees freedom of speech and freedom of information and it is the main document regulating mass media competition and activity. Lithuania legislation concerning the media is represented by the Law on Lithuanian Radio and Television and the Law on Telecommunications. The Internet content is regulated by the Law on Electronic Communications which came into force in 2004.

The media in Lithuania are not controlled by the state power, and the legislation is very liberal. There is only one kind of subsidy granted to the Lithuania media. The Fund for the Support of the Press, Radio and Television was established on 2 September 1996 on the basis of the Law on the Provision of Information to the Public, and it is financed from the state budget. The Fund provides financial assistance to those media that submit adequate cultural and educational activity programming. The Fund allocates financial support by means of the annual tenders.

The Radio and Television Commission of Lithuania is an independent institution with powers of regulation and supervision of activities of radio and television broadcasters, which is accountable to the Parliament of the Republic of Lithuania.

The Law on Competition of the Republic of Lithuania regulates relations concerning competition. It prohibits performance of actions, which restrict or may restrict competition despite their form of economic activity, with the exception of those regulated by the Law or Laws on Competition for separate spheres of economic activity. Unless otherwise provided by the law, an economic entity is considered to have a dominant position in a market when its market share makes up not less than 40 per cent.

Lithuania has no legislation for media market regulation or an anti-monopoly law. Thus, by default, the state allows both monopoly rights and cross-ownership. As a result, large sectors of the media belong to one and the same owner (Achemos grupė, MG Baltic, Rubicon).

Transparency of ownership and other kinds of influence over the media is seen as a prerequisite for any relevant political intervention against media concentration. This is a key problem in the Lithuanian mass media market. Media ownership is one of the most hidden types of data in Lithuania. The Law obliged media companies to publish exact data on their ownership structure by the 31 March each year. But it has not happened. Last year only 35 media companies declared their shares.

3. Civil Society Organizations
Main features:

■ There are two journalists' organizations in Lithuania;
■ Journalist organizations are acting as professional organizations;
■ The revised Code of Ethics of Lithuanian journalists and publishers was adopted in 2005;
■ Lithuanian journalists have an Ethics Ombudsman.

The Journalists' Union of Lithuania has over 700 members (as of January 2007), and the Journalists' Society of Lithuania (about 100 members). The trade union movement among Lithuanian journalists is almost non-existent. Journalists' Union of Lithuania the Journalists' Society of Lithuania functions both as professional organizations.

Publishers are represented by two organizations – The Lithuanian Newspaper Publishers Association regional and city newspapers publishers association. Lithuanian Centre of Journalism is the mid-career training centre for professional journalist.

The regulations of the Lithuania mass media are based on a self-regulation system. There are two regulation bodies: the Ethical and the Commission of Journalism and Publisher Ethics. The new version of the Code of Ethics of Journalists and Publishers, adopted by a journalists' meeting in 2005, lays down the main ethical provisions.

The accountability system is identified as the way the media is accountable to public. The ethics ombudsman weights the nature of the complaint basing his/her decisions on the Law on Provision of Information to the Public and Commission on the Code of Ethics of Lithuanian journalists and publishers. Both Commission and Ombudsman have direct links to the government. The Ombudsman is appointed by the Parliament and the Ethics Commission is regulated by law.

The Lithuanian self-regulation mechanism is close to ineffective. Little motivation exists from journalists and media industry to participate in critical media debates. The audiences are also not very active to say their opinion. Non-governmental organizations are too few and they do not deal with critical issues of media activity. Liberal market policy and absence of an efficient accountability mechanism have given the media, especially the press, nearly unlimited possibilities to set the agenda according to their business interests.

4. Development Trends
The Lithuanian Parliament adopted in 2006 new amendments to the Law on the Provision of Information to the Public.

A new metro-type newspaper, *15 minutes*, was successfully introduced in the Lithuanian media market and has the third highest circulation.

At the end of the 2006 the first effort was made to protect interests and social guarantees of journalists and establish a social dialogue with media owners. The leaders of Journalists' Unions signed the first collective agreements with the employers of National regional and cities publishers Association.

In 2006 Telecoms operator Teo LT started to provide Internet digital television services. Teo provides these services under the name of GALA, offering more than 50 different channels to the clients.

References & Sources for Further Information

Online resources

Department of Statistics to the Government of the Republic of Lithuania (Statistics Lithuania 2005). http://db.stat.gov.lt/sips/Database/sipsen/databasetree.asp.

Lietuvos spaudos statistika (Lithuanian publishing statistics). ISSN 1822-3028 (electronic version).

http://www.lnb.lt/lnb/selectPage.do?docLocator=0422A897883711DAA310746164617373&inlanguage=lt.

Radio and Television Commission of Lithuania. http://www.rtk.lt/en/.

TNS–Gallup: http://www.tnsgallup.lt/en/disp.php/en_surveys/en_surveys_48?ref=/en/disp.php/en_surveysfilterby=en_surveys_grp2&subm.http://www.vz.lt/lyderiai.

Valstybės žinios (Official Gazzette) 2004 Nr.69–2382.

THE POLISH MEDIA LANDSCAPE

Ania Lara

Poland, situated in Central Europe, has a population of 38.5 million. Administratively the country is divided into sixteen provinces called *województwa*. Poland is ethnically and religiously homogeneous (Poles – 96.7 per cent, Roman Catholics – 89.8 per cent).

The Polish media landscape is a product of the country's political and economic transition resulting from the fall of communism in 1989. The main post-communist media developments include: privatization of the press sector, transformation of the state radio and television into public broadcasting organizations, licensing of the private broadcasters, influx of foreign capital on the Polish media market and European integration of audio-visual media policies.

1. The Market

A. The Print Media
Main features:

■ Press market is dominated by foreign ownership, the only big domestic competitor is Agora S.A.
■ Gradual decline in sales of national and regional daily press
■ Increased specialization of the magazine sector, yet continuing dominance of women and opinion magazines

Poland has more than 5,400 press titles including national and regional dailies (167), weeklies (827), monthly magazines (2,401) and specialized press. None of the Polish dailies comes out on Sunday or has a second print run in the afternoon. The 2006 data on the readership rates show that 90 per cent of Poles read the written press, 78 per cent declare reading dailies, 68 per cent – weeklies and 41 per cent – monthly magazines. Recent statistics show a gradual decline in sales of national dailies (except *Gazeta Wyborcza*), regional dailies and opinion weeklies. This negative trend is foreseen to continue.

The press market in Poland is dominated by foreign, mostly German owners such as H. Bauer (operating in Poland as Wydawnictwo H. Bauer LTD.) Verlagsgruppe Passau (Polskapresse), and Axel Springer (Axel Springer Polska LTD.) Another important foreign publisher is Norwegian Orkla Press (Presspublica). The only domestic competitor with similar circulations is Agora S.A. There are also smaller domestic press owners.

Fakt, launched in 2003 and owned by Axel Springer, has fast become leader on the Polish daily press market. In 2005 its average circulation came to 519,000 copies. Modelled on the German *Bild, Fakt* is considered a moderate version of western tabloids. In contrast to quality papers such as *Gazeta Wyborcza* and *Rzeczpospolita*, *Fakt* targets medium- to low-income groups and Poles of lower educational levels.

Gazeta Wyborcza, launched in 1989 and owned by Agora S.A., was the first totally independent newspaper in post-communist Poland. *Gazeta Wyborcza* had been the top Polish national daily with the highest circulations for over a decade until *Fakt* recently took the lead. In 2005 the average circulation of *Gazeta Wyborcza* amounted to 447,800 copies. The newspaper consists of the national edition, regional inserts and topical supplements. It is also renowned for uncovering the country's corruption scandals such as the notorious 'Rywingate'.[1]

In April 2006 Axel Springer launched their second national daily – *Dziennik*. During the first four months of its publication, the daily has come third on the Polish daily press market with circulation of 239,900 copies. *Dziennik* has been promoted as a quality paper reporting on "Poland, Europe, [and] the World" in an innovative way.

Super Express – another Polish national daily of a tabloid format – is owned by Media Express LTD. – whose shareholders are the Polish Zjednoczone Przedsiebiorstwa Rozrywkowe and the Swedish AB Marieberg from the Bonnier's group. In 2005 *Super Express* reached an average circulation of 216,100 copies.

Rzeczpospolita has two shareholders: the Norwegian Presspublica and the Przedsiębiorstwo Wydawnicze Rzeczpospolita S.A. – the publishing house owned by the State Treasury. In 2005 circulation of *Rzeczpospolita* came to 182,700 copies. *Rzeczpospolita* is considered a quality newspaper known from its focus on law and economy and thus designed for academics, diplomats and businesspeople.

More specialized national dailies include *Przegląd Sportowy*, focusing on national and international sport events, and two business/economic newspapers, *Gazeta Prawna* and *Puls Biznesu*.

The fall of communism with its tendency for centralized national press, as well as administrative division of the country into *województwa* contributed to the emergence of many regional daily titles. Circulations of the regional dailies range from 20,000 to 100,000 copies. The top regional papers with circulations similar to that of top national dailies are *Dziennik Zachodni* (Silesia region), *Gazeta Pomorska* and *Dziennik Bałtycki* (Pomerania region).

The Polish magazine sector can be divided into segments according to their audience and their topics (women, men, children, teenagers, Catholics, opinion, computing, economic, gossip magazines and TV guides). As a result of recent saturation of the market for these most popular magazine segments, more specialized publications appeared.

Among opinion weekly magazines the leader is *Polityka* with an average circulation of 176,300 copies in 2005. *Polityka*, published since 1957, had been taken over by its staff who formed a cooperative – Spółdzielnia Pracy Polityka in the post-communist privatization process. *Wprost* – another opinion weekly – comes second with a circulation of 153,600 copies in 2005. *Wprost*, published since 1982, had also been taken over by its staff and is currently published by Agencja Reklamowo-Wydawnicza Wprost. The Polish version of *Newsweek* was launched in 2001 by Axel Springer and has quickly succeeded in reaching top circulations within the segment – 151,200 copies in 2005.

In 2005 the Polish press sector accounted for 34.8 per cent (1.05 billion euros) of total media advertising revenue – 2.97 billion euros, out of which dailies accounted for 18 per cent and magazines for 16.8 per cent. While the advertising revenue of national dailies has increased compared to previous years, particularly in case of the top dailies such as *Fakt*, *Gazeta Wyborcza* and *Rzeczpospolita*, the revenue of regional and local daily press has declined. Within the magazine sector, opinion weeklies and women's magazines earned most on advertising. When considering media as a whole, growth of press advertising has been slower than that of radio, TV and the Internet.

B. The Broadcast Media
Main features:

- Public and private duopoly
- Dominance of public broadcaster in terms of audience and advertising shares
- Competition between two main commercial channels
- Private radio include two leader nationwide stations, Catholic radio station, three over-regional stations and numerous local networks
- Cable market is dominated by six operators with significant foreign capital

- Two digital television satellite platforms
- Governmental strategy for the transition from analogue to digital broadcasting via 'digital islands' until the complete analogue switch-off in 2014
- Planned tender for applicant multiplex operators and licensing process for TV channels to broadcast within the multiplexes

Following the fall of communism, the Polish audio-visual media sector has grown rapidly and led to the establishment of a public and private broadcasting duopoly. There are 74 television channels and 235 radio stations in Poland. An average Pole watches television 3 hours and 30 minutes and listens to radio 2 hours and 45 minutes per day. Ninety-five per cent of Polish households own at least one television. Fifty per cent of these households are accounted for by terrestrial transmission, 30 per cent subscribes to cable and 20 per cent subscribes to digital satellite platforms.

The Polish television market is the largest among post-communist countries of Central and Eastern Europe and one of the largest in Europe. Telewizja Polska (TVP) S.A. – owned by the State Treasury – continues to dominate the market more than any other European public broadcaster. The combined audience share of TVP channels accounts for more than 50 per cent of total audience share. The two reasons for dominance of TVP are viewer's loyalty (the former state TVP was the only existing television under communism and in the immediate post-communist period) and post-communist broadcasting regulation (until recently foreign investment in the private sector was heavily regulated).[2]

TVP S.A. operates three terrestrial channels: nationwide TVP1 and TVP2, and TVP3 via a network of twelve regional broadcasters. In 2006 the audience shares of TVP 1 and TVP 2 were 25.4 and 20.8 per cent respectively, while the regional TVP3 reached approximately 5.2 per cent. The public broadcaster also runs two satellite channels, TVP Polonia, designed to broadcast PBS to Poles abroad, and TVP Kultura, dedicated to cultural programming.

The main players on the commercial television market in Poland are nationwide Polsat with an audience share of 15.9 per cent and multi-regional TVN – 15.1 per cent. Polsat is owned by Telewizja Polsat S.A. controlled by a Polish businessman, Zygmunt Solorz-Żak. However, in 2006 Solorz-Żak declared his willingness to sell 45 per cent of his company's shares. Hitherto it is speculated that the German Bertelsmann will buy out the shares. TVN is owned by ITI Holding S.A. whose main shareholders are two Poles: Jan Wejchert and Mariusz Walter. TV4, owned by Polskie Media S.A., which in 2004 joined the Polsat Group in terms of programming and advertising sales cooperation, is the third most popular commercial TV channel in Poland.

In 2005 the Polish television sector accounted for 54 per cent (1.6 billion euros) of total media advertising revenue – 2.97 billion euros. The combined shares of TVP1 and TVP 2 were almost 33.1 per cent. The main commercial broadcasters, Polsat and TVN, came second and third with 28.1 and 24.7 per cent, respectively. The reasons behind TVP's success in attracting advertising revenue is not only its large audience share, but also its relatively low advertising rates, which the public broadcaster additionally supported through licence fees and grants from the state budget can afford. Polsat, TVN and Agora filed a complaint to the Office of Competition and Consumer Protection (UOKiK) alleging that TVP's advertising pricing policy creates unfair market conditions. In April 2006 the UOKiK launched an antitrust investigation in this matter.

The Polish national public channels are of general nature offering a wide variety of programmes, while still fulfilling their programming obligations stipulated by the Broadcasting Act.[3] The main difference between the two is that TVP1 broadcasts more political discussion types of programmes, while TVP2 devotes more of its programming to culture, education and entertainment. Regional TVP3 broadcasts more information and fewer films than the public national channels. The three main commercial broadcasters: Polsat, TVN and TV4 are more commercially oriented with greater programme output in entertainment, advertising and self-promotion, and less of information, education (except TVN), theatre, documentaries and religious programmes.

Other private terrestrial TV channels in Poland include two Roman Catholic channels, TV Trwam and TV Puls, and seven local channels. The audience share of each of these channels does not exceed 1 per cent.

The Polish public radio broadcaster – Polskie Radio (PR) S.A., owned by the State Treasury, operates five national radio stations: Program 1 of a general nature, Program 2 devoted to high culture, Program 3 known for its music and news services, Polskie Radio BIS targeting young listeners and Radio Parliament broadcasting parliamentary sessions. PR S.A. also runs seventeen regional radio stations and Radio Polonia – targeting Poles abroad. In 2005 the combined audience share of public radio was approximately 26 per cent of the total radio audience share and 17 per cent of the total radio advertising share.

Commercial radio broadcasters include two top nationwide stations Radio RMF FM and Radio Zet. The two have the highest radio audience shares (21.4 and 18.8 per cent) and the highest radio advertising revenues (26 and 20 per cent). Both networks cover 95 per cent of the country via terrestrial transmitters and are additionally available on the satellite digital platforms and the Internet. Radio RMF-FM is owned by Holding FM – controlled by its chairman, Stanisław Tyczyński, and Radio Zet is owned by Eurozet LTD – a company of Polish and foreign shareholders.

Catholic Radio Maryja, with an audience share of 2.5 per cent, is the third most popular national non-public radio broadcaster in Poland. The station is run by the Redemptionist Fathers and is classified as a social broadcaster.

The three over-regional private radio stations operating transmitters in major Polish cities are Radio Wawa of a general nature and owned by WAWA S.A, Radiostacja, targeting the young and owned by Eurozet LTD., and Radio TOK FM, owned jointly by Agora S.A. and Spółdzielnia Pracy "Polityka", that broadcasts mainly political news and commentaries.

The local commercial radio stations in Poland are either universal or thematic. Most of them operate as networks monopolized by the biggest media groups including Eska (37 stations), Agora S.A. (27 stations), ZPR Group (26 stations) and Ad.point (13 stations). Some of the local radio stations are run by independent broadcasters, examples of which are universities and local governments.

Poland is the third biggest cable television market in Europe with approximately 4.5 million subscribers (Open Society Institute 2005). The market is dominated by the biggest operators with significant foreign capital: UPC, Vectra, Multimedia Polska, Aster City Cable, TOYA, TK Poznań, etc., the combined market share of which is 60 per cent. Most of these operators offer radio and TV broadcasting, the Internet and telephony services.

There are two digital television satellite platforms in Poland: Cyfra+ and Polsat Cyfrowy. Cyfra+ is owned by Telewizja Polska Korporacyjna S.A, whose shareholders are Canal+ Group (49 per cent of shares), UPC Polska, and Polcom Invest S.A. It offers 71 Polish language radio and TV channels and has 800,000 subscribers. Polsat Cyfrowy is owned by Telewizja Polsat S.A. and offers 45 Polish-language radio and TV channels, and has 700,000 subscribers.

In May 2005 the Strategy for a transition from analogue to digital broadcasting with respect to terrestrial TV was adopted. This document set the framework for Poland's transition until the complete analogue switch-off in 2014. The approved scenario of conversion is based on the launch of digital TV in particular provinces ('digital islands') until full national coverage can be achieved. Launch of digital broadcasting will start in Warsaw (multiplex 1) and in five towns of Wielkopolska province (multiplex 2) covering 16 per cent of Poland's population. The available frequencies will be allotted to applicant multiplex operators in a tender organized by the The Office for Electronic Communication (UKE). The KRRiT will grant licences to TV channels to broadcast within the multiplexes.

The strongest digital operators in Poland are TP Emmitel and the Polish Television Operator (PTO) – founded in November 2005 by TVN S.A. and Telewizja Polsat S.A. The public broadcaster TVP S.A appealed to the UKE to be automatically granted one of the two first multiplexes, yet the final decision on the matter has not yet been taken.

C. The Internet Media

Main features:

- Growth in the percentage of households with Internet access, yet disproportions among different sectors of society persist
- Dominance of analogue over broadband
- The most popular online media are *Gazeta* – online equivalent of top Polish daily and services by two commercial nationwide radio stations

The percentage of households with Internet access in Poland came to 30 per cent in 2005 compared to 26 per cent in 2004. Despite the growth, the access is still disproportionate among different sectors of society. Households with the lowest net income and located in rural areas are the most disadvantaged. With regards to type of Internet connection, in 2005 percentage of households with Internet access using a faster and more secure broadband connection came to 16 per cent compared to 8 per cent in 2004. The majority of Polish households still use analogue modems.

In 2005, 28.5 per cent of Poles declared that they use the Internet. Thirteen per cent of them mentioned reading online press as their main reason for using the Net and 6 per cent cite – listening/watching online radio and TV broadcasts. The most popular online medium is Gazeta – online equivalent of Gazeta Wyborcza regularly visited by 57 per cent of Internet users. The other most popular online media are respectively: Radio RMF FM, Radio Zet and Rzeczpospolita. Popularity of news websites available exclusively on the Internet has been growing. The most visited news portals are *Onet*, *Wirtualna Polska* and *Interia*.

D. News Agencies

Main features:

- Major news agency is the public Polish Press Agency
- Smaller private information service providers

The major news agency in Poland is the Polish Press Agency (PAP) owned by the State Treasury. The PAP operates national and foreign offices as well as receives information from agencies from all over the world. The agency offers general news service, specialized services and English-language news service. The Catholic Information Agency (KAI), set up by the Polish Episcopate, specializes in gathering information for the Catholic press. There are also several smaller, private information and photograph service providers in Poland.

2. State Policies

Main features:

■ Constitutional guarantees of freedom of the press
■ The Press Law
■ The Broadcasting Act
■ The National Broadcasting Council – main broadcasting regulator

The Polish Constitution guarantees freedom of the press and prohibits both preventive censorship and licensing of the press. It also proclaims that the main task of the National Broadcasting Council (KRRiT) is to safeguard the freedom of speech, the right to information and the public interest in radio and TV.

The 1984 Polish Press Law, which was subsequently amended, applies to dailies, periodicals, press agencies, radio and television. The law obliges the press to protect journalistic sources (except for the cases involving national security and murder), to publish the corrections of untrue or inaccurate information and to publish official statements of the state and regional administration.

The 1992 Broadcasting Act, which was subsequently amended, regulates the whole broadcasting sector in Poland. The Act determines: mode of appointment, responsibilities and competences of the KRRiT, general tasks of broadcasters, status of public broadcaster, licensing of commercial broadcasters, retransmission of programme services in cable and satellite networks and programming obligations.

The main legally assigned tasks of the KRRiT include: determining legal conditions of broadcasting activity, issuing and withdrawing broadcast licences, supervising activities of broadcasters and appointing the Supervisory Councils of public radio and TV.

According to the Act, both public and commercial broadcasters should: provide information and entertainment, promote national culture and facilitate education. The programmes of public radio and TV should, additionally, respect the Christian system of values, strengthen family ties, combat social pathologies and provide free-of-charge airtime to the state authorities, political parties, public service organizations and entities participating in national and local elections.

The Broadcasting Act was amended in 2004 in order to comply with the EU audio-visual policy requirements and the Television Without Frontiers (TWF) Directive. Hence, licences may be granted to foreign persons and entities resident in the EU. Licences to companies with foreign shareholders from countries other than EU may be granted if the foreign capital share does not exceed 49 per cent. Other amendments included the protection of minors and the promotion of the European cultural productions.

When it comes to limiting media concentration, the only provision of the Act dealing with the issue is the vague reference to the ban on broadcaster achieving 'dominant position' in mass media. The debate on the issue of media concentration was abandoned as a result of the 2003 *Rywingate* corruption scandal over bribery in exchange for amendment that would have enabled the biggest Polish press company, Agora, to enter the television market. The parliamentary investigation of the *Rywingate* scandal exposed the illicit broadcasting policy practices of the government, the governing parliamentary party – the Democratic Left Alliance (SLD), the main broadcasting regulator – the KRRiT, and the media businesses. The long-term 'politicization' of the KRRiT by means of appointing its members not on the basis of media expertise but rather political affiliation, and its resulting 'politicized' decisions such as appointment of the 'politically loyal' management of public broadcasting organizations, came into the spotlight.

The National Broadcasting Council (KRRiT) regulates the content of public and commercial broadcasting related to protection of minors, harmful content, advertising restrictions, etc.

3. Civil Society Organizations
Main features:

■ Two major national journalist associations
■ Associations of publishers, audio-visual producers, Internet and digital telephony providers, and advertisers
■ Codes of ethics enacted by the public broadcasters, the two national journalist associations and the main publisher association
■ The Council of Media Ethics provides advice on an ethical media performance

The major journalist professional organizations in Poland are the Polish Journalists Association (SDP) and the Journalists' Association of the Republic of Poland (SDRP), which run their regional offices in major Polish cities.

The major press publishers' organizations are the Polish Chamber of Press Publishers (IWP), which represents the interests of 120 publishers of over 460 titles, and the Association of the Local Press Publishers (SGL), which unites 58 publishers of 73 regional and local titles. The Press Circulation Audit Union (ZKDP) collects and analyses data on press circulation in Poland.

In the audio-visual sector, the National Chamber of Audiovisual Producers (KIPA) unites 100 production companies, both public and private, as well as represents major Polish TV broadcasters such as TVP S.A. and Canal+ Polska. The Convent of Radio Stations of the National Industrial Chamber of Electronics and Telecommunications (KIGEIT – KSR) represents commercial interests of 29 private radio stations. The Polish Chamber of Electronic Communications (PIKE) unites 140 companies operating broadcasting, Internet and digital telephony industries.

The main advertising organizations are the Polish Advertising Chamber and the Association of Advertising Agencies.

Most of Poland's media studies research is conducted in the Institute of Journalism – University of Warsaw and the Centre for Press Research – Jagiellonian University.

The Polish Chamber of Press Publishers (IWP) formulated its own code of professional ethics and established a system of interior courts, the sanctioning powers of which range from order to cease illegitimate practices to dismissal from the Chamber. The two biggest journalist associations also developed their internal codes of ethics and systems of journalists' courts. The Press Freedom Monitoring Centre monitors and reports on cases of Polish media freedom violation.

Additionally, public broadcasters formulated their own codes of ethics. The Commissions of Ethics guiding observance of these codes have no sanctioning powers but act as advisory bodies to the TVP and RP Boards of Management.

In 1995 Polish media owners and professionals adopted the Media Charter and established the Conference of Media, which in turn appoints the Council of Media Ethics. The Council publicly adjudicates upon the issues of observing the Charter, yet it constitutes an advisory body with no sanctioning powers.

The main Polish civic organizations participating in media ethics debate include the Association of Polish Consumers (with its 2004/05 Safe Internet campaign) and various Catholic movements and associations (III Poland's Congress of Catholic Movements and Associations 2005–2007 with the Media as a Forum for Evangelization campaign).

4. Development Trends
Main features:

- Reform of the KRRiT's mode of appointment
- Debates on requirements for and implications of the digital switch–over
- Debates on broadcasting legislation amendments: the ownership concentration and the PSB
- Poland's position on the revision of the TWF Directive

The 2005 parliamentary elections were won by the right-wing Law and Justice party and the 2005 presidential elections were won by Lech Kaczyński of the same party. The first issue on the new right government's agenda was the reform of the KRRiT's mode of appointment. In December 2005, together with its coalition partners the nationalist/Catholic League of Polish Families and the populist Self-Defence, the Law and Justice party voted for adoption of the Act on Transformations and Modifications to the Division of Tasks and Powers of State Bodies Competent for Communications and Broadcasting.

The act has reduced the number of members of KRRiT from nine to five; two of them were to be appointed by the Sejm, one by the Senate and two by the President. The chairman was to be nominated and dismissed by the President. The new mode of appointment was strongly criticized by the opposition parties: the centre Citizens Platform and the Democratic Left Alliance, which claimed that the real motivation behind the amendment was control of the new KRRiT by the Law and Justice and its coalition partners. The opposition also claimed that political motive behind the haste with which the new law was adopted was dismissal of the incumbent Council and the appointment of the new Council by January 2006, when the Supervisory Councils of public radio and TV were to be nominated. In March 2006 the Constitutional Tribunal pronounced the new law to be unconstitutional on the following points: President's right to nominate and dismiss the KRRiT's chairman and the KRRiT's responsibility to control observance of journalistic ethics. In April the act was amended again according to the Tribunal's ruling.

The broadcasting legislation in Poland needs to be updated in order to catch up with the ongoing technological and market changes. Although Poland has already adopted provisional strategy for the digital switch-over, the issues of compression standards, "must carry" programming, licensing and state financial involvement are not legally resolved. With regards to the Internet, there is essentially no legal framework to regulate online media. The legislation is also lacking when it comes to regulating ownership concentration. Legislative works on the issue were to a huge extent discontinued post to the *Rywingate* scandal. When it comes to PBS, existing legal provisions relating to its status, management and mode of financing have become obsolete. The Ministry of Culture and National Heritage, responsible for audio-visual policy, and the Ministry of Transport, responsible for telecommunications, are working on drafting these relevant amendments.

Polish media have been moving away from universal content to more targeted content as a response to growing audience fragmentation. There is a growing number of specialist press titles launched every year. In case of broadcast media, the shift has been lengthier. Apart from universal channels available via terrestrial transmission, the two main commercial broadcasters, Polsat and TVN, have launched thematic channels dedicated to sport, news, health, style, etc., available via cable and digital satellite platforms. Both plan to launch more thematic channels as a part of their transition strategy from analogue to digital broadcasting. The public broadcaster, TVP S.A., has also been preparing to enrich their programming offer with the launching of a few thematic channels.

With regard to the European integration of audio-visual media policies, Poland has submitted its position on the issue of revision of the TWF Directive to the European Commission and participates in debates on the topic. Poland's position paper emphasized the issues of material and territorial competence of the Directive, the promotion of European and independent audio-visual production, regulations regarding advertising and protection of minors.

Notes

1. See section on state policies.
2. See section on state policies.
3. See section on state policies.

References & Sources for Further Information

- National Broadcasting Council (KRRiT) http://www.krrit.gov.pl/
- Office of Electronic Communication (UKE) http://www.uke.gov.pl/
- Press Research Centre of the Jagiellonian University (OBP UJ) http://www.obp.pl/
- *Zeszyty Prasoznawcze* published by the OBP UJ
- Open Society Institute. *Television across Europe: Regulation, Policy, and Independence*, Country Report on Poland, vol. 2, 2005.

The Romanian Media Landscape

Alex Ulmanu

With a population of 22 million and a total area of 237,500 sq km, Romania is the largest Eastern European country after Poland. After missing the first EU integration wave partly because of the reform-shy governments which ruled the country after the ousting of communism in 1989, Romania, a NATO member since 2004, joined the European Union in 2007.

In the fall of 2004, the Social Democrat Party (PSD), seen by many as a continuator of the former communist party, lost the elections to the 'Justice and Truth' alliance comprised of the National Liberal Party (PNL) and the Democrat Party (PD), which later formed the government together with the Conservative Party (PC) and the Hungarian Union (UDMR). The new president, Traian Basescu, has won the electoral battle against Adrian Nastase, the former social democrat prime minister.

Romanian is the official language, with almost 90 per cent of the population formed of ethnic Romanians. According to official figures, the largest minority groups are the Hungarian (6.6%) and the Roma (2.5%). About 50 percent of the population lives in rural areas, which causes distribution problems for print media. Newspapers are almost exclusively being sold in urban communities. Penetration of cable TV and the Internet is also much lower in rural areas.

1. The Market

A. The Print Media
Main features:

- Vast number of titles in the market
- The quality of top newspapers has been increasing, with better print, more pages, more diverse coverage, supplements and Sunday editions
- There is a trend toward changing to tabloid formats
- Sales figures are decreasing, while advertising revenue is on the increase; however, the print media share from the advertising pie has been further cut in favour of TV
- There is a trend toward concentration around several strong groups, but also one toward fragmentation due to the increasing number of titles on the market

The Romanian print media is characterized firstly by the vast number of titles on the market. In total, there are more than 2,000 publications being printed in Romania, more than 70 of which being daily newspapers – according to data from the Romanian National Library. In 1989, before the fall of communism, there were only 36 dailies and 459 other periodicals, according to the National Institute of Statistics.

In the past years, daily newspapers have started to market themselves along the lines of 'quality' vs. 'tabloid' media outlets. Although one of the most constant trends has been toward more popular content and layout, most top newspapers call themselves 'quality' or 'reference' newspapers. Apart from improving their design and print quality, top newspapers have in the past two years started to increase the number of pages and develop special sections and weekly supplements. Business, sports and lifestyle are starting to get more coverage, as newspapers which tended to be highly politicized are shifting their focus toward other subjects.

Many newspapers have turned toward more compact/tabloid formats lately. Only a few of the top newspapers have maintained a broadsheet format. Others have moved to formats such as berliner, tabloid, or the American long format. Niche publications such as financial or sports newspapers have proved successful in some cases.

The best-selling newspaper is *Libertatea*, a soft tabloid which sells around 260,000 copies a day. The two main sports dailies, *Gazeta Sporturilor* and *ProSport*, stand at about 70,000 to 100,000 copies sold each day. *Jurnalul National* and *Evenimentul zilei* sell 60,000 to 80,000 copies each; they market themselves as quality newspapers, but can rather be considered mid-market by content and style. *Romania Libera*, a conservative, old-fashioned newspaper, which leads the classifieds market, sells around 50,000 to 60,000; *Gandul*, a recently launched newspaper preoccupied especially with social and political issues sells 30,000 copies a day; while *Adevarul*, one of the oldest newspapers on the market, sells about 23,000 copies.

The most successful regional newspaper is *Gazeta de Sud*, distributed in four counties in southern Romania, which sells about 30,000 copies a day.

As for many newspapers circulation is not audited by the Romanian Audit Bureau of Circulation (BRAT); it is difficult to estimate the general circulation for dailies. However, it probably stands at a little more than one million copies a day. The weeklies market is not as vivid. Most of the best-selling weeklies are Sunday editions of the top dailies. As a general trend, both sales figures and readership figures have been in decline for most dailies and weeklies in the past few years, due partly to market fragmentation. An analysis by *Gazeta Sporturilor* marketing manager Dochita Zenoveiov, quoted by the blog gustiroman.ro, of the sales figures of the top ten dailies shows a decrease from 900,000 copies a day in 2004 to 700,000 copies a day in 2006.

A particular aspect of the Romanian newspaper market is the great gap between the number of sold copies and readership. According to the National Audience Survey (Studiul National de Audienta – SNA), readership is in some cases nine or ten times larger than the sales figures. This is due to the fact that often one copy is read by more people, and also to the fact that the survey also takes into account Internet readers. However, readership figures are also on the decline. With a few exceptions, local publications are also losing readers.

There is a booming glossy market, with more than a dozen women's magazines, a few men's magazines, as well as auto, computers, cooking and other niche products.

In spite of the falling circulation, advertising figures are on the rise, for both national and local publications. The amount of money spent in the print media by advertisers increased by 10 per cent in 2005, according to the Media Fact Book (MFB) 2006 by Initiative Media. The advertising volume for the entire media for 2005 is estimated at 250 million euro (25 per cent above the 2004 figure), and 8.9 per cent of that money went towards print media. However, the print ratio has decreased from 10.5 per cent in 2004. Initiative estimates that all media companies will have advertising worth 321 million euro in 2006, and experts expect the print ratio to further diminish, although the sum invested in print ads would increase again.

In terms of ownership, there is a trend towards concentration around several strong groups.

B. The Broadcast Media
Main features:

- Television is a favourite pasttime for Romanians;
- Almost 90 per cent of the advertising pie goes to TV;
- Most Romanians are being reached by TV through cable networks;

- Big local and international groups own the most successful TV and radio stations;
- The radio scene is dominated by private FM stations in cities and by national or regional public broadcasts in rural areas.

Television remains the most popular means of entertainment for most Romanians, and, lately, the major players have moved to diversify their channel offer and consolidate their positions on the market. A number of niche channels have been developed, and there are plans to open further more.

As television took an 88.3 per cent chunk (145.9 million euro) from the 250 million invested in advertising in the whole Romanian media in 2005, national channels have been mostly after the urban population aged 18 to 49, the most attractive segment for advertisers. Members of this age group watch TV, on average, 36.4 hours a week, one of the highest levels in Europe.

The most popular station is ProTV, associated with the Media Pro group and part of CME, an American-based TV holding running stations in several Central and Eastern European countries. Antena 1, belonging to the Voiculescu family, is the challenger. Both ProTV and Antena 1 put a strong accent on entertainment. TVR1, the first public channel, is number three in terms of audience, closely followed by Acasa TV, another CME television station, oriented mostly toward feminine audiences. Smaller nationwide televisions include Prima TV (owned by Scandinavian company SBS), which focuses on reality shows such as a Romanian version of *Cheaters*, or, in previous years, a Romanian version of *Big Brother* (which proved to be a failure, making only a few points of rating).

Most Romanians receive their TV programmes via cable.

According to a study by market research institutes CSOP/TNS and IMAS in June 2006 through May 2007, and cited by "Cartea Alba a Presei III – probleme economice ale presei" ("The Carte Blanche of the Press III – economical problems of the press", Media Monitoring Agency, Bucharest, 2007), more than 82 per cent of TV sets in the urban areas are connected to cable, compared to only 53.9 per cent in the rural areas. Around 5 per cent of urban TV sets receive TV programmes in the DTH system (Direct to Home, or digital television), compared to 20.6 per cent in the villages. And just 4.9 per cent of the households in the urban areas use individual antennas, compared to 18.1 per cent in the rural areas.

There are two main companies which have managed to swallow almost all competitors and which share the market in almost equal chunks: RDS/RCS and UPC. Several years ago, the cable operators have started to upgrade the network by installing fiber optics, which has allowed them to offer not only TV packages but also Internet and phone services.

The media groups which have invested in the print media have also oriented their money toward the TV and radio scene. Sorin Ovidiu Vantu has invested in a news channel called Realitatea TV, which has positioned itself as a quality product and leads the news TV niche. Vantu's company, Realitatea Media, renamed Realitatea-Catavencu after a merger, has also started a business channel and has taken over soap opera station Romantica, planning to raise its profile in order to compete with Media Pro's house and women's channel Acasa TV. According to some media reports, Realitatea-Catavencu will continue to start new broadcast channels, including a generalist TV station.

Scandinavian company SBS owns Prima TV, and also two FM radio networks. American-based CME owns the Media Pro International group, including the largest commercial stations ProTV, Acasa TV, ProCinema and ProTV International, which broadcast through the Internet and satellite to Romanian audiences outside Romania. The company owns InfoPro, a news and music radio network broadcasting nationwide on dozens of FM frequencies, plus another FM radio network, ProFM, focused on music and entertainment. Very recently, the group has acquired TV Sport, rebranded it as Sport.ro and relaunched it together with a new website also called sport.ro.

French-based group Lagardere owns the most important news and music FM network, Europa FM, as well as a youth FM radio network, Radio 21. Lagardere also plans to launch two TV stations: a general interest one and a youth station. Although they had been announced for the summer of 2007, the launch has been postponed.

Voiculescu's Intact group owns the second largest commercial television, Antena 1, news channel Antena 3, a new lifestyle TV station called Euforia (designed to compete with Acasa TV), and has recently launched Antena 2, dedicated mostly to male audiences. The company also owns a radio station, Romantic FM, in addition to its ventures in the print media.

The radio scene is dominated by FM stations in the urban areas, with more than 300 licences for FM radio stations having been issued by the National Broadcasting Council. In rural areas, radio is seen as the most important information medium, as newspapers have not been able to establish distribution networks to reach villages in a comprehensive manner. The public news station Radio Romania Actualitati, which is not bound by geographically limited FM frequencies, is most popular in such rural areas, together with regional stations belonging to the public network. No private non-FM stations are operating in Romania.

Digital Radio and Television are still in infancy in Romania. The national phone operator Romtelecom, owned by the Greek company OTE, has recently announced it had aquired a system which would allow it to deliver digital television.

C. The Internet Media
Main features:

- Over six million people are online, and broadband is growing at a rapid pace;
- Online advertising is bringing more money to the industry, hence, competition is growing more fierce;
- Most traditional media outlets have online versions; newspaper sites are moving from shovelware content to content developed or adapted for the Web by teams of online journalists;
- Blogs are becoming more popular.

About six million Romanians use the Internet. Broadband is on the rise, as well as home use. According to the National Authorities for Communications quoted by underclick.ro, high-speed Internet has grown by 96 per cent in the past two years, amounting to over 750,000 broadband connections. The Communications minister has estimated there will be four million broadband users by 2009. The broadband penetration rate is 3.46 per cent, which places Romania in first place in south-eastern Europe in terms of broadband growth.

The online medium is becoming ever-more competitive, as online advertising is gaining momentum. It is estimated that between 2 and 3.5 million euros was invested in online advertising in 2005, and estimates for 2006 vary between 4 and 7 million.

The most popular traffic service, trafic.ro, is being used by advertisers as a standard audit tool for websites popularity. However, the new developments have prompted the Romanian Audit Bureau of Circulation (BRAT) to initiate its own website audience tracking tool, which has been operational since autumn 2007.

Most traditional media outlets are present online. Until recently, the newspapers websites were mostly shovelware (print content being put online, without any special treatment for the Web), while TV and radio websites were rather presentation websites than news sites. However, as users turn to the online media in greater numbers, news sites are starting to improve and adapt their content to the Web.

The most popular news site is gsp.ro, sports daily *Gazeta Sporturilor*'s website. According to trafic.ro, the site has as of the autumn of 2007 an audience of more than 800,000 unique visitors a week. Other popular news sites are Prosport.ro, the website of the other large sports newspaper, *ProSport*, or evz.ro, the website of the *Evenimentul zilei* daily newspaper.

A number of newspapers and television stations have recently created special journalistic departments to take care of their online presence, an important development for Romanian online journalism. Some exclusively online news outlets have also managed to capture large audiences. The most popular such website is hotnews.ro, ranked in the news sites top ten by trafic.ro.

Weblogs or blogs are becoming more popular and influential. There is no official statistical data on Romanian blogs, but according to the 2007 RoBloggersSurvey, a poll of several hundred bloggers, conducted by Internet experts Carmen Holotescu and Cristian Manafu, shows there are several dozen Romanian blogs active at present. Most of them have appeared in the past years. In addition, a growing number of news sites have developed blog sections.

D. News Agencies
Main feature:

■ Competition is growing as new private press agency appeared

The news agency scene is becoming crowded. The supremacy of *Mediafax*, a private news agency which is part of the Media Pro group, has remained uncontested for almost ten years. Meanwhile, *Rompres*, the heir of the communist official agency *Agerpres*, has been considered as rather poor in terms of reporting quality. However, lately, *Rompres* has started to improve its coverage and its low-price policy has allowed it to gain some contracts from local newspapers which turned off their more expensive *Mediafax* subscriptions.

The Realitatea-Catavencu group has started in the summer of 2006 a new press agency, *NewsIn*, with an initial investment of more than three million euro according to media reports. *NewsIn*, which has been recruiting journalists from other media outlets, including *Mediafax*, in addition to starting its own training programme for junior reporters, is considered as an important potential challenger of *Mediafax*'s position on the market.

Smaller agencies include *Click News*, a cooperation between several local newspapers, and Bucharest-based *AM Press*, which specializes in political reporting.

2. State Policies
Main features:

■ The National Broadcasting Council is the main watchdog of the audio-visual, as well as the institution responsible to issue broadcasting licences;
■ Libel and slander have recently been decriminalized;
■ 'Masked subsidies' in the form of advertising in chosen newspapers from state entities has disappeared after social democrats lost the elections;
■ The public channels are being supported through a licence fee, as well as money from the state budget and advertising.

There is no media law in Romania as such. However, there are other laws which affect the media. The right to information is recognized by the Romanian Constitution and (since the end of 2001) by the Law on Access to Public Information, which obliges government institutions to announce any information of public interest.

Libel and slander have recently been decriminalized, which contributed to a significant reduction in the number of trials opened against journalists.

The audio-visual field is regulated by the Audiovisual Law adopted in 1992, with the National Broadcasting Council established in 1990 as the sole supervisor of the Romanian TV and radio stations. The NBC has eleven members appointed by the Parliament, the Government and the President. Recent media reports have accused the authorities of having the intention to further politicizing the council by adding two more members to the eleven. The council issues and withdraws broadcasting licences, prepares rules and regulations and monitors the stations to see if the rules are respected – and issues fines or recommendations regarding the content of broadcasts. It makes sure that no 'indecent' content is being broadcast before 22h00, it sanctions hidden advertising, pornography, racist and violent behaviour, as well as foul language.

There is an ongoing debate on the need to depoliticize the Romanian public radio and TV stations by changing the law by which these institutions function, but the Parliament has so far been unwilling to take steps in that direction. The two public institutions, each running several channels, are led by the Councils of Administration whose members are named by political parties and by the government.

The public stations are being financed through a licence fee, but also receive money from the state budget and from advertising. There are no government subsidies to independent print and broadcast media. 'State advertising' was considered as masked subsidy in 2000–2004, but the practice to place large sums of advertising money in certain newspapers has stopped with the new government.

3. Civil Society Organizations
Main features:

- Although unions exist, there is no representative organization for all Romanian journalists;
- The Romanian Press Club is an organization representing the interests of the media owners;
- The advertising industry is represented by the Romanian branch of the IAA;
- BRAT is the institution which certifies circulation and readership data for newspapers;
- Ethics codes have been developed by various organizations;
- There is no overall self-regulating body to sanction foul play;

■ Some NGO's have started to run campaigns in order to raise awareness on professional issues for both journalists and media consumers.

A confederacy of journalists' and typographers' unions has promoted and negotiated a collective labour contract for the media industry. Signing the collective agreement with the ownership in the spring of 2004 was considered a great success by the union, as it guarantees for the first time certain rights for journalists, such as the right to invoke the clause of consciousness when they feel they received an unethical assignment. The contract also regulates working hours, holidays and minimum wages.

There are over 40 media organizations, but none of them can claim to represent a large part of the Romanian journalists. Some of these organizations, from local unions to training centres, have been gathered under an umbrella called the Convention of Media Organisations, an initiative of the Media Monitoring Agency and the Centre for Independent Journalism.

The most prominent organization of the Romanian media, however, is the Romanian Press Club, in fact, an employers' association protecting and promoting the economic interests of several central media institutions, and not those of the journalists working there. Cristian Tudor Popescu, a journalist and shareholder in the newspaper *Gandul*, resigned on 20 November 2006, from the position of RPC president, issuing an open letter in which he said the organization should not represent both the owners and the journalists.

The Association for Protecting and Promoting Freedom of Expression offers juridical assistance to journalists being sued for what they publish and trains lawyers and judges in European media law.

The advertisers are grouped within the Romanian branch of the International Advertising Association (IAA – Romania). It includes about 85 members, including advertisers like Coca-Cola, advertising agencies, media, research, PR and marketing companies.

One of the most important organizations in the media industry is BRAT (The Romanian Audit Bureau of Circulation), which is seen by the advertisers as an essential instrument to certify and study the print run, sales and audiences of newspapers. The organization counts over 150 print publishing houses, nine online publishers, almost 30 advertising agencies and nine advertisers such as Vodafone or Procter&Gamble. Besides certifying the print run and sales figures, the bureau has been commissioning the National Audience Survey, detailing the number and profiles of readers for its members. The Romanian ABC has started, in the autumn of 2007, a similar service to survey the website's audiences.

The Romanian Press Club has its own ethics code, which should be respected by all its members and has issued a set of editorial policy principles stating that the editors, and not the owners, should decide the editorial policy.

The Convention of Media Organisations also drafted a code of ethics which it recommends to Romanian newsrooms. Few Romanian media outlets have their own ethics codes and style guides. The CMO also has an emergency board which issues press releases of public condemnation each time it considers professional and ethical standards have been breached by media outlets.

An NGO formed in 2005, called the Association of Media Consumers, has taken upon itself to act on behalf of Romanian readers, listeners and viewers. It reacts to what it considers harmful to the public by press releases and various forms of attracting attention, and it organiZes round tables with the media. However, the association does not have a high profile yet.

4. Development Trends

Main features:

- Local journalists have often been victims of political and economic pressure;
- Competition is becoming more fierce due to new investments;
- More titles concentrate around several big groups.

Especially in the local media, journalists are still often subject to pressures from local oligarchs and media owners – who sometimes are the same people. The phenomenon, which often led to biased stories and also to self-censorship, took epic proportions during the PSD regime in 2000–2004, and it hasn't ceased after the social democrats lost the elections – in some areas, the media owners changed sides, or the media outlets they used to control changed hands, being transferred to the political victors.

However, the most spectacular developments in the Romanian media in the past years have been triggered by an unprecedented influx of money. New players have challenged the positions of more established companies. The process has led to concentration, as more outlets are grouped around a handful of media groups, but also to fragmentation due to the launching of new titles.

Swiss-owned Ringier Romania, which prints the best-selling *Libertatea*, as well other successful titles such as *Evenimentul zilei, Capital* and a host of glossy magazines has been the most successful print media group. Throughout the past couple of years, however, many top managers and journalists from Ringier have moved to other groups.

Media Pro, which groups a vast number of publications, the *Mediafax* news agency and several commercial stations including the champion ProTV, has also seen many of its professionals move to the competition. However, it has remained one of the most solid groups on the market. Media reports indicate that toward the end of 2007 the company has paid more than eight million euros to buy sports newspaper *ProSport* back from Ringier. Five years ago, Media Pro had sold *ProSport* to Ringier, but at present the company is heavily banking on sports content.

A traditional competitor for Media Pro has been Intact, a media group belonging to the Voiculescu family, which owns, besides commercial TV stations Antena 1, Antena 3 and Euforia, some of the most successful titles on the newspaper market, such as *Jurnalul National* and *Gazeta Sporturilor*. The company has been expanding rapidly in the past couple of years.

But the most spectacular developments in terms of media ownership in both print and broadcast media have at the centre controversial figures like Sorin Ovidiu Vantu and, lately, Dinu Patriciu.

Vantu, whom the media accused of nationwide scams after thousands of people lost their savings when an investment fund he founded went down a few years back, is one of the richest men in Romania, with an estimated fortune of 500 million to one billion US dollars. After making some investments in the media in the 90s, he backed away and said he would rather invest in something else. However, he has revealed recently that he had been the hidden owner of the most successful TV news channel in Romania, Realitatea TV, and has since built an ever-growing media empire including a TV business channel and a news agency. Vantu's group, Realitatea Media, has also acquired, in recent months, one of the most respected media companies in Romania, Catavencu, which is the publisher of several premium publications and the owner of a network of FM radios called Guerrilla. The new company created through the merger is called Realitatea-Catavencu. Sorin Ovidiu Vantu has caused quite a stir in the Romanian media scene and behind it, not only through daring acquisitions of media outlets and initiatives to launch new ones, but also through an aggressive strategy to attract professionals from the competition – at both the editorial and the management level.

The newest player on the Romanian media scene is Dinu Patriciu, the president of Rompetrol, an oil company. Patriciu too has been having trouble with the prosecutors, being put under accusation for fraud. He has recently acquired the majority package in the Adevarul publishing house – which owns the *Adevarul* daily, and plans to further expand both in print and broadcast. In October 2006, Patriciu also bought the newspaper *Averea* (a business daily turned tabloid several months ago, whose sales figures, not audited by the Romanian ABC, are said to stand at around 30,000 or 40,000 copies a day). Like Vantu, Patriciu has started an aggressive campaign to attract professionals. On 17 October almost the entire staff of the best-selling tabloid *Libertatea*, owned by Ringier, quit the paper in order to join *Averea*. The tabloid was afterwards rebranded as *Click*, with a format and style extremely similar to *Libertatea*'s.

As a direct result of such moves, we are witnessing a somewhat paradoxical situation: although a healthier economic climate would normally lead to fewer but better titles on the market, the reality is quite the contrary. There is now a growing number of media institutions, but the number of good professionals in the business is not increasing at the same pace. As media analyst Iulian Comanescu noted, the overall quality of Romanian journalism is decreasing because the same number of professionals are being fought over by an increasing number of media institutions. Good journalists and publishers are in great demand, and wages are up. A new wave of investments is good news to media people and bad news for media consumers, who are bound to get more diverse but poorer quality products.

References and Sources for Further Information

The School of Journalism and Mass Communication Studies at the University of Bucharest and the Tritonic publishing house publish Jurnalism si Comunicare, a scholarly journal dedicated to communication and society in the post-communist period in Romania.

Among the few synthesis texts about post-communist media in Romania, one could mention Peter Gross (1991, 1995, 1996), Ion Dragan, J. P. Lafrance (1994), Mihai Coman (1994 and 1995).

The National Audiovisual Council periodically publishes bulletins with a more technical content.

There are several publications dedicated to media and advertising, such as AdMaker.

Information about aspects of media-related law and freedom of expression can be found at the website of FreeEx (www.freeex.org).

For media monitoring, and the Media Monitoring Agency's reports on press freedom, please visit www.mma.ro.

The South East European Network for Professionalisation of the Media (SEENPM) has published reports on "Media Ownership and Its Impact on Media Independence and Pluralism" in eighteen countries in the region. The report on Romanian media, written by journalist Manuela Preoteasa, can be found at http://www.mirovni-institut.si/media_ownership/romania.htm.

THE SLOVAKIAN MEDIA LANDSCAPE

Andrej Školkay

Slovakia is a small nation with 5.4 million inhabitants. There are two important minorities: about half a million of Hungarians and about 350,000 Roma. This makes any generalizations about national media output and consumption based on per capita statistics potentially slightly misleading.

On the one hand, obviously, many ethnic Hungarians do watch broadcasting or read media in Slovak language, in addition to broadcasting or media for minorities in their language, but almost all of them also watch broadcasting from Hungary.

On the other hand, although there are some media for Roma in Roma language in Slovakia, but the dominant source of information and entertainment for Roma seems to be television broadcasting in Slovak language or in Hungarian language. There is some limited broadcasting in Roma in both public radio and television broadcasting too.

Almost all ethnic Slovaks are bilingual in Slovak and Czech languages. This makes the penetration of Czech programmes easier, especially in television broadcasting. Although programmes for children were translated from Czech language into Slovak language for about a decade, it was quite common to broadcast foreign programmes with Czech dubbing in Slovak electronic media. However, this has changed due to new law passed in summer 2007. From January 2008, all broadcast must be in Slovak language or with Slovak subtitles – the only exceptions are original Czech movies as well as programmes dubbed in Czech language till 1 January 2008.

1. The Market

A. The Print Media
Main features:

- The number of published daily newspapers has stabilized in the last few years;
- There is trend of decline in circulation and readership of daily newspapers;
- There is an increase in circulation and readership of weeklies, both newspapers and magazines, but this is largely due to a number of new weeklies. Overall, circulation per weekly declines.

There were 1,424 newspapers and magazines published in 2005 in contrast to 886 newspapers and magazines published in 2004 and 1,100 journals and magazines published in 2003. Obviously, many newspapers and magazines are short-lived. While there is a continuous trend of decline in total number of circulated newspapers, as well as in circulation of daily newspapers, there is a continuous increase in circulation of weeklies in general. In particular, there has been an increase in popularity of regional and local newspaper weeklies. These weeklies were regularly read by 38 per cent of citizens (November 2005). Despite the fact that the daily newspapers are read by 91 per cent of citizens at least once in a two-week period, they were read on regular basis by 48 per cent in early 2006, with decreasing interest.

The total circulation of daily newspapers was less than 100 million copies in 2006 (sold copies), while it was 191 million copies in 2004 and 216 million copies in 2003. There was an increase in circulation of weeklies from 154 million copies in 2003 to 166 million copies in 2004 and then again an increase to 184 million in 2006. The total circulation of newspapers and magazines was about 300 million copies in 2006, while it was 385 million copies in 2004 and 464 million copies in 2001.

There were nine national or multiregional independent daily newspapers in Slovakia in 2006 (a network of daily regional newspapers is considered to be statistically only one daily) and two city evening newspapers. The story of publishing of evening newspapers shows a negative trend, while the number of published daily newspapers has stabilized in the last few years.

There were the following national daily newspapers in Slovakia in 2006: *Nový čas* (Ringier, circulation 190,000), *Pravda* (Northcliffe International Ltd, 75,000), *Sme* (Verlagsgruppe Passau, 73,000), *Šport* (Slovak owner Šport Press), one fully advertising daily, *Avízo* (Northcliffe International Ltd, 11,000), Hungarian language daily *Új Szó* (Verlagsgruppe Passau, 25,000) and *Hospodárske noviny* (Dow Jones and Handelsblatt, 20,000). In September 2006, a new tabloid entered the scene – daily *Plus Jeden Deň* (SPOLOČNOSŤ 7 PLUS, s.r.o., 55, 000).

In addition to these national dailies, there were two evening city newspapers (*Prešovský večerník* and *Košický večer*) and a regional network of newspapers which shared the common title *Východoslovenské noviny* and subtitle *Korzár* (and additional subtitles) and some common pages with the daily *Sme*. Their total circulation was 32,000. Their specific feature is their location in the eastern part of Slovakia. Then there is a number of regional weekly newspapers, most of them published by Verlagsgruppe Passau.

Finally, there is the daily newspaper *Blikk*, a Hungarian-language tabloid imported from Hungary, as well as some imported Czech daily newspapers like *Blesk, Mladá fronta dnes* and *Lidové noviny*.

The two most successful publishers of magazines in Slovakia belong to Swiss Ringier (60% market share) and the Slovak company Spoločnost 7 Plus. Some specialized magazines and journals are published by Dow-Jones/Handelsblatt.

Among the weeklies published by the Swiss company Ringier are the women's weekly *Nový čas pre ženy* (250,000 copies), the family weekly *Život* (150,000 copies), the TV programme weekly *Eurotelevízia* (140–150,000 copies).

Among the weeklies established and published by the Slovak company Spoločnost 7 Plus was *Plus 7 dní*, for several years the most popular weekly magazine in Slovakia (170–180,000 copies). In addition to this general interest weekly, there was the women's magazine *Báječná žena* (150–160,000 copies).

B. The Broadcast Media
Main features:

- Three-quarters of Slovaks watch television every day;
- Both public television and public radio enjoy a high level of public trust and enjoy relatively high ratings.

Three-quarters of Slovaks watch television every day. More than half (56%) of Slovak households own only one TV set, one-third have two TV sets and one-tenth of households have three and more TV sets. While older people watch television broadcast for information, younger people prefer more television entertainment.

Historically, public radio broadcasting has always had the highest quality of cultural programmes, while Slovak Television broadcasts, as well as broadcasts of the most important private television, *Markíza*, had been heavily influenced by politics in the late 1990s.

Both public television and public radio enjoy relatively a high level of public trust. The most trusted medium in the past fifteen years has always been the public Slovak Radio.

In the period between December 2001 and April 2005 the level of public trust in the institution of public radio was between 74 and 78 per cent.

The Slovak Television, due to long-term (1994–1998) political bias, has enjoyed a lower level of trust, both historically and comparatively. Yet, it has increased its level of trust from 51per cent in March 1999 to 71 per cent in April 2005.

However, in general, more than half of Slovaks consider TV as the most trustworthy source of information, followed by radio (19%), newspapers (15%) and Internet (12%). At the same time, TV news programmes are fully trusted only by 22 per cent of viewers. Almost 40 per cent believe that TV stations inform correctly only sometimes or never do so. Almost 60 per cent believe that news reporting of private TV stations is equally trustworthy as news reporting of public television.

There were 23 radio stations in Slovakia in 2006, in addition to five domestic public radio stations and one international broadcast of public radio. This has been almost a fixed number in the last few years, although, obviously, some radio stations were established and some vanished or changed their names.

More than 85 per cent of the population aged above 14 years listen to radio broadcasts according to long-term research. Thus, it is the second most popular medium after television broadcast in Slovakia.

The first channel of public Slovak Radio, historically a long-term radio leader, has lost its first rank in popularity when the private Rádio Express became for the first time in Slovak history the radio leader in 2005. Rádio Express was listened by 21 per cent of listeners in contrast to 20 per cent listeners of the public radio´s first channel, *Rádio Slovensko*, in 2006. The private radio Fun Rádio was at the third position (9%), followed by the public regional radio channel Rádio Regina (7%) followed by Rádio Okey (7%), the music channel of public radio Rádio FM (4%) and the Christian *Rádio Lumen* (4%).

Among foreign radio broadcasts, the most popular ones were the Hungarian private radios *Danubius Rádio* and *Slágerradio* (2.5%). *Rádio Patria* broadcasts for national minorities. *Radio Slovakia International* is an international broadcast in foreign languages, including broadcast in Slovak language for the Slovaks living abroad. It has limited its foreign broadcast significantly in the summer of 2006.

There is the public television Slovenská televízia (Slovak Television, STV) with two channels, (1) Jednotka and (2) Dvojka. Then there are the national private terrestrial/satellite digital/cable television stations Markíza (CME Media Enterprises B.V., A.R.J. and Media Invest) and terrestrial/cable Joj (J&T Bank) and satellite/cable/terrestrial news television TA3 (J&T Finance Group). J&T Banka and J&T Finance Group are linked together. Then there are some specialised national or multiregional television stations. There is one national TV station, NAUTIK TV, which broadcasts only via satellite. Its programme was originally focused at everything related to water issues. In 2006 it expanded its programme with music, life-style programmes and some current affairs programmes. Then there is the teleshopping TVA television channel which broadcasts in major cities. TV MUSIC BOX/NAŠA broadcasts only music programmes digitally via satellite and then through KDS technology. Moooby TV broadcasts music and entertainment via satellite. ETV – medicus broadcast educational programmes via satellite. There is also TV Ring, which broadcasts, only 50 hours a week, TV games and interactive erotic programmes.

In addition to these multiregional stations, there are over 100 local/city television stations, info channels and teleshopping channels.

The most popular channel in 2006 was Markíza (between 31–36% market share), STV1 Jednotka (18–21%), Joj (15–17%), STV2 Dvojka (5–6%) and TA3 (1.3–2%). Czech television stations attracted about 10 per cent, Hungarian TV stations about 7 per cent and the other TV stations about 8 per cent of viewers.

The public Slovenská televízia has its main source of income from licence fees and commercials. The Slovak Television broadcasts for a Hungarian minority (89 hours in 2004 and 123 hours in 2005 and 140 hours in 2006) and in German, Roma, Ukrainian and Ruthenian languages (together 44 hours in 2005 and 78 hours in 2006).

The first channel broadcasts 60 per cent of domestic programmes and 40 per cent of foreign programmes, while the second channel broadcasts 89 per cent of domestic programmes and 11 per cent of foreign programmes in 2005.

The first channel (Jednotka) has become very similar to commercial stations, with no significant difference from other Slovak commercial stations in quality of its entertainment programmes. The second channel (Dvojka) is more focused on information, education and social as well as political issues in general. There is a plan to establish digital broadcasting of the third sport channel in 2008, starting during the Olympic Games.

TV Markíza has been broadcasting since August 1996. It has become a market leader in a relatively short time, both in viewership and profit-making. Markíza´s majority owner is Central European Media Enterprises (CME B.V., Netherlands – in fact, an American company). It covers terrestrially 85 per cent of the country but it also broadcasts via satellite. TV Joj has been broadcasting since March 2002. It has significantly increased its viewership with its tabloid-infotainment strategy in the last years. Then there is the national news television TA3, perhaps unique in small countries. TA3 has similar programmes to CNN or BBC World. It has been in operation since September 2001 and broadcasts via satellite, in cable networks and in some areas also terrestrially since early 2006. It has limited viewership of about 1–2 per cent and it broadcasts seventeen hours on weekdays and fifteen hours during weekends.

C. The Internet Media

Main features:

- There is an increasing trend towards pay-per-read services in case of commentaries and longer articles of journals;
- There are several specialized news portals;
- Almost two-thirds of citizens do not use Internet at all;
- Less than one-quarter of all citizens have access to Internet at home, but more than one-third of those who do not have access to the Internet at home do have access to the Internet at work.

All daily newspapers have their own websites. However, increasingly their older issues in electronic archives are getting closed for unrestricted access after some time. The daily *Sme* was the first daily that established its own site for bloggers in 2004/2005. Some articles from this site are being published in this daily. Some weeklies have a special (different from print version) electronic version of their publications, but there is an increasing trend towards pay-per-read services, at least in the case of full versions of some articles and content protected by copyright. Most media websites offer limited versions of their regular content, but some, particularly with very low circulation like *Slovo*, publish online full texts of all articles. However, even these Internet-free media close their access to these articles after a week's time or so.

There are several specialized news portals in Slovakia: bleskovky.sk produced by *Nový čas* is the most popular news portal in Slovakia, webnoviny.sk (produced by *SITA* news agency) and the more recent and professional news portal aktualne.sk.

In contrast to print media, electronic media increasingly put full-length versions of their selected programmes on the Internet. These programmes include mainly news and current affairs programmes.

Overall, 62 per cent of citizens do not use Internet at all. Internet use is Slovakia is considered to be expensive and many people do not speak foreign languages, needed for wider use of Internet. About half of the population do not see any reason why to use the Internet at all.

There has been approved and introduced a controversial policy which should make Internet use more accessible to young people. According to this plan, under certain conditions young people can have state-sponsored Internet at home for up to two years.

The media webpages with most frequent "unique visitors" are *Sme* (950,000 unique visitors in August 2007), *bleskovky* (913,000), *aktuality* (500,000), *Markíza* (451,000), *Pravda* (428,000), aktualne.sk (262,000), eTrend.sk (245,000).

As far as listening to radio through the Internet is concerned, 45 per cent of those who use the Internet sometimes listen to radio via the Internet, but this is on daily and almost daily basis only by every fifth Internet user. Out of those who use Internet on regular basis, 11 per cent access Web-based radio and/or television stations, as well as 46 per cent log-in online versions of print media.

D. News Agencies
Main features:

- There are two major domestic news agencies: the private *SITA* and state-supported *TASR*;
- There is the specialized Roma News Agency *RPA*.

There are two major domestic news agencies: the private *SITA* (Slovak Information and Press Agency), established in January 1997, and the state-supported *TASR* (Press Agency of the Slovak Republic) founded in 1992. In addition to these two universal news agencies, there is the specialized Roma News Agency *RPA*.

TASR employs 167 staff and 75 external reporters. Also, it has only one foreign correspondent – in Brussels. There is a general decline of interest among media in service of *TASR*. There is some increase in demand for voice and picture production of *TASR* as well as increasing demand for news from *TASR* among news portals. Although there were attempts to prepare a new legislation for *TASR* in early 2006, there was no political consensus about the future of *TASR* in 2005/2006.

SITA has over 100 permanent staff members and dozens of external contributors. *SITA* produces over 400 news items per day and dozens of specialized bulletins in various languages. *SITA* has expanded its services in 2001 with specialized services for the business sector and institutions. *SITA*'s main target is business services.

RPA specializes at Roma issues. In addition to news, *RPA* produces a weekly e-bulletin for self-government with focus on topics related to grant possibilities for Roma communities and two specialized monthly bulletins for the NGO sector. The first one is focused at life of Roma women and the second one informs about cultural issues. Most services of *RPA* are free of charge.

2. State Policies
Main features:

- A number of specialized/minority periodicals are being sponsored by various state bodies;
- There is slow process of preparation for the digitalization of radio and television broadcasting;
- The main regulatory bodies for electronic media are the Council for Broadcasting and Retransmission, the Council of Slovak Television as well as the Radio Council.

There is freedom of expression in the media in Slovakia. However, there have been cases that public figures sued successfully the media even in cases of cartoons. Also, there is a strict law and quite tough policy that does not allow denying the Holocaust or making racist remarks.

The main regulatory bodies for electronic media are the Council for Broadcasting and Retransmission, the Council of Slovak Television as well as the Radio Council. There is also the Press Council. Allocations of licences and frequencies are a responsibility of the Council for Broadcasting and Retransmission.

The Ministry of Culture supported financially 44 periodicals with a total circulation 200,000 copies and the amount of 25 million Slovak Crowns (1 euro equals 37 SKK in 2005). The Ministry of Social Affairs supported 28 periodicals with 6.5 million Slovak Crowns in 2005. The Office of the Government supported eighteen journals with 3.5 million Slovak Crowns in 2005.

In the last few years, the government agreed to pay for debts of both public service broadcasters in millions of euros, in hope to revitalize both institutions. There is also regular but decreasing state subsidy to the *TASR*.

The first experimental digital broadcasting was in 1999. There have been some pilot projects for radio and television digital broadcasting in major cities.

The professional and ethical behaviour of electronic media is being supervised primarily by the Council for Broadcasting and Retransmission, and less so by the Council of Slovak Television and the Radio Council.

3. Civil Society Organizations
Main features:

- There is one major professional organization for journalists the Slovak Syndicate of Journalists;
- There are various state and non-governmental bodies which monitor ethical and professional behaviour of the media and journalists;

ganization for journalists, the Slovak Syndicate of
Journalists, currently with 1,200 members. This is a politically independent organization.
Then there is the Slovak Association of Journalists with about 500 or less members. This
is a more politically oriented organization, but with almost no publicly visible activity.
There is also Slovak Union of Journalists-Seniors (Retired) with about 300 members.
This organization is also not really publicly active.

Other professional organizations include the Association of Independent Radio and
Television Stations, the Association of Publishers of Periodical Press, the Association of
Providers of Cable Television and the Association of Local TV Stations – Lotos.

There is a voluntary non-state Ethics Commission which deals with unethical behaviour
of advertisers or with controversial ads. The most recent political initiative with respect
to advertising was to stop the practice of louder broadcasting of ads during commercial
breaks.

An Ethics Code has been approved by the Slovak Syndicate of Journalists in 1990. Yet
its real implementation began in 2002, when the Press Council of the Slovak Republic
was established. The Press Council resumed its activities in autumn 2005 after somehow
slow activity in 2004 and in the first half of 2005. The Press Council is little known
among the wider public and not very known even among quite many journalists.

There is also MEMO´98, an NGO which monitors fairness in media reporting. This
organization monitors media fairness and objectivity mostly through quantitative
methodology. There is also an *ad hoc* project, Slovak Press Watch, which monitors
fairness and quality of the media reporting in qualitative terms.

Finally, there is also ABC Audit Office which regularly publishes verified data about
printed and sold publications. However, it covers only those publications and publishers
which voluntarily agreed to join this system.

4. Development Trends
Main features:

- Political influence
- New Press Law
- New PBS Law
- New legal framework for Digital TV

Indirect political influence in television and radio councils remains present because even
the so-called independent candidates elected in the Radio Council in early 2006 as well

as in the Council of Slovak Television in September 2006 were in fact close to political parties. However, there is some positive trend because the majority of new members have some experience with the media.

The Government Platform has promised to create a new legislative, financial and organizational framework for public service media. It has also promised to pass a new law for the *TASR* agency as well as a new press law and announced legislation and proper financial conditions for digital broadcasting. There is also political aim to give some support for audio-visual works and European co-production as well as more use of Slovak dubbing.

Among very specific goals of the government is the idea to prepare a concept paper for media education. There has been a law passed for the protection of audio-visual and multimedia works. Lastly, there is new draft law which would link licence fees for public radio and television services to consumption of electricity. Until now licence fees are linked to ownership of TV and radio sets.

References & Sources for Further Information

Statistical Office of the Slovak Republic, www.statistics.sk
The Media Research Department of the Slovak Radio.
Yearbook of *TASR* 2005.
www.24hod.sk
www.abcsr.sk
www.aktuality.sk
www.aktualne.sk
www.medialne.sk
www.radia.sk
www.strategie.sk
www.culture.gov.sk
www.rada-rtv.sk
www.slovakradio.sk
www.stv.sk
www.ssn.sk
www.memo98.sk
www.radia.sk
www.trsr.sk

THE SLOVENIAN MEDIA LANDSCAPE

Marko Milosavljevič

Slovenia is a member of European Union and NATO that was part of former Yugoslavia until independence in 1991. In 2004, Slovenia, with a population of 1.96 million, had a per capita GDP of €16,112 112 ("the richest ex-communist state", according to the *Financial Times*) and a GDP growth rate of 4.3 per cent.

After fourteen years of coalitions where Liberal Democrats (LDS) played main role, a new government was formed after parliamentary elections in 2004 with only right-wing parties in the ruling coalition for the first time since 1992. This also reflected in changes of media policy and many changes in Slovenian media, ownership and editorial policy.

There are currently 877 media outlets registered in the country. Gross value (without discounts) of the advertising pie in Slovenian media in the first half of 2006 was €177 million.

1. The Market

A. *The Print Media*
Main features:

- There are eight daily newspapers in Slovenia with a circulation of approximately 263,000 copies;
- After the fall of socialism in the beginning of 1990s foreign investors were not present on the Slovenian market for almost a decade;

■ After 2000, important foreign media actors on Slovenian market are Bonnier AG, Dagens Industri (Sweden), Styria Verlag, Leykam (Austria) and Burda (Germany).

The Slovenian newspaper market was for a long time quite unique among all post-socialist countries. Ever since the fall of socialism in 1990, there were almost no foreign investments in the print media, unlike in Hungary, the Czech Republic or Poland. All the print media were privatized, however, they were bought by Slovenian companies and in most of the print media not even one foreign owner, either company or person, was present, even as a minor shareholder. Although some interest had been shown in the beginning of the 1990s (from Robert Maxwell and some German publishing houses), no investments were made as it was considered that the Slovenian market had already reached a level of saturation where no new successful newspapers were possible and where old newspapers had enough income, profit and economic strength, and, therefore, did not need any foreign investors.

At the same time, the privatization of the print media has not been completely finished as state-owned trusts and companies still own important part of the shares and, thus, also exert managerial and editorial influence. This reflected particularly after the change of the government after the parliamentary elections in November 2004: editors-in-chief and managers at three daily newspapers (*Delo*, *Primorske novice* and *Večer*) were changed after representatives of state-owned trusts and companies in the supervisory boards, who appoint them, were first changed.

There are eight daily newspapers in Slovenia. Since it is a small country, there are problems with defining a newspaper as national or regional. Dailies and their supplements had a 19.2 per cent share of gross advertising pie in the first half of 2006. The two dailies with the highest circulations are the broadsheet *Delo* (average circulation 67,000) and the tabloid *Slovenske novice* (average circulation 89,000) owned by the same holding company, Delo d.d.. They share a number of common special interest supplements (*Ona, Polet, Delo & Dom, Vikend*), while on Sunday they publish *Nedelo* (circulation 70,000; format changed from broadsheet to tabloid in May 2002). Together the company *Delo* and its two newspapers control more than 50 per cent of the market for daily newspapers in the republic. Delo also publishes weekly magazine *Mag*.

Two other quality dailies are both regional, each controlling about 20 per cent of the market: in the capital, Ljubljana, there is *Dnevnik* (48,000 copies; it also publishes the popular weekly tabloid *Nedeljski dnevnik* with an average circulation of around 250,000 and weekly tabloid *Hopla*) and *Večer* in the north-eastern town of Maribor (46,000 copies; it also published general weekly magazine *7D*). *Večer* shares a supplement, *Bonbon*, with another regional daily, *Primorske novice*, from another region of Slovenia, while in autumn 2005, *Dnevnik* started to publish the tabloid titled *Direkt*. All these newspapers, with the exception of the two tabloids (*Slovenske novice* and *Direkt)*, already existed in socialist Slovenia.

In 2000, the four existing dailies were first joined by two new dailies, both specialized: the sports newspaper *Ekipa* became a daily with a circulation of 30,000, while the business newspaper *Finance* was re-launched as daily in February 2001 with a print-run of around 5,000 (in the first half of 2006, its sold-circulation is 12,000). The sold copies circulation of all daily newspapers in Slovenia altogether is 263,000 copies.

As mentioned earlier, there were no foreign investors present on the Slovenian newspaper market in the 1990s. This changed in 2000 when the Swedish corporation Bonnier AG and its partner, Dagens Industri, invested approximately three million euro in the re-launch of the newspaper *Finance*. *Styria Verlag*, from Austria, bought more than 25 per cent of the Ljubljana daily *Dnevnik*. Some other foreign companies are present in the magazine market, for instance, Burda of Germany and once again Styria and Leykam of Austria. Burda publishes a number of Slovenian versions of foreign titles, such as *Playboy*, *Elle*, *Lisa* and *Men's Health*, as well as successful weekly tabloid *Nova*. Styria publishes a free weekly, *Žurnal*, in Ljubljana, while *Leykam* publishes a free weekly, *Dober dan*, in Maribor. The company Dnevnik is at the moment discussing a joint venture with the German company WAZ; however, no final deal has been announced yet. However, print media and radio still remain predominantly in the hands of Slovenian companies, unlike commercial television where the three largest stations are owned and controlled by foreigners.

The main publisher of magazines in Slovenia remains Delo Revije with a number of highly read magazines, mostly for women and tabloid in nature: *Lady*, *Jana*, *Obrazi*, *Anja*, *Eva*, *Modna Jana*, *Ambient* and *Stop* are just some of them. Another important publisher is Salomon, the publisher of the bi-weekly *Salomon Oglasnik*, the sports daily *Ekipa* and some others. Burda, as mentioned above, is another important publisher of magazines.

Magazines had 11 per cent share of the gross advertising pie (according to estimates) in the first half of 2006.

B. The Broadcast Media
Main features:

- There are five television channels, private and public, out of 39 that can be seen by more than 75 per cent of the Slovene population;
- Unlike the print media market, foreign media owners play an important role in the Slovenian commercial television. Three of the largest commercial channels are owned by foreign companies;
- On average, 11 per cent of the population (or 221,500 people) watched television every day in 2004. Each viewer watched television for an average of 249 minutes per day;
- Television had a 54.6 per cent share of the advertising pie in the first half of 2006. There are no reliable estimates for radio for listeners' consumption and advertising revenue;

- In Slovenia there are 81 radio channels in total (eight are part of the public broadcaster Radio-television Slovenia; 73 are in private ownership);
- The digitalization of radio (DALET) started in 1998, and the gradual digitalization of television began in 1999; however, there are no digital platforms available in Slovenia and there are no plans for such platforms in the near future.

Approximately 98 per cent of all Slovenian households have one or more television sets. According to estimates, in 2003 the net turnover of the Slovenian television advertising market was €40–50 million. Fifty-six per cent of the households have cable; this level of penetration is similar to other countries in Central and Eastern Europe.

There are four domestic public service broadcast channels (Slovenia 1, Slovenia 2, Television Koper and Television Maribor) and 35 domestic commercial television channels, owned by 31 television stations in Slovenia. There are five television channels, private and public, that can be seen by more than 75 per cent of the Slovene population: Pop TV, Slovenia 1, Kanal A, Slovenia 2, POP TV, and TV3. Other television programmes cover local and regional areas.

TV Slovenia is the largest television station and most important in terms of diversity and quantity of its production. In 2004, it had an audience share of 37.6 per cent. Historically, SLO1, the national first public service channel, dominated the market. The other national channel, SLO2, provides complementary programming: SLO1 is mainly dedicated to news, current affairs, children's programmes, prime-time entertainment and films. SLO2 broadcasts mostly sports, documentaries and arts. SLO1 reaches nearly all of Slovenia's television households and SLO2 reaches 97 per cent of Slovenia's television households.

Unlike print media, foreign owners play an extremely important role in commercial television. Three of the largest commercial channels are all owned by foreign companies: Pop TV, Kanal A, as well as TV3, Pop TV and Kanal A, are owned by the same company, American-owned Central European Media Enterprises (CME), while TV3 was established by Slovene Catholic Church, but later sold to Croatian entrepreneur Ivan Ćaleta who at that time also owned Television Nova in Croatia and OBN in Bosnia and Herzegovina. He sold TV3 in the summer of 2006 to Swedish company Modern Times Group MTG AB. The first programme of the national public television and the commercial programme *Pop TV* have the largest audience among all television broadcasters in Slovenia, both in general and during prime time.

Twenty television channels are transmitted only through cable systems. A number of specialized channels also broadcast, such as Čarli Television (popular music) and Television Petelin (folk music). A franchised network, MTV Adria, started broadcasting in autumn 2005, with broadcasts and production from Slovenia and other countries from the Balkan region. Foreign channels are available through cable and satellite; some, such as National Geographic, Discovery, Hallmark and HBO, broadcast their programmes with Slovenian subtitles, as local affiliates of the transnational channels.

Eight radio channels compose the radio part of the public service broadcaster Radio-Television Slovenia (Radio Slovenia 1, 2 and 3, Radio Koper, Radio Maribor, Radio Capodistria for the Italian minority in Slovenia, Pomursko-Hungarian Radio for the Hungarian minority in Slovenia and Radio Slovenia International). Radio Ljubljana, the forerunner of Radio Slovenia, went on air as early as 28 October 1928. There are some 73 other radio channels in private ownership. Only three radio channels (all of them public service broadcasters) cover the entire country with their signal: Radio Slovenija 1, 2 and 3.

Radio broadcasting has been quite deregulated since 1991, however, there is no commercial national radio station or network, although a number of stations until recently got their news programmes from television company Pro Plus (producing programmes *Pop TV* and *Kanal A*) and their radio news production team.

No foreign investor is at the moment present in Slovenian radio broadcasting, at least not publicly, while a number of stations are owned by the same or connected persons or companies, thus making it highly possible that in the future they could merge and form common programmes with nationwide reach. As no commercial or local station has nationwide reach, their highest rating achieved is a little more than 5 per cent. Public radio stations have an important advantage regarding ratings, with the second programme of Radio Slovenija, called Val 202, reaching by far the highest ratings, followed by the first programme, called Slovenija 1.

Public stations derive their revenue mainly from licence fees, but with an important share of advertising income. Local stations are financed from advertising, but also through local communities, financing their 'non-commercial' programme, including arts and local information. Commercial stations are financed mostly from advertising.

According to the proposed *Strategy on RTV Slovenia 2004–2010* (May 2004), RTV Slovenia should provide additional specialized digital television and radio channels of informative, parliamentary, educational, sports and archival character, and also trans-border television for minority programmes using satellite broadcasting. One of the most important tasks of public service broadcasting, according to the *Strategy*, will be archive digitalization.

At this time, RTV Slovenia is obliged to archive in-house radio and television production, but would prefer that the state would take over the part of the burden for the archive. The public service broadcaster should also find a proper way to enable the public to access the archive. This kind of approach could eventually ensure additional income.

However, there are few plans for switching from analogue to digital signal and almost no public debate on the digitalization of broadcasting. The digitalization of radio (DALET) started in 1998, and the gradual digitalization of television began in 1999, however, there are no digital platforms available in Slovenia and there are no plans for such platforms in the near future. Digitalization is mostly present as digitalization of transmissions by the public broadcaster and other changes in production, while there are few digital television sets or digital decoders in use.

Slovenian public broadcaster RTV Slovenia received its first digital frequencies at the end of April 2006 from Broadcasting Council.

C. The Internet Media
Main features:

- The percentage of households that have access to the Internet reached 54 per cent in 2006, which is slightly above the EU average;
- All Slovenian daily newspapers have their websites, as well as the two most important television channels, RTV Slovenia and Pop TV;
- RTV Slovenia and Pop TV short news is also available through mobile phones with WAP technology.

According to the Report of the Slovenian Agency for Telecommunications, Radio Diffusion and Post Services for 2003, the Slovene telecommunication market ranks among medium-sized European markets with an annual turnover of 139.1 billion SIT/€579 million. This is 2.6 per cent of the national GDP. According to the data provided by the Association of Slovene Cable Operators, Slovenia had in May 2004 more than 230,000 cable television subscribers. Approximately 24,000 subscribers used this platform also for access to the Internet.

The Report on "The Use of Internet" by the Research Institute of Slovenia (RIS) shows that the percentage of households that have access to the Internet reached 54 per cent in 2006, which is slightly above the EU average.

All Slovenian dailies have their websites (www.delo.si, www.dnevnik.si, www.vecer. si, www.finance-on.net, www.direkt.si, etc.) that are quite popular (the reach of www. delo.si is over 150,000 users, while www.vecer.si and the website of weekly magazine *Mladina*, www.mladina.si, had a reach of almost 150,000, in the first half of 2006), as well as RTV Slovenia and Pop TV, the largest television stations. The public service broadcaster is expanding its online offer to include real-time transmission of radio and television programmes and a range of additional services.

RTV Slovenia short news is available through mobile phones with WAP technology. The two largest mobile phone operators, Mobitel and Si.Mobil, offer this service on their platforms, entitled Planet and Vodafone live, respectively. The website rtvslo.si features content from both Radio and TV Slovenia. Its recent domestic production, including news, is available online in video and audio.

Pop TV's website (24ur.com) features regular updates and video. In January 2005 it received Izidor, the newly established Slovenian award for websites for the best Internet presentation of news and current affairs. Online had a 1.1 per cent share of the gross advertising pie (according to estimates) in the first half of 2006.

D. News Agencies
Main features:

- There is one main news agency in Slovenia – *Slovenska tiskovna agencija* (*STA*), which is almost completely owned by the State.
- STA is an important source of information for smaller media, especially radio stations.

There is only one main news agency in Slovenia, *Slovenska tiskovna agencija* (*Slovene press agency*) or *STA*. It is almost completely, more than 95 per cent, owned by the State, which puts it under direct government influence when it comes to the appointment of the general manager and editor-in-chief., especially radio stations who don't have large or any news staff, but main daily newspapers also publish plenty of their news and reports. However, Slovenia is such a small market that the press agency is not likely to become a profitable company and this is also the main reason why its previous private owners sold their shares back to the State.

2. State Policies
Main features:

- The main broadcasting regulatory bodies today are the Ministry of Culture – including the Media Inspector and the Ministry's special Directorate for Media (established in autumn 2004); the Agency for Post and Electronic Communication (APEK) and the Broadcasting Council (SRDF);
- Owners can be involved in either radio or television broadcasting, and not in both. The owner of a radio or television channel can control up to 20 per cent of a daily newspaper and vice versa;
- Public broadcasting RTV Slovenia is governed by its Programming Council, while its financial operations are controlled by a supervisory board.

The main broadcasting regulatory bodies today are the Ministry of Culture – including the Media Inspector and the Ministry's special Directorate for Media (established in autumn 2004); the Agency for Post and Electronic Communication (APEK) and the Broadcasting Council (SRDF). The Agency's most important tasks are ensuring the implementation of the Law on Electronic Communication and monitoring the compliance of radio and television stations with the restrictions on their programming defined in the Mass Media Act. It issues broadcast licences on the basis of a binding instruction of the Broadcasting Council, which is an independent body that, among other things, supervises the adherence of broadcasters to the obligations contained in their licences. The Ministry of Culture supervises the implementation of the Mass Media Act, with the ministry's Media Inspector investigating breaches of the act on its own initiative or following complaints from the public.

The Ministry of Culture prepares laws regulating public service broadcasting and commercial media, including all broadcasters, and supervises the implementation of the Mass Media Act. In autumn 2004, a special Directorate for Media was established within the Ministry. Based within the Ministry of Culture is the Media Inspector who deals with breaches of the Mass Media Act on his/her own initiative or after complaints from the public. A complaint cannot be anonymous. According to the Mass Media Act, the Inspector has no mandate for any monitoring, as his mandate is only for administrative proceedings in supervising the implementation of the act. He can propose to the Broadcasting Council to request the APEK to monitor certain programmes or channels, but he/she has no mandate or competency to conduct monitoring.

Potential investors have to receive permission from the Ministry of Culture if they intend to acquire 20 per cent or more of the proprietary shares or the voting rights in newspaper, television or radio companies. The Mass Media Act foresees that the Ministry must consult the Agency for Post and Electronic Communication (APEK) before ruling on such requests.

The Ministry is also obliged to refuse approval if this would enable an investor to obtain a monopoly over advertising revenues. Under the Mass Media Act, a monopoly means gaining control over more than 30 per cent of radio or television advertising time, or gaining frequencies that exceed 40 per cent of all of the nationally available frequencies. As a monopoly is defined in terms of advertising time, rather than revenue, and by all of the nationally available frequencies, rather than viewer share or coverage, this means that no television station or channel holds a monopoly.

In accordance with the Mass Media Act 2001, owners can be involved in either radio or television broadcasting, and not in both. The owner of a radio or television channel can control up to 20 per cent of a daily newspaper and vice versa. There are no limits regarding cross-media ownership of magazines and radio or television channels. Advertising agencies cannot own or control more than 20 per cent of radio or television channel. Telecommunications companies cannot own a radio or television channel.

The EU "Television Without Frontiers" Directive (hereafter, TWF Directive) is, to a certain extent, mirrored in Article 92 of the Mass Media Act 2001, which lists the following requirements for RTV Slovenia: European audiovisual production must account for the majority of airtime of annual public service broadcasting.

Commercial broadcasters in Slovenia have almost no public service obligations. They do not have to broadcast news, current affairs, education programmes, documentaries or religious programmes. Since they are not obliged by law to broadcast programmes for minorities in their own languages, or to provide any airtime for other social groups, they do not broadcast such content.

Slovenian television stations, both public and commercial, will have a problem to adhere to the obligations determined in the EU TWF Directive. Already there is a problem meeting Slovenian quotas, especially when it comes to domestic audio-visual works, which is in relatively short supply. Slovenia is a small country and the Slovenian language is little used outside the country's borders, meaning that there can be few benefits from economies of scale. Slovenian production is much more expensive than programmes bought from the USA, Latin America or the rest of the EU. To adhere to EU quotas, most television stations rely on cheap formats, such as talk shows, studio interviews and music videos.

3. Civil Society Organizations
Main features:

- There are two main organizations in Slovenian journalistic landscape: The Slovenian Union of Journalists (more than 650 members) and The Association of Slovenian Journalists (more than 1550 members);
- There is a National Chamber of Advertisers (*Slovenska oglaševalska zbornica*) and an Association of PR Practitioners, which are not particularly active, because there are almost no cases of unethical practice in advertising or public relations exposed or sanctioned by these organizations;
- There are also two codes of ethics: First is a general Code of Practice for Slovenian Journalists and the second is RTV Slovenia's in-house code of ethics;
- Two types of sanctions can be used against journalists for not upholding professional standards: Public warning issued by the Journalistic Court of Honour, an internal committee that discusses particular cases or a civil court case and demands for financial compensation.

There are two main organizations: The Slovenian Union of Journalists and The Association of Slovene Journalists. They have over 650 and 1550 members, respectively. Most members of the Union are also members of the Association. There are also almost 100 retired journalists among the members of the Association. There is no organization of media producers or editors. There is also no organization of media proprietors, however, some of the print media are members of the Print Section at the Slovenian Economy Chamber (Sekcija za tisk pri Gospodarski zbornici Slovenije).

Between the NGO's that are also involved in media research and publishing is Mirovni inštitut-Peace Institute, which regularly publishes reports and research, particularly on media ownership, censorship, but also on issues of national, religious, sexual and minorities. Many of these research papers are published in the Slovenian and in the English language, often in association with other Central and Eastern European organizations.

There are also two codes of ethics: first is a general Code of Practice for Slovenian Journalists (2002) and the second is RTV Slovenia's in-house code of ethics (2000).

At RTV Slovenia, its Programming Council acts as a sort of ombudsman at the moment, discussing complaints regarding biased or unprofessional reporting or programmes. However, to date no such case brought before the Council has resulted in penalties or sanctions. RTV Slovenia's code of ethics foresaw the appointment of an ombudsman to monitor and safeguard adherence to professional standards and ethical principles. There are also currently no independent and effective mechanisms to improve public accountability regarding programmes and their contents.

Two types of sanctions can be used against journalists for not upholding professional standards. Journalists can be summoned to the Journalistic Court of Honour, an internal committee that discusses particular cases and issues public warnings. If, as sometimes happens, the Court rules that a journalist has acted unethically, the judgment should be published in the same outlet where the unethical act took place. However, since this is a self-regulatory system adopted by journalists and not accepted by all publishers (or all journalists), it is not binding. Some media do not publish the decisions of the Court of Honour or at least not those related to themselves. The Mass Media Act also regulates the rights of reply and of correction, which are very detailed and can result in a civil court order to a publisher to publish a reply or correction. Another way to address violations of professional standards is to file a civil court case and demand financial compensation.

4. Development Trends
Main feature:

■ Introduction and implementation of new Broadcast Law

On 1st of April 2005, a new law on Public Broadcasting was presented. The law was extremely controversial, as it proposed dominant role of the state and of the government in appointing both the Programming Council and Supervisory Board, where previously different institutions from civil society (universities, association of writers, sports organizations, etc.) held dominant influence. The draft law was criticized by domestic media experts, but also by a number of international organizations and institutions, among others by the International Federation of Journalists, Article 19 and Council of Europe. However Slovenian government refused to accept any important changes, refused the opinion by Council of Europe as "legally incorrect, wrong and politically missed from the start", while Karol Jakubowicz, the chairman of the Steering Committee on the Media and New Communications Services of the Council of Europe, who said that the draft law is "a catastrophe", was labelled by Slovenian minister of culture Vasko Simoniti as "a third-rate public servant from Poland". The law was adopted in November 2005, after a special referendum for this law was held and after the law passed with a 50.2 per cent majority.

The new law on mass media was adopted by the parliament in the summer of 2006. The new law extends the "right of correction", by which anybody who would be upset or offended by what was written or said or implied about him/her, including comments, and would want to present different, "opposite" facts, could demand a "correction", and this correction will have to be published in the same place (including front page) and occupying the same space or even larger, since this correction could be longer than the original article. This means that even if every data or quote in the article is correct, somebody can demand this "correction". This presents an opportunity particularly for government institutions and large companies (many of which are connected with or owned by the government) to demand all sorts of "corrections", thus limiting editorial independence and journalistic freedom to criticize. Indeed a number of such controversial "corrections" were published, including one in a main culture magazine on public television and one in a magazine spread over two pages of that magazine.

The new law also increases state help and subsidies for media. Thus, local, regional or national media who are important for "the pluralism" of Slovenian society (the first criteria to establish whether they are important for "the pluralism" is whether they regularly cover and report on political parties and government) will receive from the Ministry of Culture €4 million annually.

References & Sources for Further Information

Agency for Post and Electronic Communication (2005), Annual Report for 2004. Ljubljana.

Agency for Telecommunications, Radio Diffusion and the G. P. O. (2004), Annual Report for 2003, Ljubljana.

Bašić Hrvatin, Sandra/Lenart J. Kučić (2004), Report on Slovenia. In Brankica Petković (ed.), *Media Ownership and its Impact on Media Independence and Pluralism*. Ljubljana: SEENPM and Peace Institute. http://www.mirovni-institut.si/media_ownership/pdf/slovenia.pdf (accessed 22 June 2005).

Bašić Hrvatin, Sandra/Marko Milosavljevič (2001), Media Policy in Slovenia in the 1990's. Ljubljana: Peace Institute.

Broadcasting Council (2002), Annual Report 2001/2002, Ljubljana.

Broadcasting Council (2001), Radio and TV Programmes in Slovenia. Ljubljana: Broadcasting Council.

Central European Media Enterprises (2004), Annual Report 2003. ftv://www.sec.gov/edgar/data/925645/000101540204000664, 12 March 2005.

Jakubowicz, Karol (2005), Katastrofa. In: Delo, 11 June 2005, Ljubljana, p. 11.

Kmet Stare/Bučar Zupanič (2004), Slovenia – On The Way To The Information Society. Office for Macro-economic Analysis and Development, Ljubljana, June 2004.

Media Services AGB (2005), Research on 2004. Ljubljana.

Ministry of Culture (2004), *Poročilo Ministrstva za kulturo Republike Slovenije za leto 2003* (*Annual report of Ministry of Culture 2003*), Ljubljana.

Nacionalna raziskava branosti (2004), *National research of readership*, data for 3rd quarter of 2004, Ljubljana.

Research Institute of Slovenia (Raziskovalni inštitut Slovenije – RIS) (2004), Uporaba interneta v gospodinjstvih v letu 2003, (Report on The Use of Internet in Households for the year 2003). Ljubljana: RIS.

RTV Slovenia (2004), Annual Report 2003. Ljubljana.

RTV Slovenia (2004), Dopolnitve dolgoročne strategije razvoja RTV Slovenija 2004–2010 (Annex to the long-term development strategy of RTV Slovenia 2004–2010). Ljubljana: RTV Slovenia.

RTV Slovenia (2005), Delovno gradivo za letno poročilo za leto 2004 (working material for the Annual Report of RTV Slovenia for 2004). Ljubljana: RTV Slovenia.

CONCLUSIONS

CONVERGING MEDIA GOVERNANCE ARRANGEMENTS IN EUROPE

Johannes Bardoel

In this final chapter, I will attempt to give, first, an evaluation of the current media governance arrangements that exist all over Europe, and, subsequently, I will try to draw some conclusions to see to what extent there is a convergence of media governance arrangements across Europe. Governance according to EU consists of the "rules, processes and behaviour that affect the way in which powers are exercised, particularly as regards openness, participation, accountability, effectiveness and coherence" (European Commission 2001). The also fairly new concept of 'media governance' seems an appropriate term to cover – even 'avant-la-lettre' – the pluricentric power relations and various regulatory regimes that altogether shape the media performance. This situation does not result from recent insights on the subject matter but is, first and foremost, a product of a long and strong tradition of freedom of expression in most European countries. This tradition has prevented most governments to really intervene in the press sector ever since the abolition of the press stamp. In communication sectors, where governments did not have the choice not to intervene, such as broadcasting and telecommunication, authorities were usually eager to keep a distance and not to interfere directly with content matters. These different policy practices have resulted in media governance arrangements that grew incrementally, varying considerably from medium to medium (cf. press versus broadcasting policies), and lacking a clear common legitimacy or logic. Even the notion that the media have a strong sense of social responsibility is not uncontested in the media sector. Social responsibility is interpreted in terms of both 'responsibility', indicating the media's responsibility with regards to society, and 'responsiveness', indicating the manner in which the media listen to and consider the public. McQuail (2000) defines media responsibility as the 'obligations and expectations' that society has regarding the media. He distinguishes between four types of responsibility: assigned, contracted, self-assigned and denied responsibilities. According to Hodges (1986) 'responsibility' has to do with defining proper conduct, and 'accountability' with compelling it. To put it differently: responsibility is the theory, and accountability its practice. In the last decade, we note a clear shift among communication specialists from more general and abstract thinking about media responsibility to more practical and concrete interpretations of these concepts (from responsibility to accountability), in which the emphasis is shifting from a negative approach (liability) to a positive one (answerability). In line with McQuail (2000) and Lange & Woldt (1995), I (Bardoel 2001, 2003) distinguish four accountability mechanisms for the media: 1) political; 2) market; 3) professional and 4) public. To varying degrees all these mechanisms have been used to organize the relationship between the media and society and all have their (dis)advantages in realizing social responsibility in the media (Bardoel 2003). That may be the reason why in media governance regimes in most countries these mechanisms are combined.

1. Current Media Governance Arrangements in Europe

Market Accountability

Inarguably, the market is the oldest vehicle for ensuring the social accountability of the media. Although nowadays not everyone immediately associates the market with securing freedom and responsibility, in past centuries it has shown itself to be a reliable tool for evading the grasp of the established powers of church and state. Today as well, market activity is usually an effective mechanism for organizing the free exchange of goods and services, including those of a symbolic nature. As McQuail (2000, 185) argues, the market is extremely flexible, which allows it to serve people quickly and without prejudice. Thus, in many respects, the media market encourages openness and equality and is usually not coercive. In the United States, the theory and practice of media policy – for both the press and broadcasting – are largely based on the concept of the '*free marketplace of ideas*' (Napoli 1999). Also, in the other countries that belong to the North Atlantic or Liberal model (Hallin & Mancini 2004), the market dominates in the media sector, although countries like Britain and Ireland also have a strong public broadcasting system. At the same time Britain was the first country, by the 1950s already, to open up its broadcasting system for private competitors. Countries with a large private sector and an early development of capitalism usually have a long tradition of press freedom and an established position of liberal institutions. They were also the first to liberalize their media and telecommunications policies starting in the early 1980s, but at the same time tried to control the deregulation by organizing independent supervision authorities. At the same time we notice that in countries with weaker markets and later capitalist development the deregulation of media markets often developed in a rather unregulated way, also because of alliances between politics and the private sector, politicization of regulatory authorities and more, in general, the lack of liberal institutions.

Besides the advantages of market-driven media, however, we have also witnessed the drawbacks of the market in recent decades. There is always a looming danger of concentration and monopolization; markets show a preference for mainstream content and audiences and in the end, citizens are always treated as consumers, based on their purchasing power. These aspects of the market detract from any pretences of freedom of choice and unhindered competition. Market accountability is primarily aimed at the owners and shareholders of media companies, but it also refers to serving audiences and target groups, for which market research and marketing play an important role ('consumer sovereignty'). Such activities make it possible to determine and meet a variety of preferences and tastes, specifically with reference to popular culture, which in a public system are widely ignored. In addition, as a result of competition, market activity claims to handle the resources available more efficiently. For this reason, quasi-market relations have been introduced within many public media organizations (cf. the BBC's 'Producer Choice'). The nature of market accountability is, however, free of obligations and non-binding; the trend of 'corporate governance', in which companies hold themselves accountable to society for non-economic transactions as well ('people, profit and planet'), seems largely to have passed the (commercial) media world by thus far.

At the same time, it has to be noted that the 'social responsibility theory of the press' has existed for 60 years now (Hutchins Commission 1947). This theory defines the press and, indeed, the media, as being not only a commodity, but also a 'public trust' that was formulated more than half a century ago in the United States in answer to rising commercialization and monopolization. In the post-war period this theory has also found wide resonance all over Europe, not so much because of commercialization but as a result of the propagandistic role mass media had played before and during World War II. In many European countries, due to the tradition of social, not-for-profit media organizations, many press companies functioned more as a public trust though than as a commercial media enterprise, but in the current, competitive media market there seems continually less room for such an approach.

Professional Accountability

The first and most important supplement to and correction of the market model in the media has come from the journalistic profession. From the moment journalism became an independent profession in the nineteenth century, freeing itself from printers, publishers and newspaper owners, Anthony Smith (1980) writes that journalists began to develop their own, more moral connection with the public. In order to be able to properly fulfil their social obligations, journalists began to claim a freer, more independent position for themselves. These days, journalists are part of an open professional group in which acting responsibly is part of its professionalism. Journalistic professionalization has its earliest and deepest roots in liberal countries, whereas in countries with a stronger role for the state professional autonomy only got the change to develop later. In this tradition journalism in liberal countries considered itself as the watchdog of democracy and has chosen an informational and fact-oriented style of writing. Journalists in countries with a more political and partisan press tradition were more geared towards advocacy journalism and a commentary writing style.

When it comes to giving account of the professional activities of journalists, print media have shown a clear preference for self-regulation above any form of imposed regulation or government intervention. Most professional associations have conformed to the well-known 'Code of Bordeaux' (1954, completed and adopted in 1986) as an international standard for professional conduct. In addition to this, in many countries additional national codes have been introduced, often initiated to enforce self-regulation and to prevent possible government intervention. In addition to such 'paper' codes, editors have developed active rules (of play) to dictate how to react to commercial pressure, such as editorial statutes and ethical guidelines. This not only fulfils an internal need for the editorial offices, which have gotten bigger and have consequently seen a drop in the effectiveness of informal rules and social control by colleagues, but it is also a reaction to regular incidents and increasing external pressure. Many countries also have press councils, which primarily function to set standards and usually only pass judgment without penalty. Also, here we see that Liberal and Corporatist countries, in this rank order, have the longest and strongest traditions in this respect, while in the countries in the south and the east the arrangements for securing journalistic autonomy are still relatively weak.

Despite its limited professional institutionalization, journalism ranks as an important public service for carrying out the media's social responsibilities. It is also, however, a public service which is traditionally based on informal practices, its own editorial culture and self-regulation. At the same time, this means that the freedom and responsibility of journalists is institutionally guaranteed to a limited extent only, which makes it very vulnerable, especially in the increasingly cold, commercial climate that has emerged in the media world in recent decades ('market-driven journalism').

Political Accountability

Government intervention is an important but from a historical viewpoint relatively recent tool for organizing the media's social responsibility and accountability. Strictly speaking, government intervention is old news, having existed since the 1920s and 30s, when public monopolies were formed in both the telephone and broadcasting systems. However, these interventions were primarily evoked by a scarcity of distribution means, due to which the government felt itself forced to intervene. Van Cuilenburg and McQuail (2003, 186) call this pre-war period the phase of rising industrial communications policy, in which the media are mainly regulated in line with their technical and national-strategic significance. A more deliberate, active and content-oriented media policy – Van Cuilenburg & McQuail call this the period of public service media policy – only came into existence after World War II, in parallel with the rise of the welfare state. But also here there are considerable differences between countries. The Liberal countries attributed a limited role to the state, while in the Corporatist countries the state has taken an ever more important role in the post-war period, also to substitute the eroding political parallelism and a growing market orientation in the media. In the Mediterranean and post-Communist models the state remained to play a much more dominant role, even to the extent that several authors speak about 'state paternalism'. Not surprisingly, public service broadcasting has the strongest position and is organized at 'arms length' in the Liberal and Corporatist countries, and a much weaker, more politicized position in the latter countries where it often is effectively in the hands of the political majority of the day. Notions of general interest and public service have a shorter tradition here. In the Liberal and Corporatist countries state authority has a much stronger rational-legal base and, therefore, the public trust in political institutions, and also in public broadcasting, is relatively high in these countries. More in general, public trust is an important prerequisite for proper media performance.

Despite the often very pretentious aims of media policy since the 1970s, in practice state intervention has remained rather modest in many countries for two reasons: one the one hand, the basic principle of the freedom of expression only allows a limited space for government interference; and, on the other hand, in media affairs, the ideological visions of the ruling political parties involved usually differ to such an extent that, especially in countries with coalition governments, it is very difficult to come to terms in media matters. Consequently, government policy with reference to media is often 'incremental', occurring in small steps (Bardoel 1994). According to McQuail (2000, 19–20), political accountability through legislation and regulation does offer the advantage that it establishes the public will in a clear and binding manner. In practice, however, such policy is usually aimed at accommodating existing actors (Krasnow & Longley 1978, 102) and thus takes more account of the interests of media institutions than it does serve the needs of media users. Another shortcoming of the current political accountability of the media is its limited scope. In most countries media policy is primarily aimed at the public broadcasting system and much less so at commercial broadcasting, the press and new media. Consequently, it is not possible to develop a full-fledged media policy that stimulates a pluralist media offer, that fights the concentration of media ownership and predominant opinion power and that protects media consumers across the board. Even in the domain where political accountability is strongest, public broadcasting, the scope of political accountability is rather limited. Despite the fact that the legal obligations imposed on the public broadcasting system seem firm, in practice they are hardly feasible due to incompatibility with the freedom of communication (which discourages interference with regards to content) and problems to operationalize them properly. This supports the general observation that media policy lends itself to interference on a structural level, but that it is much more difficult to apply to content-related issues. Altogether, this implies that the steering power of politics and the government in relation to the media should not be overestimated.

Public Accountability

Public accountability is a relatively new phenomenon and primarily directed at strengthening the relationship with citizens and civil society more directly. It has become an attractive policy option mainly in public broadcasting but also the press. In the broadcasting domain, the advent of private broadcasters has opened alternative options and partnerships for politicians and governments, also since new entrants often promised to be less critical and cynical towards politics than PSB journalism deemed necessary. Part of the explanation for this recently more critical and distant attitude between politics and PSB probably lies in the forced tango that national politics and public broadcasters have danced for many decades, simply because of the lack of other, private partners. Moreover, public broadcasters in many continental European countries have gained independence in recent decades, due to a decline in 'political parallelism' and a rise in the professionalism and autonomy of journalists, especially in countries with a corporatist tradition. More in general, the liberalization of policies has caused a distancing on both sides and a search for new policy instruments for public broadcasters to become less dependent of politics and the government of the day. Especially since the 1990s, after the introduction of commercial broadcasting companies in many European countries, did 'public' broadcasting companies feel themselves forced to go back to worrying about their legitimacy and roots in civil society (Bardoel & Brants 2003). Once they did, they came up with new accountability instruments in order to give the citizens more involvement in PSB policies. As it happens, as Sondergaard has pointed out, this phenomenon has come up in public broadcasting corporations throughout Europe: 'Competition has above all forced public service media to be more responsive to their audiences than previously in the sense that viewers and listeners' wishes and desires now carry more weight than society's desires regarding cultural or social functions. The dissolution of the monopolies meant the death of the kind of paternalism previously associated with public service media.' (Sondergaard 1996, 24).

Although the European Commission (2001) explicitly and correctly includes 'professional associations' in its definition of civil society, journalists and their professional organizations were often part of this paternalistic complex, sharing the same pedagogical, top-down approach. These new forms of public accountability, though, such as organizing interaction platforms, public hearings and better complaints procedures, are aimed more at establishing a direct dialogue and interaction with the individual citizen and have been developed in recent years by public broadcasters in Liberal and Corporatist countries, partially in imitation of the active accountability policy practiced by the BBC (Woldt 2002) and other public broadcasting companies in Europe. This new focus on public accountability can also be seen as an attempt to compensate for public broadcasting's unilateral political dependence (through political appointments and following the public funding of TV licensing fees – cf. the experiences of the BBC under Thatcher). In the press sector, public accountability is used to improve the relationship with the reader (examples: more discussion pages, ombudsmen, reader's editors, et cetera), as well as to parry criticism of the introverted journalistic system and to halt the drop in

ORGANIZATION OF SOCIAL RESPONSIBILITY OF THE MEDIA

MECHANISM	Principle	Decision	Participation	Instrument	Effects
MARKET	Competition, companies	Demand and supply	Purchasing power, money	Market share, market research	Economic growth, flexibility, but: bias towards 'mainstream'
POLITICS	Hierarchy, bureaucracy	Law and regulation	Authority, force	Budget, annual review, contract/ charter	Social justice, but: slow, steering of 'content' problematic
PROFESSION	Professionalism, ethics	Self-regulation	Education, 'peer review'	Reflection, code, Council for Journalism	Independence, but: lack of representativity
PUBLIC	Voluntarism, associations, pressure groups	Discussion, dialogue	Commitment	Openness, feedback: hearings, ombudsmen	Shaping of public opinion, social capital, but: voluntarism

Reference: Bardoel (2003)

Figure 1.

newspaper circulation. Additionally, following the participative journalism movement in the 1970s, starting in the 1990s there were once again movements to make journalism more 'citizen-oriented' – through 'public' or 'civil journalism', especially strong in the US (Carey 1999). Of course, these new practises presuppose a favourable social context, i.e. the presence of a vital civil society and a spirit of public service among both media professionals and the public, which is, of course, absent in countries where clientelism still prevails over citizenship.

Figure 1 offers an overview of the main social responsibility mechanisms as described in this paragraph.

2. Convergence of Media Governance Arrangements in Europe

In the previous paragraph we have seen that the market is clearly the oldest media governance arrangement and that it initially had a primarily emancipatory function. Over time, this was supplemented by the professional accountability of journalists and publishers, who started to see themselves as belonging to a respected public tradition. As a result of the increasing concentration of the print sector in the post-war period, the commercialization of the press sector slowly but surely increased, allowing less room for the 'public spirit' of publishers and the professional autonomy of journalists.

Though it would be possible to say that commercial publishers were 'socially responsible entrepreneurs' even before the term existed, they still have hardly taken up the trend of corporate governance, which is currently fashionable in other business sectors. The same applies to commercial broadcasting that has, as we have seen, hardly established an accountability system of its own.

Professional accountability has gradually gained ground, in parallel with the establishment and (semi-)professionalization of journalism. A delayed, late professionalization occurred in many corporatist countries, which only gained the upper hand since the 1960s and 1970s through the erosion of political parallelism and the shift from a vertical orientation, built around political affiliation, to a more horizontal orientation, focused on journalistic peer review. With this background of late independence in many countries, journalism is still quite wary of new forms of (public) accountability. In the meantime, however, the profession is being subjected to increasing pressure and criticism. Journalism is being reproached for its questionable quality and transparency, as well as for not being able to sufficiently counterbalance commercial public relations or political spin doctoring.

As has been said, political accountability in the form of media-related government policy has only relatively recently arrived on the scene, due in part to friction with the freedom of the press. Such policy is primarily directed at (public) broadcasting. In relation to the press, government policy has always remained discrete, resulting in a limited range of intervention. From the 1980s, governments once again made motions to step back (the deregulation and privatization of the broadcasting and telecommunications sectors). Currently, the movement away from government and toward the market seems to have passed its peak, and politicians are seeking a new policy paradigm.

Every media system and all media governance arrangements are the product of a given society, as this book clearly illustrates. Resulting from a comparison of media and political systems in several western countries, Hallin and Mancini (2004) have developed three 'ideal types' that, as you will have noticed, also constitute the structure of this book: 1) the 'Liberal model', mainly to be found in Great Britain and the former British colonies (United States, Ireland and Canada); 2) the 'Polarized Pluralist model' with considerable levels of politicization, state intervention and clientelism in the Mediterranean countries; and 3) the 'Democratic Corporatist model' in the Scandinavian countries, the Netherlands, Austria, Switzerland, Belgium and Germany strongly relying on the role of organized social groups in society, against a more individualistic concept of representation in the Liberal model. This book introduces a forth category that can, according to Jacubowicz in his introduction, most adequately be called the 'post-Communist model'. The country studies in this book clearly show, in my view, both the conceptual and analytical value of this relatively new typology as well as the great variation of national media governance arrangements, within and between the four models.

Assessing the analogies and differences of these models in relation to the actual national policy practises presented in this book, I am inclined to the conclusion that instead of four models we can also think of two main clusters that have much in common and are quite different from one another: the Liberal and the Corporatist models in one cluster, and the Mediterranean and post-Communist models in the other cluster. The decisive distinction here is the difference between old and young democracies, with a strong versus a weak formal-legislative authority and the presence or absence of a well-developed public sphere and civil society. Looking at the history of the respective countries we further notice a difference between, roughly speaking, the Protestant cultures of north-western Europe with strong Enlightenment roots and individualistic reading traditions as opposed to the Catholic cultures of southern and eastern Europe with roots in the Counter Reformation and more collective cultures and stronger image cultures and viewing habits.

In their recent study, 'Broadcasters and Citizens in Europe; trends in media accountability and viewer participation', Baldi and Hasebrink (2007) make a distinction between (1) 'most-advanced countries', being the UK, Ireland, Germany, Scandinavian countries and the Netherlands, (2) 'less-advanced countries' like France, Italy, Spain and Greece and (3) 'under construction countries' comprising all the post-Communist countries. This divide shows a considerable overlap with both Hallin & Mancini's typology and the structure of this book, and it also introduces a rank order in terms of advancement or progress. Several other authors see similarities between the Mediterranean and the eastern European model, and Jacobowicz also poses the question to what extent the difference between these models is of a fundamental or rather of a gradual or temporal nature.

Recent regulatory changes at both national and, first and foremost, EU level undoubtedly show a tendency to stimulate a market-orientated approach (Steemers 2003; Murdock and Golding 1999) and consequently favor a convergence towards the Liberal model. Based on the EU-policy driven imperative to separate policy and supervision, administrative accountability via independent supervisors has risen sharply since the 1990s. Such relatively independent supervision, disassociated from the government policy of the day, is intended to ensure an equal level playing field for public and commercial players in the 'dual' media landscape. In practice, it undoubtedly stimulates more open and transparent conduct from and playing rules for media companies. In the same line, the European Commission has stipulated in its Communication on the application of state aid rules to public service broadcasting (2001) that the definition of the public service mandate should be as precise as possible. Moreover, on the basis of 'subsidiarity' the European Commission leaves it to the Member States to formulate the task – broad or small – of public service broadcasting, while at the same time making it clear that as far as the Commission is concerned this mandate cannot be concrete enough. Also this emphasis on harmonization of regulation on the basis of explicit and precise rules in order to create equal rules of play for all public and partners involved in effect favors the formal-legislative authority that goes with the Liberal model and disfavours the incremental working procedures that are predominant in corporatist and clientelist cultures. The same holds for the European Commission's preference for transparent divisions between public and private financing that favours the BBC model of separate bookkeeping and disfavours the mixed-income model of dual funding systems – public and advertising money – that characterizes most PSBs on the European continent. At the same time we have to realize that, as Williams (2005) points out, EU media policy remains a constant power struggle between liberals and dirigistes, between economic and cultural objectives and between the development of a pan-European culture and the protection of national cultures, where the first have indeed the upper hand in the policy-making process, but where at the same time the recognition of the latter interests seems to increase. Kevin Williams concludes his book with the interesting observation that "it is possible to argue that EU media policy is bringing about the opposite to what it states it is trying to achieve. Rather than promoting Europeanness, the strategy of liberalization is creating more commercial channels, which are dependent on American programming. Americanization may be the unintended consequence of television without frontiers in Europe" (Williams 2005: 149).

Next to, and even more than, EU policies, other major trends in the media and in society at large – like modernization, globalization and commercialization – have enabled, what Hallin and Mancini (2004, 251) call, the homogenization of media systems and the triumph of the Liberal model. In fact, all these trends go hand in hand and it is not easy to determine what is the chicken and what is the egg. In general it means that the patterns of political communication have changed considerably, from party-centered patterns with strong relations to collectively organized social groups to more media-centered patterns where politics is personalized and the support of the electorate of individual citizens is increasingly organized via political marketing (Hallin & Mancini 2005: 252–253). Hallin & Mancini call this increasing separation or 'differentiation' between media and political institutions a principal characteristic of the Liberal model, in which a distinctive 'media logic' comes to prevail over the 'political logic' that dominated the media scene in Europe for such a long time. The media's ever-larger role in political communications can also be explained as a result of major changes amongst citizens or within the general public. According to Bardoel (2003, 12),

deinstitutionalization and individualization are the key words to describe the evolutions that have taken place within the public arena over the last few decades. This growing individualization goes along with self-reinforcing phenomena such as increased education, income and mobility, which have weakened the power and influence of older, collective vehicles for self-improvement in favour of the citizens' individual ability to choose to improve their own destiny. In Giddens' words, 'emancipatory politics' loses out to 'life politics' (Giddens 1991, 210, ff.; Faulks 1999, 169). This has resulted in smaller families, limited participation in traditional church, political party and trade union activities, and on average less of a connection with the values of a group to which one belongs. As such, the old, institutionally-anchored system of external pluralism has fallen away, making room for shifting public preferences based on age, level of education and '*lifestyle*'.

In this context, some authors even speak of the emancipation or liberation of the public (Bardoel 1997, 190; Mazzoleni & Schulz 1999, 253). All this means that the role of organized social groups in society, which is characteristic for the Democratic Corporatist model, has given way to a more individualistic conception of representation that is central to the Liberal model.

We have seen the many different media governance arrangements that have arisen from the tension between freedom and responsibility of the media in various geographical and historical contexts. At the same time, the basic principle of freedom of expression does not make it easier either to develop effective governance arrangements for the media in future. In my opinion, as I have stated earlier (Bardoel 2003), in the future there must be a balanced intervention mix of governance arrangements to ensure the public interest.

There seems to be a growing consensus that the increasing 'power' or, better, 'influence' of the media has to be counterbalanced by greater media transparency and accountability. However, there is no consensus on how the latter should be achieved. *Governments* are often considered as the classic guarantee for a sound media system, but they have proven to be quite ineffective in preventing media monopolies in the press or broadcasting industries and in stimulating the plurality of media content. They experience, also, problems with the organization of public broadcasting 'at arm's length.' More, in general, media regulation proves to be rather ineffective in the management of content. In the 1980s and 1990s, media *markets* were seen as a new panacea for the problems of public and/or government-controlled media: inefficiency, inflexibility and bureaucratization, paternalism and lack of interest for popular taste and culture, lack of innovation, et cetera. Over the last decade, the dark side of market-driven media is getting more attention again: its mainstream orientation, its interest in consumers (not citizens), the influence of advertisers and sponsors, et cetera.

The trend of 'less government' and 'more market' also sheds new light on the position of the media *professionals*: they have become the 'guardians' of the quality of media output, while at the same time the public spirit of and the public space for professional journalists and other creative people tend to diminish. Media professionals want to work 'for the people', but often see accountability to the public and to society as no less threatening than the forces of the market or the state. More than ever in the past, the *citizen* becomes an active part of the (mass) communication process, due to the potential of new technologies, more competition between media and, last but not least, a more self-conscious and better educated citizenry. Involvement of citizens and civil society can also provide a 'fourth' way to organize social responsibility in the media, next to the primacy of either the market, the state and/or the professional. There is, in other words, a growing awareness that an adequate media and communications 'ecology' can best be organized, not by exclusively relying on one of these parties or mechanisms, but by way of interrelated and multileveled 'governance' arrangements in the media system. This also corresponds with new approaches in the reflection on public policies and business strategies.

In political science several new concepts have emerged that imply a change of, and not an end to, state responsibility for the public domain (cf. Hoffmann-Riem et al. 2000; WRR 2005). These and other authors (cf. Schulz & Held 2004) make a distinction between state regulation, co-regulation and self-regulation and demonstrate that, both in the literature and in the policy practice, many alternative forms of regulation on the continuum between state and market and based on collaborative arrangements between public and private partners have been elaborated recently. The idea that market forces can simply replace government regulation has proven to be naïve. Instead of deregulation, we should speak about re-regulation. Also the European Commission (2001) has been reflecting on new forms of regulation and governance: Its aforementioned White Paper, 'European Governance', emphasizes that co-regulation will be more and more put in practice. Consequently, in the media and telecommunications sector, a transformation of statehood is taking place that can be traced by trends such as a change from protectionism to promotion of competition, the separation of political and operative tasks (i.e., independent regulatory authorities), the shift from vertical (sector-specific) to horizontal regulation, the transition from national to supra- and international regulation and the change from state to self- and co-regulation in which private and societal partners are becoming more actively involved in regulation. Looking at the future of media policy in Europe it is interesting, as we have tried to do, to assess the analogies and differences between media policy models and to address the question if there is a convergence of these models, but in my view it is much more important to look for new governance arrangements that include a proper balance of market, state, profession and, last but not least, the public.

References

Baldi, P. & U. Hasebrink (eds.) (2007), *Broadcasters and Citizens in Europe. Trends in Media Accountability and Viewer Participation*. Bristol: Intellect Books.

Bardoel, J. & L. d'Haenens (2004), Media meet the citizen. Beyond market mechanisms and government regulations, *European Journal of Communication* 19 (2), 165–194.

Bardoel, J. (2003), 'Macht zonder verantwoordelijkheid? Media, mediabeleid en de kwaliteit van de openbare informatievoorziening' [Power without Responsibility. Media, media policy and the quality of public communication]. *Tijdschrift voor Communicatiewetenschap*, 32 (1), 79–99.

Bardoel, J. & K. Brants (2003), 'From Ritual to Reality. Public Broadcasters and Social Responsibility in the Netherlands'. In: G. F. Lowe & T. Hujanen (eds.), *Broadcasting & Convergence: New Articulations of the Public Service Remit*, Nordicom, Goteborg, 167–187.

Bardoel, Jo (2001), "Open Media, Open Society. Rise and Fall of the Dutch Broadcast Model: A Case Study". In: Y. Zassoursky & E. Vartanova, *Media for the Open Society* (pp. 98–121). IKAR Publisher/Faculty of Journalism, Moscow State University, Moscow.

Bardoel, J. L. H. (1997), *Journalistiek in de informatiesamenleving*. [*Journalism in the Information Society*]. Otto Cramwinckel Uitgever, Amsterdam.

Carey, J. W. (1999), 'In Defense of Public Journalism'. In: Th. L. Glasser (ed.), *The Idea of Public Journalism*. The Guilford Press, New York, 49–67.

CEC Commission of the European Communities (2001), *Application of State Aid Rules to Public Service Broadcasting*. Brussels: C 320/04.

European Commission (2001), European Governance, A White Paper, Brussels, 25.7.2001, COM(2001) 428 final, p. 8 and 14 respectively.

Available from: http://eur-lex.europa.eu/LexUriServ/site/en/com/2001/com2001_0428en01.pdf.

Faulks, K. (1999), *Political Sociology. A Critical Introduction*. Edinburgh: Edinburgh University Press.

Giddens, A. (1991), *Modernity and Self-Identity. Self and Society in the Late Modern Age*. Stanford University Press, Stanford.

Hallin, D. C. & P. Mancini (2004), *Comparing Media Systems. Three Models of Media and Politics*. Cambridge: Cambridge University Press.

Hodges, L. W. (1986), 'Defining press responsibility': a functional approach. In D. Elliot (ed.), *Responsible Journalism* (pp. 13–31). Beverly Hills, CA: Sage.

Hoffmann-Riem, W. & W. Schulz, T. Held (2000), *Konvergenz und Regulierung. Optionen fuer rechtliche Regelungen und Aufsichtsstrukturen im Bereich Information, Kommunikation und Medien*. Baden-Baden: Nomos.

Hutchins Commission (1947), *Report of the Commission on the Freedom of the Press. A Free and Responsible Press*. University of Chicago Press, Chicago.

Krasnow, E. G. & L. D. Longley (1978), *The Politics of Broadcast Regulation*. St. Martin's Press (2nd edition), New York.

Lange, B. P. & R. Woldt (1955), The results and main conclusions of the international comparison. In: J. Dries & R. Woldt (1996), *The Role of Public Service Broadcasting in the Information Society*. Düsseldorf: European Institute for the Media, (pp. 463–503).

Mazzoleni, G. & W. Schulz (1999), 'Mediatization' of Politics: A Challenge for Democracy?' *Political Communication*, 16, 247–261.

McQuail, D. (2000), *McQuail's Mass Communication Theory*. Sage (4th edition), London.

Rowland, W. D. (1986), 'American Telecommunications Policy Research: its contradictory origins and influences'. *Media, Culture and Society*, 8, 159–182.

McQuail, D. (1992), *Media Performance. Mass Communication and the Public Interest*. Sage, London.

Murdock, G. & P. Golding (1999), Common Markets: Corporate Ambitions and Communication Trends in the UK and Europe. *Journal of Media Economics* 12: 117–132.

Napoli, P. M. (1999), 'Deconstructing the Diversity Principle'. *Journal of Communication*, 49/4, 7–34.

Schulz, W. & T. Held (2004), *Regulated Self-Regulation as a Form of Modern Government. An analysis of case studies from media and telecommunications law*. Eastleigh: John Libbey/University of Luton Press.

Siebert, F. S., T. Peterson & W. Schramm (1956), *Four Theories of the Press. The Authoritarian, Libertarian, Social Responsibility and Soviet Communist Concepts of what the Press should be and do*. University of Illinois Press (6th printing, 1971), Urbana.

Smith, A. (1980), *Goodbye Gutenberg: the newspaper revolution of the 1980's*. Oxford University Press, Oxford.

Søndergaard, H. (1996), 'Public Service after the Crisis'. *Nordicom Review*, 1, 107-120.

Steemers, J. (2003), Public service is not dead yet. Strategies in the 21st century. In G. F. Lowe & T. Hujanen (eds.), *Broadcasting & Convergence: New Articulations of the Public Service Remit* (pp. 123–137). Goteborg: NORDICOM.

Van Cuilenburg, J. J. & D. McQuail (2003), 'Media Policy Paradigm Shifts: Towards a New Communications Policy Paradigm'. *European Journal of Communication*, 18 (2), 181–207.

Williams, K. (2005), *European Media Studies*. London: Hodder.

Woldt, R. (2002), 'Selbstverplichtungen bei der BBC: Ein Modell für Transparenz im öffentlich-rechtlichen Rundfunk?' [Self-regulation in BBC; a model for transparency in public broadcasting?] *Media Perspektiven*, 5, 202–209.

Wetenschappelijke Raad voor het regeringsbeleid [Scientific Council for Government Policy]. (2005), *Focus op functies. Uitdagingen voor een toekomstbestendig mediabeleid. [Focus on Functions: Challenges for a Sustainable Media Policy]*. Amsterdam: Amsterdam University Press (see http://www.wrr.nl/pdfdocumenten/r71se.pdf for a summary in English).

About the Authors

Ruken Barış is a freelance journalist. She mainly focuses on the EU-Turkey relations, human rights issues and contemporary culture.

Piet Bakker is an associate professor at the Amsterdam School of Communication Research (ASCoR), University of Amsterdam.

Johannes Bardoel is a professor of Media Policy, working with the Departments of Communication at the University of Amsterdam and the Radboud University Nijmegen, the Netherlands. At present he also is the chairman of the Media Commission of the Council for Culture, the official advisory body for the Minister of Education, Culture and Sciences.

Els de Bens is emeritus professor of the Department of Communications at the University of Gent and is the Chairwoman of the Flemish Media Council.

Joseph Borg lectures at the University of Malta, and he is the audio-visual policy consultant of the Minister of Culture.

Michael Bromley is Professor of Journalism and Deputy Head of the School of Journalism and Communication at The University of Queensland (Australia).

Nada Buric is a Croatian consultant for communication strategies. Among other tasks, she was involved in developing communication strategy projects with the European Commission and the Croatian Government.

Fernando Correia is an associate professor at the Universidade Lusófona (Lisbon) and teacher at CENJOR. He is also the editor of the culture magazine *Vértice* and editor of the periodic publications for Editorial Caminho.

Dan Hallin is a professor of Communication and adjunct professor of Political Science at the University of California, San Diego.

Mario Hirsch is Director of the Institut Pierre Werner.

Karol Jakubowicz is a member of the Independent Media Commission in Kosovo and was, until recently, Director, Strategic Planning and Analysis Department, National Broadcasting Council of Poland, the broadcasting regulatory authority. His academic pursuits have included a teaching post at the University of Warsaw and Visiting Professorships at the University of Dortmund and the University of Amsterdam.

Per Jauert is an associate professor at the Department of Information and Media Studies, University of Aarhus. The television section is written by Henrik Søndergaard, associate professor at the Department of Film and Media Studies, University of Copenhagen.

Anna Maria Jönsson is a senior lecturer at the University College of Södertörn.

Dr Jyrki Jyrkiäinen is a senior lecturer at the Department of Journalism and Mass Communication, University of Tampere.

Ildikó Kaposi is an assistant professor of communication at the American University of Kuwait.

Hans J. Kleinsteuber, Professor, Institute for Political Science, University of Hamburg, Germany.

Maria Kontochristou teaches at the Greek Open University.

Bernard Lamizet and **Jean-François Tétu** are professors at the Institut d'Etudes Politiques, Lyon.

Ania Lara is a project manager at Europe's World journal.

Urmas Loit is the Managing Director of the Association of the Estonian Broadcasters and a lecturer at the University of Tartu.

Paolo Mancini is a professor at the Dipartimento Istituzioni e Societa, Facolta di Scienze Politiche, Universita di Perugia.

Carla Martins is Media Analyst at Entidade Reguladora para a Comunicação Social (ERC) and Communication and Journalism Studies Professor at Universidade Lusófona.

Denis McQuail is Honorary Research Fellow and Professor Emeritus, Amsterdam School of Communication Research, University of Amsterdam. He is an editor of European Journal of Communication and former member of the EuroMedia Research Group. He is author of *McQuail's Mass Communication Theory* (2005) and other books on media theory, policy and research.

Werner A. Meier is senior researcher and lecturer at the Institute for Mass Communication and Media Research (IPMZ) at the University of Zürich.

Marko Milosavljevič is an associate professor at the Faculty of Social Sciences at University of Ljubljana. (This text was finished in 2006.)

Audronė Nugaraitė is an associate professor at the Institute of Journalism, Vilnius University.

Helge Østbye is a professor at the Department of Information Science and Media Studies, University of Bergen.

Rúnar Pálmason has been a reporter at *Morgunblaðið* since 2000.

Stylianos Papathanassopoulos is a professor at the Faculty of Communication and Media Studies, National & Kapodistrian University of Athens.

Ramón Salaverría is a lecturer of Journalism at the School of Communication, University of Navarra.

Andrej Školkay is a media analyst based in Slovakia.

Milan Šmíd is a lecturer of Journalism and Media History at the School of Social Sciences, Charles University, Prague, Czech Republic.

Ilze Šulmane is a lecturer at the Department of Communication Studies, Faculty of Social Sciences, University of Latvia.

Vessela Tabakova is an associate professor at the Faculty of Journalism and Mass Communication of Sofia University "St. Kliment Ohridski".

Georgios Terzis is an associate professor at Vrije Universiteit Brussel seconded to Vesalius College in Belgium.

Barbara Thomass, Professor, Head of the Institute for Media Studies, University of Bochum, Germany.

Fabrizio Tonello is a professor of Public Opinion Studies at the University of Padua.

Josef Trappel is the head of IPMZ transfer, Centre for knowledge transfer and applied media research at the Institute for Mass Communication and Media Research at the University of Zurich.

Wolfgang Truetzschler is a Senior Lecturer in Communications at the Dublin Institute of Technology.

Alex Ulmanu is teaching at the University of Bucharest.

Myria Vassiliadou is the director of Mediterranean Institute of Gender Studies.

Peter Vasterman is an associate professor at the Department of Media Studies at the University of Amsterdam.

Lennart Weibull is a professor of Media Research at the Department of Journalism and Mass Communication at Göteborg University.